AF479298

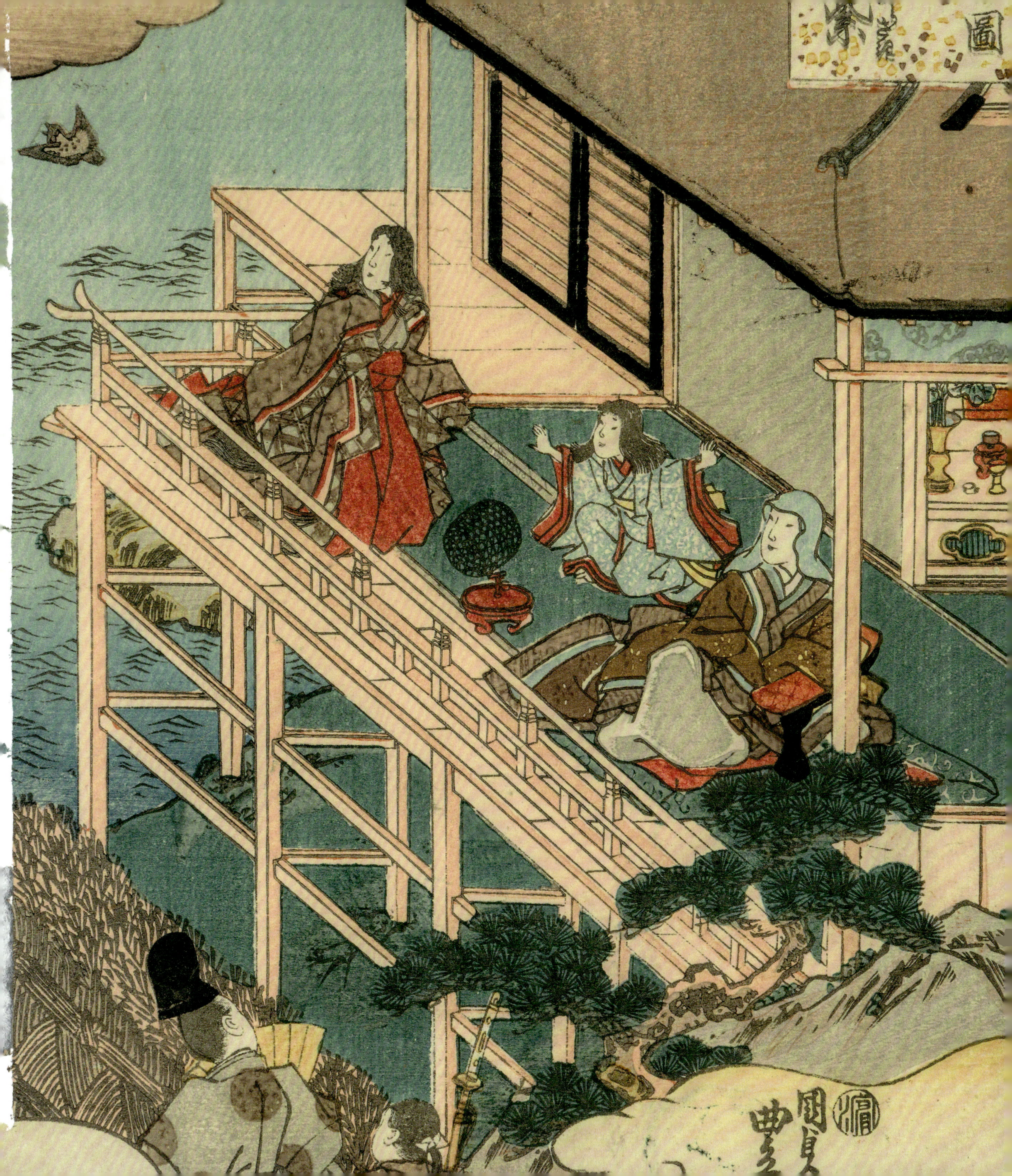
圖
国貞

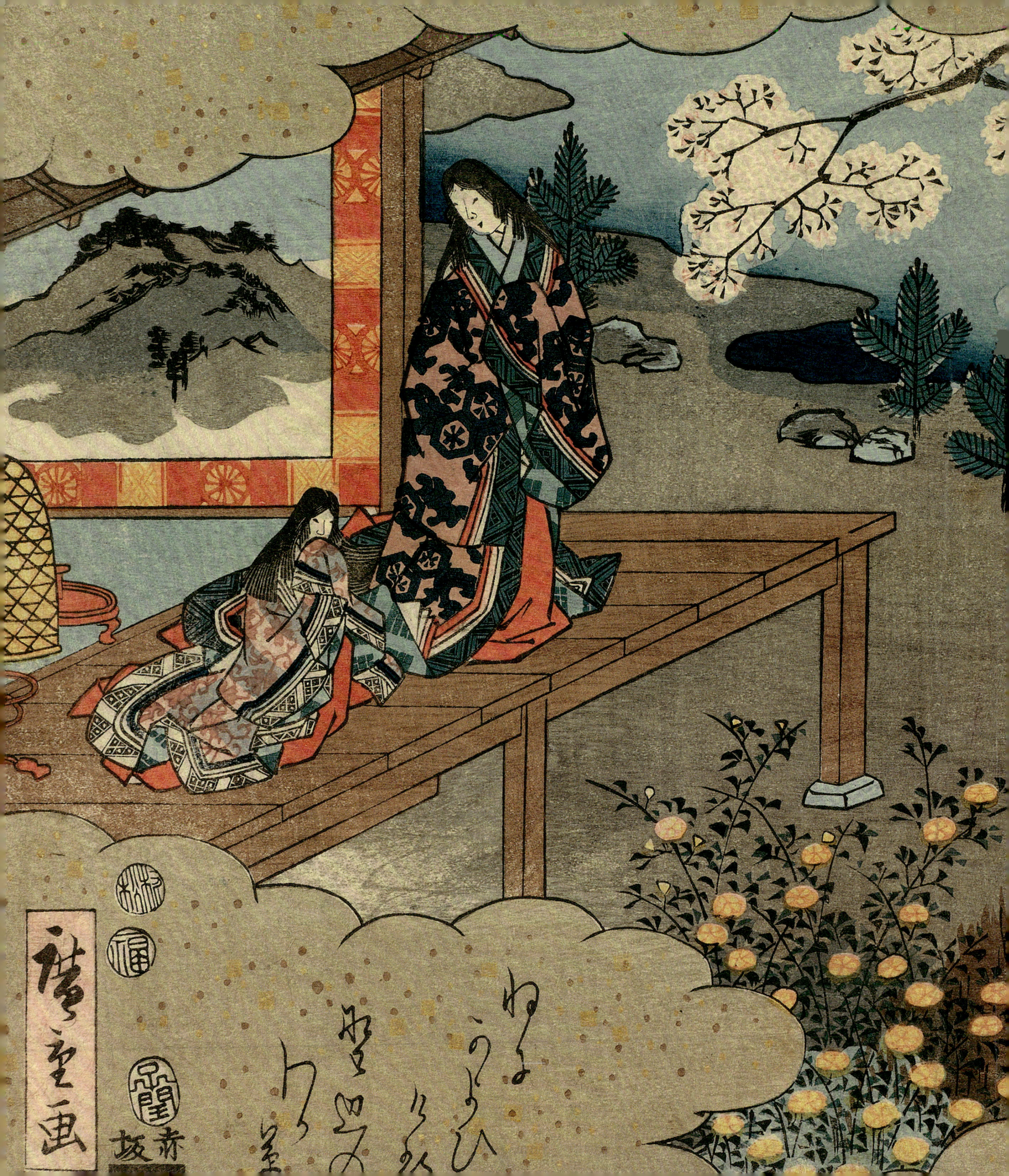
廣重画
赤坂

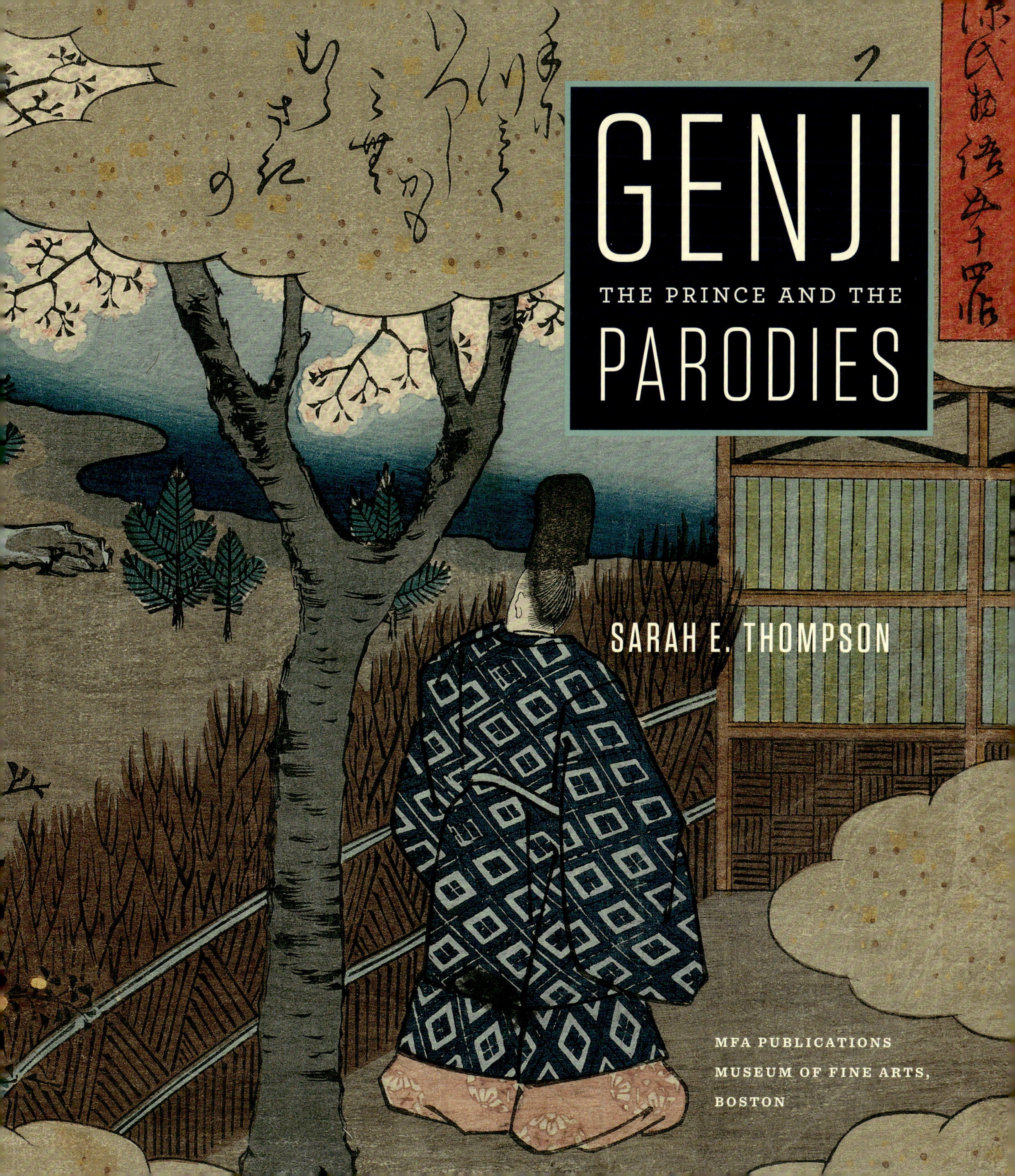
GENJI
THE PRINCE AND THE
PARODIES
SARAH E. THOMPSON
MFA PUBLICATIONS
MUSEUM OF FINE ARTS,
BOSTON

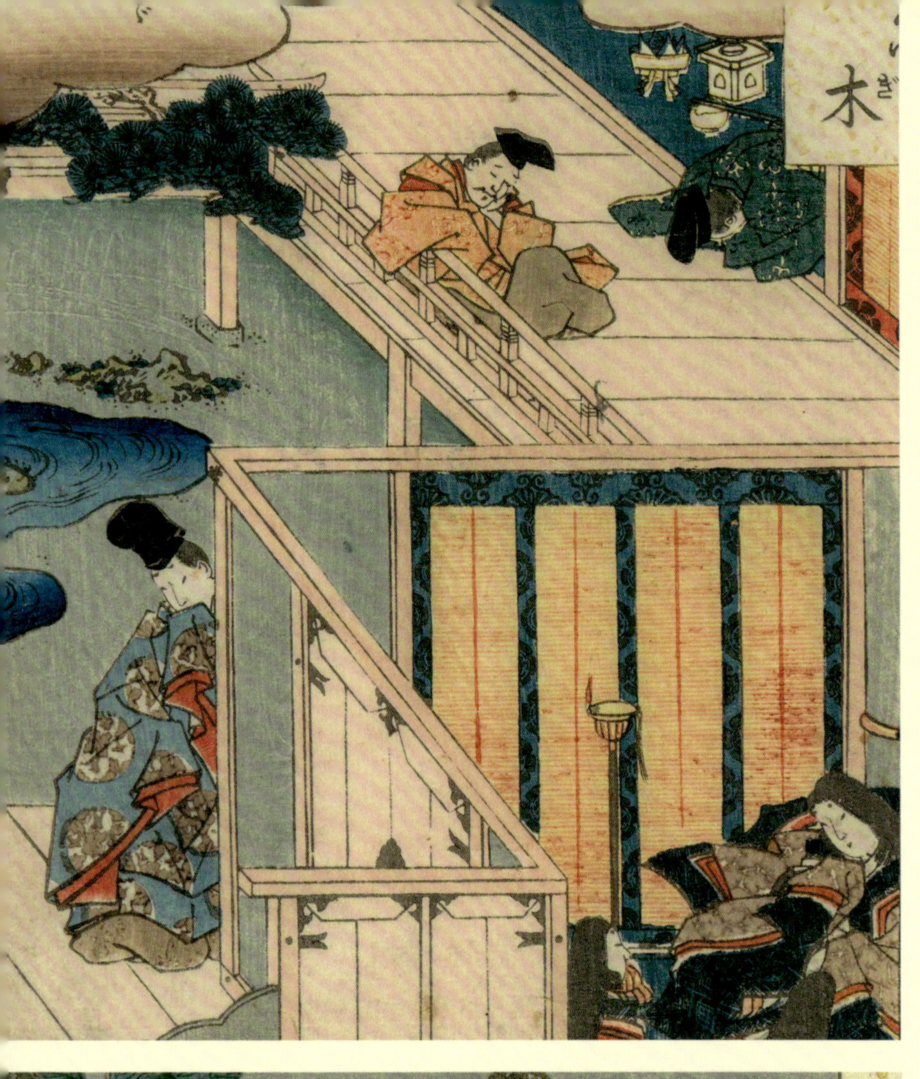

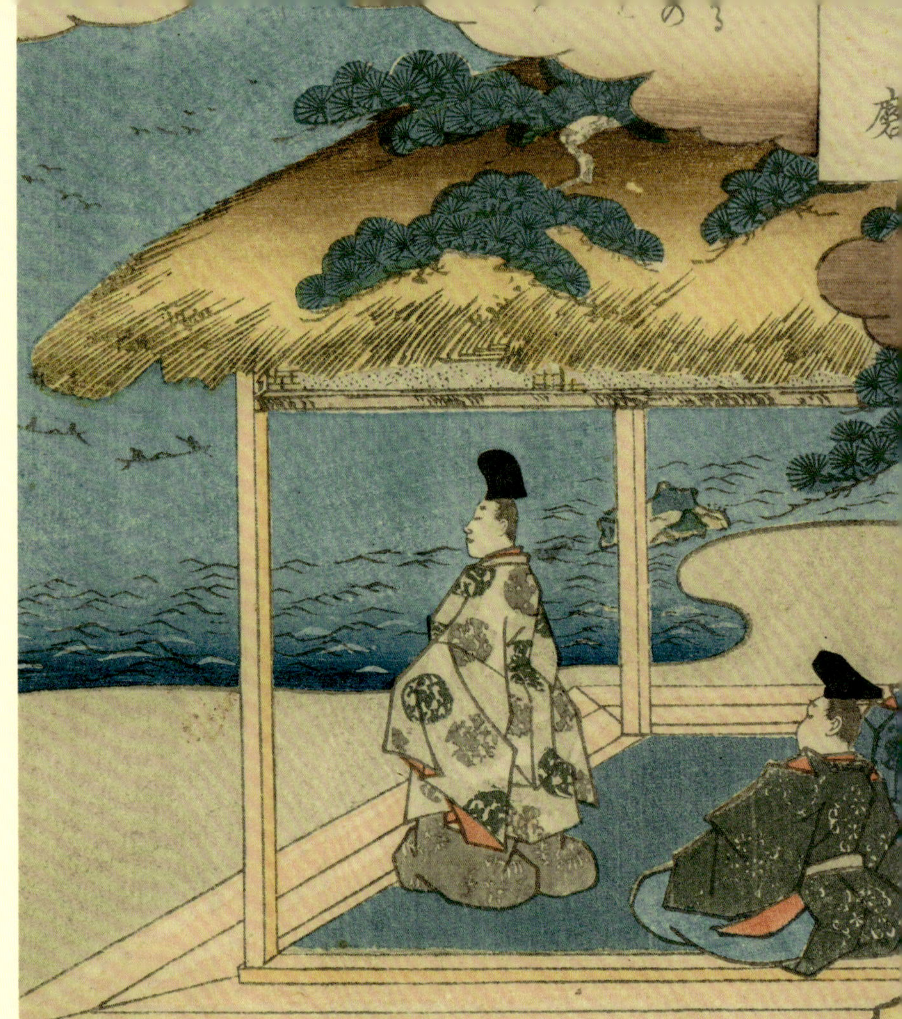

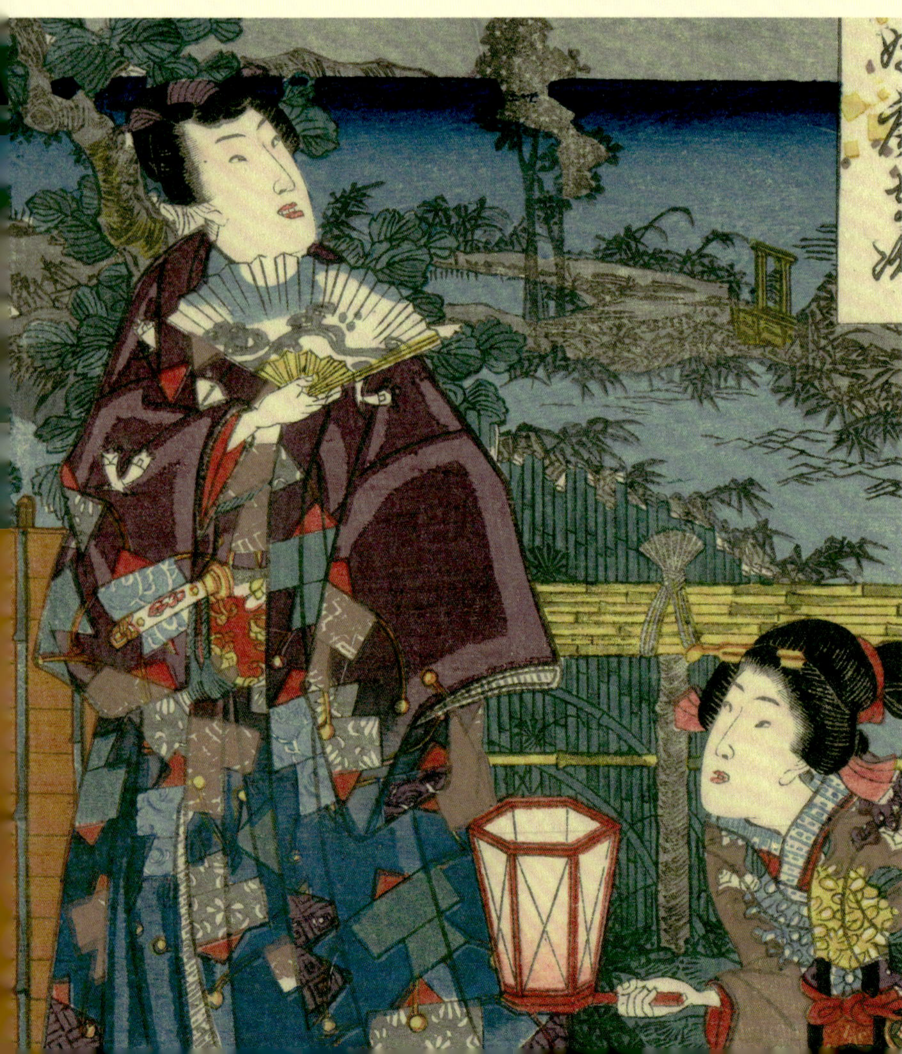

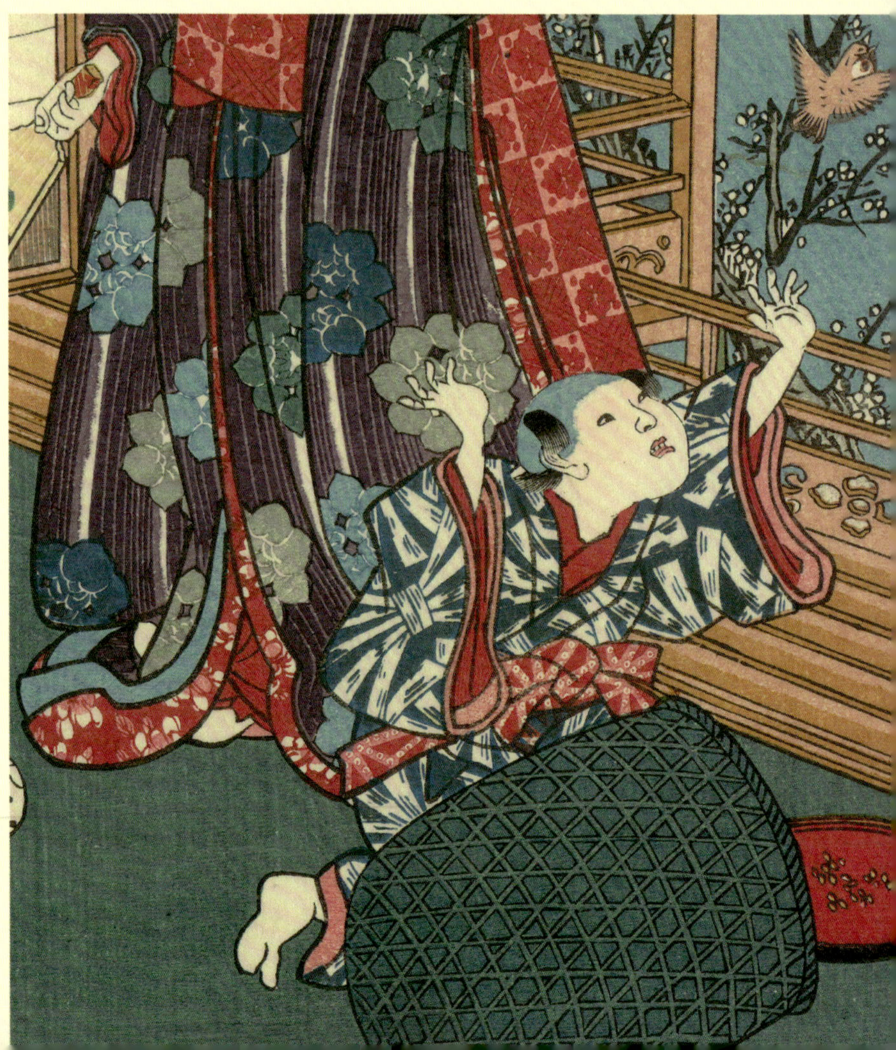

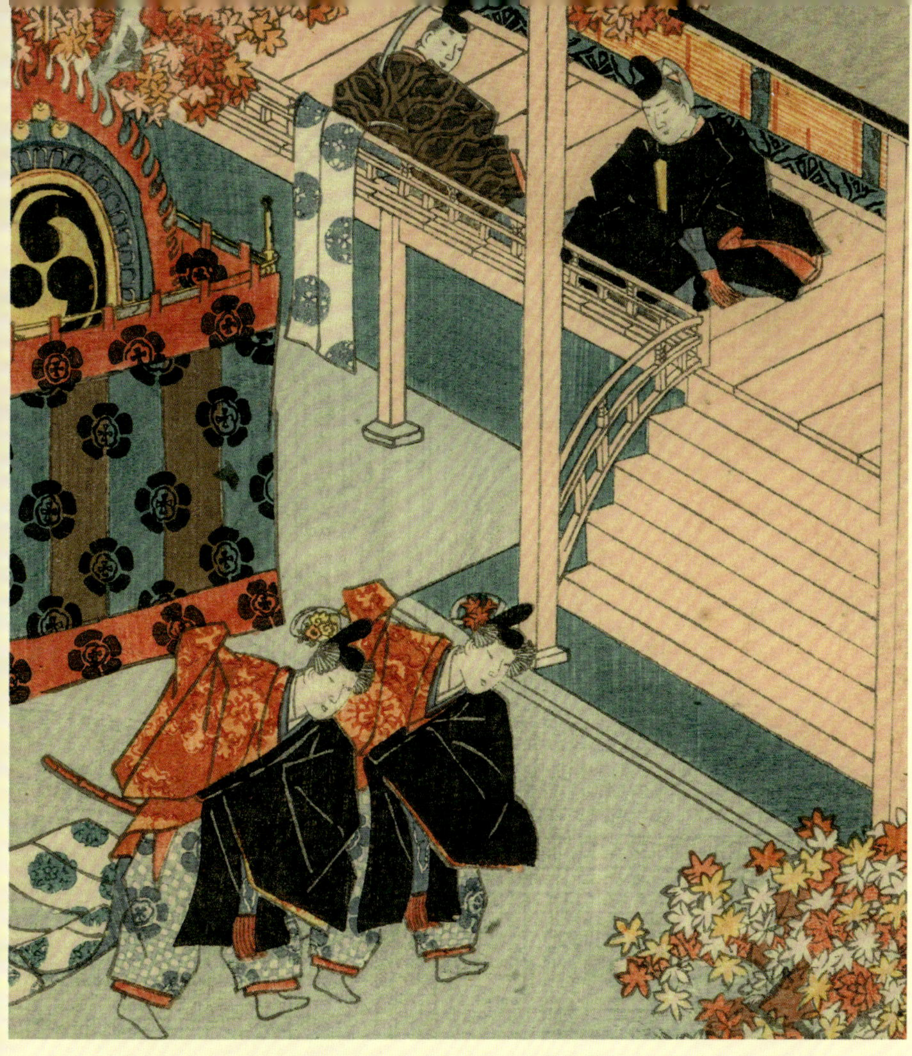

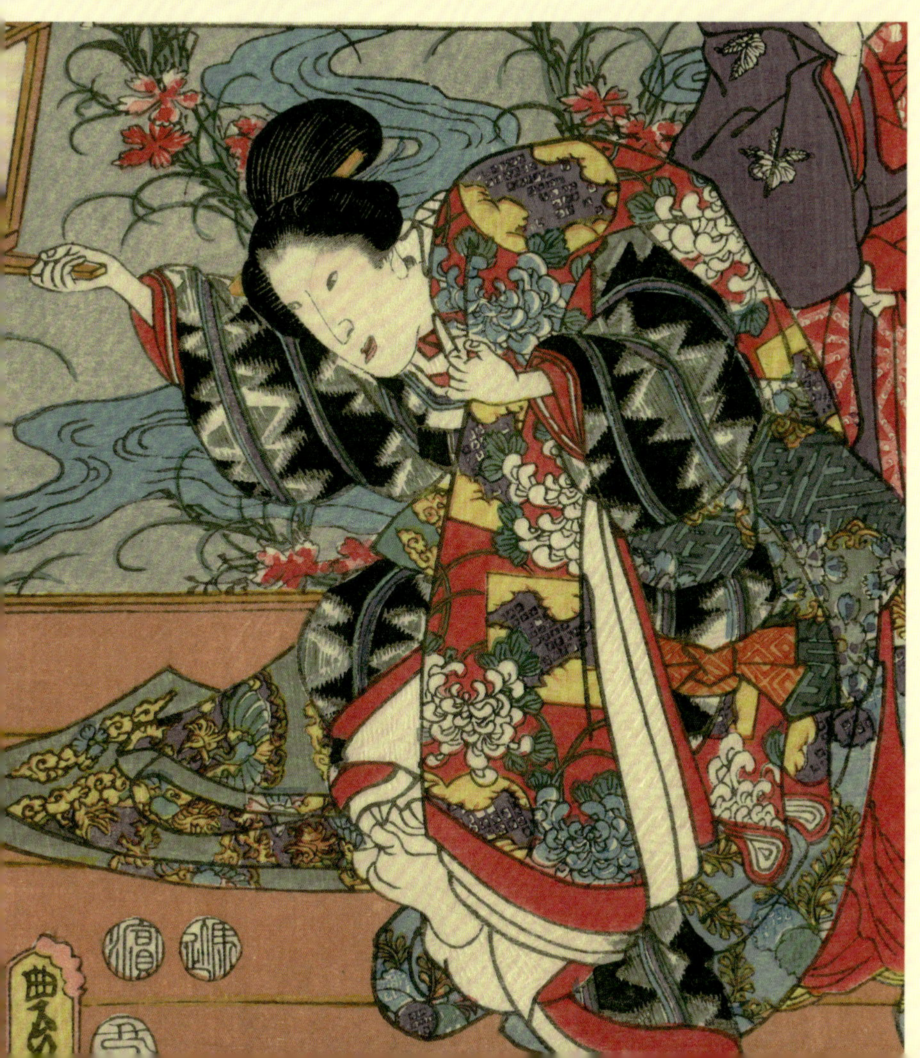

Contents

The Shining Prince and the Floating World 7

Genji: The Prince and the Parodies 27

List of Illustrations 191

Further Reading 204

Acknowledgments 207

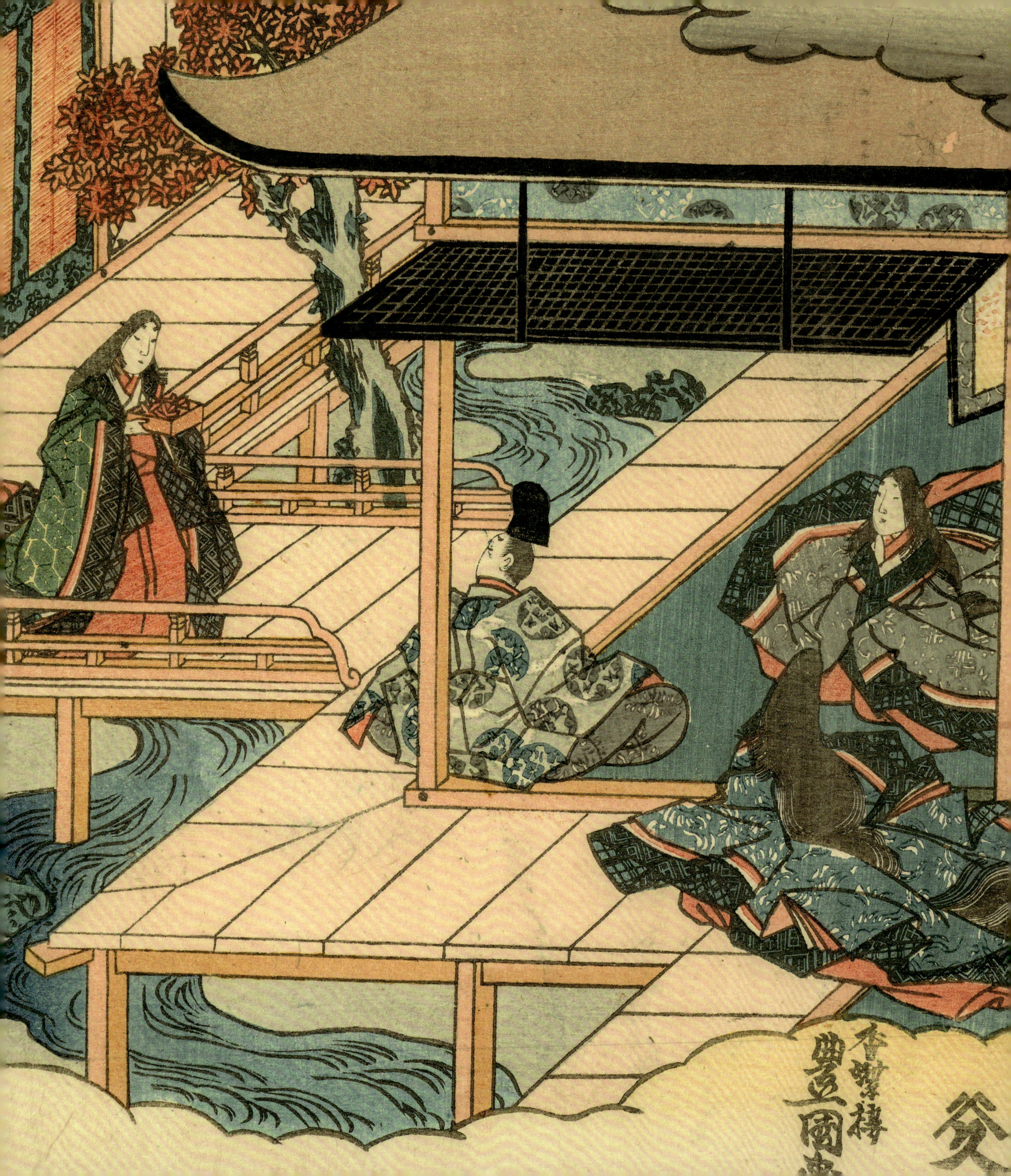
香蝶楼
豊國

The Shining Prince and the Floating World

The *Tale of Genji* (*Genji monogatari*) is universally recognized as the greatest classic of Japanese literature, and indeed one of the major masterpieces of world literature. A novel of manners, it was written at the beginning of the eleventh century C.E. by a lady-in-waiting at the imperial court known to us only by her nickname and title, Murasaki Shikibu (literally Lady Purple; about 978–about 1014). In fifty-four chapters, totaling over one thousand pages in English translation, the book follows the life and loves of the eponymous Prince Genji and his descendants, in perceptively described emotional detail. The story of the Shining Prince, as his creator called him, remains very readable as a novel even a thousand years later on the other side of the world; there have been four major English translations so far, published between 1925 and 2015, as well as translations and studies in numerous languages, drawing on a millennium of Japanese scholarship. Lady Murasaki brought her characters so vividly to life that a global readership is still happily debating their personalities, their motivations, and their ethics.

The works reproduced in this book are woodblock prints of the Edo period (1615–1868), with a few additional works of the Meiji era (1868–1912), that can be described as "Genji pictures" (Genji-e). When writers and artists of the Edo period created original tales and pictures of life in the Floating World (ukiyo), as the urban popular culture was called, they often drew on the heritage of older literature for inspiration and playful allusions. The new "low culture" of the urban commoners appropriated the traditional "high culture" of the elite for its own purposes, in fiction, drama, and the visual arts. The school of pictorial art associated with this hybrid popular culture became known as ukiyo-e or "Pictures of the Floating World," which included paintings, book illustrations, and single-sheet woodblock prints such as those illustrated in this book.

The works that follow fall broadly into three categories: (1) straightforward depictions of the original *Tale of Genji*, following long-established conventions for illustrations of courtly literature; (2) humorous reworkings of the original story, including modern updatings or parodies, and comparisons to other stories suggested by the chapter titles; and (3) scenes from the greatest parody of all, the bestselling popular novel of nineteenth-century Japan, *The False Murasaki's Rustic Genji* (*Nise Murasaki inaka Genji*) by Ryūtei Tanehiko (1783–1842), published serially from 1829 to 1842, with several later sequels by other authors. In this retelling, the hero is a kind of James Bond figure, fighting

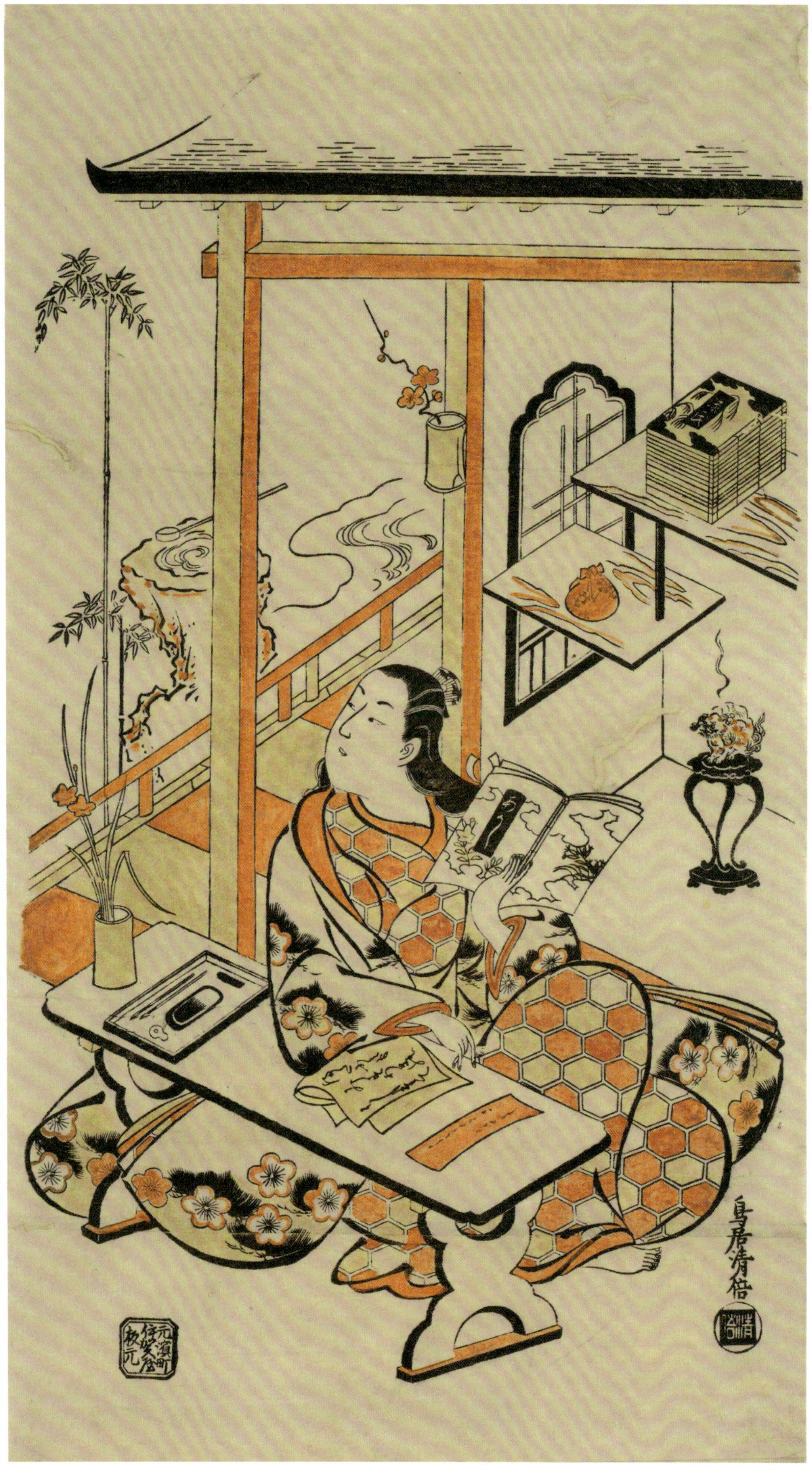

plots against the shogunate while having affairs with many women. *Inaka Genji* was profusely illustrated by Utagawa Kunisada I (1786–1864), the most prolific and financially successful of all ukiyo-e print designers, whose imaginative designs for elaborate costumes and interiors in an allegedly historical fifteenth-century setting contributed greatly to the success of the book. Kunisada and other artists later designed large numbers of color prints based on the black-and-white illustrations found on almost every page of the book.

This book focuses on two complete series both designed by Kunisada, each with fifty-four sheets. *Genji Incense Pictures* (*Genji kō no zu*), published sometime between 1844 and 1847, presents scenes from the Heian-period novel in a traditional style derived from the printed Genji books of the seventeenth century that seem to have been Kunisada's models. *The Color Print Contest of a Modern Genji* (*Ima Genji nishiki-e awase*), published in 1852–54, is an *Inaka Genji* series in the ukiyo-e style. Both series are in the small chūban format (roughly the same as one standard sheet of printer paper) and depict one scene for each of the fifty-four chapters of the original *Tale* (although in the case of *Inaka Genji* these chapter numbers do not correspond exactly to the content of the book, which includes an action-adventure plot as well as the parody elements and so has more chapters per episode than the Heian *Tale*). The two series will be compared in detail, chapter by chapter, with additional comparisons of one or more prints that may be from any of the three main categories noted above. Of course, there is significant overlap between the various categories; for example, the poems associated with the chapter titles of *The Tale of Genji*, often accompanied by small illustrations, may be included in prints of the second and third categories as well as the first. The translations of the poems given here are by Royall Tyler.

FIG. 1 | Torii Kiyomasu I (active about 1696–1716), Woman reading the Akashi chapter of *The Tale of Genji*, about 1710s

The Original *Tale of Genji*

The Tale of Genji circulated in manuscript form for many centuries, typically with each of the fifty-four chapters in the form of a paper-bound booklet with its own title; a full set might be housed in a small chest of drawers built for the purpose. One of the earliest ukiyo-e prints to depict a Genji-related theme, a hand-colored print designed by Torii Kiyomasu I (active about 1696–1716), shows a modern woman of the early eighteenth century reading a booklet whose title identifies it as the Akashi chapter of the *Tale*; more such booklets are on a shelf behind her (fig. 1). Her pose, at a writing desk overlooking a scenic garden, with a cusped window in the background, shows that this scene is inspired by the well-known image of Lady Murasaki at Ishiyama Temple, where she was supposedly inspired to begin her great masterpiece.

The first readers of those manuscript booklets were the courtiers who were members of the author's own social circle. Following the shift of political power from the nobility of the imperial court (kuge) to the warrior clans (buke, or samurai) in the late twelfth century, the book was all the more cherished by the nobles as a reminder of their days of glory; while at the same time, the warriors sought to prove that they, too, were people of culture by studying courtly literature such as *The Tale of Genji* and commissioning manuscript copies and illustrations. Since the book is very long, and the classical courtly language of the eleventh century was becoming increasingly difficult to understand, numerous commentaries and digests began to appear. Illustrations of the story, in formats ranging from small album paintings, handscrolls, and fan paintings to large folding screens and sliding-door panels, were commissioned by both the nobility and the warriors as cultural status symbols.

The earliest surviving illustrations of *The Tale of Genji* date from the early twelfth century, about a century after the book itself was written, and consist of handscrolls with excerpts from the full text followed by pictures, with one to three such units per chapter. The painting style exemplifies what came to be called yamato-e or Japanese painting: black outline drawings with brilliant colors lavishly applied; for the major characters, round faces with simply indicated features, so that the viewer can more easily identify with the characters or project onto them her own ideas of their appearance; a relatively shallow, flattened pictorial space; and a special compositional technique known as the blown-off roof (fukinuki yatai), in which the roof of a building is removed so the viewer can observe simultaneously what is taking place in different rooms, or both inside and outside a building.

Over the centuries, artists experimented with various ways of representing the *Tale*, occasionally including the technique of time-based continuous narration seen in other Japanese picture scrolls, with the same figure reappearing at different moments as the scroll is rolled along by the viewer. For this story, however, a more static form of illustration seems most appropriate, with poignant moments that capture the reader's emotions frozen into single images on the pictorial surface. By the early seventeenth century, the most typical Genji illustrations were albums of paintings made by artists of the Tosa school (the main practitioners of the yamato-e style at this time), with one illustration for each chapter, often among the luxury goods featured in the dowry of an upper-class bride (fig. 2). These small paintings often preserved much older stylistic and compositional features, and they in turn became the basis for the earliest printed Genji illustrations.

An important development in the appreciation of *The Tale of Genji* was the emphasis on the numerous poems that are included in it, since exchanges of five-line waka poems were an important feature of Heian-period courtship and personal life in general. In 1193, almost two centuries after the *Tale* was written, the noted poet and critic Fujiwara Shunzei (1114–1204) famously remarked that "to compose poetry without having

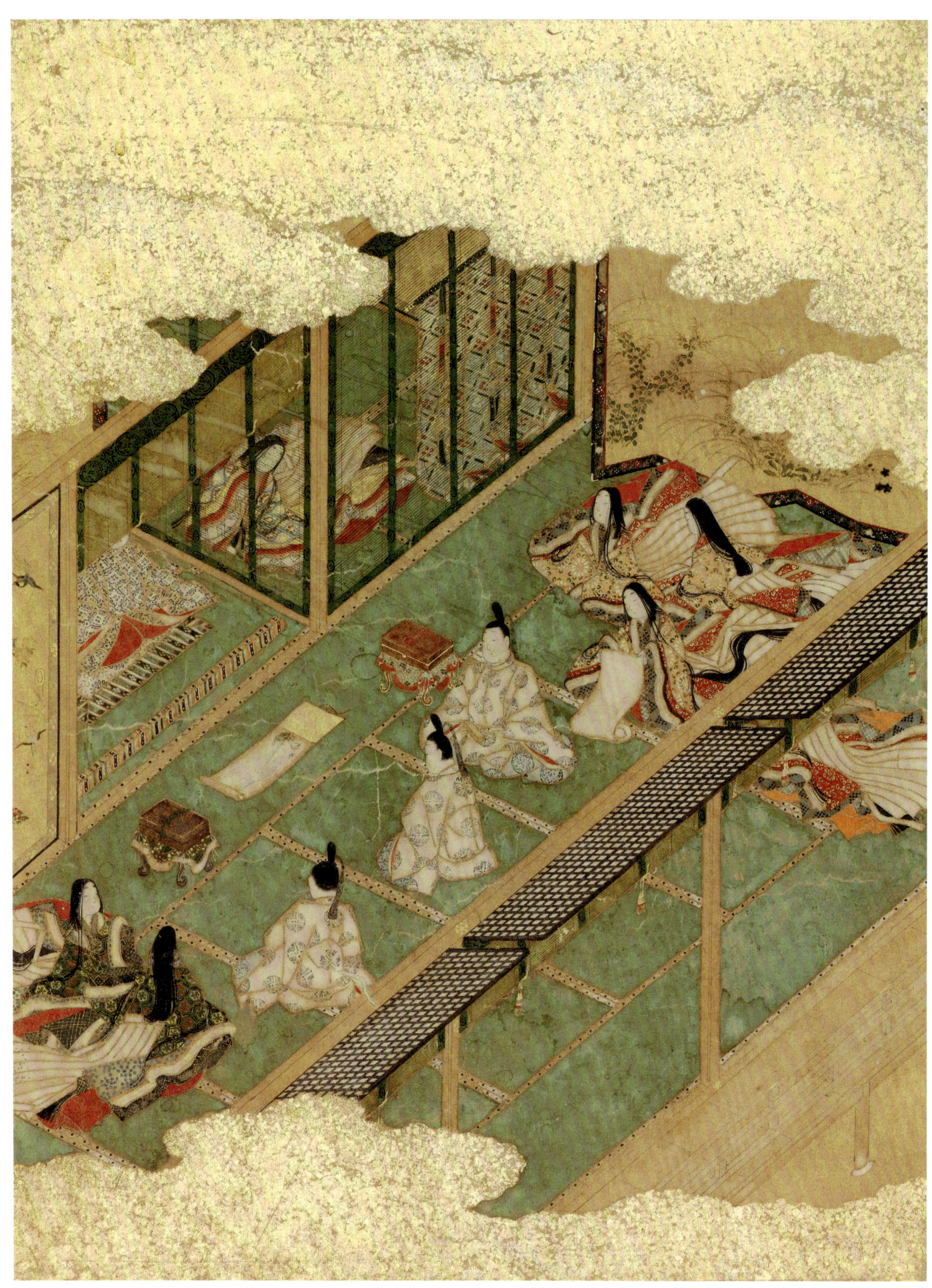

FIG. 2 | Unknown artist, The picture contest from *The Tale of Genji*, 17th century

read *Genji* is simply inexcusable" (as translated by Thomas Harper). The implication seems to be that the sensibilities expressed in the book are those that appear in poetry as well, rather than that the poems in the book are unusually good, since a number of other classical poets were recognized as better at poetry than Murasaki. Nevertheless, this comment led to an increased emphasis on the poetry in the book, and the scenes chosen for illustration are often those related to the composition of poems, particularly poems related to the titles of the individual chapters. Treating the very long novel as a kind of poetry anthology also made it easier to master and enjoy its complex contents.

Around the beginning of the seventeenth century, a third group of potential readers and art patrons became important: the newly affluent merchants and artisans in the major cities, who although they did not belong to either of the two elite groups were also eager to acquire cultural capital by cultivating knowledge of the classics. After a century of civil wars, the country was reunited under the Tokugawa shoguns, who established the city of Edo (modern Tokyo) as their center of rule, while maintaining a figurehead emperor and his court in the old capital of Kyoto. Peace and relative prosperity led to the rise of a middle class with enough disposable income to enjoy the pleasures of city life, such as the kabuki theater and the Yoshiwara brothel district, and a high enough rate of literacy to make commercial publishing viable. The woodblock printing technology that had already been used for centuries to make multiple copies of Buddhist texts and images was now applied to books for sale to the general public.

Printed editions of classical literature such as *The Tale of Genji* spread this prestigious knowledge to far more people than ever before. Commentaries explicating the now-difficult classical language of the texts spread from manuscript culture to print culture, and abbreviated guides to the content of the books appeared in reference books for commoners, especially young

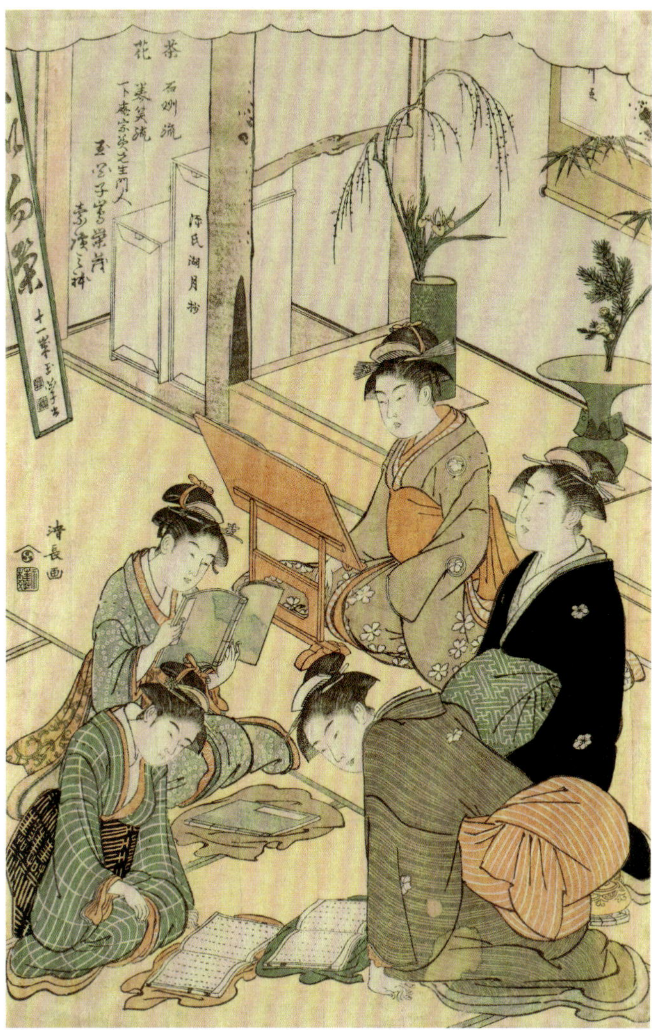

FIG. 3 | Torii Kiyonaga (1752–1815), Child prodigy Gyokkashi Shima Eimo giving a reading lesson, about 1785

women, who wished to appear highly cultured — including both the daughters of affluent families and the top-ranked courtesans of the Yoshiwara, who were admired not only for their beauty but for their cultural accomplishments in fields such as calligraphy, poetry, painting, and music.

A charming color print designed by Torii Kiyonaga (1752–1815) in the 1780s shows a young girl, the child prodigy Gyokkashi Eimo, sitting at a lectern as she delivers a lesson on a difficult text to several other young women (fig. 3). The text is most likely *The Tale of Genji*, since in the background we see a large wooden box labeled *The Moon on the Lake Commentary* (*Kogetsushō*), an annotated edition of the complete *Tale of Genji*, with extensive headnotes and interlinear reading aids, that was first published in 1673 in sixty

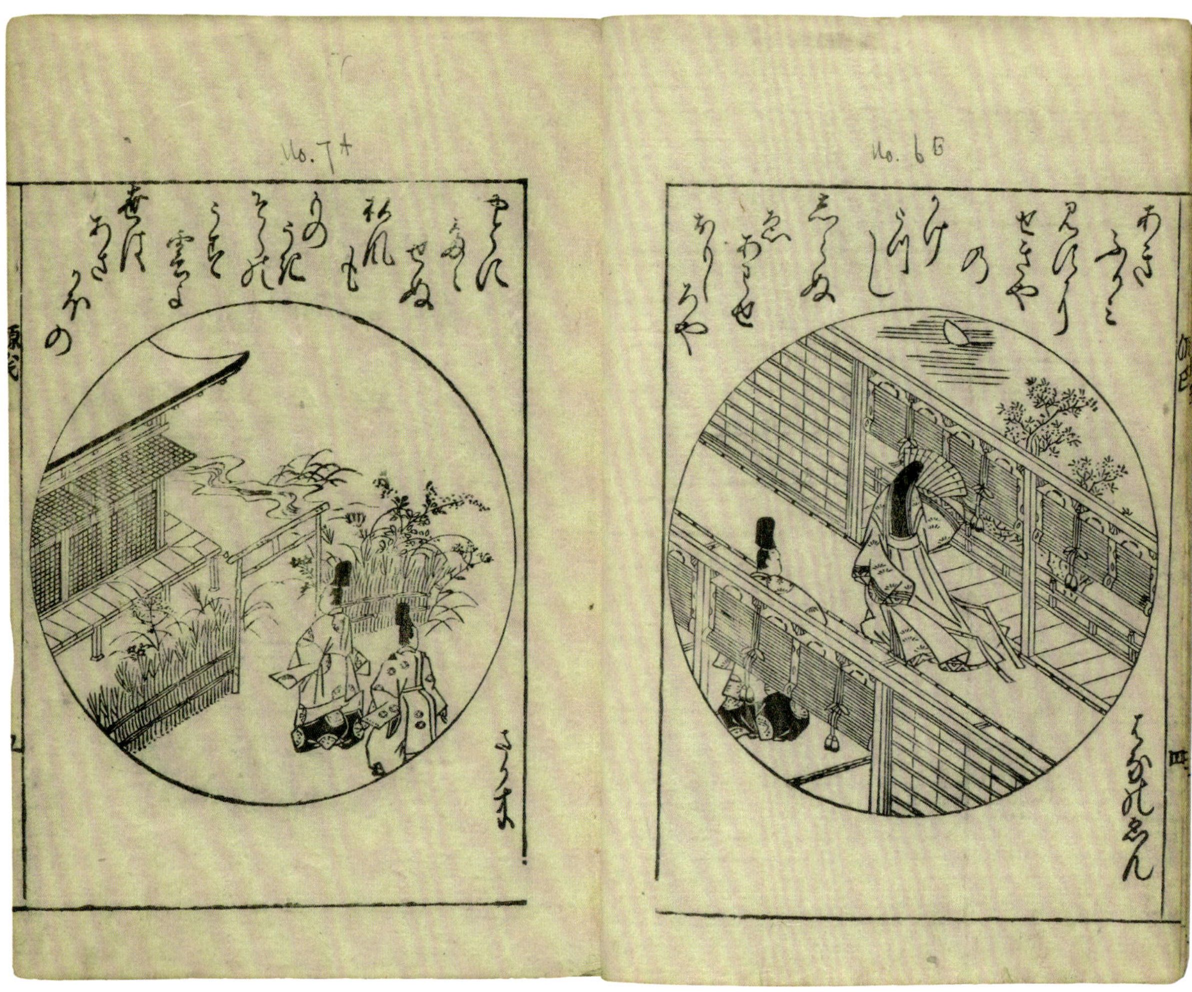

FIG. 4 | Hishikawa Moronobu (died 1694), *Picture Book of The Tale of Genji*, 1685

volumes (one for each chapter, plus additional reference material) and became the standard edition used throughout the Edo period. A number of other prints representing elegant interiors include a boxed set of *Kogetsushō* as an indicator of learning and refinement.

The *Kogetsushō* did not, however, include pictures, nor did the earliest printed editions of *The Tale of Genji* published in the first half of the seventeenth century. The first printed illustrations seem to have been the set designed by the Kyoto lacquer artist Yamamoto Shunshō (1610–1682) for the 1650 publication *The Illustrated Tale of Genji* (*E-iri Genji monogatari*), a very influential work that went through several editions (the pictures were even reproduced in the 1976 English translation by Edward Seidensticker) and influenced many later Genji illustrations. This work included the full text of the novel, in sixty volumes with one chapter per volume, including several full-page illustrations inserted into each chapter, plus six additional volumes of explanatory material (like the somewhat later *Kogetsushō*).

Later printed books of Genji illustrations, from the second half of the seventeenth century, did not include the full text. Instead, they consisted largely of pictures, generally just one per chapter, with only short captions or excerpts from the novel, all contained in two or three volumes. Important examples include *The Little Mirror of Genji* (*Genji kokagami*) of 1657 and *The Sidelock Mirror of Genji* (*Genji binkagami*) of 1660, both of which were used as references by nineteenth-century print designers such as Kunisada. The pictures in

FIG. 5 | Hishikawa Moronobu (died 1694), *New Collection of Pictures of Beauties*, about 1684–87

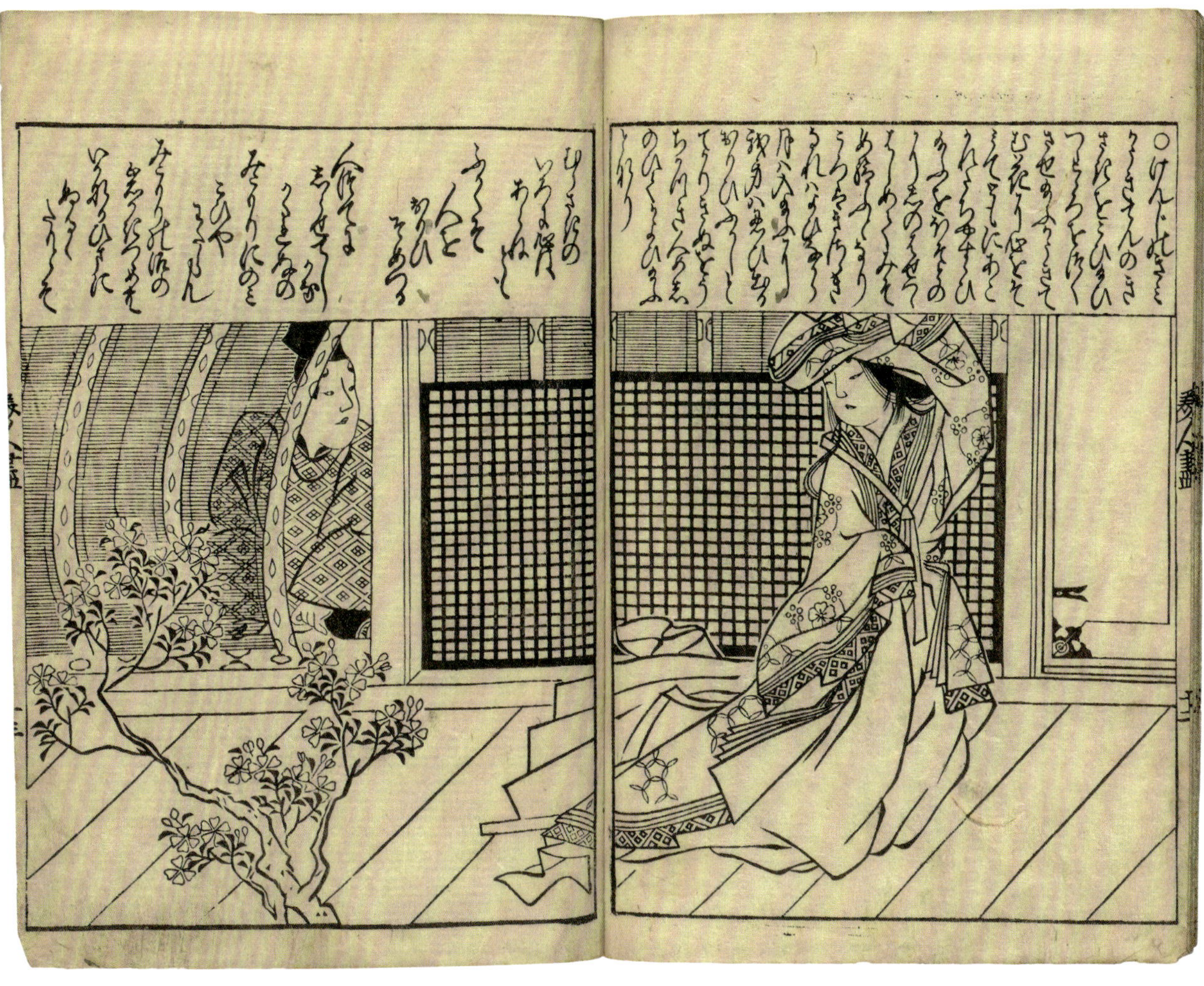

all of these works were woodcut versions of the traditional painted Genji albums in the Tosa style, which continued to be made for those who could afford them even as much cheaper printed versions proliferated.

The birth of the ukiyo-e style of paintings and prints can be seen clearly in a comparison of Genji illustrations by the first ukiyo-e artist whose name is known, Hishikawa Moronobu (died 1694). His *Mirror of Genji in Japanese Pictorial Style* (*Genji yamato-e kagami*) of 1685 shows traditional illustrations in circular medallions, with short captions, that preserve the basic qualities of the Tosa style: palatial interiors with figures seen from a distance, often from above, using the blown-off roof technique to show two rooms at once, or simultaneous indoor and outdoor views (fig. 4). But his illustrations for *A Collection of Pictures of Beauties* (*Bijin e-tsukushi*), undated but also published in the mid-1680s, are done in the new ukiyo-e style that he pioneered. Among various scenes from the history and literature of both China and Japan that focus on people who were considered especially good-looking (primarily women, but attractive men are also included) are three scenes from *The Tale of Genji* (fig. 5). In the ukiyo-e style, the figures become much more prominent; their bodies and faces, their elegant clothing, and their interactions with each other are now the focus of attention.

In single-sheet Genji prints as opposed to book illustrations, noteworthy examples of traditional designs can also be found. The prolific Okumura Masanobu (1686–1764), an artist and publisher responsible for a number of technical and stylistic developments in the first half of the eighteenth century, designed both parodies (see 6B) and serious Genji images, such as a complete series of small hand-colored prints based on the compositions of Moronobu's *Genji yamato-e kagami* but showing each picture as part of an imagined collage of pictorial and calligraphic works, perhaps to be pasted onto a folding screen or other surface; the set in the MFA has been mounted as a small album, although the prints were most likely issued separately (fig. 6).

The most gorgeous of all of the hand-colored Genji prints is the series designed half by Nishimura Shigenaga (1697?–1756) and half by Torii Kiyomasu II (1706–1763), undated but probably published in the 1730s (see 9B, 18C, 21B). In addition to lavish hand-painting including metallic pigments, the series boasts stenciled backgrounds with colorants sprayed over paper cutouts in appropriate shapes. The publisher's advertisement at the right edge of each print explains that the pictures may be cut out and pasted onto sewing boxes (haribako). Like the small paintings that they mimicked, the prints could also be used to decorate folding screens or sliding door panels, although cutting out the central fan-shaped pictures would have meant losing the lovely stenciled patterns of the backgrounds.

Color printing in ukiyo-e prints gradually replaced hand coloring in the 1740s and came into full flower after the perfection of full-color printing (defined as five or more color blocks in addition to the black-outline key block) in 1765. During this time almost all Genji-related prints were parodic updatings. Around 1800, however, Kunisada's teacher Utagawa Toyokuni I (1769–1825) created a small chūban-sized series based on early book illustrations in the Tosa style, probably a major source of inspiration for his pupil's later *Genji Incense* series (see 10B, 23B). By this time full-color printing had been taken for granted for over thirty years, and some artists were experimenting instead with a restricted color scheme known as benigirai (literally red hating or red avoiding) that used a deliberately subdued palette of grays and purples, sometimes with a few other colors as well; it was this type of coloring, considered especially elegant at the time, that Toyokuni I chose for his series.

Toyokuni I's reason for designing a series of traditional Genji pictures is unknown, but his student Kunisada seems to have become interested in the history of illustrations of the original *Tale of Genji* as a result of research connected with his illustrations for *Inaka Genji*, the better to link the parody novel to its source. Kunisada's first experiment with Genji prints designed in a version of the traditional Tosa style, strongly influenced by ukiyo-e, was a set of triptychs published in 1839–42; each of the nine known designs represents a well-known scene from a single chapter, expanded into the larger three-sheet format. This experience with the older style stood him in good stead when he designed the *Genji Incense* series sometime between 1844 (when he changed his art name from Kunisada to Toyokuni, after his late teacher) and 1847 (when the system of censors' seals used on the prints changed).

It seems very likely that the *Genji Incense* series was published at this time precisely because Edo consumers had just been deprived of their favorite novel, *Inaka Genji*, which was banned in 1842 as a part of the Tenpō Reforms, an ongoing attempt at economic reorganization that resulted in widespread censorship of anything deemed frivolous or improper. Fans of the parody novel had to settle for the original instead, and Kunisada obliged them. He himself had been hard hit by the reform movement, since the actor prints that were his main specialty were also (temporarily) banned. His colleague Utagawa Kuniyoshi (1797–1861), who specialized in prints of historical warriors, also took advantage of public interest in the original *Tale of Genji* to produce a series of warrior prints matched with the chapters of Genji in about 1845–46 (see 24B, 41C, 52B). The third member of the troika of top Utagawa-school artists,

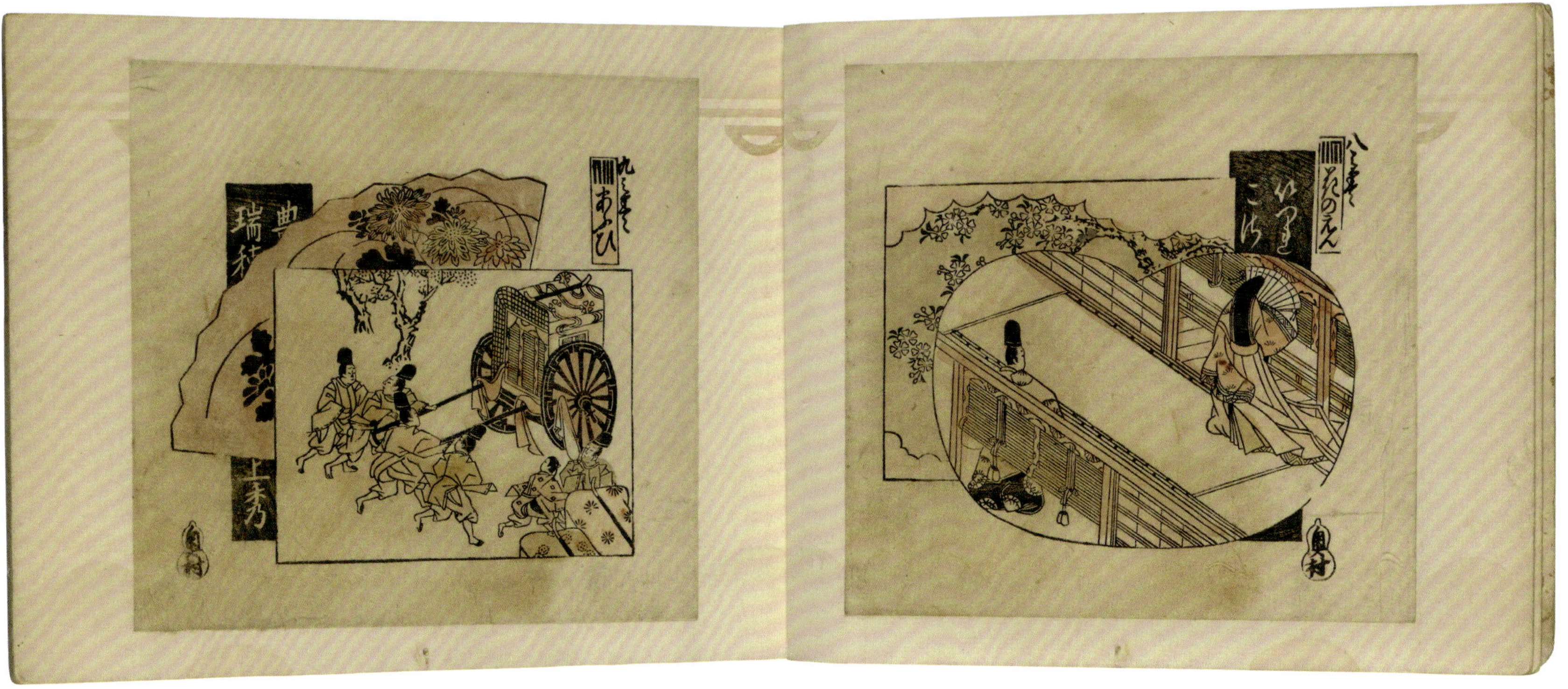

FIG. 6 | Okumura Masanobu (1686–1764), Untitled album of prints of *The Tale of Genji*, about 1730s

Utagawa Hiroshige I (1797–1858), best known for his landscapes, also produced a beautiful Genji series in the traditional style, published in 1852 (see 1B, 3B, 5B). By this time, however, the beloved *Inaka Genji* was once again available in the form of sequels. Hiroshige's series, based on early printed Genji illustrations but expanded into the full-size ōban format with high-quality, full-color printing, does not seem to have been as successful as Kunisada's series, since it was discontinued after only five designs.

The *Genji Incense* series takes its name from an aristocratic game that seems to have developed in the early seventeenth century in the Kyoto social circles surrounding the imperial court. In the Genji incense game, five sets of five scents are prepared and randomly mixed. Each player tests five packets of incense and must determine whether the scents tested are the same or different. They might be all the same, all different, or some combination. The possibilities are indicated by small diagrams, known as Genji mon (crests), consisting of five vertical lines, with identical scents connected across the top by horizontal lines. Mathematically, there are exactly fifty-two possibilities for such combinations, and so each little diagram is given the name of a Genji chapter (with two of them repeated for the first and last of the fifty-four chapters). The answer that each contestant submits is the name of the Genji chapter whose mon corresponds to the pattern they perceived.

Sets of equipment for the incense game typically included small booklets showing the mon and the matching chapter titles, usually accompanied by an abbreviated pictorial motif symbolizing the events of the chapter, and sometimes also the poem associated with the chapter title. Such booklets are depicted in two later print series that match the chapters with completely different stories, one by Kuniyoshi that shows miniature scrolls (see 24B, 41C, 52B), and one by his pupil Utagawa Yoshiiku (1833–1904) that shows an accordion-folded booklet (see 31B, 43C, 45B, 53C).

The Genji mon, and/or the pictures that often accompanied them, became popular motifs in the decorative arts, appearing on textiles, lacquerware, and so on. They were also utilized on the playing cards for a card game that involved matching the

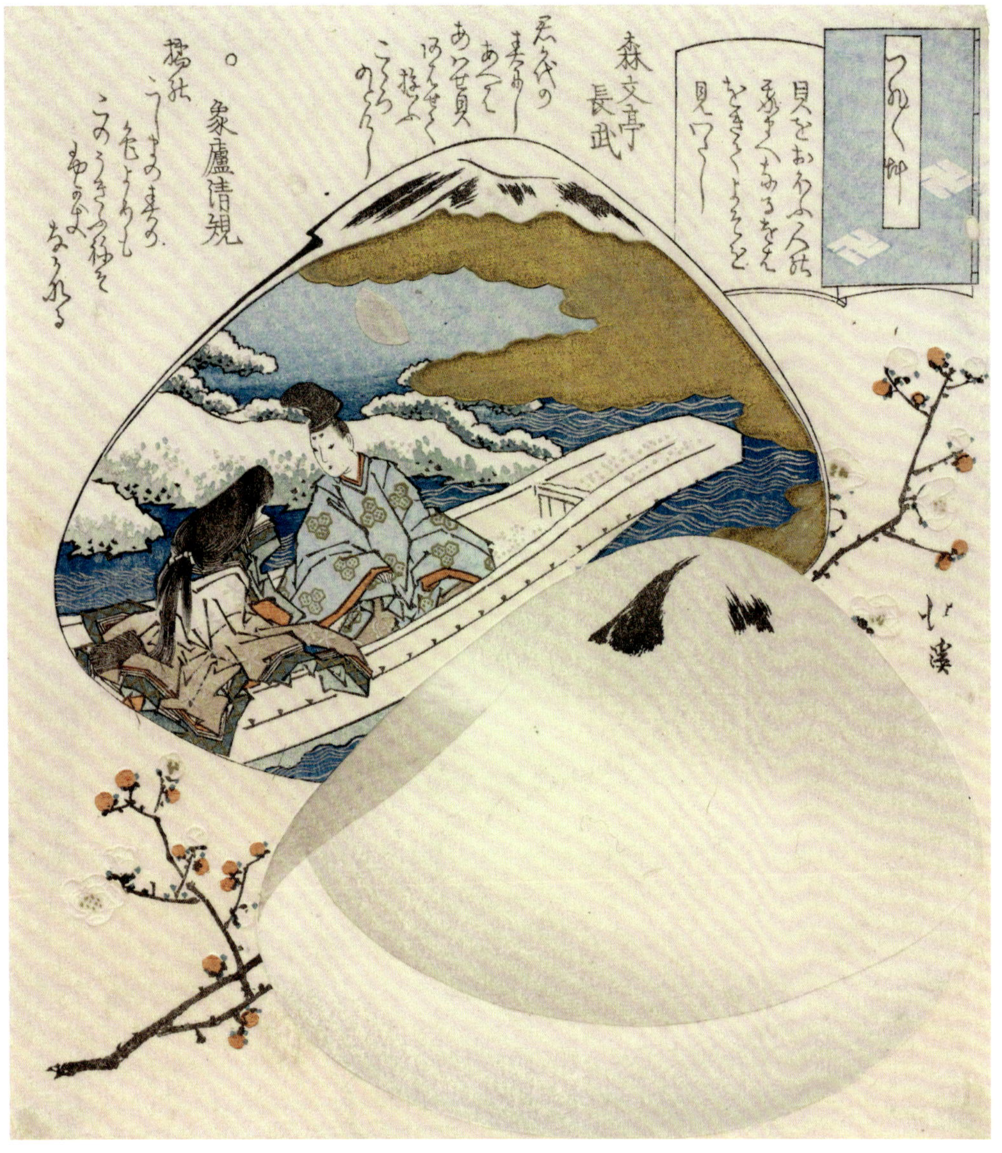

Fig. 7 | Totoya Hokkei (1780–1850), *The Shell-Matching Game* from the surimono series *Essays in Idleness*, about 1831–32

first and last halves of the poems representing the chapters, a variation of the much more famous card game (still played today) based on the classical anthology *One Hundred Poems by One Hundred Poets* (*Hyakunin isshu*). These card games, in turn, had developed from an earlier aristocratic game of matching the halves of clamshells painted with scenes from literary classics such as Genji (fig. 7). The Genji poem-card game seems to have been very popular, and in 1811 a set of four prints, intended to be cut apart and mounted as playing cards, was designed by Katsushika Hokusai (1760–1849). A series of elegant women by Kikukawa Eizan (1787–1867) uses Genji playing cards — in paired sets with the first half and last half of each poem — as title cartouches for the individual prints (see 20B).

Throughout the 1850s and 1860s, the popularity of *Inaka Genji* prints eclipsed those depicting the original story, although these parody prints sometimes included pictorial references to the original *Tale*. In the Meiji era, however, the original story came to the fore once again. The modernization of Japan and the efforts of the new government to establish their nation as equal in cultural achievement to the European countries led to a rediscovery of the Japanese classics and the establishment of a literary canon in which Murasaki's *Tale of Genji* featured prominently. Parodies and updatings gradually disappeared, and by the late Meiji era, prints illustrating the story presented historically accurate scenes of Heian-period life done in a new, semi-Westernized style, as, for example, in a series by Ogata Gekkō (1859–1920) published in 1892.

Toward the end of the Meiji era, in the first decade of the twentieth century, ukiyo-e prints ceased to be the primary medium for popular visual culture, replaced by new media such as photography and lithography, and new formats such as illustrated magazines and picture postcards. Included in this book are selections from two sets of late Meiji postcards depicting the chapters of Genji: an anonymous set that includes the Genji mon of the incense game, poems, and small pictures, in much the same way as the old Genji playing cards (see 14C, 26B); and a set by Kajita Hanko (1870–1917), a prominent illustrator of contemporary fiction, who reimagined scenes from the *Tale* in a pared-down, modern style (see 15B, 48B). A similar reimagining can be seen in the woodblock illustrations designed by Nakazawa Hiromitsu (1874–1964) for the first translation of Genji into modern Japanese, by the celebrated woman poet Yosano Akiko (1878–1942), which appeared in two volumes in 1912 and 1913, the end of the Meiji era and the beginning of the Taishō era.

Parodies, Updatings, and Other Humorous Takes on *The Tale of Genji*

Prior to the Edo period, illustrations of classical literature including *The Tale of Genji* were almost always serious in tone, a completely understandable situation given the two social groups that were the patrons of such art: the kuge (imperial nobility) who saw it as their own precious heritage, and the buke (warrior clans) who wanted to present themselves as equally cultured. The Edo-period commoners who created the Floating World and its visual arts had a more complicated relationship to the classics and felt free to experiment with humorous approaches as well as traditional ones. In my opinion, they were not so much mocking the high culture as claiming it for their own, subject to the same carefree attitude they prized within their own culture. In the case of works such as Genji that were strongly associated with the imperial court, for commoners to identify with the characters might also have carried a hint of resistance to the rule of the warrior class, a sentiment that could never be expressed openly.

The kinds of humor often seen in Edo-period visual references to the classical high culture are referred to by modern scholars under the blanket term mitate, loosely translated as parody. But within this broad category, several very different kinds of humor can be found. The common thread is the establishment of a link of some kind between the classical past and the fashionable present, sometimes understood as a contrast between the elegant high culture (ga) and the vulgar low culture (zoku). Such comparisons may take the form of a detailed reenactment of a scene from an original story, or more loosely, a modern scene that is related to the classical one only through a vague similarity of theme, perhaps a modern illustration of the sentiments expressed in a classical poem. From the late eighteenth century on, a second kind of humorous reinterpretation of the classics appears, in which a theme such as the chapters of *The Tale of Genji* is incongruously matched with completely different stories, related to each other by a visual similarity or a play on words.

Alfred Haft has argued persuasively that these different types of humor can be distinguished by the terminology of their titles, which use words such as fūryū (stylish, elegant), yatsushi (disguised, informally presented), or, later, mitate (selected, matching), although the issue is confused by the fact that other words are also used for the same kinds of prints. The term yatsushi is especially interesting since it is related to a kabuki plot device in which a hero of high birth disguises himself as an urban commoner. The idea that historical or literary heroes might become denizens of the Floating World — as opposed to modern people superficially taking on the appearance of such heroes — may have been a bit too subversive for comfort when expressed visually in prints, since yatsushi went out of use and was replaced by mitate.

Although the first printed Genji pictures are book illustrations in a very traditional style, the earliest known single-sheet Genji print is a parodic work of the 1680s in the Tokyo National Museum, unsigned but attributed to Moronobu's contemporary Sugimura Jihei (active about 1681–1703). It is an updated version of the famous cat incident in chapter 34, Young Shoots Part 1 (Wakana I), with the characters dressed in contemporary clothing. This particular scene would have been recognizable even in parody form because it was one of the few episodes from Genji that appeared in kabuki, as a scene inserted into other plays.

Okumura Masanobu, already mentioned for his traditional Genji illustrations, also created at least two witty parody series in the 1710s, uncolored monochrome prints showing modern versions of scenes from various chapters — identified by titles, since they might otherwise have been hard to identify (see 6B). The most gorgeous of his many Genji pictures is a hand-painted print of the 1740s, a modern version of the boating scene in chapter 51, A Drifting Boat (Ukifune), that shows a contemporary couple (either an actor and a courtesan, or possibly two actors, one of whom is dressed as a courtesan) enjoying a boat ride in moonlight. The scene has so few visual links to the original version that it is clearly identifiable only because of the title written on the print itself, together with the lyrics of a suggestive song (see 51D).

The first artist to design ukiyo-e prints that were printed in full color, Suzuki Harunobu (died 1770), drew numerous parodies showing scenes from classical literature acted out by attractive young people of his own time. Unlike Masanobu's works, which are identified by titles included in the design of each print, Harunobu's prints are often untitled, suggesting that his intended audience was sufficiently well educated to recognize the visual allusions even without verbal clues. Some of the ideas for the parodies may in fact have come from his patrons, the wealthy amateur poets who financed the development of full-color printing. Harunobu's version of the meeting of Genji and Yūgao in chapter 4 is a typical example: the modern young couple interact in person rather than through servants, and Genji's carriage is represented by a bamboo insect cage in the shape of a carriage, held by a boy servant (see 4B).

When Harunobu died suddenly in 1770, Isoda Koryūsai (1735–1790) became the leading designer of prints of fashionable beauties. Unusually for an ukiyo-e artist, Koryūsai was a member of the samurai class; he used his elite education in combination with a trendy desire for novelty in print-publishing to create prints featuring witty allusions to the classics. His series *Genji in Fashionable Modern Guise* (*Fūryū yatsushi Genji*) presents attractive young people in modern clothing, in situations vaguely suggested by the chapter title poems inscribed above (see 28B, 36B, 44B).

A double parody is the basis for two series whose main subject is contemporary beauties, one from the late 1790s by Chōbunsai Eishi (1756–1829) — also born into the samurai class and well educated in classical literature — and one from the mid-1810s by Kikukawa Eizan, both entitled *Eight Views of Genji* (*Genji hakkei*). The Eight Views theme, originally referring to "Eight Views of the Xiao and Xiang Rivers" as depicted in Chinese ink landscape paintings with accompanying poems, became a much-parodied subject in ukiyo-e prints. Here, the eight different themes that make up the Eight Views (sailboats returning to harbor, clearing weather after a storm, and so on) are applied to appropriate scenes selected from *The Tale of Genji*. But the Genji landscapes, shown in small insets next to the titles, are not the main subject; they are merely the second layer of literary allusion, and the real subject is the fashionable contemporary women whose poses and accessories are only vaguely associated with either Genji or Chinese painting (see 11B, 12B).

Perhaps the most beautiful of all of the Genji parodies is the elegant set of triptychs by Eishi, featuring the elongated figures typical of the 1790s (see 7B, 18B, 33B, 34B). The title, *Genji in Fashionable Modern Guise* (*Fūryū yatsushi Genji*), suggests the pleasures that Prince Genji might enjoy if he was magically transported into the Edo period. In each triptych, a single male figure in Heian-period clothing is surrounded by women in high-fashion modern outfits, in situations that suggest the plot of the original *Tale* but do not follow it exactly. To heighten the effect of subdued elegance, the series uses a deliberately limited color scheme consisting primarily of grays and purples that was fashionable at the time; the same unusual coloring is seen in Toyokuni I's series of small traditional illustrations done just a few years later in about 1800.

In the nineteenth century, the trend in Genji pictures shifted from fashionable updatings to humorous matches, often based on puns or other wordplay rather than on plot elements. Kikukawa Eizan, the designer of one of the *Eight Views of Genji* series, also created a slightly later series, made in the late 1810s or early 1820s, of close-up images of beautiful young women matched with Genji chapters indicated by small inset pictures of Genji poem cards (see 20B). A similar idea was used by Hiroshige for his series *Famous Places in Edo and Murasaki's Genji* (*Edo Murasaki meisho Genji*), which shows well-dressed women at Edo

12B | (detail)

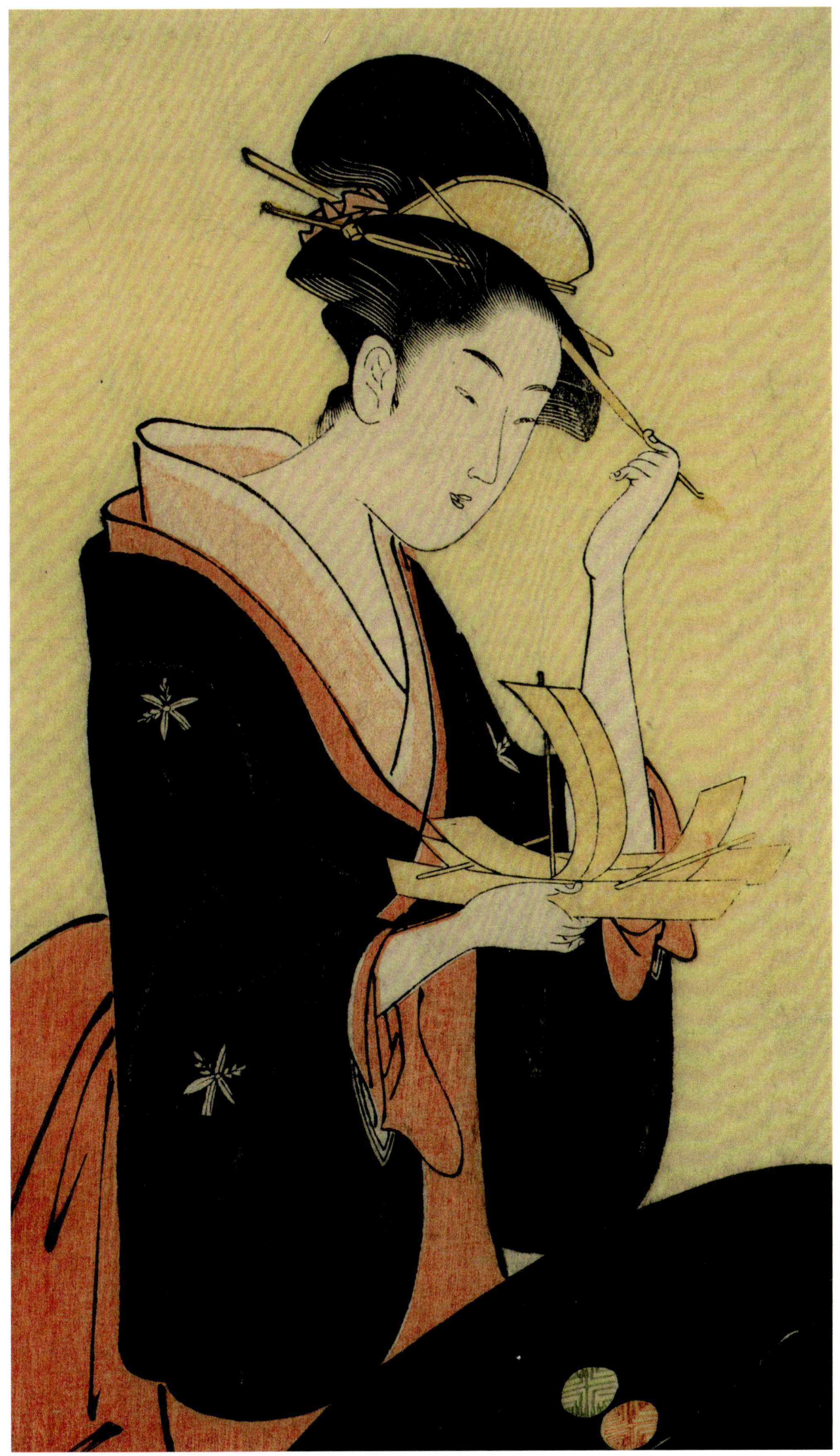

locations loosely correlated with Genji chapter titles, such as the famous plum garden at Kameido for the chapter A Branch of Plum (Umegae) (see 32B). This series was published in the mid-1840s, at about the same time as Kunisada's *Genji Incense* series and probably for the same reason: appealing to the many fans of the now-unavailable book *Inaka Genji* through references to the original *Tale of Genji* that the banned bestseller had parodied. The title panel of Hiroshige's series includes a drawing of a clamshell to suggest the courtly shell-matching game, but the text is a description of the place depicted rather than anything to do with Genji.

The most successful of these series matching unrelated subjects to the Genji chapters through far-fetched correspondences was the one designed by Kuniyoshi, also in the mid-1840s (see 24B, 41C, 52B). This series catered to the clandestine desires of print buyers in two ways: the upper register showing a miniature scroll with the chapter title poem and a small picture for each chapter, though ostensibly an educational reference to the original *Tale of Genji*, implicitly referred to *Inaka Genji* as well; while the main images below, though presented as historical scenes, were drawn mainly from the kabuki theater in response to the ban on actor prints that was part of the Tenpō Reform regulations. This formula was so successful that it was repeated in 1863–64, long after the reform movement had faded away, by Kuniyoshi's pupil Yoshiiku in his series *Modern Parodies of Genji* (*Imayō nazorae Genji*), with a new selection of matching scenes and accordion-fold booklets rather than scrolls depicted in the upper register (see 31B, 43C, 45B, 53C).

Toyohara Kunichika (1835–1900), one of the many artists turning out *Inaka Genji* triptychs during the 1850s and 1860s, also did a complete series of modern scenes matched with the chapters of Genji in 1884–85, possibly the last Genji mitate series. In the punning title *Fifty-Four Chapters in Modern Times* (*Genji gojūyojō*), the first word is pronounced "Genji" but is written

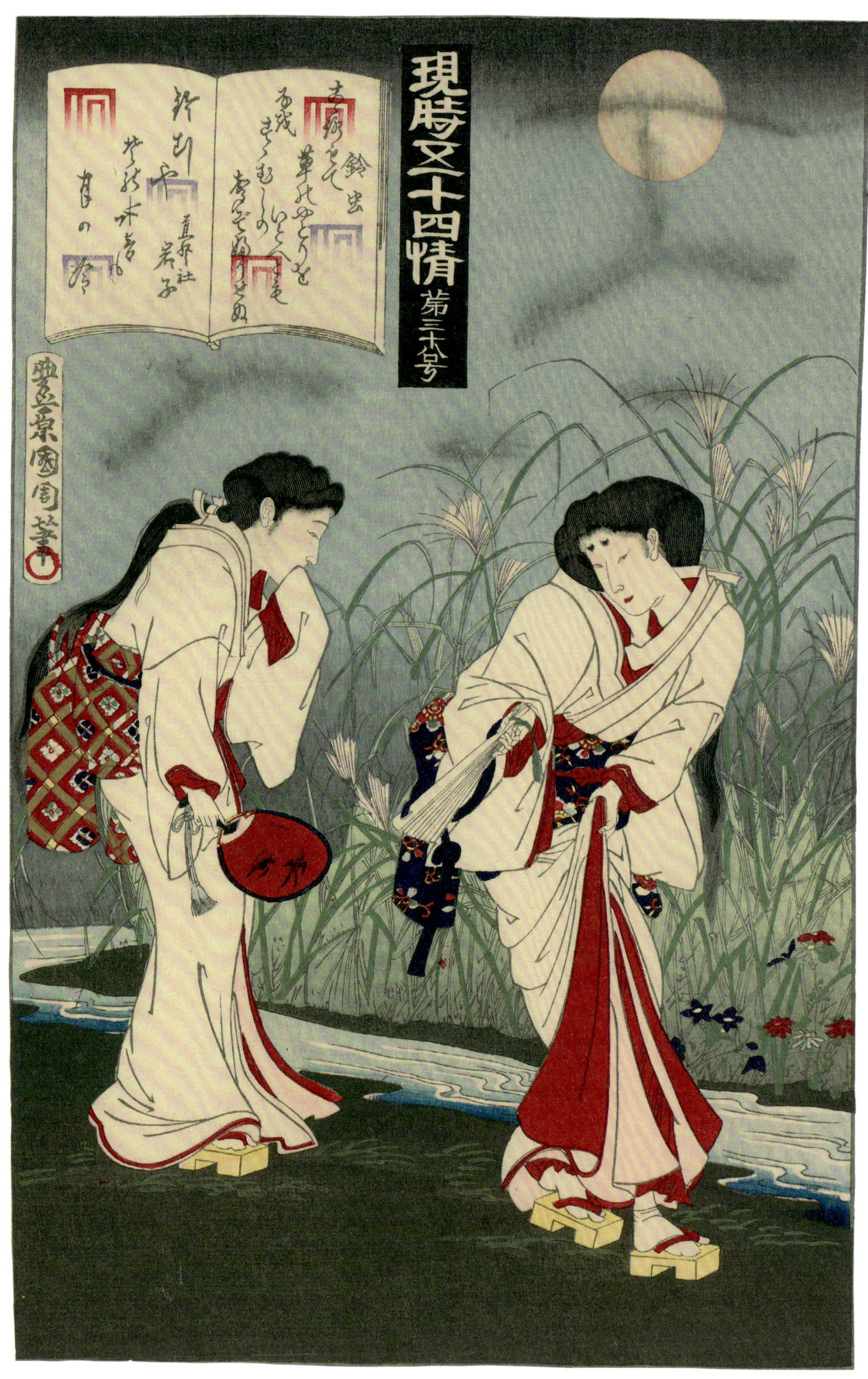

FIG. 8 | Toyohara Kunichika (1835–1900), *Suzumushi* from the series *Fifty-Four Chapters in Modern Times,* 1884

with characters meaning "modern times" (fig. 8). In many of the designs for this series, Kunichika catered to the current interest in scenes alleged to represent the actual court of the Meiji emperor. The modern women who stand in for Genji's paramours are ladies-in-waiting at the Meiji imperial court, wearing traditional court makeup with eyebrows painted high on the forehead, and a hairstyle that includes a long ponytail suggesting the floor-length hair of Heian women. This kind of subject matter would have been illegal during the Edo period, when depictions of the real upper class (even artists' imaginary conceptions) were strictly banned; the gorgeous *Inaka Genji* triptychs of the late Edo period had responded to public desire for such images by showing fictional nobility in an earlier historical period.

Prints of *Inaka Genji*

While *The Tale of Genji* dealt with the private lives of imperial courtiers, with attention to realistic emotional detail, *Inaka Genji* is not so much a meditation on life as a fast-moving page-turner that combines violent thriller-style action with romantic intrigue in a historical setting, all in the context of a clever parody of the great classic. Three very different periods of Japanese history are combined in *Inaka Genji*. Though based on a work of the early eleventh century, the story is ostensibly set in the late fifteenth century, at the court of the Ashikaga line of shoguns during the Muromachi period (1336–1573); yet the manners and customs depicted in Kunisada's illustrations are the contemporary ones of the Edo period, albeit with a fantastic touch justified by the quasi-historical setting.

The Muromachi-period setting was a standard device used in many Edo-period works of popular fiction and drama as a way of circumventing censorship regulations that banned any mention of upper-class persons who lived after 1573 (the time when the ruling Tokugawa line of shoguns began their rise to power). It was especially suitable for a Genji parody, since during the fifteenth century both the imperial court and the court of the Ashikaga shoguns were located in the ancient capital city of Kyoto. Thus the adventures of the hero Mitsuuji, the younger son of a shogun, could take place in many of the same locations as the activities of his prototype Prince Genji, the younger son of an emperor. Despite the humorous title that Tanehiko gave his story, Mitsuuji is anything but rustic; yet the historical displacement and the Kyoto setting served to deflect suspicions that the author-artist team were depicting the contemporary shogunal court in Edo.

The *Inaka Genji* story, published a chapter at a time with several chapters appearing each year, had covered the events of thirty out of the fifty-four chapters that make up the original *Tale of Genji* when it came to an abrupt halt in 1842. In the end the false historical setting was not enough to avert censorship, and the book was banned as part of a widespread crackdown on popular publishing included in the Tenpō Reforms. No official reason was given, but contributing factors may have been the possible interpretation of the lavish lifestyle depicted in the book as a criticism of the actual shogunate; the existence of two under-the-counter, technically illegal erotic books by the very same author-artist team (under transparent pseudonyms) that presented explicit scenes of Mitsuuji and his lovers omitted from the main book; and embarrassment over the fact that Tanehiko, himself a member of the ruling samurai class, had sunk so low as to write a popular bestseller. The unfortunate Tanehiko died mysteriously and is widely believed to have committed suicide under orders from the head of his clan.

By 1847, five years after the initial banning of *Inaka Genji*, the reform movement had died down and the regulations were being loosened or quietly ignored. At this point the story of Mitsuuji and his many ladies was continued in the form of a sequel, *A Related Rustic Image (Sono yukari hina no omokage)*, though with the hero's name prudently changed to Terumoto; this book continued to be published in serial form, in twenty-three chapters, until 1862. In 1850, however, there was apparently a rift of some sort in the publishing world, since two more sequels began to appear from competing publishers. *Ashikaga Robes Hand-dyed in Purple (Ashikaga-ginu tezome no Murasaki)* — sixteen chapters published serially from 1850 to 1861 — began at the same point in the story as chapter 6 of *Rustic Image* but took the plot in a different direction; while *Pale Purple Dawn at Uji* (*Usumurasaki Uji no akebono*) — eight chapters published serially from 1850 to 1856 — skipped ahead to the last part of the original *Tale of Genji*. To confuse the issue even further, in 1851 a fourth sequel appeared, the short-lived *A Purple Story in Edo Tie-dyeing* (*Edo kanoko Murasaki-zōshi)*, with only a single known chapter. Although all four of these books were issued by different publishers, all of them were illustrated by Kunisada, at least initially, with his pupils in some cases taking over the later chapters.

During the 1830s, when Tanehiko's *Inaka Genji* was being published chapter by chapter, Kunisada concentrated on designing the illustrations for the book itself, often based on sketches by the author. At this time he designed only a few color prints based on the story, the earliest of which seems to have been a triptych showing characters from chapter 6 of *Inaka Genji* (equivalent to chapter 5 of *The Tale of Genji*) posed against a landscape background (see 5D). A series of fifteen known designs from the late 1830s also depicts *Inaka Genji* characters, while four prints made in about 1839–40 reproduce paintings donated to the Kameido Shrine near Kunisada's home (three of the original paintings, showing scenes of the four seasons, are now in the collection of the Museum of Fine Arts, Boston).

In the early 1840s, as noted above, Kunisada and other artists turned to color print illustrations of the original *Tale of Genji* (or at least works that referred to it, such as Kuniyoshi's mitate series), probably in an attempt to satisfy popular demand for Genji material of some kind after the banning of *Inaka Genji*. After 1847, however, the return of the story in the form of sequels by other authors was accompanied by a flood of color woodblock prints by Kunisada and other designers. About 1,300 such prints are known, about half of them designed by Kunisada himself. In fact, there are enough of these works to constitute an identifiable subgenre in ukiyo-e prints of the 1850s and 1860s. The popularity of the frequently reprinted books and the prints illustrating them was so great that for many readers, the parody eclipsed the original work; to them, Genji meant Tanehiko's Mitsuuji rather than Murasaki's Shining Prince. The fame of the story was spread even further when parts of it were dramatized for the kabuki stage, first in 1838, again in 1851, and later (see 4D, 4E, 7D).

In addition to numerous color print triptychs, Kunisada designed three complete, or almost complete, *Inaka Genji* series with one print for each of the fifty-four chapters of the original *Tale*. In chronological order, they are: the horizontal ōban series *Magic Lantern Slides of That Romantic Purple Figure* (*Sono sugata yukari no utsushi-e*), published in 1850–52; the vertical chūban series reproduced in this book, *The Color Print Contest of a Modern Genji* (*Ima Genji nishiki-e awase*), published in 1852–54 with many reprints indicating its popularity; and a beautifully printed, deluxe series of vertical ōban diptychs based in part on the color cover designs of the *Inaka Genji* books, *Lingering Sentiments of a Late Collection of Genji* (*Genji goshū yojō*; a pun on "Fifty-Four Chapters of the Tale of Genji"), jointly issued by several publishers from 1857 to 1861 (fig. 9).

All three of these series faced the same problem in correlating the fifty-four chapters of Murasaki's *Tale of Genji* to the thirty-eight chapters of Tanehiko's *Inaka Genji*, plus its sequels. Because Tanehiko introduced new plot elements in addition to his parody of the original story, additional chapters are needed, so that the thirty-eight chapters published during his lifetime correspond to only thirty chapters of the original story. The sequels issued by competing publishers confuse the situation even further, since some of

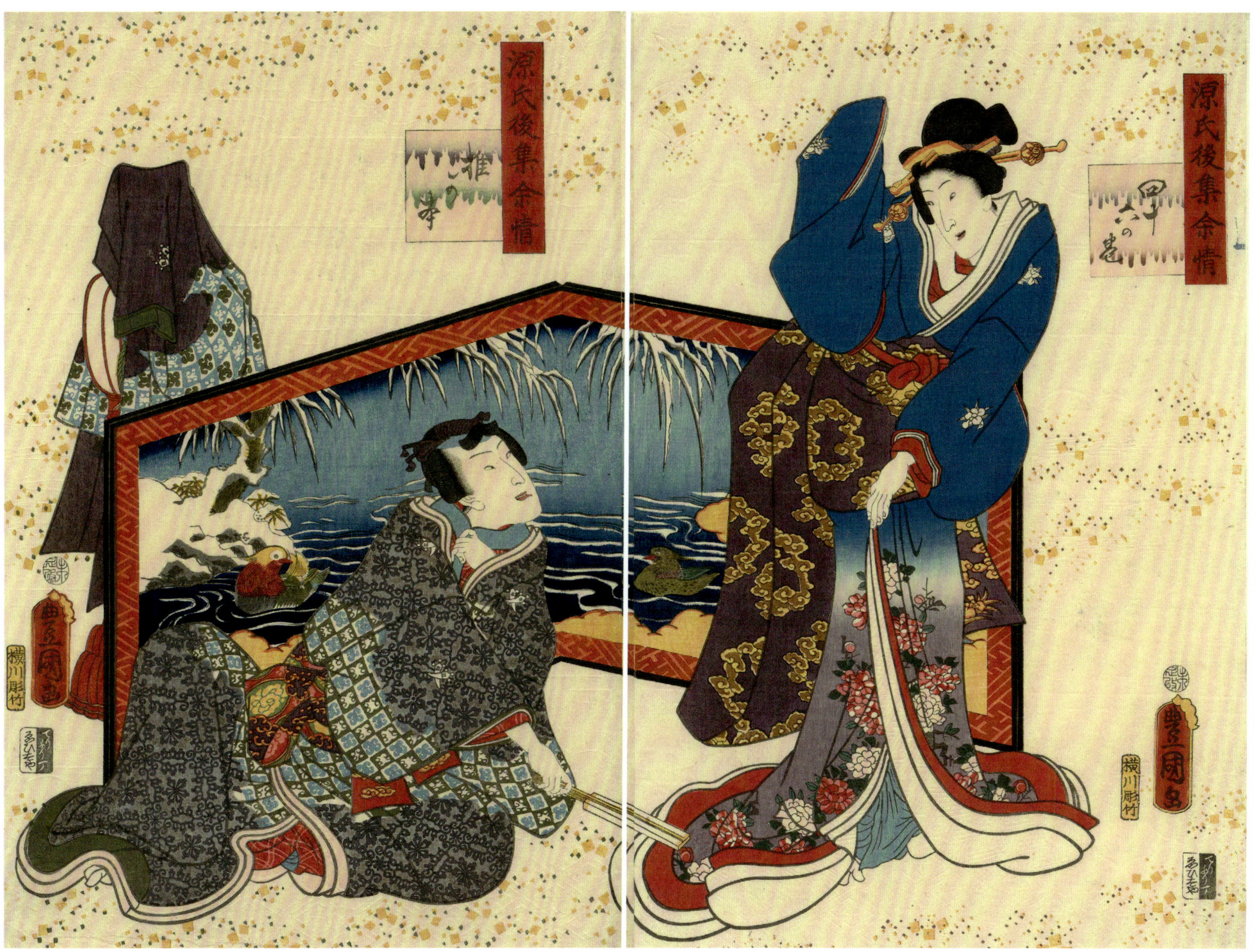

FIG. 9 | Kunisada, *Shiigamoto* from the series *Lingering Sentiments of a Late Collection of Genji,* 1859

them cover the same material in different ways, and none of them cover all of the chapters of the original. For the horizontal ōban series, Kunisada simply produced color versions of scenes from *Inaka Genji* and the first of its sequels, *A Related Rustic Image*, more or less in chronological order. In the vertical ōban diptych series, confusingly, he added the chapter titles from the original *Tale* but matched them with the chapter numbers from *Inaka Genji* (continuing with the chapter numbers from the first sequel, *A Related Rustic Image*, from number 39 on). Only thirty-seven diptychs out of a possible fifty-four are known (scattered from number 1 to number 51), together with a title sheet showing Murasaki at her writing desk, and it is possible that the series was never quite finished.

The Color Print Contest of a Modern Genji does not have the series title written on the individual prints. It is known from a title page for the series published in the online database of the Art Research Center (ARC) at Ritsumeikan University, together with a preface by Ryūtei Senka (1806–1868), the author of chapters 12–14 of *A Related Rustic Image* as well as chapters 6–15 of *Ashikaga Robes* and chapters 7–8 of *Pale Purple Dawn*. Many of the prints are known in three different states, indicating that the series was so popular that it went through several editions: one with a red rectangle containing the chapter title alone, one with a red rectangle containing the chapter title and its number added after the title, and one with the number in a yellow circle.

In addition to the red rectangle containing the chapter title and possibly the number on each print, there is also a larger rectangle decorated with yellow flecks suggesting the sprinkled metallic flakes traditionally used on paper for fine calligraphy (seen also on some of the *Inaka Genji* book covers and in the backgrounds of the later diptych series), each with a kyōka poem related to the content of the chapter. The composition of kyōka poems, a light-hearted version of classical five-line waka poems, was a favorite hobby of Edo-period intellectuals and was strongly associated with the production of surimono, privately commissioned prints that often featured especially lavish printing techniques (see fig. 7 and 14B, 17B, 22B, 25B, 51B). I have not attempted, at this stage, to translate the poems or identify the pseudonymous poets, but further research in this area will no doubt shed light on the circumstances of the publication of the series. Although it is clearly a commercial series, and a very successful one, the high quality of the printing is reminiscent of surimono; perhaps some private funding, as well as commercial investment, was involved in its production.

Unlike the other two chapter-by-chapter series by Kunisada, *The Color Print Contest* series does follow the order of events in Murasaki's *Tale of Genji*, matching each named chapter with equivalent events in the *Inaka Genji* version of the story. In addition to designs based on *Inaka Genji* and *A Related Rustic Image*, it includes a few images derived from *Ashikaga Robes* (chapter 37) and *Pale Purple Dawn* (chapters 40 and 51). The fourth sequel, *A Purple Story*, does not seem to have been used for the color prints, but more in-depth research on the sources of the designs for the *Color Print Contest* series may turn up unsuspected connections. The care with which Kunisada selected the illustrations to match the subjects of the original Genji chapters shows the level of attention he had already paid to the classical work while designing his earlier, serious illustrations, including the *Genji Incense* series and the 1830s triptych series.

Two more complete series of *Inaka Genji* pictures in fifty-four chapters were designed by Utagawa Kunisada II (1823–1880), the pupil who was allowed to use the Kunisada name after 1844, when Kunisada I took the name of his teacher. *Lady Murasaki's Genji Cards* (*Murasaki Shikibu Genji karuta*), published in 1857, refers in its title to the Genji poem card game but has a title cartouche on each print in the shape of the clamshells used for the predecessor of the card-matching game (see 16C, 26D, 28D, 30C, 31D, 36D, 37D, 39C, 54C). *Traces of Genji in Fifty-four Chapters* (*Omokage Genji gojūyojō*), published in 1864–65, was co-designed with Utagawa Hiroshige II (1826–1869), who had inherited the name of his teacher when Hiroshige I died in 1858 (see 40C, 47C, 50C). Both of these series take the same general approach to the selection of illustrations as Kunisada's *Color Print Contest*, picking scenes from the world of *Inaka Genji* that relate to the corresponding chapters of Murasaki's *Tale*.

The *Traces of Genji* series is, in a way, a combination of both the original *Tale* and the *Inaka Genji* story, since over a third of each print consists of a folding fan design by Hiroshige II, with the poem for that chapter and a small illustration. The prominence given here to the classical work hints at the trend in the late nineteenth century, when *Inaka Genji* fell out of favor, although the existence of Meiji-era reprints from Edo-period woodblocks suggests that the book still had loyal fans. New Genji pictures of the late nineteenth and early twentieth centuries were illustrations of the original *Tale of Genji*, now celebrated as a treasure of the nation.

Visions of Genji in Current Popular Culture

More recently, the kind of creative adaptation of the great classic that was practiced by Tanehiko and Kunisada, in a (very successful) effort to appeal to a contemporary audience, has begun to appear once again. In the second half of the twentieth century a number of manga (graphic novel) versions appeared, of which the most successful was *Fleeting Dreams* (*Asaki Yume Mishi*) by Yamato Waki (born 1948), published serially from 1979 to 1993. In keeping with its origins as a comic for teenage girls, Yamato's version presents the story in terms of sweet romances, while later manga versions emphasize more explicit sex scenes, particularly those by Maki Miyako (born 1935), aimed at adult women, and by Egawa Tatsuya (born 1961), intended for male readers. These additions to the original text are reminiscent of the technically illegal, underground erotic versions of *Inaka Genji* that may have been one reason for Tanehiko's sad fate.

From 1951 to 2020, there have been at least nine film versions of parts of *The Tale of Genji*, both live-action and animated, and at least nine television programs. Many of these works add new characters or plot elements to the story, just as Tanehiko did in *Inaka Genji*. An especially inventive example was the 2001 production *Love of a Thousand Years: The Tale of the Shining Genji* (*Sennen no koi: Hikaru Genji monogatari*), which included fantastic elements such as an underwater love scene and had Genji — who is repeatedly described by Murasaki as so pretty that he should have been a girl — played by a woman, a star in male roles from the famous Takarazuka all-female musical theater. The numerous stage productions based on parts of *The Tale of Genji* include a 1989 Takarazuka performance celebrating the troupe's seventy-fifth anniversary.

Perhaps the most unusual Genji-related production in the performing arts was the ice show "Hyōen 2019: Tsuki Akari no Gotoku" ("Drama on Ice 2019: Like the Moonlight"), which featured a cast of international figure-skating stars (including a blonde Russian as Murasaki) combined with popular singers (with a retired Takarazuka actress playing a cross-dressing pirate chief who falls in love with the shipwrecked Genji), and special lighting effects provided by the interdisciplinary art group Team Lab. The story of magic and court intrigue is only tenuously related to the original *Tale*, but Tanehiko and Kunisada would no doubt have enjoyed it immensely. Clearly *The Tale of Genji* is alive and well in the hearts of the Japanese public and continues to be a source of inspiration for many different art forms.

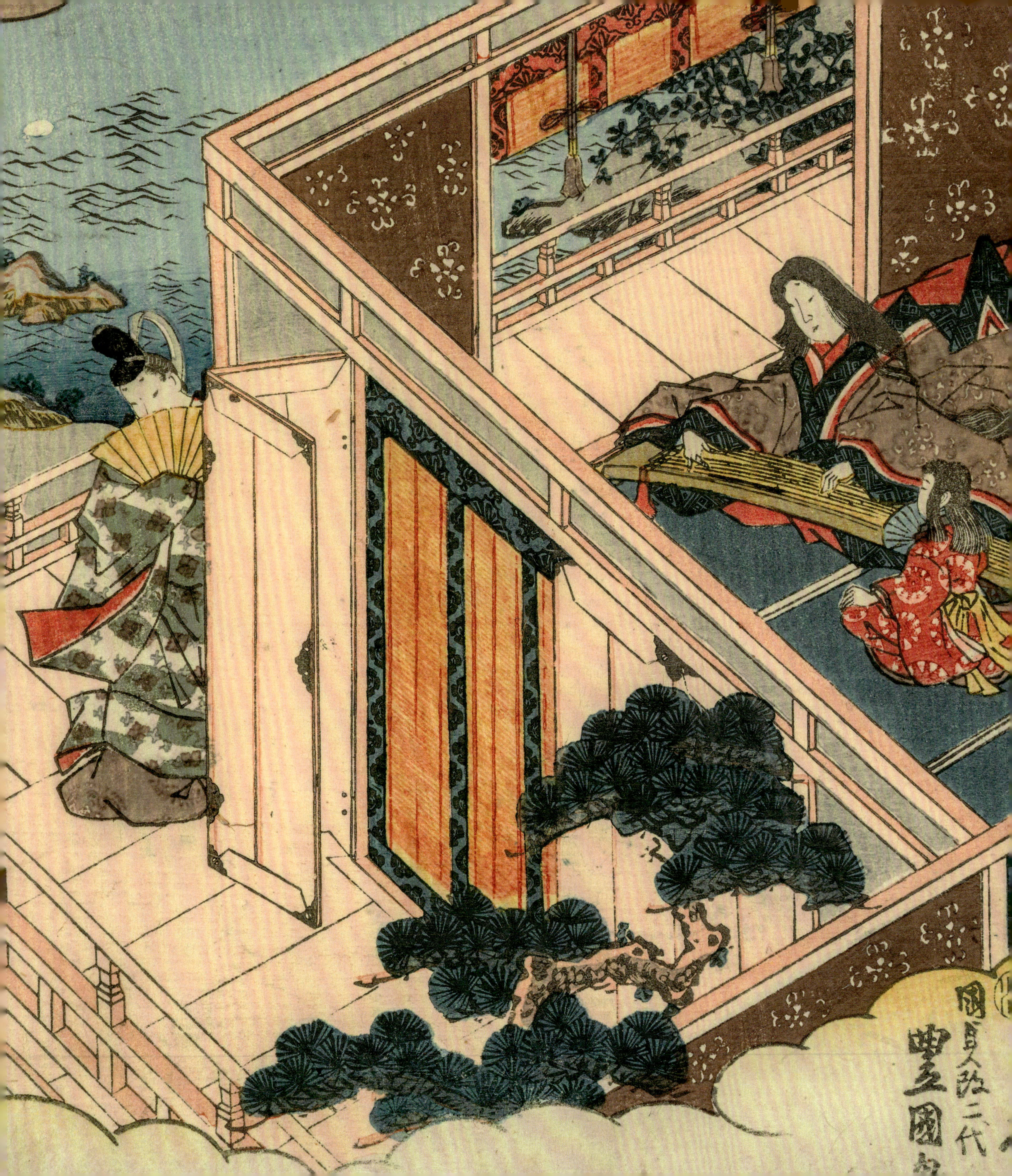
国貞改二代
豊国

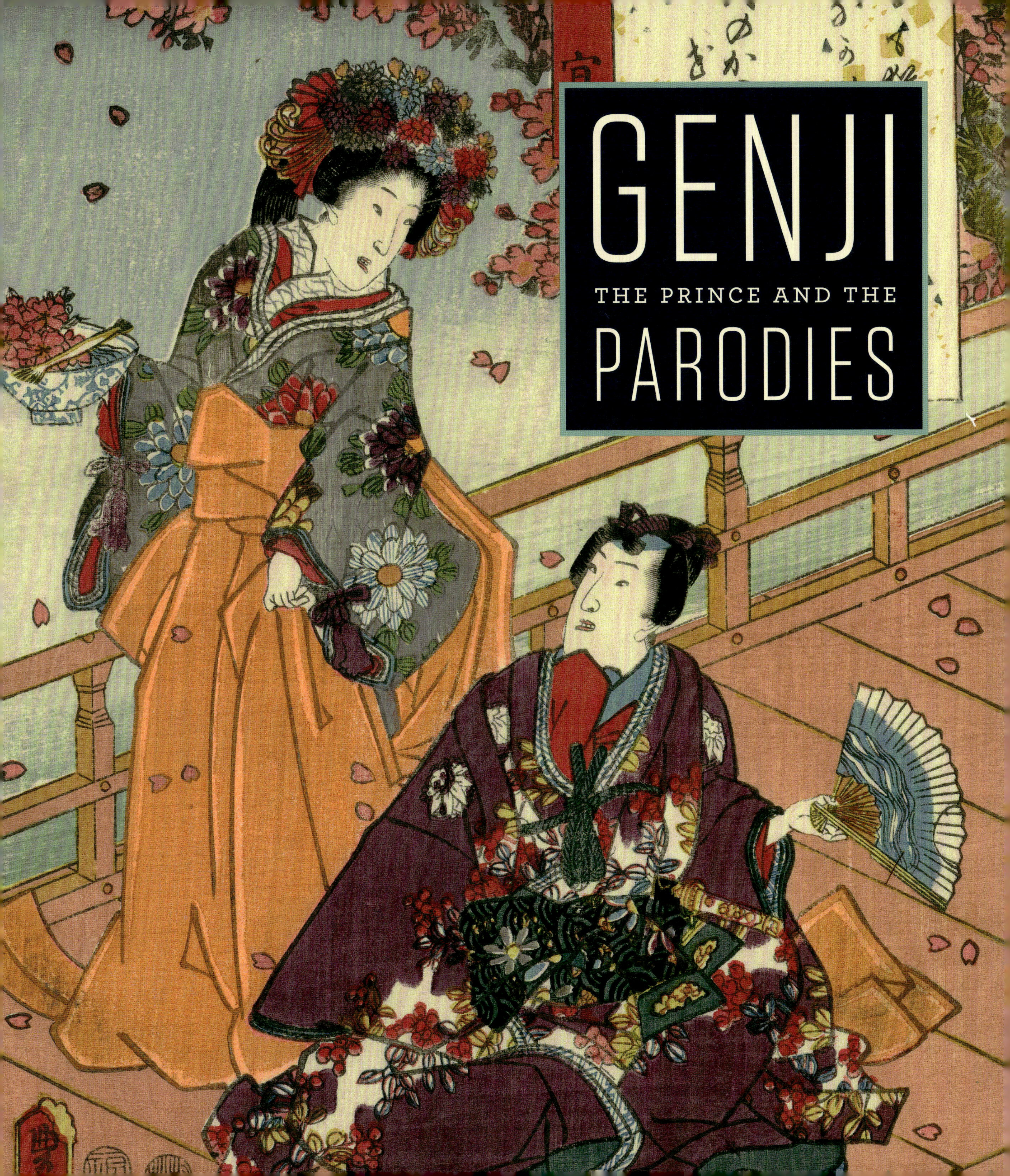
GENJI
THE PRINCE AND THE
PARODIES

1

The Paulownia Courtyard (Kiritsubo)

Prince Genji is a younger son of the emperor by the Lady of the Paulownia Courtyard (Kiritsubo), who is beautiful and accomplished but does not come from a politically powerful family. She is tormented by the other court ladies, who are jealous of the emperor's love for her, and she dies young. Little Genji is his father's favorite son, but because he lacks strong family backing, his father takes him out of the imperial succession and instead plans a career for him as a prominent courtier.

Kunisada's *Genji Incense* series introduces the reader to Genji at his coming-of-age ceremony at the age of twelve, seated among other courtiers as he waits to exchange his child's hairstyle for an adult's upswept hairdo and hat (1A). Genji's imperial father (seated on a curtained dais) and the Minister of the Left (bowing before him) exchange congratulatory poems and arrange a marriage for Genji with Aoi, the Minister's daughter (who is not present on this all-male occasion). Hiroshige shows instead the first presentation of the baby to his father, in his mother's rooms off the Paulownia Courtyard in the palace (1B). Both prints use the ancient convention of showing respect for an emperor — even a fictional one — by concealing his face behind hanging bamboo blinds.

Into that first knot
to bind up his boyish hair
did you tie the wish
that enduring happiness
be theirs through ages to come?

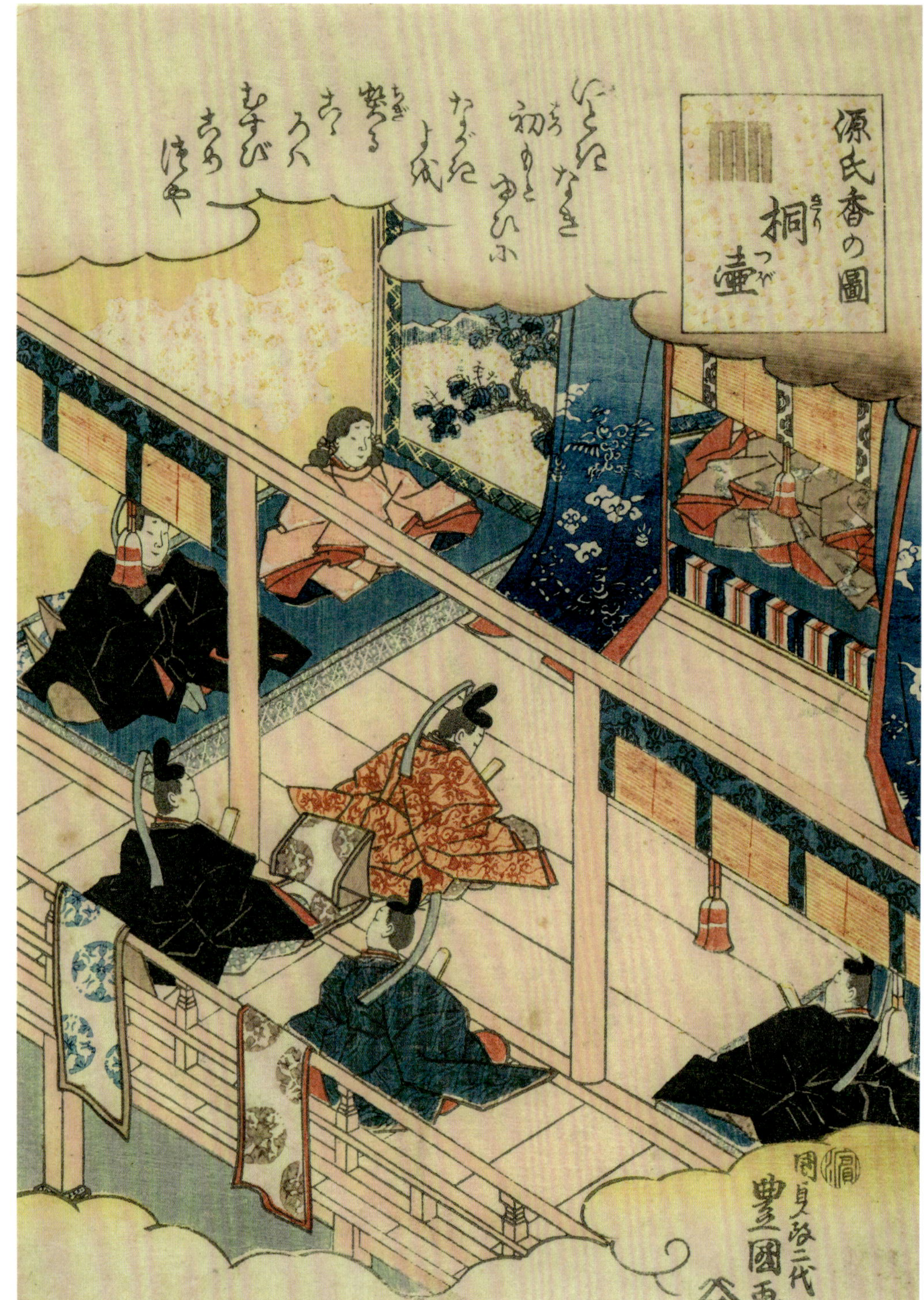

1A | Kunisada, *Genji Incense Pictures*, 1844–47

Mitsuuji, the hero of *Inaka Genji,* is also a younger son of a ruler — in this case, a fictionalized version of the real-life shogun Ashikaga Yoshimasa (1436–1490). His mother, Hanagiri (Paulownia Flower), is also the target of nasty practical jokes by jealous competitors, such as spreading smelly fish guts in the corridor she walks through each night to visit the shogun. Kunisada's illustration shows the lady's attendant trying to take away her soiled kimono and bring a replacement, stepping high to avoid the mess on the floor, which the artist tastefully refrains from showing (1C). The shogun identifies the culprit and forces her to change rooms with his beloved — and that very night, a mysterious assassin breaks in and kills the guilty woman, mistaking her for Hanagiri. This incident begins the complicated tale of courtly intrigue and deadly conflicts that is intertwined with the Genji parody.

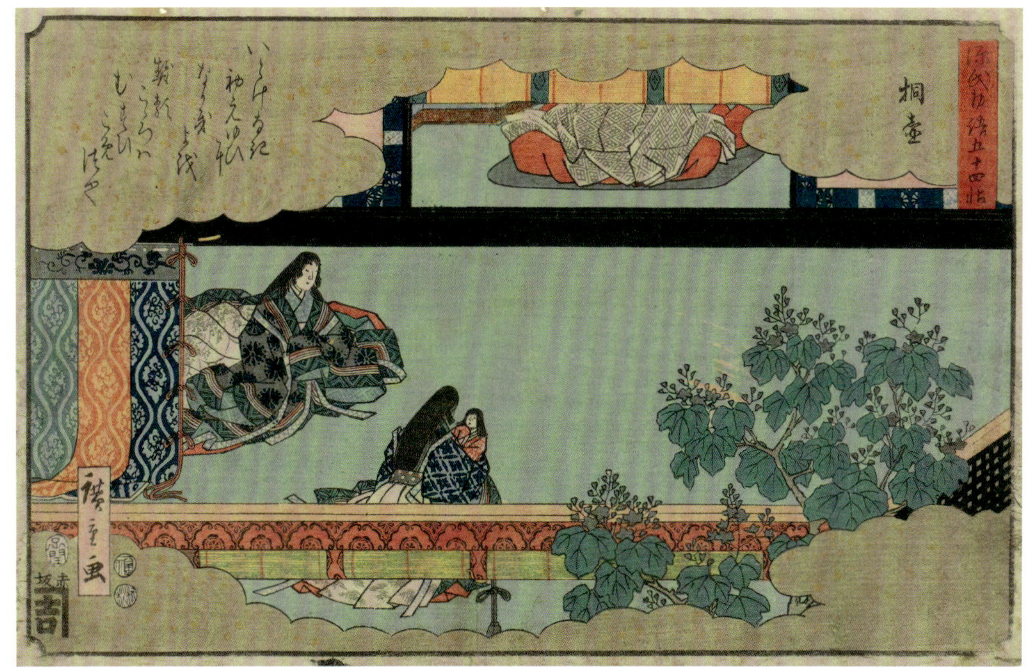

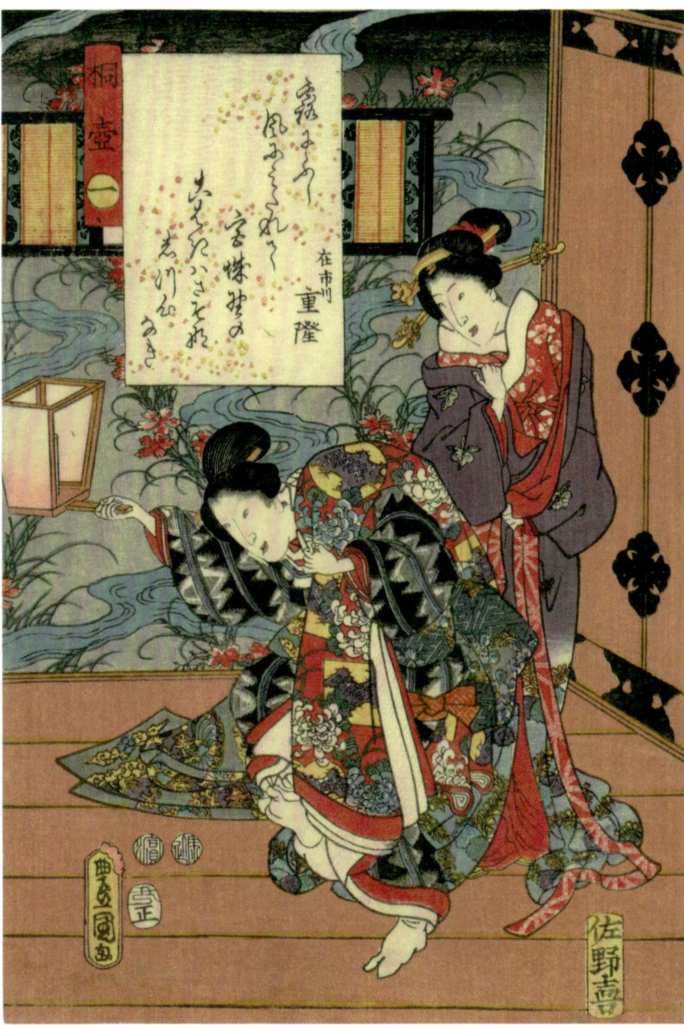

1B | Hiroshige, *The Fifty-Four Chapters of the Tale of Genji,* 1852

1C | Kunisada, *The Color Print Contest of a Modern Genji,* 1853

2

The Broom Tree (Hahakigi)

The most famous scene in this chapter is the comparison of women's qualities (shinasadame), also called the rainy-night discussion, when Genji, his brother-in-law Tō no Chūjō, and two other young male friends spend a rainy evening talking about real women they have known and ideal women that they imagine. Incidents and ideas from this conversation will echo throughout the book.

Kunisada's diptych of 1855 shows a gender-reversed parody: a group of courtesans take some time off to enjoy eating sushi and sipping sake, playing with the cat, trimming toenails, reading books and love letters, and of course talking about men (2B).

Soon afterward, Genji begins his first recorded extramarital affair, with a lady known as Utsusemi (Cicada Shell), the young wife of a provincial governor, whom he meets when he visits the house of her adult stepson. The *Genji Incense* series shows Genji eavesdropping on the women of the household, who excitedly discuss the handsome prince they think is asleep in the next room (2A). After one night of secret romance, Utsusemi has second thoughts

Stricken with regret
to have it known she was born
in a humble home,
the broom tree you briefly glimpsed
fades and is soon lost to view.

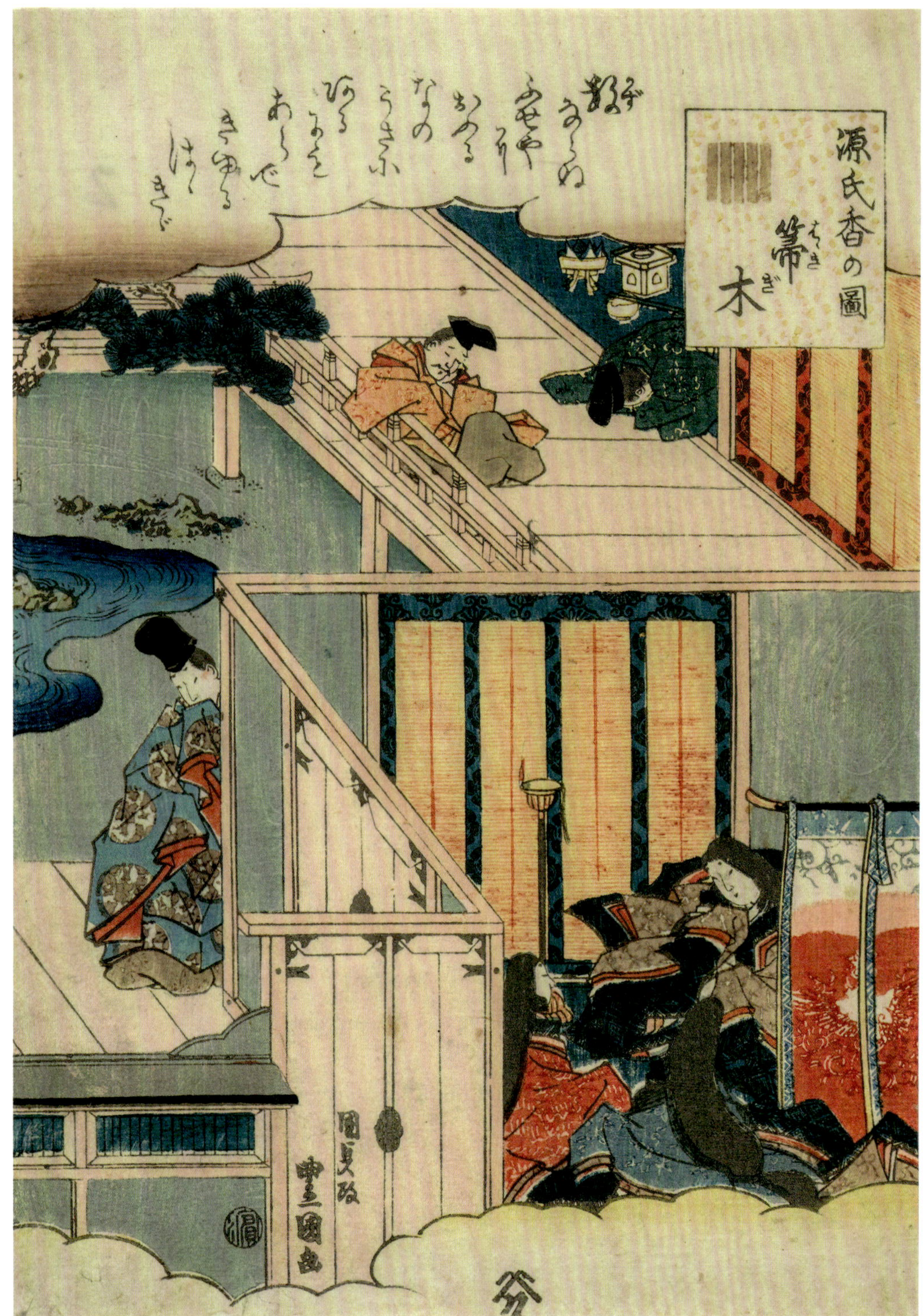

2A | Kunisada, *Genji Incense Pictures*, 1844–47

and is reluctant to continue the liaison. In a wistful exchange of poems, Genji compares her to a magical tree that disappears when one approaches it, the source of the chapter title.

In chapter 3 of *Inaka Genji*, the teenage Mitsuuji and his friends also discuss women on a rainy night. Kunisada illustrates the story-within-a-story told by Umanojō, who quarreled with his lover after a cherry-blossom-viewing party (2C). When he swatted her with a souvenir branch of blossoms, she defended herself by using a clothes-scenting rack — a piece of furniture resembling a large basket, which would be placed over an incense burner to perfume clothing draped on it.

Meanwhile, in order to foil the plots of the villain Yamana Sōzen (who has no equivalent in the original *Tale of Genji* and is loosely based on a historical samurai who rebelled against the Ashikaga shogunate), young Mitsuuji pretends to have an adulterous affair with the shogun's latest wife, Fuji no Kata, echoing the top-secret affair between the original Prince Genji and his stepmother Fujitsubo.

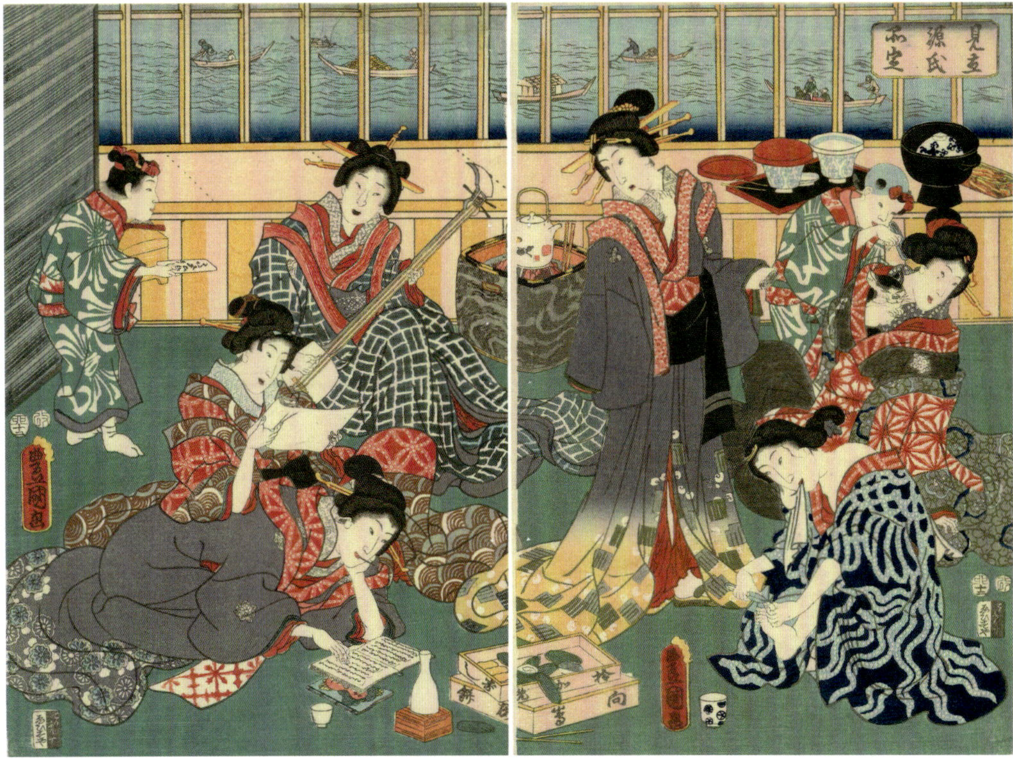

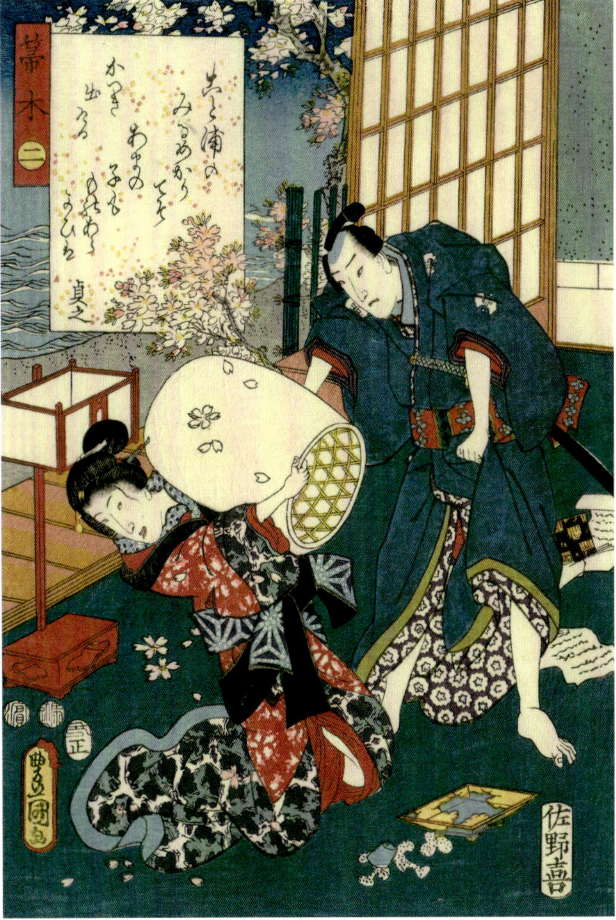

2B | Kunisada, *Parody of The Tale of Genji*, 1855

2C | Kunisada, *The Color Print Contest of a Modern Genji*, 1853

3

The Shell of the Cicada (Utsusemi)

The incident that gives Utsusemi her nickname Cicada Shell occurs in this chapter. Still hoping to continue their affair, Genji — accompanied by Utsusemi's little brother — spies on her as she plays a game of *go* with her attractive stepdaughter, who is close to her in age (3A). That night, when he comes to her room, she evades him by slipping out of her outer robe and leaving it behind, as shown in Hiroshige's design (3B). Genji spends the night with the stepdaughter instead, but he still yearns for Utsusemi and writes a poem comparing her empty robe to the discarded shell of a molting cicada.

Underneath this tree,
where the molting cicada
shed her empty shell,
my longing still goes to her,
for all I knew her to be.

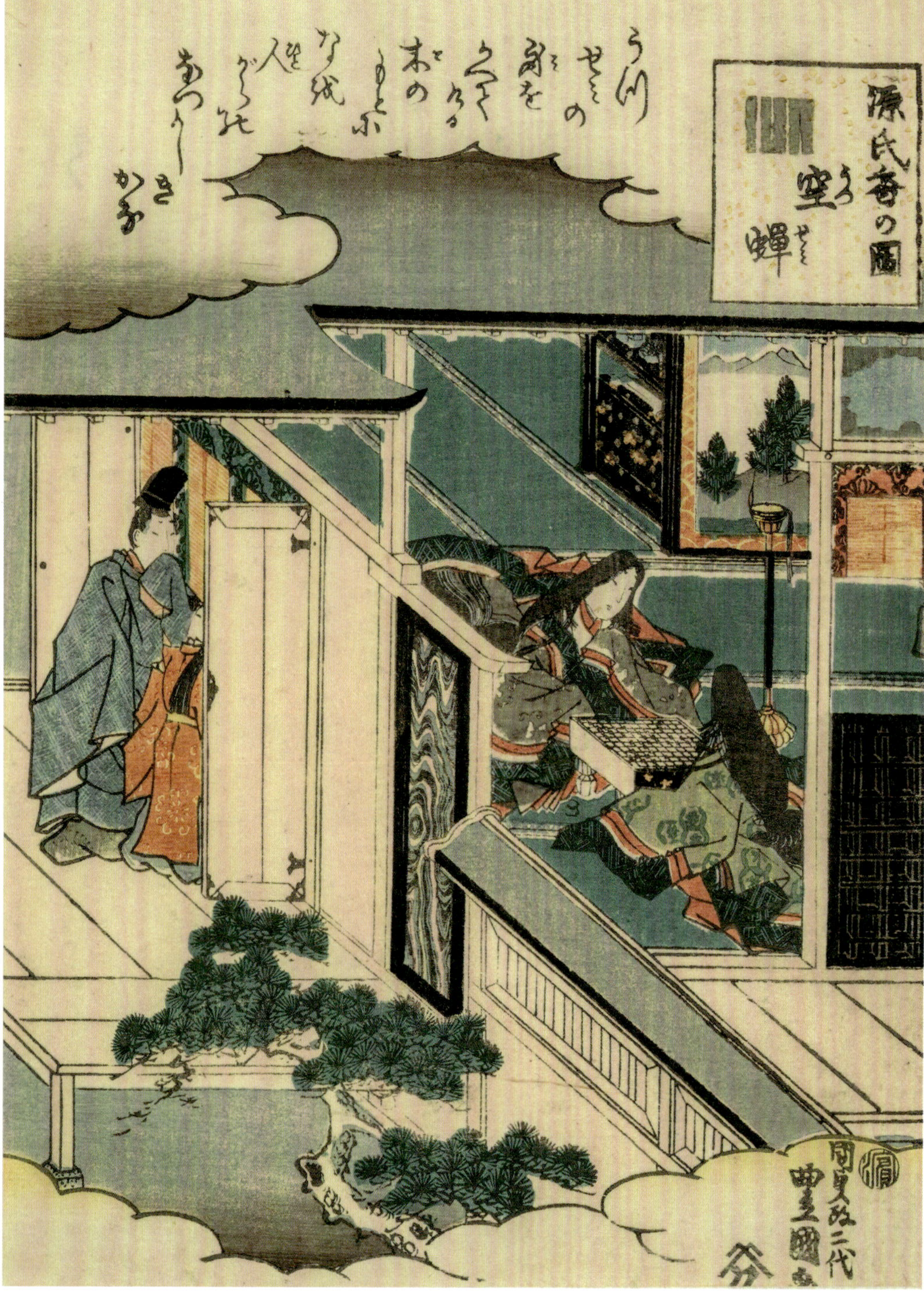

3A | Kunisada, *Genji Incense Pictures*, 1844–47

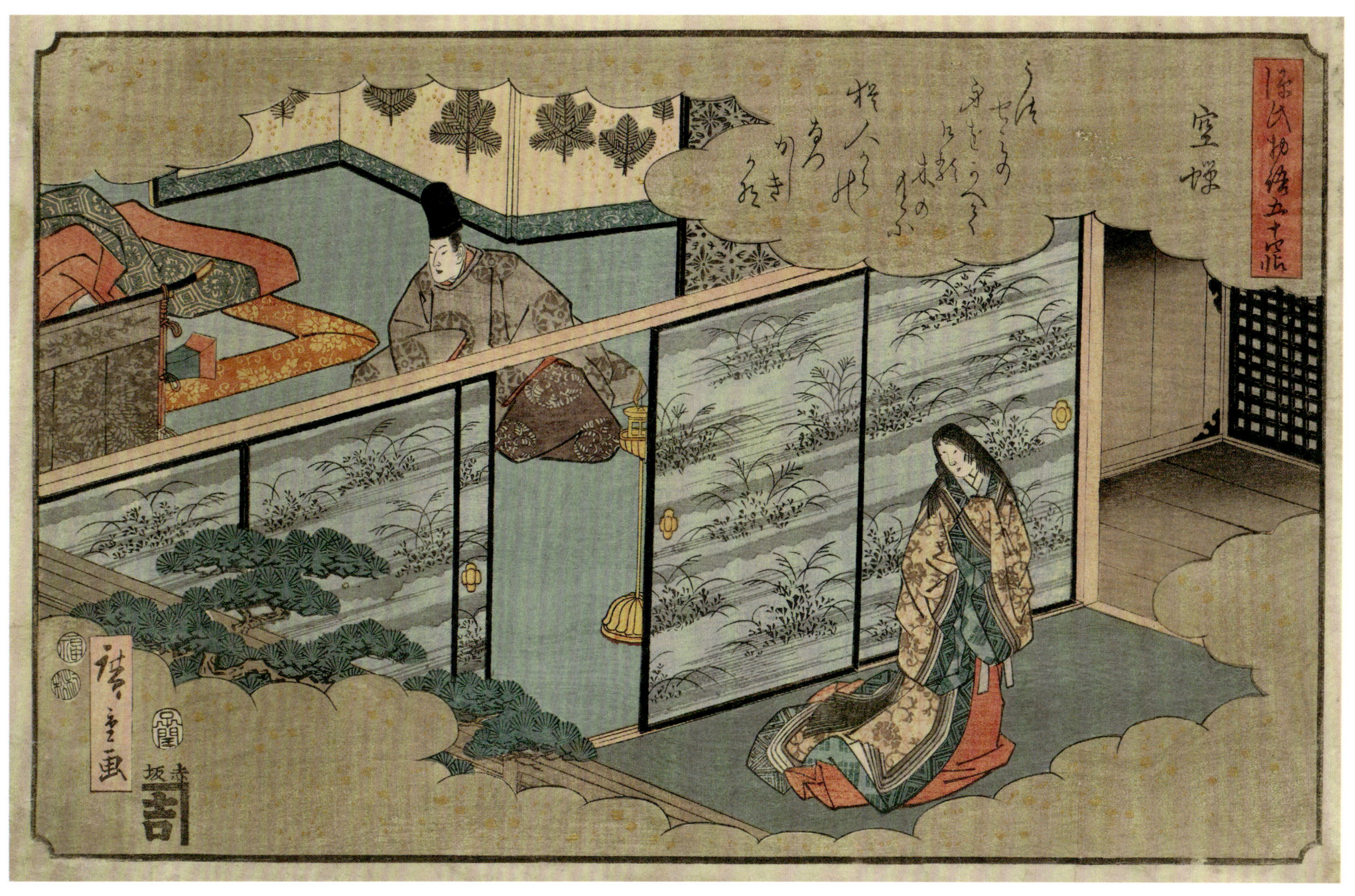

3B | Hiroshige, *The Fifty-Four Chapters of the Tale of Genji*, 1852

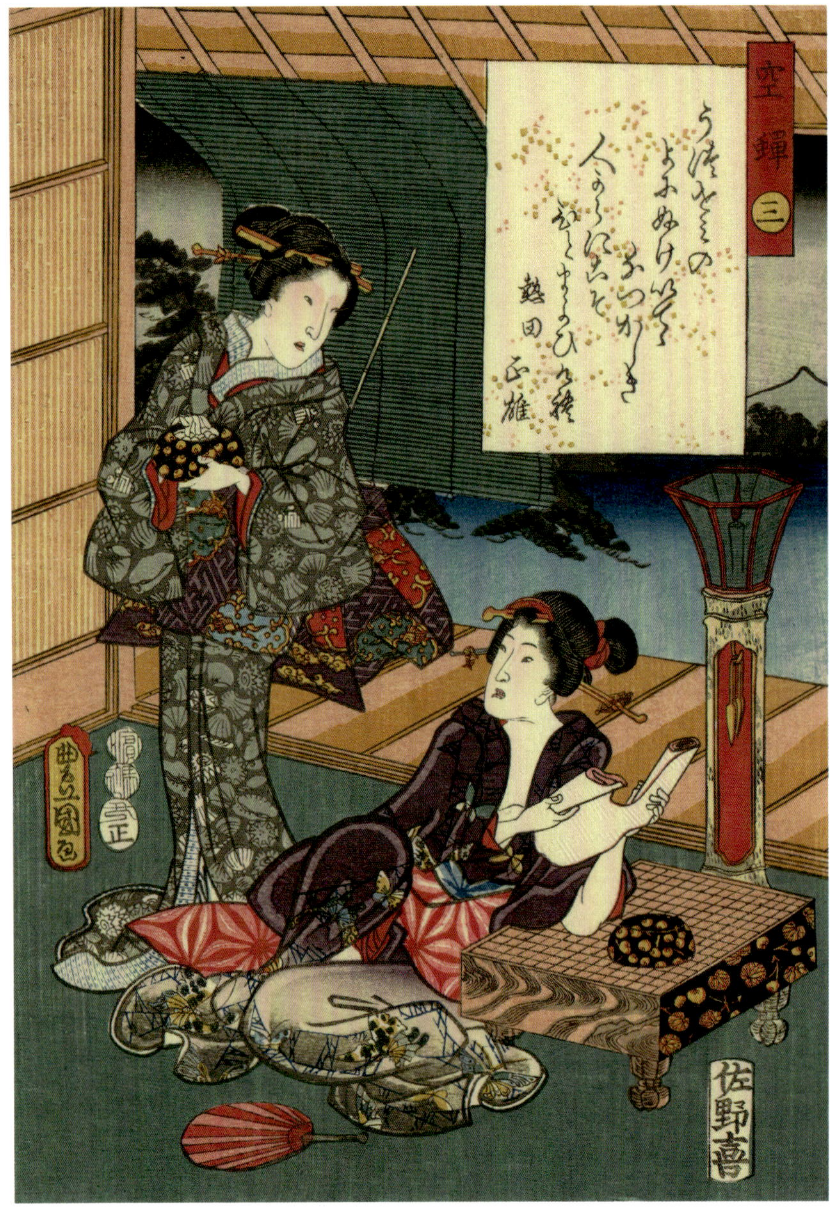

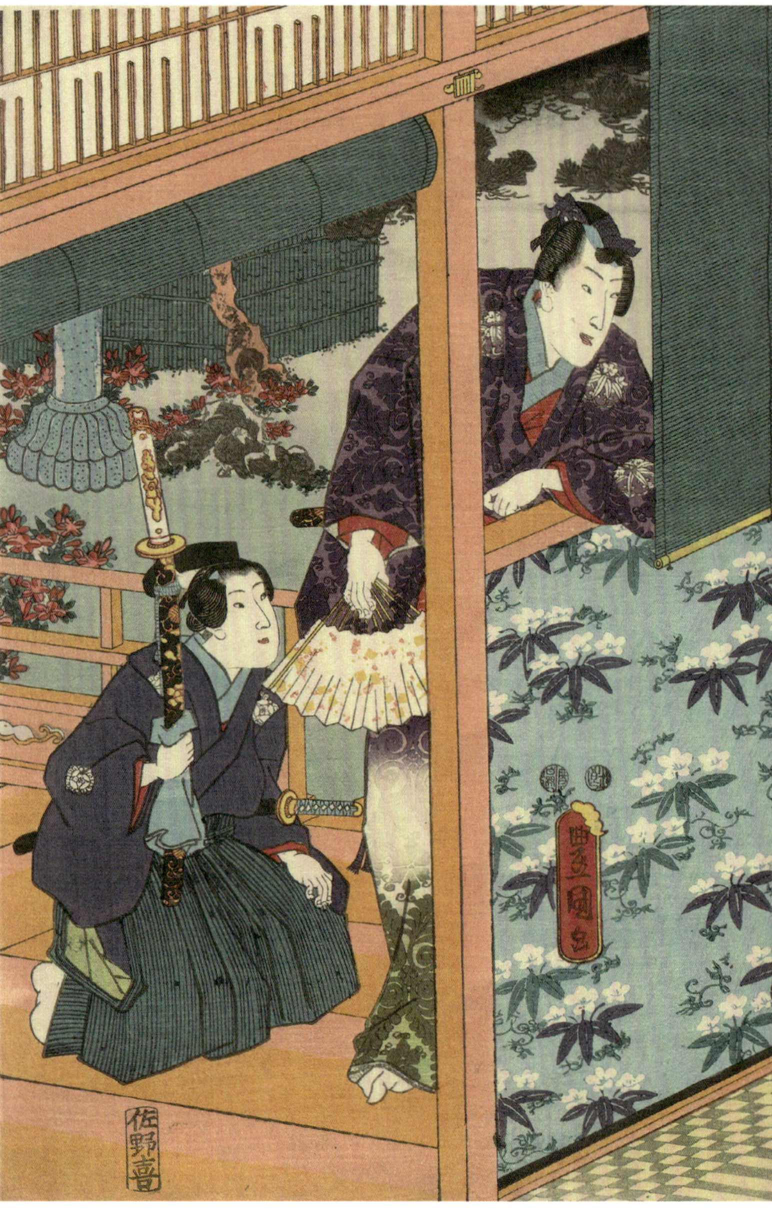

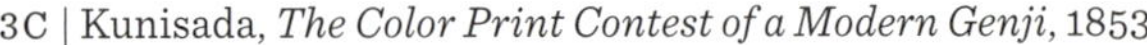

3C | Kunisada, *The Color Print Contest of a Modern Genji*, 1853

3D | Kunisada, *Figures in Edo Purple*, 1847–52

Because *Inaka Genji* has additional plot elements, the scenes that parody the original *Tale of Genji* are often spread over more than one chapter, with the added events interspersed between them. Thus the rainy-night discussion takes place at the beginning of chapter 3 of *Inaka Genji* (rather than chapter 2 as in the original). While it is going on, a mysterious woman steals a precious sword from the treasury of the shogun's palace, leaving behind a torn bit of her sleeve. The guardsman who tries to stop her, Nikki Kiyonosuke, is the husband of Karaginu (Empty Robe, the equivalent of Utsusemi); Muraōgi is his daughter by a previous marriage and is about the same age as Karaginu.

In *Inaka Genji*, the case of mistaken identity unfolds in the opposite direction, and the sequence of events is also reversed. Mitsuuji thinks that he is sleeping with the stepdaughter Muraōgi when he is actually

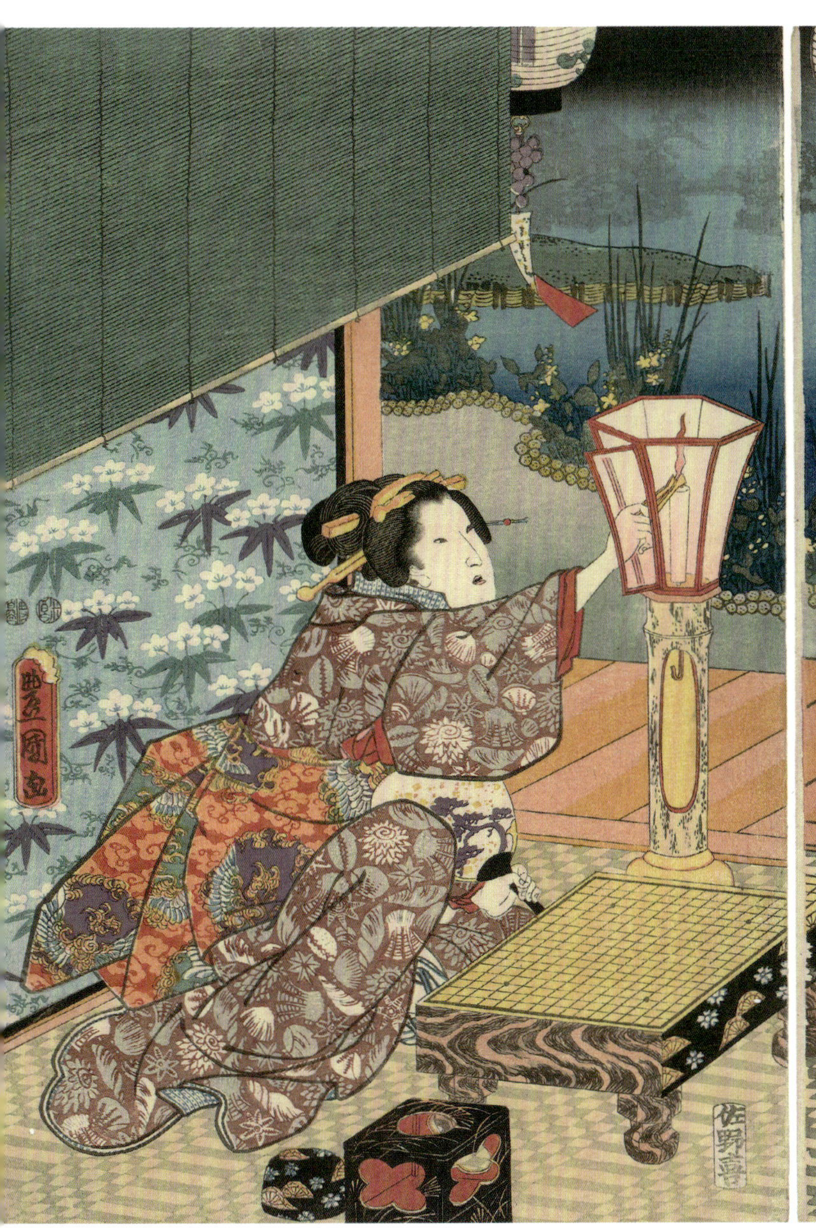

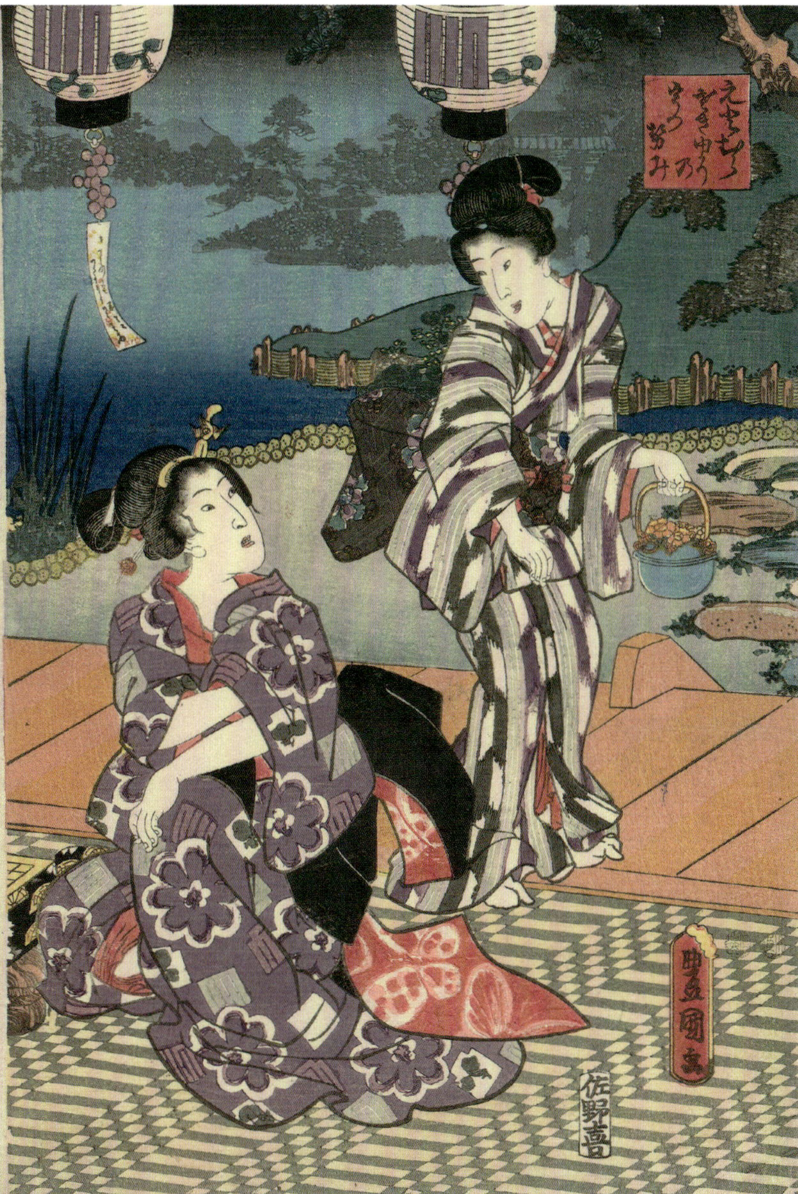

with Karaginu, who has taken her place. Only later, when he secretly watches the *go* game between the women, does he learn of the substitution. As the two women prepare for their game, Muraōgi reads a love letter addressed to her by Mitsuuji, which puzzles her because as far as she knows, she has never met him (3C). The following scene, in which Mitsuuji watches the two women playing their game, was also the subject of a triptych by Kunisada (3D).

4

Evening Faces (Yūgao)

The most frequently illustrated incident in *The Tale of Genji* is the encounter that begins Genji's tragic love affair with the lady known as Yūgao (Evening Faces), the name of the flowering vine that grows on the fence of her dilapidated house. On the way to visit his secret lover, the high-ranking Lady Rokujō (Sixth Avenue, from her address), Genji stops to visit his old nurse, the mother of his servant Koremitsu. While waiting in his oxcart, he notices the beautiful flowers on the house next door and sends Koremitsu to pick some for him. Meanwhile, the lady inside has been observing Genji through the blinds. She sends out her own servant, who offers a fan to put the blossoms on (4A).

When he returns home, Genji discovers that the mysterious lady has written a poem on the fan indicating her interest in him. He responds with the chapter title poem, and they begin an affair that ends with her sudden death at Genji's villa, apparently due to the malice of the jealous spirit of Lady Rokujō. In Heian-period Japan, it was believed that strong emotion could result in ghost-like emanations even from people who were still alive. Yūgao was one of the former lovers mentioned by Tō no Chūjō in the rainy-night discussion, and their daughter Tamakazura, currently a baby being cared for by her nurse, will become an important character later in the story.

Let me then draw near
and see whether you are she,
whom glimmering dusk
gave me faintly to discern
in twilight beauty flowers.

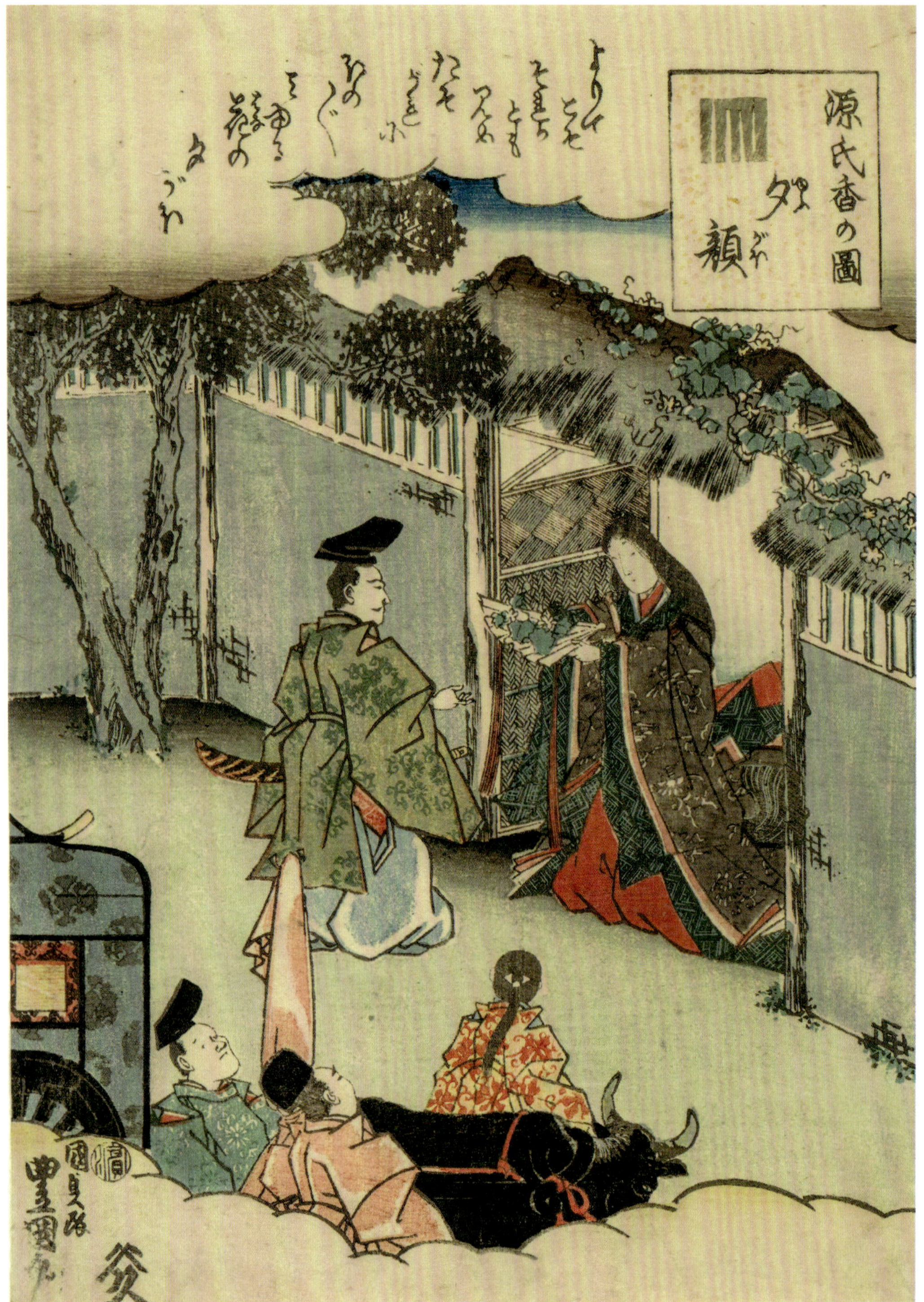

4A | Kunisada, *Genji Incense Pictures*, 1844–47

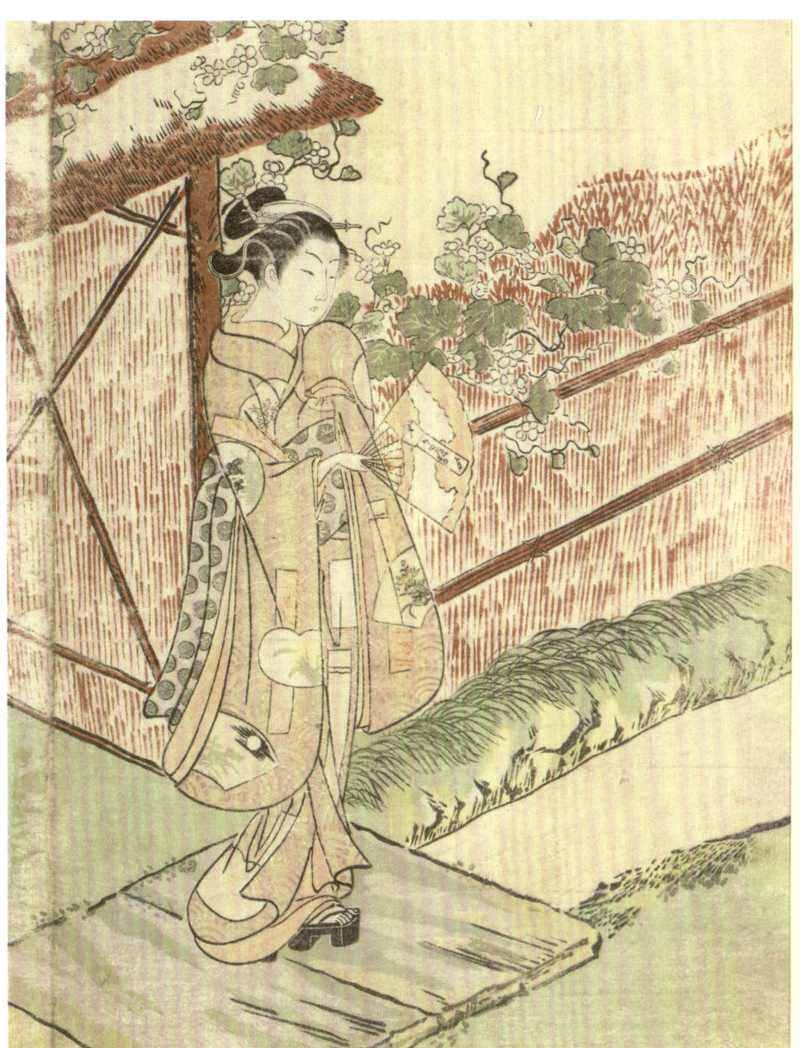
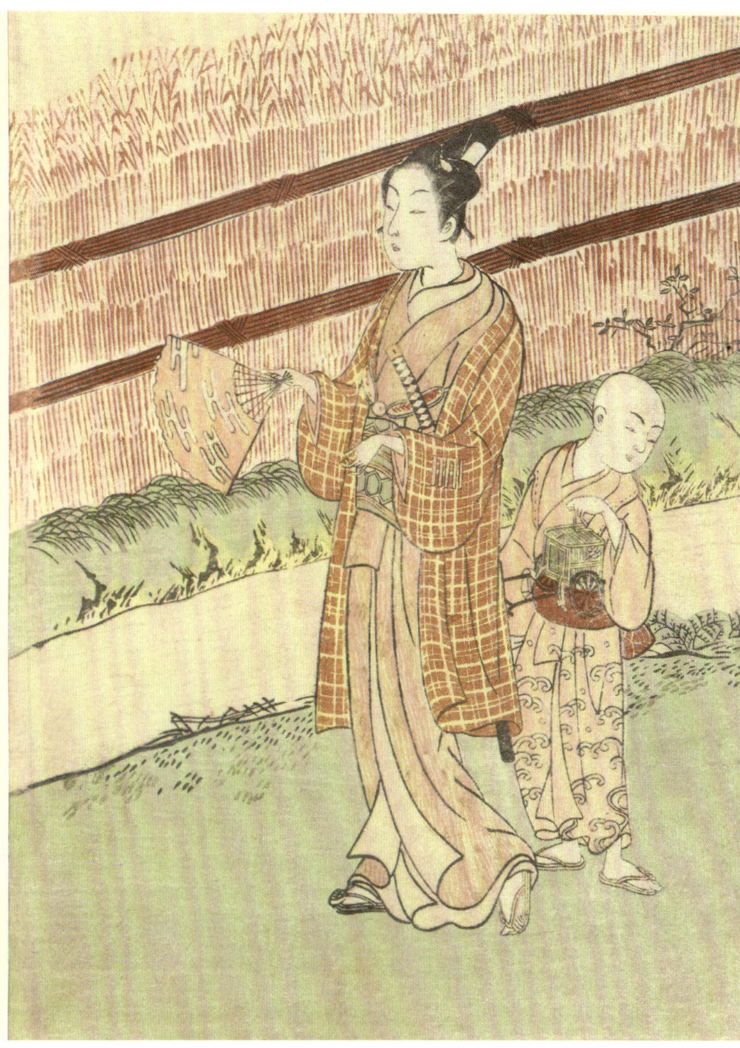

4B | Suzuki Harunobu, Parody of *The Tale of Genji*, about 1766

Harunobu's charming parody shows a contemporary teenage couple of the 1760s interacting with each other directly, rather than through servants (4B). The flowers remain on the vine, and the fan offered by the young woman has a folded love letter attached to it. The oxcart is represented by a tiny cage for singing insects held by the young man's boy servant.

The version of this story retold in chapters 4 and 5 of *Inaka Genji* is an especially successful merging of the parodic romantic plot and the interpolated action-adventure plot. The iconic first encounter is visually parodied in a black-and-white illustration in the book that Kunisada later reworked as a full-color triptych (4D). Mitsuuji leans against a palanquin, the standard means of transportation used by the *Inaka Genji* characters in place of the courtly oxcarts of *The Tale of Genji*. Similarly, the flowers are placed on a flat fan rather than a folding fan.

The beautiful young woman standing in the gateway holding a fan is Tasogare (Dusk), the daughter of the dancing teacher Shinonome (who has no equivalent in the original *Tale of Genji*). Mitsuuji begins an affair with Tasogare, and he also becomes involved with the courtesan Akogi, the equivalent of Lady Rokujō (a sly nod to the

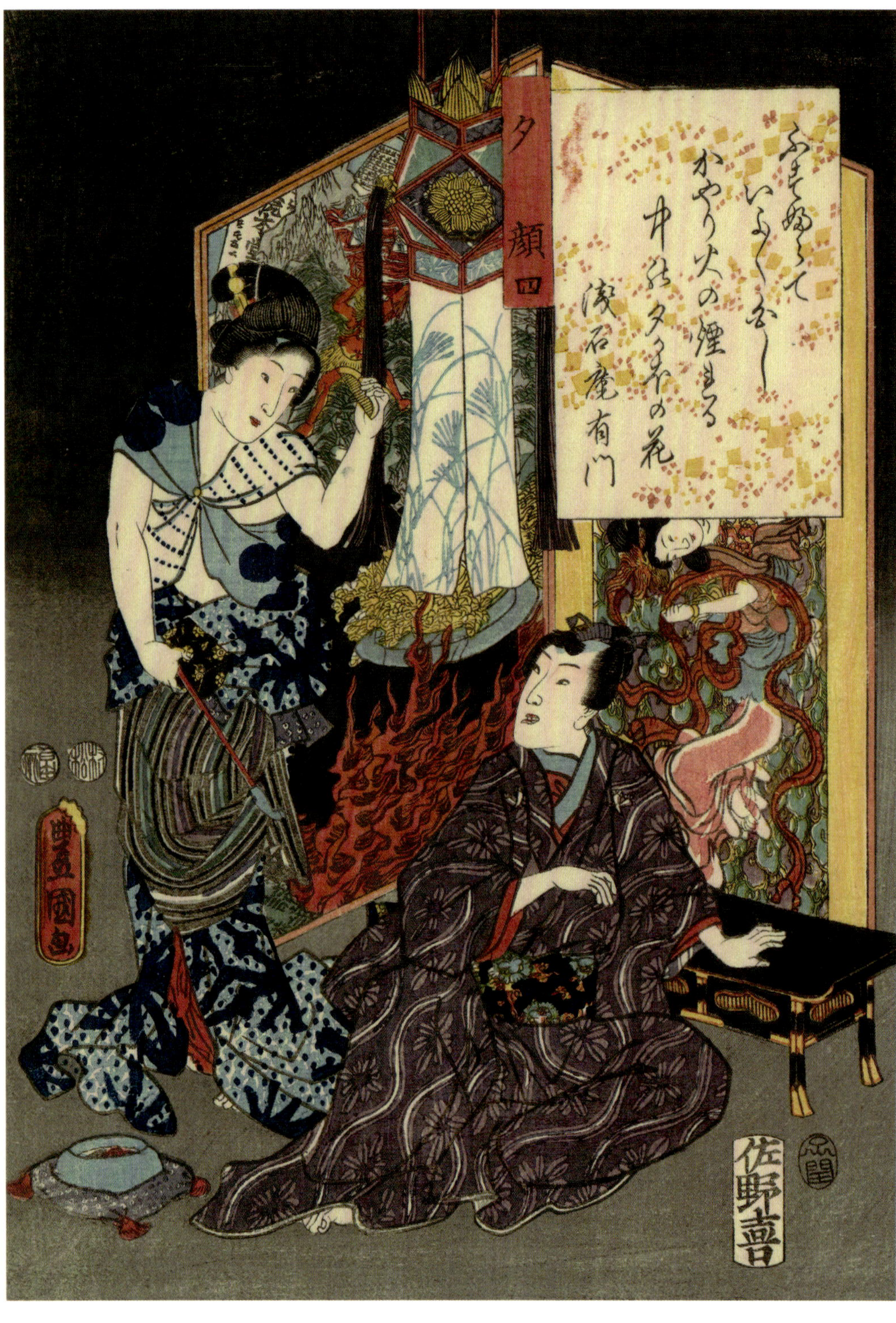

4C | Kunisada, *The Color Print Contest of a Modern Genji*, 1852

evolution of Sixth Avenue, the area where Genji's lover lived, into the location of the Kyoto pleasure quarter).

Mitsuuji is especially interested in Tasogare because he has noticed a newly washed garment on the drying board outside her house (in the right sheet of the triptych) that has the same pattern as the torn sleeve of the sword thief. Her mother, Shinonome (lurking around the corner, just behind the drying board), was in fact the thief and is now plotting to kill Mitsuuji, but he and Tasogare escape and make their way to a ruined temple (4C). On the way, Mitsuuji wraps himself in an old bamboo blind to hide the glitter of his sword fittings in the moonlight (4E). The change of scene parallels the original Genji's decision to take his lover Yūgao from her own noisy neighborhood to a more secluded villa of his own — with fatal results for her.

Mitsuuji and Tasogare encounter not just one but two hostile female entities. The living ghost of Akogi menaces Tasogare (seen in 4E), and shortly afterward she is attacked again by a demonic figure that claims to be the resentful living ghost of Mitsuuji's neglected wife Futaba (= Aoi) but is actually her own mother, Shinonome, in disguise. In the end both Tasogare and Shinonome commit suicide out of remorse, but the sword is still missing.

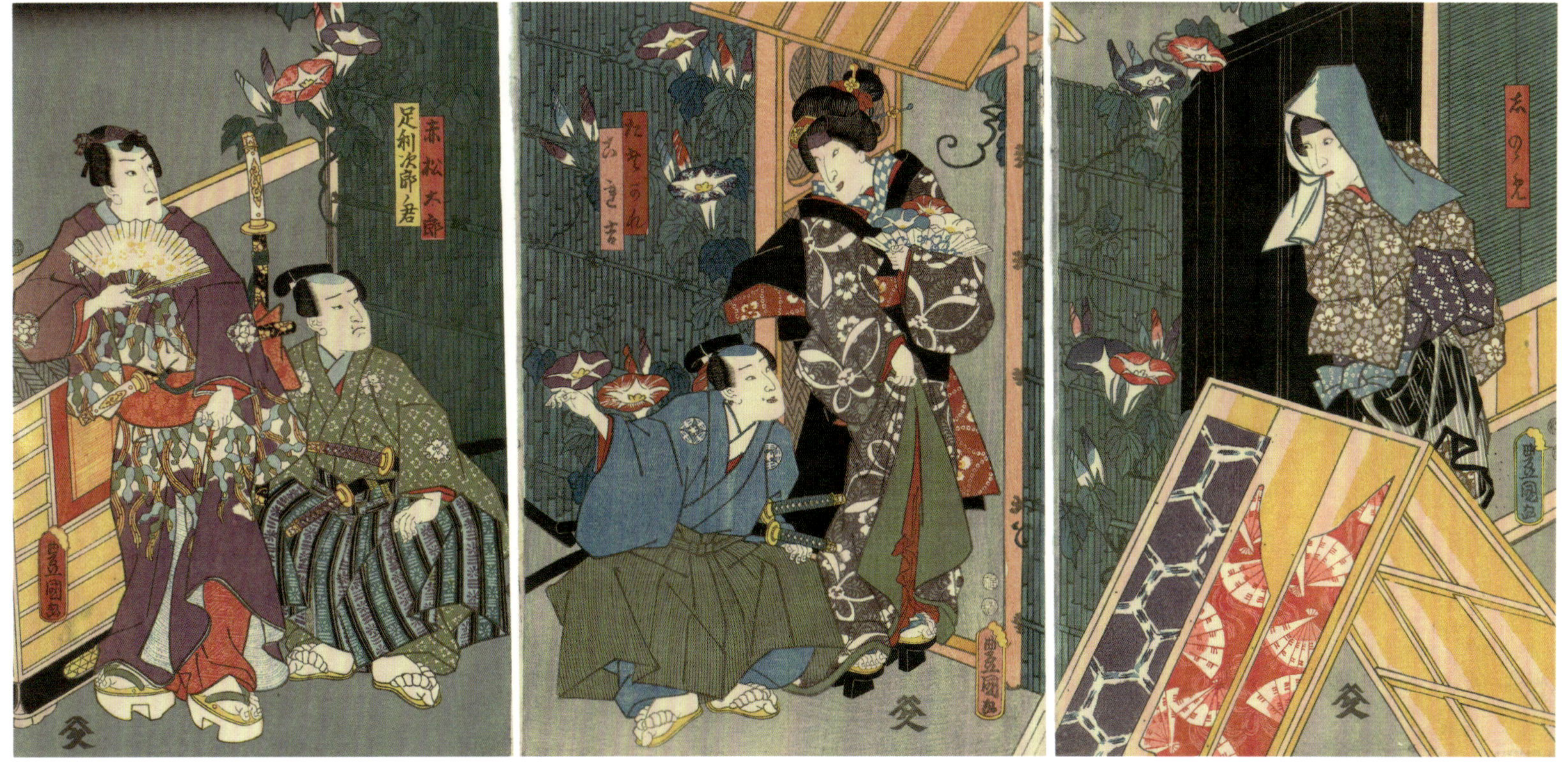

4D | Kunisada, Actors in *Higashiyama Sakura Zōshi*, 1851

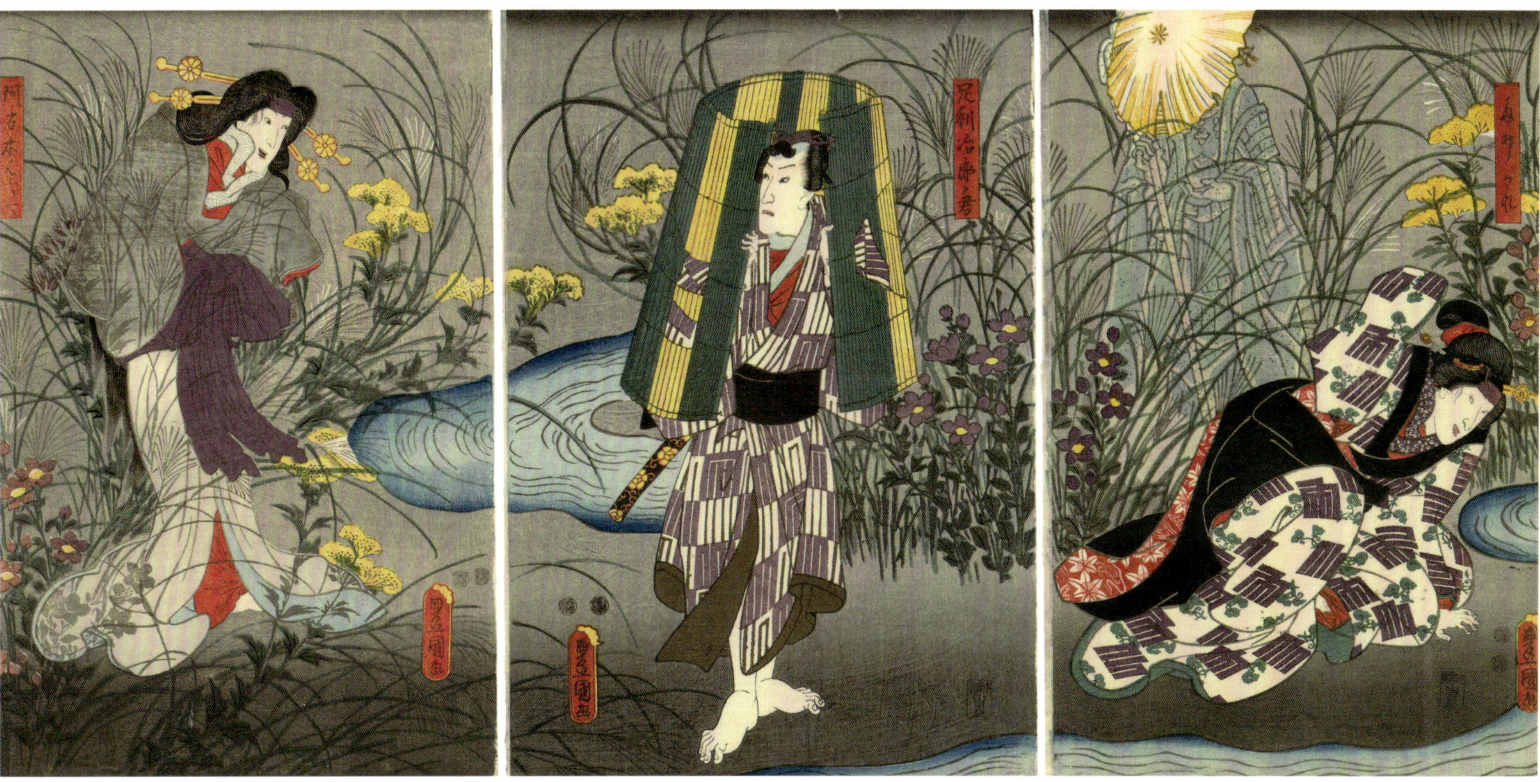

4E | Kunisada, Actors in *Higashiyama Sakura Zōshi*, 1851

5

Young Lavender (Wakamurasaki)

Another very famous scene is Genji's first glimpse of the greatest love of his life, Murasaki (Lavender), who shares a nickname with the book's author. Suffering from recurring fevers, eighteen-year-old Genji visits a miracle-working priest in the mountains of Kurama, north of Kyoto, and spends the night there. He peeps through the brushwood fence of a nearby house and witnesses the scene so often depicted: a charming ten-year-old girl with her grandmother and serving women, upset because a clumsy attendant has knocked over a wicker birdcage (similar in appearance to a clothes-scenting rack) and accidentally released the baby sparrows she was keeping as pets. Both Kunisada and Hiroshige depicted this well-known incident in a traditional manner (5A, 5B).

How glad I would be
to pick and soon to make mine
that little wild plant
sprung up from the very root
shared by the murasaki.

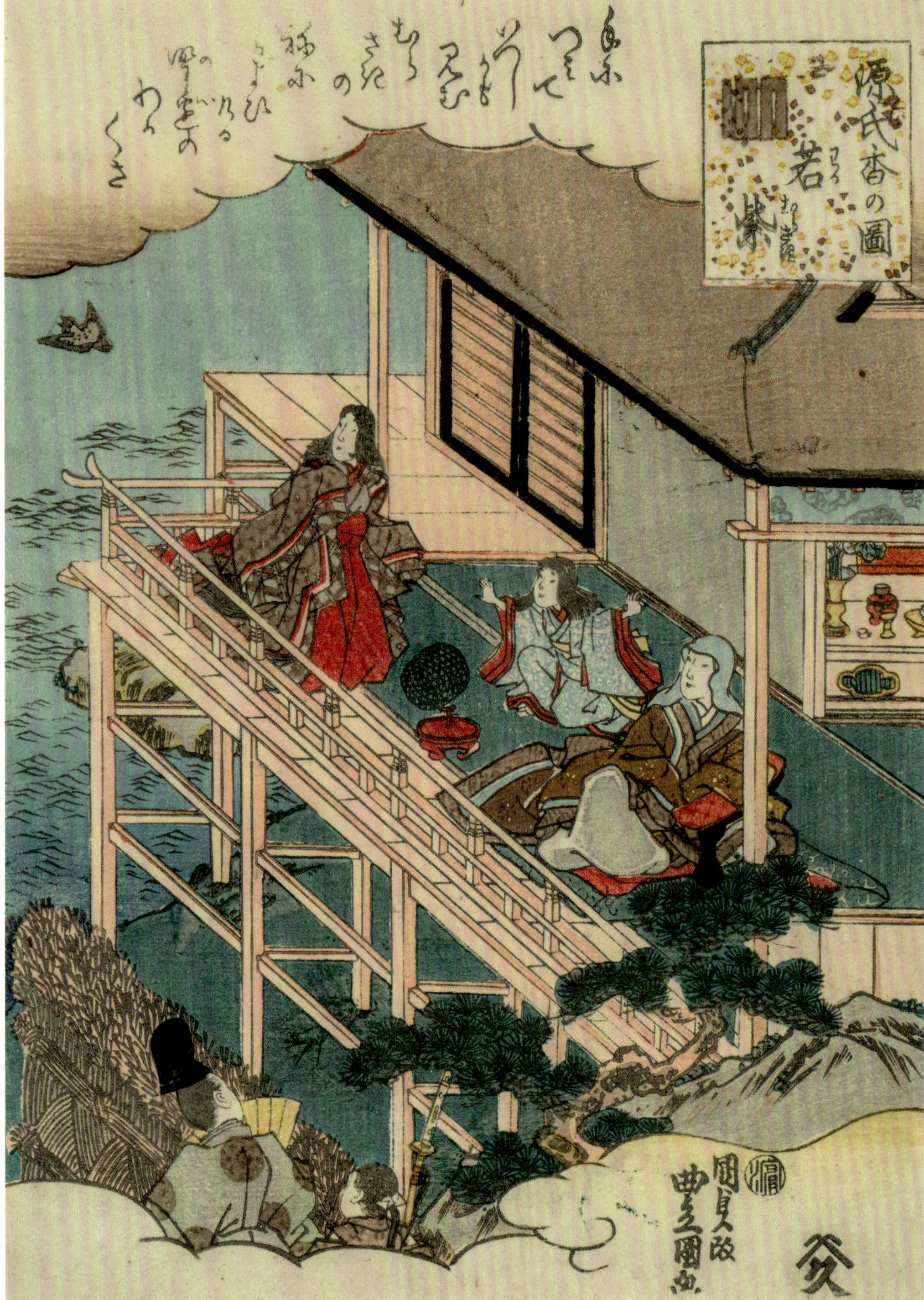

5A | Kunisada, *Genji Incense Pictures*, 1844–47

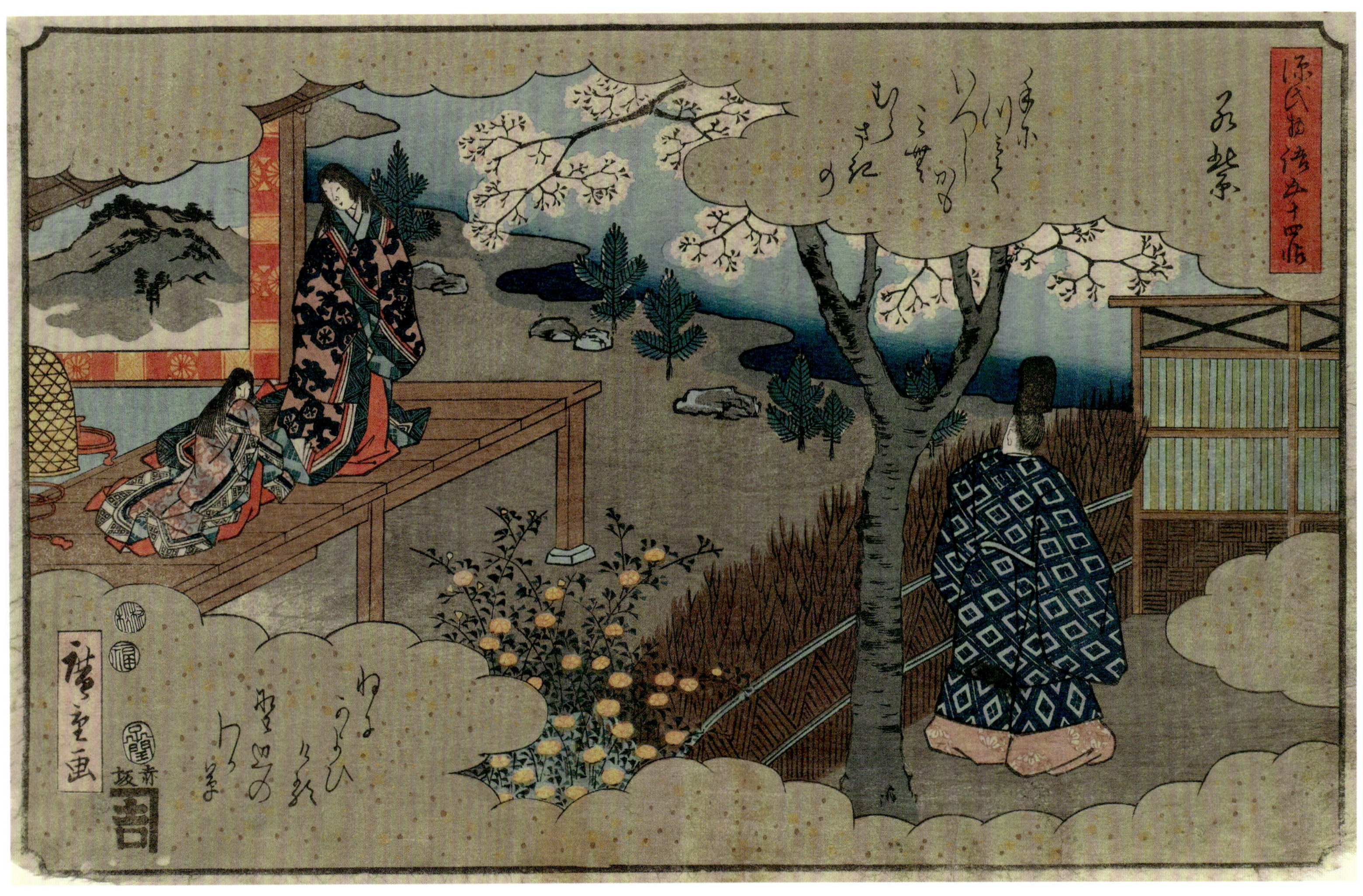

5B | Hiroshige, *The Fifty-Four Chapters of the Tale of Genji*, 1852

Genji learns that little Murasaki, who like him lost her mother at an early age, is the unacknowledged and somewhat neglected child of a prince. In the end Genji takes Murasaki to his own home to bring her up to be an accomplished woman (and no doubt a beautiful one). In this chapter Genji also manages to arrange a secret meeting with his stepmother Fujitsubo while she is away from court visiting her own family, and she becomes pregnant as a result.

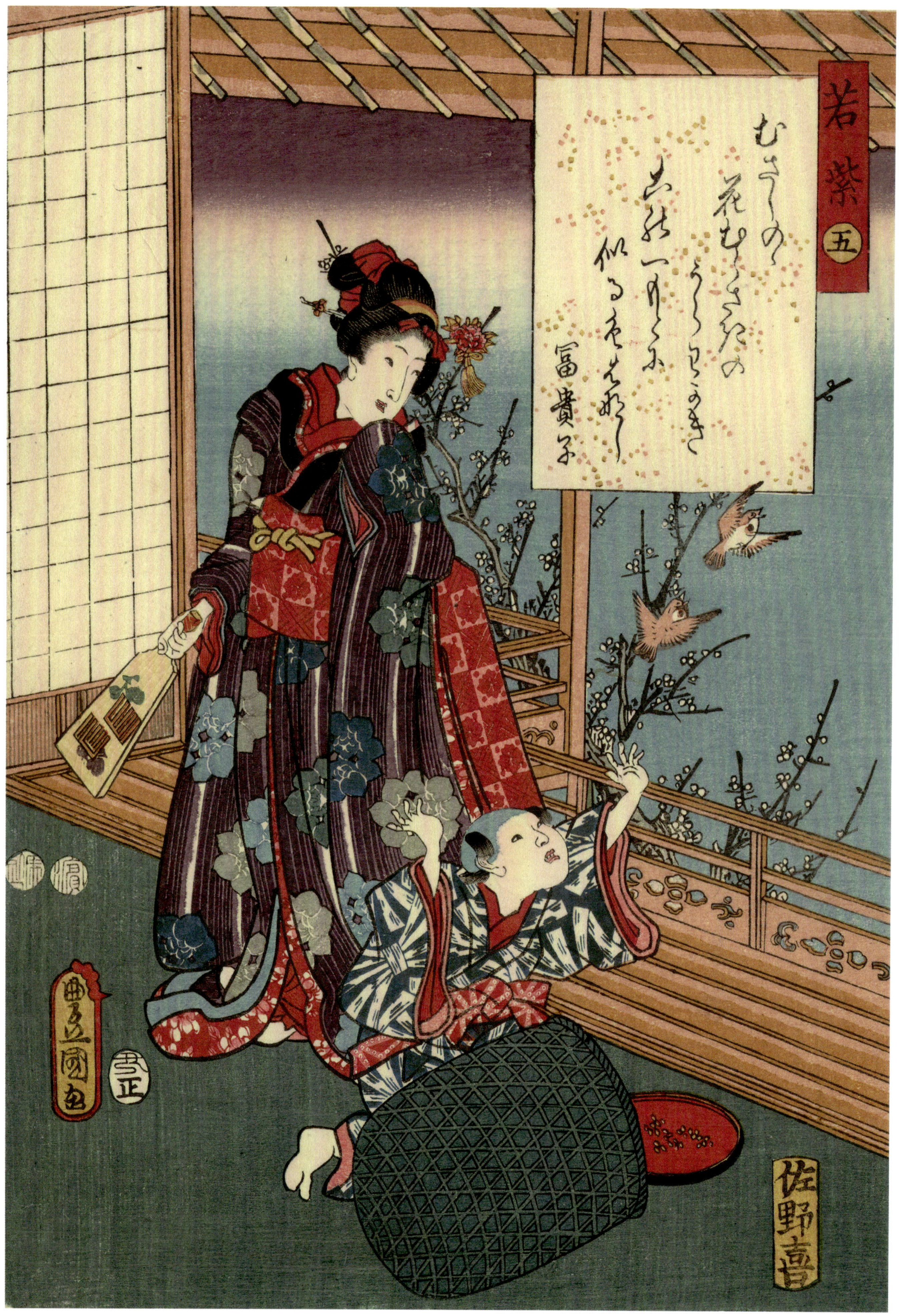
若紫 五
豊国画
佐野喜

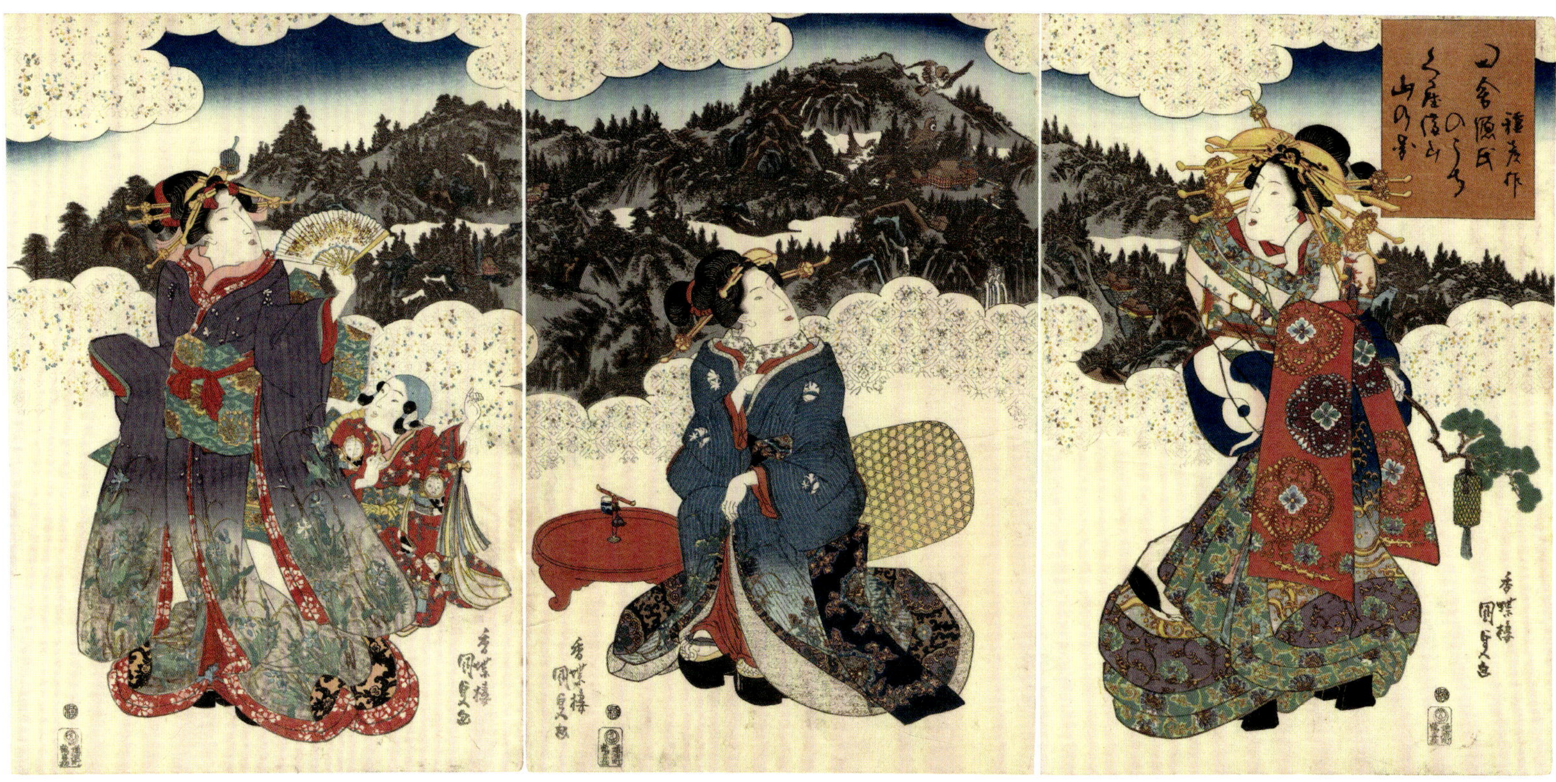

5D | Kunisada, *Mountain Scenery of Mount Kurama*, 1830s

Like modern readers, Edo-period readers of *The Tale of Genji* were uncomfortable with the fact that the love interest in this chapter is still a child — although it should be noted that Genji does not consummate the relationship for several years, waiting patiently until Murasaki is well into adulthood by Heian standards. They tended to reinterpret traditional illustrations of the scene by identifying the standing adult figure on the veranda, watching the escaping sparrows, as Murasaki rather than her servant. *Inaka Genji* follows this new interpretation and makes Murasaki slightly older, so that she is an adolescent. The little girl in the *Inaka Genji* pictures is the child attendant who overturned the birdcage (5C).

Because the exciting events at the ruined temple leading to the deaths of Mitsuuji's lover Tasogare and her mother, Shinonome, took up most of chapter 5 in *Inaka Genji*, the parody of the first meeting with Murasaki occurs in chapter 6. Like Genji, Mitsuuji travels north to Mount Kurama in search of healing. He learns that the area is a retreat for people from the pleasure quarters; little Murasaki, although of illustrious descent, is being raised there because she is destined to become a courtesan, the only way that her impoverished grandmother could provide for her. Mitsuuji buys out Murasaki's contract with the brothel and repairs her grandmother's old house so that she can live there for the time being.

While at the mountain retreat, Mitsuuji also meets with his lover, the courtesan Akogi. She heals his illness by using a magical amulet, actually a calligraphic inscription by a former emperor that is one of three great treasures stolen one at a time from the shogun's household; the other two are an heirloom mirror and the sword taken by Shinonome. In an early triptych thought to be Kunisada's very first color print based on *Inaka Genji*, he includes Akogi in the scene of the overturned birdcage, even though she was not actually present, with the mountain scenery of Kurama in the background (5D).

5C | Kunisada, *The Color Print Contest of a Modern Genji*, 1853

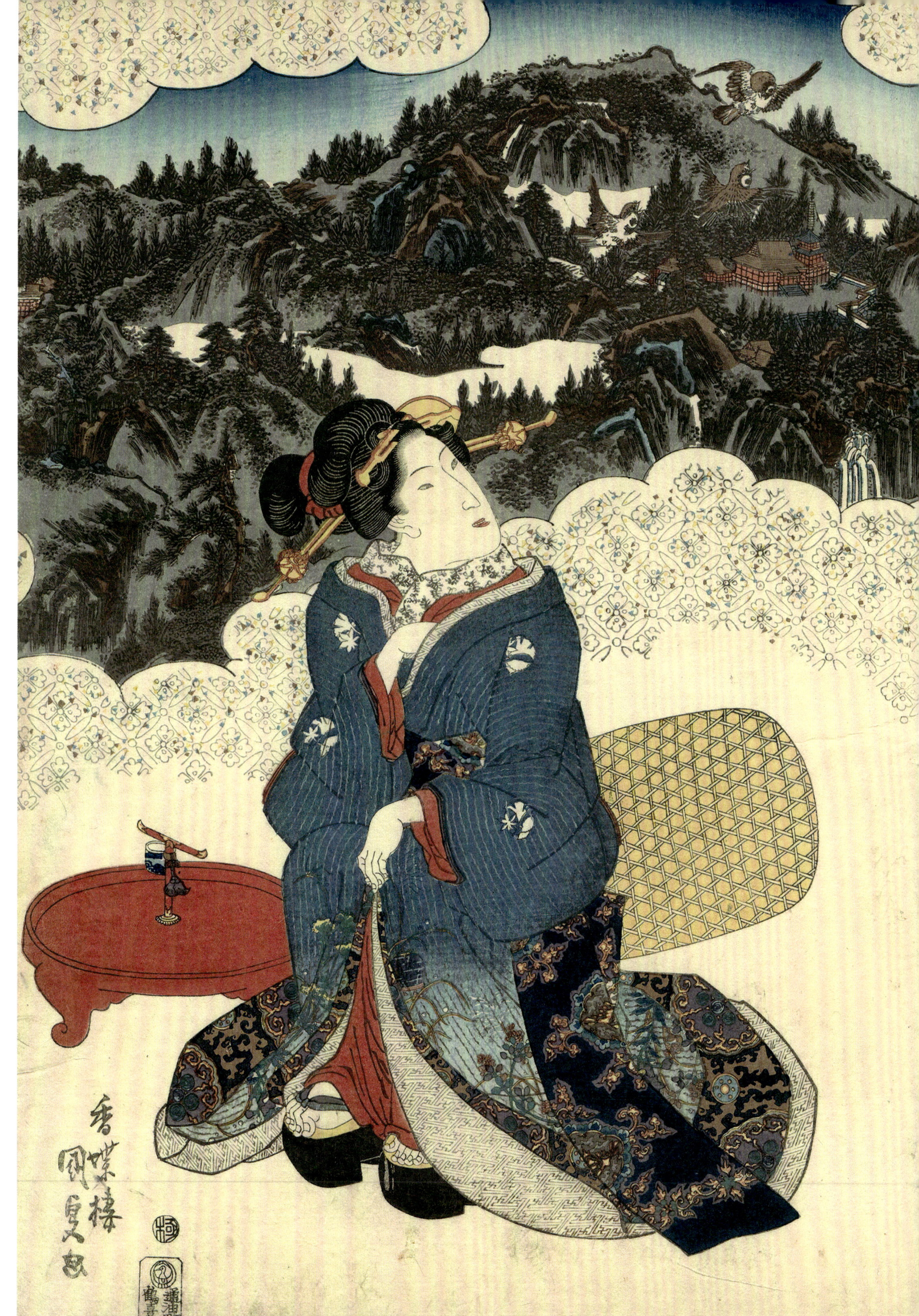
香蝶楼
国貞画

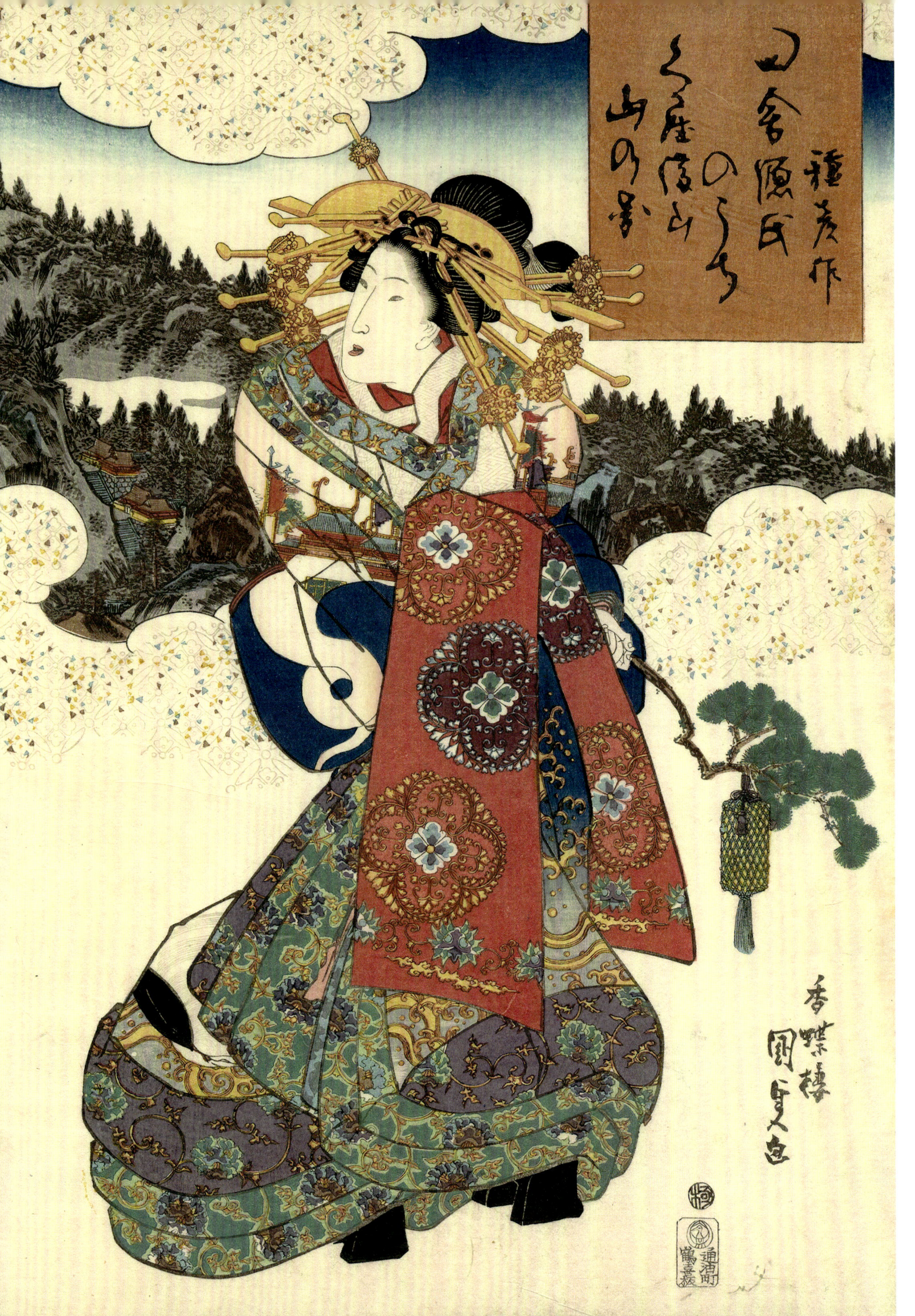
種彦作
田舎源氏のうち
山の景
香蝶楼国貞画
通油町
鶴喜

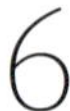

The Safflower (Suetsumuhana)

The rainy-night discussion in chapter 2 leaves Genji with a fondly imagined vision of an ideal romantic situation: a lovely young woman living in obscurity, waiting to be discovered by a lover. Hearing of an orphaned princess who is a skilled koto player, he secretly visits her one night (6A). On the morning after their tryst, when he sees her face in full light for the first time, he discovers that she has a large, red nose that reminds him of the red dye made from safflower. Furthermore, her poetry and the gifts of clothing that she sends him afterward are embarrassingly dated.

This is not at all
a color to which I warm;
what then did I mean
by letting myself brush sleeves
with a safflower in full blush?

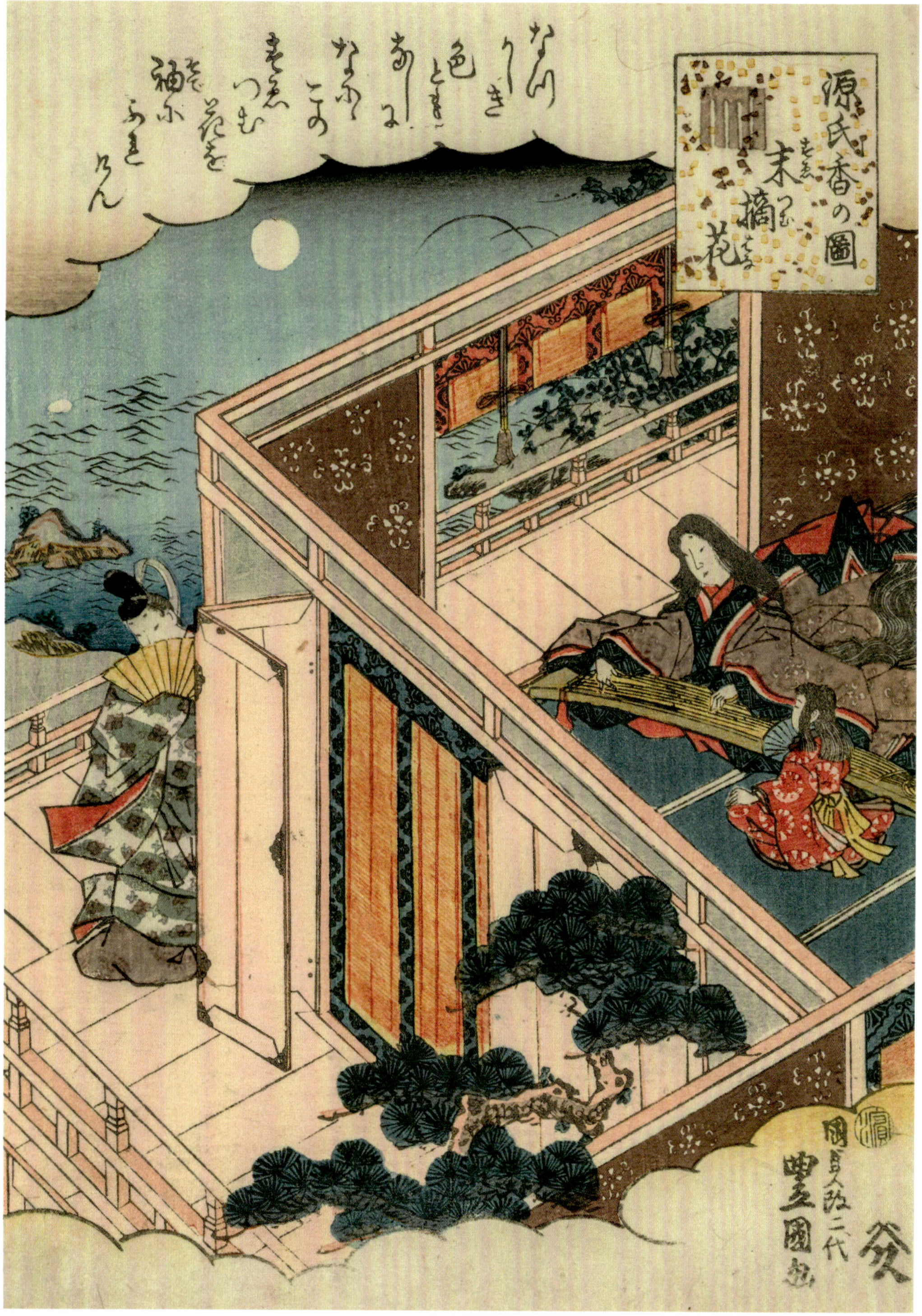

6A | Kunisada, *Genji Incense Pictures*, 1844–47

Okumura Masanobu's parody shows a modern version of Genji ruefully contemplating the princess's unfashionable gifts (6B). While struggling to write a polite reply, Genji composes the safflower poem instead. However, he is kind to the princess in person, concealing his disappointment and continuing to treat her with courteous attention.

In *Inaka Genji,* Mitsuuji is intrigued by the koto playing of Lady Inabune, the young daughter of a former shogun. He eventually learns that Inabune is currently disguised as the maidservant Kurenai (Crimson), while the real Kurenai — a homely, red-nosed servant girl — has temporarily taken her place to thwart possible kidnapping by the scheming Yamana clan.

In chapter 10, Mitsuuji visits Lady Inabune's house on a snowy day and asks her attendants to clear the snow from tree branches in the overgrown garden (echoing a winter visit of Genji to Suetsumuhana in chapter 6 of the original book) (6C). He later watches secretly as would-be suitor Yamana Saburō Munekiyo, son of the villain Yamana Sōzen, storms off in disgust after seeing the ugly face of the false lady.

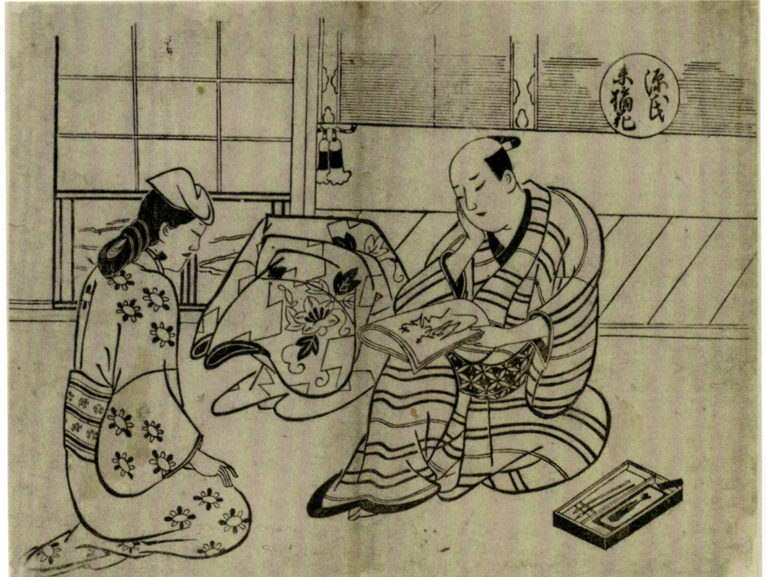

6B | Okumura Masanobu, *The Suetsumuhana Chapter*, about 1710

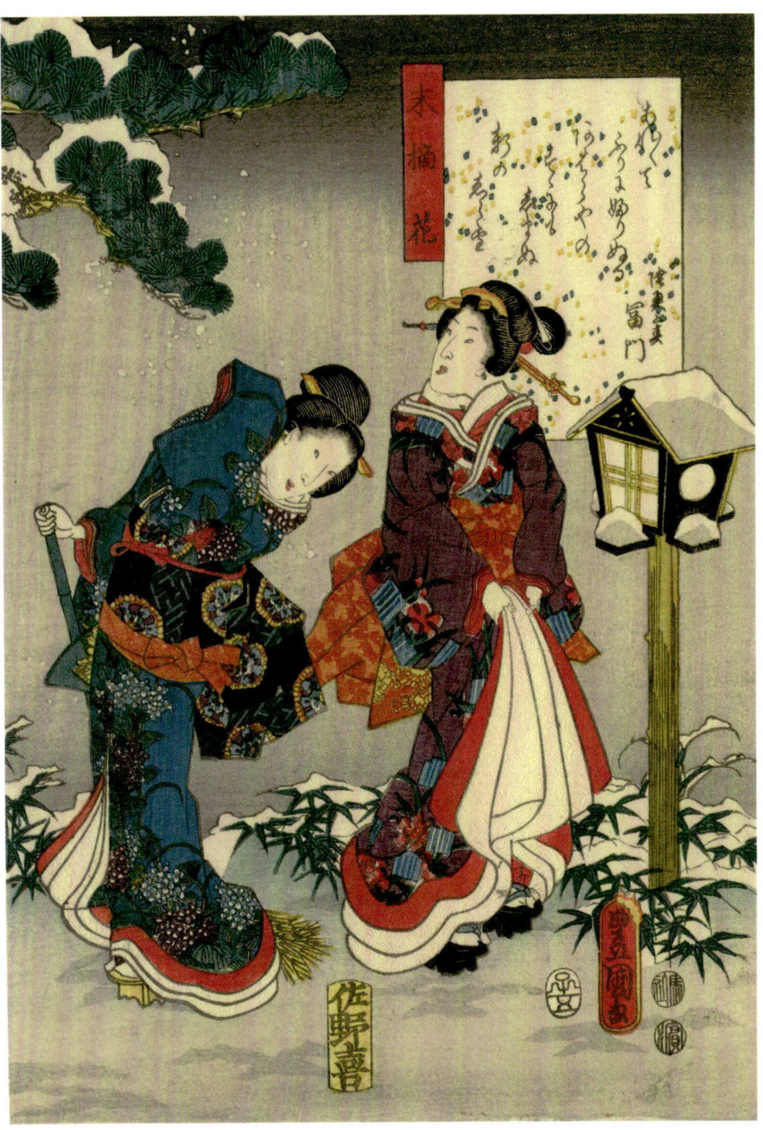

6C | Kunisada, *The Color Print Contest of a Modern Genji*, 1852

7

An Autumn Excursion (Momiji no ga)

In the fall of Genji's eighteenth year, his father the emperor hosts a maple-leaf-viewing excursion with lavish entertainments at the Suzaku Palace. The highlight of the event is a performance by Genji and his best friend, Tō no Chūjō, of the dance Waves of the Blue Sea. The spectacle is observed with mixed emotions by Lady Fujitsubo, Genji's stepmother and secret lover, who is painfully aware that the child she carries was fathered not by the emperor but by Genji.

My unhappiness
made of me hardly the man
to stand up and dance;
did you divine what I meant
when I waved those sleeves of mine?

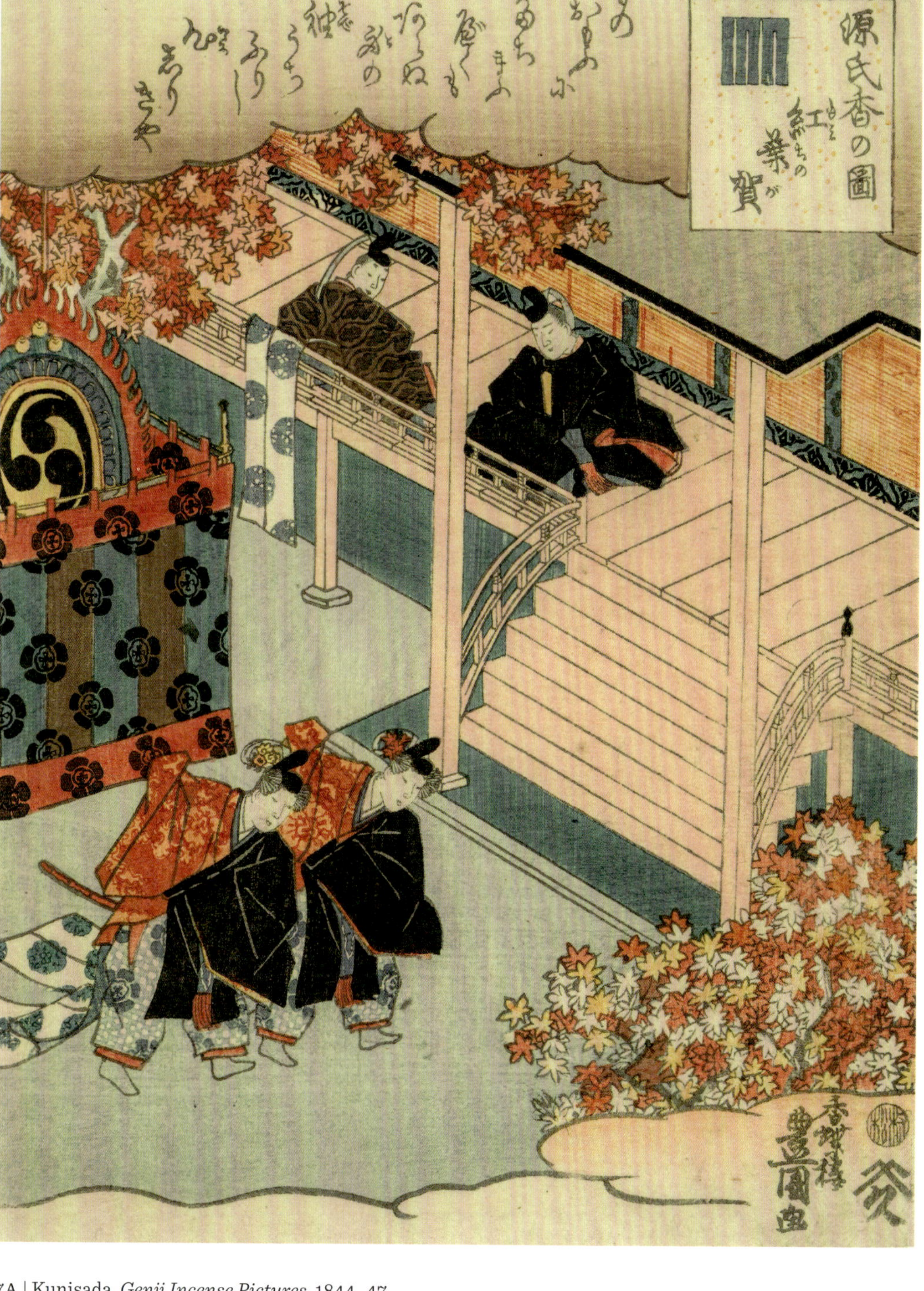

7A | Kunisada, *Genji Incense Pictures*, 1844–47

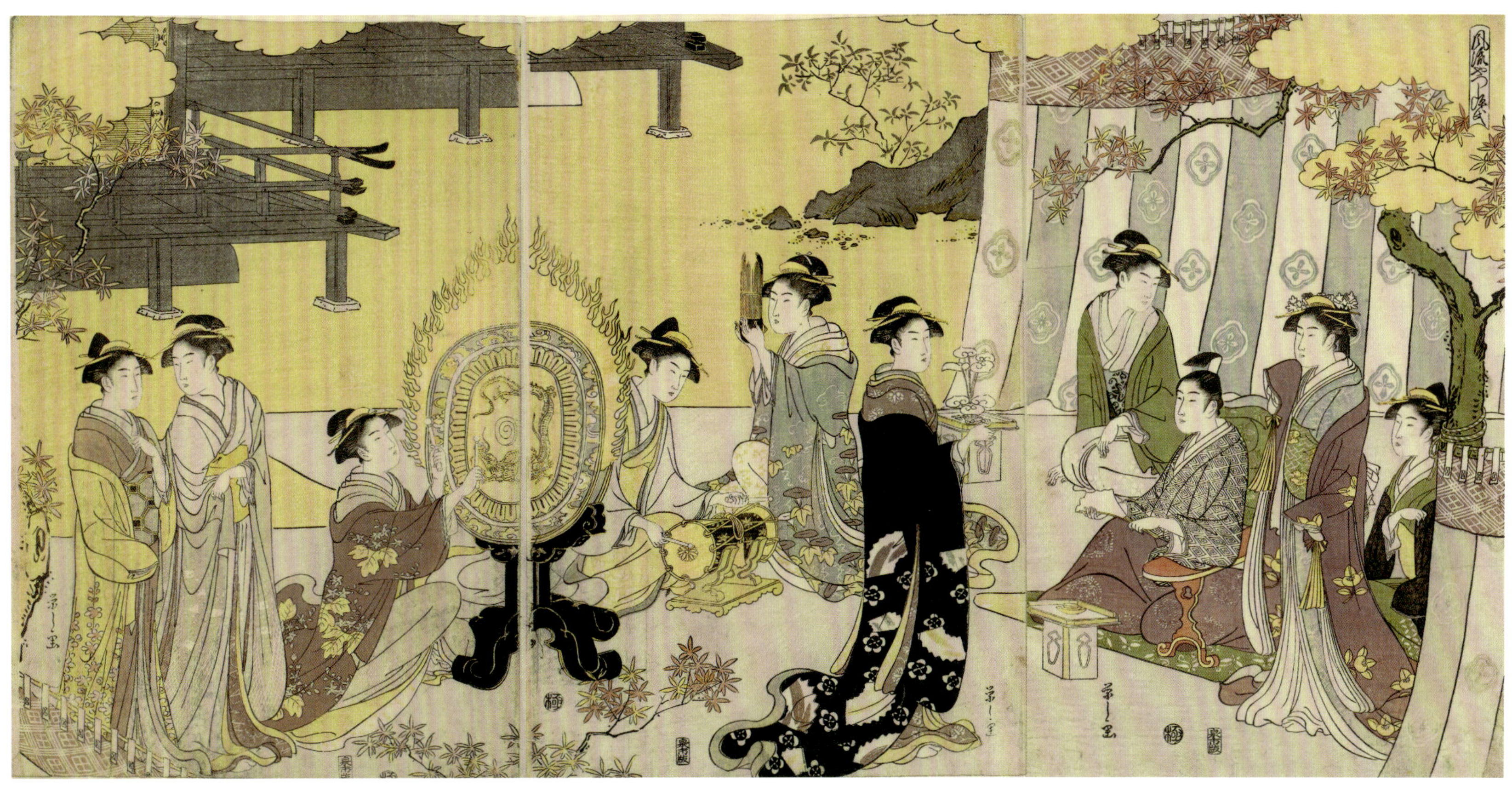

7B | Chōbunsai Eishi, *Genji in Fashionable Modern Guise*, about 1792

The print from the *Genji Incense* series follows earlier models in showing the two dancers, dressed as imperial guards, performing in front of the stairs of the palace veranda, where the emperor and his entourage are seated behind closed bamboo blinds (7A). Eishi's elegant updated design comes from a series of ten triptychs that show a young man surrounded by ladies in the high-fashion modern kimono of the 1790s, in lavish settings that allude to the original *Tale* (7B). The series' color scheme is mainly gray and purple, with areas of blue, green, and yellow; here, red has been added to highlight the maple leaves and the male figure's armrest.

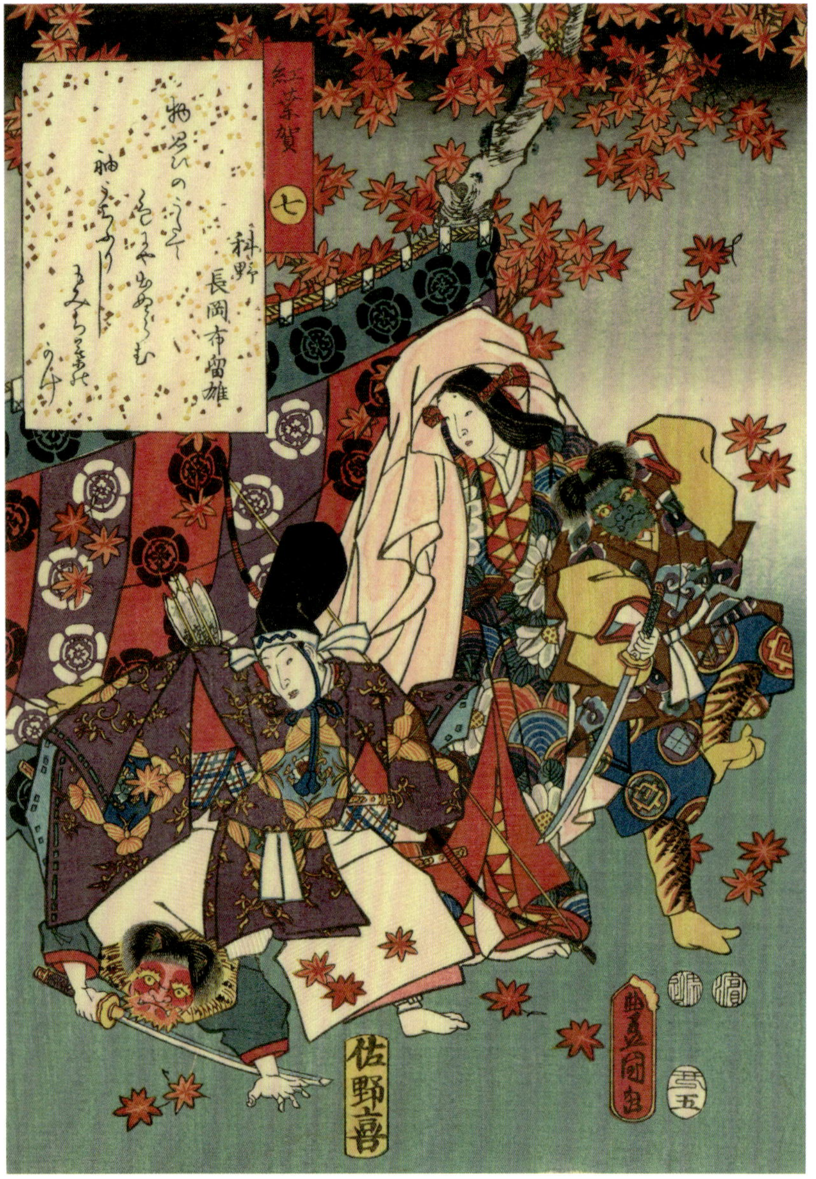

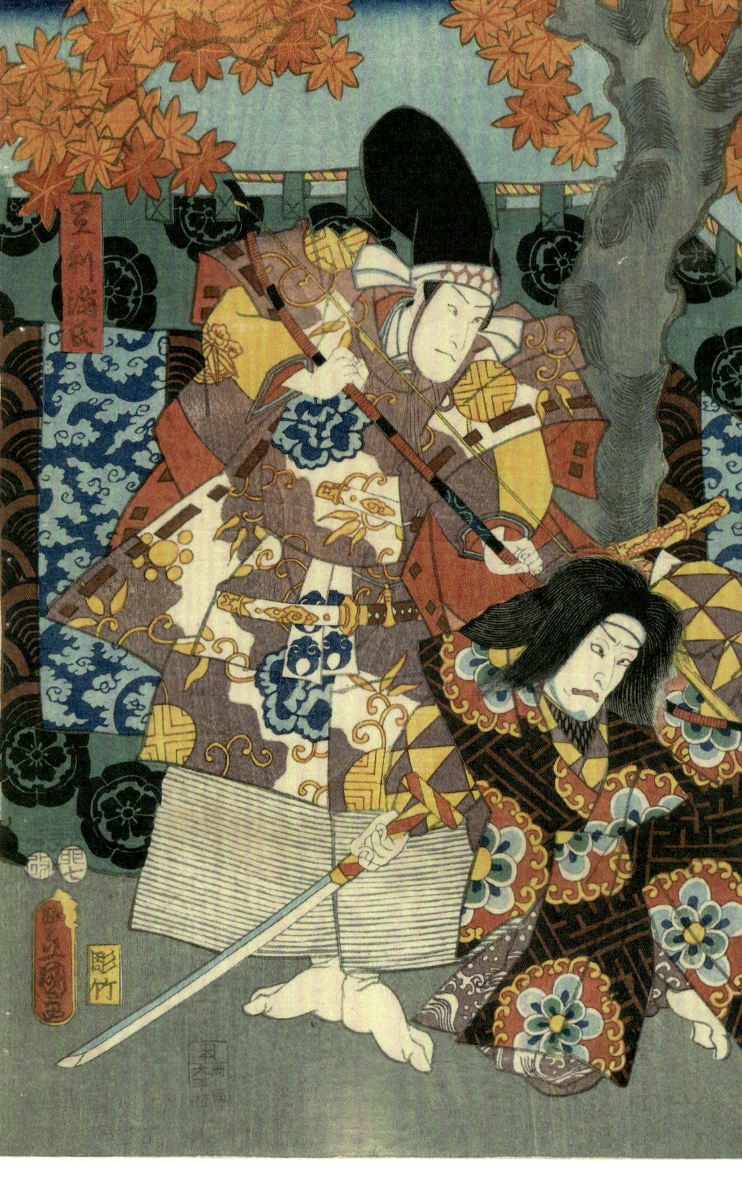

7C | Kunisada, *The Color Print Contest of a Modern Genji*, 1853

7D | Kunisada, Actors in a scene based on *Higashiyama Sakura Zōshi*, 1855

In *Inaka Genji*, the shogun's leaf-peeping party is held at one of the most famous scenic spots of Kyoto, the Tsutenkyō bridge spanning a deep gorge on the grounds of the Zen temple Tōfuku-ji (in the Higashiyama area of Kyoto) that is still famous today for its gorgeous autumn foliage. The plot elements that correspond to chapter 15 of the original *Genji* appear in chapters 15 and 16 of the parody, with the autumn excursion described in chapter 16. Mitsuuji and his stepmother Fuji no Kata are not lovers, although they have deliberately spread a rumor that they are in order to foil the evil plans of their enemy Yamana Sōzen, who is plotting to overthrow the shogun. Sōzen sends assassins, disguised as dancers in demon masks, to kill Mitsuuji; with his superb martial arts skills, our hero easily defeats them (7C).

Parts of *Inaka Genji* were dramatized for the kabuki stage as early as 1838, but the 1851 production at the Nakamura Theater was especially memorable because it included an entirely new plot combined with the Genji parody plot under the title *Higashiyama*

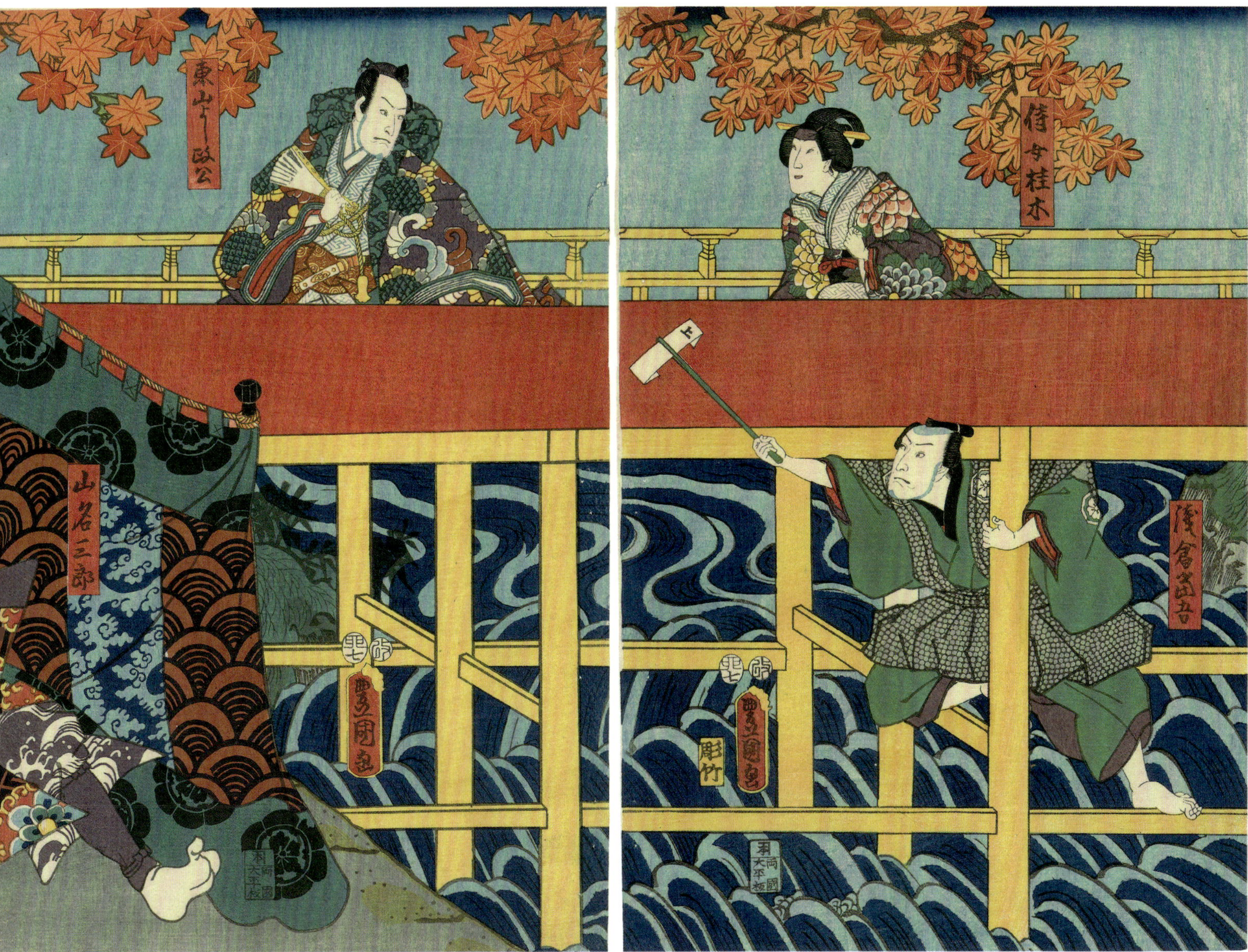

Sakura Zōshi (A Story of Cherry Blossoms in the Eastern Hills). The new story was based on a historical incident of 1653, with names altered to avoid censorship. Very unusually for a kabuki play, the hero was not a samurai or townsman but a member of the peasant class. Asakura Tōgō (in real life, Sakura Sōgō), the mayor of a rural village that is suffering terribly from the greed and cruelty of the local ruler, decides to petition the shogun for help — even though he knows that it is a capital crime for commoners to approach the shogun directly. In the play, the hero returns as a ghost after his execution, haunting the evil lord and achieving vengeance from beyond the grave.

The two interwoven plots of the play intersect in the scene of the dance by Mitsuuji and his brother Yoshihisa. During the performance, the hero Asakura climbs up under the bridge to give his petition to the shogun (7D). This triptych, based on the staging of the 1851 play, shows an imaginary recasting with different actors, possibly for a planned production that never actually occurred.

The Festival of the Cherry Blossoms (Hana no en)

As a tipsy Genji makes his way through the palace after the court celebration of the cherry blossoms, he encounters a beautiful young woman who will take her nickname from the circumstances of their first meeting: Oborozukiyo, or Misty Moonlit Night. He begins an affair with her, although she does not initially respond to Genji's poetic query about her identity (8A). Unfortunately for him, she turns out to be the younger sister of his hostile stepmother Kokiden, who is hoping to make a match between Oborozukiyo and Kokiden's own son, the Crown Prince, and is furious at Genji's interference with her plans.

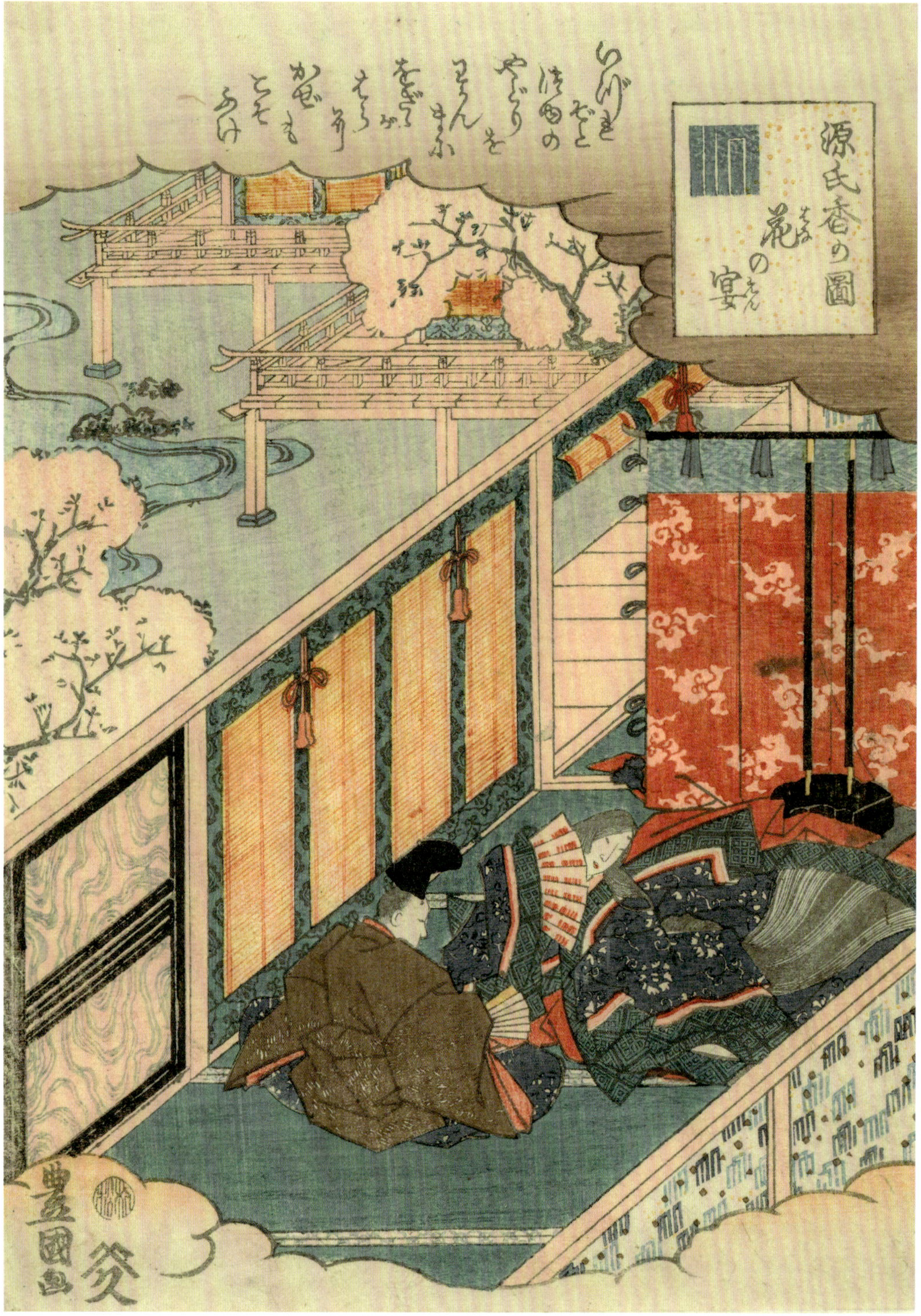

While I strove to learn
in what corner I should seek
my dewdrop's dwelling,
wind, I fear, would be blowing
out across the rustling moors.

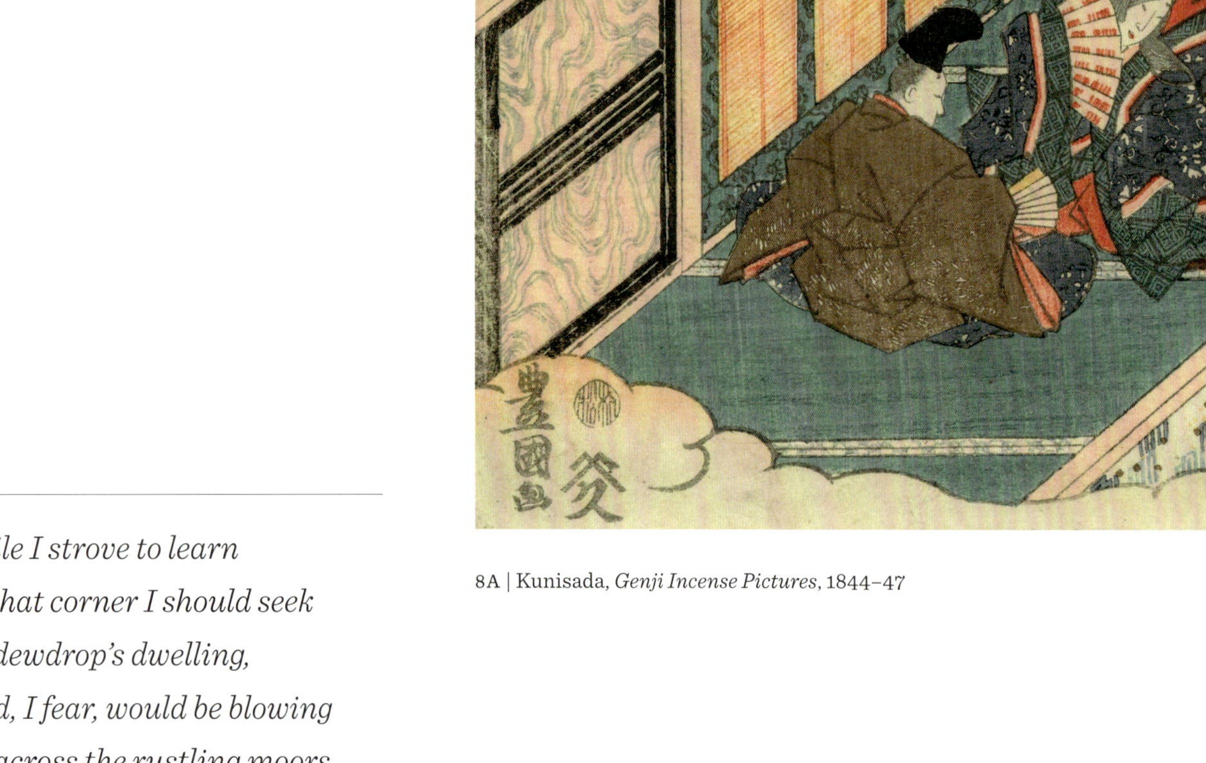

8A | Kunisada, *Genji Incense Pictures*, 1844–47

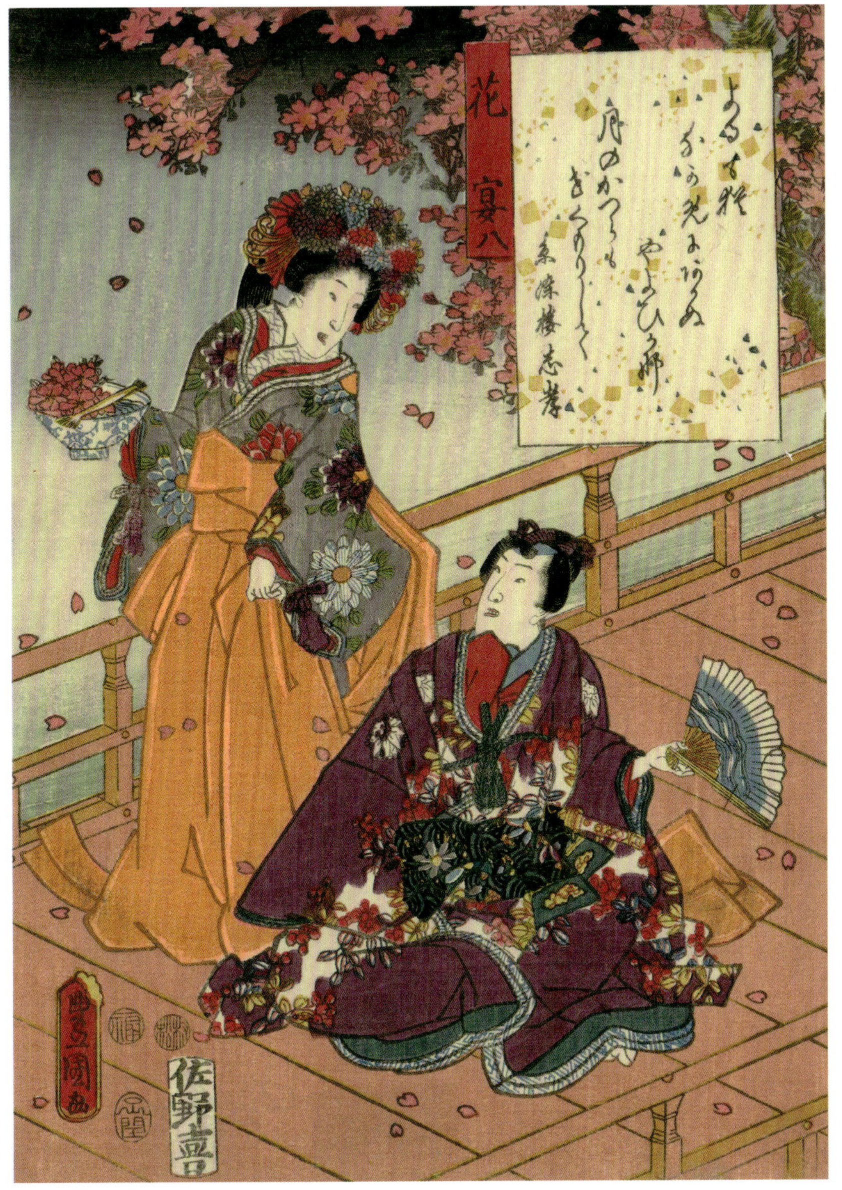

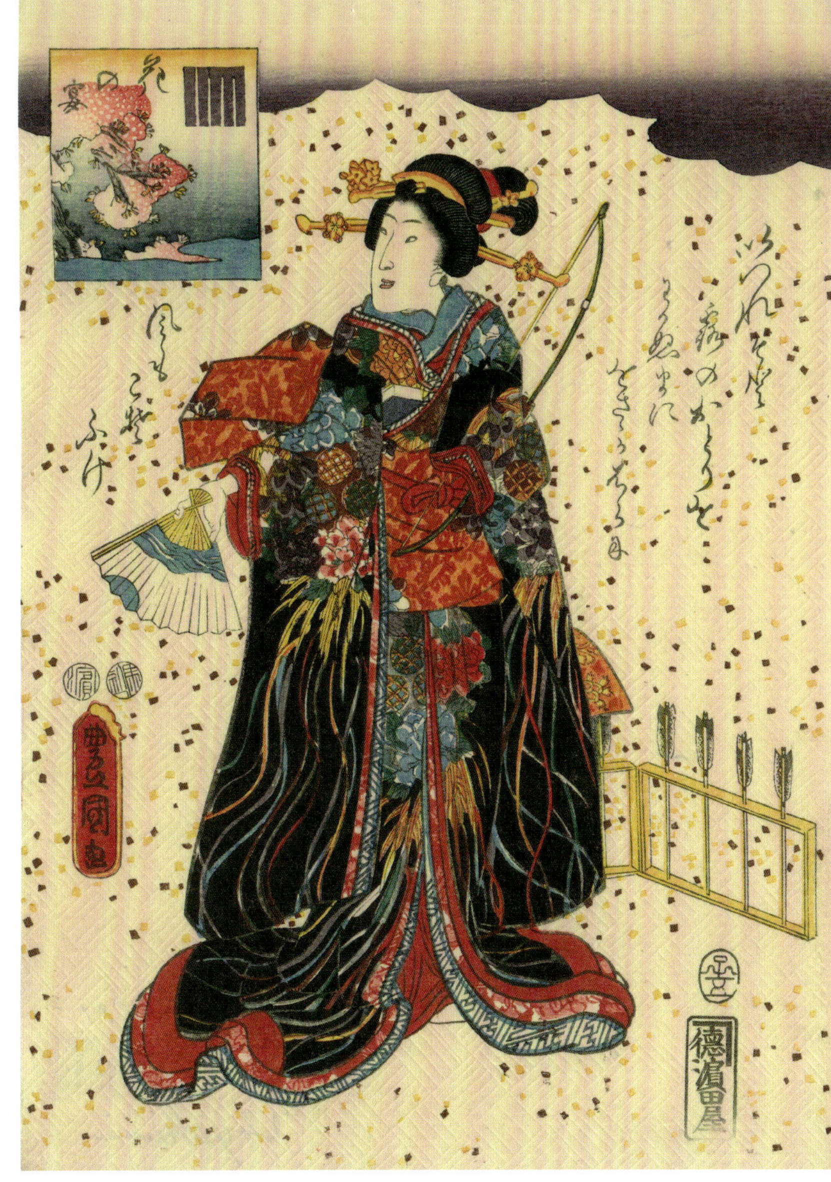

8B | Kunisada, *The Color Print Contest of a Modern Genji*, 1852

8C | Kunisada, untitled series of Genji pictures, 1852

Mitsuuji's experience on a misty moonlit night after the cherry blossom festival takes place in chapter 12 of *Inaka Genji*, when he enters the quarters of his stepmother Lady Toyoshi (the Kokiden equivalent), the mother of his older brother Yoshihisa, through an unguarded gate. On the veranda he meets Toyoshi's niece Katsuragi (= Oborozukiyo), who is now hoping for a relationship with Yoshihisa but was formerly involved with Mitsuuji's supposedly murdered friend Umanojō (8B). (Their stormy relationship had been described during the rainy-night discussion, and the reader later learns that Umanojō is in fact still alive and working undercover for Mitsuuji.) Mitsuuji scolds Katsuragi for not being faithful to the memory of Umanojō; she takes his message all too seriously and decides to become a nun. To dissuade her from this plan, her doting father hosts a jolly party with various amusements, including her favorite parlor archery games, as shown in an untitled but exquisitely printed Genji series with embossed backgrounds (8C).

9

Heartvine (Aoi)

This chapter includes several very important events in Genji's life: the birth of his legitimate son, Yūgiri; the death of his first wife, Aoi; and the beginning of his marriage to Murasaki. Yet the scene most frequently illustrated is an episode near the beginning of the chapter, known as the battle of the carriages. Genji is to appear in the parade for the Kamo Festival at the beginning of summer, and the women in his life all turn out to view the spectacle, which they will watch through the bamboo blinds of their ox-drawn carriages parked along the parade route. Rokujō arrives first and secures a good place, but she and her attendants are rudely pushed out of the way when the entourage of Genji's very pregnant wife, Aoi, arrives (9A, 9B). As no poems are composed on this occasion, the poem representing this chapter comes from a different scene, in which Genji admires young Murasaki's beautiful long hair as he trims it in preparation for the festival.

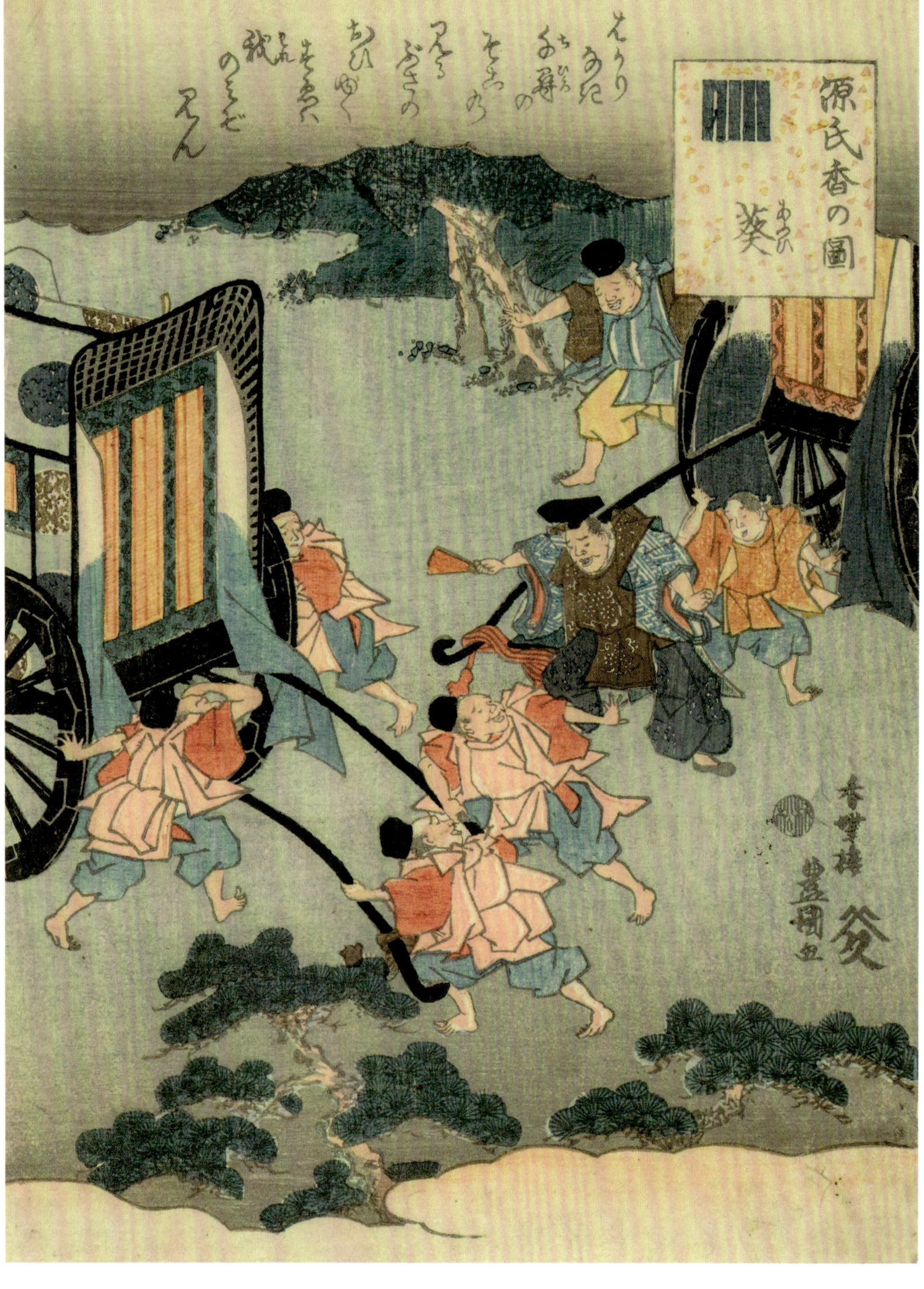

9A | Kunisada, *Genji Incense Pictures*, 1844–47

Rich seaweed tresses
of the unplumbed ocean depths,
a thousand fathoms long,
you are mine and mine alone
to watch daily as you grow.

9B | Nishimura Shigenaga, *Genji in Fifty-Four Sheets*, about 1735

9C | Kunisada, *The Color Print Contest of a Modern Genji*, 1852

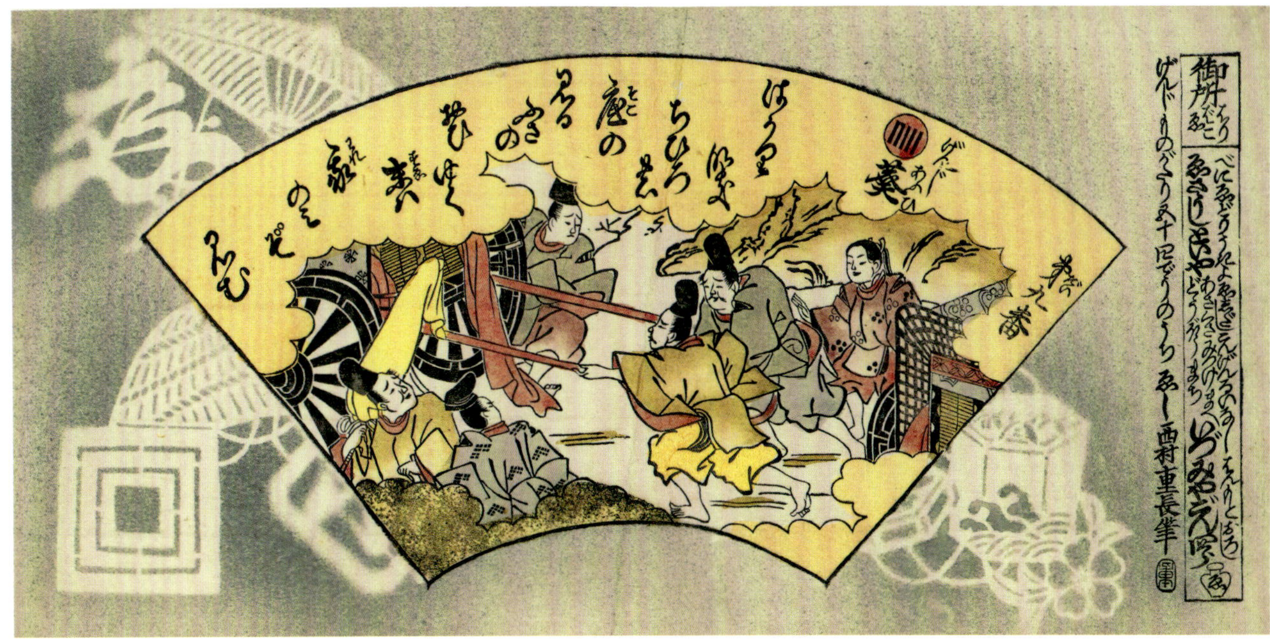

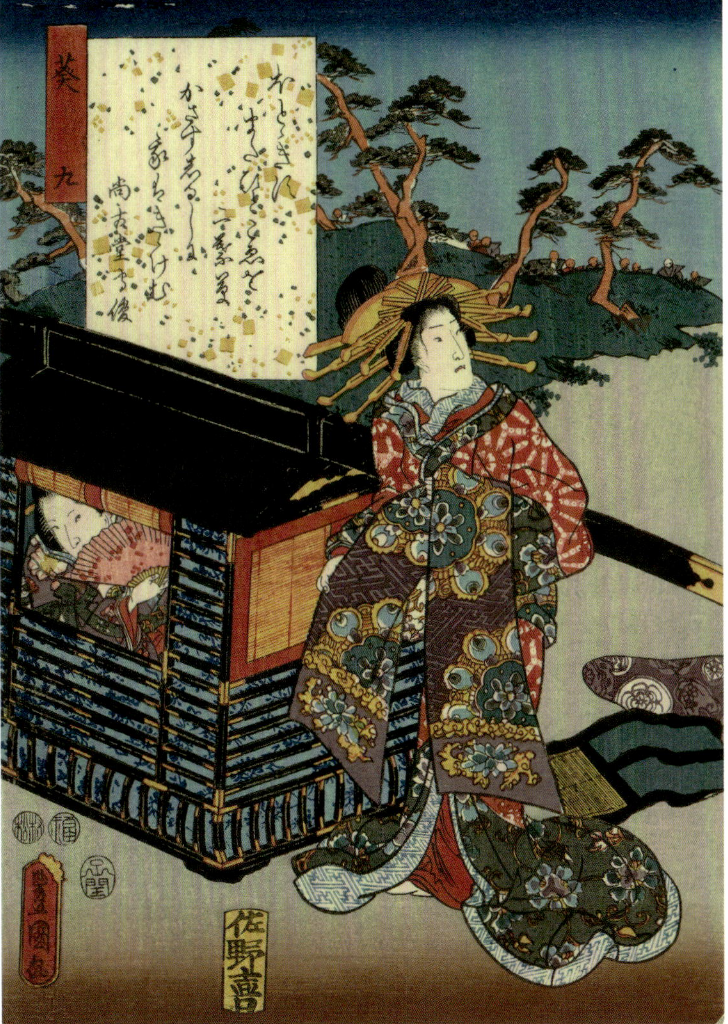

Soon after the festival, Aoi goes into labor and is tormented by an evil spirit that cannot be exorcised. Genji realizes to his horror that it is the living ghost of Rokujō. Aoi rallies long enough to deliver a healthy baby boy and then dies.

In chapter 12 of *Inaka Genji*, palanquins stand in for courtly oxcarts. When the courtesan Akogi and her daughter Isona try to view the Kamo Festival parade, their palanquins are roughly pushed aside and overturned by the servants of Mitsuuji's wife Futaba. Kunisada's print shows a distraught Akogi speaking to another spectator, who helps her and her daughter to get home afterward (9C). In the following chapter, Futaba meets the same sad fate as her prototype, Aoi.

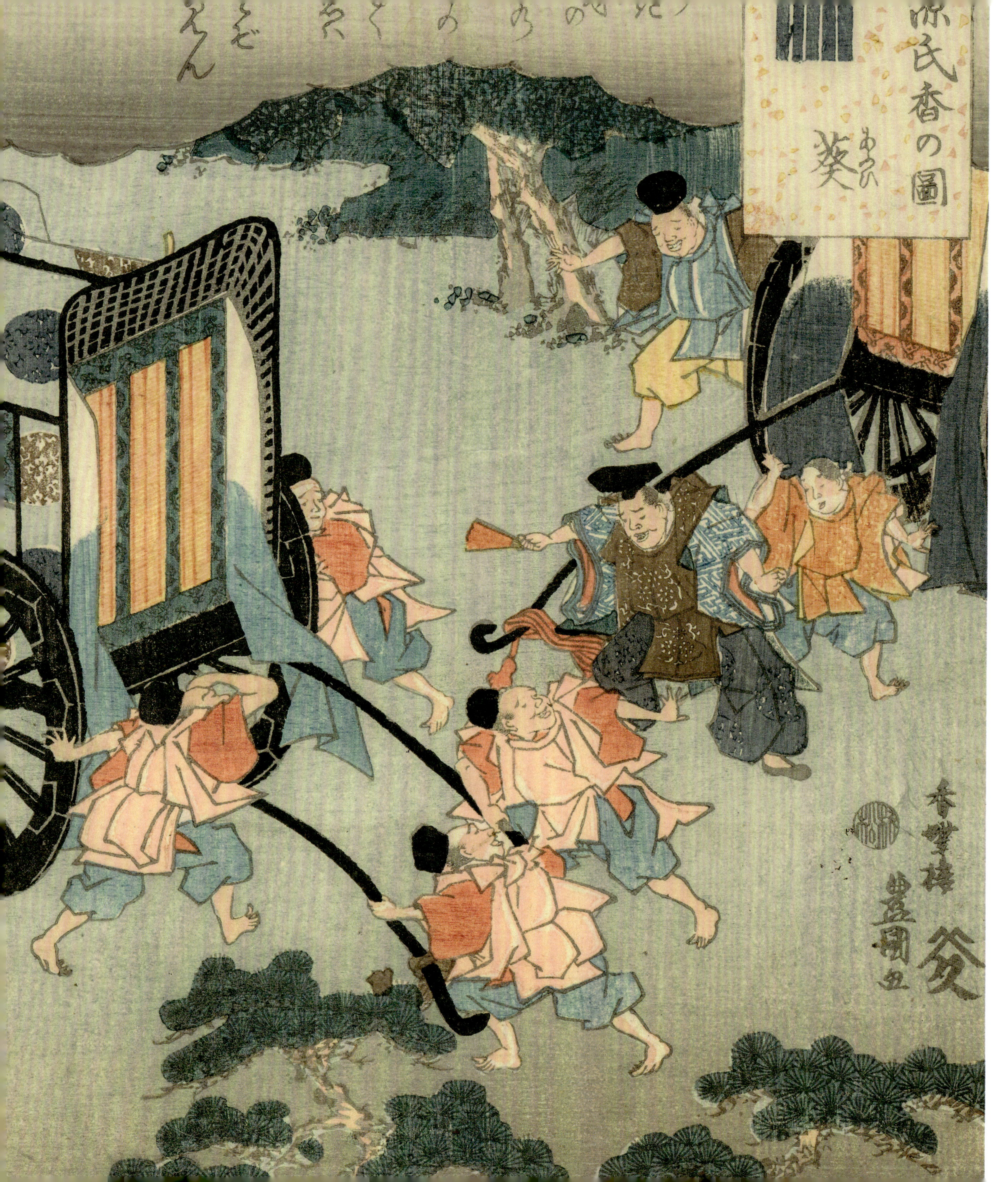

氏香の圖
あふひ
葵
香蝶楼
豊國画

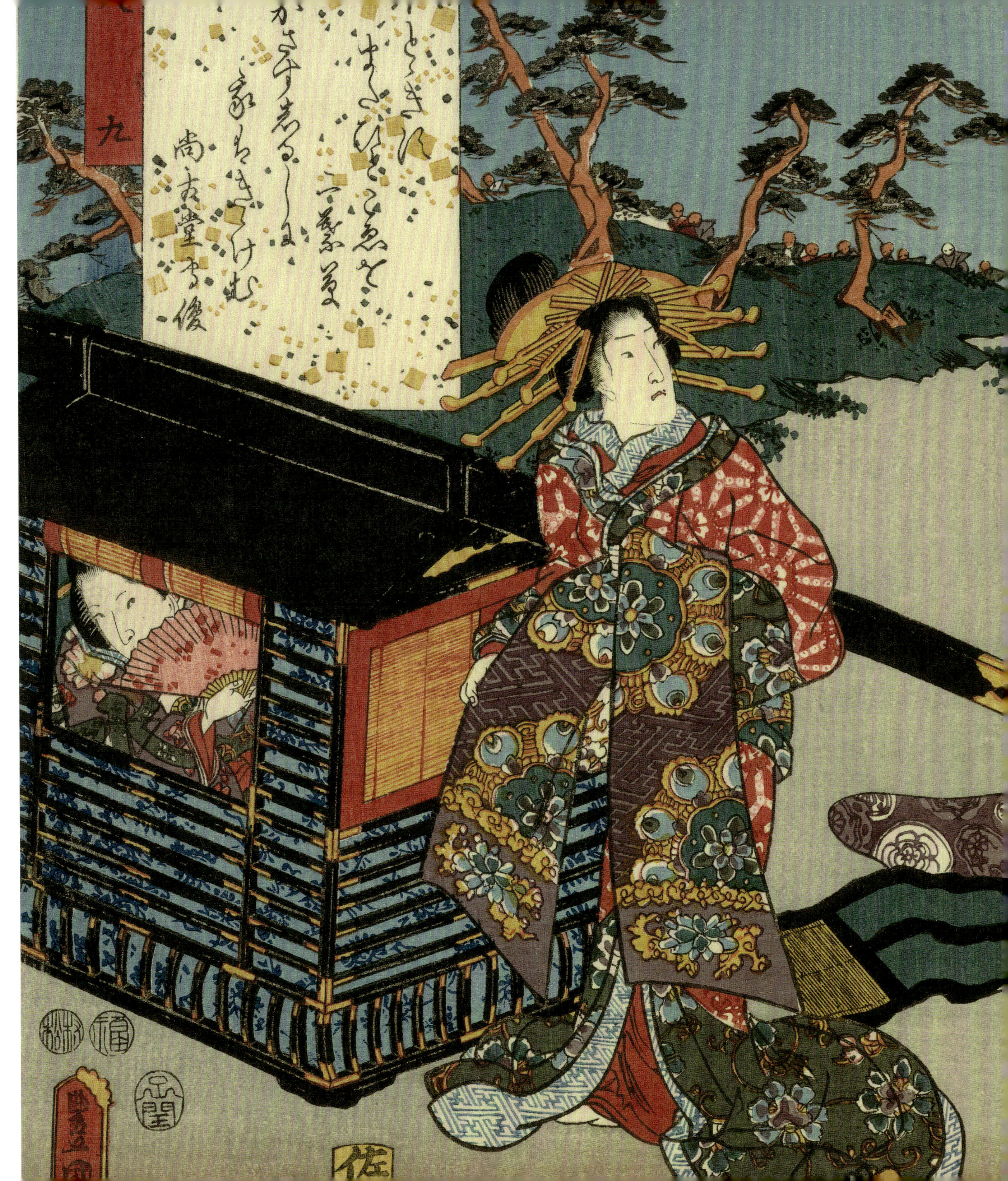
九
尚古堂
佐

10

The Sacred Tree (Sakaki)

Lady Rokujō's daughter (later known as Akikonomu) has been designated the new high priestess of the Ise Shrine, and her mother plans to go with her to Ise as an escape from all the unhappiness of her affair with Genji. While preparing to depart for Ise, the two ladies are staying at the Nonomiya Shrine, known for its unusual entrance gate with the bark still on the wooden pillars. Genji visits one night to say goodbye, announcing his arrival by sliding into the room a branch of the sacred tree called sakaki, an evergreen with shiny oval leaves often used as an offering at Shinto shrines (10A). Kunisada's teacher Toyokuni I had depicted the same episode in a small-scale traditional Genji series with a restricted color scheme that may have been one of the inspirations for Kunisada's later *Genji Incense* series; he showed the scene from the opposite viewpoint, with Genji approaching the bark-covered gate while Lady Rokujō waits inside the building (10B).

When no cedar trees
stand as though to draw the eye
by the sacred fence,
what strange misapprehension
led you to pick sakaki?

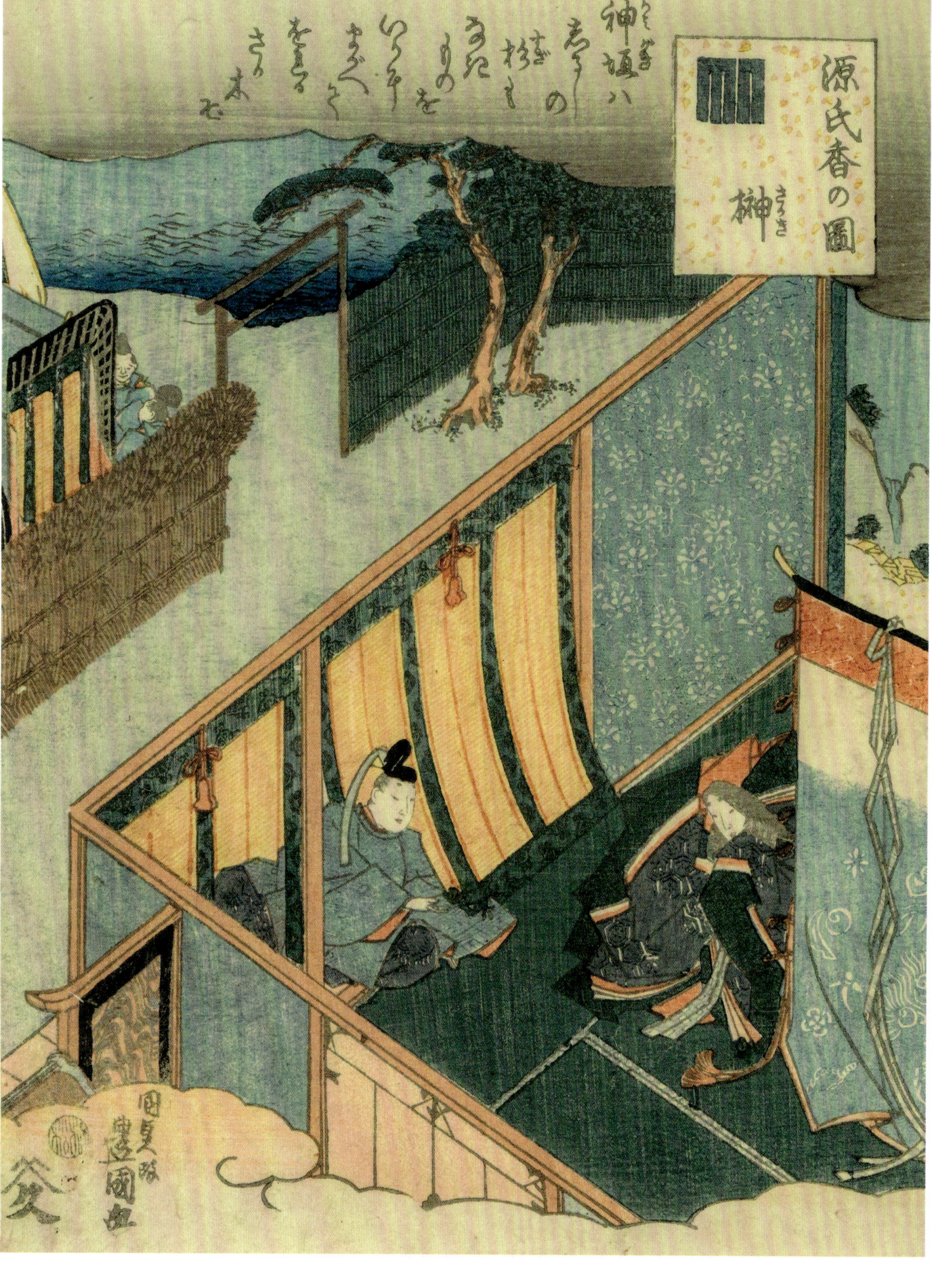

10A | Kunisada, *Genji Incense Pictures*, 1844–47

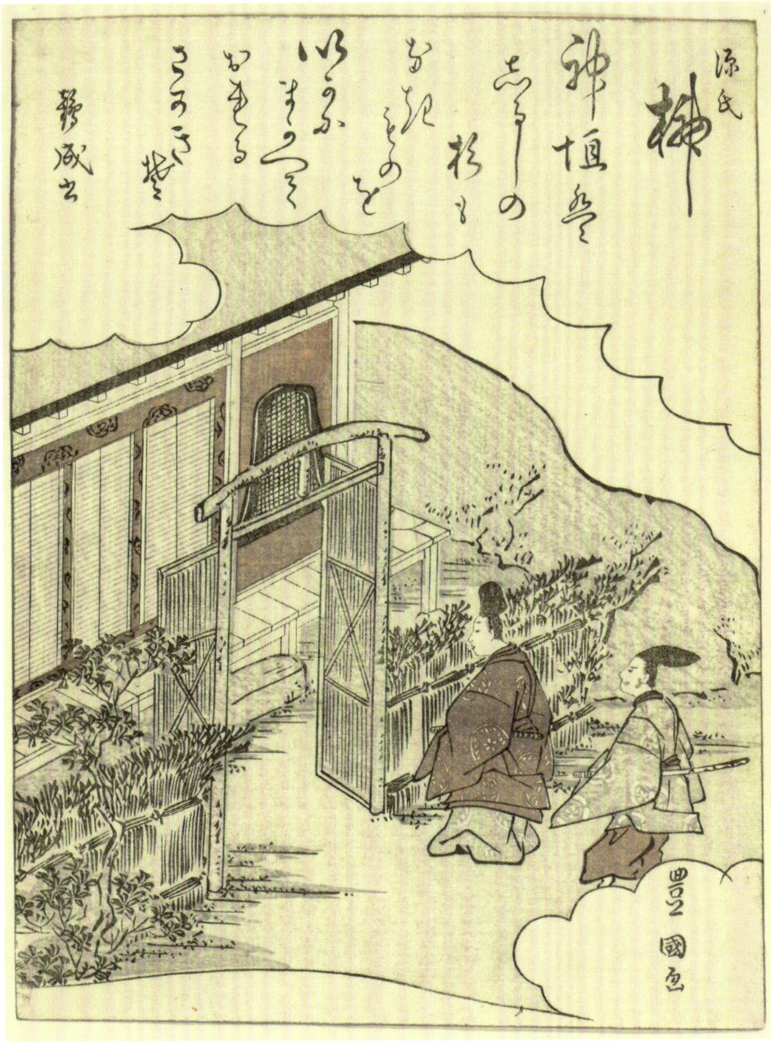

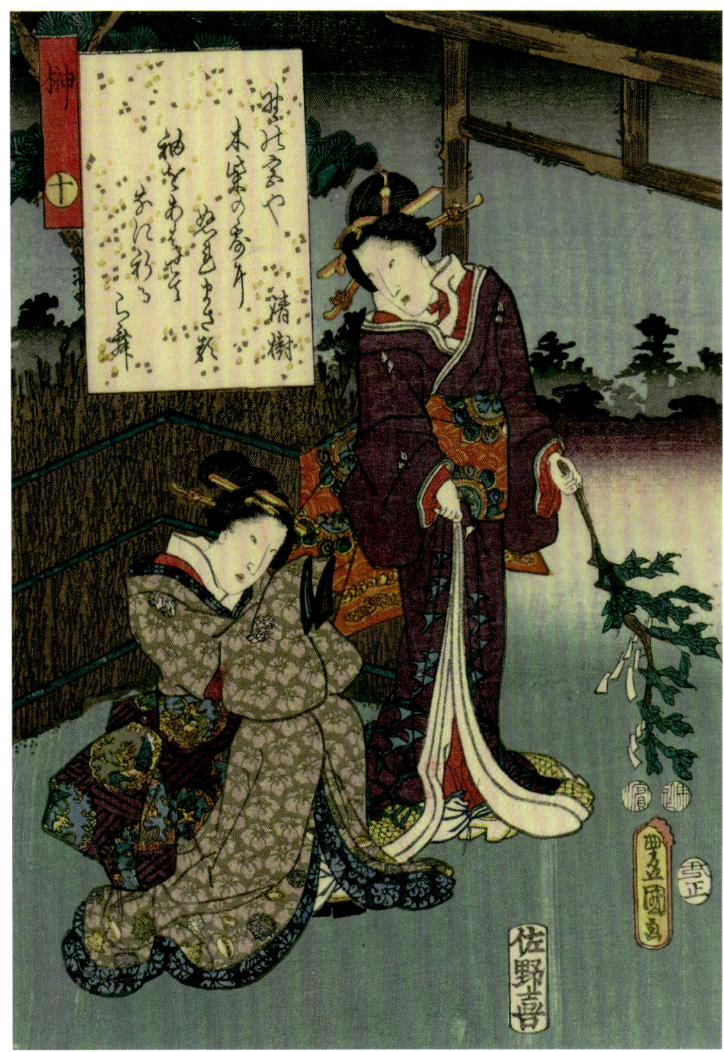

10B | Toyokuni I, *The Tale of Genji*, Edo period

10C | Kunisada, *The Color Print Contest of a Modern Genji*, 1853

The sad mood continues throughout the chapter, with the death of Genji's father, the former emperor, and Fujitsubo's decision to become a Buddhist nun. Worst of all for Genji's future, an indiscreet visit to Oborozukiyo results in the exposure of their illicit affair to her older sister Kokiden, Genji's stepmother, who has always disliked him.

In chapter 12 of *Inaka Genji*, Mitsuuji decides to send Nikki Kiyonosuke and his wife Karaginu (= Utsusemi) to Ise to foil the plots of the Yamana clan in that area; he also plans to take Akogi and Isona (= Rokujō and her daughter) out of the brothel and send them to Ise as well. While waiting to go to Ise, they will stay at Kiyonosuke's villa in the neighborhood of Nonomiya. In chapter 14, shortly before their departure for Ise, kindhearted Karaginu asks Mitsuuji to come and visit Akogi, who is very unhappy. In a scene based on the opening illustration of chapter 14, Kunisada shows Akogi and Karaginu beside the shrine gate (10C). Akogi holds a branch of sakaki, decorated with white paper streamers that mark it as a sacred object.

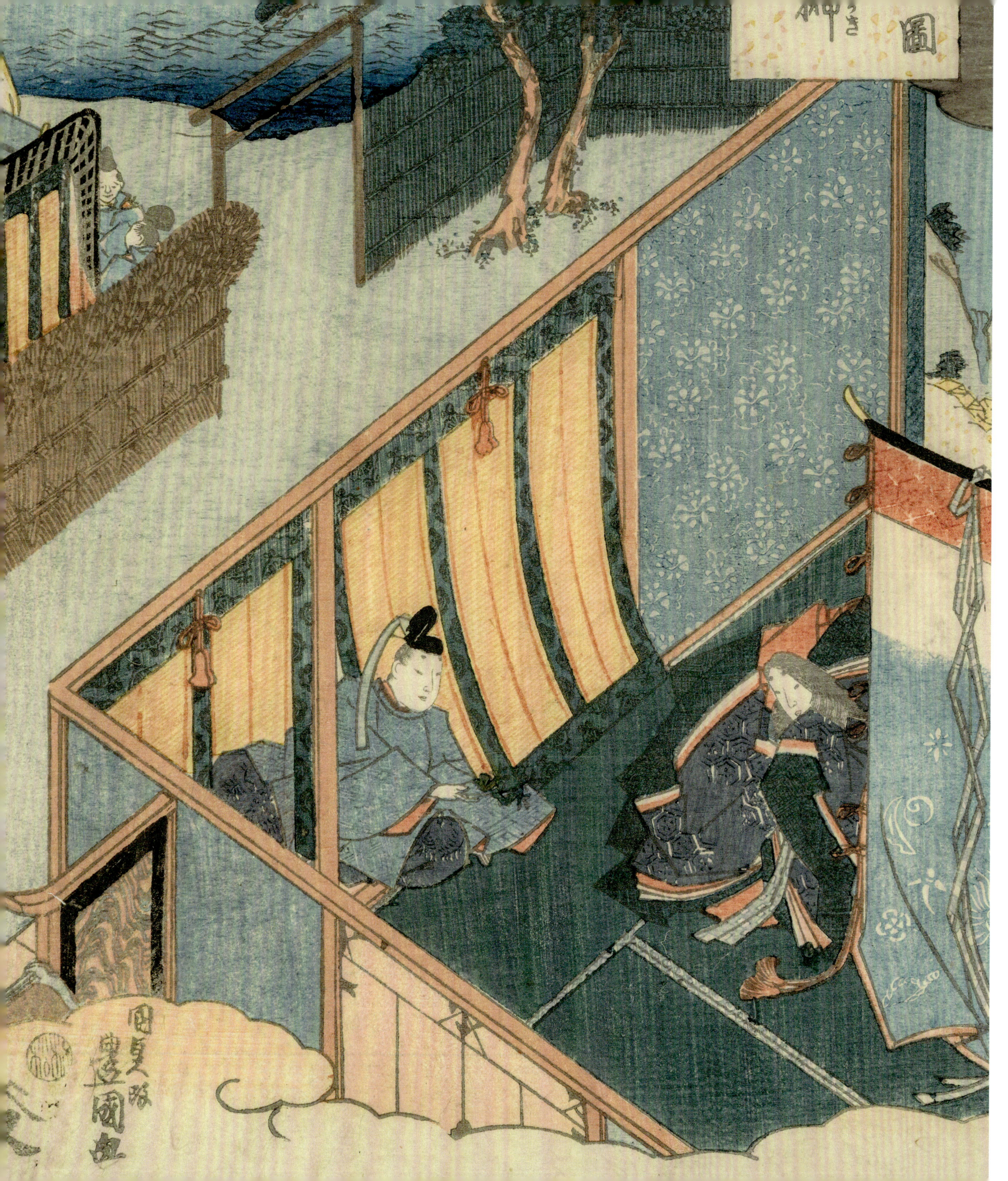
圖
国貞改
豊國画

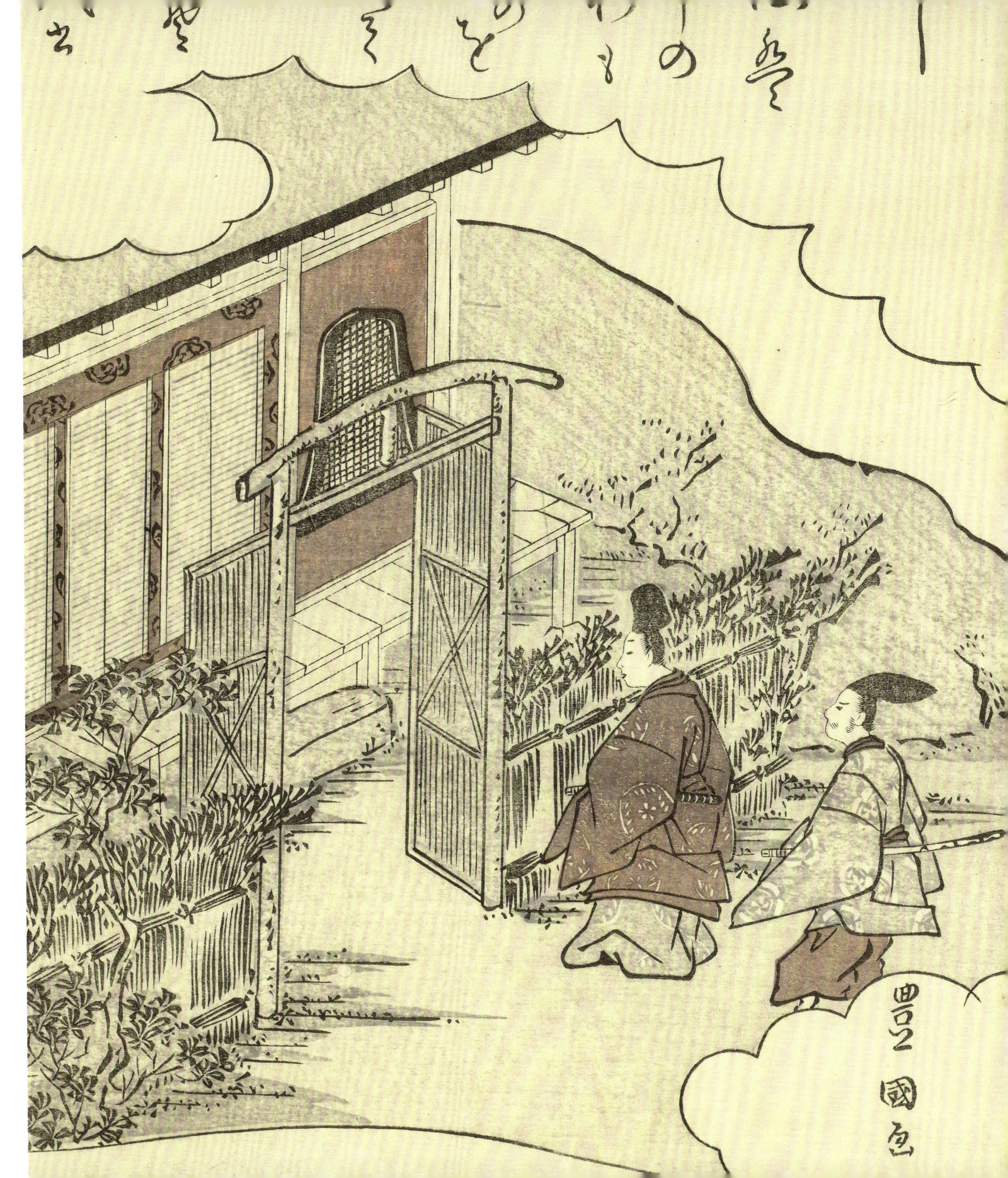
豊国画

11

The Village of Falling Blossoms (Hanachirusato)

Genji takes time off from his increasingly troubled personal life to visit two sisters living in a quiet village near the city: Reikeiden (one of his late father's ladies) and her younger sister (a former lover of Genji himself), whose nickname comes from their residence, Hanachirusato, the Village of Falling Flowers; in this case, the flowers are fragrant orange blossoms. On the way, Genji stops at the residence of another, unnamed lady, but he is not received there and continues on to the home of the sisters (11A).

The visit takes place during a lull in the rainy season of early summer, and so this scene was selected by Eizan to represent the "clearing weather" theme in an *Eight Views* series ostensibly based on Genji but focusing primarily on noted courtesans of the day, with the implication that they are as beautiful and charming as Genji's ladies (11B). The motif of Eight Views came from Chinese ink paintings imported into Japan during the fourteenth and fifteenth centuries; it referred originally to *Eight Views of the Xiao and Xiang Rivers*, showing famous scenic spots in China in eight different circumstances, such as clearing weather after a rainstorm, autumn moonlight, sailboats returning to harbor, and so on, with

Many fond yearnings
for an orange tree's sweet scent
draw the cuckoo on
to come to find the village
where such fragrant flowers fall.

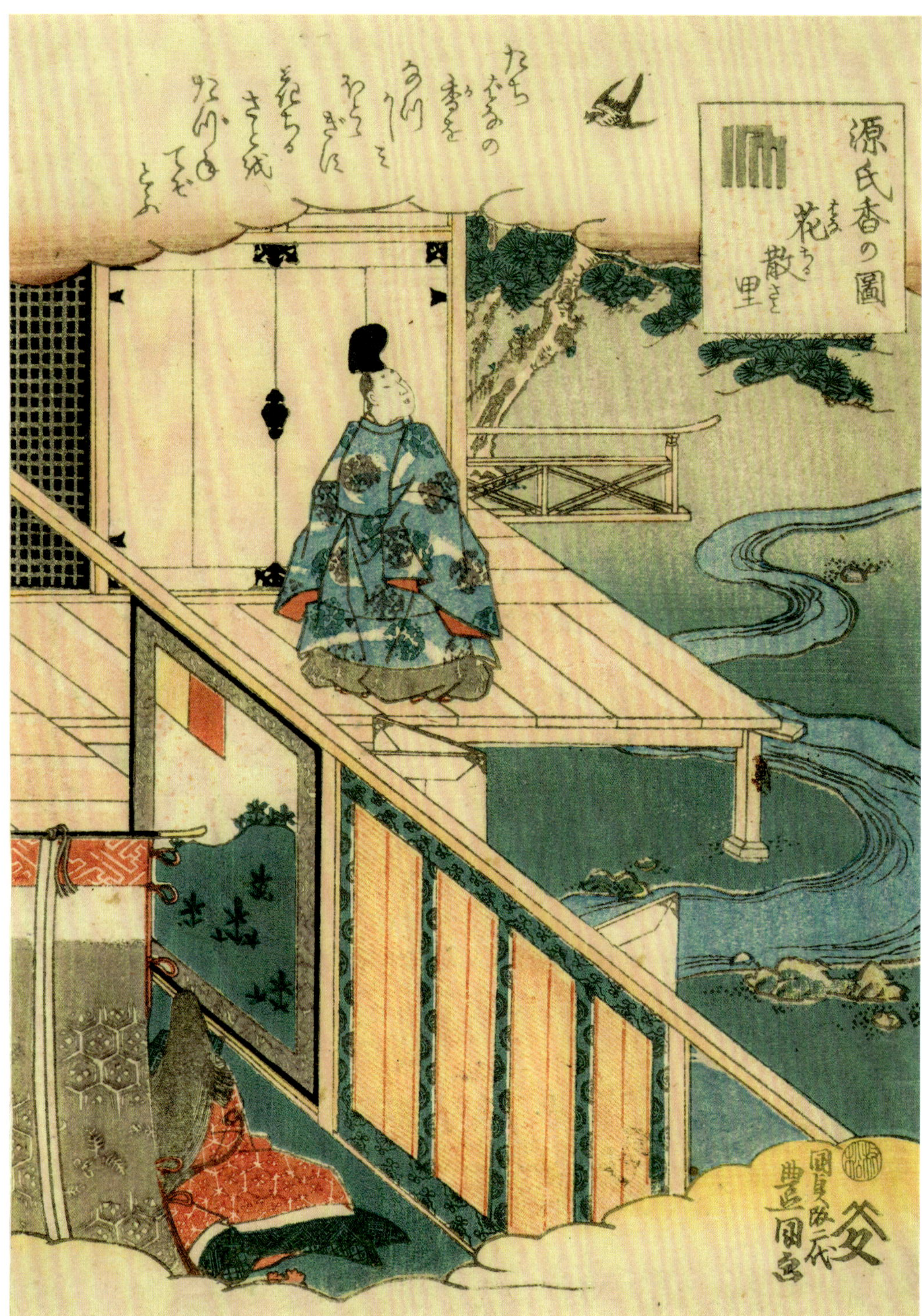

11A | Kunisada, *Genji Incense Pictures*, 1844–47

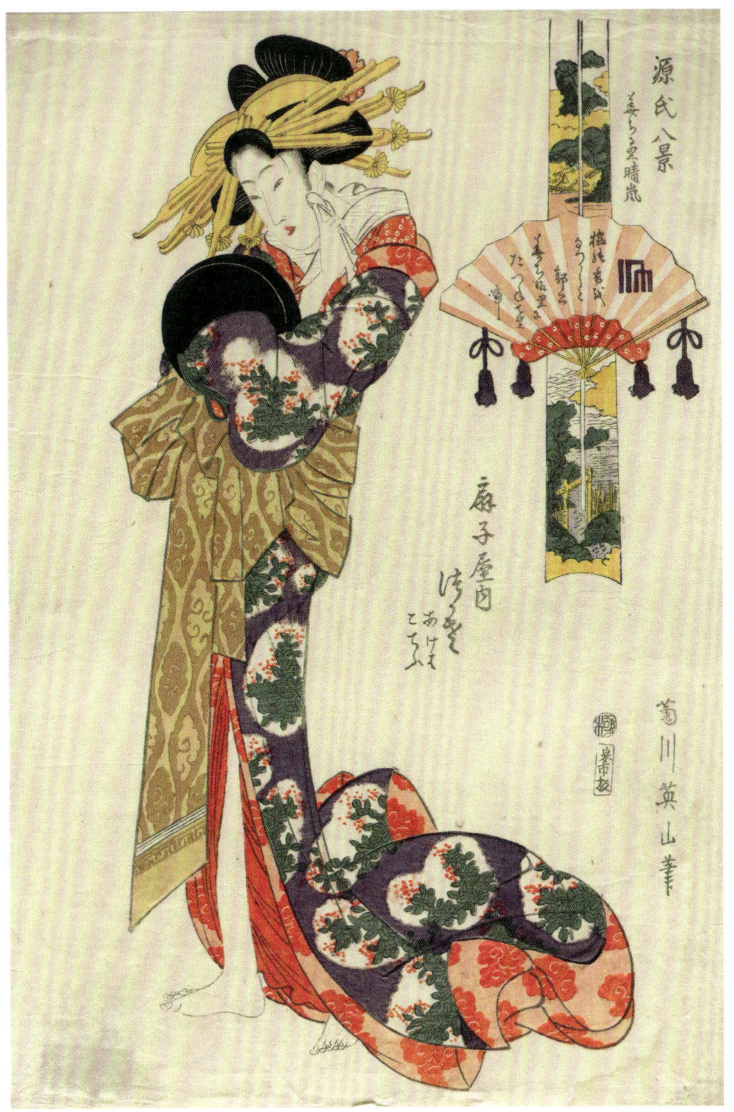

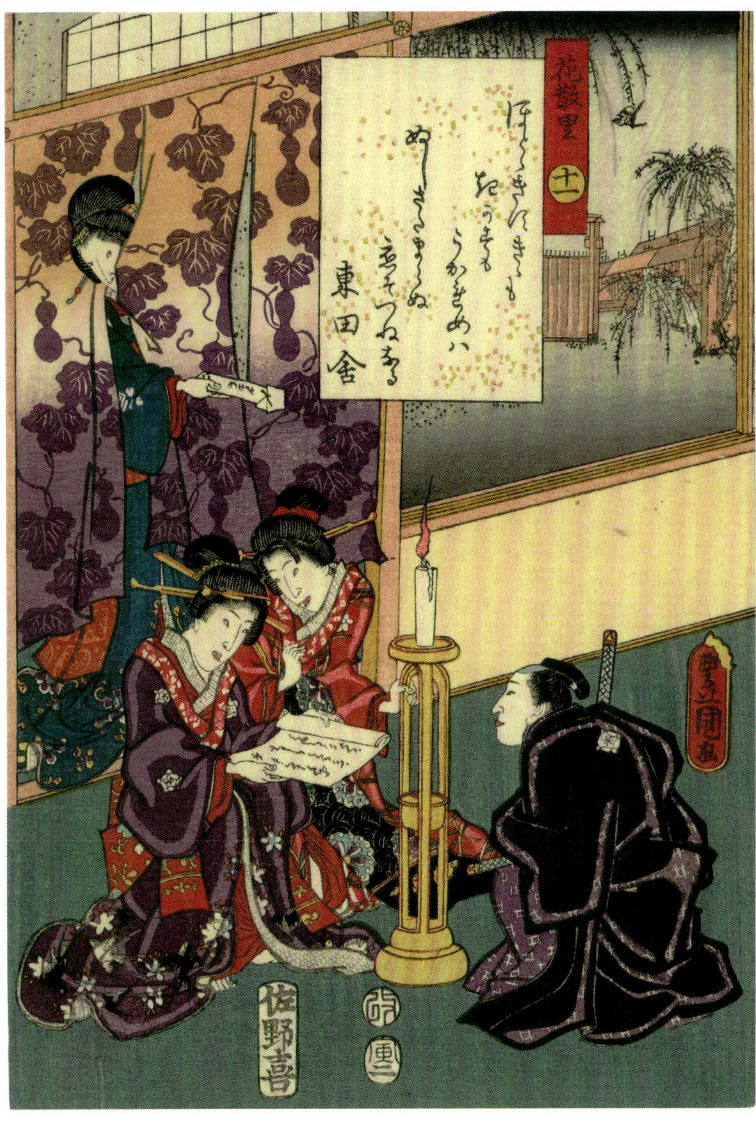

11B | Kikukawa Eizan, *Eight Views of Genji*, about 1814–17

11C | Kunisada, *The Color Print Contest of a Modern Genji*, 1854

accompanying poems. The same concept was subsequently used by Japanese artists to create *Eight Views of Ōmi Province*, and ukiyo-e print designers gleefully parodied the basic theme in many different ways.

The corresponding scene in *Inaka Genji* is in chapter 16, when Mitsuuji makes some visits in anticipation of his departure from Kyoto. He first stops off at a house of courtesans and has his servant Korekichi (the equivalent of Genji's Koremitsu) deliver a note to someone. As shown in Kunisada's print (based on an illustration in the book), the women study the note and send a reply (11C). Readers will later discover that this incident was not an unsuccessful flirtation, as in the original novel, but an arrangement for a future secret meeting.

Mitsuuji goes on to visit his father's former concubine and her younger sister Hanazato (= Hanachirusato), who had a fling with Mitsuuji when she worked for Lady Inabune (see chapter 6). Mitsuuji appears to spend the night with Hanazato, but this is actually a ruse concealing his meeting with Muraōgi, who has managed to recover the shogun's stolen sword and return it to him, so that Mitsuuji now has all three of the lost treasures.

12

Suma (Suma)

Since many powerful people are angry with him, Genji decides that it would be wise to get out of town for a while. Leaving Murasaki in charge of his home in the city, he moves to the seacoast of Suma (present-day Kōbe) with just a few loyal retainers. There he passes the time playing the koto, sketching the scenery, composing poetry, and writing melancholy letters to his friends; a response from Lady Rokujō, now at Ise, is the chapter title poem. Kunisada shows Genji gazing out at the boats of the fisherfolk (12A). In Eishi's gentle parody, two lovely ladies pose with a toy boat that appears to be made of strips of poetry paper, representing the Eight Views theme of sailboats returning to the harbor (12B). A koto and several books hint at Genji's other elegant pursuits.

Give thought when you can
to the Ise saltmaker
gathering sorrows,
you who are of Suma shore,
where I hear the brine drips down.

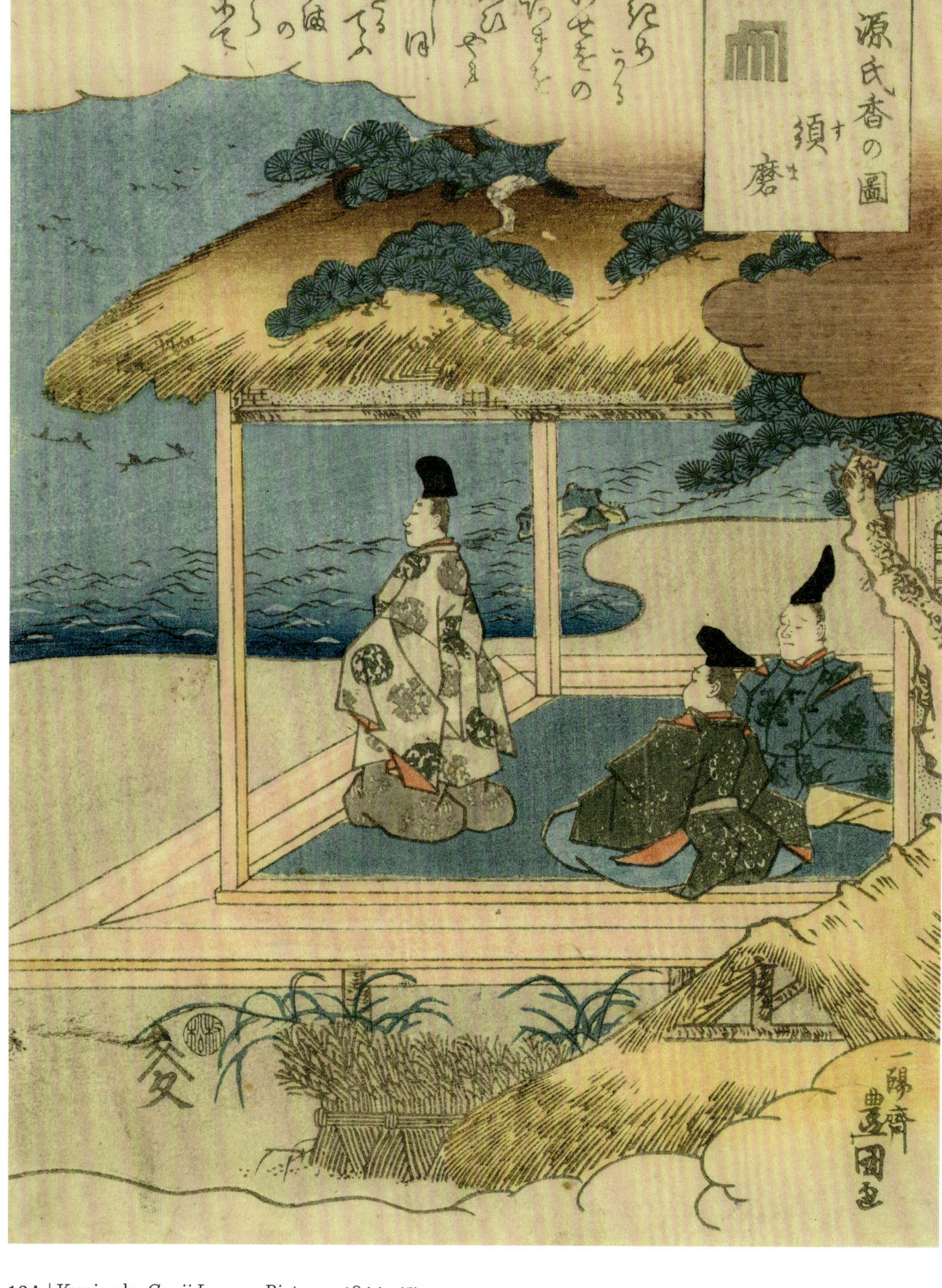

12A | Kunisada, *Genji Incense Pictures*, 1844–47

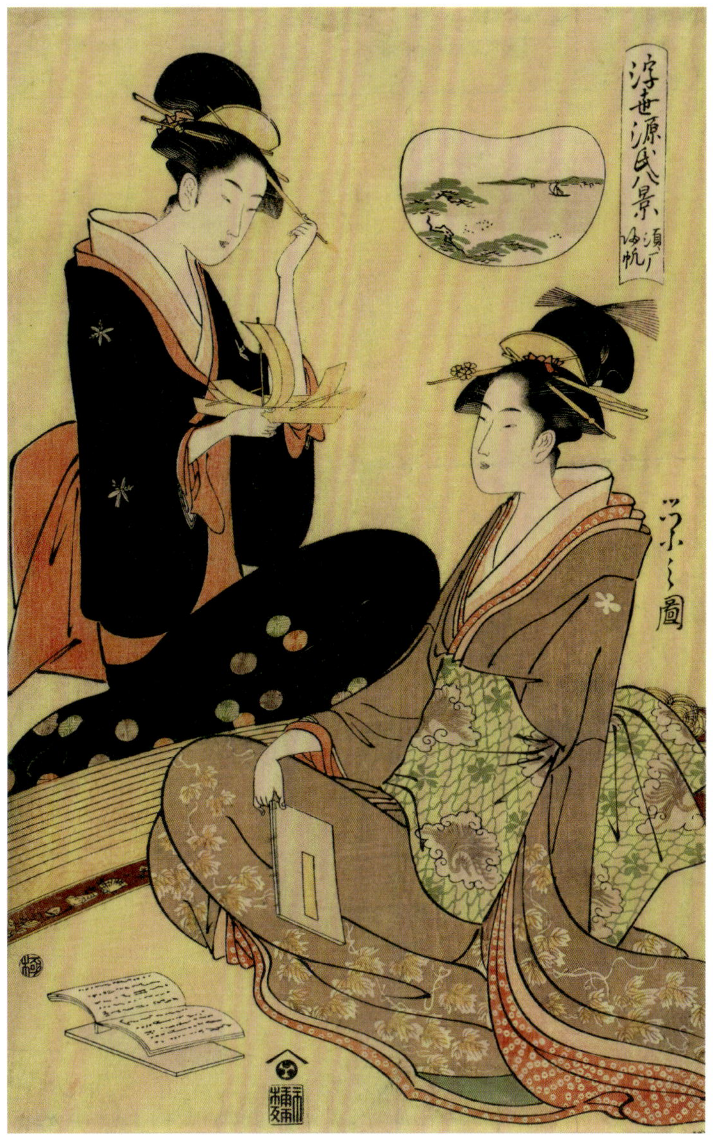

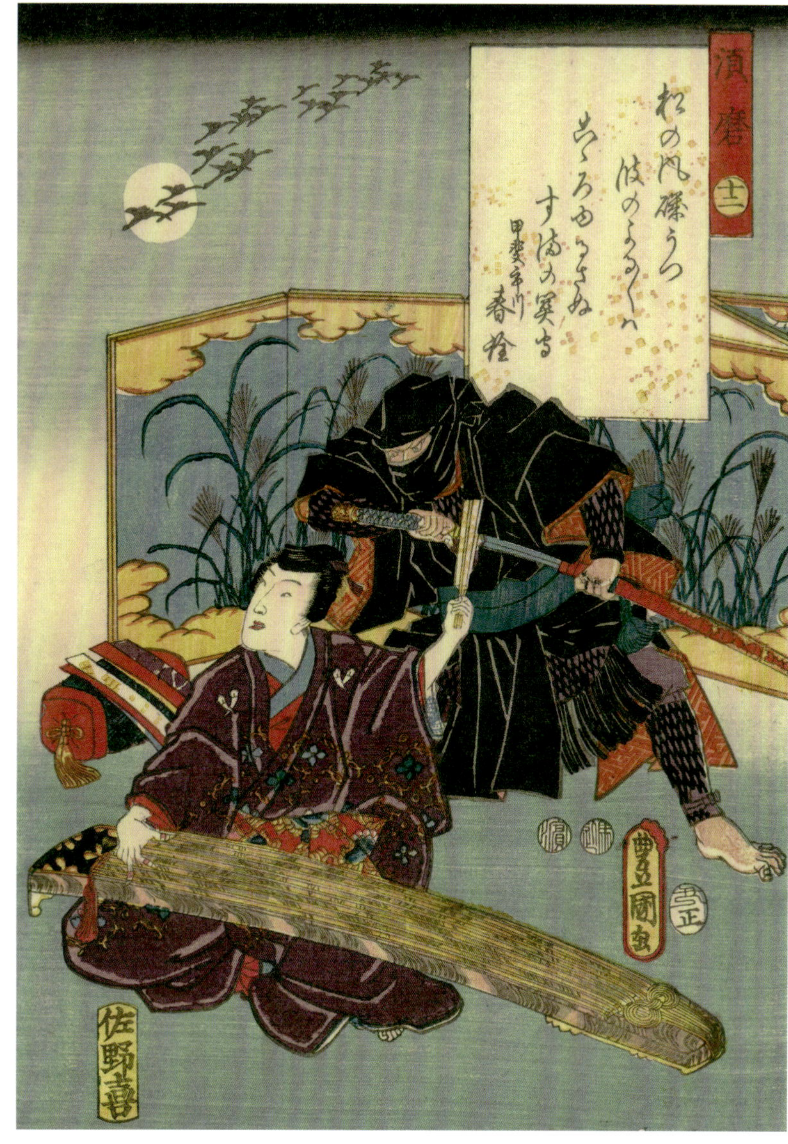

12B | Chōbunsai Eishi, *Eight Views of Genji in the Floating World*, about 1797–99

12C | Kunisada, *The Color Print Contest of a Modern Genji*, 1853

In chapter 17 of *Inaka Genji*, Mitsuuji moves to Suma in Harima Province, ostensibly to escape the consequences of his alleged affairs, but really in order to help thwart the rebellion of the Yamana clan, who are fighting the Otogawa clan (the family of Fuji no Kata). On the way to Suma, Mitsuuji is the target of an attempted assassination by the villain Kawajirō (the wicked stepson of Karaginu, who has no equivalent in the original *Tale*) that ends with Kawajirō himself drowning when he falls into the river wearing his armor. In chapter 18, at the villa in Suma, Mitsuuji is attacked again as he plays the koto one night; but his martial arts skills are so outstanding that he is able to trounce the attacker with his left hand while continuing to strum the koto with his right (12C). The geese flying overhead — probably understood to be seen through opened sliding doors in the room where the attack occurs — show that the season is autumn.

13

Akashi (Akashi)

News of Genji's arrival in Suma has reached the inhabitants of nearby Akashi, including a retired governor who has taken Buddhist vows but is still searching for a suitable husband for his daughter. He invites Genji to visit him, and Genji exchanges poems with the daughter; but the young lady is understandably nervous about the difference in their ranks and is hesitant to go further. On a moonlit autumn night, her father arranges for another visit, and Genji, accompanied by his retainers, rides across the beach to Akashi in the most frequently illustrated scene of the chapter (13A). Although he does not yet know it, this event marks the beginning of a great upswing in Genji's fortunes, for the Akashi lady will bear him a daughter who will one day become empress. At the end of the chapter, Genji is pardoned for his offenses and recalled to the court.

In the world of *Inaka Genji*, the lay priest at Akashi is Yamana Sōnyū, a younger brother of Yamana Sōzen who does not support his treasonous brother. He hopes to make a match between Mitsuuji and his daughter Asagiri (Morning Mist). Although Mitsuuji is very attractive, Asagiri has the same kind of reservations as her prototype in the original *Tale*; but at last, she agrees, persuaded by her maid Chidori.

On this autumn night,
O steed with coat of moonlight,
soar on through the skies,
that for just a little while
I may be there with my love!

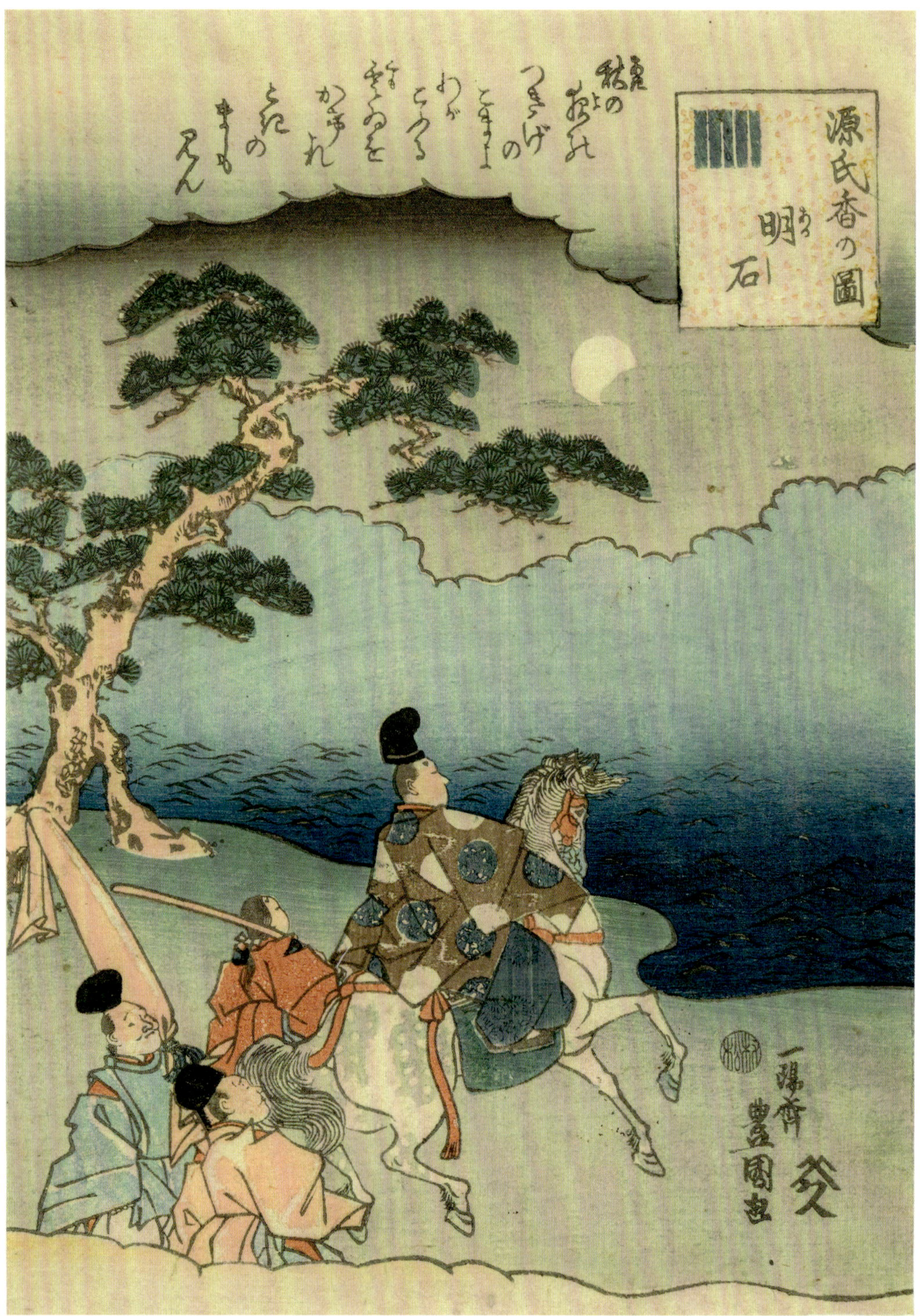

13A | Kunisada, *Genji Incense Pictures*, 1844–47

13B | Kunisada, *The Color Print Contest of a Modern Genji*, 1852

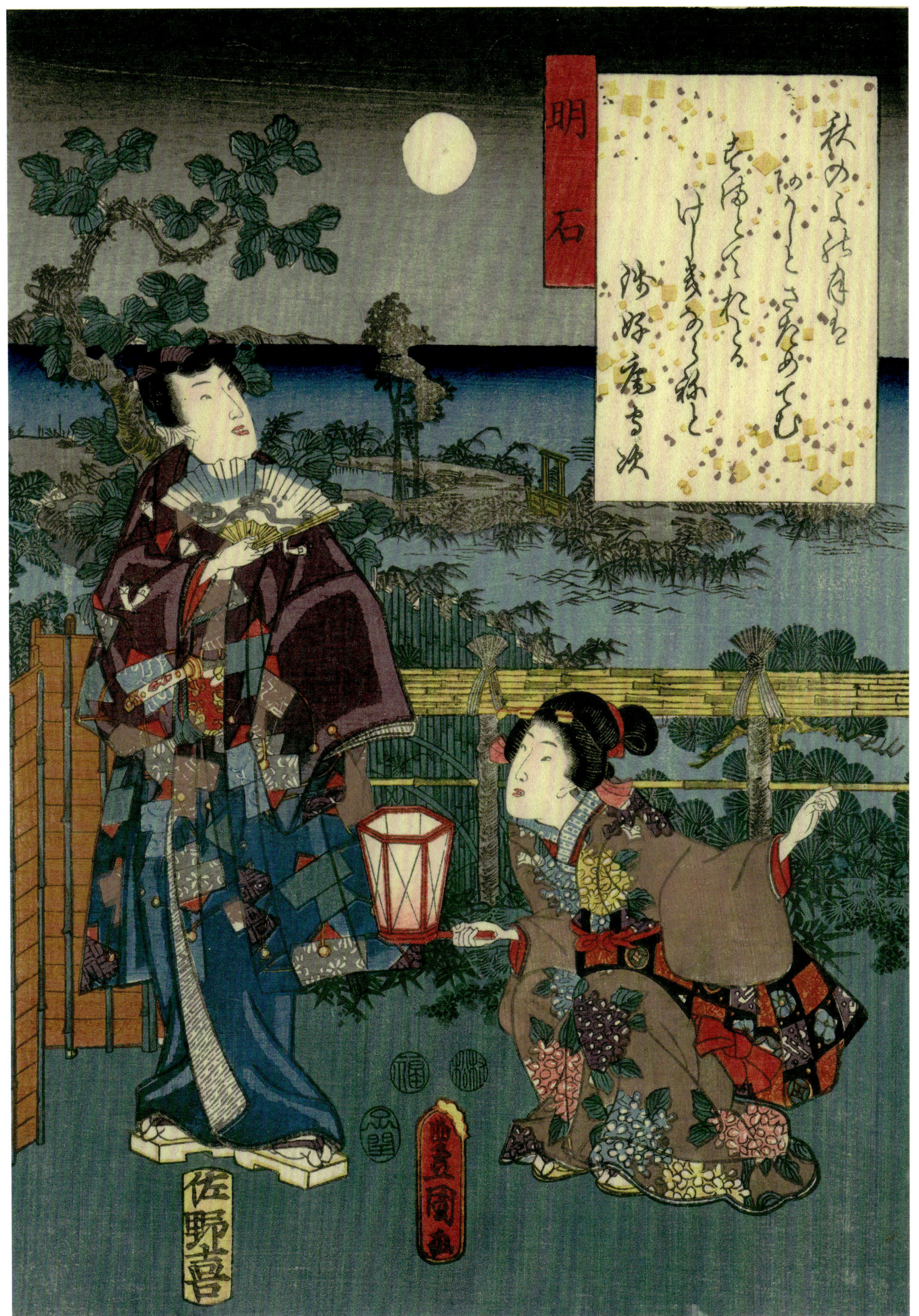
明石
豊國画
佐野喜

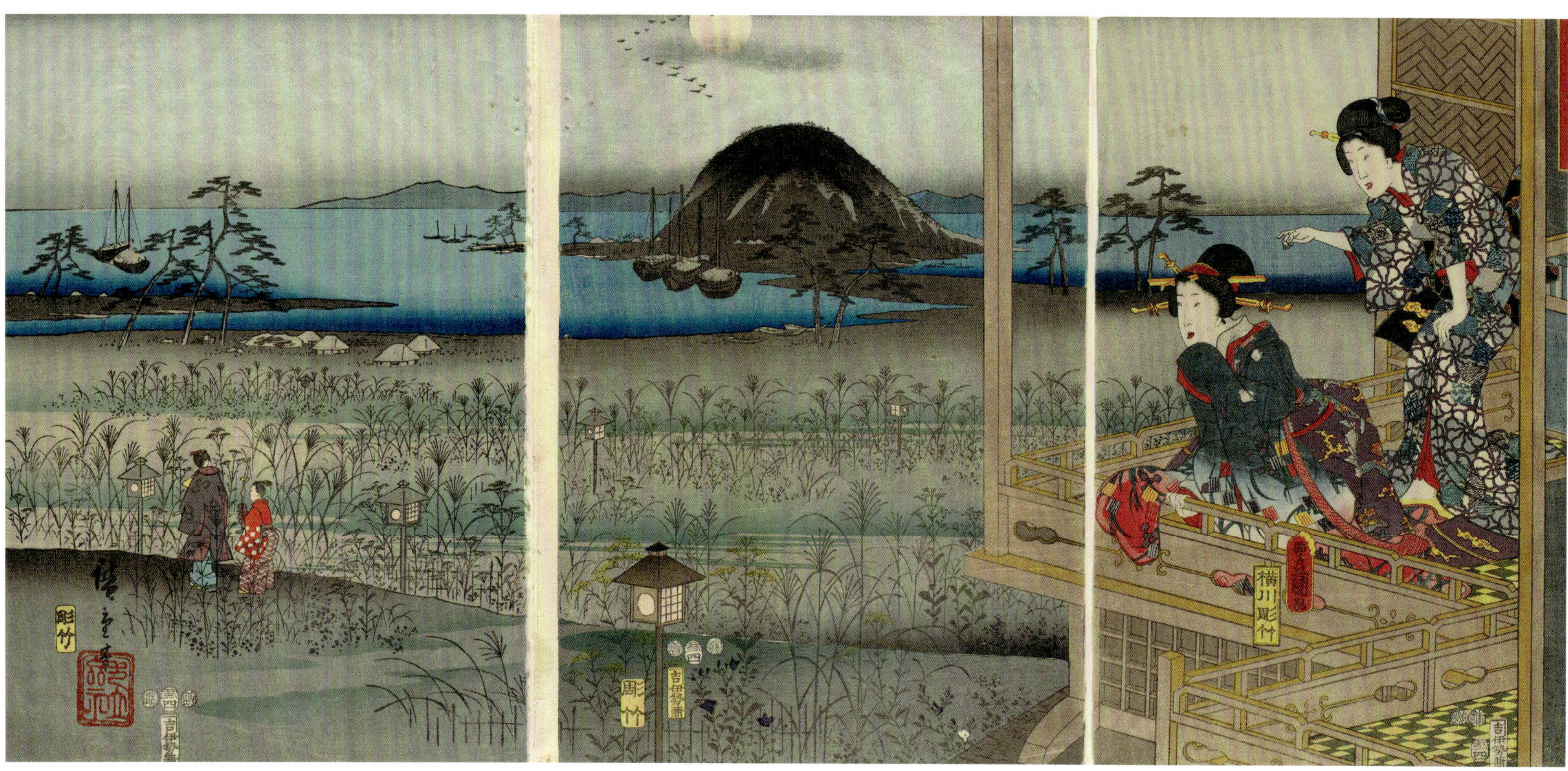

13C | Kunisada and Hiroshige, *Fashionable Genji*, 1853

Mitsuuji makes his way to the lady not by riding a horse along the beach, but by walking through the garden wearing "horse clogs" (komageta), led by Chidori (13B). Months go by, and in chapter 22, Mitsuuji is recalled to the capital by his brother the shogun, following the defeat of the Yamana clan. Mitsuuji spends one last night with Asagiri and leaves before dawn; a triptych co-designed by Kunisada and Hiroshige shows him walking back through the garden as Asagiri and Chidori watch him go (13C).

A special feature of Yamana Sōnyū's palatial estate at Akashi is the two-story bathhouse, with water brought up on a pulley from a well on the lower level. Kunisada illustrated the bathhouse in a double-page frontispiece at the beginning of chapter 21, which he later reworked as a spectacular six-sheet color print design (13D). The full image is actually a pair of triptychs that just happen to fit together, since at the time it was technically illegal to publish designs of more than three sheets. The Akashi bathhouse is not described in the text until chapter 26, when it is compared with another building; this delay suggests that the idea may have originated with the illustrator, and the author liked it so much that he wrote it into the story later.

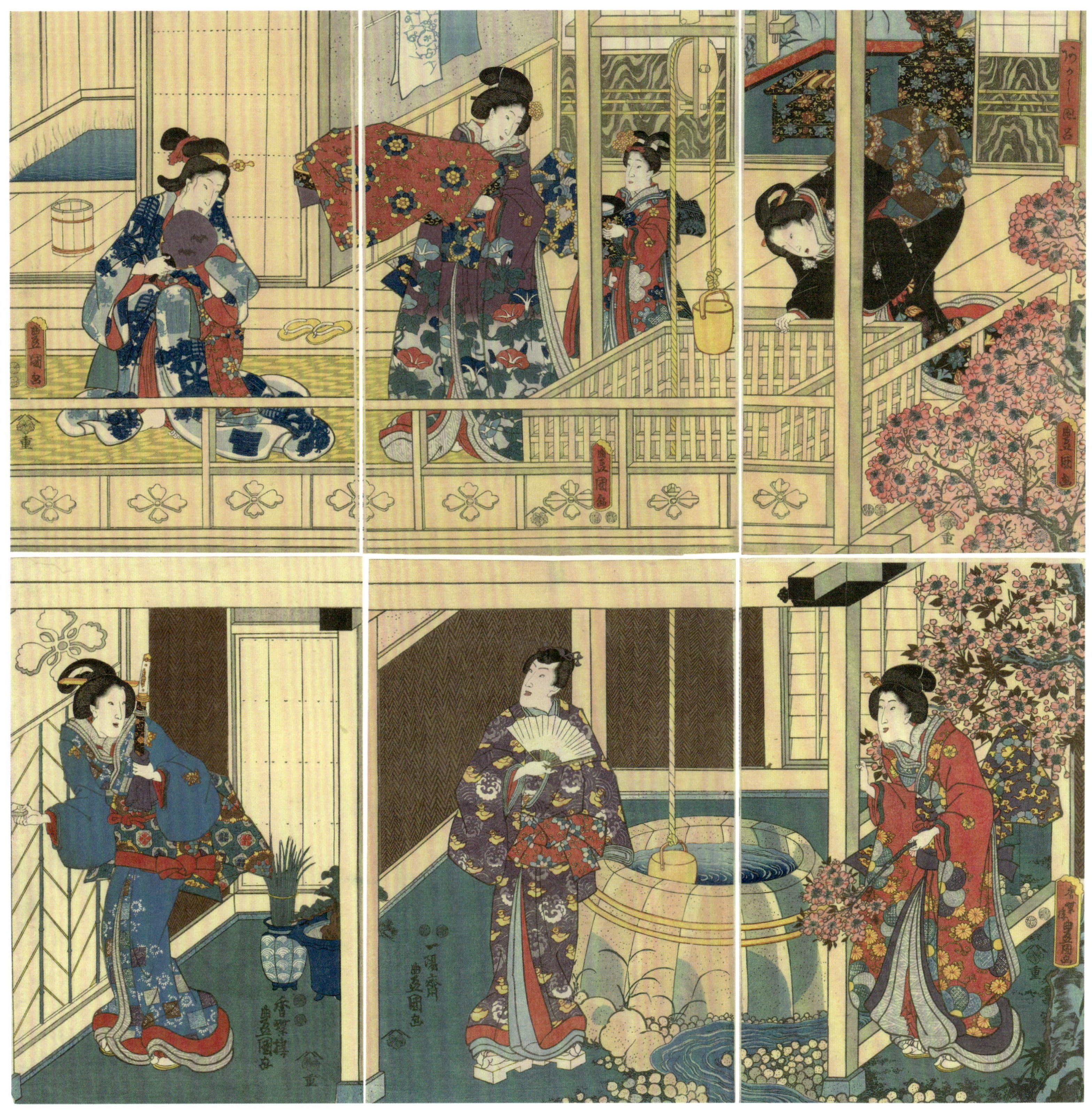

13D | Kunisada, *The Akashi Bathhouse*, 1847–52

14

Channel Markers (Miotsukushi)

Genji makes a pilgrimage to the Sumiyoshi Shrine (in present-day Osaka) to give thanks to the God of Sumiyoshi for the restoration of his high position. He travels from Kyoto by oxcart, with a large and splendid retinue. By coincidence, the Akashi lady, who has recently given birth to Genji's child, also plans to visit the shrine on the same day, coming from Akashi by boat. But the crowds on the beach are so great that she is unable to complete her own pilgrimage that day, leaving her saddened by the gap between Genji's exalted rank and her own more humble position. The same scene, with Genji's carriage in the foreground and the lady's boat in the distance, is illustrated both in the *Genji Incense* series and in an anonymous surimono (privately commissioned print) from the 1830s that makes lavish use of gold- and silver-colored metallic pigments to simulate a Tosa-school album painting (14A, 14B).

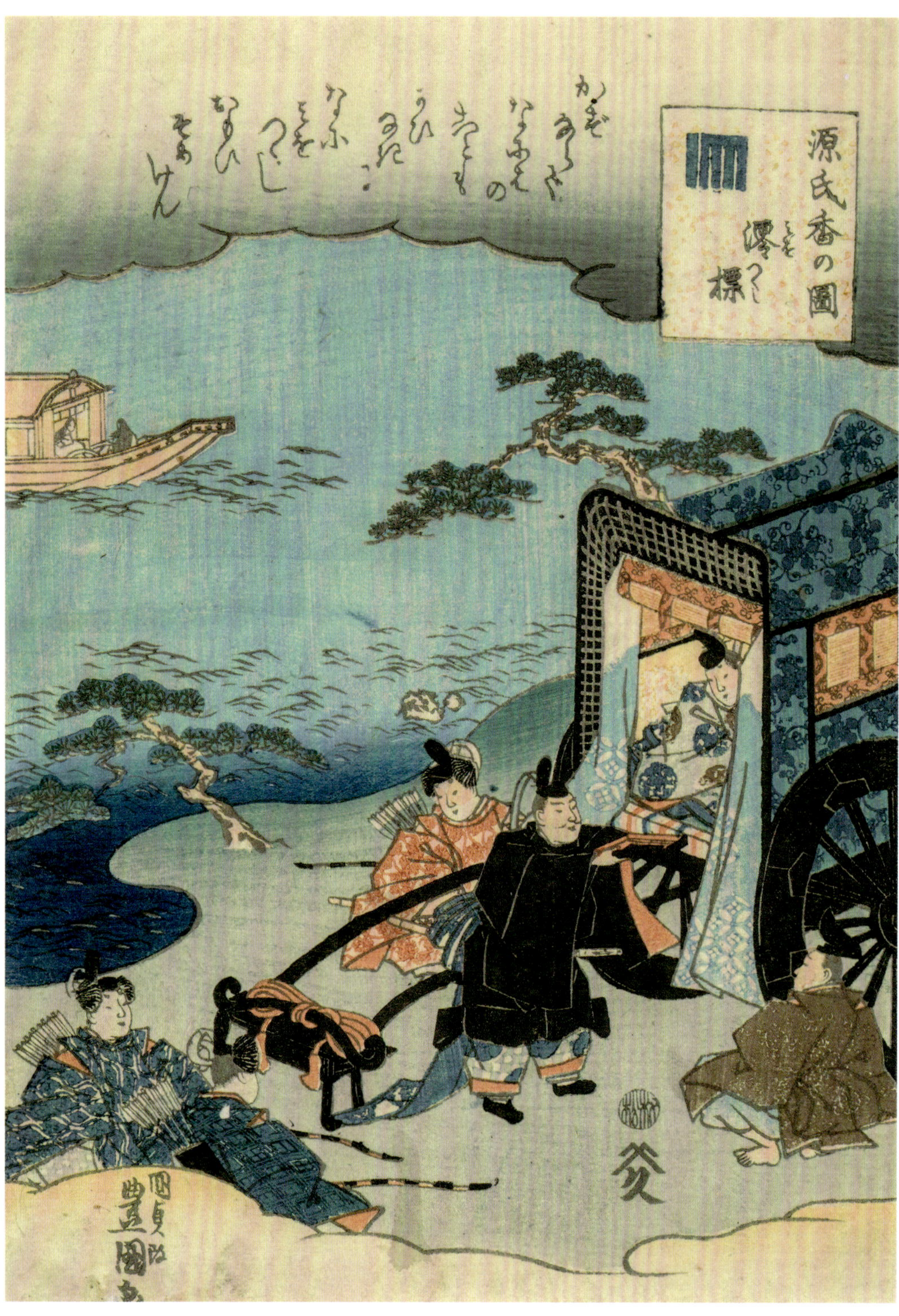

14A | Kunisada, *Genji Incense Pictures*, 1844–47

Lacking any worth,
I have no title to claim
any happiness;
what can have possessed me, then,
so to give my all for love?

14B | Unknown artist, untitled Genji surimono series, about 1836–37

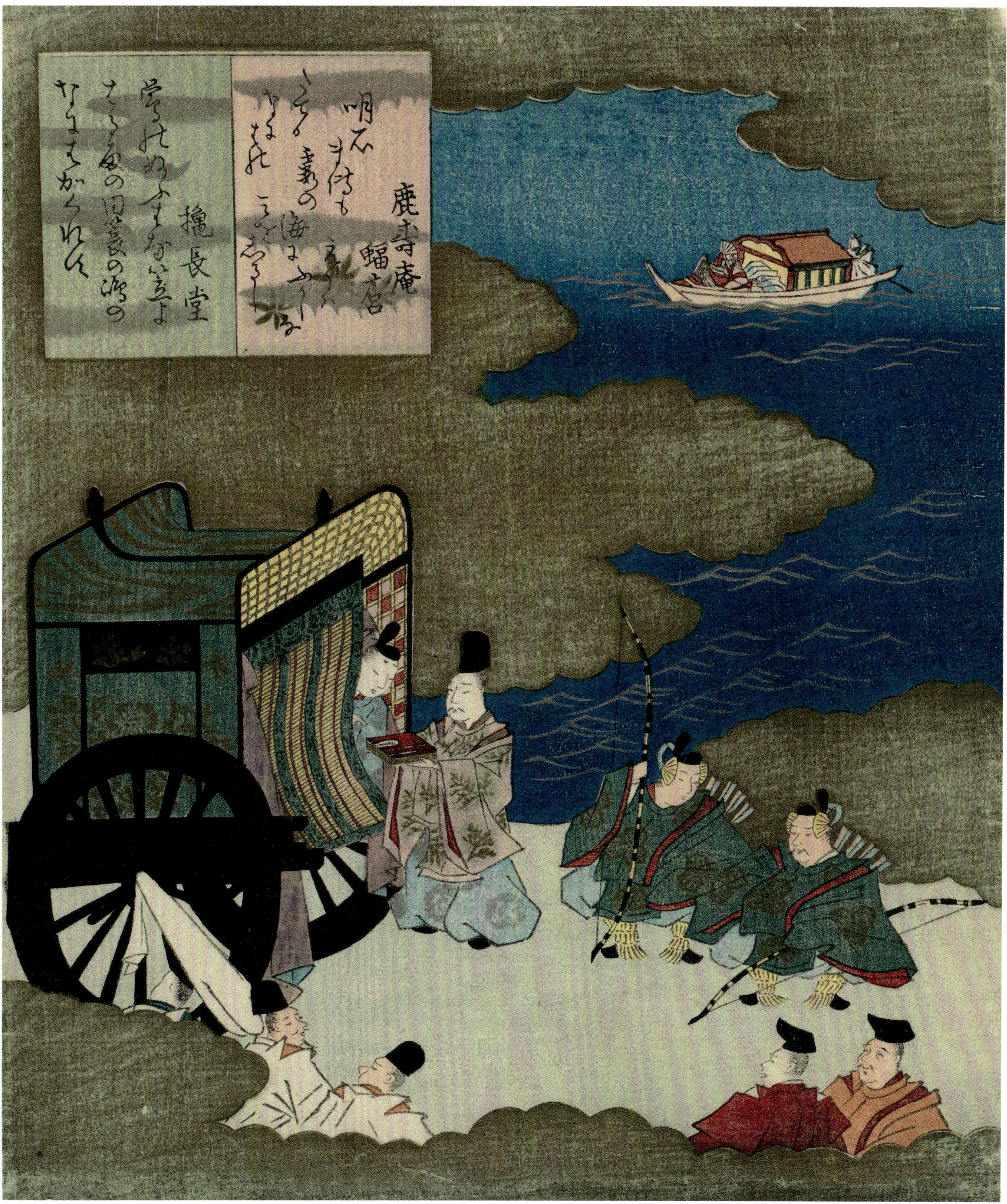

14C | Unknown artist, untitled Genji postcard series, late Meiji–Taishō era

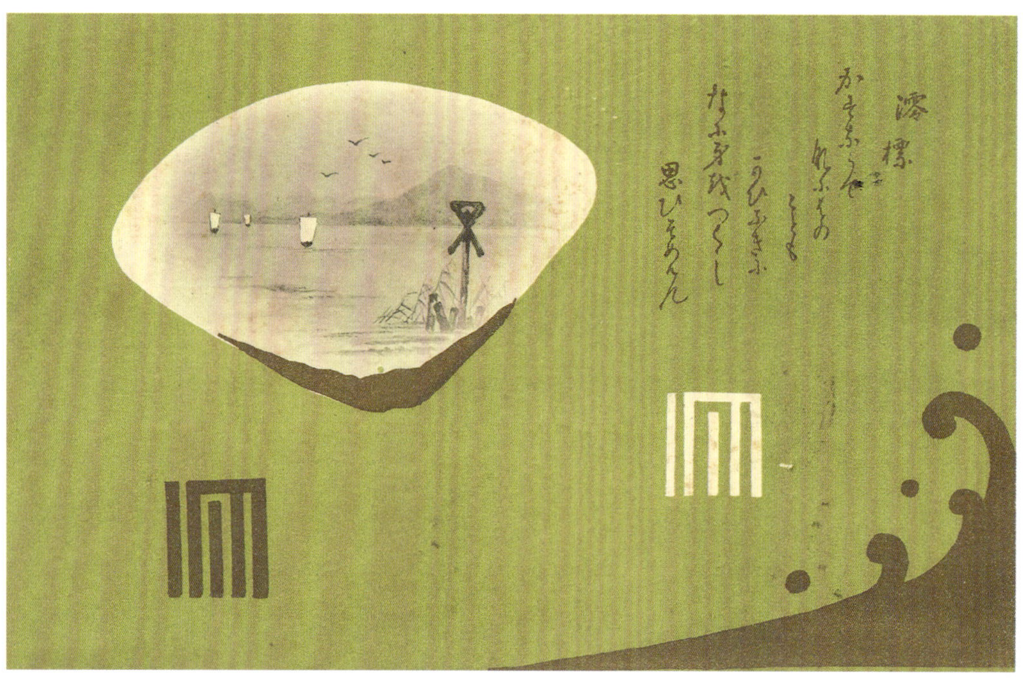

Genji hears of Akashi's plight and exchanges poems with her, with wordplay on the term for the famous channel markers at Naniwa, miotsukushi, which can also mean "to throw oneself away" (that is, either to love too intensely, or to commit suicide by drowning). In more recent times, the distinctively shaped markers became a symbol of the city of Osaka; two of these markers are clearly depicted in an early twentieth-century postcard from a set of Genji cards by an unknown artist illustrating the chapter title poems with small vignettes (14C). In most earlier illustrations, however, they are shown as simple pillars.

For the purposes of his own storyline in *Inaka Genji*, Tanehiko rearranged the order of the next few chapters of *Genji monogatari*. The events corresponding to Yomogiu (15) take place from chapter 22 to chapter 24 of the parody, while Miotsukushi (14) and Sekiya (16) are combined in chapter 24. Asagiri, the lady from Akashi, brings her newborn daughter for the child's first visit to the Sumiyoshi Shrine, accidentally choosing the same day as Mitsuuji's pilgrimage. She travels most of the way in a large sailing ship but transfers to a small boat for the final approach to the shrine. Kunisada shows her as she disembarks, holding the baby in her arms (14D).

14D | Kunisada, *The Color Print Contest of a Modern Genji*, 1853

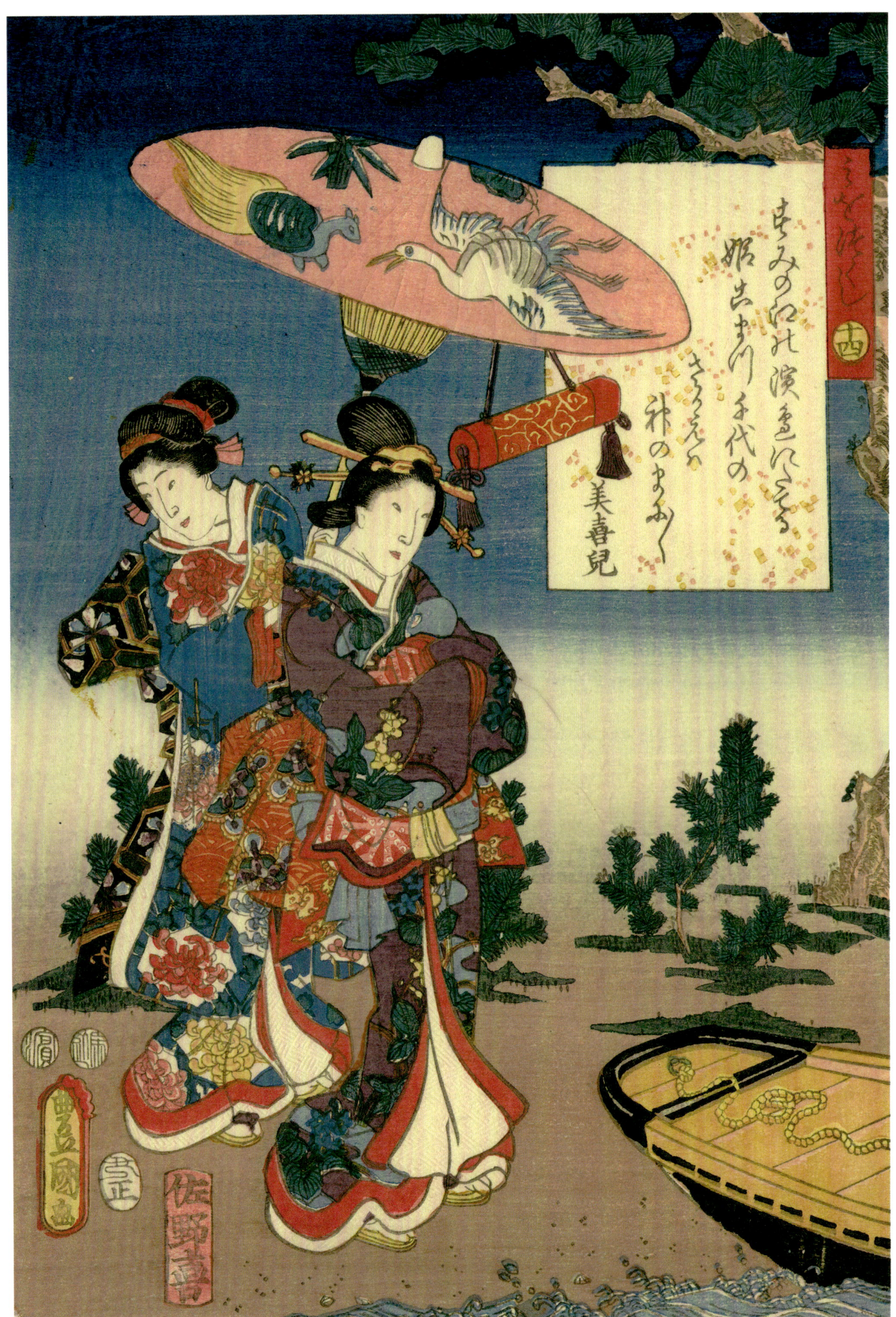
みをつくし
美喜児
豊国画
佐野喜

15

The Wormwood Patch (Yomogiu)

While Genji was away in Suma, the unfortunate red-nosed princess Suetsumuhana grew even more impoverished, but she resisted her obnoxious aunt's grudging offer of lodging and stayed on in her shabby mansion. Now back in the city, Genji is passing by one night and suddenly recognizes the dilapidated house. He makes his way inside, with Koremitsu going ahead to brush away the raindrops from the plants in the overgrown garden (15A). This scene, with much the same composition, had appeared repeatedly in Genji illustrations as far back as the earliest surviving depictions of the novel from the twelfth century; Kunisada's print echoes these earlier examples.

A postcard by Kajita Hanko, created in 1905, brings a twentieth-century design sense to the same traditional image (15B). The figures are partly obscured by driving streaks of rain, and by the large, red umbrella that hides Genji's face. Its round shape is echoed by another bold arc at the lower left that may be a stylized representation of the bark roof of the princess's home. Genji, who feels responsible for the welfare of all of his former lovers, has the princess's house repaired and later invites her to move into his enormous mansion to be honored as one of his ladies.

Now that I am here,
I myself shall seek her out
through her trackless waste,
to see whether all these weeds
have left her as she was then.

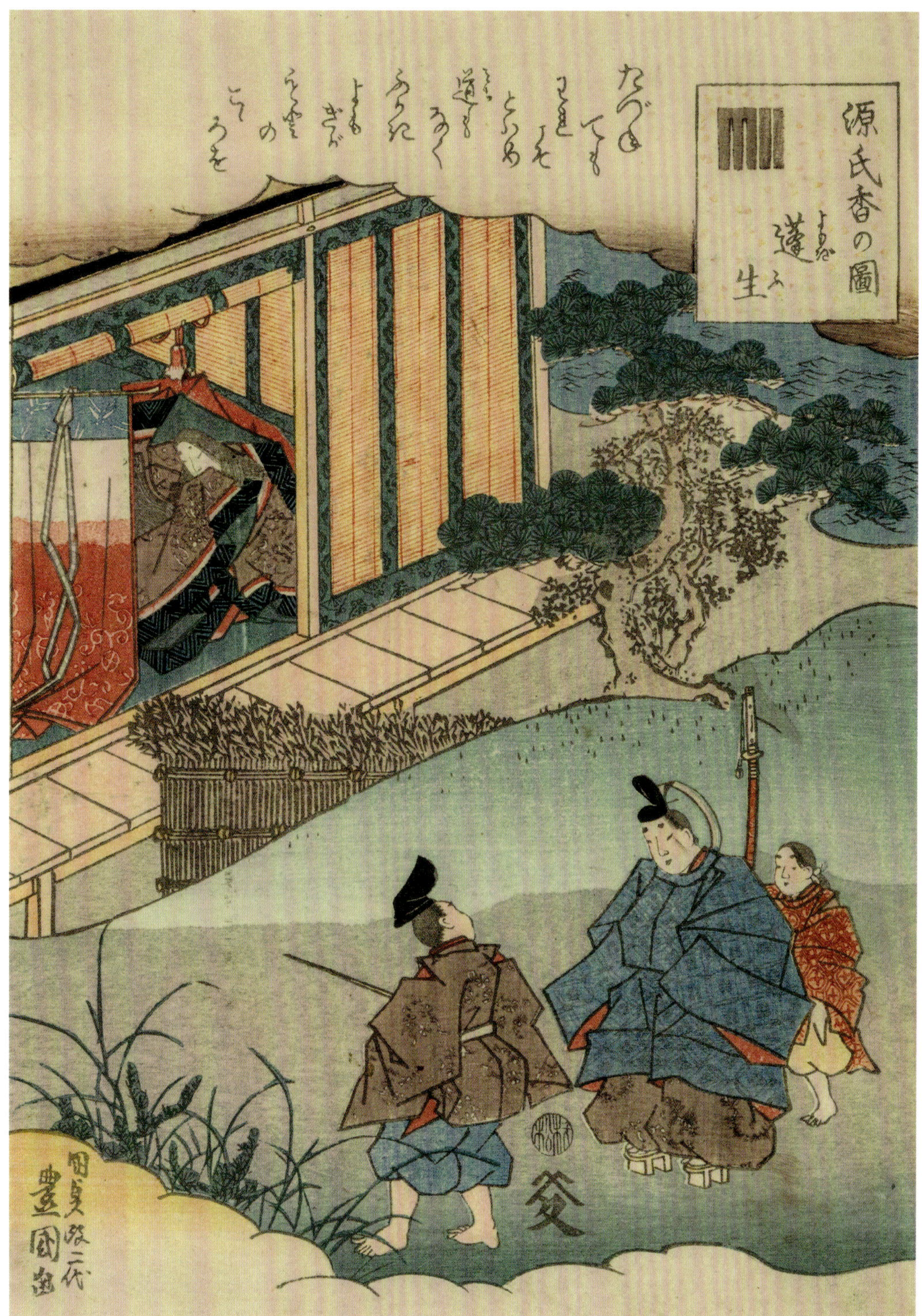

15A | Kunisada, *Genji Incense Pictures*, 1844–47

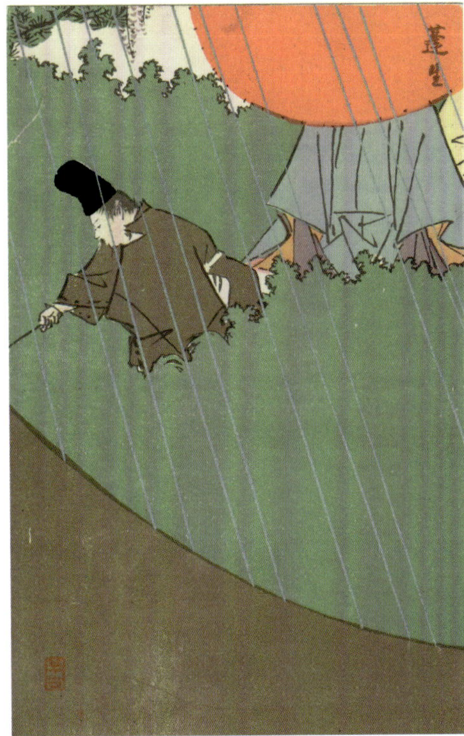

15B | Kajita Hanko, *The Tale of Genji*, 1905

Lady Inabune of *Inaka Genji*, the daughter of a former shogun who was rumored to be one of Mitsuuji's early conquests but was actually only a friend, also suffered financially in the absence of her benefactor. She even received an insulting offer from the upstart Lady Sagawa, who wanted to employ Inabune as a companion for her daughters. Mitsuuji finds her on his return, in a scene modeled on Genji's rediscovery of Suetsumuhana, and sees to it that she receives the fortune of the defeated Yamana clan and marries a distinguished husband. In the end Sagawa and her daughters find themselves in the service of Inabune. In a design taken from one of the illustrations for chapter 22, Inabune passes on a letter from Sagawa (just out of sight at the far left) to one of her attendants, who has agreed to go to work for Sagawa in place of Inabune herself (15C). Another attendant speaks to Sagawa through the decrepit bamboo lattice of a folding screen, indicating the current sorry state of the furnishings of Inabune's house.

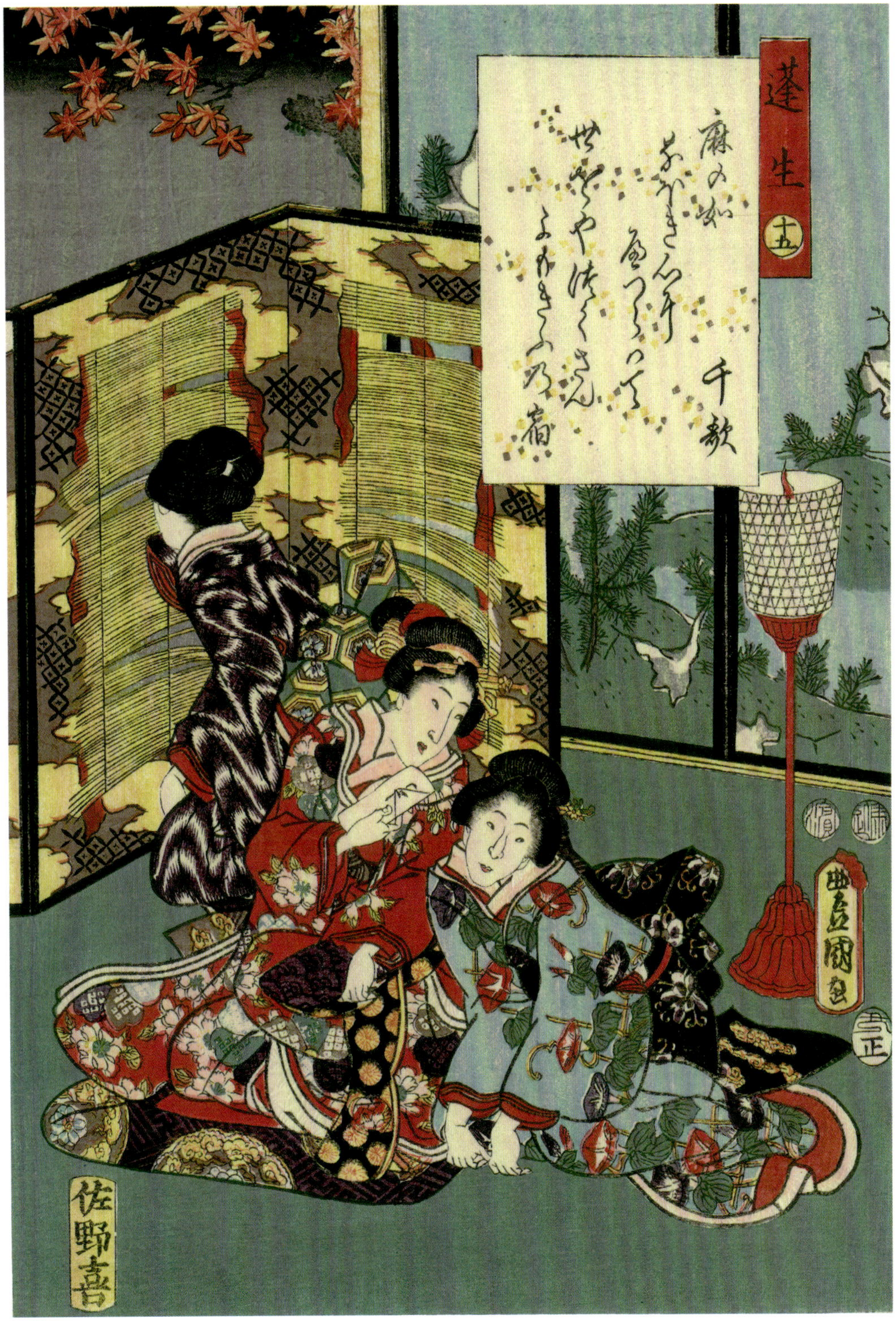

15C | Kunisada, *The Color Print Contest of a Modern Genji*, 1853

16

The Gatehouse (Sekiya)

This chapter is frequently illustrated, since it features both a beautiful autumn landscape and a poignant meeting between former lovers. Utsusemi (see chapters 2 and 3) and her husband are returning to the capital after years in the provinces. By chance, their procession of carriages and retainers passes the even more splendid entourage of Genji, who is on his way to make a pilgrimage to nearby Ishiyama Temple (the very place where the author, Lady Murasaki, is said to have begun writing the tale). At the barrier gate controlling traffic to and from the city, they pull aside to let him pass. Genji and Utsusemi remain inside their carriages while her younger brother, who still remembers Genji fondly, delivers poetic messages between them (16A). After her husband's death at the end of the chapter, Utsusemi becomes a nun.

In chapter 24 of *Inaka Genji*, Karaginu (= Utsusemi) and her husband Nikki Kiyonosuke are returning to Kyoto just as Mitsuuji sets out on his pilgrimage to Ishiyama. Mitsuuji goes to the palanquin of Karaginu, but it seems to be unoccupied; and when he opens the door, he finds only a branch of maple leaves with a poem attached. Karaginu has slipped out of the door on the other side and hidden among her attendants, in a playful reference to

---

O what can it be,
the Osaka Barrier,
that in just this place
one must make one's mournful way
through a forest of sorrows?

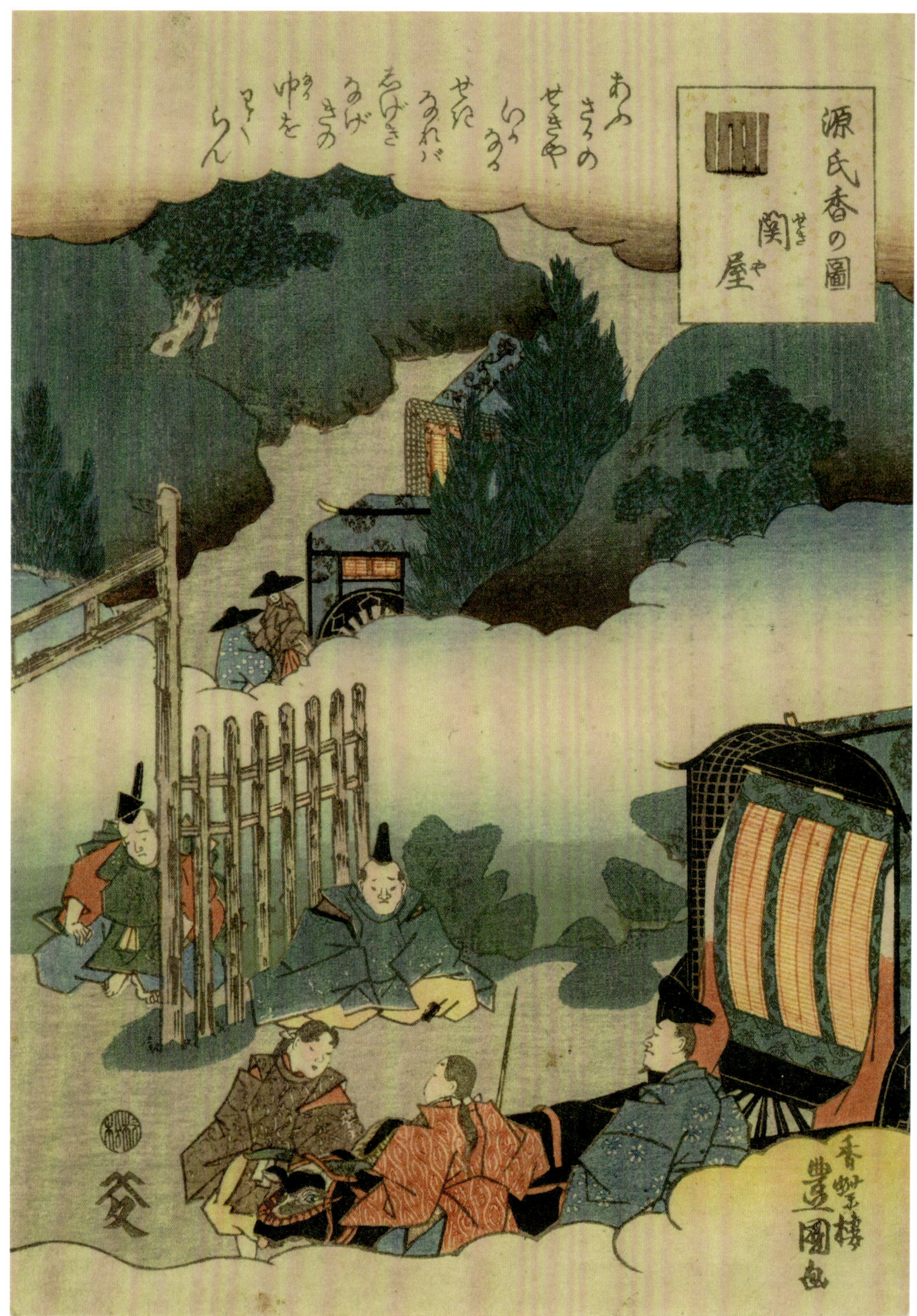

16A | Kunisada, *Genji Incense Pictures*, 1844–47

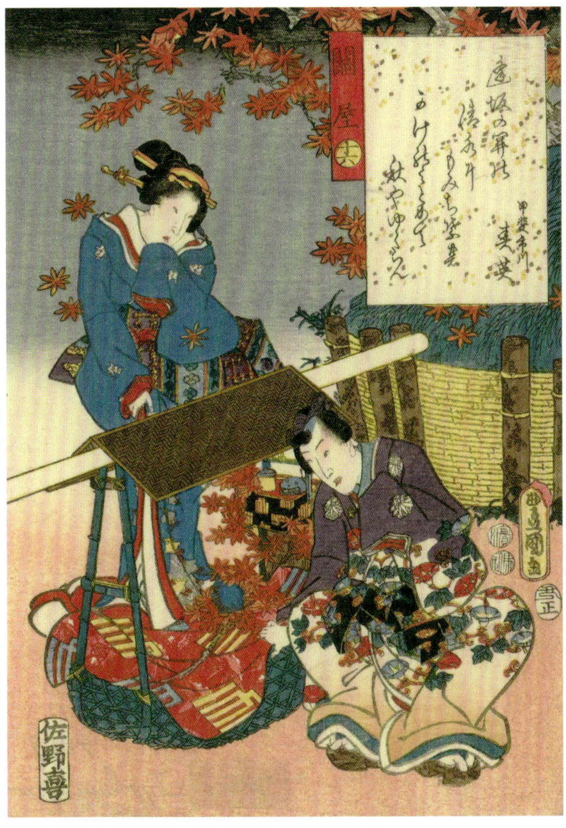

16B | Kunisada, *The Color Print Contest of a Modern Genji*, 1853

their long-ago games. Kunisada II shows the scene almost exactly as Kunisada had illustrated it in the book (16C), whereas Kunisada himself takes greater liberties with his own work, removing the figures of the attendants and drawing not a closed palanquin but a simpler, open one (16B).

In addition to reuniting the one-time lovers, the meeting also allows Mitsuuji to reconcile Kiyonosuke with his son Yoshikiyo, now that the villainous Kawajirō, the former heir of the Nikki family, is dead.

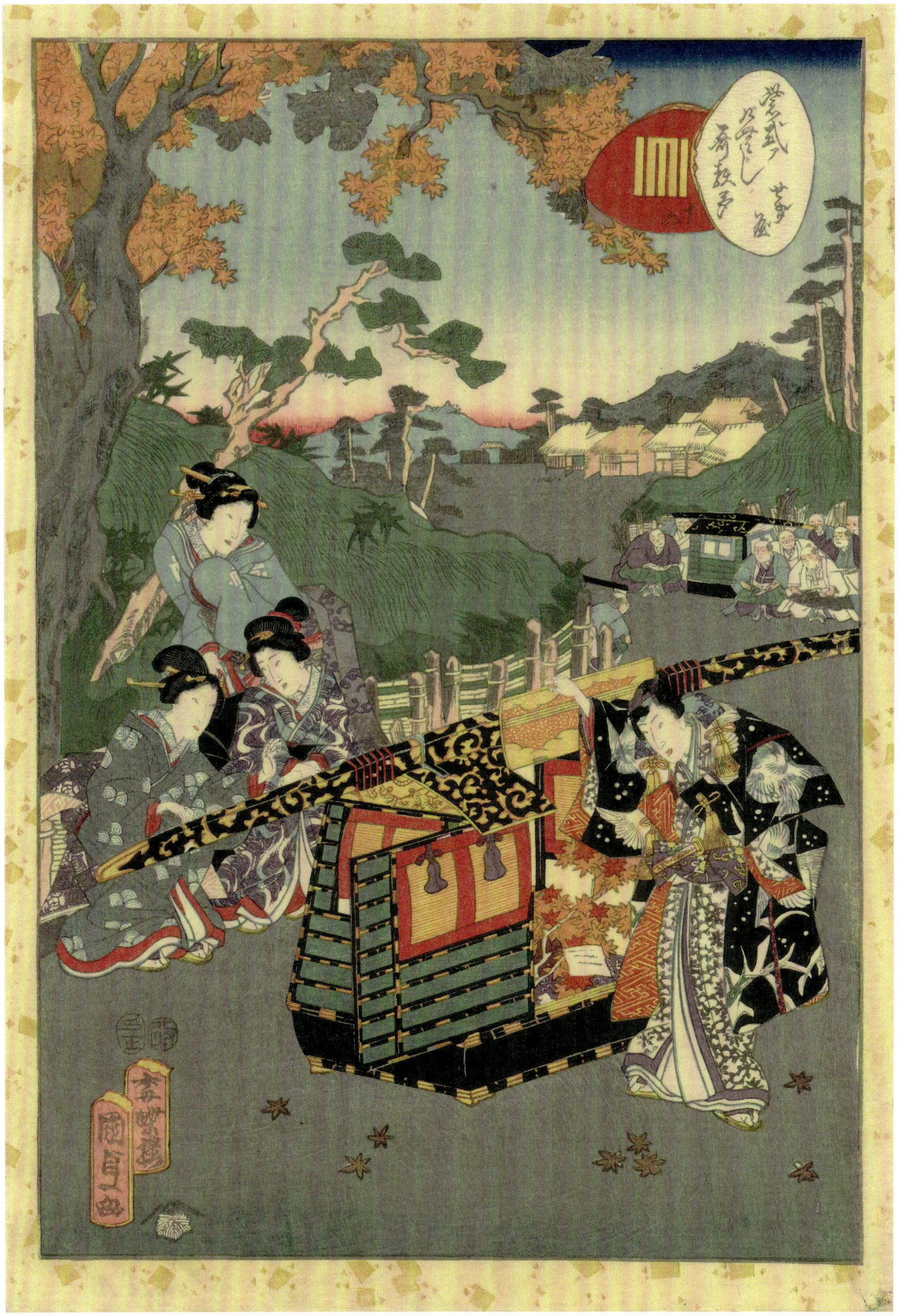

16C | Kunisada II, *Lady Murasaki's Genji Cards*, 1857

17

The Picture Contest (Eawase)

At the beginning of chapter 14, Genji's older brother, the Suzaku emperor, abdicated in favor of Fujitsubo's twelve-year-old son (Genji's secret child), who is now the Reizei emperor. The young emperor has not yet chosen an empress from among his ladies, but Genji's ward Akikonomu (the daughter of his deceased lover Rokujō) is a strong candidate. Also in the running is a daughter of Tō no Chūjō. Since the emperor is fond of illustrated stories, the two sides compete to please him in a picture contest: Genji brings out heirloom treasures to loan to Akikonomu, while Tō no Chūjō commissions fashionable artists to make paintings for his daughter. In the end the contest is won by Genji's own drawings of his exile at Suma, described in the chapter title poem.

Still more vividly
than in those sad days now past,
when I suffered them,
those ordeals return to mind,
bringing with them many tears.

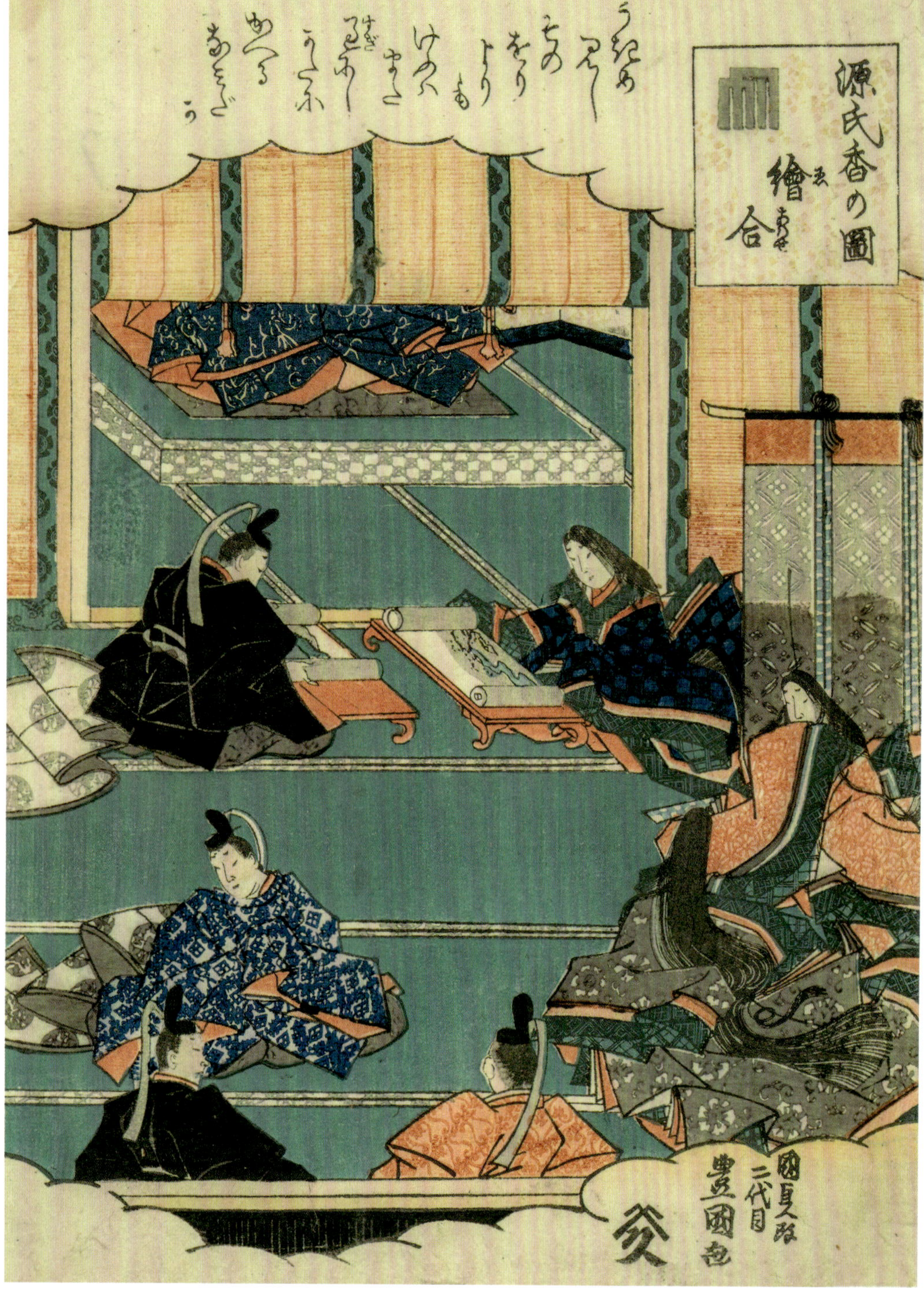

17A | Kunisada, *Genji Incense Pictures*, 1844–47

There are actually two rounds of competition, an informal one with Fujitsubo as the judge and a formal presentation before the emperor, judged by Genji's cousin Prince Hotaru. Kunisada shows this final round of the contest, with the usual convention of hiding the emperor's face behind a bamboo blind (17A). A charming surimono by Shunman jokingly turns the courtly painting contest into a competition between different kinds of ukiyo-e prints: actor portraits, both full-length and close-up; courtesans; bird-and-flower designs; and landscapes (17B).

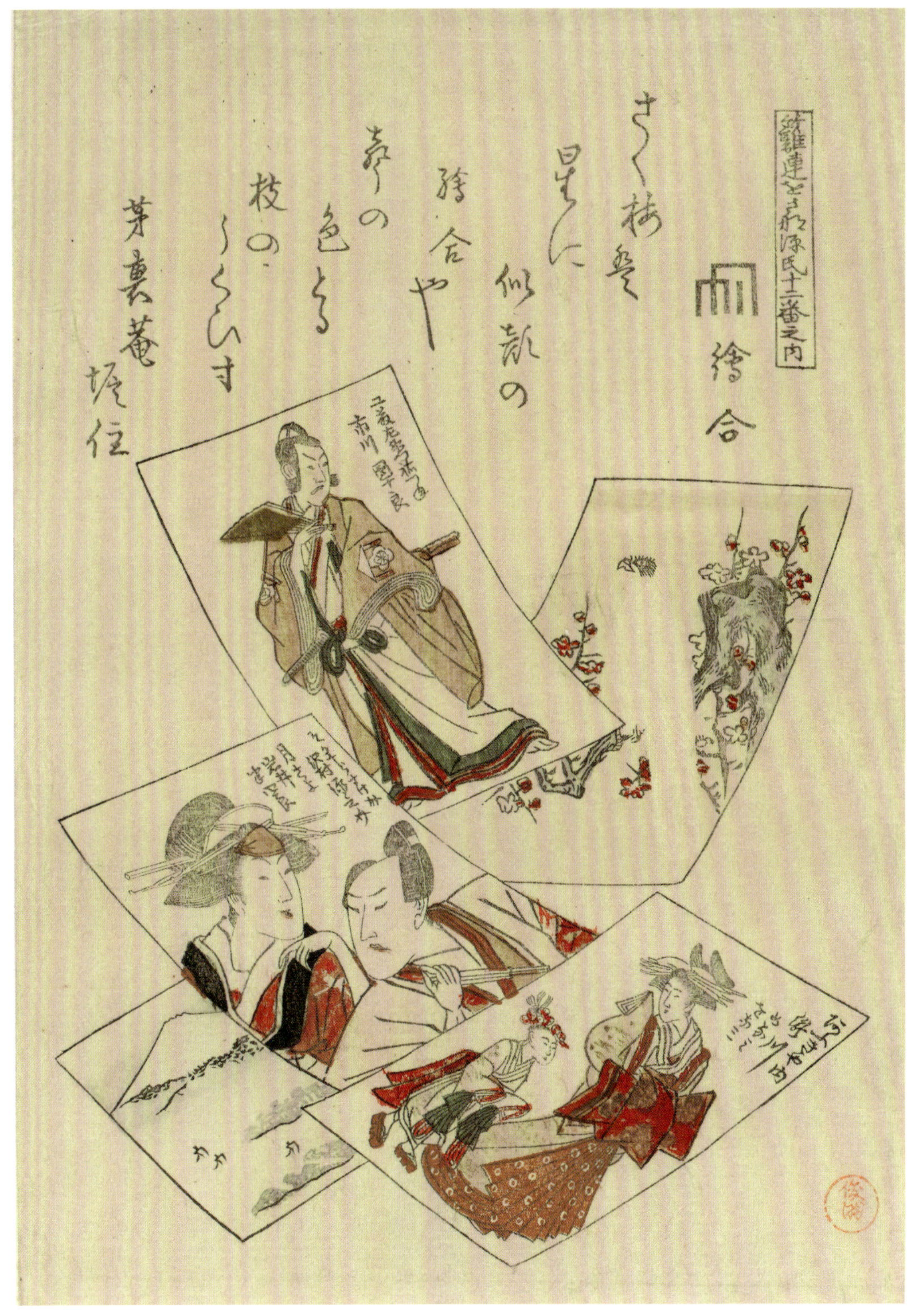

17B | Kubo Shunman, *Twelve Designs from a Children's Genji*, about 1801–18

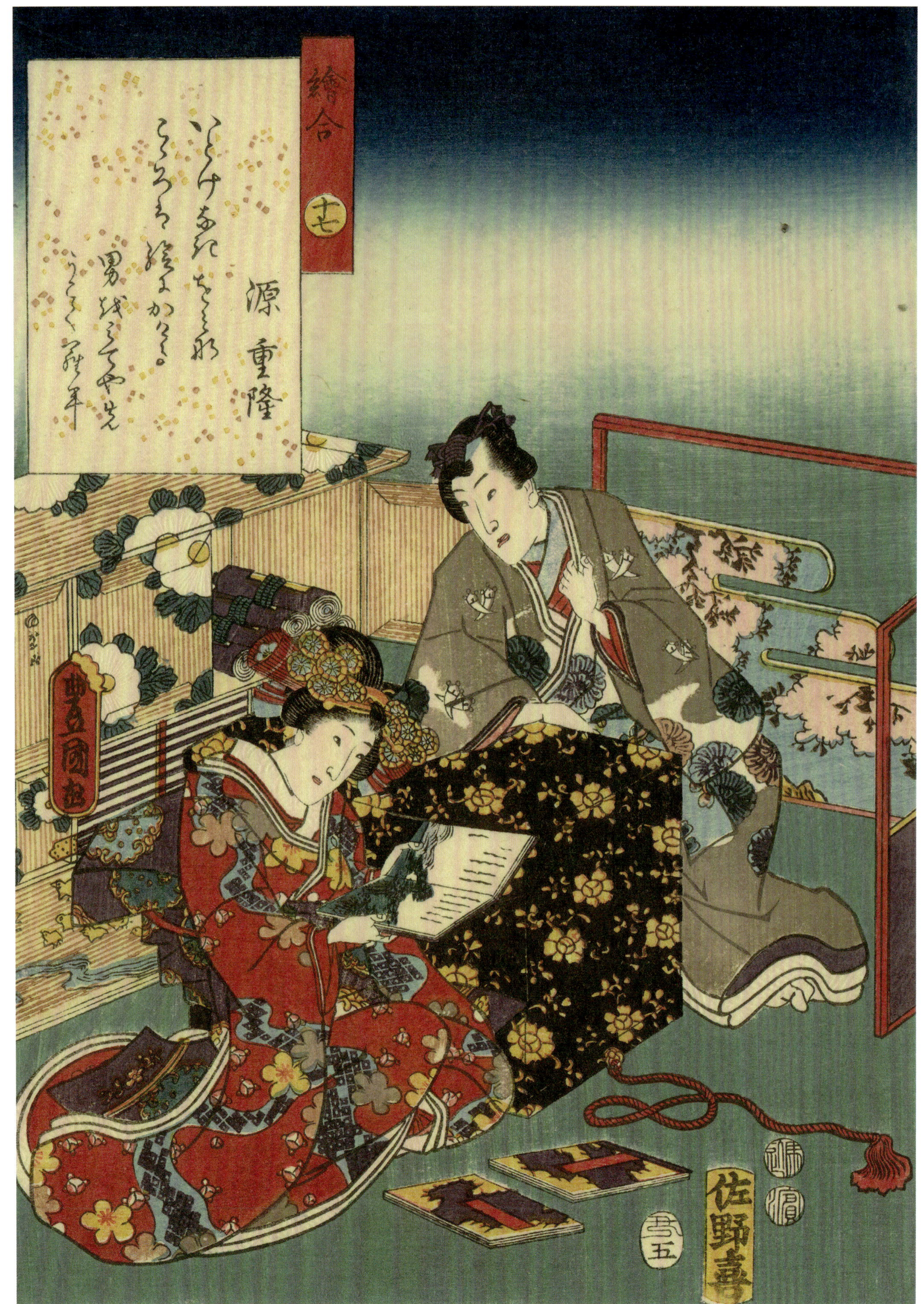
繪合
十七
源重隆
豊国画
佐野喜

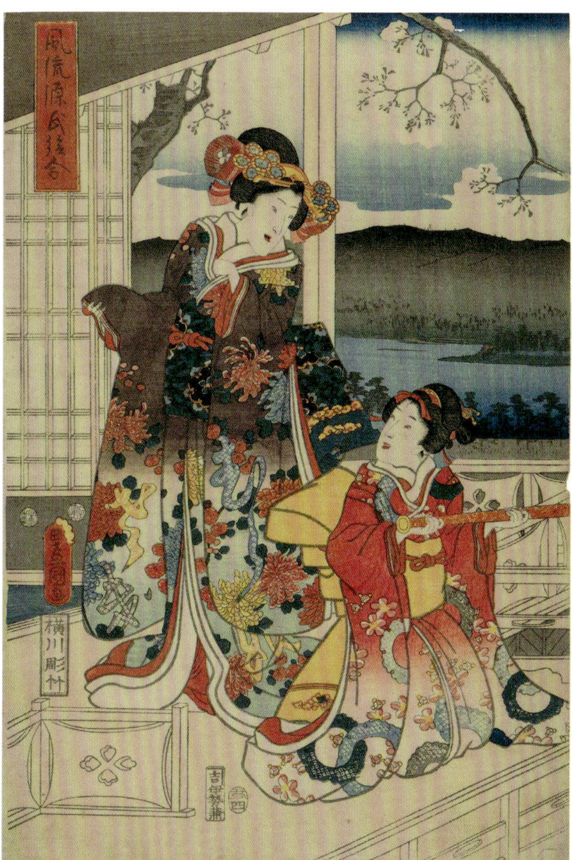
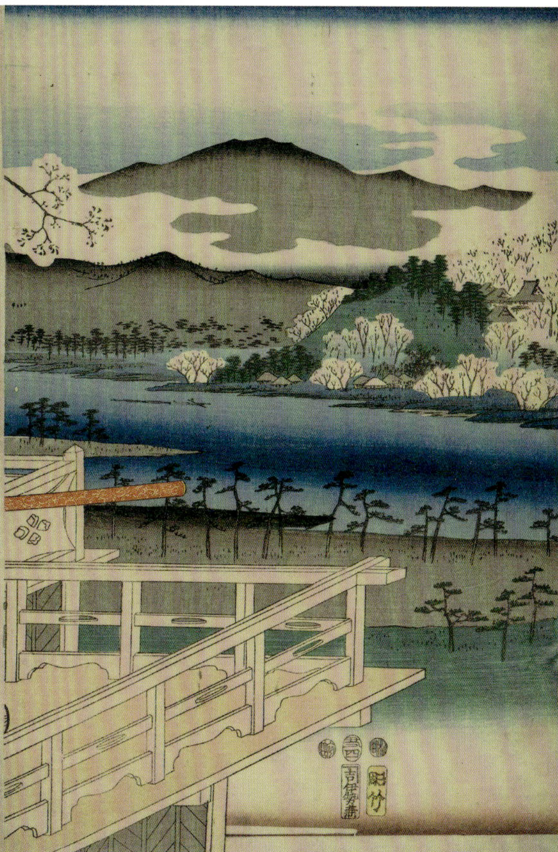
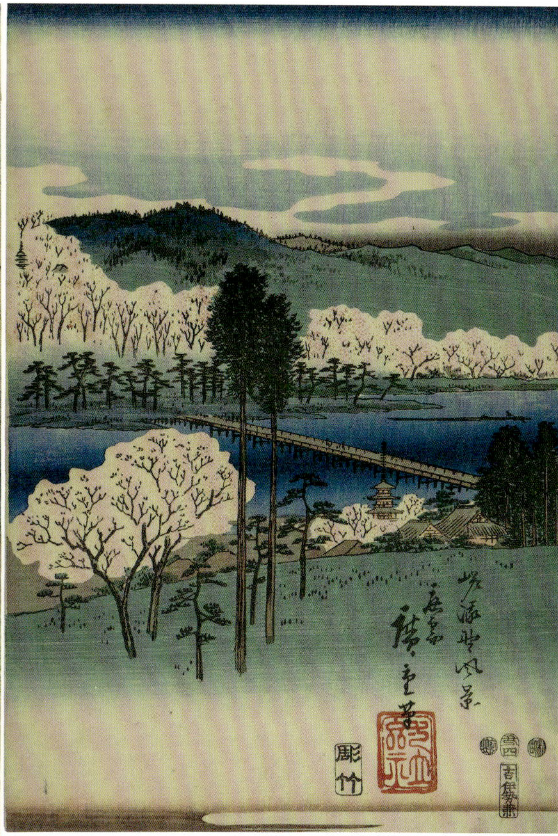

17D | Kunisada and Hiroshige, *Fashionable Genji*, 1853

The picture contest in chapters 25 and 26 of *Inaka Genji* closely follows its prototype, with Isona — the daughter of the late Akogi, now adopted by Mitsuuji — and Tomiyo — daughter of Mitsuuji's friend Akamatsu Takanao (= Tō no Chūjō) — competing for the favor of the child shogun Yoshitane. Kunisada's print depicts Mitsuuji and Murasaki selecting pictures for the contest (17C).

Soon afterward, Mitsuuji builds a Buddhist temple near his mansion in Saga and enlarges the mansion itself to accommodate the various ladies who are dependent on him. An illustration for chapter 26 of the book shows Murasaki and her ladies using a telescope (not mentioned in the text) to observe the new temple; this image inspired a triptych that Kunisada co-designed with Hiroshige, displaying the talents of the great landscape specialist in a beautiful view of the river and rolling hills in western Kyoto, with cherry blossoms just coming into bloom (17D).

17C | Kunisada, *The Color Print Contest of a Modern Genji*, 1853

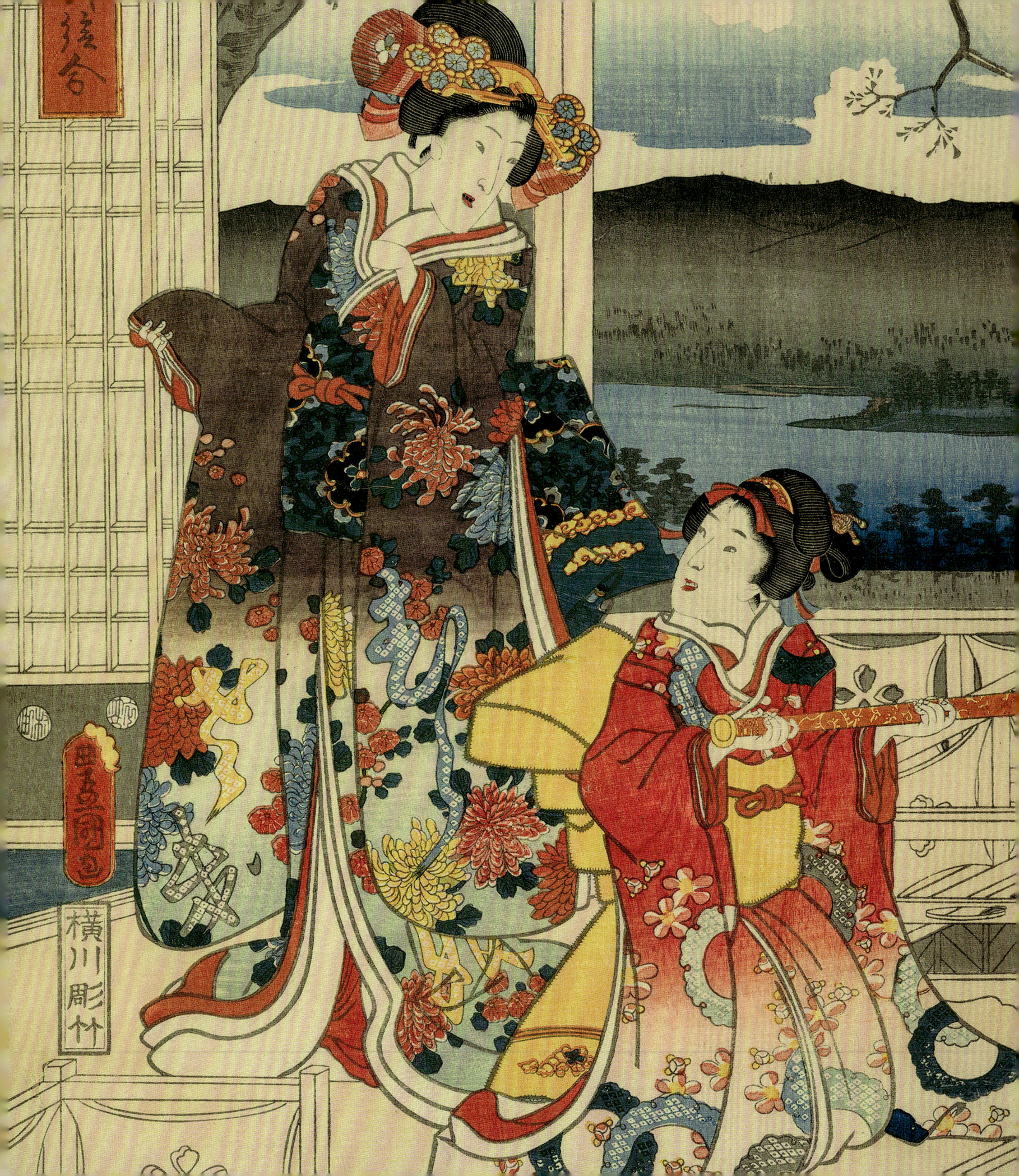
絃合
豊国画
横川彫竹

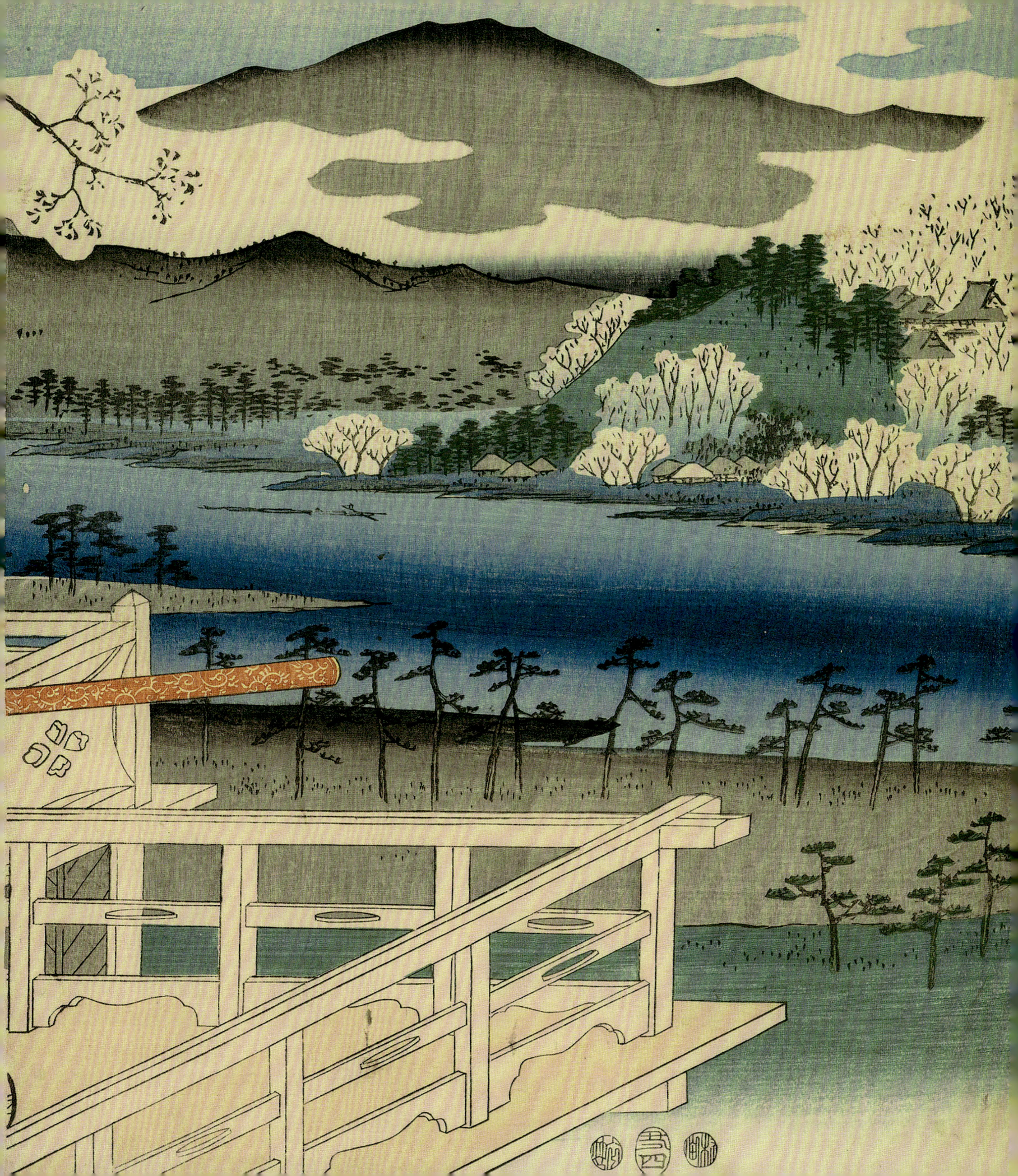

18

The Wind in the Pines (Matsukaze)

Genji wants the Akashi lady to come to the capital with their daughter, but she is reluctant to move into Genji's mansion for fear that her provincial upbringing will put her at a disadvantage relative to the other ladies there. Fortunately, her father owns a villa at Ōi, in the western part of Kyoto, and he has it refurbished for her. Leaving her father behind in Akashi, the lady moves to Kyoto with her little daughter and her mother the nun. Genji visits occasionally, but the lady is often lonely, passing the time by playing the koto and exchanging poetry with her mother. The *Genji Incense* series shows one of Genji's rare visits (18A). Eishi's modernized triptych also shows a visit from Genji in the deliberately subdued color scheme known as benigirai that avoids the use of red (18B). Shigenaga depicts the actual composition of the chapter title poem by the Akashi nun, a response to a poem by her daughter (18C).

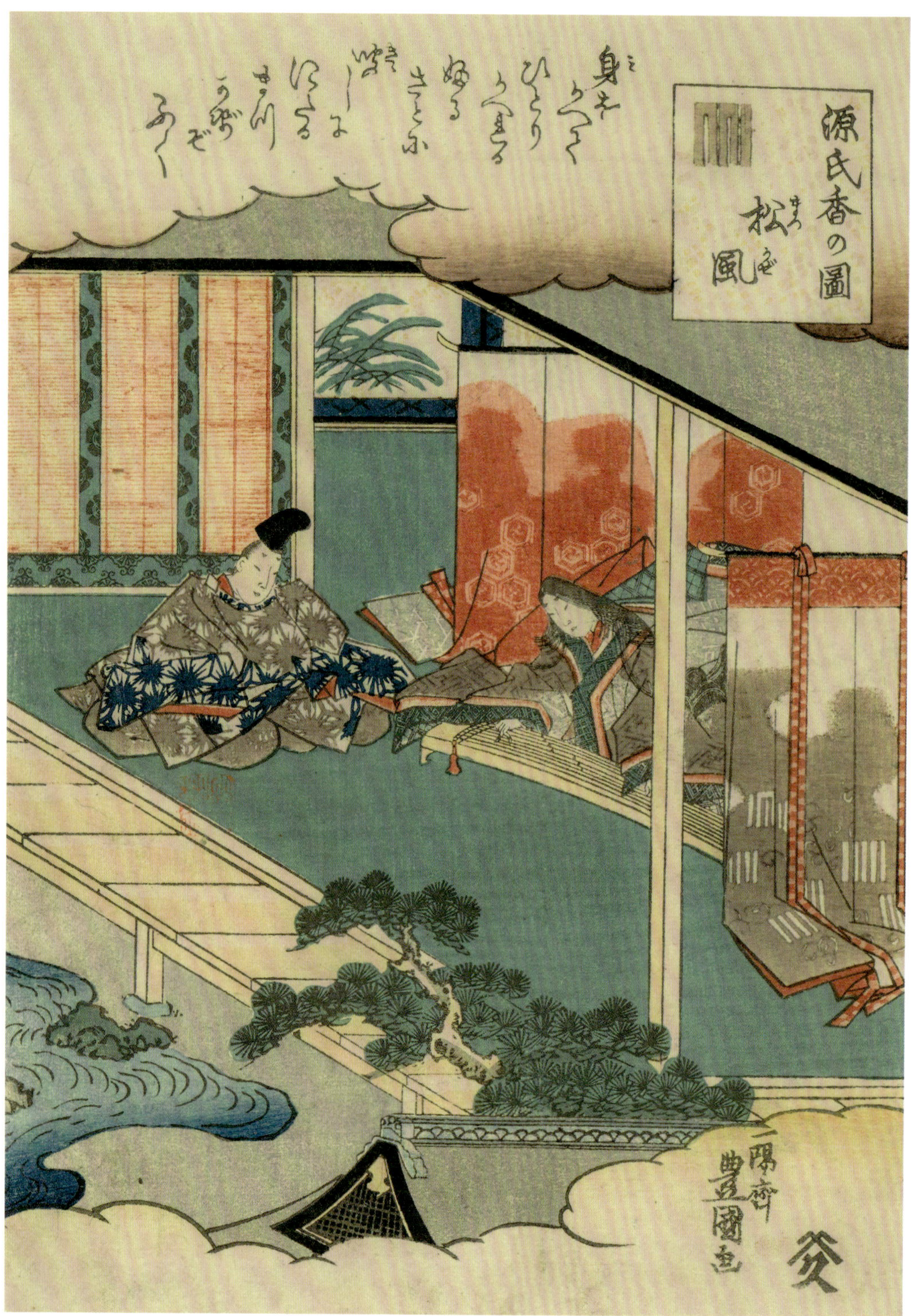

18A | Kunisada, *Genji Incense Pictures*, 1844–47

Here at my old home,
where I have returned
alone and in changed guise,
I hear blowing through the pines
a familiar-sounding wind.

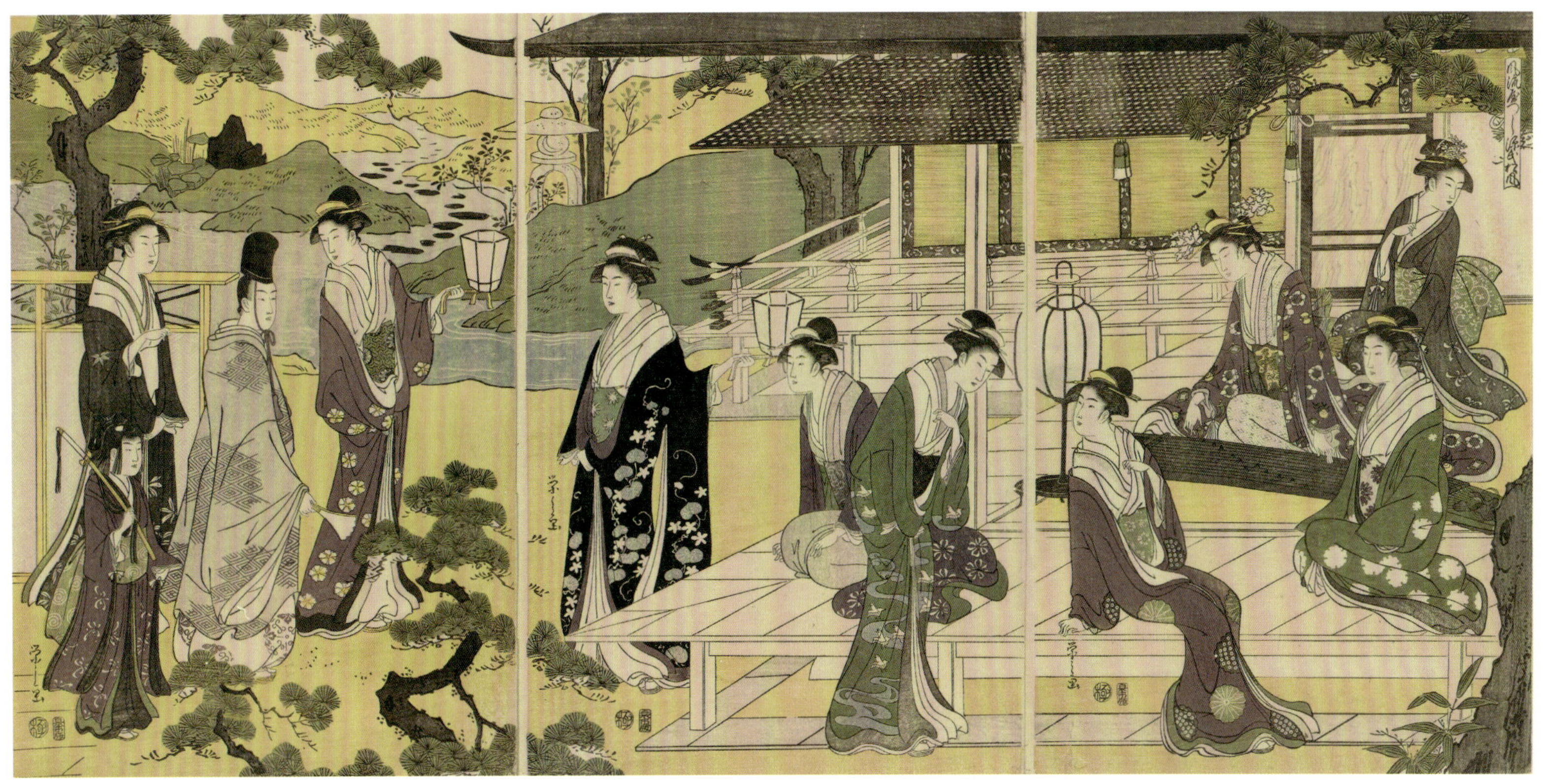

18B | Chōbunsai Eishi, *Genji in Fashionable Modern Guise*, about 1792–93

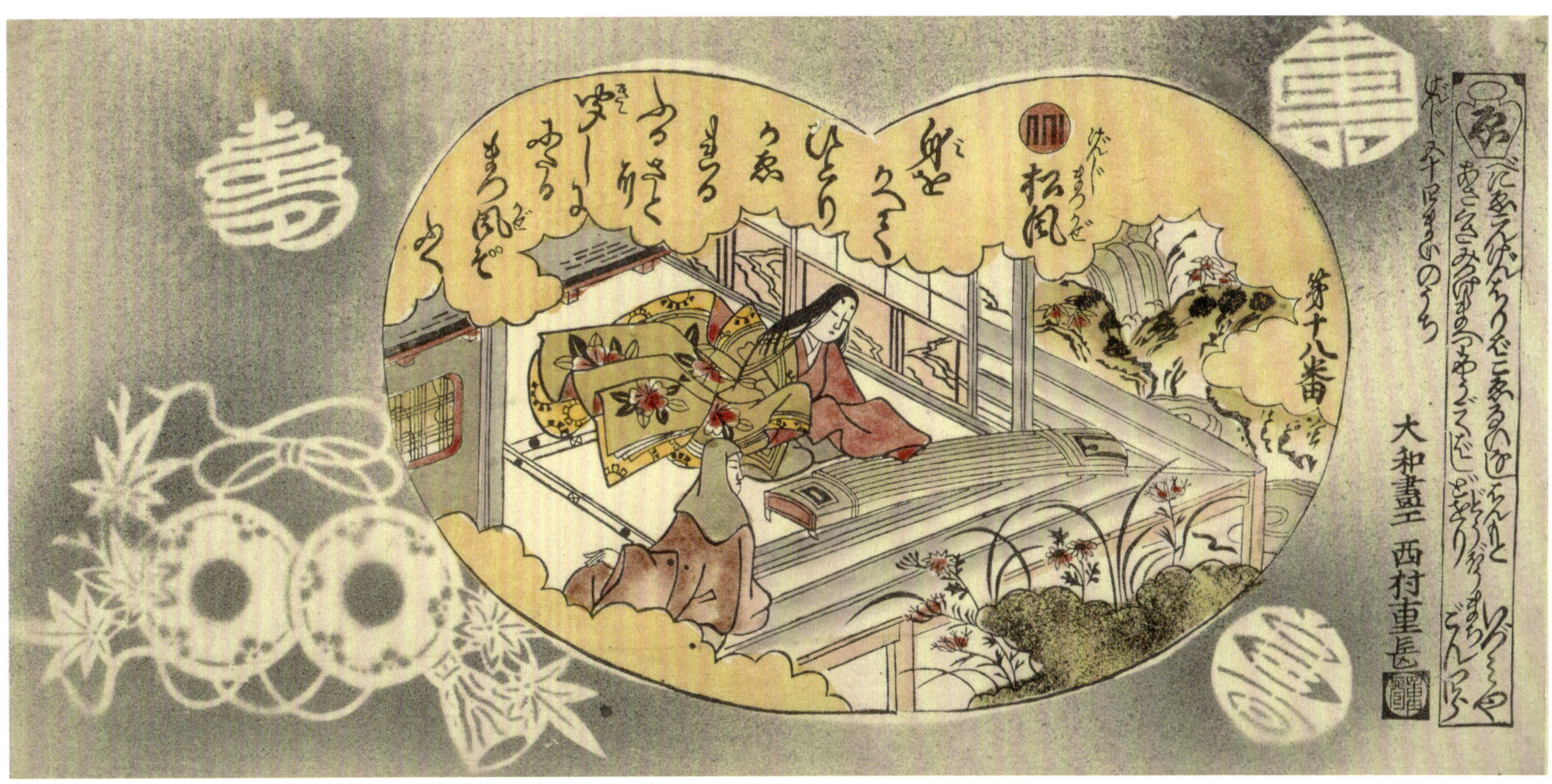

18C | Nishimura Shigenaga, *Genji in Fifty-Four Sheets*, about 1735

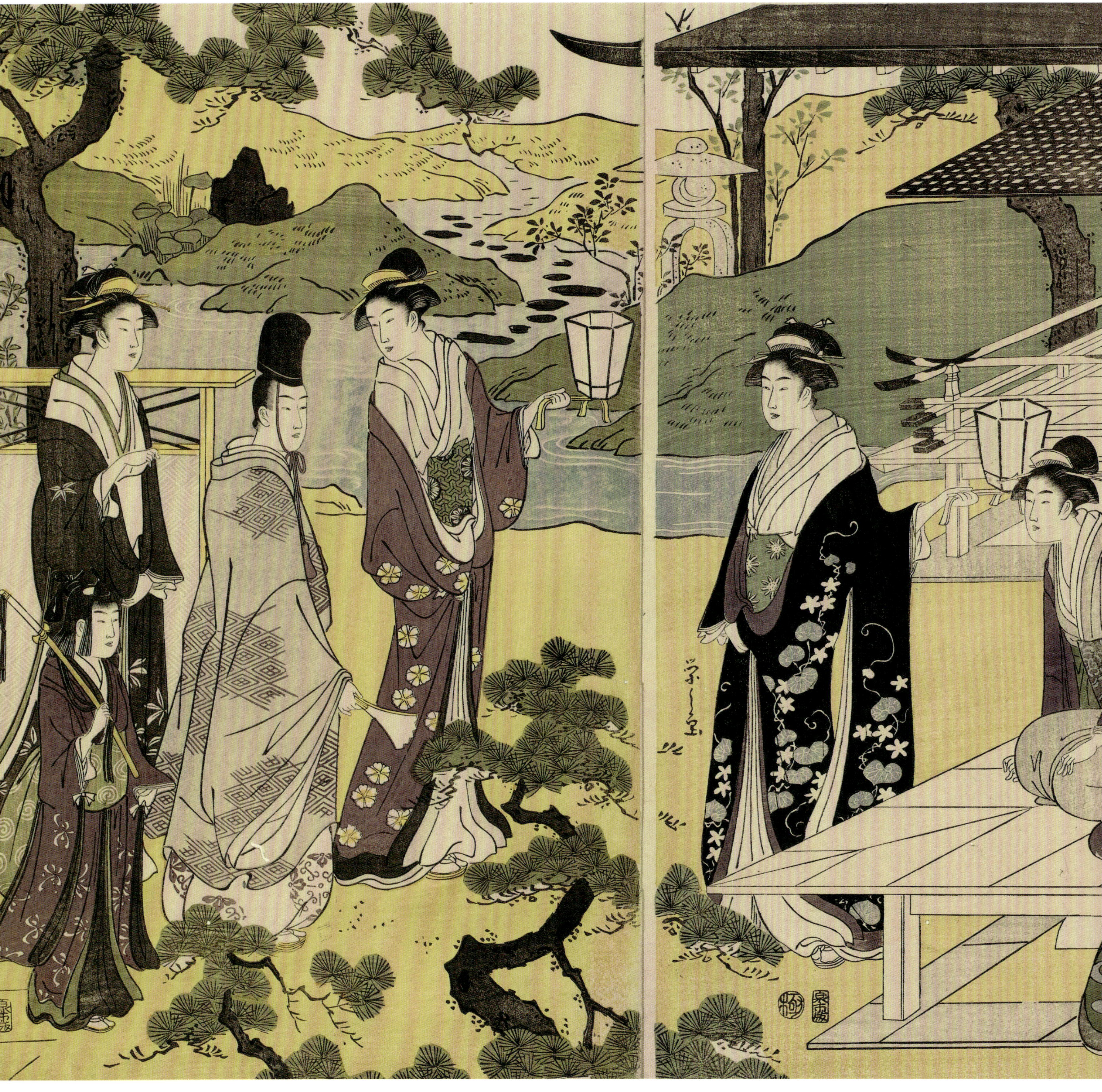

The corresponding events in *Inaka Genji* are a close parallel. In chapter 26, Yamana Sōnyū makes plans for his daughter Asagiri to take his granddaughter (named Akashi after her birthplace) to Kyoto, to be closer to the child's illustrious father. He has his old house in Ōi rebuilt, so that it is as beautiful and comfortable as the estate in Akashi. Special mention is made of the bathhouse, which draws its water directly from the Ōi River, as compared to the two-story bathhouse and well at Akashi. The frontispiece for chapter 26 of the book, subsequently reworked as a color print, shows Mitsuuji in the bathhouse with a nurse holding his little daughter, whom he has just met for the first time (18D).

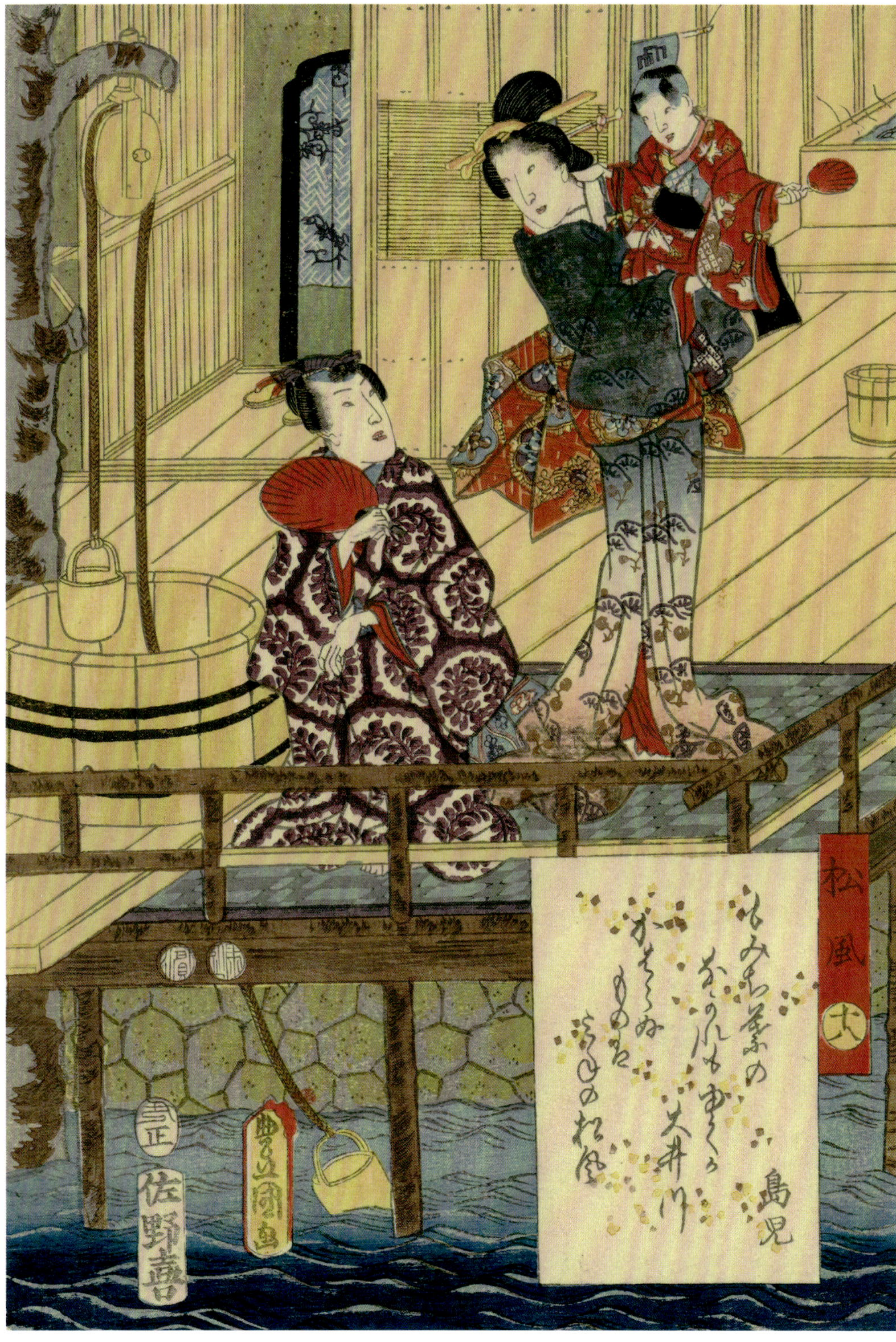

18D | Kunisada, *The Color Print Contest of a Modern Genji*, 1853

18B | (detail)

19

Wisps of Cloud (Usugumo)

This is a melancholy chapter, full of loss and emotional pain. Worst of all for Genji is the sudden death of Fujitsubo; the chapter title poem expresses his mourning for her. Earlier, Genji made arrangements for his young daughter to leave her mother and be brought up instead by the childless Murasaki. The Akashi lady is very sad but agrees that this arrangement is in the child's best interests, so that she can learn the sophisticated urban manners she will need in her future career at court. After Fujitsubo's death, an elderly bishop who had been close to her reveals to her son, now the Reizei emperor, that Genji is not his brother but his biological father. Reizei is very distressed and tries to name Genji as his successor, but Genji refuses.

Although the chapter title poem is Genji's lament for Fujitsubo, Kunisada chose to show a different scene in the chapter, in which Genji visits his daughter after she has moved to his mansion in Nijō (Second Avenue). Murasaki and the child's nurse look on as the little girl reaches out to her father (19A).

Those thin wisps of cloud
trailing there over the mountains
caught in sunset light
seem to wish to match their hue
to the sleeves of the bereaved.

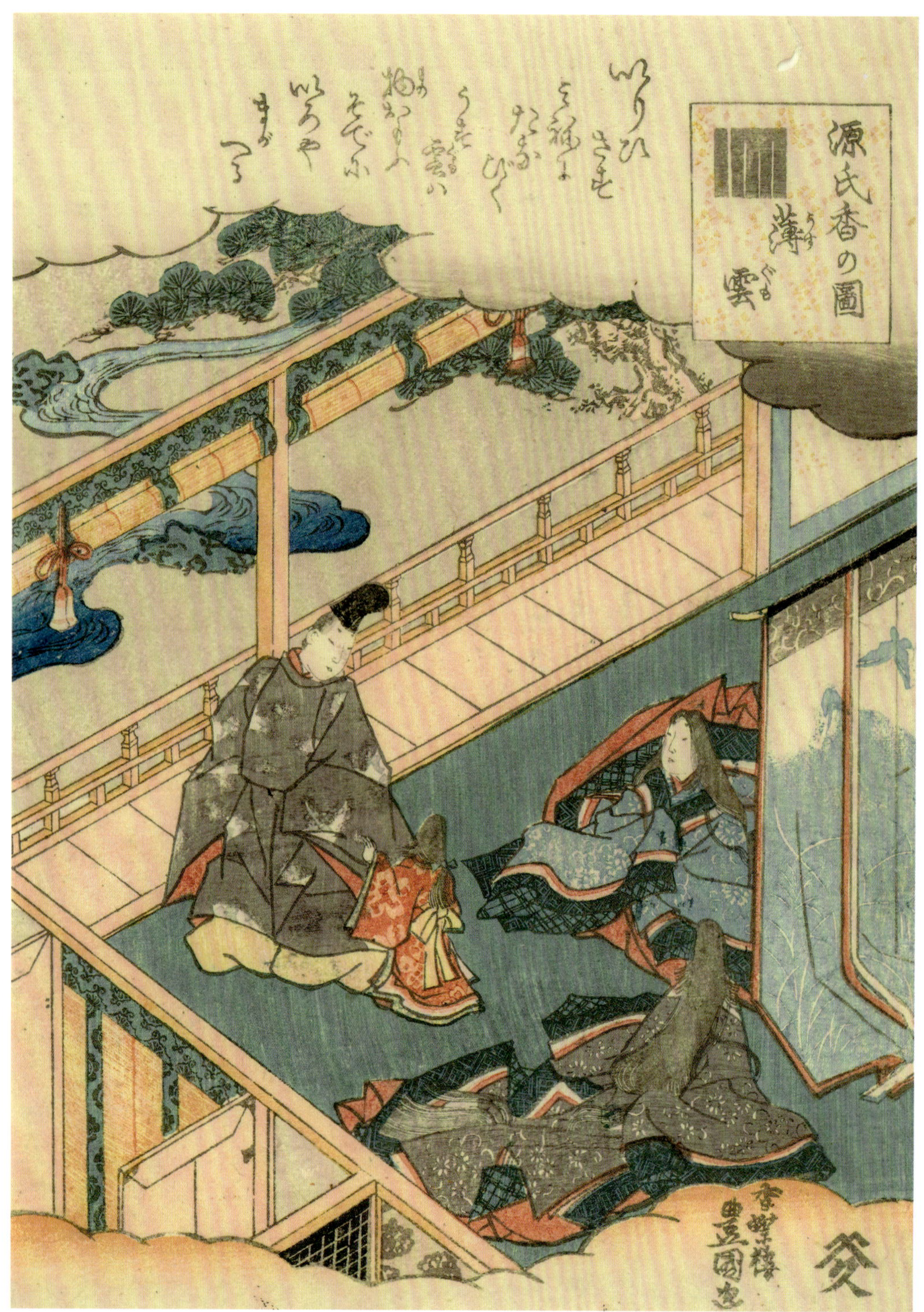

19A | Kunisada, *Genji Incense Pictures*, 1844–47

Some, but not all, of these developments occur in *Inaka Genji* as well. In chapter 28, Asagiri's daughter Akashi leaves her mother and goes to live with Murasaki at Mitsuuji's mansion, where she enjoys fabulous toys such as the indoor boat shown in a book illustration later expanded into a color triptych (19C). The scheming priest Denkan tries to cause trouble by telling the young shogun Yoshitane, incorrectly, that Mitsuuji is his real father. Unlike Fujitsubo, Yoshitane's mother, Fuji no Kata, remains alive and well, perhaps because she did not really commit adultery at all but only pretended (see chapter 2).

In the *Color Print Contest* series, the father-son motif is represented by a scene of Mitsuuji with his true son Yūgirimaru, also called Kumoinojō, based on an illustration in chapter 28 of the book (19B).

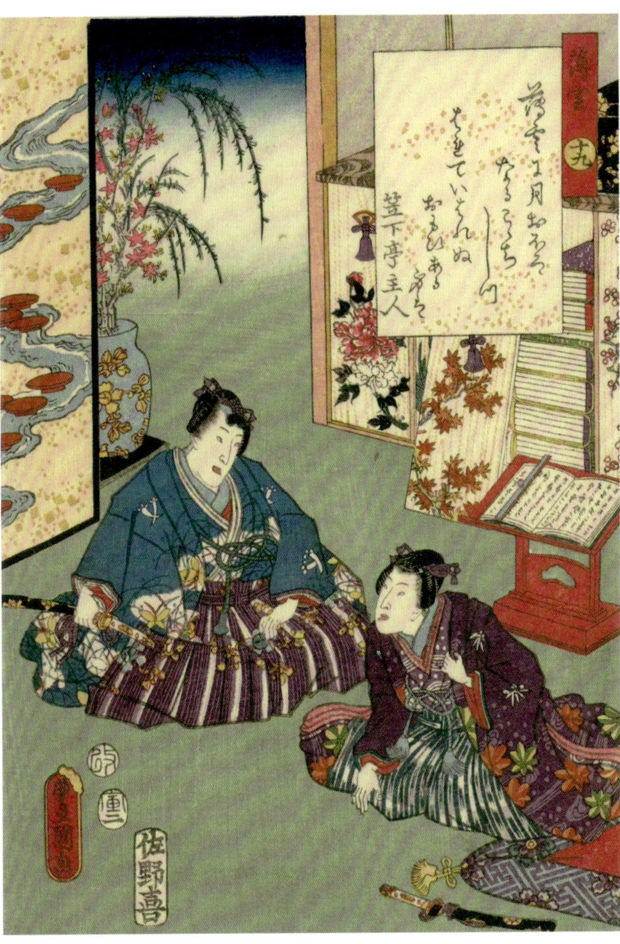

19B | Kunisada, *The Color Print Contest of a Modern Genji*, 1854

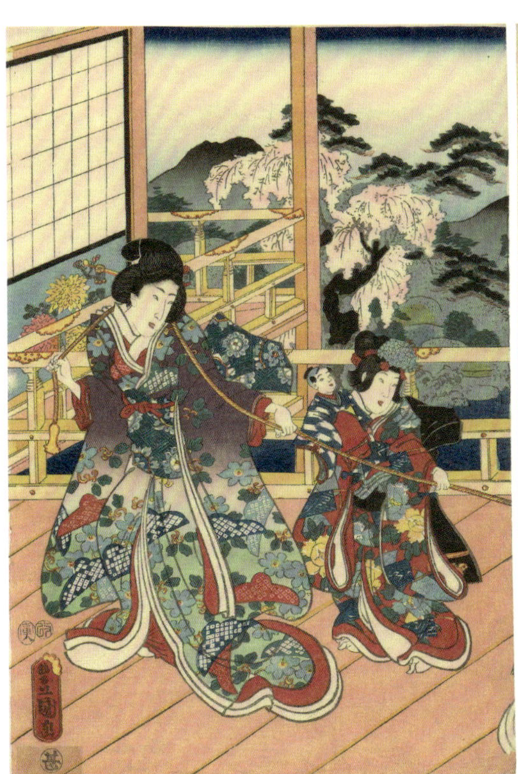

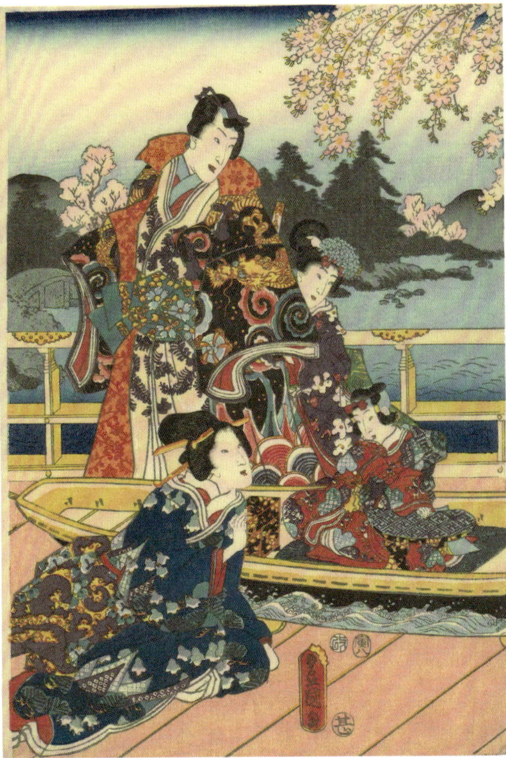

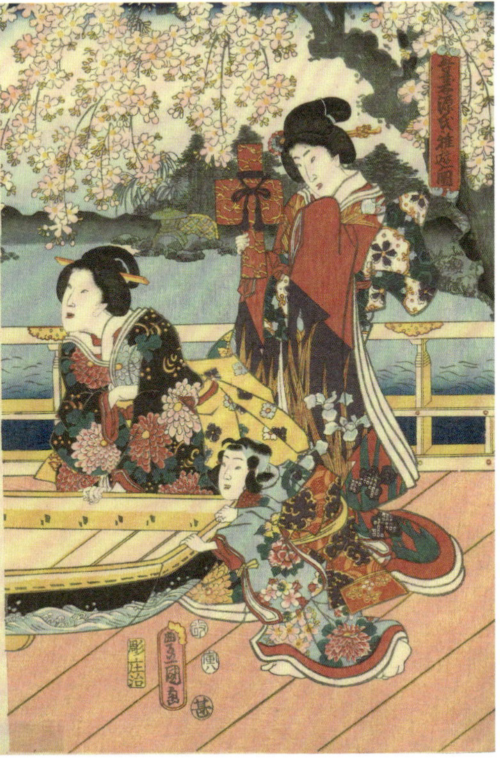

19C | Kunisada, *Elegant Amusements of Eastern Genji*, 1854

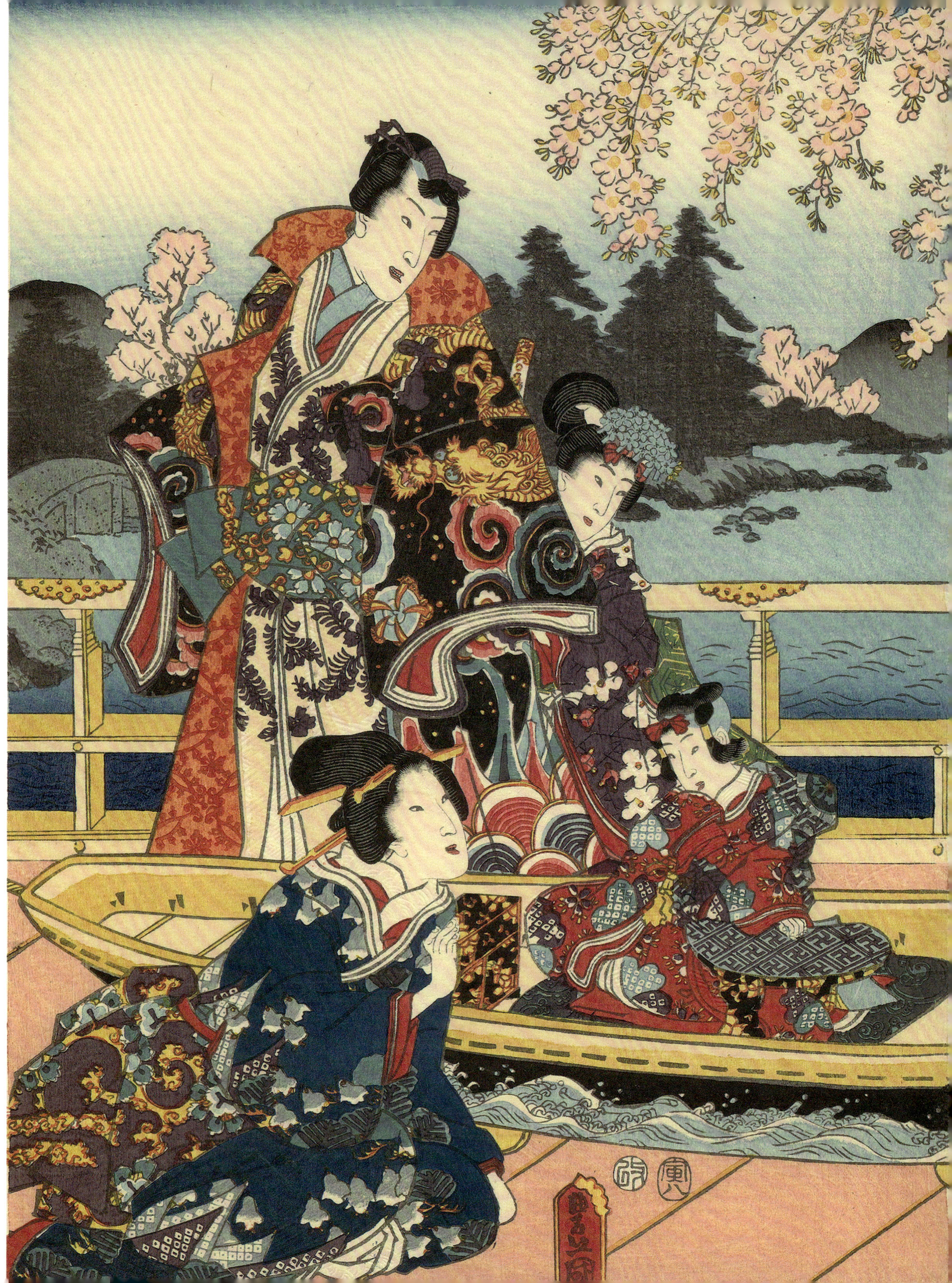

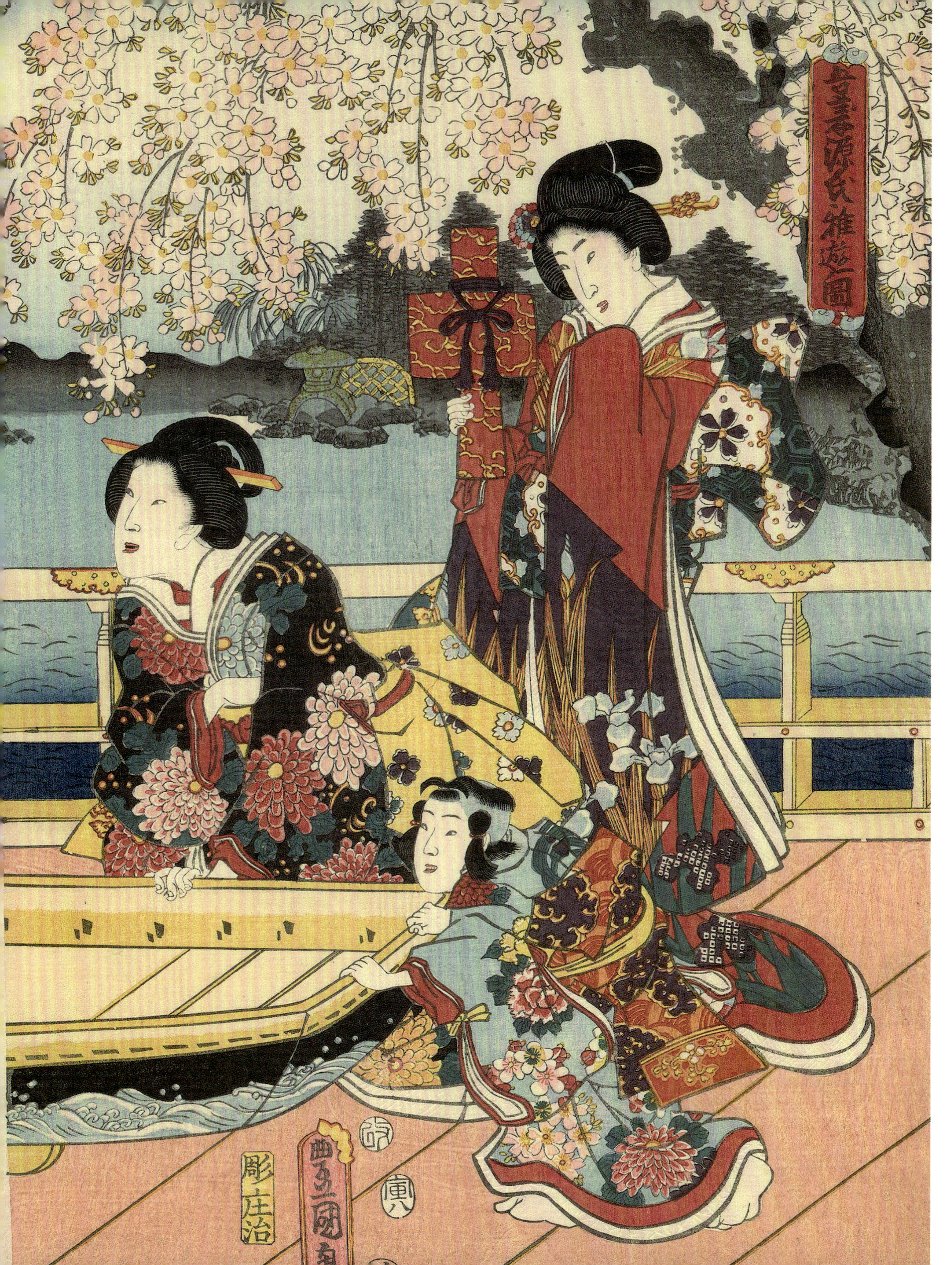
彫庄治
豊国画
寅八

20

The Morning Glory (Asagao)

For years Genji has been interested in his cousin, the princess called Asagao (Morning Glory), but she has resisted his advances. Now he flirts with her once again, sending her a faded morning glory with the chapter title poem that is the source of her nick-name; but once again she politely declines to become romantically involved with him. He returns to Murasaki, and at his mansion in Nijō the two of them watch the maidservants, some of them still children, playing in the garden after a heavy snow-fall. In this frequently illustrated scene, elegantly dressed little girls roll giant snowballs (20A).

The parody print by Eizan plays on the literal meaning of the chapter title: the term for morning glories, asagao, means literally "morning faces" (20B). A beautiful young woman looks into her mirror as she washes her face and prepares to apply makeup at the start of the day. Cosmetics decorate one of the two playing cards on which the poem is written, for use in the Genji poem card game.

Could it really be
that the bluebell I once knew
and cannot forget
no longer displays the bloom
that was hers in days gone by?

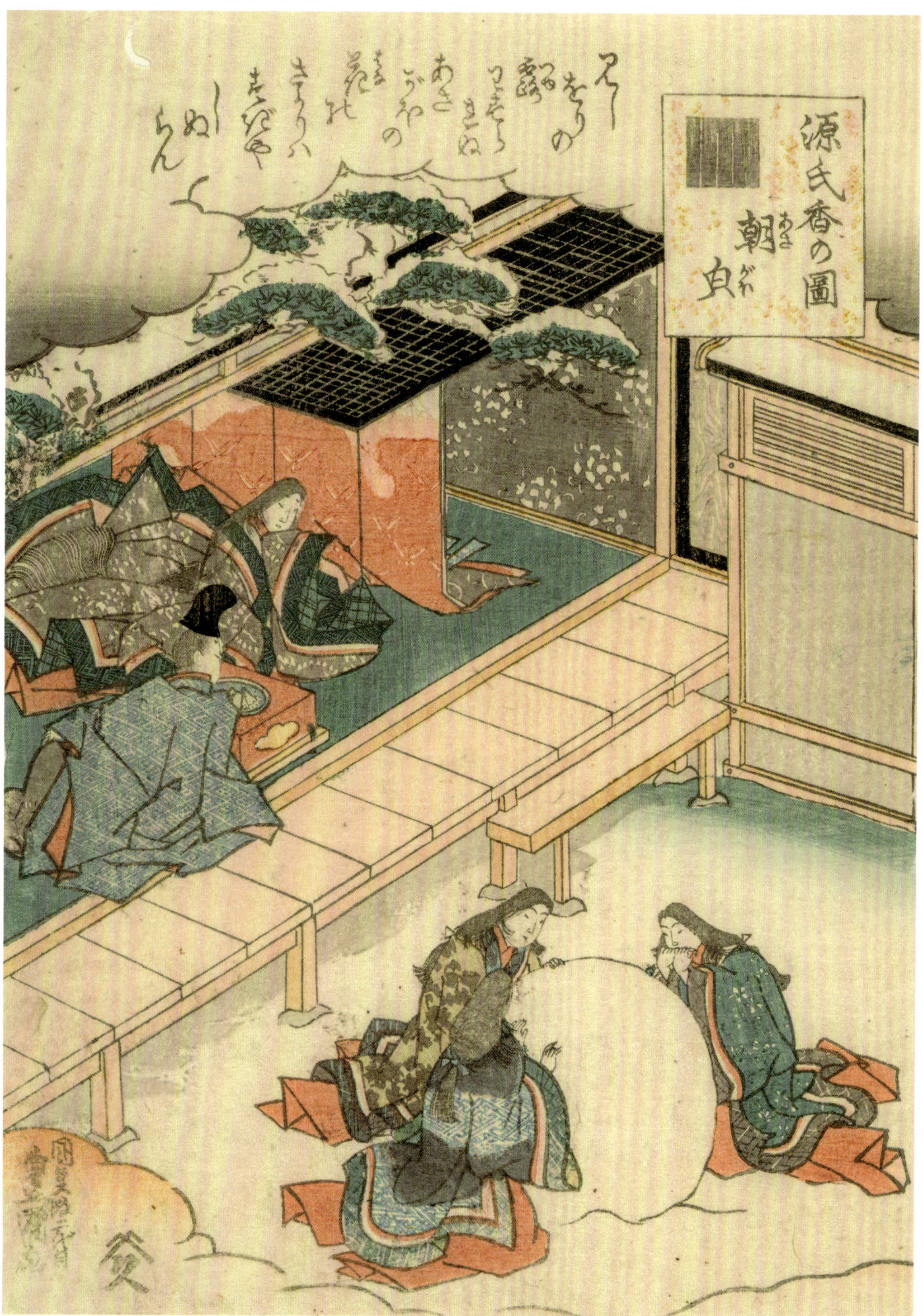

20A | Kunisada, *Genji Incense Pictures*, 1844–47

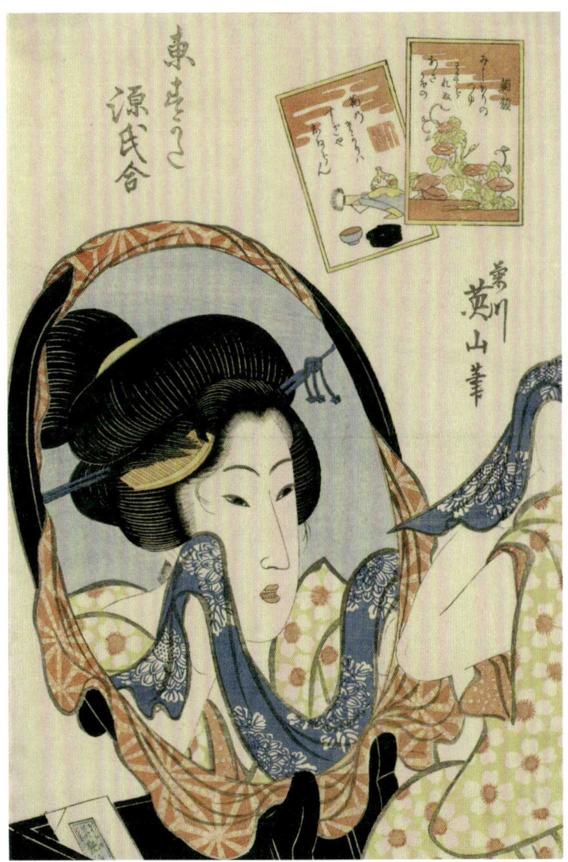

20B | Kikukawa Eizan, *Eastern Figures Matched with The Tale of Genji*, about 1818–23

The *Inaka Genji* character corresponding to Asagao is Kikuzaki, who is introduced in chapter 26 when she comes to work as a lady-in-waiting at Mitsuuji's mansion. Mitsuuji flirts with her, but eventually she returns to her mother's house. He visits her there from time to time, averting Murasaki's jealousy by telling her, falsely, that Kikuzaki is his cousin.

Finally, in chapter 29, we learn that Kikuzaki, originally named Asagao, is actually the daughter of the villain Yamana Sōzen. Her parents separated when she was still a baby, and her mother concealed the relationship. Now, Kikuzaki plans to become a Buddhist nun; but first, she returns to Mitsuuji the true missing sword (the one he claimed to have recovered earlier was a fake), as shown in Kunisada's design for the *Color Print Contest* series (20C).

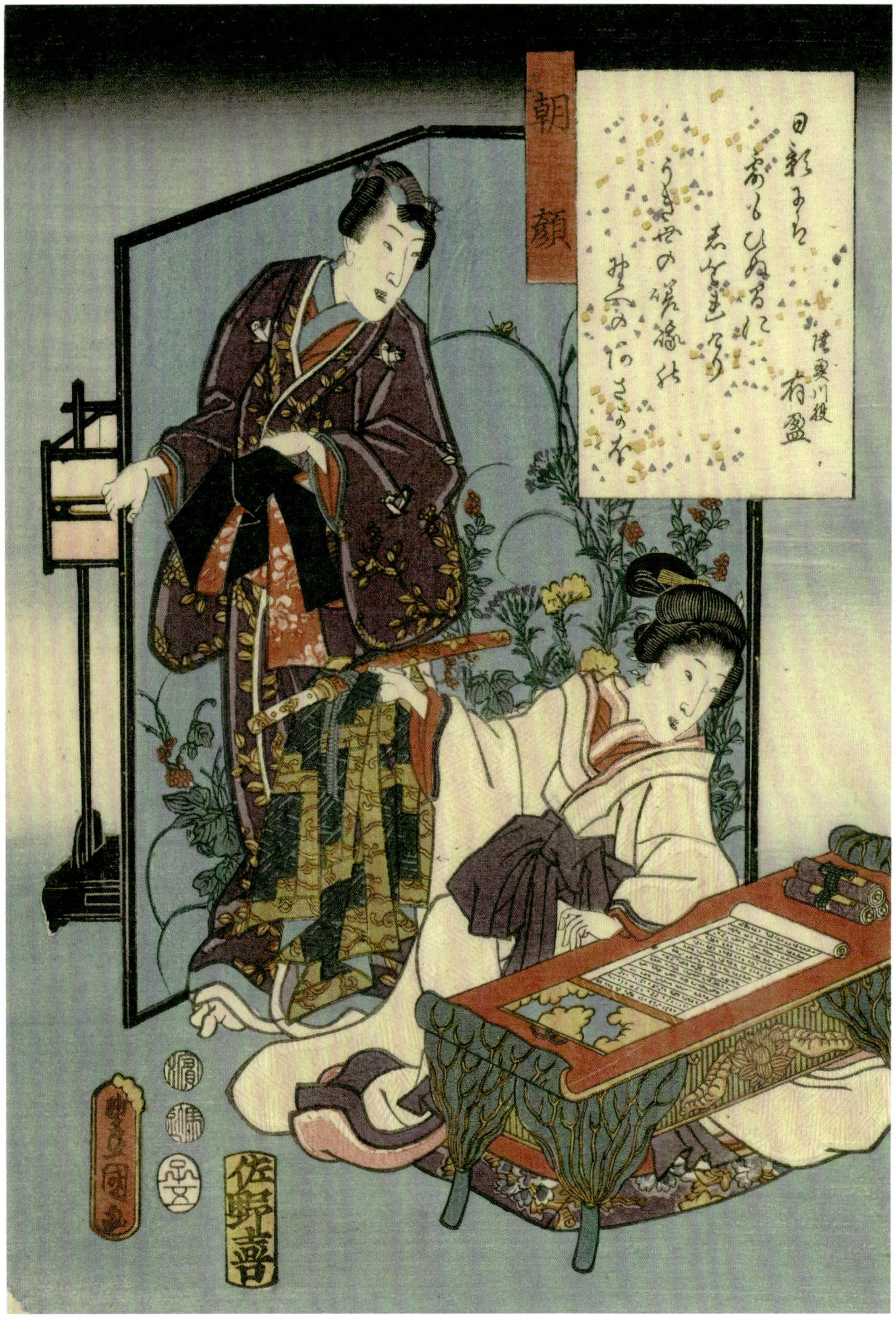

20C | Kunisada, *The Color Print Contest of a Modern Genji*, 1852

21

The Maiden (Otome)

This chapter begins the romantic adventures of the second generation of Genji's family. Akikonomu is chosen as the official empress, triumphing over Tō no Chūjō's daughter as foreshadowed in the picture contest of chapter 17. When Genji's son Yūgiri develops an interest in Kumoinokari (another daughter of Tō no Chūjō), her father discourages it, probably because he is still feeling resentful of Genji's success. Yūgiri consoles himself with the pretty daughter of Genji's right-hand man Koremitsu, who has been selected as one of the dancers at the annual Gosechi harvest festival of the court. Watching the dance, Genji himself is reminded of a past lover who was a Gosechi dancer, and he composes the title poem for her.

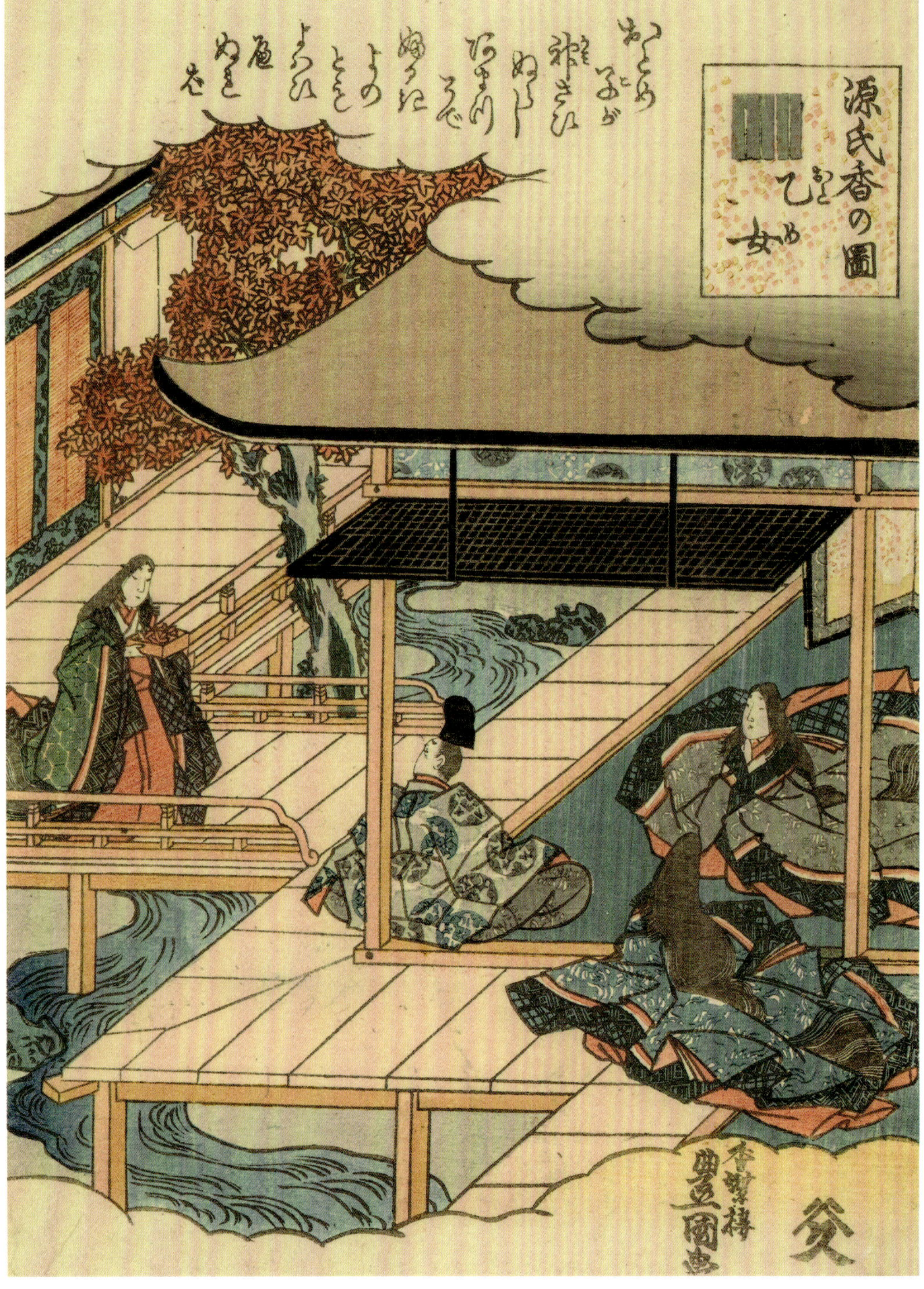

21A | Kunisada, *Genji Incense Pictures*, 1844–47

That fair dancing girl
must have grown wise in her time,
for the friend she knew
when she tossed her angel sleeves
is himself much older now.

21B | Nishimura Shigenaga, *Genji in Fifty-Four Sheets*, about 1735

21C | Kunisada, *The Color Print Contest of a Modern Genji*, 1854

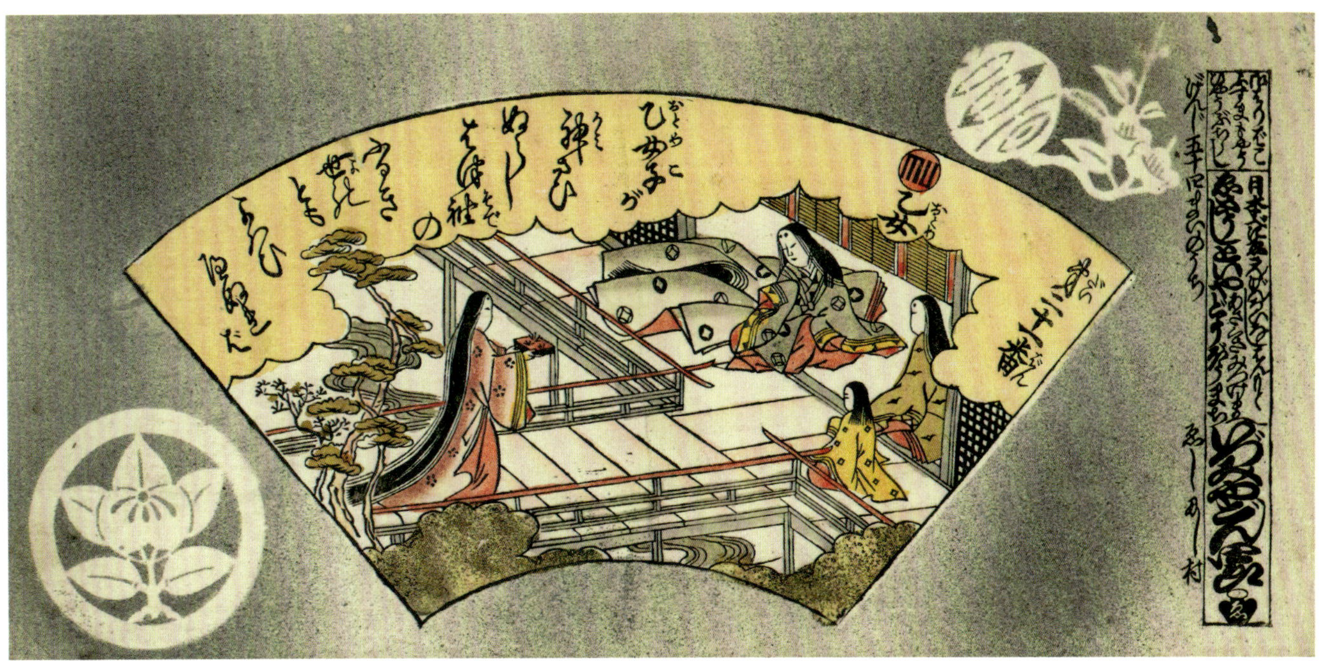

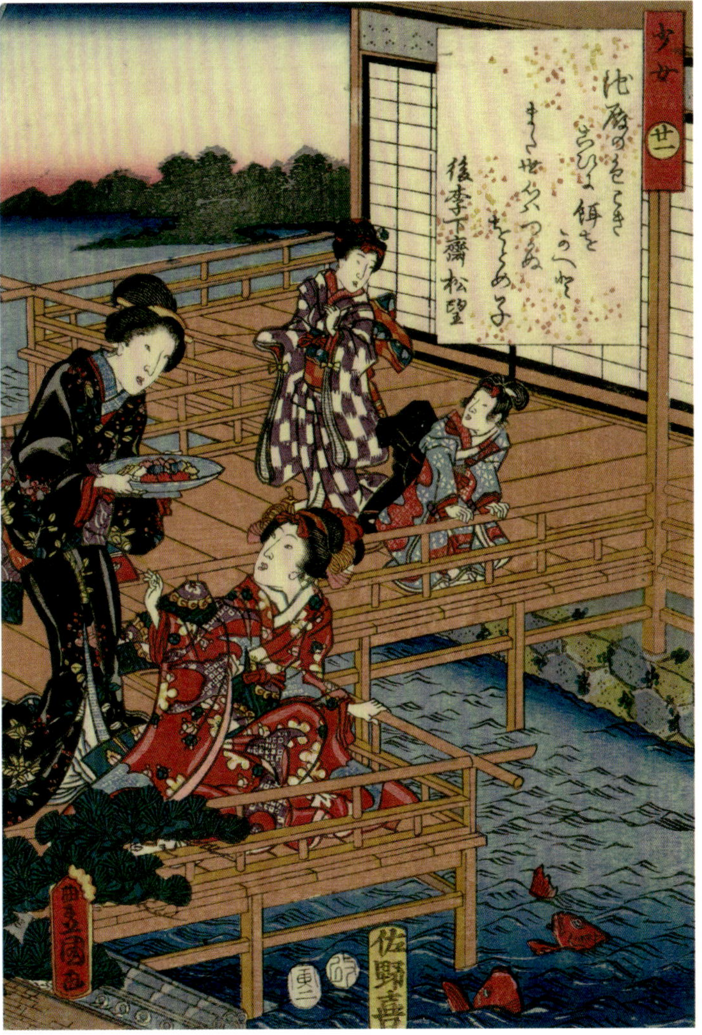

Genji moves from his mansion at Nijō to an even larger and more splendid estate at Rokujō (the area where Akikonomu's late mother once lived), with quarters for all of his ladies, including Akikonomu whenever she takes time off from her duties as empress to visit her family. In a frequently illustrated scene from the end of the chapter, Akikonomu, whose nickname means "fond of autumn," sends an elegantly dressed messenger over the walkways and bridges of the new mansion with a box of red leaves from her autumn garden as a gift to her foster mother, Murasaki (21A, 21B).

In chapter 30 of *Inaka Genji*, Mitsuuji's son Yūgirimaru comes of age and takes the names Kumoinojō and later Ujinaka. He is in love with his childhood sweetheart Karigane (= Kumoinokari), the daughter of Mitsuuji's friend and rival Akamatsu Takanao (= Tō no Chūjō), but Takanao keeps them apart. The scene of women on walkways over a koi pond is based on an illustration at the end of chapter 30 showing the Akamatsu family mansion (21C).

22

The Jeweled Wreath (Tamakazura)

Ukon, the lady-in-waiting who accompanied Yūgao on the night she died at Genji's villa in chapter 4, has remained in Genji's service for many years. Meanwhile, Yūgao's other attendants continue to care for her baby daughter, Tamakazura. When the baby-nurse's husband is appointed governor of Kyushu, the family take Tamakazura with them to the southern island. Years later, they bring the girl, now a beautiful young woman, back to the capital to find her own family. On a pilgrimage to the great temple Hasedera at Hatsuse (south of Nara) to pray for guidance, they happen to encounter Ukon. When Genji hears the story, he adopts Tamakazura and lets people think that she is his own long-lost daughter. He composes the title poem, the source of her nickname, while discussing her with Murasaki.

Most illustrations of the chapter show the dramatic meeting at Hasedera; the temple is famous for its covered staircases ascending to the main hall built out over the steep mountainside (22A). A Genji series by Shinsai includes a surimono still life of objects representing three adjacent chapters; a toy boat symbolizes Tamakazura's journey from Kyushu (22B). The next chapter, Hatsune, is represented by a gift basket and branches of pine and plum for

---

Yes, my love lives on,
just as it did long ago;
yet, O tendril wreath,
say what long and winding stem
led you all the way to me!

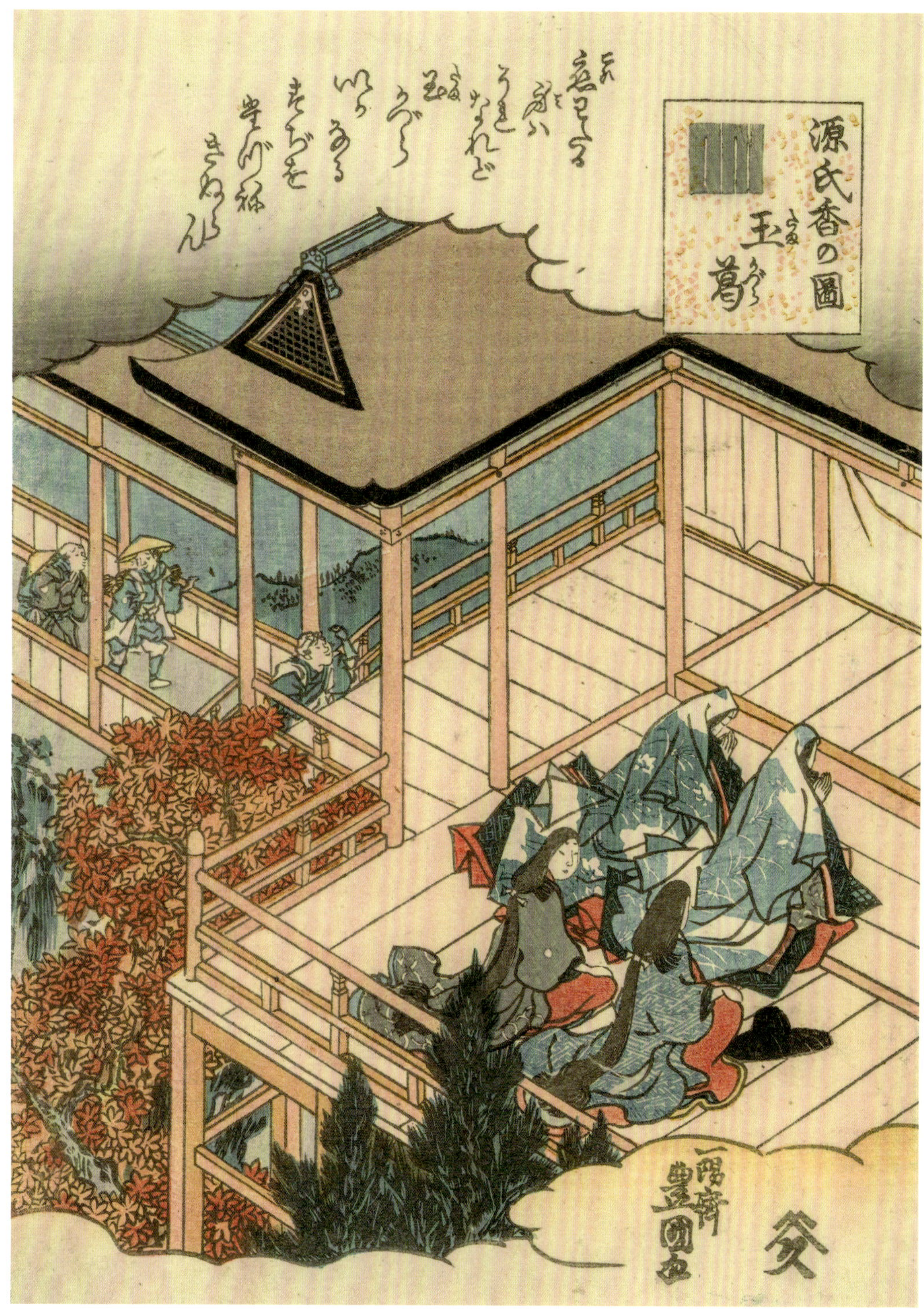

22A | Kunisada, *Genji Incense Pictures*, 1844–47

22B | (detail)

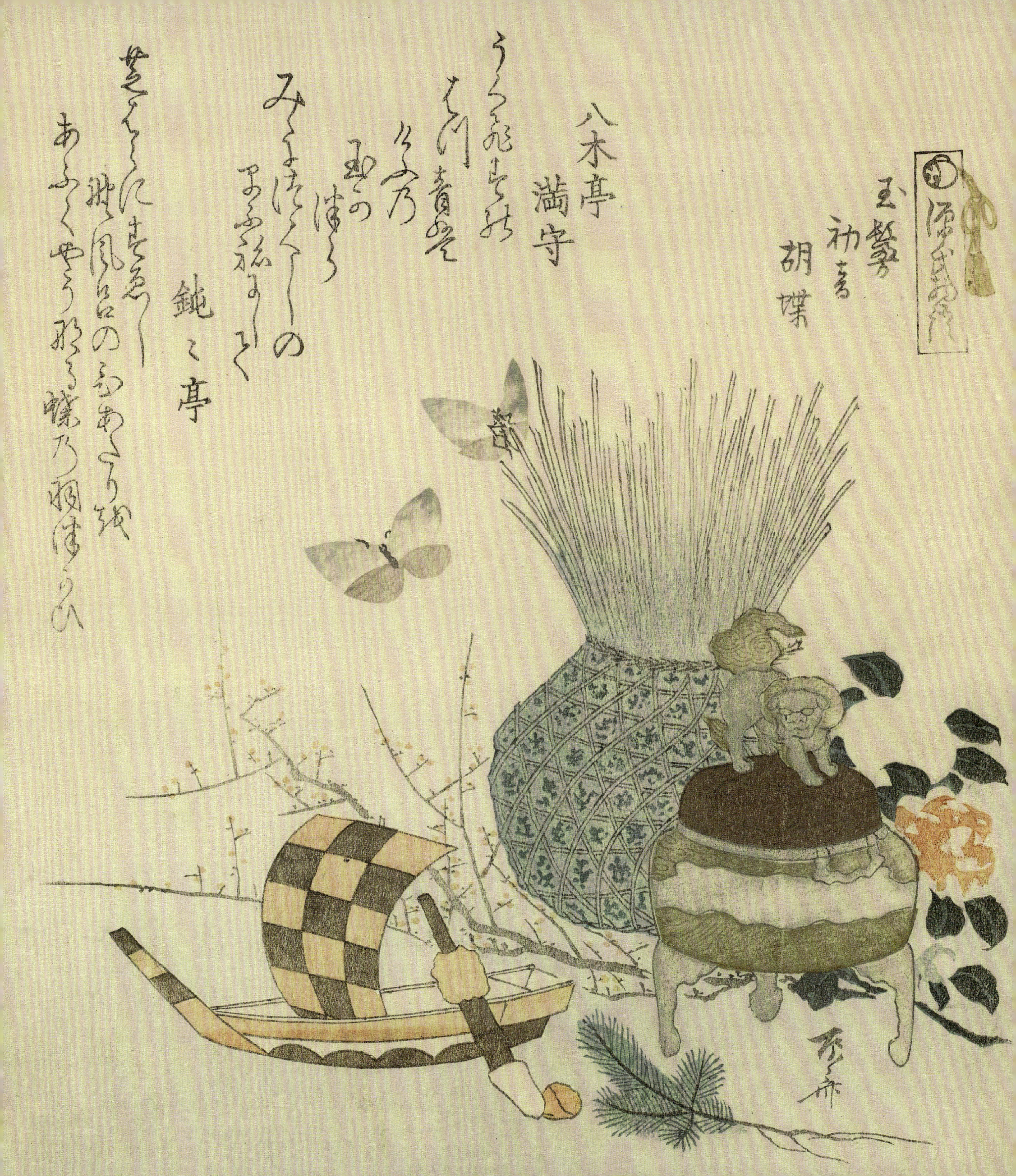
玉勢
初音
胡蝶
八木亭
満守
鈍ゝ亭

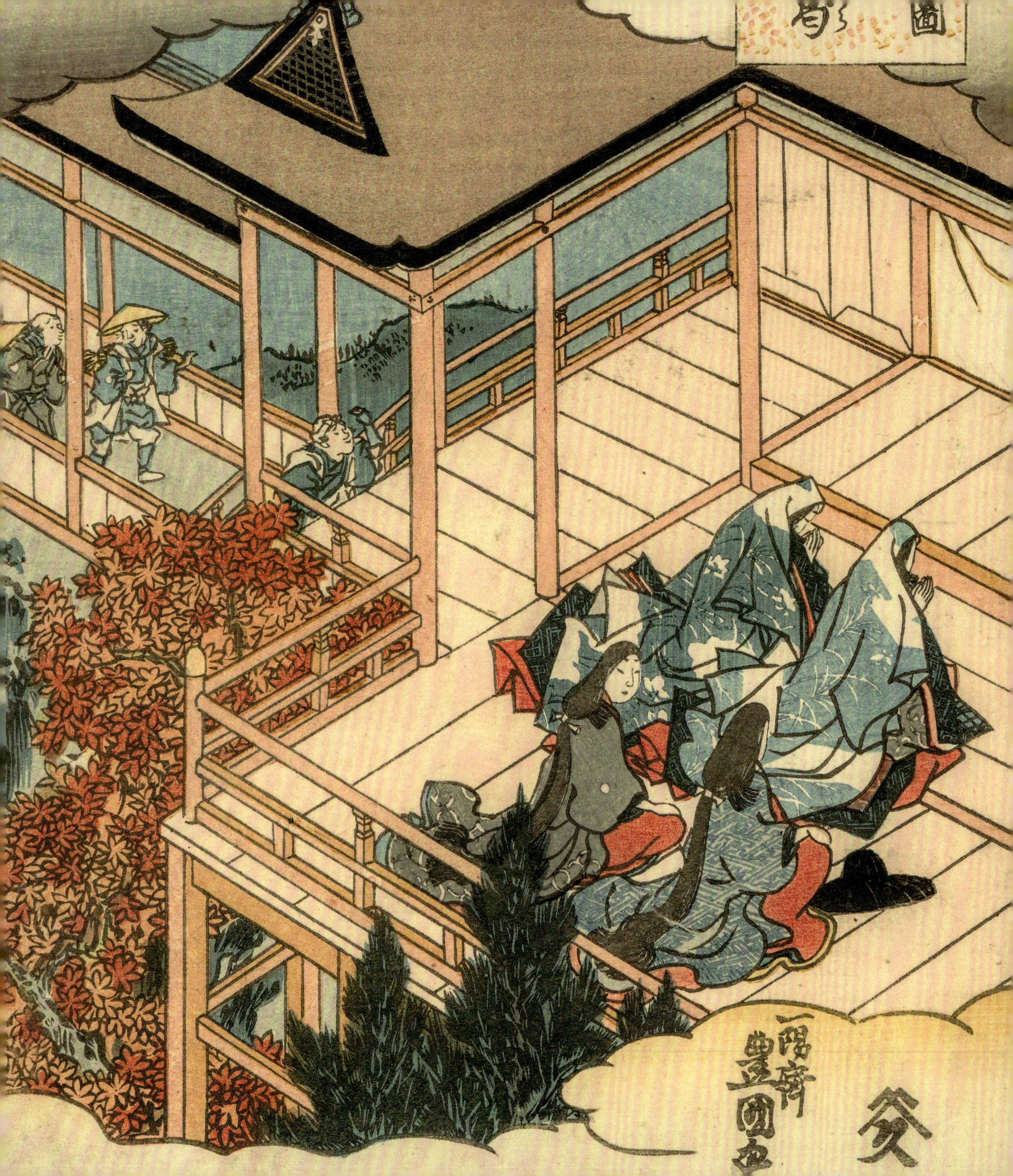
一陽齋豊國画

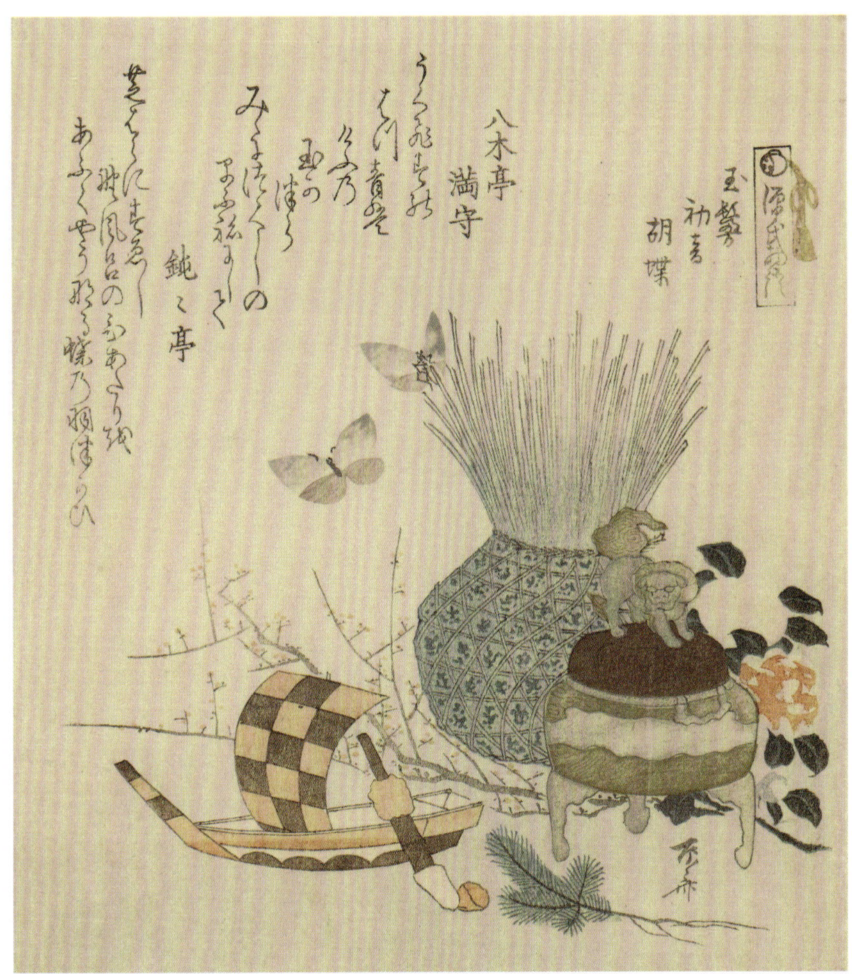

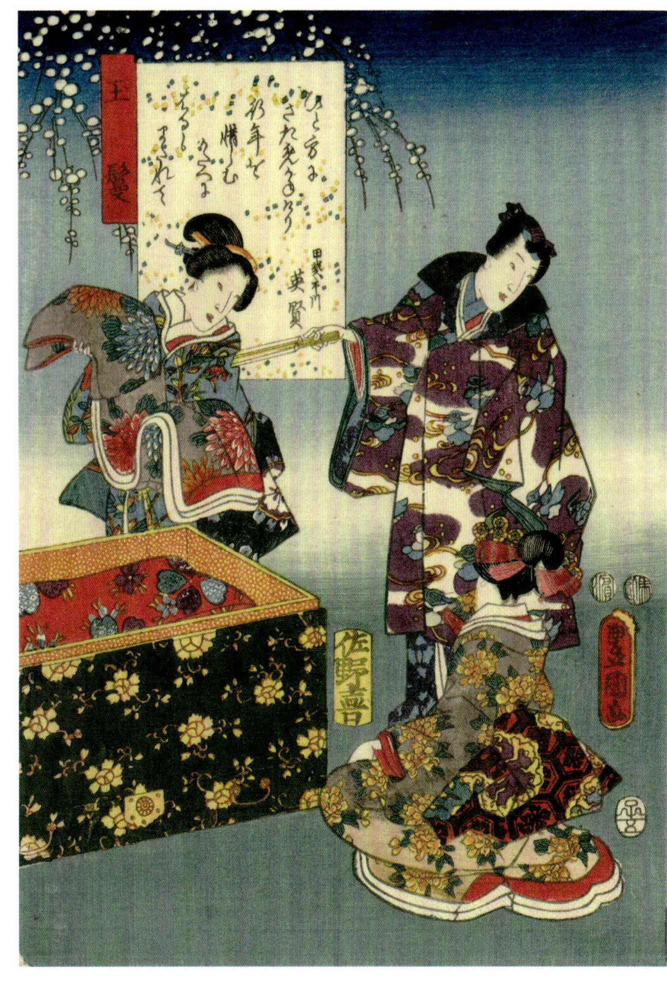

22B | Ryūryūkyo Shinsai, *The Tale of Genji*, about 1819–20

22C | Kunisada, *The Color Print Contest of a Modern Genji*, 1852

the New Year holiday, while the butterfly dance in chapter 24, Kochō, is indicated by actual butterflies. The incense burner topped with a figure of a lion could indicate the temple visit in this chapter, or the Buddhist services in Kochō.

The origin story of Tamakuzu (= Tamakazura) in *Inaka Genji* is spread across chapters 29 to 33, intertwined with plot elements from other chapters of *The Tale of Genji*. The daughter of Tasogare (= Yūgao) and Akamatsu Takanao (= Tō no Chūjō), Tamakuzu is raised in Kyushu by foster parents who bring her back to the capital to escape a provincial suitor. The fortunate meeting at Hatsuse occurs in chapter 33, and Tamakuzu then moves into Mitsuuji's mansion as if she were his daughter. The final illustration of chapter 33, which became the basis for Kunisada's color print, shows Mitsuuji and Murasaki selecting New Year gifts for Tamakuzu and the various other ladies of Mitsuuji's household (22C).

22A | (detail)

23

The First Warbler (Hatsune)

The next two chapters, Hatsune and Kochō, both occur frequently among Genji illustrations because they represent auspicious events — the New Year holiday and a spring garden party — celebrated in luxury at the highest level of society, representing a lifestyle that everyone aspired to or at least dreamed of. They are the first of seven chapters, 23 to 29, that follow the characters through a single year, with scenes of each of the four seasons.

At New Year, Genji pays calls on each of the ladies in his spacious mansion. He first visits Murasaki, who is raising his daughter. The little girl's birth mother, the Akashi lady, has sent a gift of holiday food in "bearded baskets" (a special type of basket in which the ends of the strands are not woven into the completed basket but left as a decorative fringe), together with an artificial warbler on a pine branch to symbolize the first birdcall of the year (hatsune), and a wistful poem implying how much she misses her child. Genji is close to tears as he reads the poem. Kunisada's print (23A) includes a plum tree in the garden, just coming into bloom at the time of the Lunar New Year (generally about six weeks after the modern New Year), while Toyokuni I's

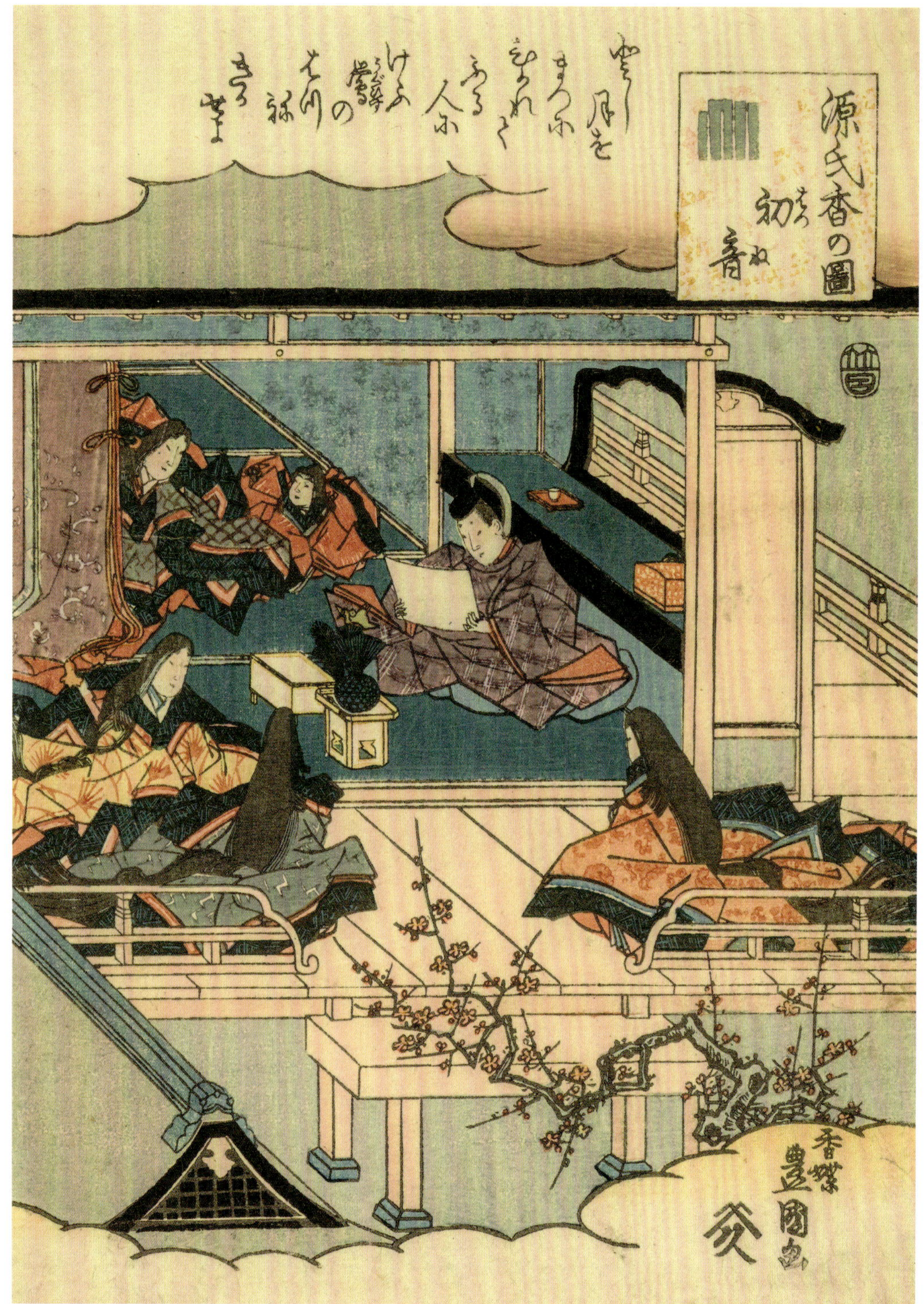

23A | Kunisada, *Genji Incense Pictures*, 1844–47

One who through the years
has clung to a single hope,
O let her today
pine no more and hear at least
the little warbler's first song!

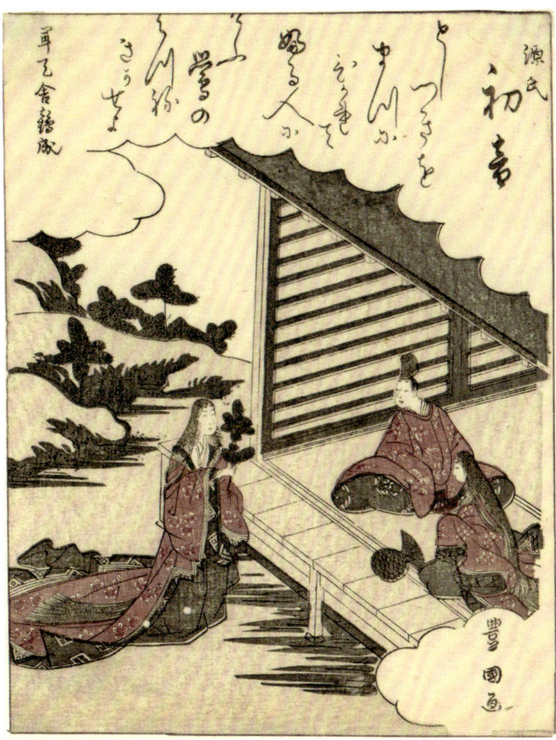

23B | Toyokuni I, *The Tale of Genji*, Edo period

earlier version in the subdued benigirai color scheme includes an attendant picking pine shoots in the garden (23B).

Perhaps because these two chapters contain little in the way of plot development, they are combined into a single chapter in *Inaka Genji*, chapter 34. In the color print based on an illustration from this chapter, Mitsuuji, Murasaki, and little Akashi admire a New Year gift from Akashi's mother, Asagiri; in this version, the baskets are miniature ones included as part of the decoration on the artificial pine branch (23C).

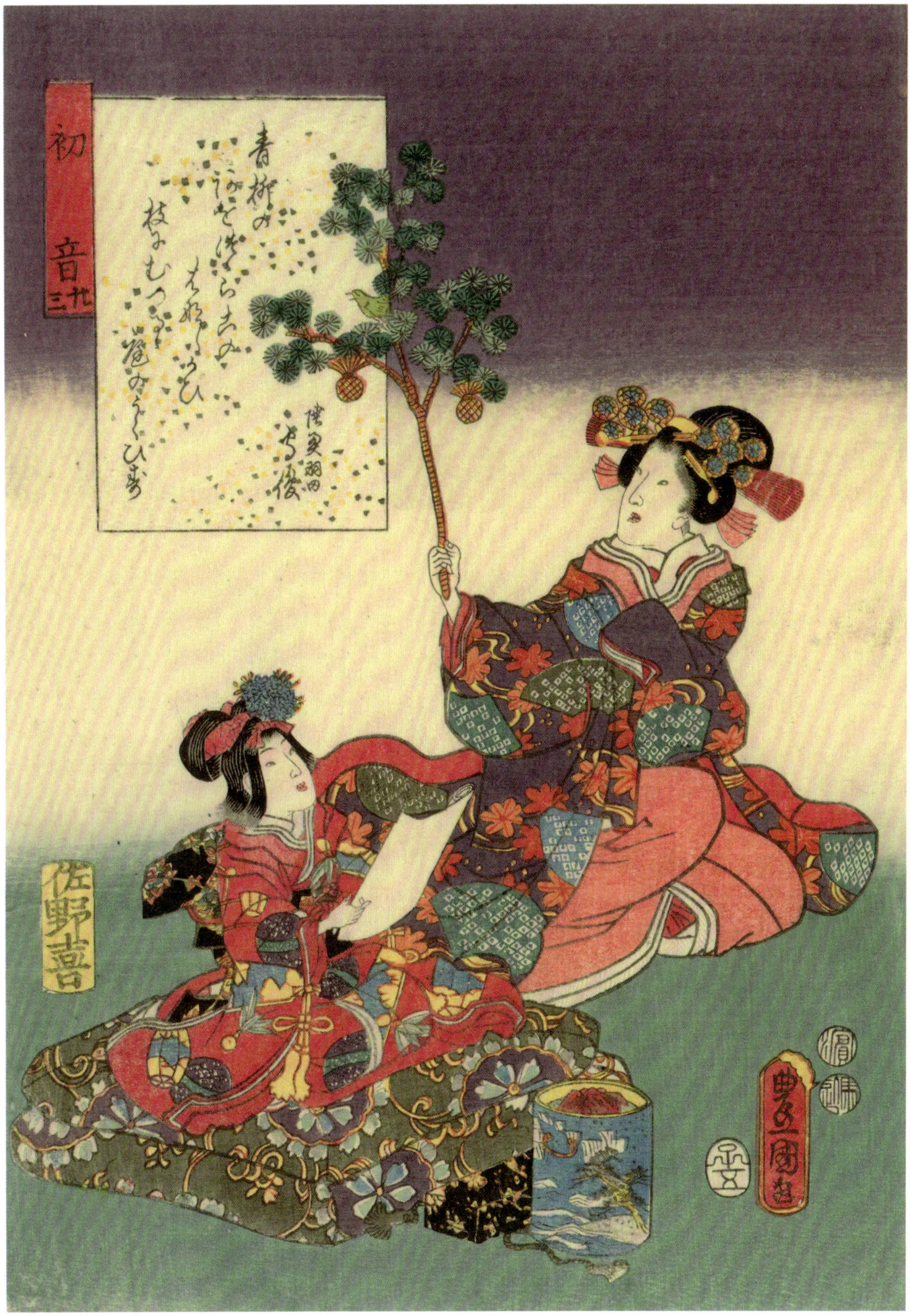

23C | Kunisada, *The Color Print Contest of a Modern Genji*, 1852

24

Butterflies (Kochō)

In the third lunar month, Murasaki's spring garden is at its height. Akikonomu is visiting, and so Murasaki invites her to an elaborately staged garden party. Guests cross the garden pond in Chinese-style dragon and phoenix boats, and there is music late into the night (24A). The following day, Akikonomu sponsors a Buddhist sutra reading. Murasaki sends floral offerings for the service, delivered by little girls dressed as birds and butterflies, who then perform a charming dance.

Kuniyoshi also uses the distinctive butterfly costumes, together with the title poem, to symbolize the chapter in his humorous Genji series of matching pictures (24B). The main image shows the young nobleman Abe no Yasuna, temporarily crazed by the death of his sweetheart, swatting at butterflies with his fan, to the bewilderment of a retainer. The scene is from a kabuki play, but since actor prints were technically illegal at the time it was made, it is presented as a real historical event. The upper part of the picture, which is similar in all of the prints in this *Genji Clouds* series, represents an unrolled handscroll containing the chapter title poems from *The Tale of Genji* — the same poems included on the prints of the *Genji Incense*

Will you look askance,
O pine cricket in the grass,
longing for autumn,
even at these butterflies
from my own flower garden?

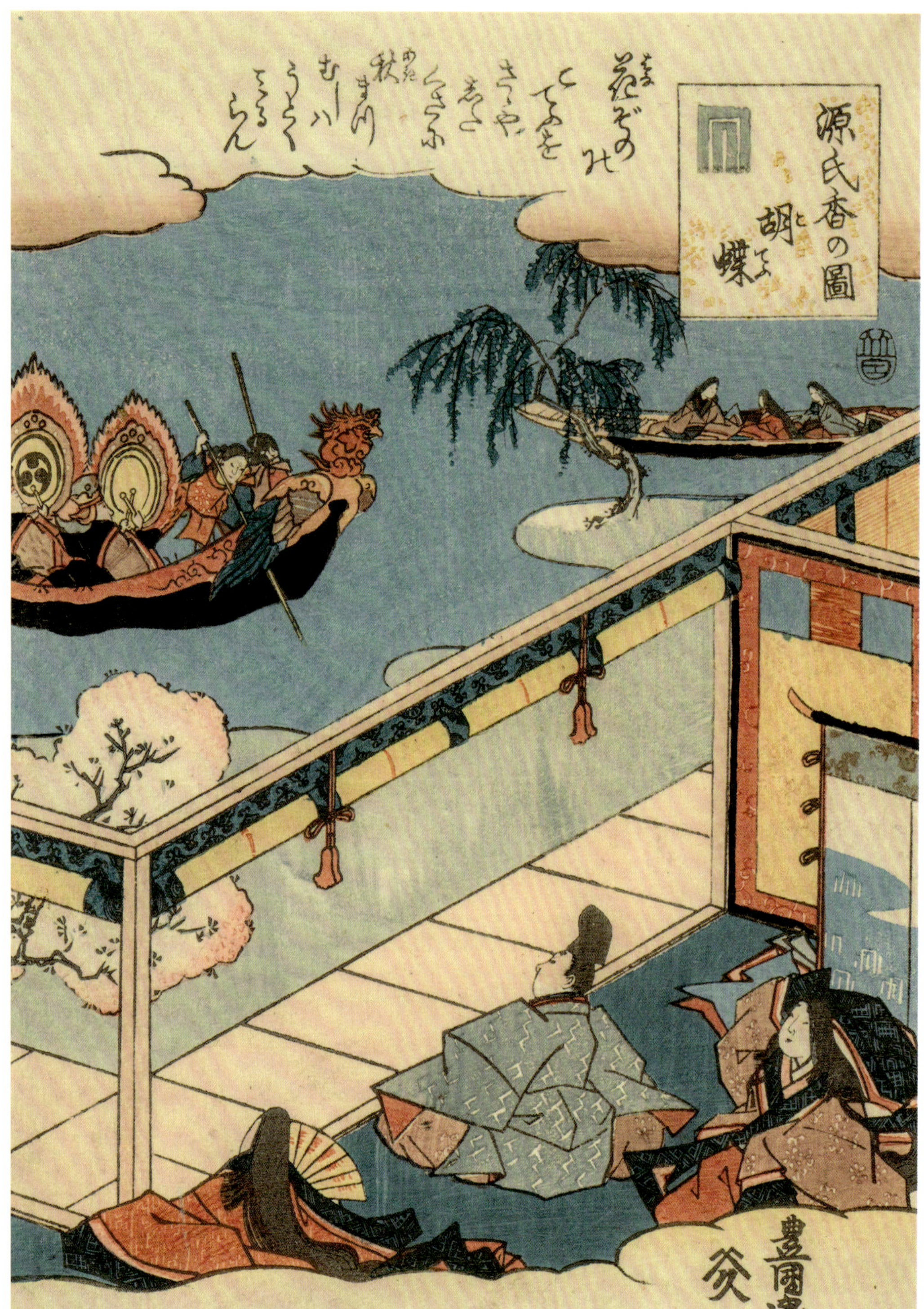

24A | Kunisada, *Genji Incense Pictures*, 1844–47

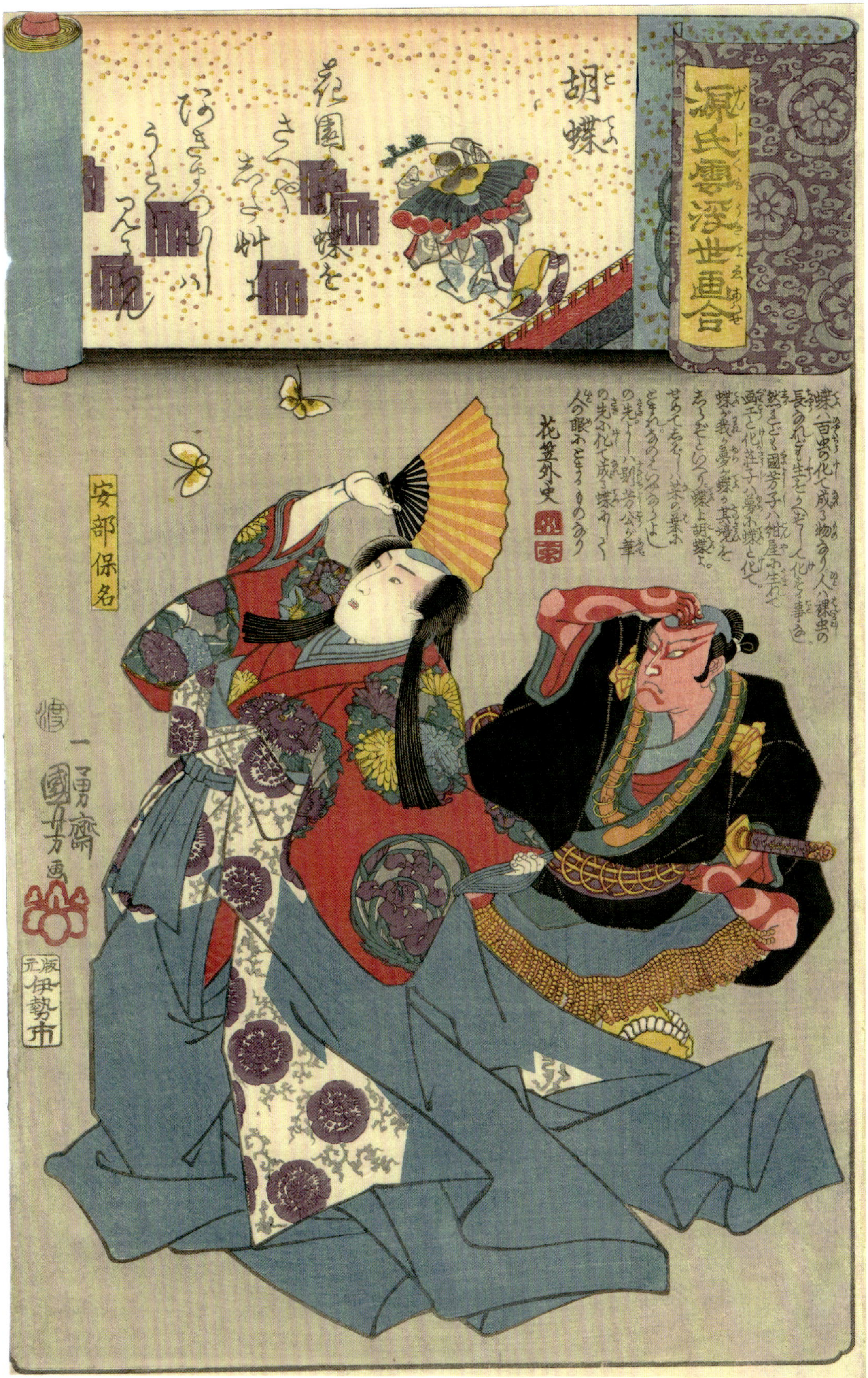

24B | Kuniyoshi, *Genji Clouds Matched with Ukiyo-e Pictures*, about 1845–46

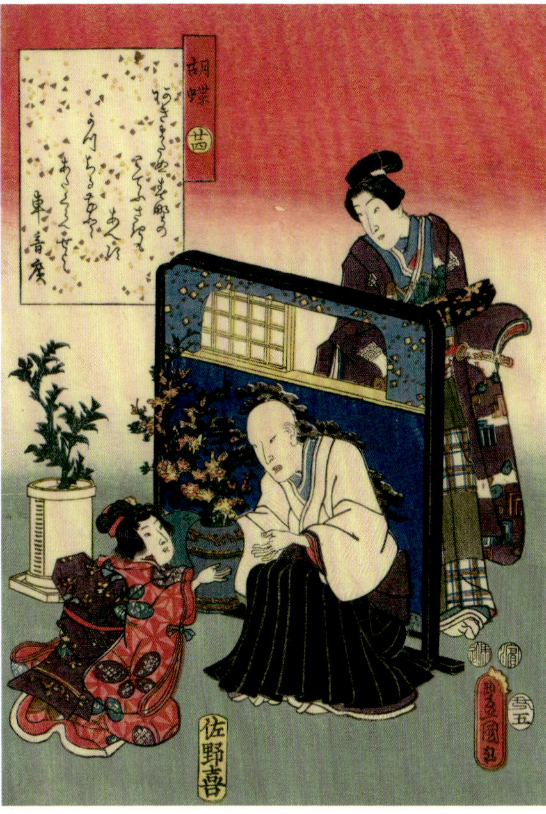

24C | Kunisada, *The Color Print Contest of a Modern Genji*, 1853

series — each decorated with a small picture and the appropriate symbol from the Genji incense game.

In *Inaka Genji*, the Buddhist service commissioned by Isona (= Akikonomu) is conducted by Zen nuns as a memorial to Isona's mother, Akogi (= Rokujō), and various other people who have died in the course of the story. The Zen nuns are a deliberate modernizing twist, since the Zen sect had not yet been introduced into Japan when the original *Tale of Genji* was written. Kunisada's print shows a nun receiving the floral offering sent by Murasaki (24C).

25

The Firefly (Hotaru)

A number of eligible young men are paying court to Tamakazura, who they believe to be Genji's daughter. Among them is the widowed Prince Hotaru (Firefly), a younger half-brother of Genji, whose nickname comes from this chapter. Women of the nobility, when they resided in private homes and not at court, were theoretically not supposed to be seen by any adult men other than their husbands or fathers, although they could converse with potential suitors through curtains or bamboo blinds, and of course, exchange written poems. Genji teasingly gives Hotaru a glimpse of Tamakazura by releasing fireflies in her darkened room, to let him know that she is beautiful as well as talented. To complicate the situation still further, Genji is becoming interested in her himself. In the *Genji Incense* print, Tamakazura shyly hides her face as Hotaru stares intently at her curtains; but the fireflies, it seems, have already made their escape and are back outside in the garden (25A).

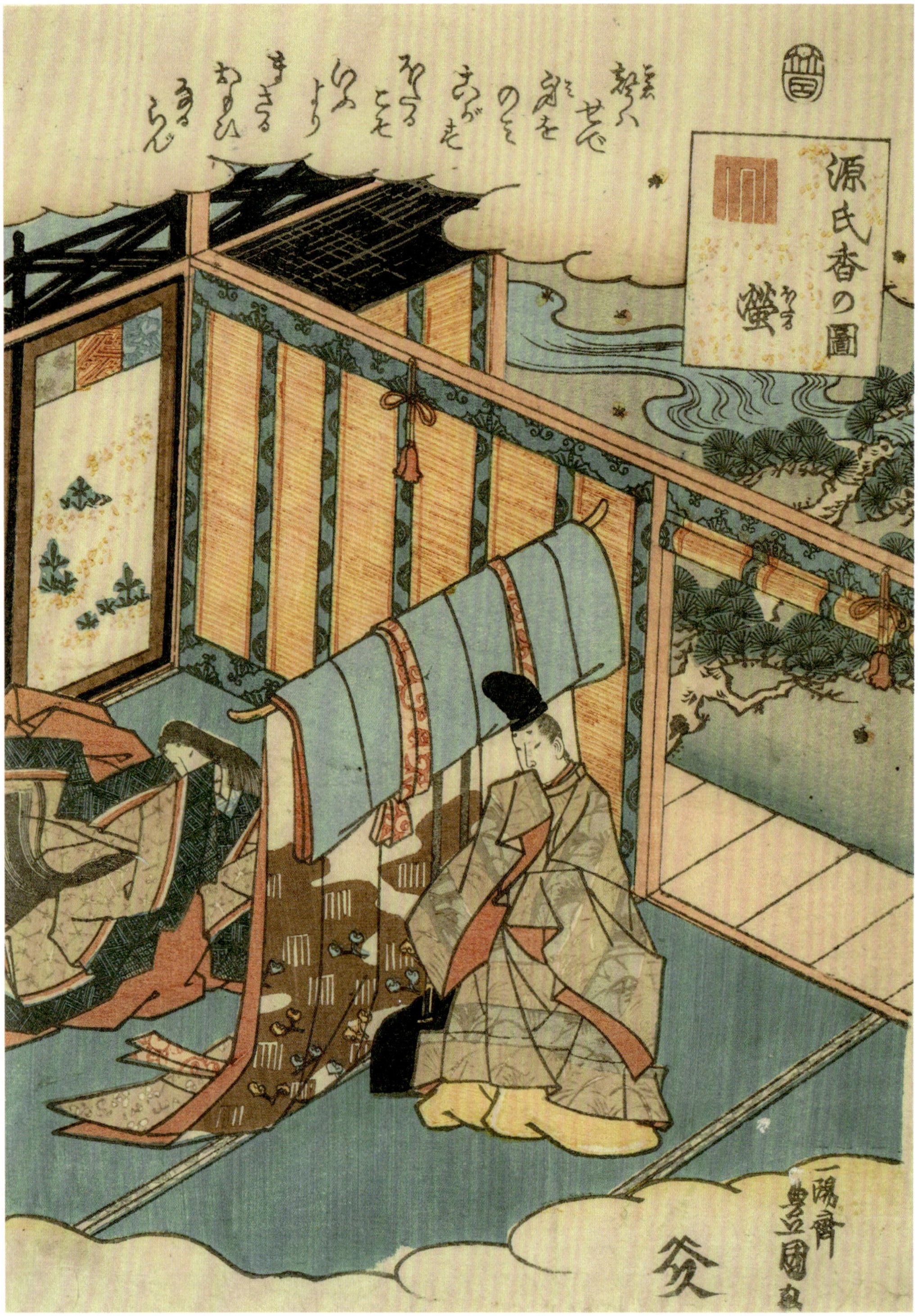

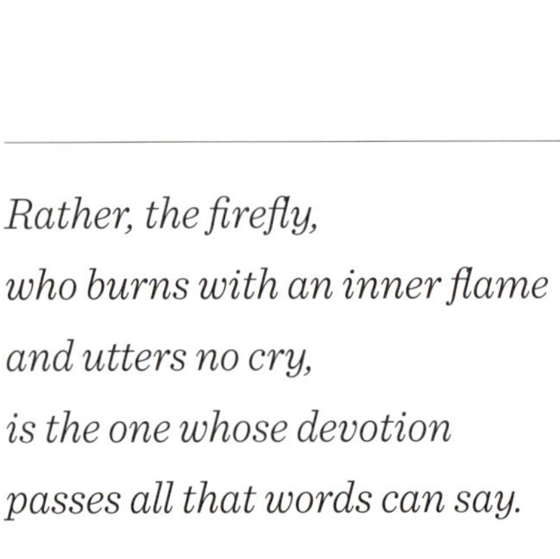

Rather, the firefly,
who burns with an inner flame
and utters no cry,
is the one whose devotion
passes all that words can say.

25A | Kunisada, *Genji Incense Pictures*, 1844–47

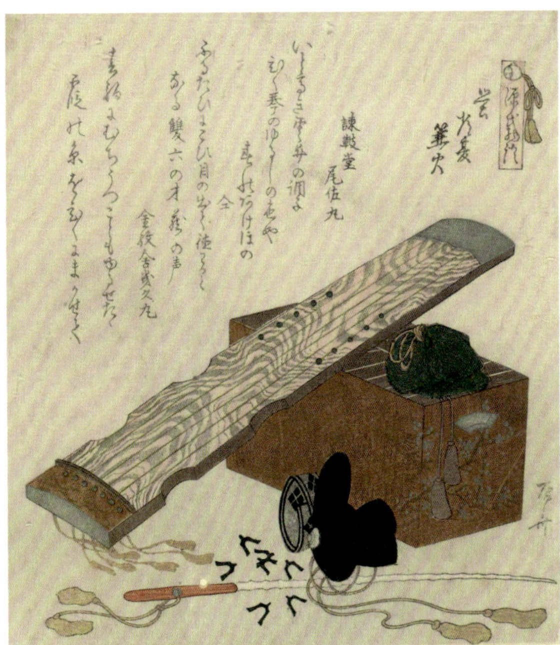

25B | Ryūryūkyo Shinsai, *The Tale of Genji*, about 1819–20

Later in the chapter, as part of the annual celebration for the fifth day of the fifth month, imperial guardsmen who are friends of Genji's son Yūgiri hold a contest of mounted archery on the grounds of Genji's mansion while the ladies enjoy watching them from behind their blinds. A surimono print from Shinsai's Genji series represents this event with a horsewhip and a guardsman's distinctive hat, together with the koto and sugoroku (backgammon) gameboard that figure in the next two chapters (25B).

The counterpart of Prince Hotaru in *Inaka Genji* is Shirō Masahisa, a younger brother of Mitsuuji. In chapter 35, Mitsuuji tries to arrange a tryst between Masahisa and Tamakuzu, using the firefly trick, but it is unsuccessful (25C). Women of the fifteenth-century warrior clans were not secluded from the gaze of men in the manner of Heian ladies; but like the noblewomen of old, they were expected to preserve their outward reputations for proper behavior, whatever they might be doing in secret.

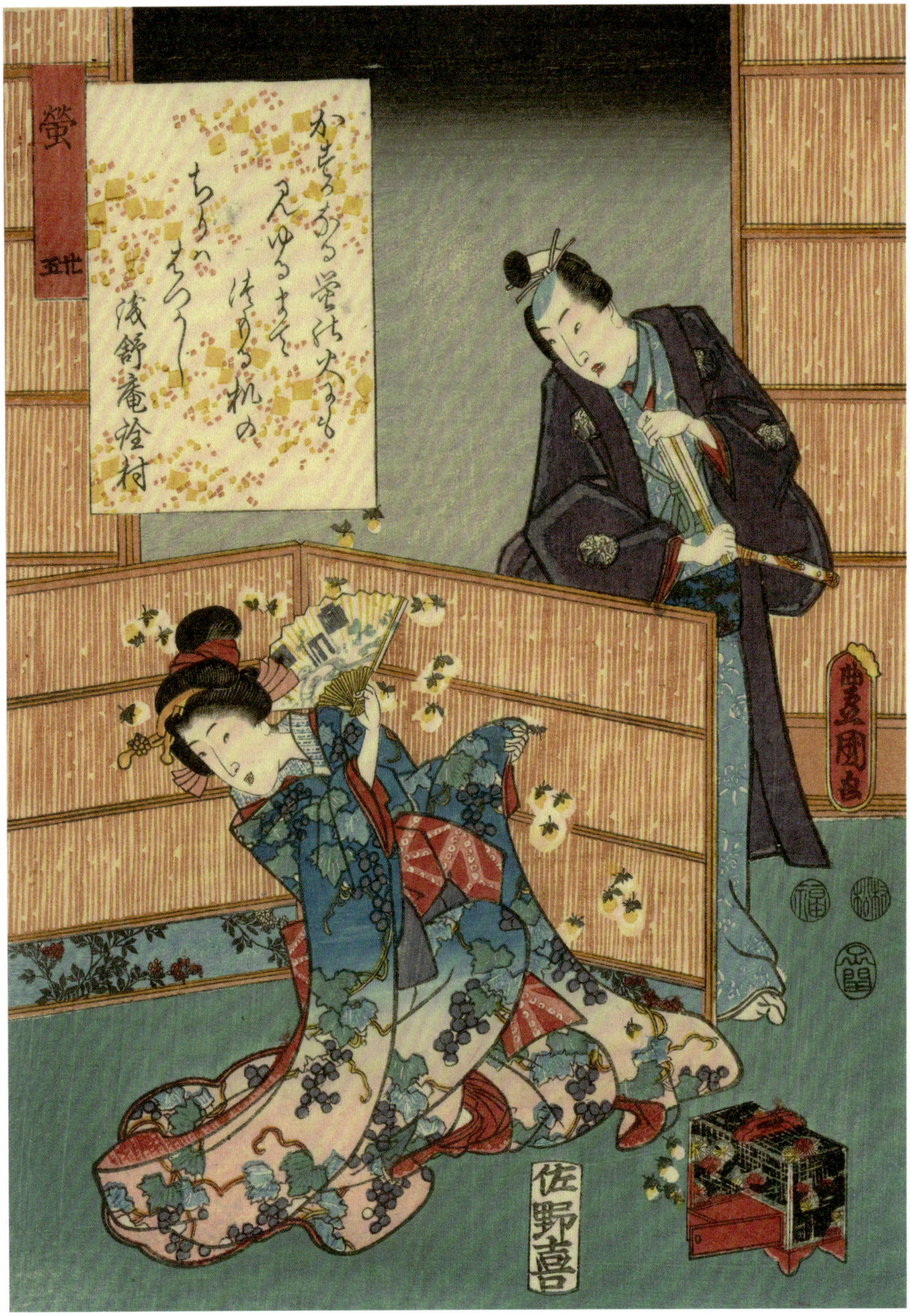

25C | Kunisada, *The Color Print Contest of a Modern Genji*, 1852

26

The Wild Carnation (Tokonatsu)

On a hot summer day, Genji and Yūgiri host a dinner of freshly caught fish with Tō no Chūjō's sons, Kashiwagi and Kōbai, who are close friends of Yūgiri. Afterward, Genji visits Tamakazura and plays the koto for her, while the young men linger in the garden. Genji wonders whether to tell Tō no Chūjō that Tamakazura is really his daughter and composes a poem comparing her to the wild carnation (tokonatsu or nadeshiko, also known as "pinks" in English), a flower that in the modern Japanese language has become a metaphor for the ideal modest, gentle, beautiful young Japanese woman (yamato nadeshiko).

Meanwhile, Tō no Chūjō has been feeling jealous of Genji's success in introducing everyone to the charming Tamakazura, and so he finds a long-lost daughter of his own, known as the Ōmi lady because she is from Ōmi Province. Alas, her manners are provincial. Toward the end of the chapter, he watches her playing backgammon with another lady and feels embarrassed by her loud voice and constant chatter. Kunisada's print shows the raucous backgammon game, while an early twentieth-century postcard focuses on the beloved flower (26A, 26B).

At the end of chapter 35 of *Inaka Genji*, Mitsuuji and his son Ujinaka enjoy a fish dinner with guests including Akamatsu Takanao's son Umenojō (= Kōbai),

---

If he were to see
all the inviting beauty
of the little pink,
he might wish to know as well
more of the gillyflower.

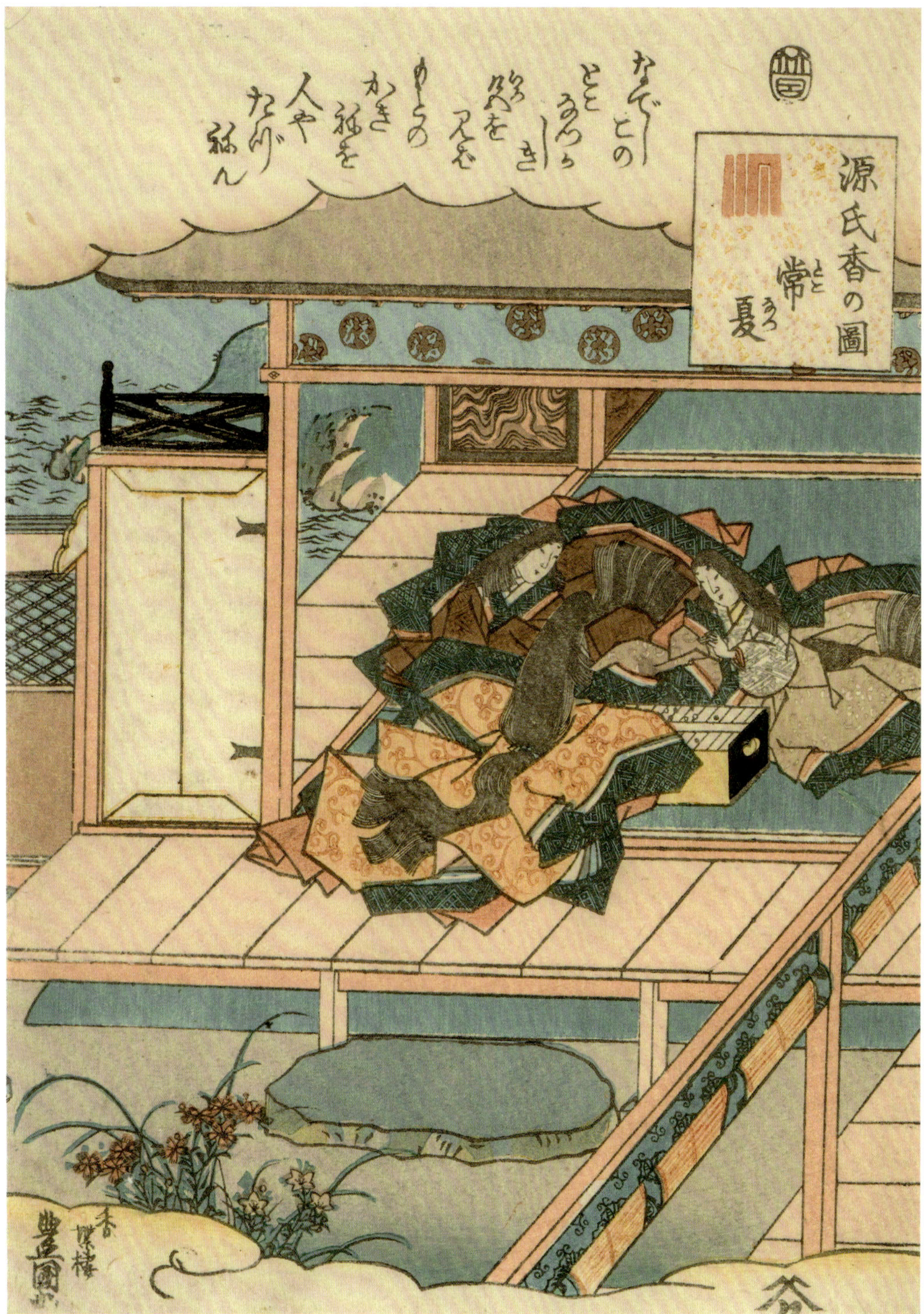

26A | Kunisada, *Genji Incense Pictures*, 1844–47

after which Mitsuuji plays the koto for Tamakuzu. Kunisada's print from the *Color Print Contest* series shows Mitsuuji and Tamakuzu admiring wild carnations in the rainy garden (26C). The backgammon game takes place in chapter 36, and Takanao's rediscovered daughter Katata sends a letter introducing herself to her sister Lady Tomiyo at the shogun's palace, attached to a bouquet of wild carnations. Kunisada II designed a color print based on the book illustration of the delivery of the letter (26D). Lady Tomiyo's young attendant, at the right, holds a lacquer box containing writing equipment that might be used to send a reply.

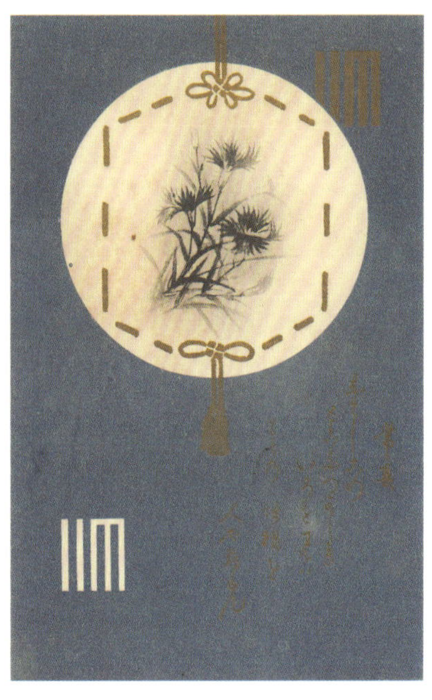

26B | Unknown artist, untitled Genji series, late Meiji–Taishō era

26C | Kunisada, *The Color Print Contest of a Modern Genji*, 1852

26D | Kunisada II, *Lady Murasaki's Genji Cards*, 1857

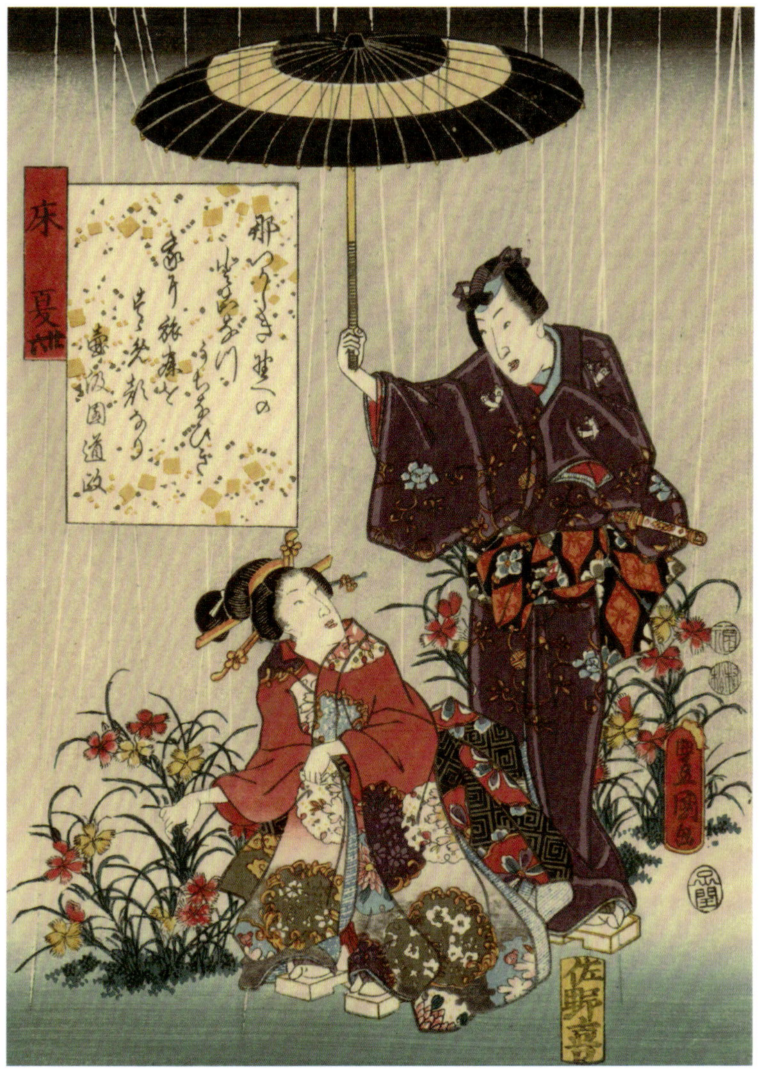

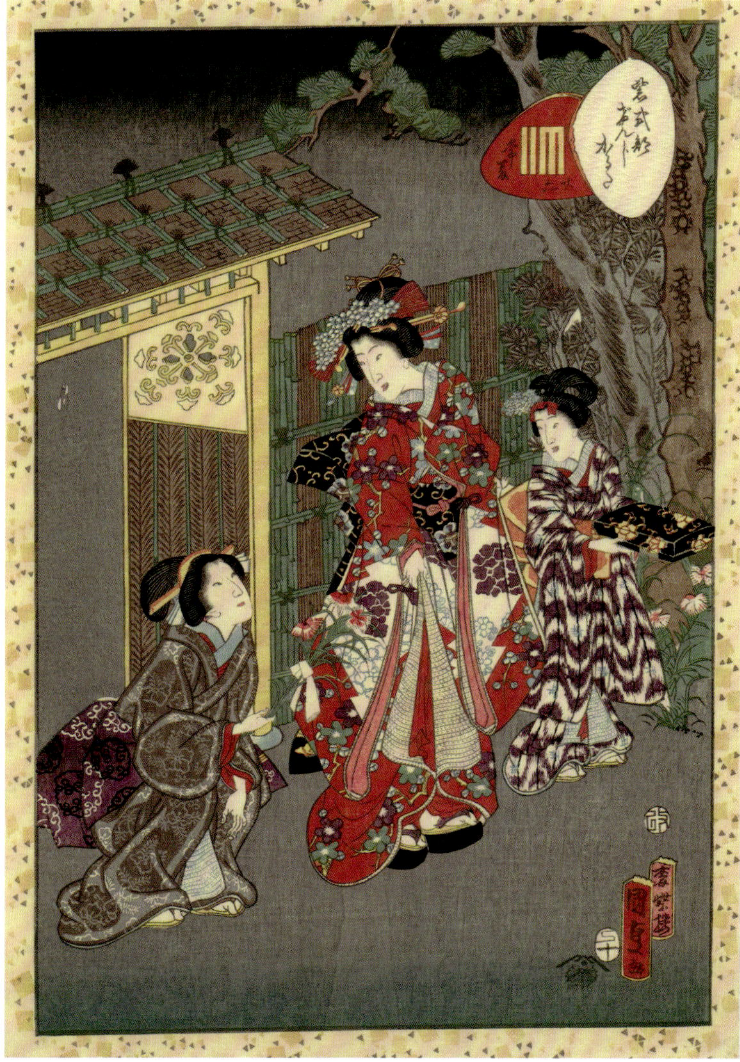

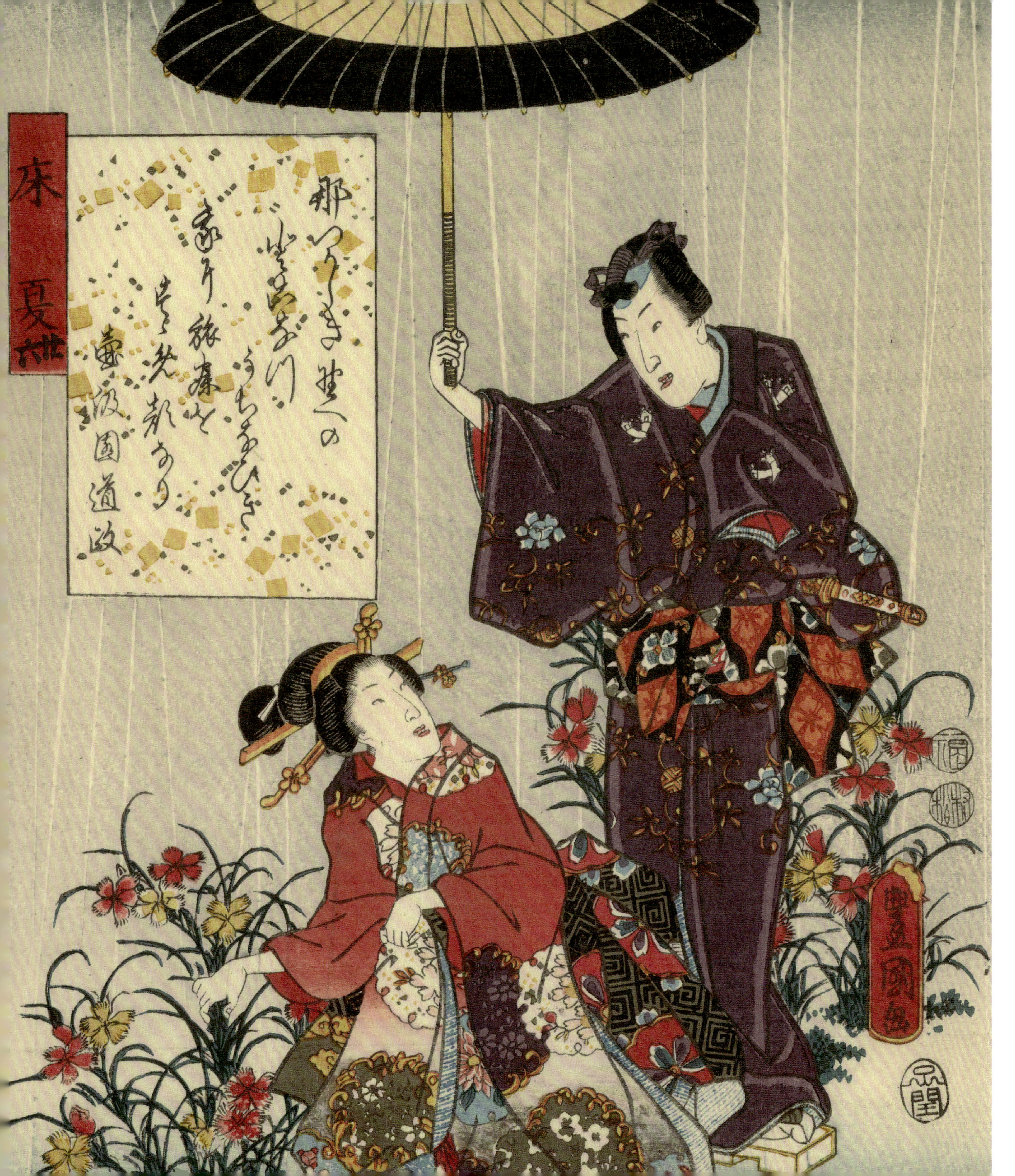
床夏
廿六
豊国画

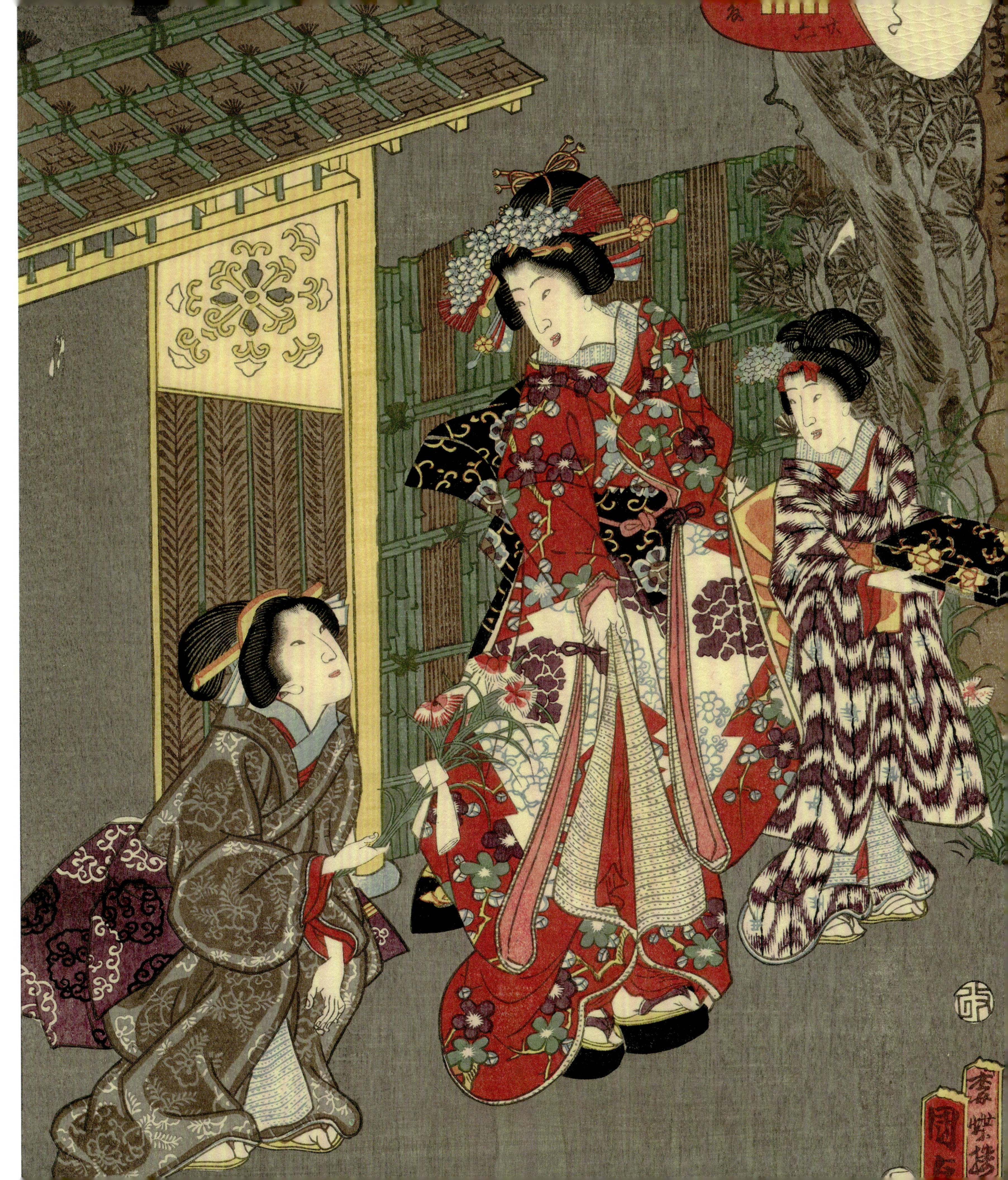

27

Garden Flares (Kagaribi)

This very brief chapter presents another romantically moody vignette of life at Genji's palatial estate. Tamakazura has firmly resisted Genji's tentative advances, but the two remain good friends. It is autumn, and flares in the form of cressets (metal baskets on poles) have been lit in the garden. Genji visits Tamakazura, and they hear Yūgiri and his friends, Tō no Chūjō's sons, playing music. Genji invites them to come and play for him while Tamakazura, decorously concealed, listens in. Tō no Chūjō's sons, especially Kashiwagi, are very interested in Tamakazura, still unaware that she is actually their sister.

In the *Genji Incense* series, Genji is shown playing the koto for Tamakazura, while outside, groundskeepers light the garden flares (27A). In traditional Genji illustrations, the cressets take the form of metal baskets hanging from curved poles. This distinctive shape makes it possible to identify the untitled triptych by Eishō, a pupil of Eishi, as a Genji parody, with the cressets at bottom left (27B).

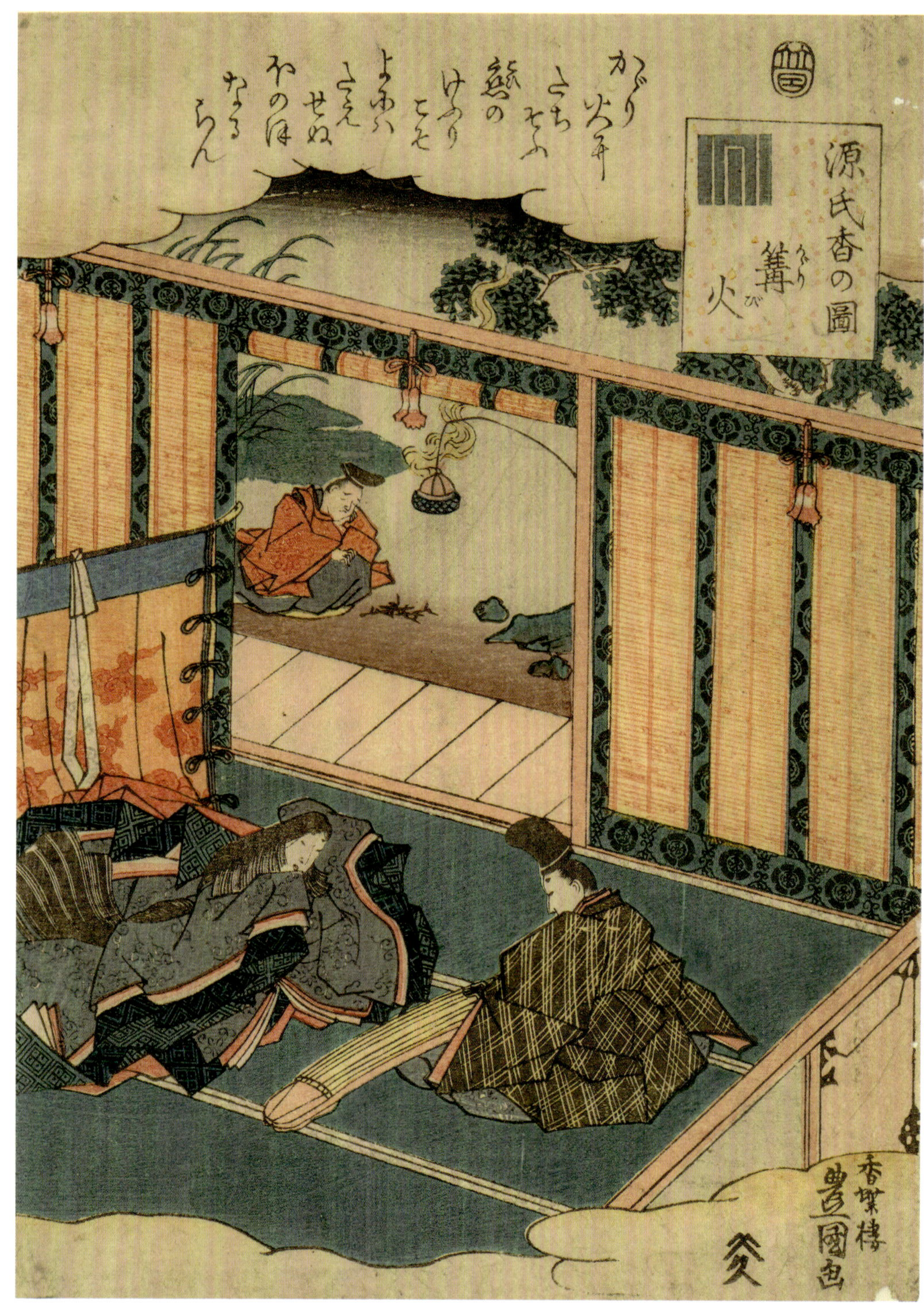

27A | Kunisada, *Genji Incense Pictures*, 1844–47

With these cressets' smoke
another rises, of desire,
from such inner flames
as I know now will burn on
for as long as this world lasts.

27B | (detail)

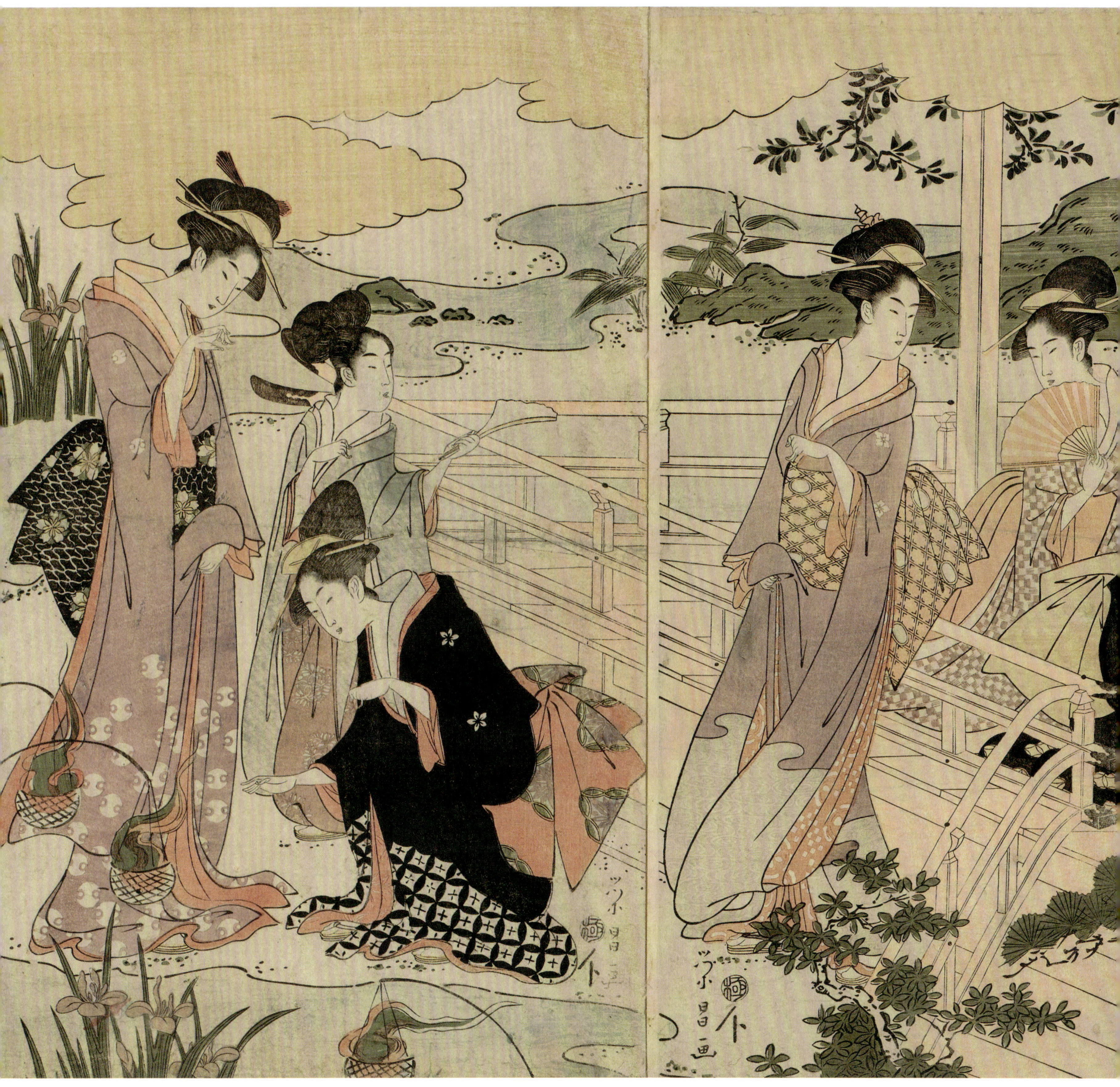

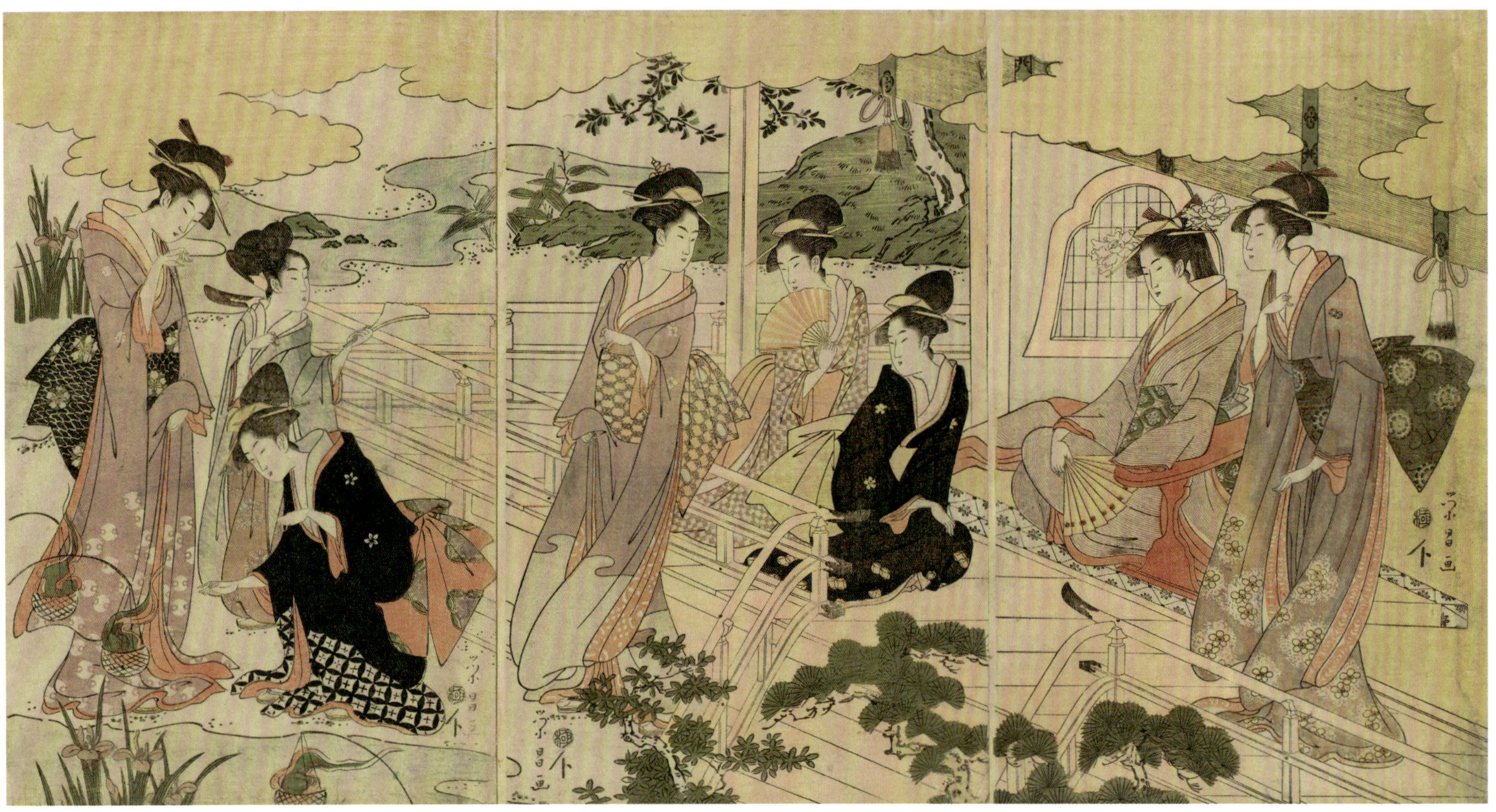

27B | Chōkōsai Eishō, Women in an iris garden, about 1794–95

The decorative window in the background on the right is another clue: windows with this pointed shape are often called "Genji windows" because there is one such window in the room at Ishiyama Temple where Lady Murasaki is said to have begun writing *The Tale of Genji*. Whereas Eishi's Genji triptychs all feature one man surrounded by women, here Eishō shows no adult men, only a temple page boy (or a girl dressed as one) in the left sheet.

A corresponding garden scene appears at the beginning of the second volume of chapter 36 of *Inaka Genji*, when Mitsuuji, playing the koto for Tamakuzu late one summer night, asks her ladies-in-waiting to refuel the flares in the garden, which take the form of lamp stands rather than hanging baskets; the gender reversal of the people tending them is also a parody element. The design for this chapter in the *Color Print Contest* series shows the figures of Mitsuuji and Tamakuzu and adds a large lantern overhead decorated with the corresponding scene from the original story (27C).

27C | Kunisada, *The Color Print Contest of a Modern Genji*, 1853

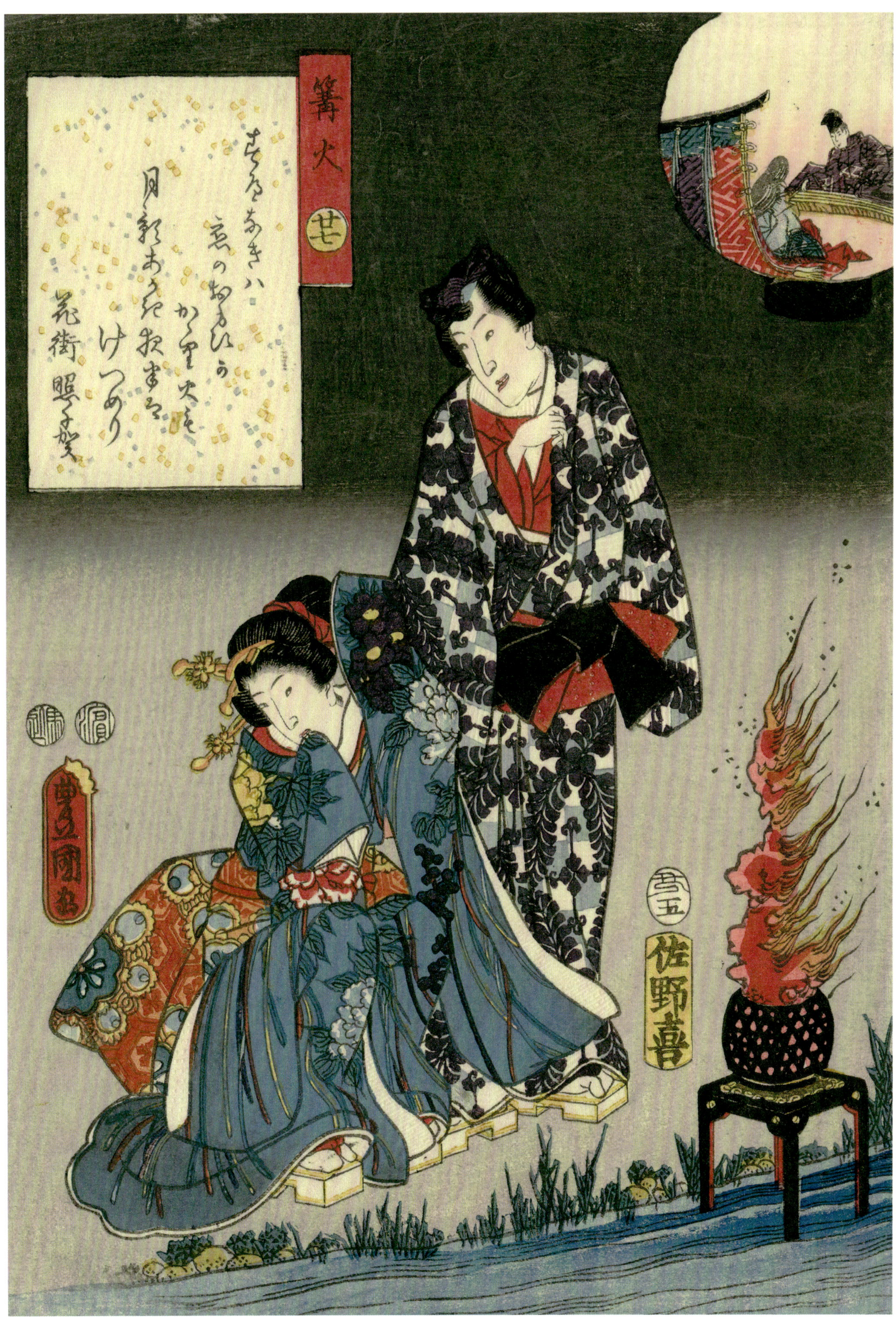
篝火
廿七
豊国画
佐野喜

28

The Typhoon (Nowaki)

Later in the autumn, the pleasant routine of life at Genji's mansion is temporarily disrupted by a typhoon. Most illustrations of this chapter show ladies struggling to control the bamboo blinds as they flap wildly in the wind. In the confusion, Yūgiri is able to catch his first glimpse of his stepmother Murasaki, and he is struck by her extraordinary beauty. The compositional technique known as the "blown-off roof" makes it possible to show both the inside and the outside of the room; the man about to enter the room is probably Genji, while Yūgiri (not pictured) watches secretly from the far end of a corridor (28A). Much as Yūgiri admires Murasaki, he still yearns for Tō no Chūjō's daughter Kumoinokari, and he writes the chapter title poem to send to her.

Koryūsai's parody version shows modern women grappling with a shōji sliding door panel (28B). Here, the motif of secret peeping and sexual titillation is hinted at by the accidental exposure of one young woman's legs as the wind blows her kimono aside — a typical theme in the genre of prints known as abuna-e or "dangerous pictures" because they teasingly pushed the limits of the obscenity laws that forbade full exposure.

Let the wild winds blow
this evening, and lowering clouds
wander the heavens,
there is no forgetting you,
no, not even when I try!

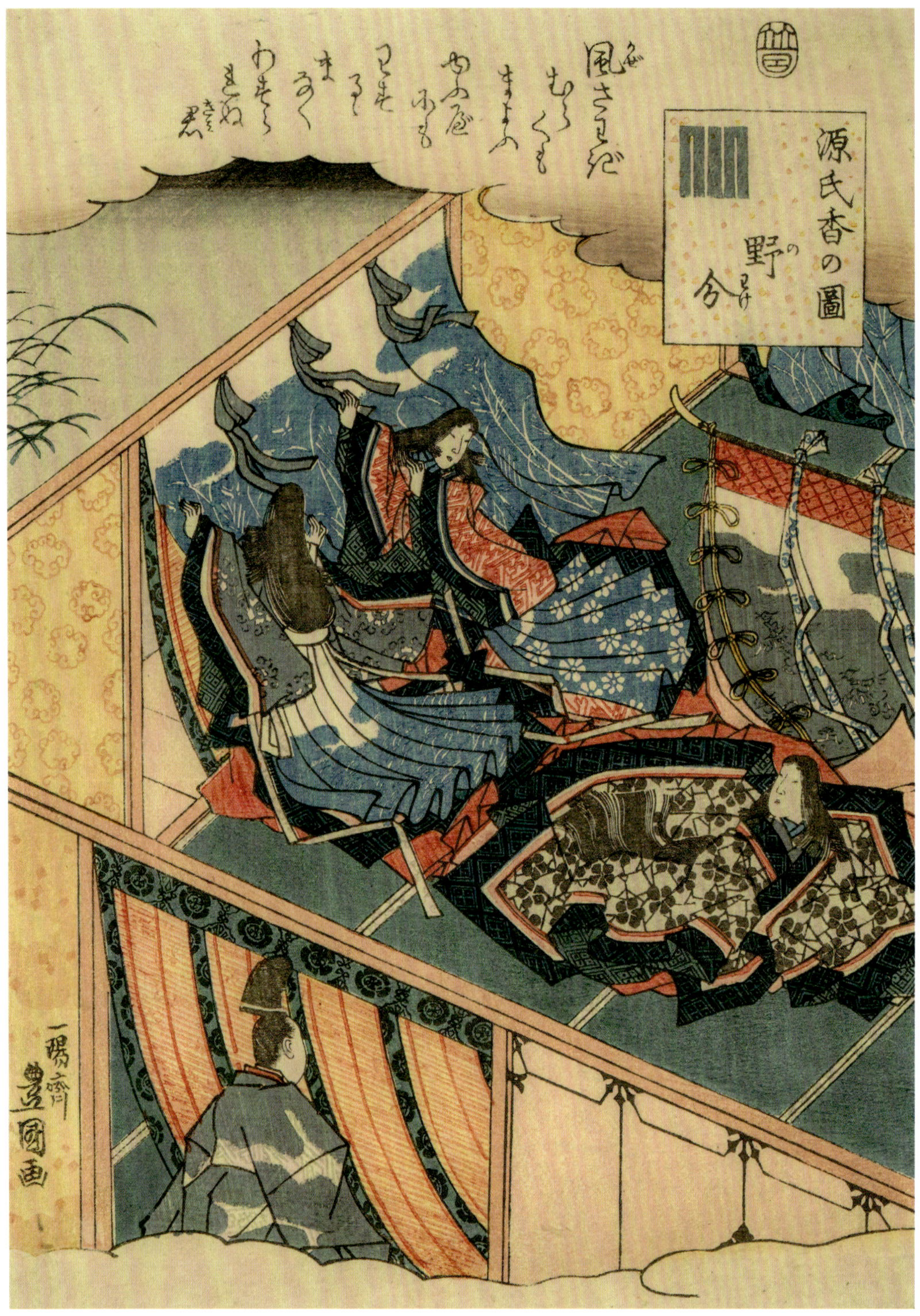

28A | Kunisada, *Genji Incense Pictures*, 1844–47

28B | Isoda Koryūsai, *Genji in Fashionable Modern Guise*, about 1770–72

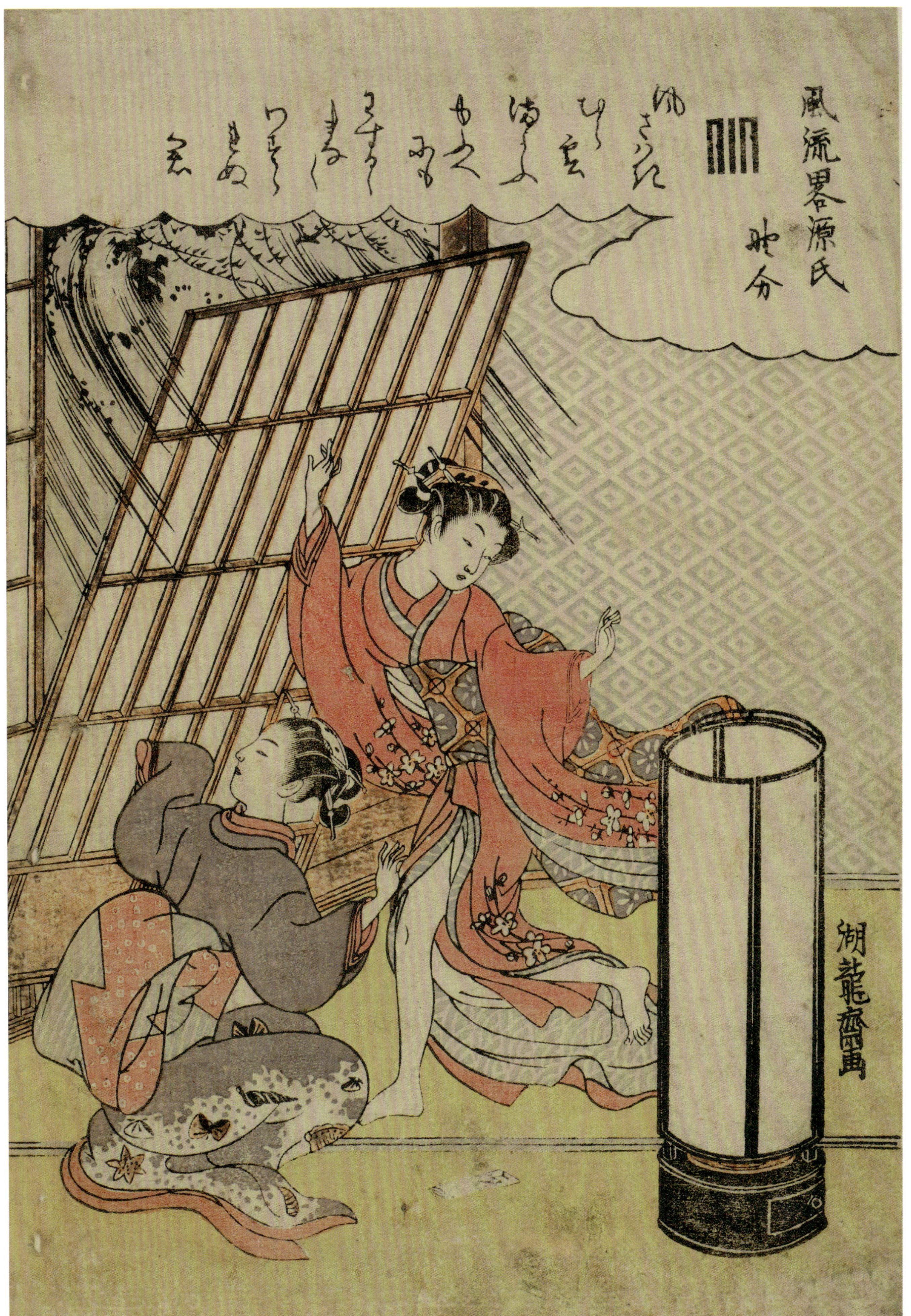
風流畧源氏
野分
湖龍齋画

The tempest of *Inaka Genji* takes place in chapter 36, with Ujinaka (= Yūgiri) having an opportunity to secretly admire his beautiful stepmother Murasaki. The design in Kunisada's *Color Print Contest* series shows Murasaki and one of her ladies (28C). The print is a simplified version of the book illustration which included Ujinaka peeping around a shōji panel in the background. A later illustration in the same chapter became the basis for a print in the *Genji Cards* series by Kunisada II: after the storm, Ujinaka observes the pretty sight of beautifully dressed young girls among the damp grasses of the garden, collecting singing insects to be kept in elaborate bamboo cages (28D).

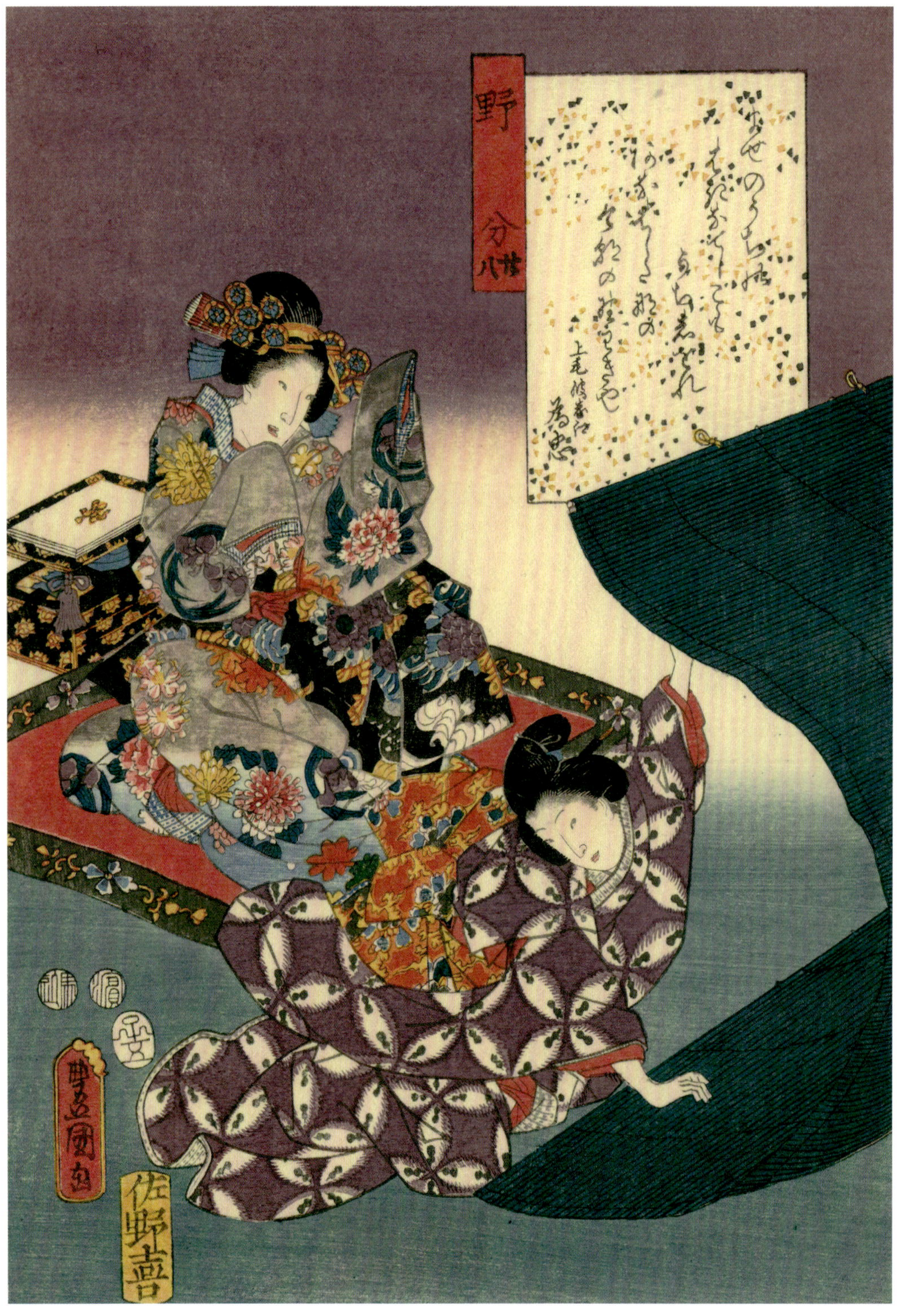

28C | Kunisada, *The Color Print Contest of a Modern Genji*, 1852

28D | Kunisada II, *Lady Murasaki's Genji Cards*, 1857

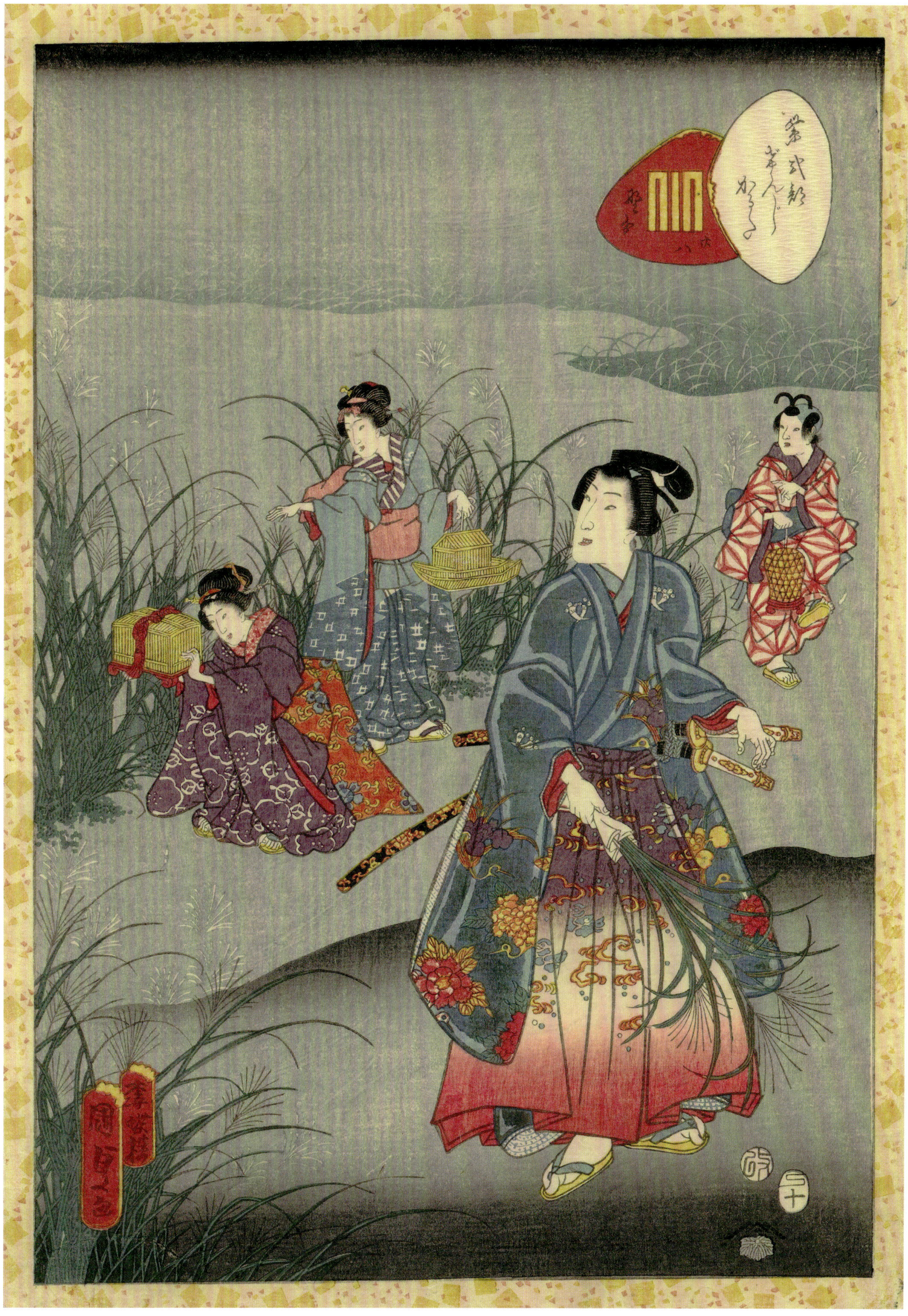

29

The Royal Outing (Miyuki)

The winter episode that completes the year is a royal excursion: a hunting party with falconry in the western suburbs of the city. Genji is unable to attend, but afterward the emperor (Genji's secret son) sends a gift of pheasants attached to a decorative branch. Genji responds with the chapter title poem, which plays on the homonyms for "royal outing" and "beautiful snow," both miyuki. In Kunisada's print, the gift is delivered to Genji by an officer of the imperial guard, who wears a guardsman's distinctive hat with fan-shaped side pieces (29A).

After the event, Genji asks Tamakazura, who now has seen the emperor as the procession passed by, whether she might like to become a lady of the imperial court. Also, at long last, he reveals to Tō no Chūjō that it is he and not Genji who is Tamakazura's real father.

In chapter 37 of *Inaka Genji*, the youthful shogun Yoshitane (who has been falsely rumored to be Mitsuuji's son but is in fact his younger brother) goes on a winter sightseeing excursion to the western part of Kyoto. Mitsuuji does not participate, but Tamakuzu, discreetly concealing her face, is among the spectators watching the splendid

O do come today
and favor again a haunt
where pheasants once rose
that time on Mount Oshio,
over the slopes deep in snow.

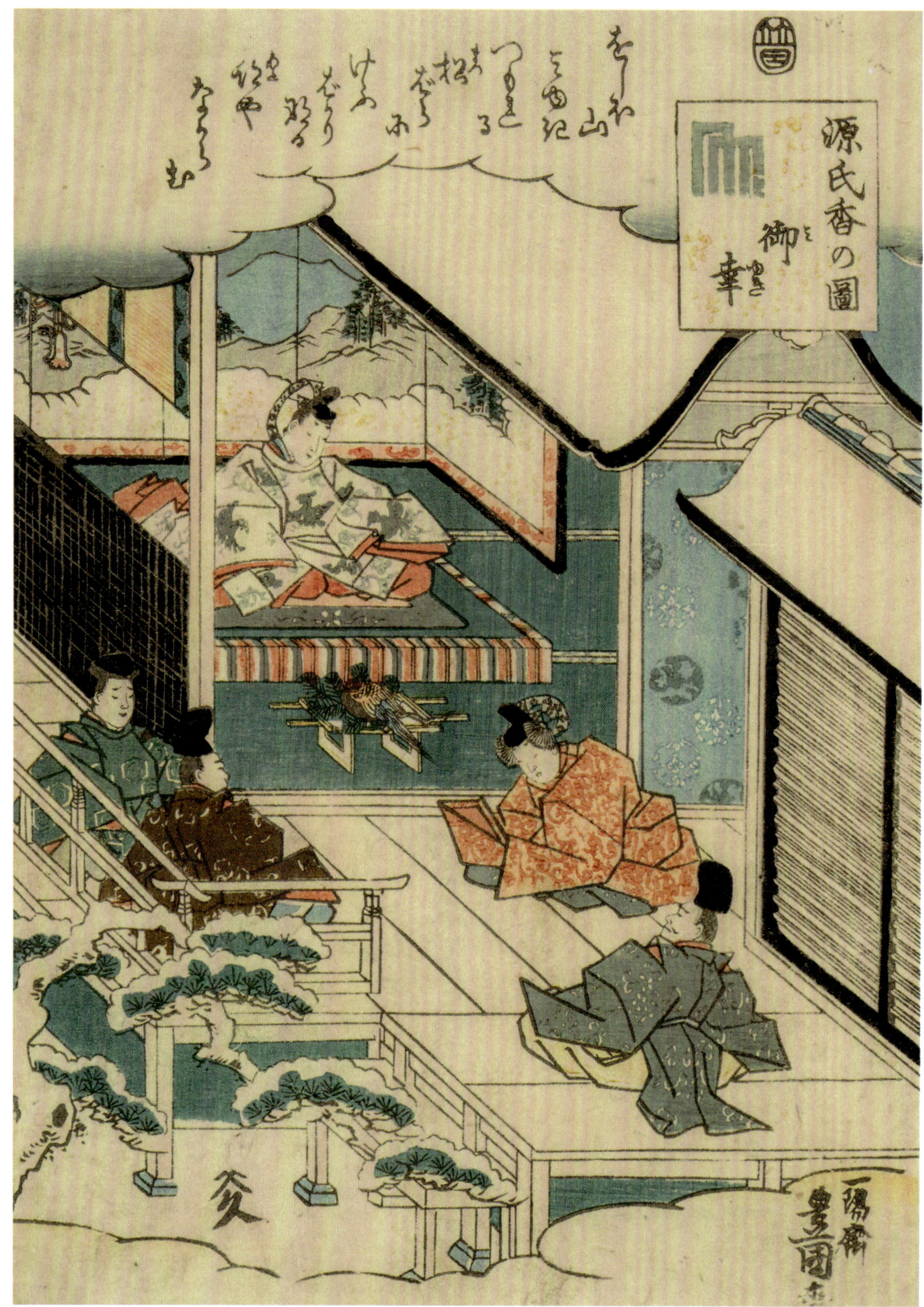

29A | Kunisada, *Genji Incense Pictures*, 1844–47

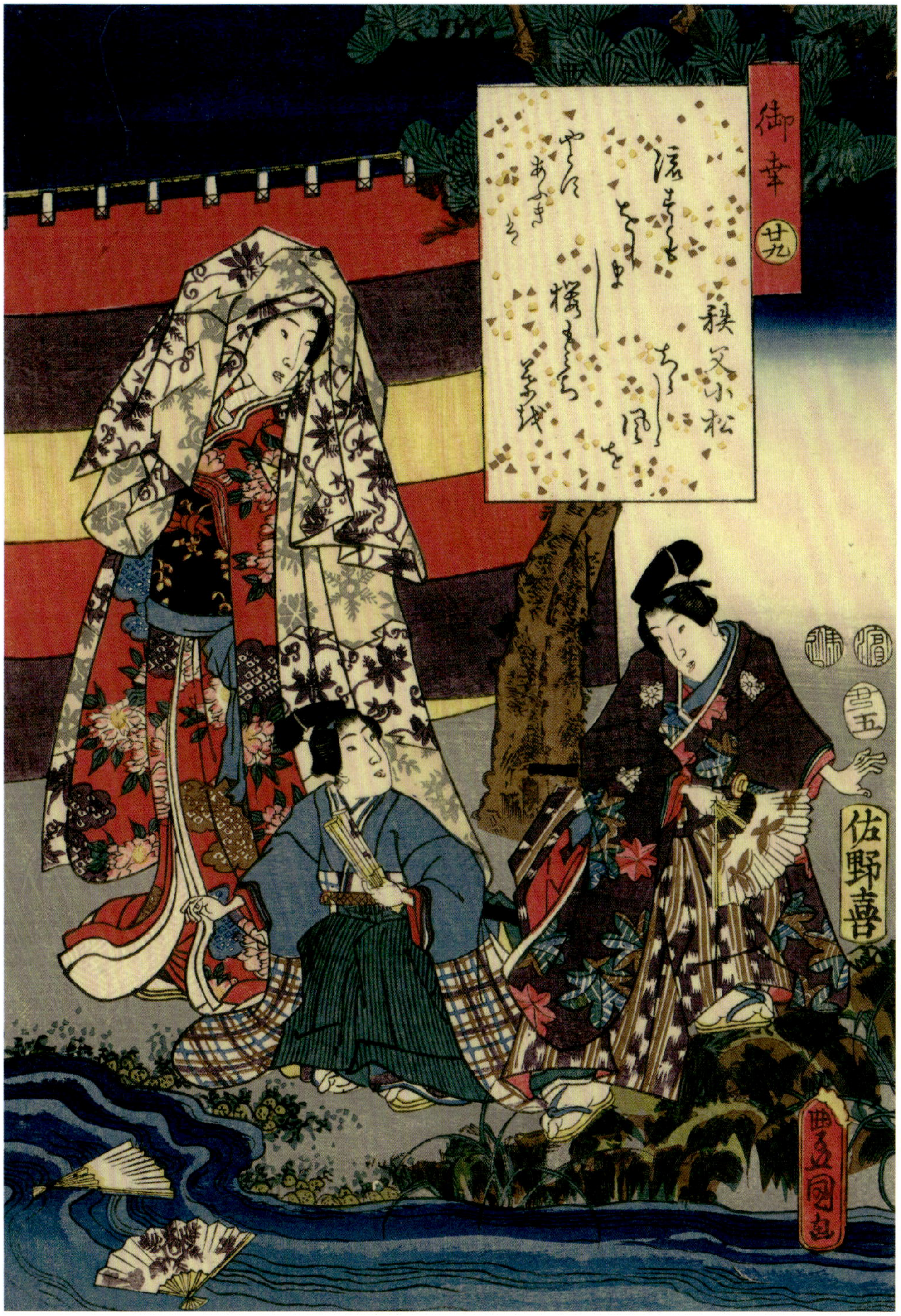

29B | Kunisada, *The Color Print Contest of a Modern Genji*, 1853

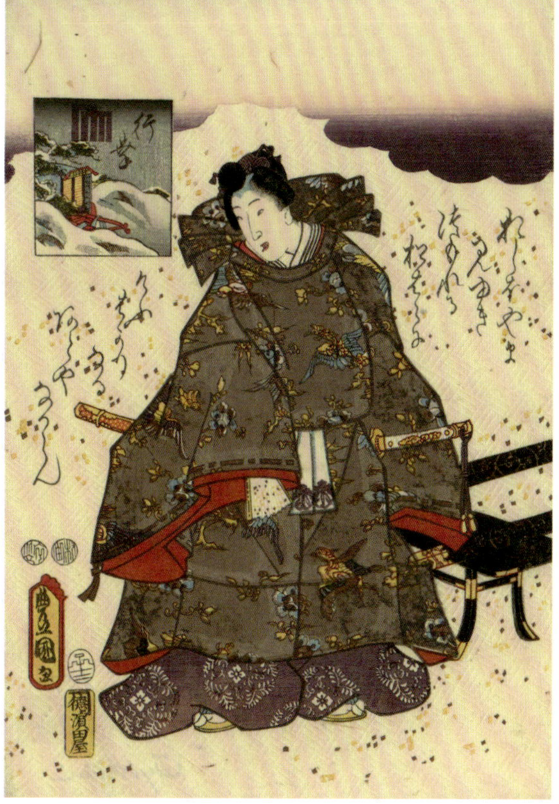

29C | Kunisada, untitled series of Genji pictures, 1852

procession go by. Later, after the procession reaches a picnic spot on the Ōi River, some of the young men amuse themselves by tossing fans into the water to see how they float, like little paper boats. For the image in the *Color Print Contest* series, Kunisada combined two illustrations in the book to show Tamakuzu, holding an extra robe over her head as an improvised veil, watching the fan-throwing game, although she was not actually present at that event (29B). The shogun himself is depicted in Kunisada's untitled series; an inset shows the imperial oxcart of the original *Tale of Genji* in a snowy landscape, but the vehicle parked behind Yoshitane is a large, elaborate palanquin (29C).

30

Purple Trousers (Fujibakama)

Now that the secret of Tamakazura's true parentage has come out, Yūgiri realizes that he is not in fact her brother and could legitimately court her. He brings her a bouquet of the autumn flowers known as fujibakama, literally "purple trousers," with the chapter title poem expressing his hopes (30A). However, long practice with Genji himself has made Tamakazura very skillful at eluding unwanted advances, and she declines Yūgiri's implied invitation.

Similarly, in chapter 38 of *Inaka Genji* — the last chapter to be published during the author's lifetime — Ujinaka presents a bouquet of purple irises to Tamakuzu, who politely rejects his offer; Kunisada's color print closely reproduces the book illustration (30B). The painted screen behind the two figures is a playful reminder of the layered chronologies of the Genji story. Folding screens made of paper on a wooden framework became common features of Japanese interiors in the fifteenth century, the time when *Inaka Genji* is set.

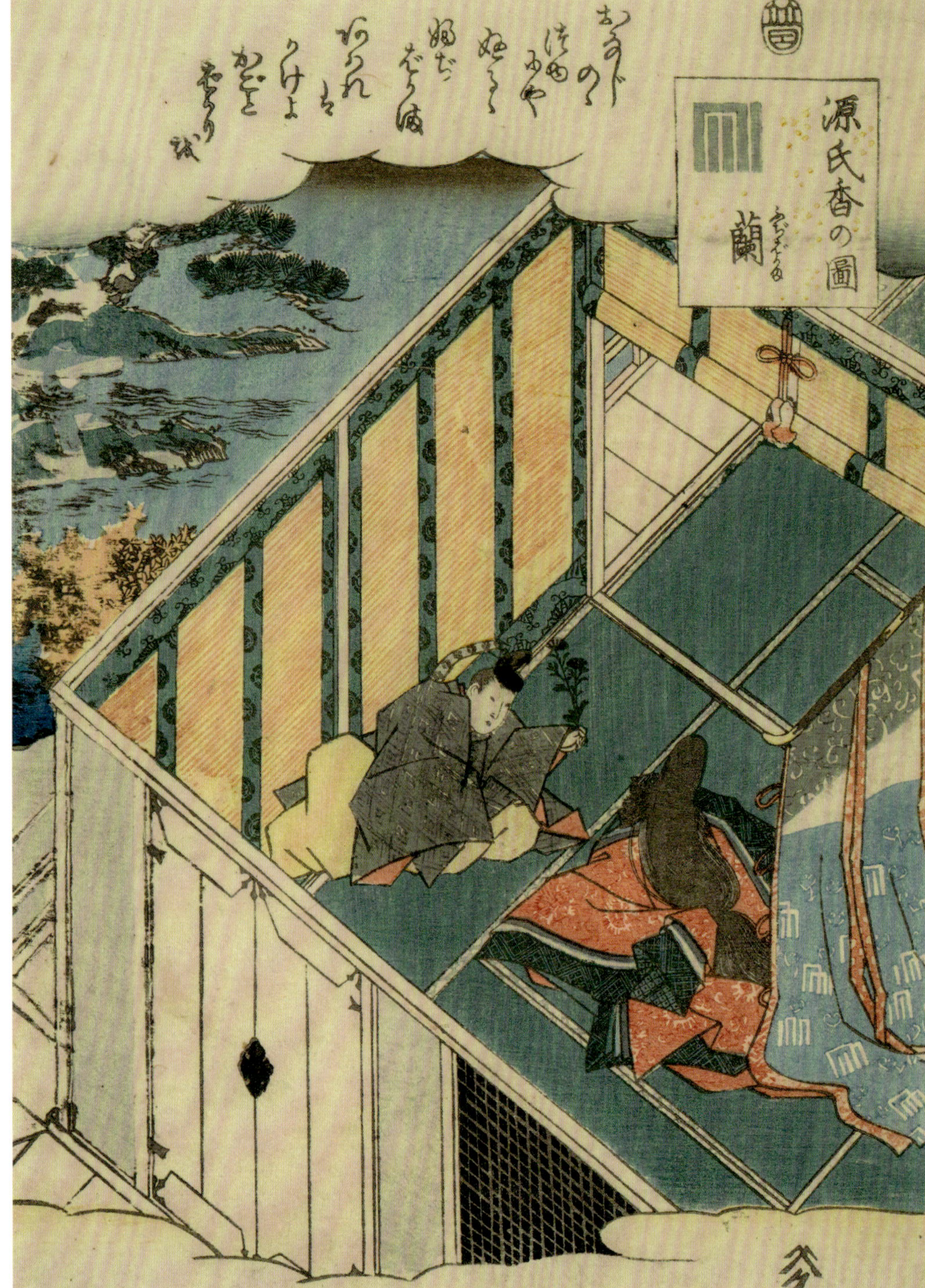

30A | Kunisada, *Genji Incense Pictures*, 1844–47

Ah, if, after all,
the dew you have brought me here
came from a far field,
then these flowers' light purple
might earn you kindness at least.

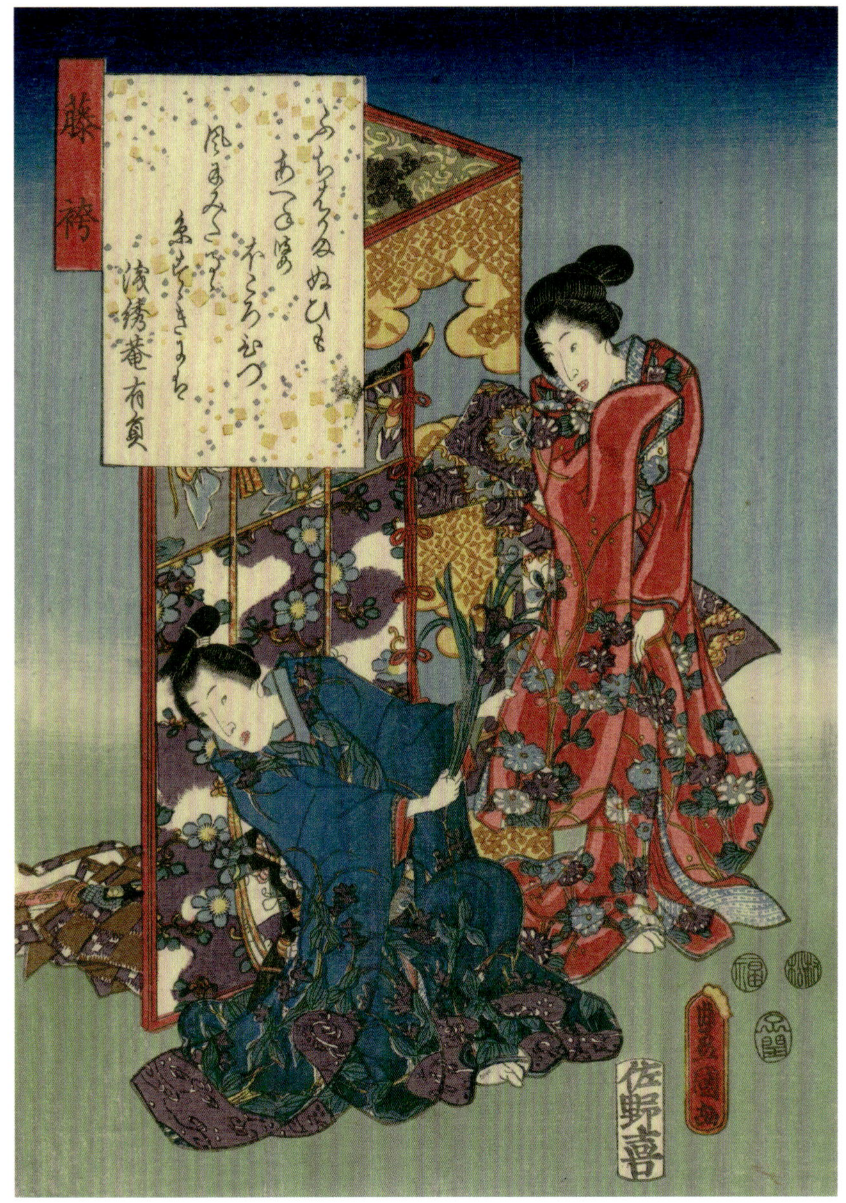

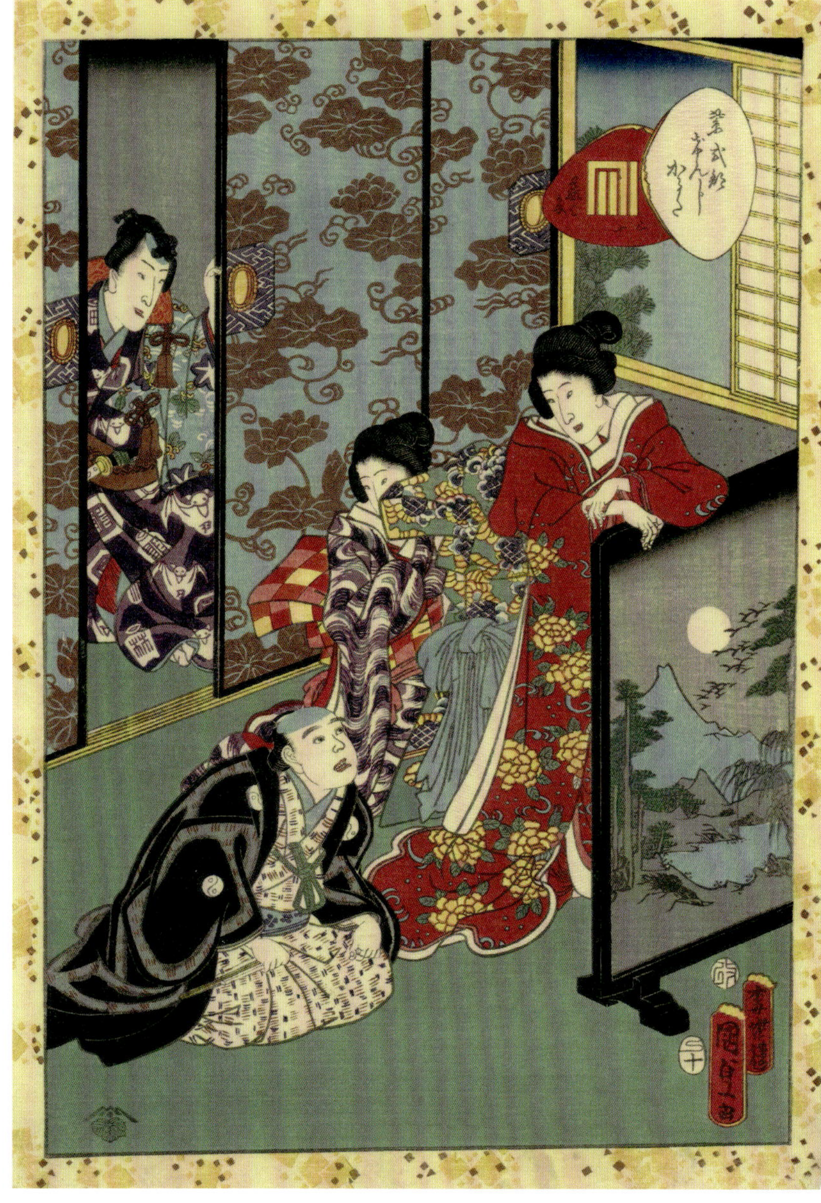

30B | Kunisada, *The Color Print Contest of a Modern Genji*, 1852

30C | Kunisada II, *Lady Murasaki's Genji Cards*, 1857

But the painting on this screen shows a Heian-period curtain stand, an earlier form of room divider that is often mentioned in *The Tale of Genji*.

Kunisada II illustrates a comic incident earlier in the chapter that is not derived from the original *Tale*. Gendayu, the obnoxious would-be suitor from Kyushu (see chapter 22), comes to Kyoto on business and arranges to meet with "Takanao's daughter" when she visits a temple. He is expecting Tamakuzu, but instead he gets Katata, the disappointing daughter from Ōmi Province (see chapter 26). In a scene based directly on the book illustration, he stares in dismay as she leans casually against a screen and chatters thoughtlessly (30C). According to the text, Mitsuuji was not involved in this scene at all; but the artist added his figure to the picture, peeking through a sliding door in the background.

31

The Cypress Pillar (Makibashira)

In the end Tamakazura surprises everyone by choosing General Higekuro (Black Beard) as her husband. Although of impeccable lineage and serious character, he is considered somewhat unattractive because of the heavy facial hair that is the reason for his nickname. He is also already married, albeit unhappily, to a half-sister of Murasaki. He would like to divorce her and has refrained so far only because of their three children. When his wife finds out about Tamakazura, she is so angry that she throws an incense burner full of hot ashes over him, and returns to her father's house, taking the children with her. Their twelve-year-old daughter, who loves her father and is afraid that she may never see him again, leaves behind the wistful chapter title poem, attached to a pillar of the house; she is nicknamed Makibashira (Cypress Pillar) because of this incident. Kunisada's print in the *Genji Incense* series shows the young girl pinning her poem to the pillar (31A).

Yoshiiku created a series of pictures pairing Genji motifs with other stories. In a scene from a bestselling fantasy novel, *The Crescent Moon Bow* (*Chinzetsu yumiharizuki*), the cypress pillar from Genji has morphed into the mast of a ship, to which the hero Tametomo clings desperately during a fierce storm at sea (31B).

I am leaving now
a home that has long been mine:
O handsome pillar,
you whom I have loved so well,
please do not forget me yet!

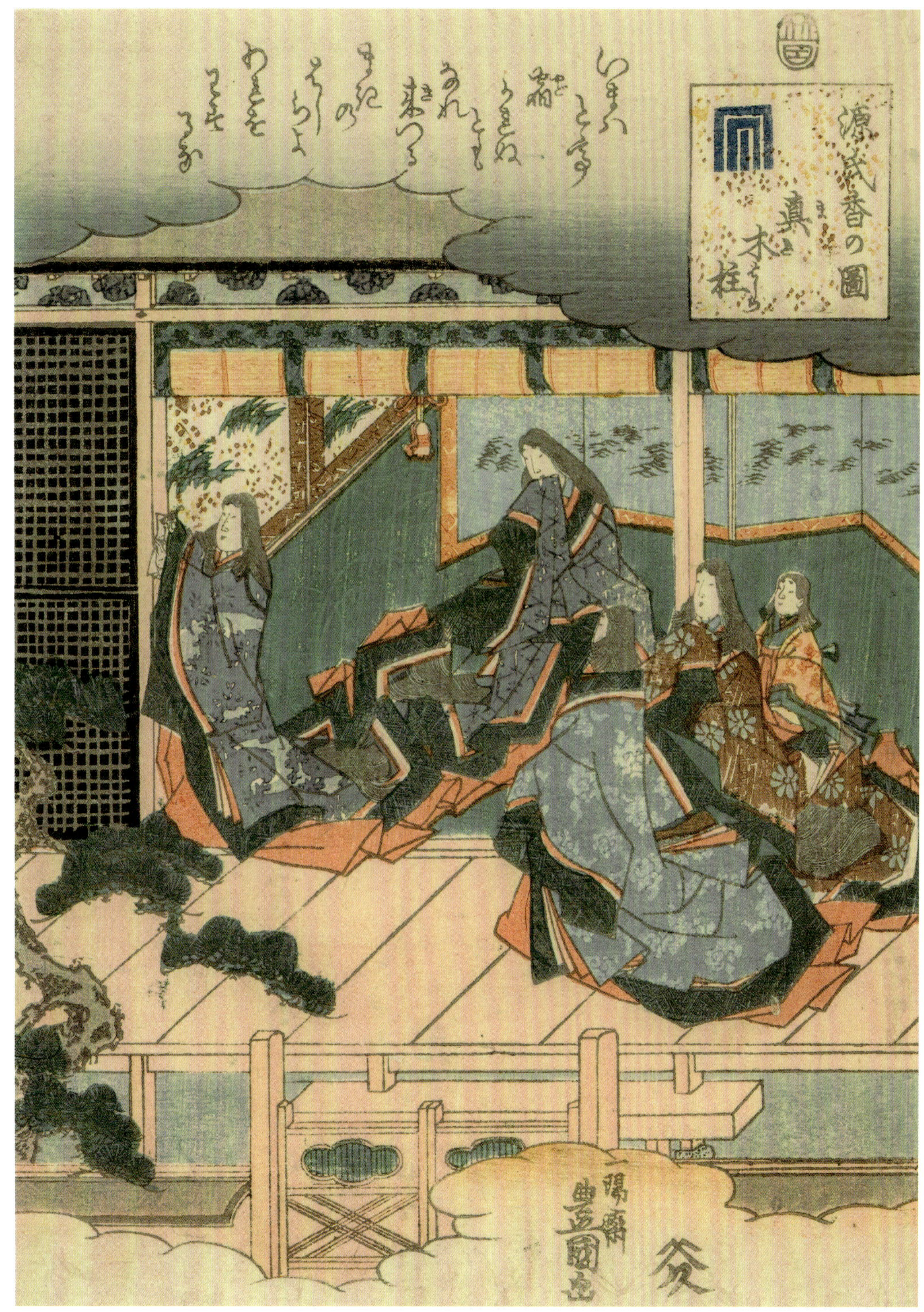

31A | Kunisada, *Genji Incense Pictures*, 1844–47

31B | Yoshiiku, *Modern Parodies of Genji*, 1864

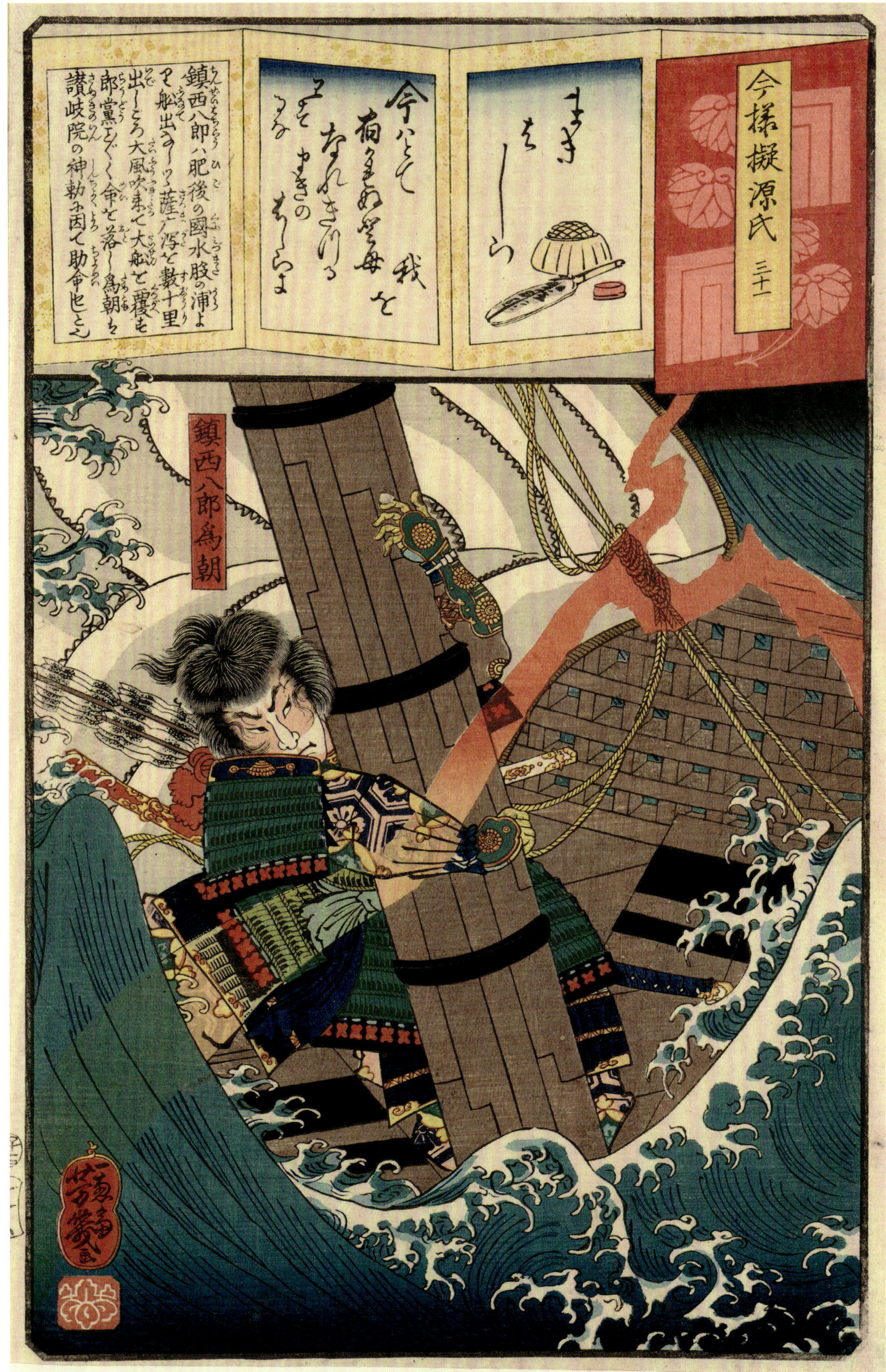

今様擬源氏 三十一
まきはしら
鎮西八郎ハ肥後の國水股の浦より船出して薩摩ノ浮を數十里出しところ大風吹来て大船を覆し郎黨ことごとく命を落し為朝も讃岐院の神勅に因て助命也とぞ
鎮西八郎為朝
一魁芳年画

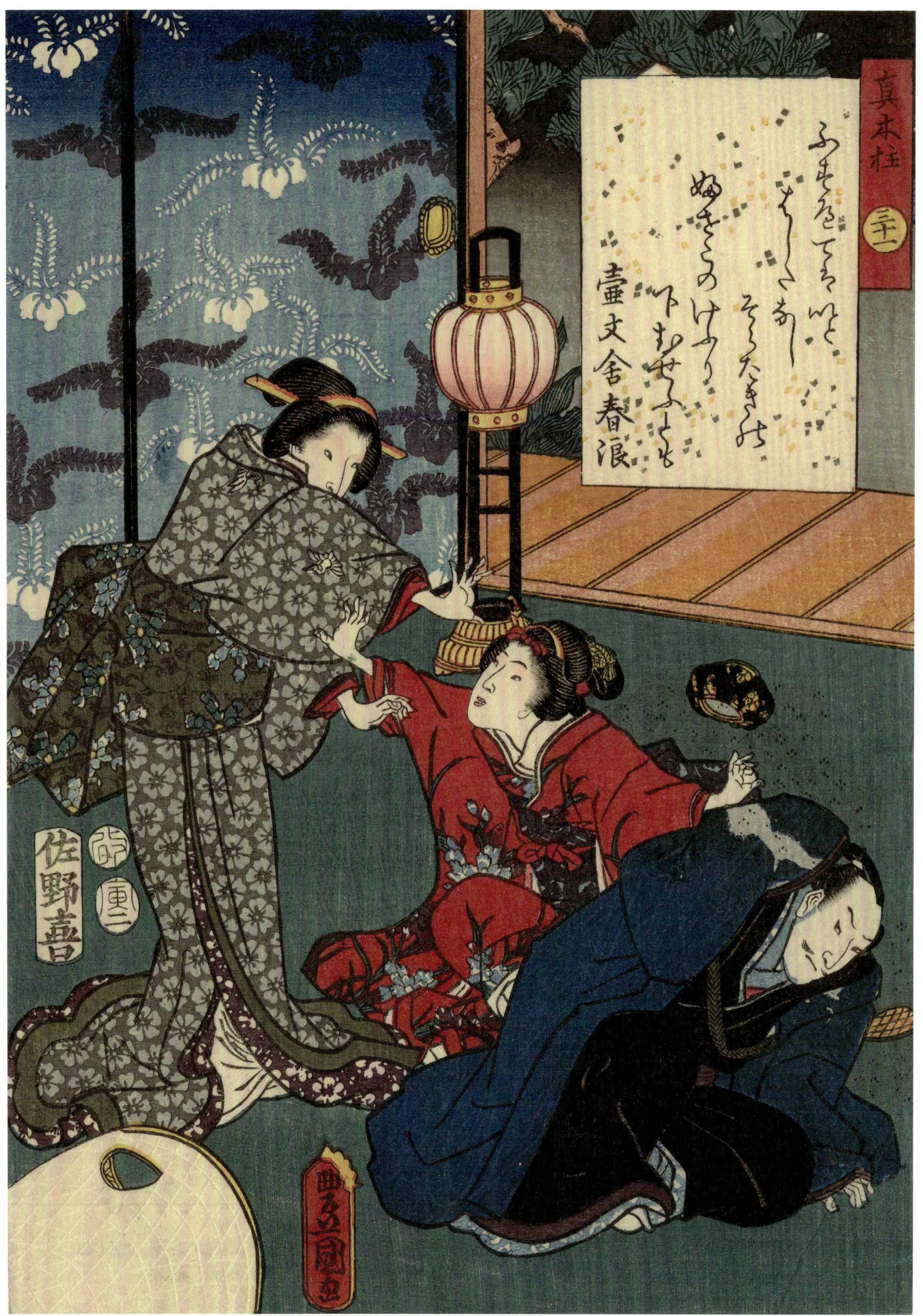

真木柱
三十一
壷文舎春浪
佐野喜
豊国画

Yoshiiku's series was no doubt inspired by the earlier series by his teacher Kuniyoshi (see chapter 24). Here, the upper part of each print in the series shows appropriate pages from an accordion-fold booklet containing the chapter title poems of *The Tale of Genji*, each with a small illustration; in Kuniyoshi's series, a handscroll of calligraphy and paintings functions in the same way.

The story corresponding to the Makibashira chapter is covered in chapters 39 and 40 of *Inaka Genji*, but those chapters were still in manuscript form in 1842, when Tanehiko died, and were not published until 1928. After the banning of *Inaka Genji* and the mysterious death of its author, there was a gap of five years — during which the *Genji Incense* series was published — before the ban on the book was tacitly rescinded and sequels by other authors began to appear. The first of these was *A Related Rustic Image* (*Sono yukari hina no omokage*), which began to appear in 1847 and, like the original *Inaka Genji*, was initially illustrated by Kunisada (though other artists took over later). The first five chapters continue the story begun by the late Tanehiko, although the names of some of the characters are now slightly changed; Mitsuuji, for example, becomes Terumoto.

The scene shown in the *Color Print Contest* series comes directly from chapter 1 of *A Related Rustic Image* and shows the scene in which the wife of Hirokado (= Higekuro) throws the incense burner at him, while their daughter Makiginu (= Makibashira) tries to intervene (31C). Kunisada II, in his *Genji Cards* series, shows Hirokado gazing fondly at two of his children: Makiginu, who is shown winding decorative cord on reels, and the older son with his sword at his side (31D).

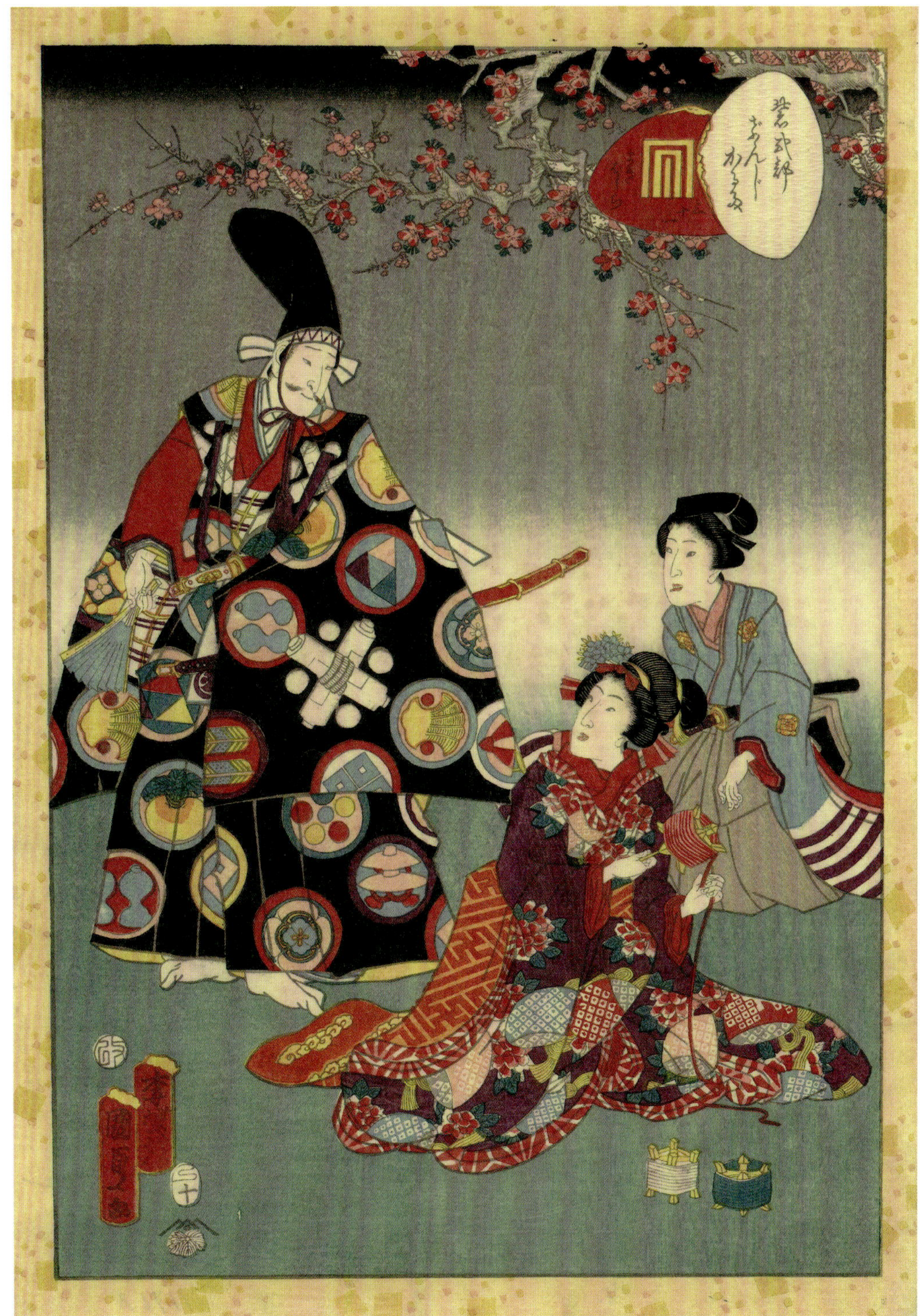

31D | Kunisada II, *Lady Murasaki's Genji Cards*, 1857

31C | Kunisada, *The Color Print Contest of a Modern Genji*, 1854

32

A Branch of Plum (Umegae)

This short chapter deals with the celebrations arranged by Genji when his daughter by the Akashi lady comes of age and takes her place at the imperial court, where she is expected to become the consort of the young Crown Prince. Genji's various ladies contribute special, rare fragrances for an incense competition (a parallel to the picture contest in chapter 17). His cousin Asagao sends a messenger with incense containers attached to a flowering plum branch, accompanied by the poem that represents the chapter. Later, at the drinking party that follows the incense competition, Genji and others join in singing an old saibara folk song, "A Branch of Plum"; this is the scene depicted by Kunisada in the *Genji Incense* series (32A).

The artist Hiroshige drew actual flowering plum branches for the Umegae chapter in a charming series that matches scenes of contemporary Edo to the Genji chapters. Published around the same time as the *Genji Incense* series, this series probably represents yet another attempt to play on public desire for the temporarily banned book *Inaka Genji*. Hiroshige shows a young woman sitting on a park bench in the famous plum garden at Kameido, which he depicted in many other prints as well (32B).

The scent of flowers
lingers not upon the bough
whence they have scattered,
but may this deeply perfume
the sleeves it will soon infuse.

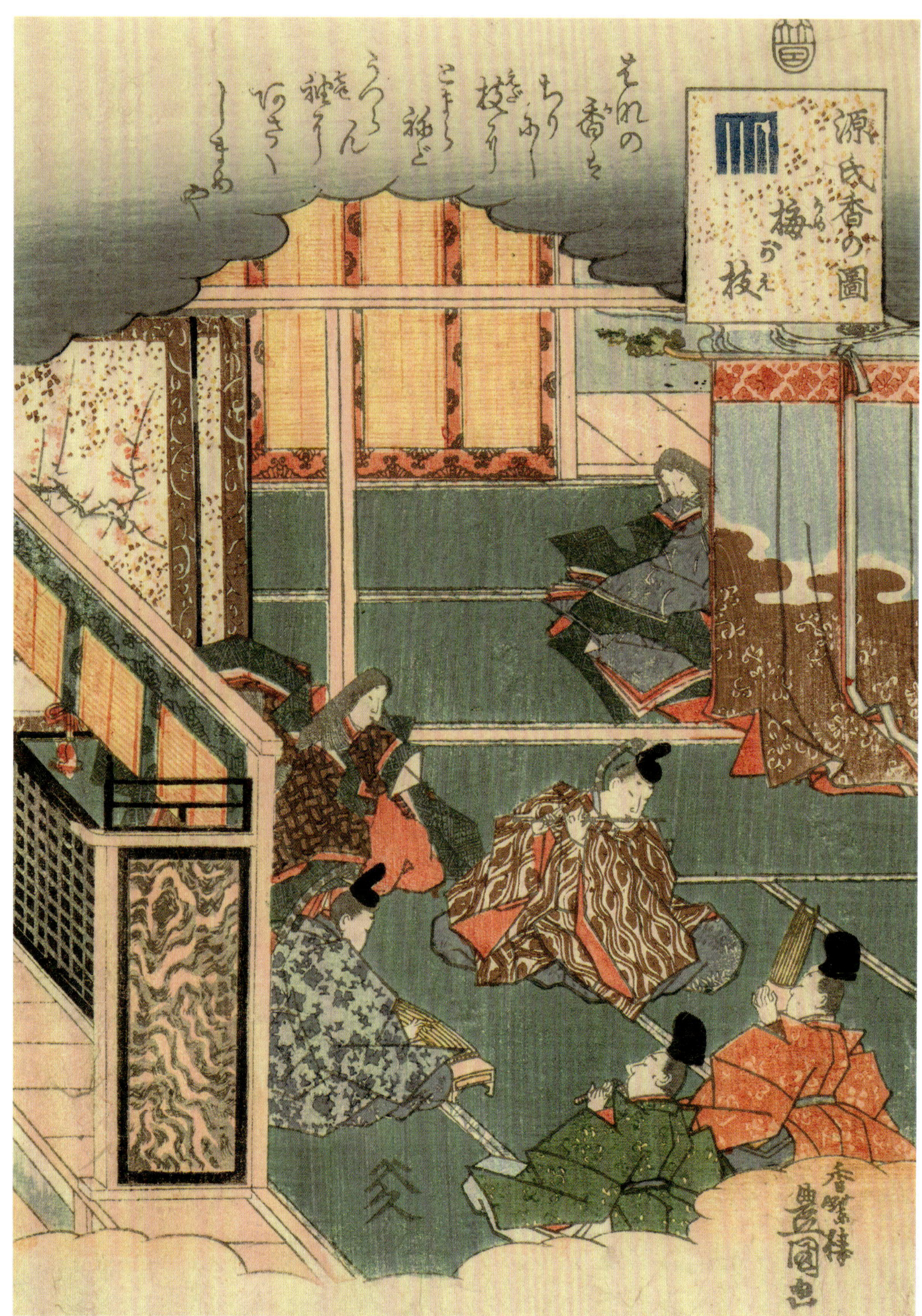

32A | Kunisada, *Genji Incense Pictures*, 1844–47

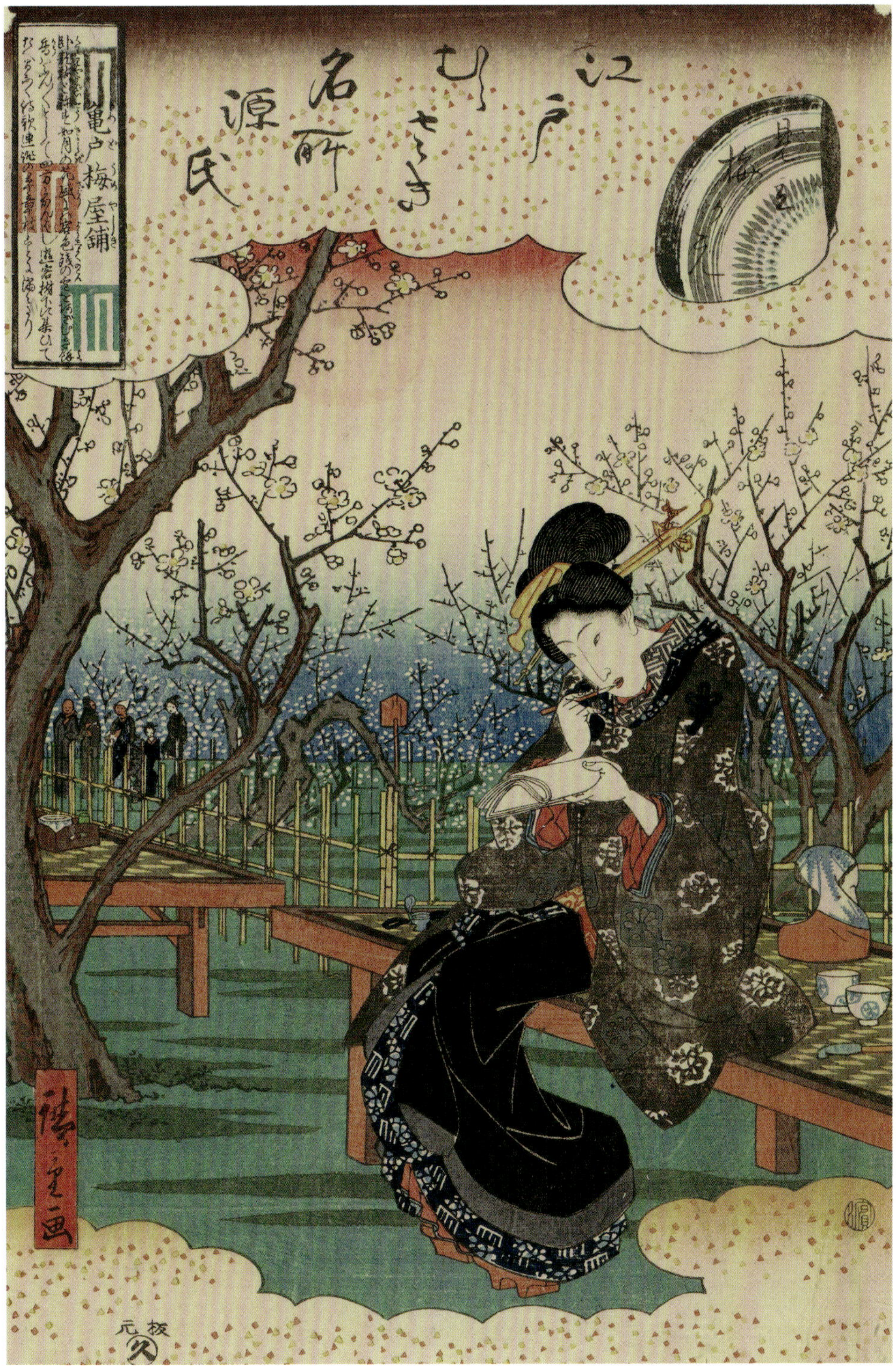

32B | Hiroshige, *Famous Places in Edo and Murasaki's Genji*, 1843–47

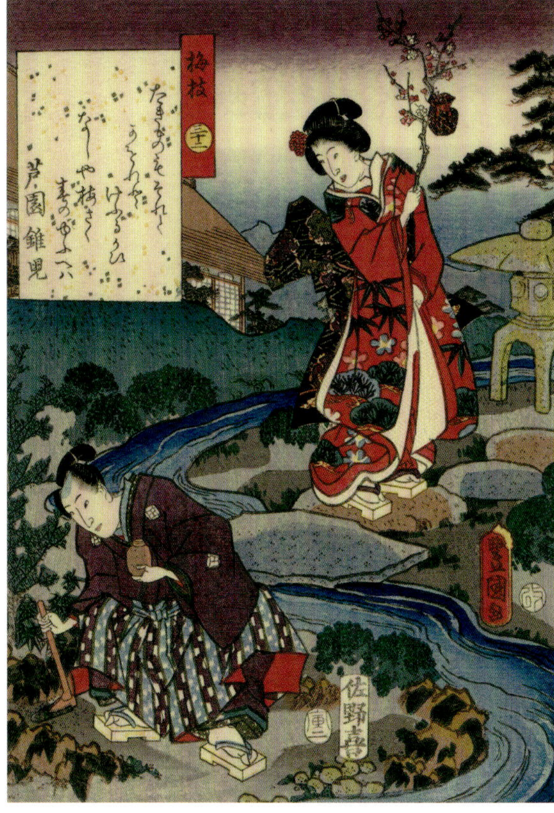

32C | Kunisada, *The Color Print Contest of a Modern Genji*, 1854

Chapter 3 of *A Related Rustic Image*, published in 1848, corresponds to the Umegae chapter and opens with Terumoto (= Genji, Mitsuuji) singing the folk song that gives that chapter its name. As in *Inaka Genji*, the sequels combine elements of action and intrigue with incidents that parody the original *Tale of Genji*. At the end of this chapter, Kashiwanosuke, the oldest son of Akamatsu Takanao (=Kashiwagi, the son of Tō no Chūjō), buries a jar of precious incense by the stream in the garden. Kunisada chose this scene to illustrate for the *Color Print Contest* series, but to tie it more closely to the chapter title, he added the figure of a lady holding the gift sent by Asagao with an incense jar attached to a plum branch (32C).

33

New Wisteria Leaves (Fuji no uraba)

The focus of this chapter is the happy conclusion of the long-delayed romance between Genji's son Yūgiri and Tō no Chūjō's daughter Kumoinokari. Tō no Chūjō relents at last and invites Yūgiri to join him and his sons for a party celebrating the wisteria blossoms at their home, with the unspoken implication that Yūgiri will be welcome to spend the night with Kumoinokari afterward. Unlike the other poems that are the source of chapter titles, this one was not written by the author in the persona of one of her characters, nor even quoted in full in the text; a tipsy Tō no Chūjō merely alludes to a famous old poem to imply that he will entrust his daughter to Yūgiri.

However, the scene shown in the *Genji Incense* series, with a man writing at a table while surrounded by women, one of whom prepares ink for him, does not correspond to the wisteria party or indeed to anything else in this chapter (33A). The closest match seems to be a scene near the beginning of the next chapter, showing the retired Suzaku emperor with his ladies shortly before he takes the tonsure. Three later prints in the *Genji Incense* series, representing chapters 35, 42, and 46, also show scenes from the wrong chapters, so this may be another such mistake on Kunisada's part.

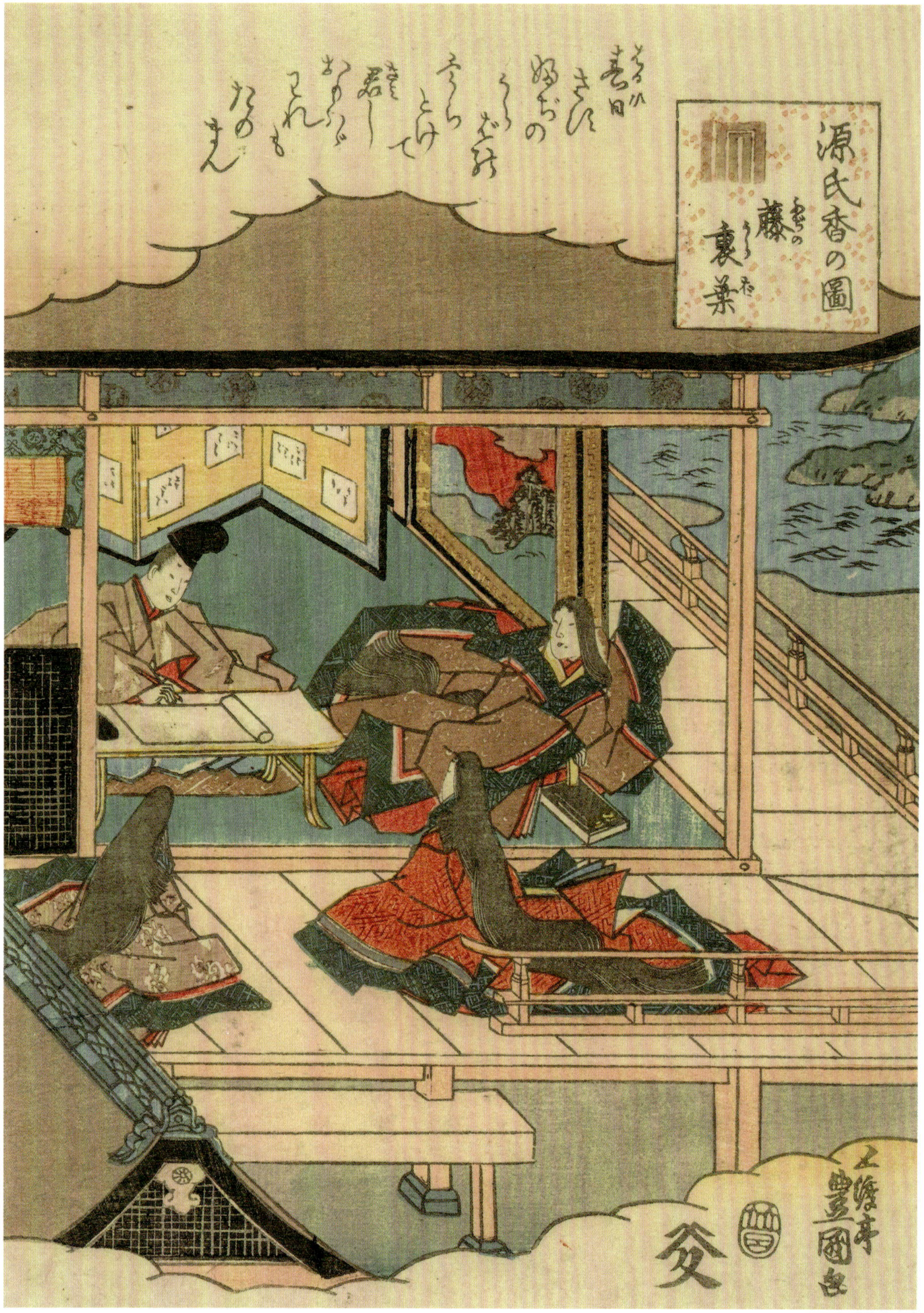

33A | Kunisada, *Genji Incense Pictures*, 1844–47

Illumined by the springtime sun,
the new wisteria leaves yield, and
if you love me, I will trust in you.

33B | (detail)

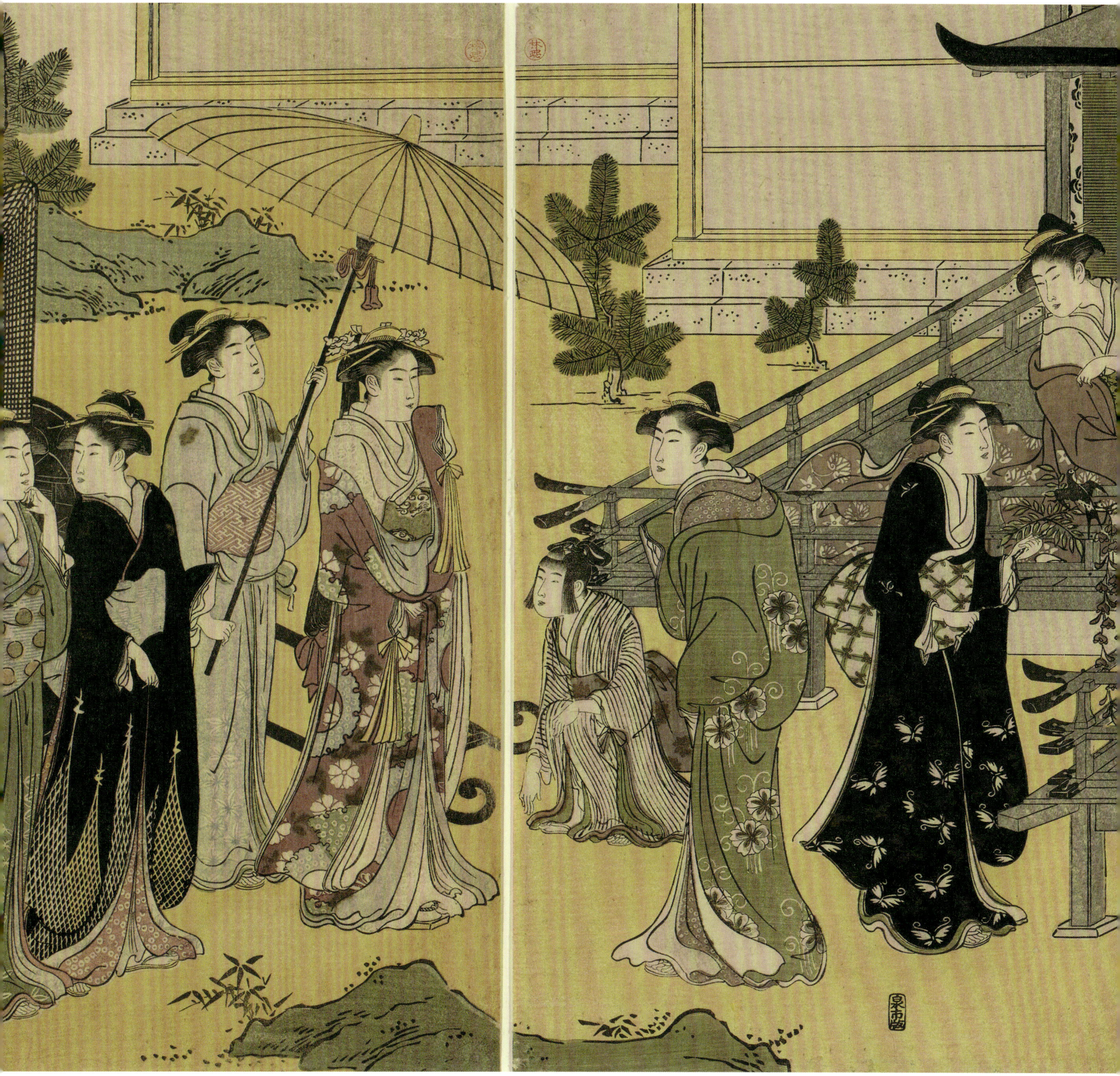

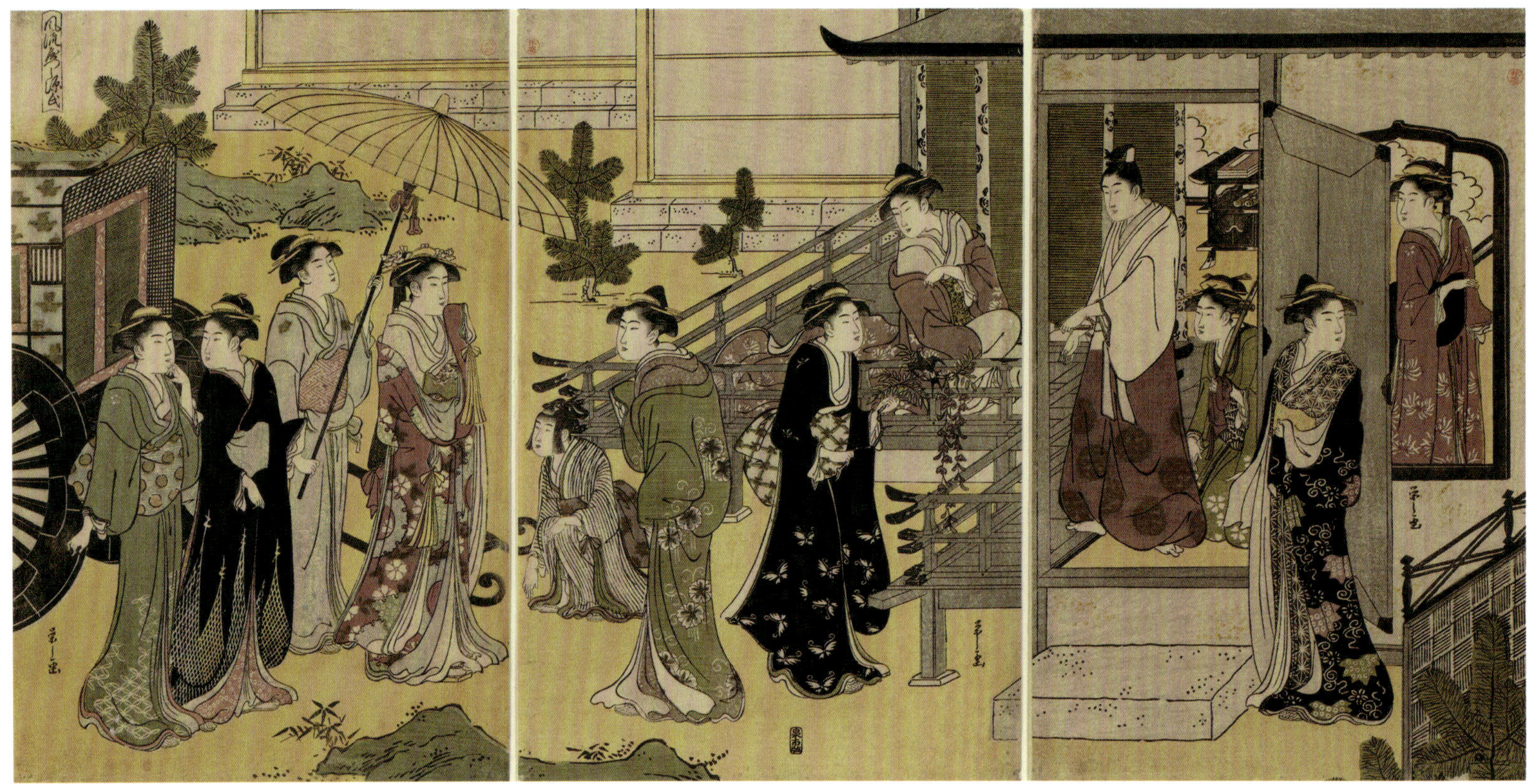

33B | Chōbunsai Eishi, *Genji in Fashionable Modern Guise*, about 1791–94

In Eishi's triptych, the wisteria branch offered to the young man identifies the scene as the long-awaited union of Yūgiri and Kumoinokari, even though we see the man at home on the right and the young woman arriving by carriage at left, in a reversal of roles from the original story (33B). Here, the benigirai (literally "red hating") color scheme lives up to its name, since the brightest color in the composition is purple, appropriate to the wisteria theme.

The marriage of Kumoinojō Ujinaka (= Yūgiri) and Karigane (= Kumoinokari) occurs in chapter 4 of *A Related Rustic Image*, at the Akamatsu mansion with its many pavilions and walkways over garden ponds (see chapter 21). In the book, the scene unfolds over four continuous pages. Under the wisteria blossoms, the Akamatsu brothers lead their friend — soon to be their brother-in-law — toward their sister's quarters. Surrounded by her attendants, Karigane awaits his arrival. For the color print, however, Kunisada condensed the longer scene from the book by removing all the other figures and showing only the two lovers gazing at each other across the garden (33C).

33C | Kunisada, *The Color Print Contest of a Modern Genji*, 1853

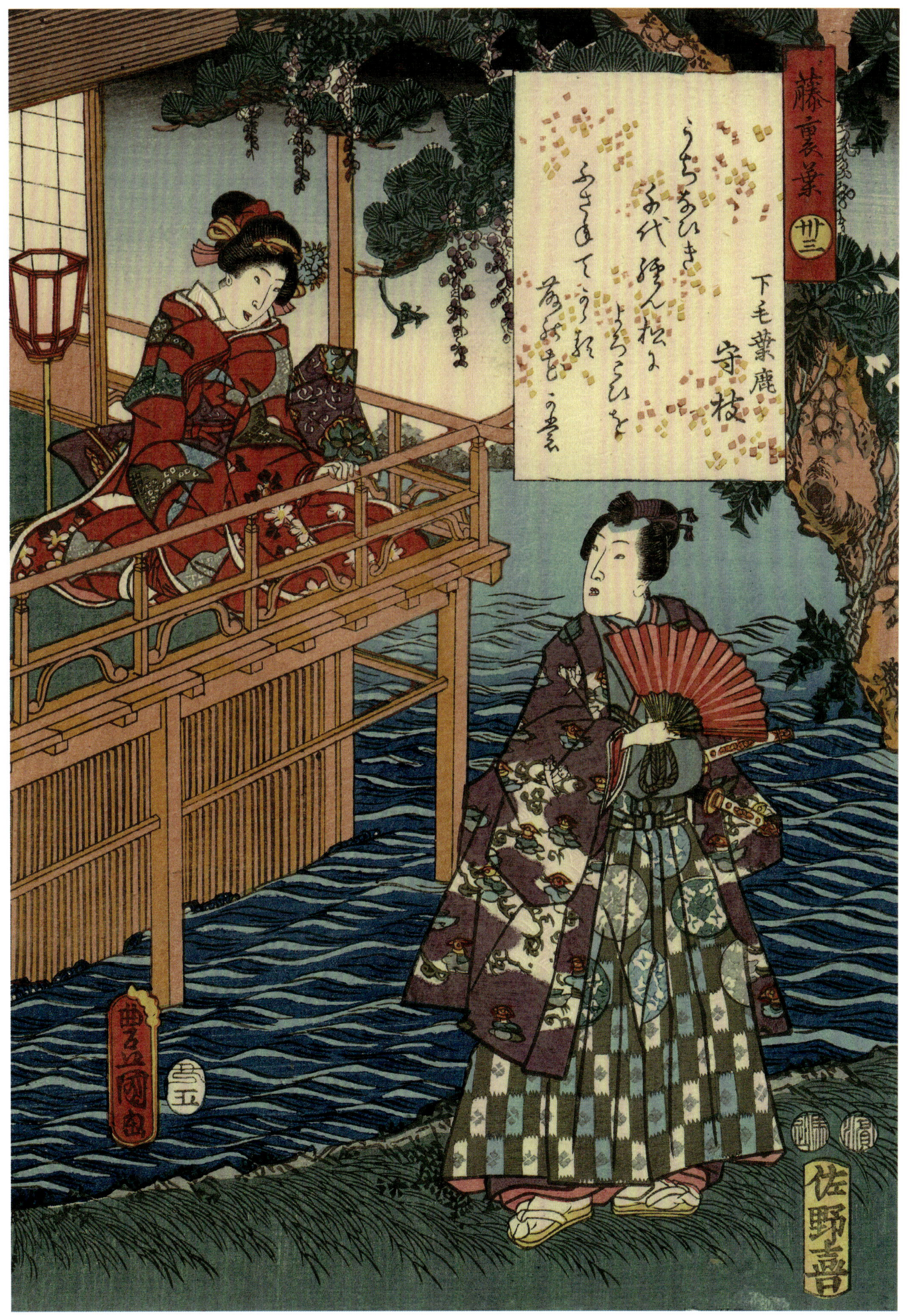
藤裏葉
廿三
下毛葉鹿
守枝
佐野喜

34

Young Shoots, Part 1 (Wakana I)

Near the beginning of this lengthy chapter, Genji makes a bad mistake that will damage his relationship with Murasaki and cast a shadow over the remainder of his life. He reluctantly accedes to the wishes of his older half-brother, now the retired Suzaku emperor, who is planning to take vows as a Buddhist monk but wants to provide for his favorite daughter, the young Third Princess, by marrying her to Genji. She is around fourteen; her half-uncle Genji is forty. After the marriage, Genji carries out his duties as the Princess's husband but finds her childish and boring; he continues to spend most of his time with Murasaki, who, although she maintains perfect courtesy, is very unhappy about the situation.

A pleasant interlude occurs at New Year, when Tamakazura comes to visit, bringing her two young sons by Higekuro. She and Genji exchange poems comparing the little boys to the fresh spring herbs (wakana) traditionally gathered and eaten at New Year. This frequently illustrated event is the source of the chapter title poem, although it is not the scene chosen for the *Genji Incense* series. Instead, Kunisada shows the visit of Genji's very pregnant Akashi daughter, now the Crown Princess, who has come home to

---

Those seedlings may yet,
plucked from such happy meadows,
draw a new shoot up
toward a still-longer span
of endlessly happy years.

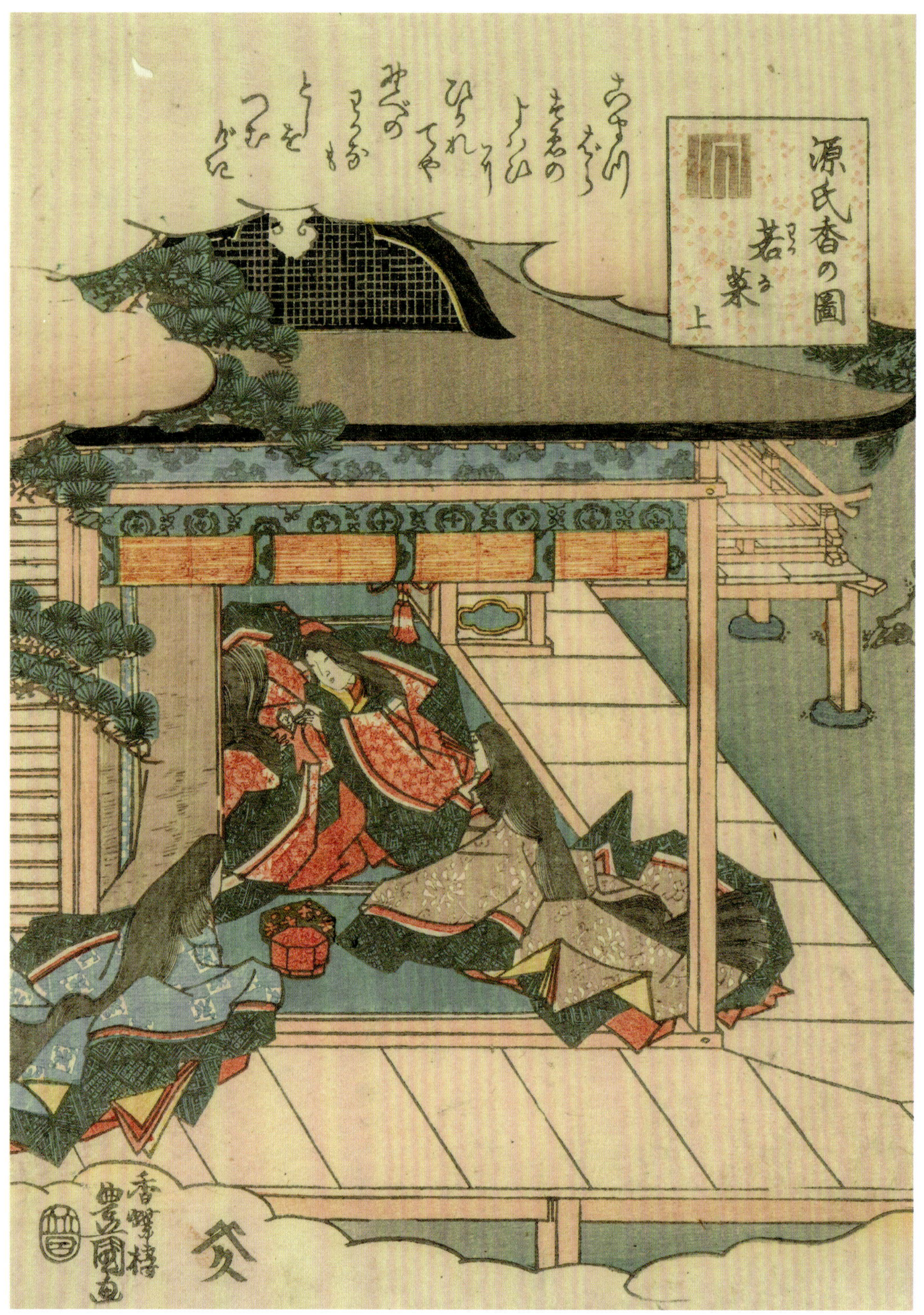

34A | Kunisada, *Genji Incense Pictures*, 1844–47

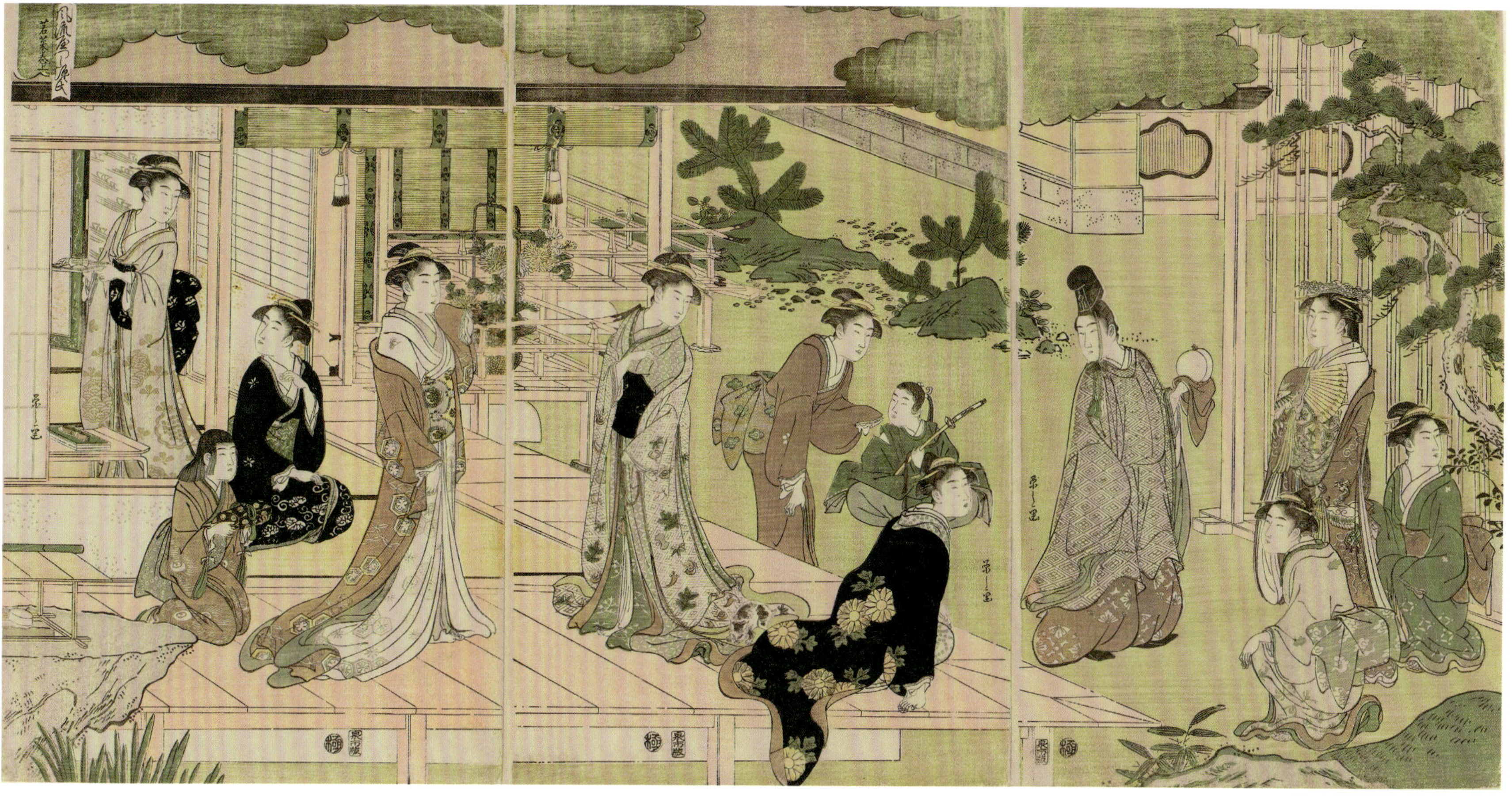

34B | Chōbunsai Eishi, *Genji in Fashionable Modern Guise*, about 1790–91

deliver her first child (34A). Still almost a child herself, she holds a doll that suggests the baby she will soon have. The poem predicting a bright future for Tamakazura's little boys applies even more strongly to the Princess's son.

The most famous event in the chapter, the notorious cat incident, occurs at the very end and has no poem associated with it. Yūgiri and his friends, the sons of Tō no Chūjō, are playing kickball in the garden while the ladies watch, concealed by their bamboo blinds as proper decorum requires. Suddenly, the Third Princess's pet cat runs out onto the veranda, pursued by a larger cat. Its leash tangles in the blinds and pulls them aside for a moment. From the garden, Kashiwagi catches a brief glimpse of the Third Princess herself and falls hopelessly in love, with disastrous consequences that will be related in the following chapters.

Perhaps because of the popularity of cats as pets, the motif of the Third Princess and her cat appears frequently in ukiyo-e paintings and prints. Often the Edo-period versions of the scene reflect confusion over the now-obsolete Heian custom of keeping women of high rank hidden away; for example, in Eishi's updated parody triptych, women stand on the veranda openly watching the young men preparing to play their kickball game (34B). The single male figure visible, representing Kashiwagi, holds a ball and stands beside a cage-like structure sometimes used for kickball games in order to avoid damage from flying balls. He and the princess gaze directly at each other with no concealment at all; the kitten on its leash is barely visible, nestled into the hem of the princess's trailing robe.

For the *Color Print Contest* series, however, Kunisada ignored cats and ballgames and turned to the basic meaning of the chapter title, the fresh young shoots that were gathered as a delicacy at New Year. Two beautifully dressed women brave the New Year snow to gather the delicate vegetables for holiday cuisine (34C).

At this point in the parody story, the posthumous continuation of Tanehiko's *Inaka Genji* forks into two different plot lines. Beginning in 1850, a second sequel began to appear, also illustrated by Kunisada. While *Rustic Image*, the first of the sequels, continued on through chapter 23, the new book, *Ashikaga Robes Hand-dyed in Purple* (*Ashikaga-ginu tezome no*

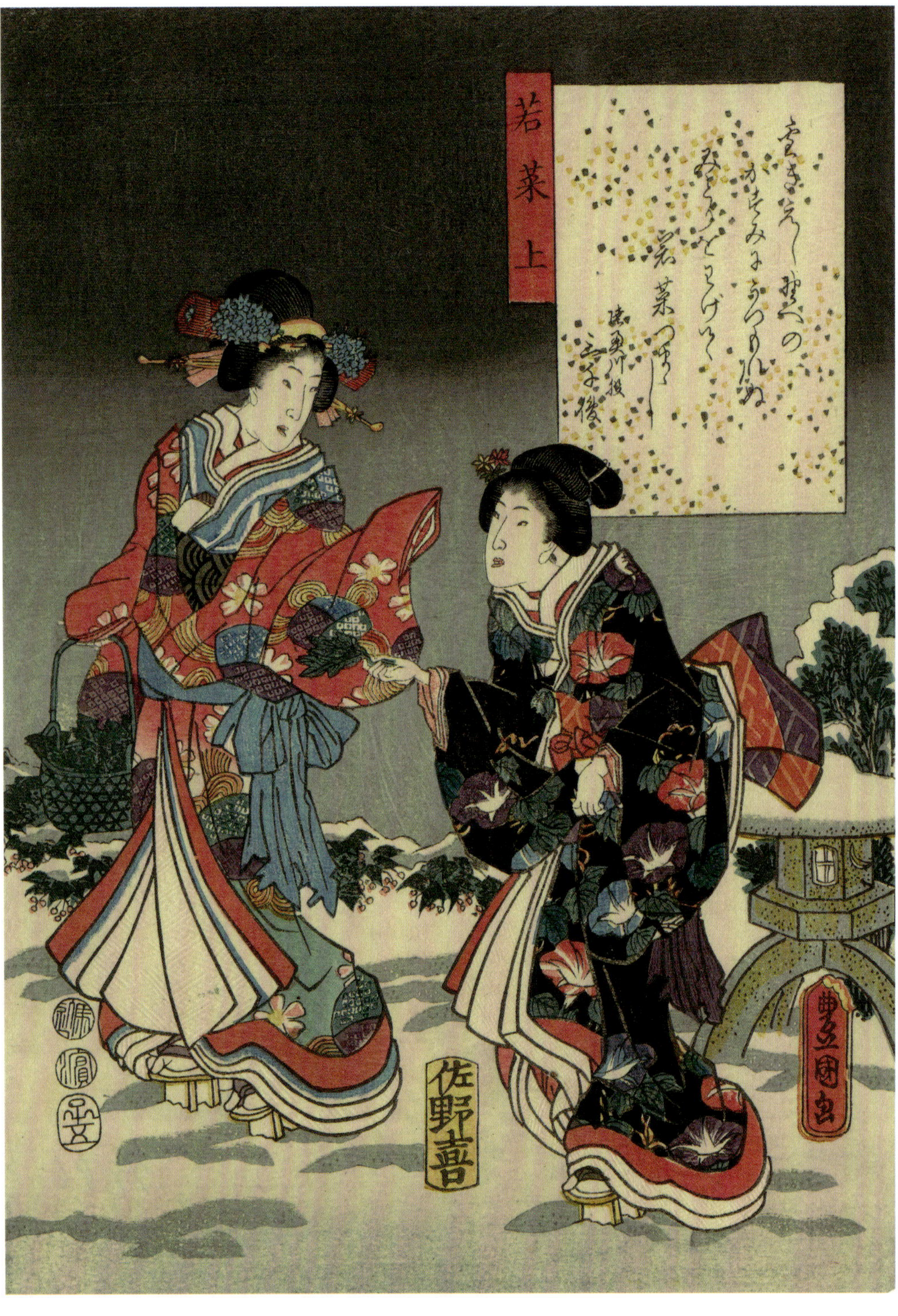

34C | Kunisada, *The Color Print Contest of a Modern Genji*, 1852

Murasaki) started the numbering of its chapters at chapter 6 — following on from the first five chapters of *Rustic Image* — and continued through chapter 21, for a total of 16 chapters.

The cat incident is illustrated in each of these books, but with different twists; and each version became the subject of a triptych by Kunisada. In the triptych based on chapter 12 of *Ashikaga Robes*, published in the fall of 1854, the kickball game is transformed into a children's handball game under the cherry blossoms, while the cat's leash pulls up the blind as in the original story (34D). Another triptych published at the end of 1854 with the assistance of Kuniteru II, *Cherry Blossoms at Genji's Rokujō Mansion*, shows the version that corresponds to chapter 12 of *Rustic Image* (34E). The ballplayers in the garden are young men, as in the original *Tale*, but the women and the cat watch openly from the balcony, with no need to pull up the blinds, just as in Eishi's earlier parody triptych. This triptych was published one month before the chapter's release, meaning Kunisada's color print could thus serve as advance publicity for the next volume of the serially published book, which was now being illustrated by his pupil Kunisada II.

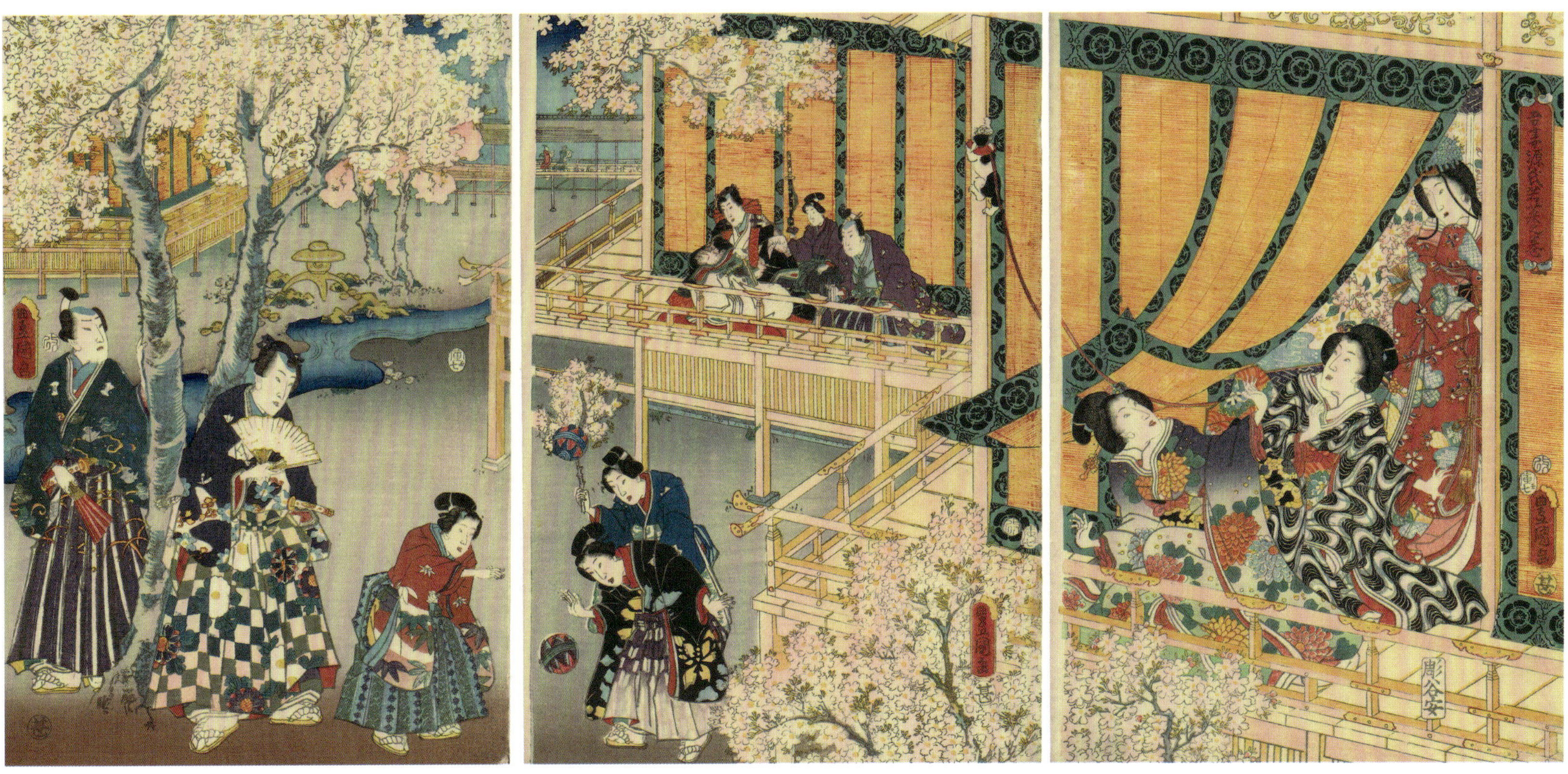

34D | Kunisada, *Eastern Genji*, 1854

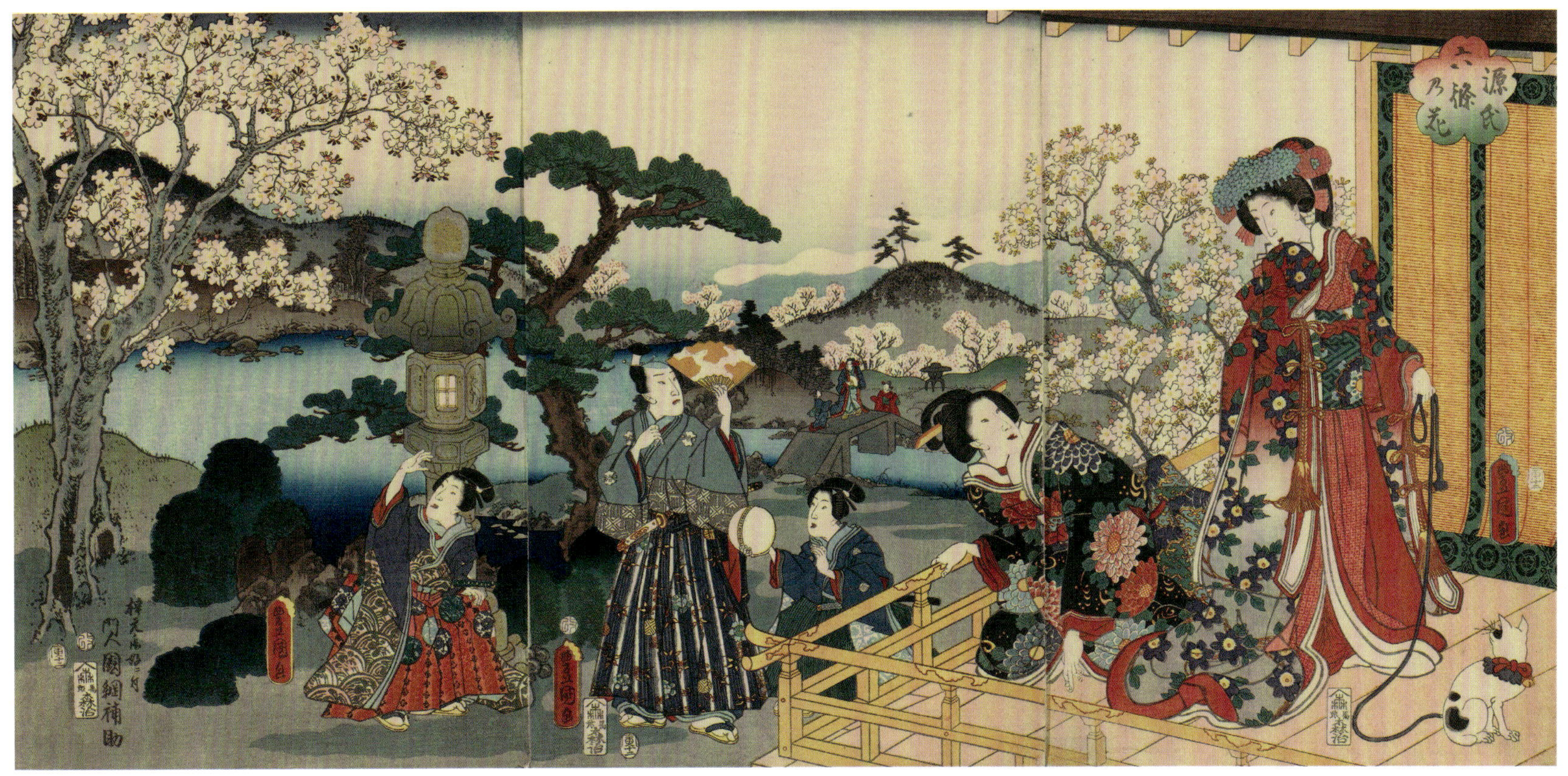

34E | Kunisada and Kuniteru II, *Cherry Blossoms at Genji's Rokujō Mansion*, 1854

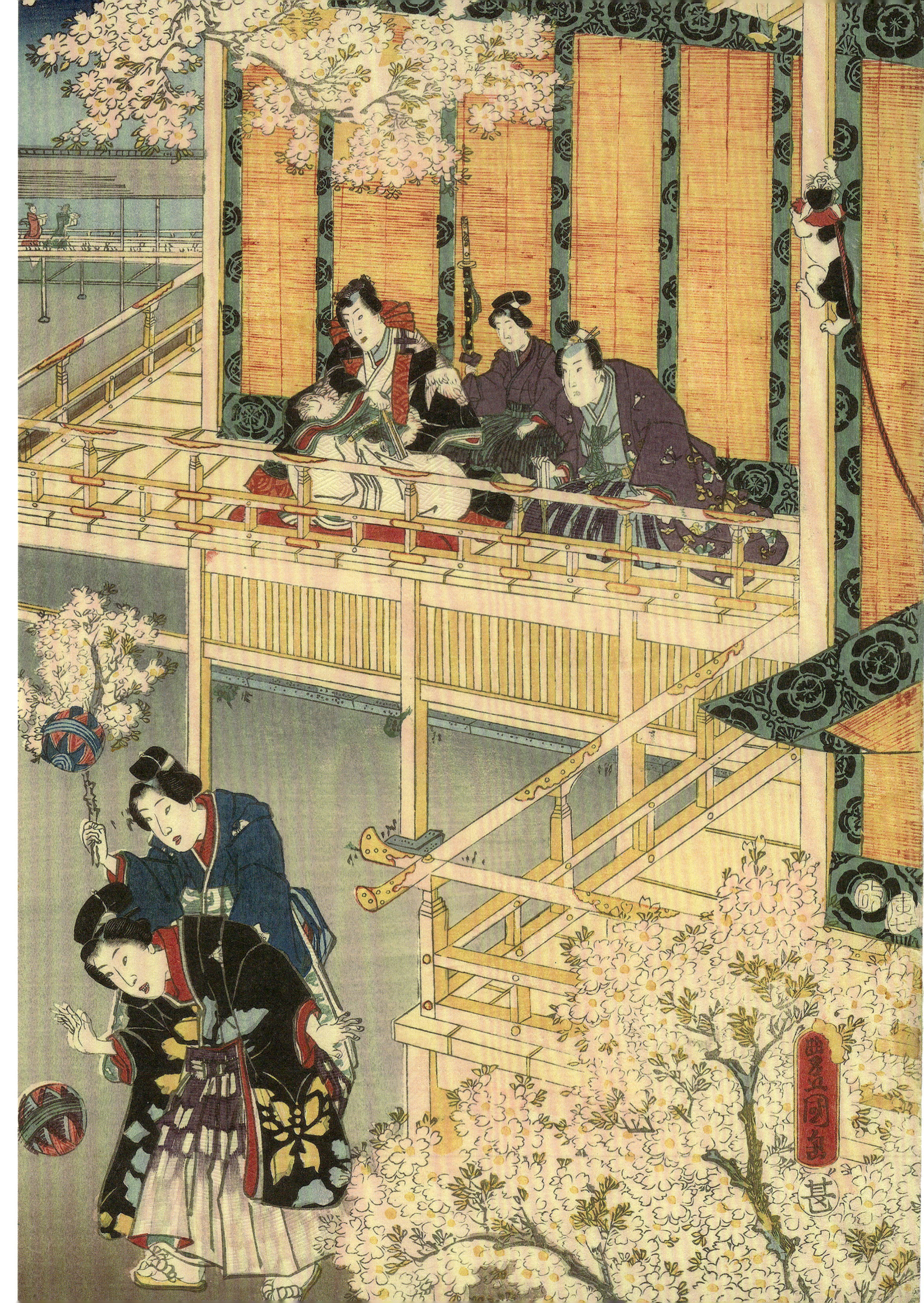
豊国画
甚

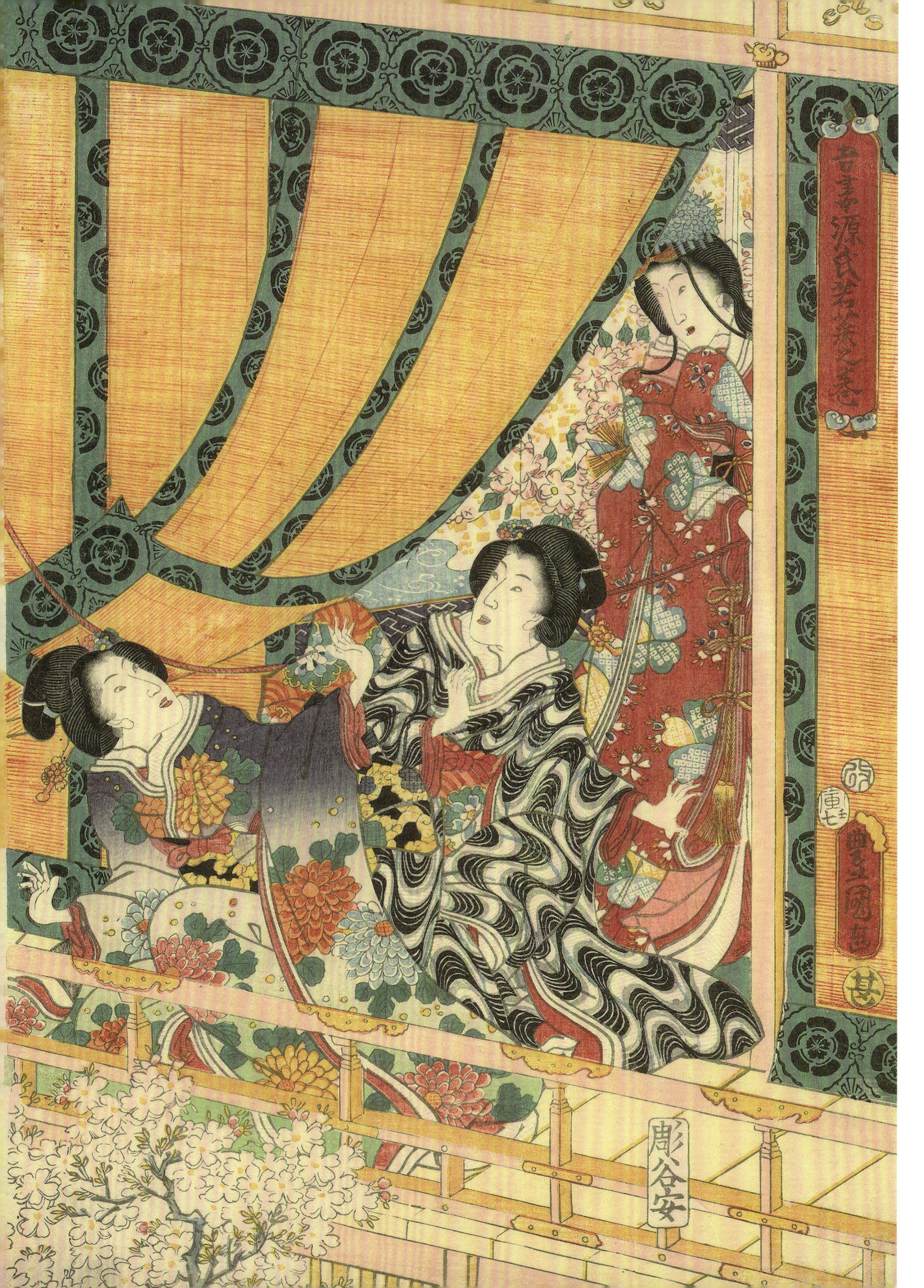

吾妻源氏若菜之巻
改
豊国画
甚
彫谷安

35

Young Shoots, Part 2 (Wakana II)

Because two chapters of the original *Tale of Genji* have the same name, artists of the Edo period sometimes seem to have confused the two. Thus Kunisada, in the *Genji Incense* series, illustrates the cat incident for the second Wakana chapter even though it actually occurred at the end of the first chapter (35A). A picture that more accurately represents this chapter was created by Kunisada's rival Kuniyoshi, famous for his own love of cats (35B). Although it allegedly illustrates a completely unrelated classical poem, the print shows a Heian nobleman holding a smug-looking cat while a servant prepares food for it. He may well represent the lovelorn Kashiwagi, who, although he has trouble gaining access to the Third Princess herself, manages to obtain her cat and enjoys cuddling it while thinking of her.

Several years go by, and Genji's Akashi daughter becomes empress, making Genji the most politically powerful man in the country. Kashiwagi marries another of Suzaku's daughters, the Second Princess, but still dreams of her sister, the cat's original owner. When Murasaki falls gravely ill, Genji spends most of his time with her and neglects the Third Princess even more than before. Kashiwagi at last finds an opportunity to spend the night with her, and she becomes pregnant as a result.

The path is shadowy
in the evening dusk:
await the moon, love, to go,
and I shall have you
that much longer!

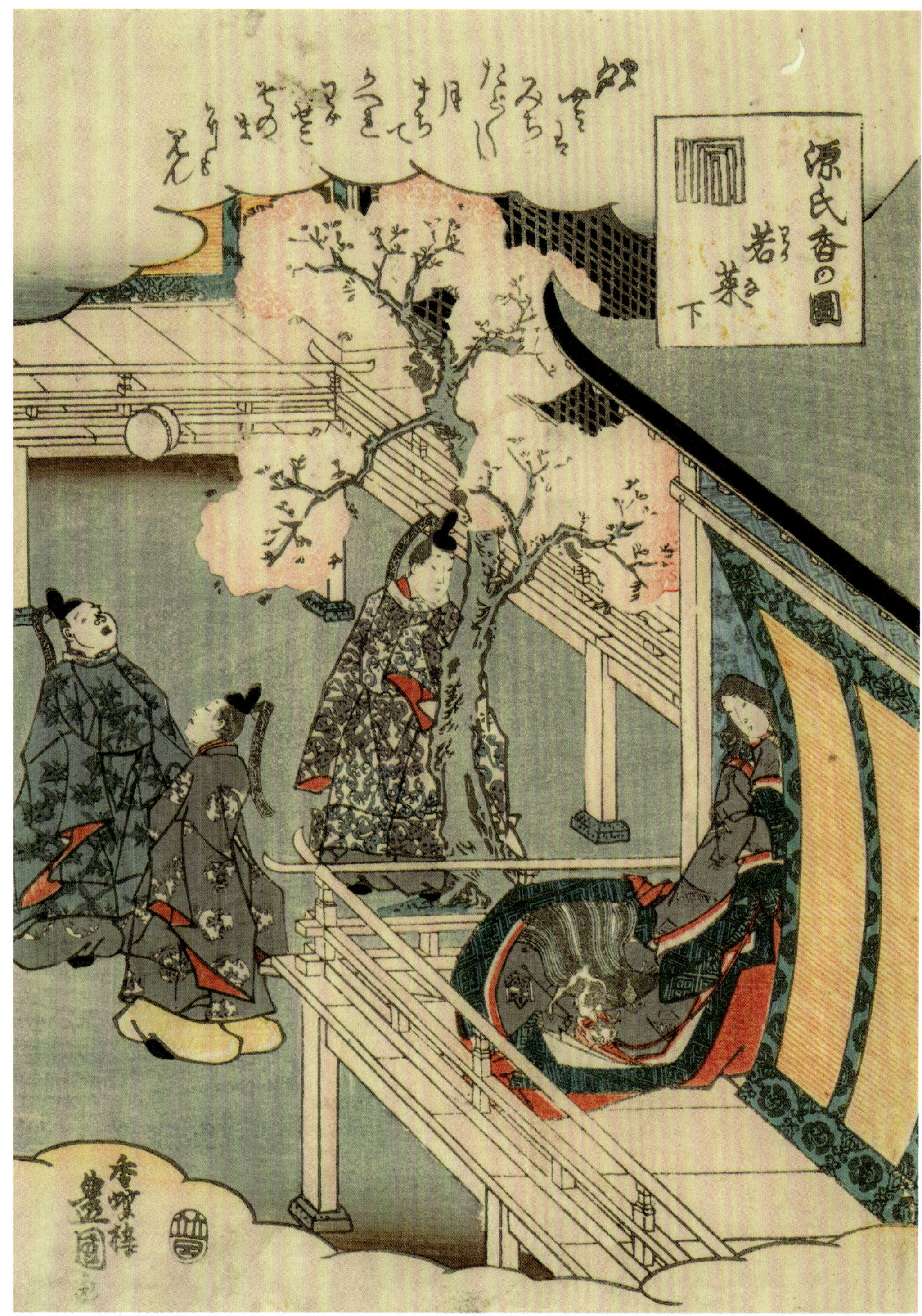

35A | Kunisada, *Genji Incense Pictures*, 1844–47

35B | Kuniyoshi, *One Hundred Poems by One Hundred Poets*, about 1840–42

35C | Kunisada, *The Color Print Contest of a Modern Genji*, 1854

With Murasaki recovering, and the Princess now apparently ill, Genji comes to visit her and alludes to (but does not quote in full) the poem that represents the chapter. As he prepares to leave the next morning, he discovers a passionate letter from Kashiwagi hidden under a cushion. Genji is of course deeply disturbed by the Princess's infidelity, but he recognizes that it is karmic retribution for his own long-ago secret affair with his stepmother Fujitsubo (see chapters 5 through 7), and decides to keep this secret as well. Kashiwagi, when he learns that Genji now knows what he did, falls ill with guilt and remorse.

The events of the two Wakana chapters are covered at length, with different twists, in both of the competing sequels *Rustic Image* (where the Genji figure is called Terumoto, later Teruuji, and the equivalent of the Third Princess is Mitsuyo) and *Ashikaga Robes* (where they become Ujimitsu and Mitsuai). The scene shown in the *Color Print Contest* series, however, does not have an exact equivalent in either book (35C). It shows two people with a cat, probably the Kashiwagi figure, Kashiwanosuke (whose name is the same in both books), and the woman of his dreams, Mitsuyo or Mitsuai.

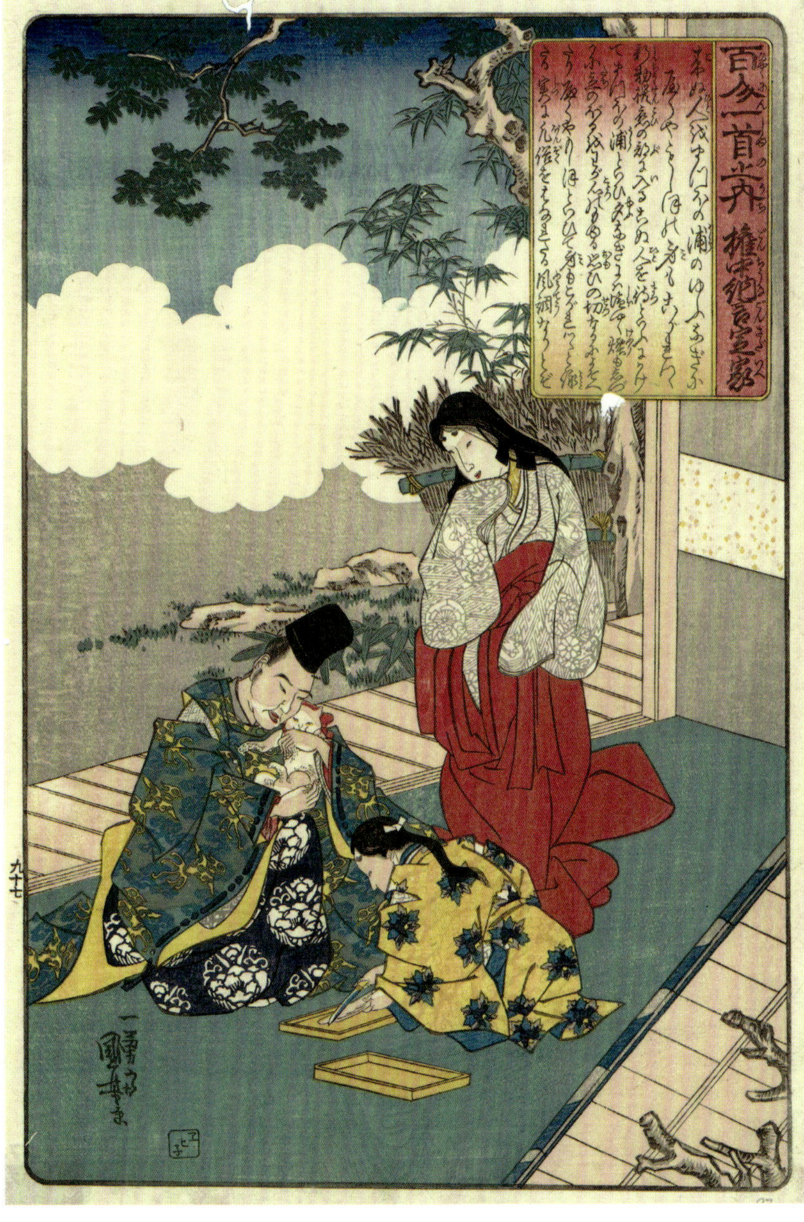

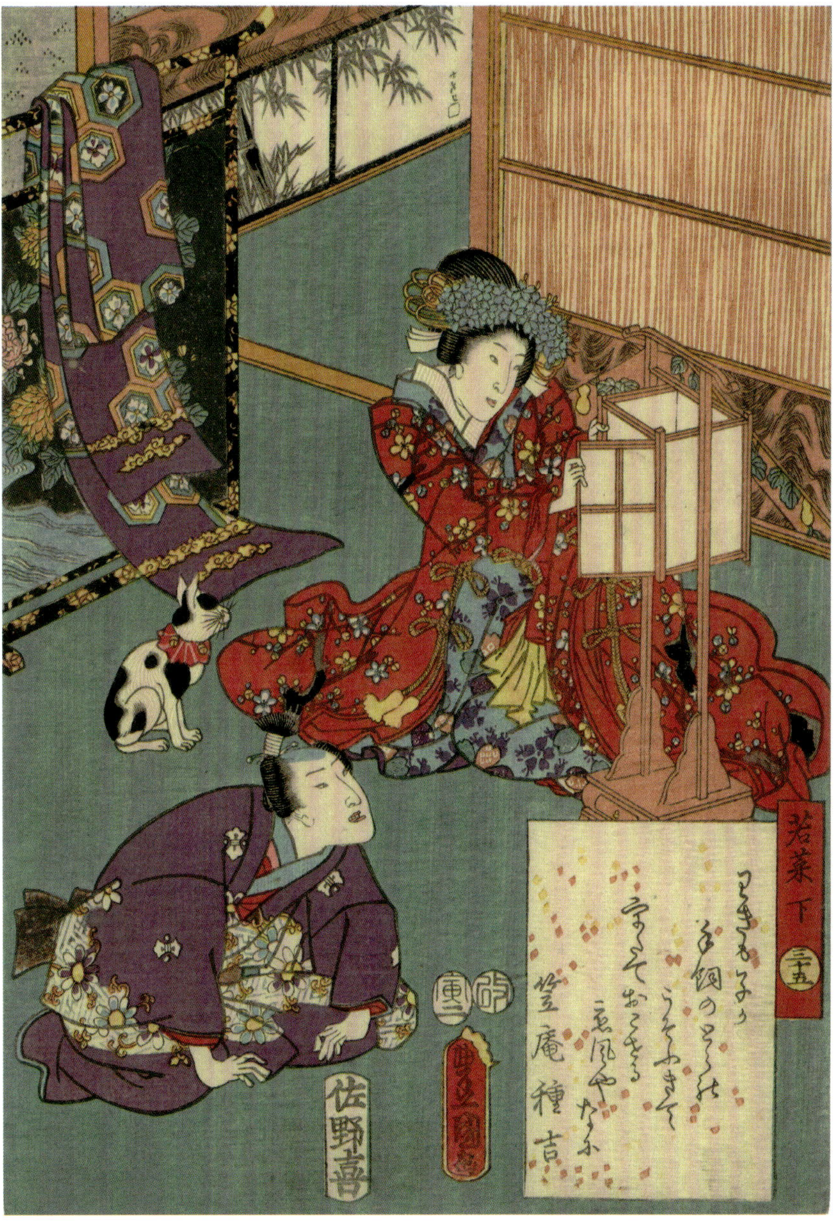

36

The Oak Tree (Kashiwagi)

Kashiwagi's illness worsens, and his final poetic message to the Third Princess is the poem representing the chapter. The Princess gives birth to her baby, the little boy who will be known in later chapters as Kaoru, and then decides to become a Buddhist nun. Kashiwagi dies and is mourned by everyone. Yūgiri, grieving for his friend, begins to pay consolation calls to Kashiwagi's widow, the Second Princess, also known as Ochiba. For many years Yūgiri has been devoted to his wife Kumoi-nokari, who has borne him seven children, but he is now starting to think seriously about another woman.

The picture in the *Genji Incense* series, showing male and female courtiers with cedarwood fans flirting with each other on a veranda, presumably represents the dying Kashiwagi's fond memory of himself with the Third Princess, even though the two of them never met as openly (36A). Koryūsai's modernized parody turns the imagined smoke of the funeral pyre into literal smoke from mosquito-repellent incense, with a young woman weeping not from grief but from acrid smoke in her eyes (36B).

When the end has come,
and from my smoldering pyre
smoke rises at last,
I know that undying flame
even then will burn for you.

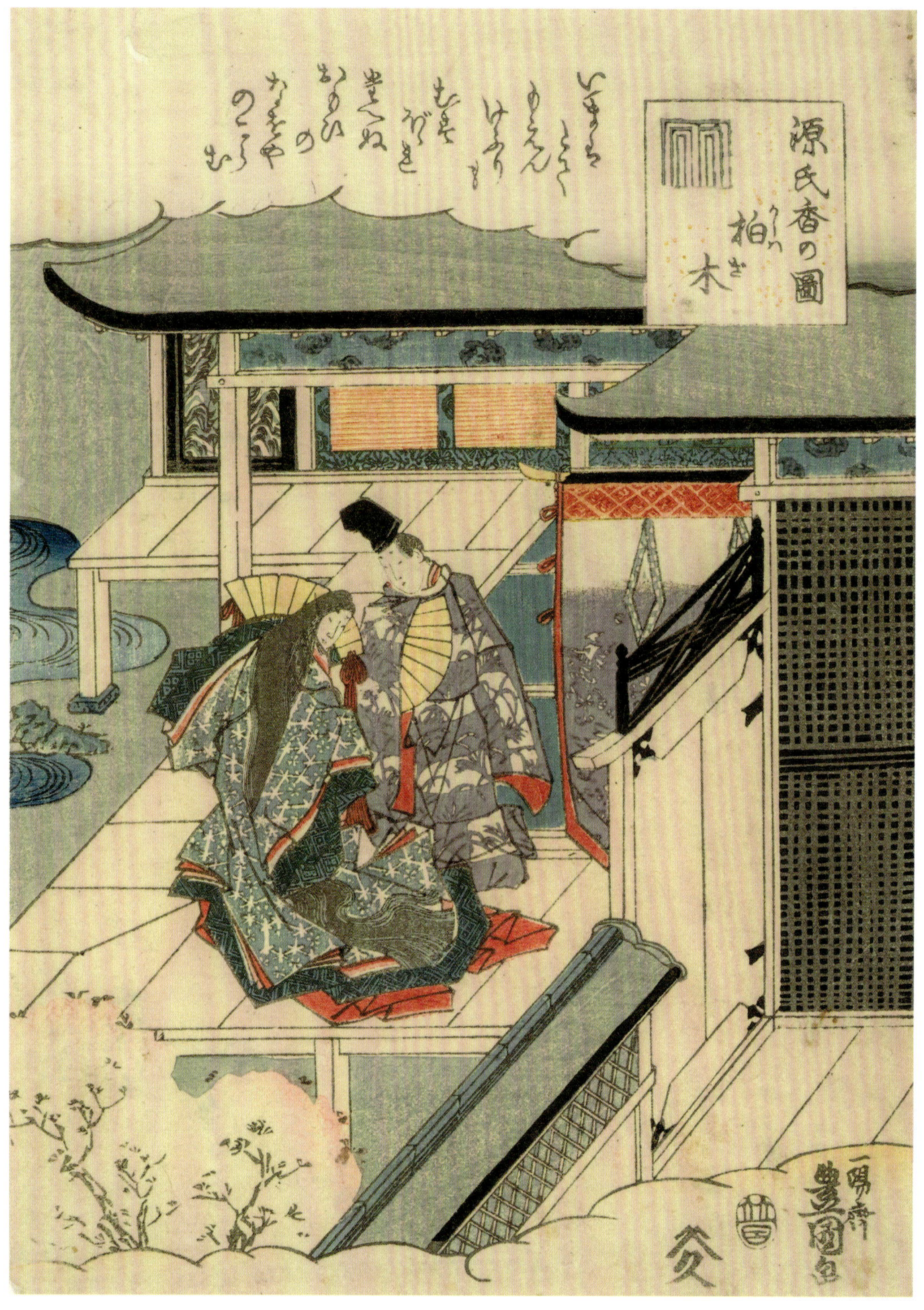

36A | Kunisada, *Genji Incense Pictures*, 1844–47

36B | Isoda Koryūsai, *Genji in Fashionable Modern Guise*, about 1770–72

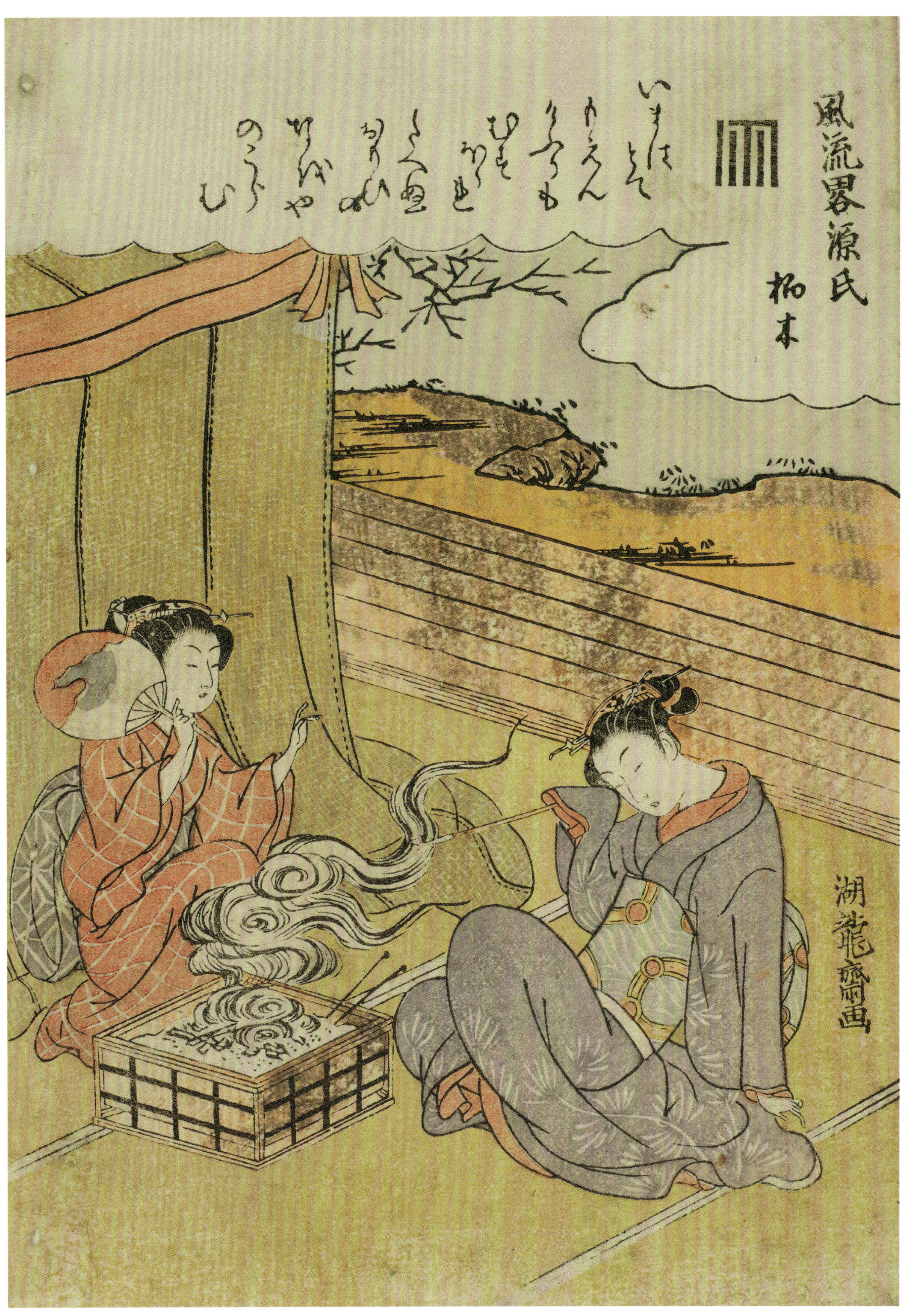
風流畧源氏
柏木
湖龍斎画

The design in the *Color Print Contest* series seems to refer not to the Kashiwagi chapter but to events of Wakana II, when Genji discovered the incriminating letter; here, Mitsuuji/Terumoto finds a letter under the bedding, while the lady and her attendant in the next room seem to be wondering anxiously what he is doing (36C). The *Genji Cards* series by Kunisada II presents yet another version of the cat incident from Wakana I. In this reworking of the story, the lady behind the blinds sends her cat out to carry a love letter to the young man she has been eyeing, thus reversing the romantic power dynamics and giving much greater agency to the female partner than the original narrative does (36D). Kashiwanosuke is holding a football, but he seems to have forgotten all about the game as he stands on the step gazing at the beautiful young lady.

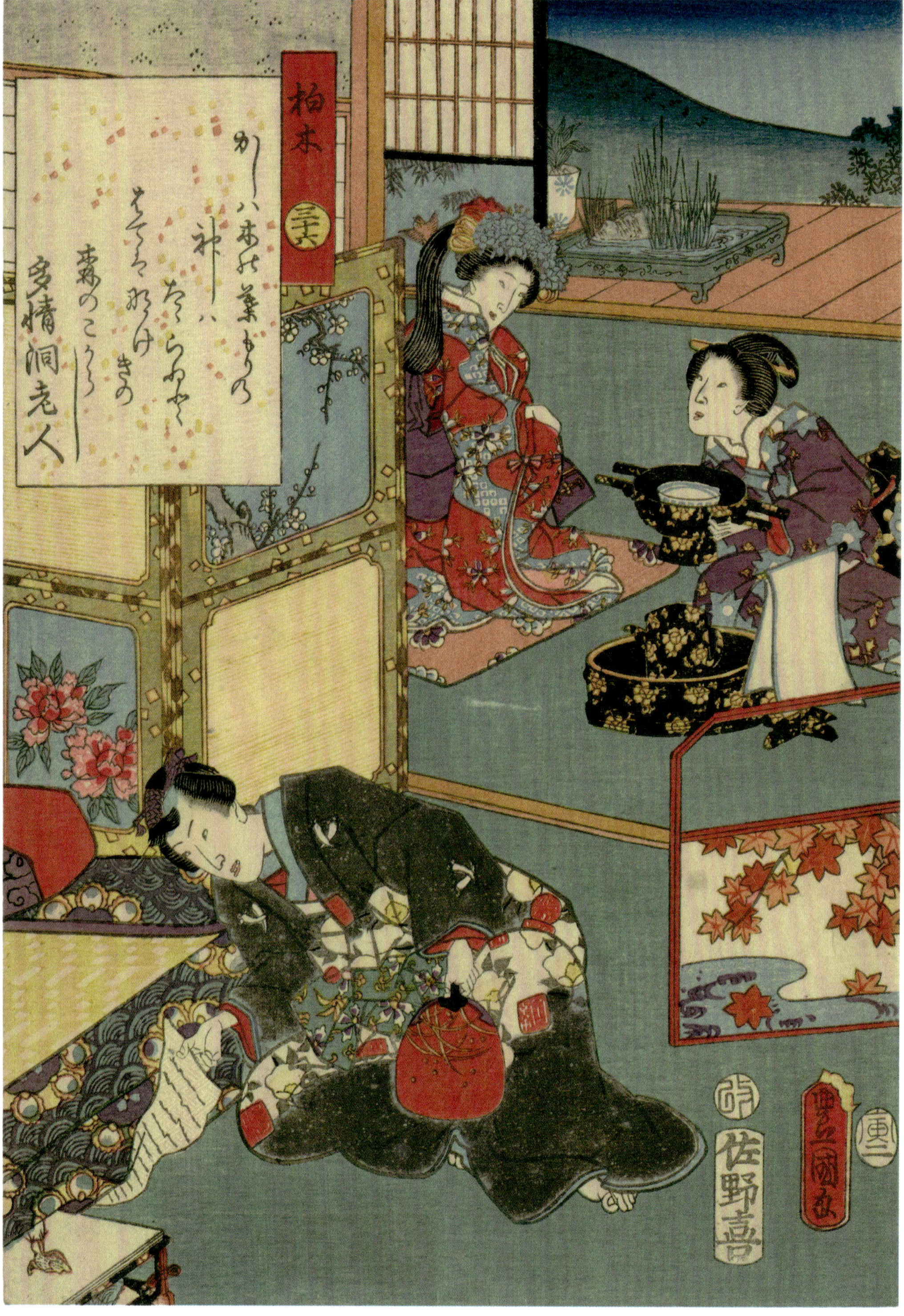

36C | Kunisada, *The Color Print Contest of a Modern Genji*, 1854

36D | Kunisada II, *Lady Murasaki's Genji Cards*, 1857

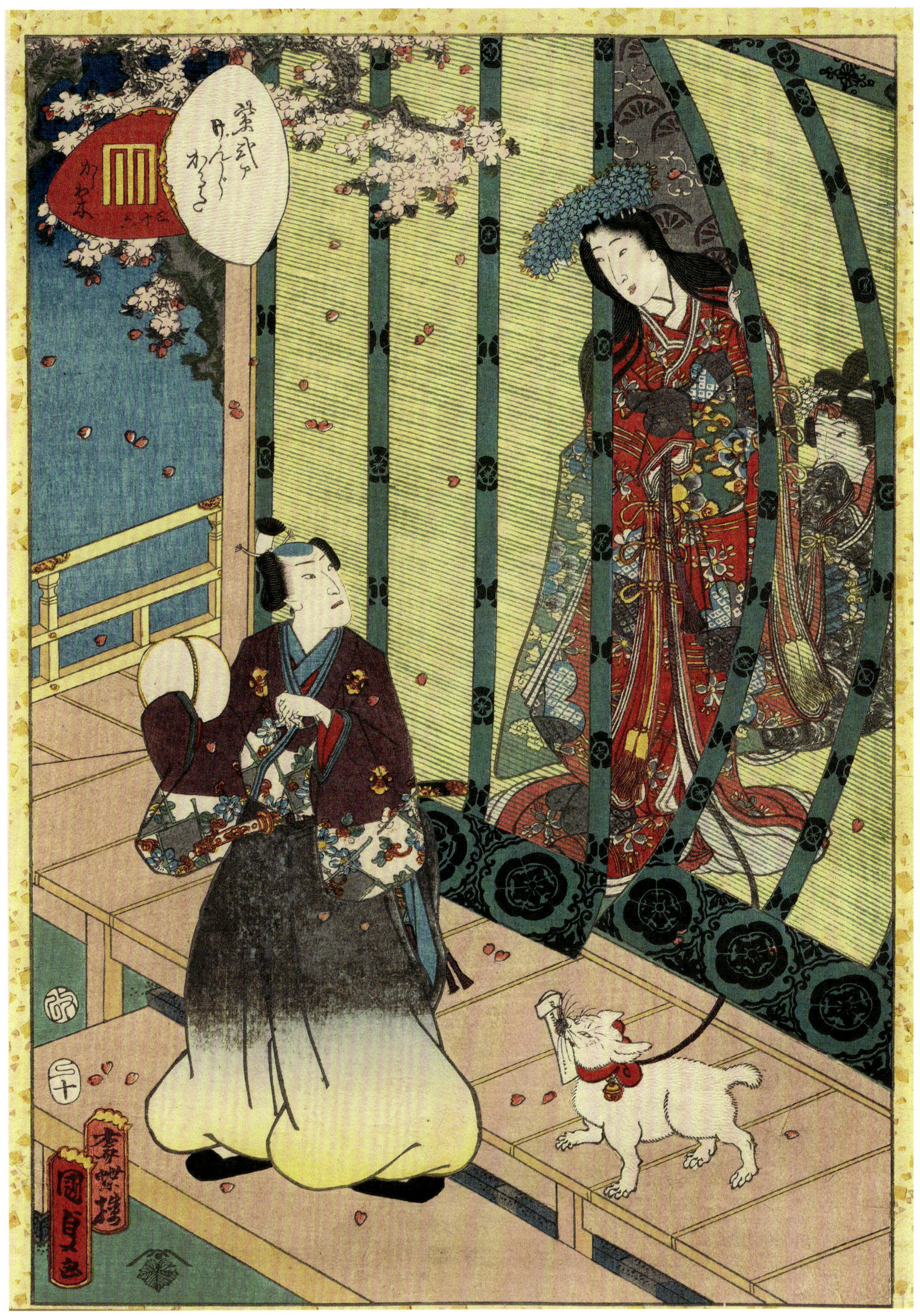
かしわ木
三十六
香蝶楼
國貞画

37

The Flute (Yokobue)

Little Kaoru is now a toddler, living with his mother at Genji's sprawling mansion in Rokujō. When Genji visits them at the beginning of the chapter, the child grabs a bamboo shoot out of a bowl to use for teething; a postcard from the series designed by Kajita Hanko in 1905 shows the beautiful but melancholy young mother with her son clutching the bamboo shoot (37B).

Meanwhile, Yūgiri continues his visits to Kashiwagi's widow, Ochiba (the Second Princess). On one such visit, Ochiba's mother gives Yūgiri a flute that had belonged to Kashiwagi, and he responds with the chapter title poem. That night, Kashiwagi appears to him in a dream and tells him that the flute should go to "my heirs" — although as far as Yūgiri knows, Kashiwagi had no children.

At the end of the chapter, Yūgiri visits the Rokujō mansion, where he encounters the Akashi Empress and her two younger sons. As shown in the illustration from the *Genji Incense* series, he picks up the three-year-old Third Prince (later known as Niou), and the Second Prince demands to be picked up too (37A). Kaoru is also present, and Yūgiri plays with him as well; he begins to wonder about the true ancestry of this appealing child, although he has no proof for his suspicions. When Yūgiri tells his father, Genji,

---

Nothing much has changed
in the music of the flute,
but that perfect tone
missing ever since he died
will live on forevermore.

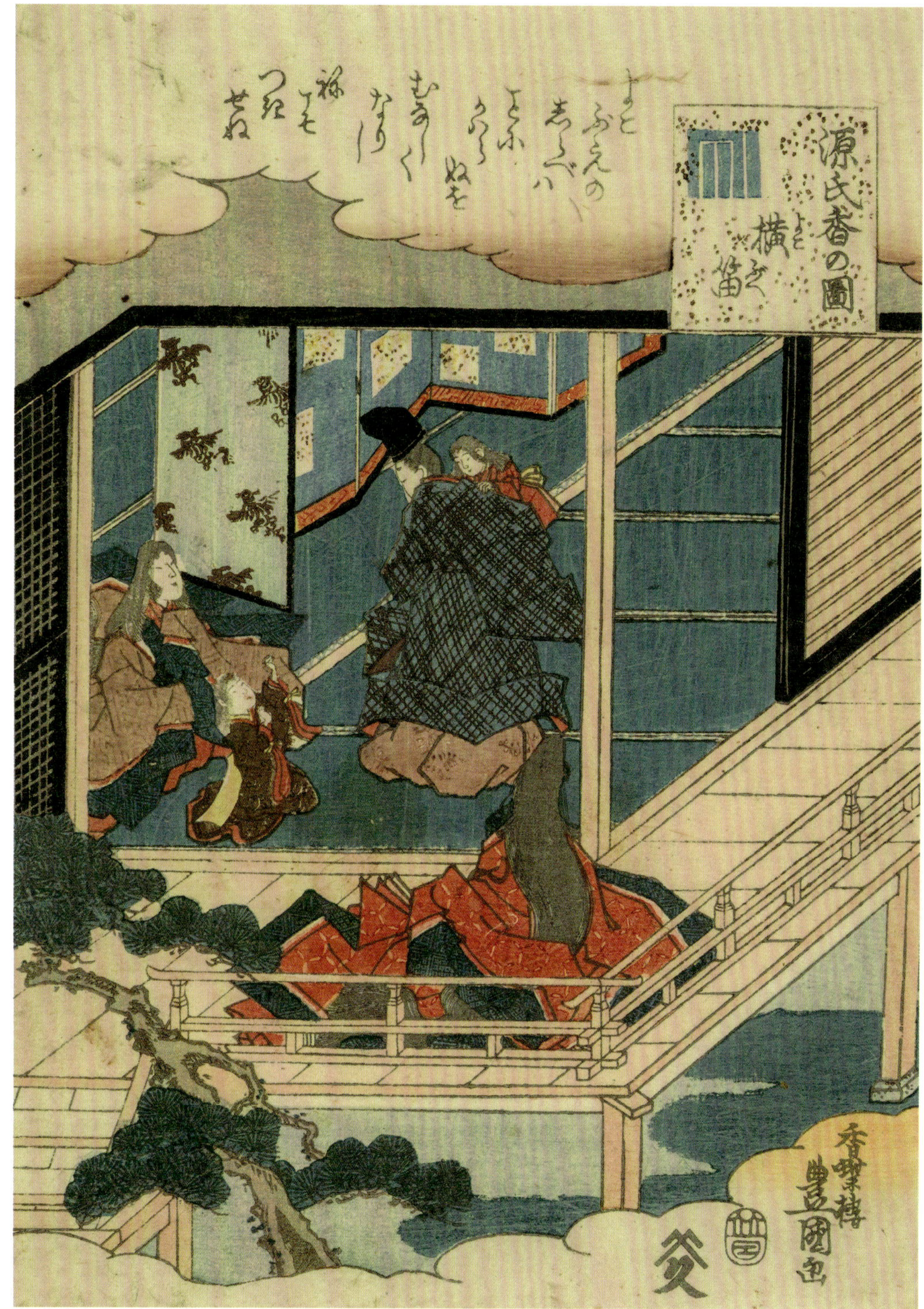

37A | Kunisada, *Genji Incense Pictures*, 1844–47

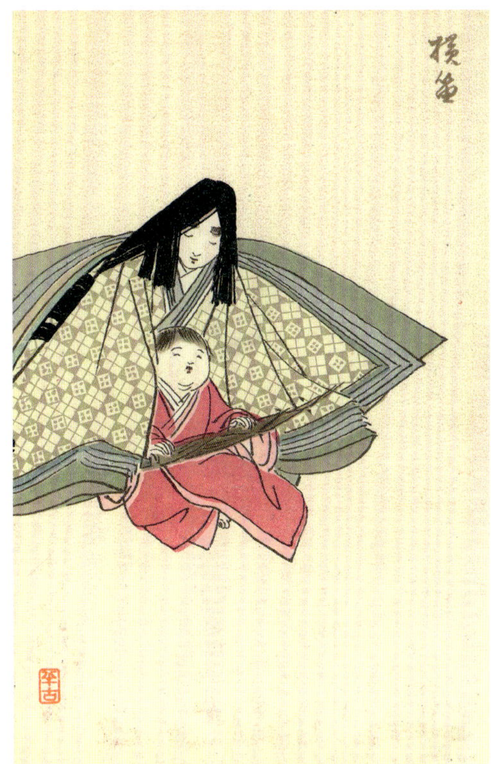

37B | Kajita Hanko, *The Tale of Genji*, 1905

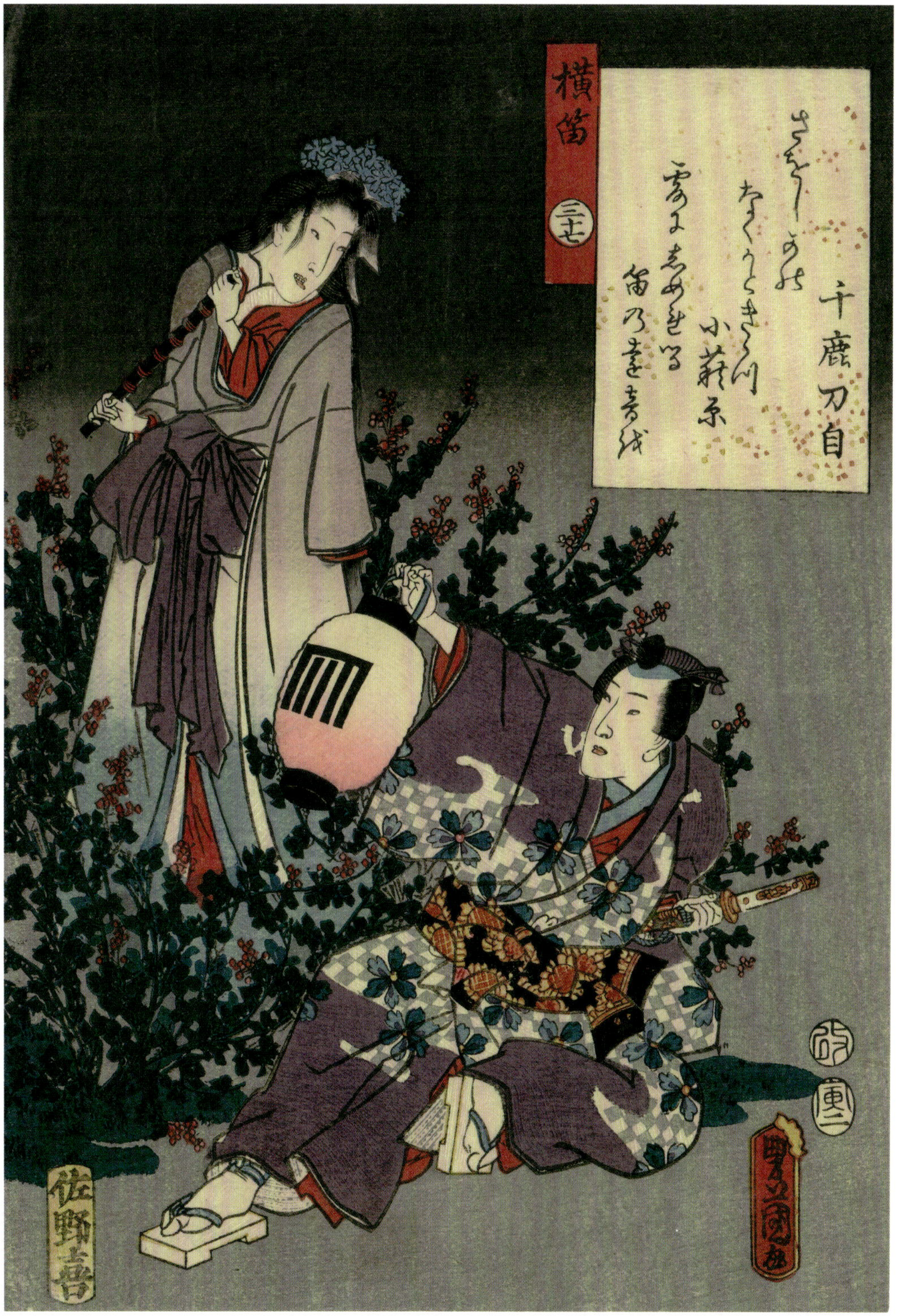

about the dream, Genji — who suspects that Yūgiri may know the truth — says that he will take charge of the flute himself.

The scene depicted in the *Color Print Contest* series is based on an illustration in the very first chapter of *Ashikaga Robes*. The ghost holding the flute, whose figure dissolves into mist below the knees, is that of a woman named Osan, who is part of the action-adventure plot interwoven with the Genji story and has no direct equivalent in the original *Tale*. She may be a kind of dark counterpart to Lady Mitsuyo or Mitsuai (= the Third Princess), since all of these names include the character for the number three. Startled by the appearance of the ghost, the man — holding a lantern out toward the ghost and clutching the hilt of his sword as he pulls back in surprise — does not appear in the book illustration but can be identified by the double-clove crest on the shoulders of his kimono as Kumoinojō Ujinaka (= Yūgiri) (37C).

37C | Kunisada, *The Color Print Contest of a Modern Genji*, 1854

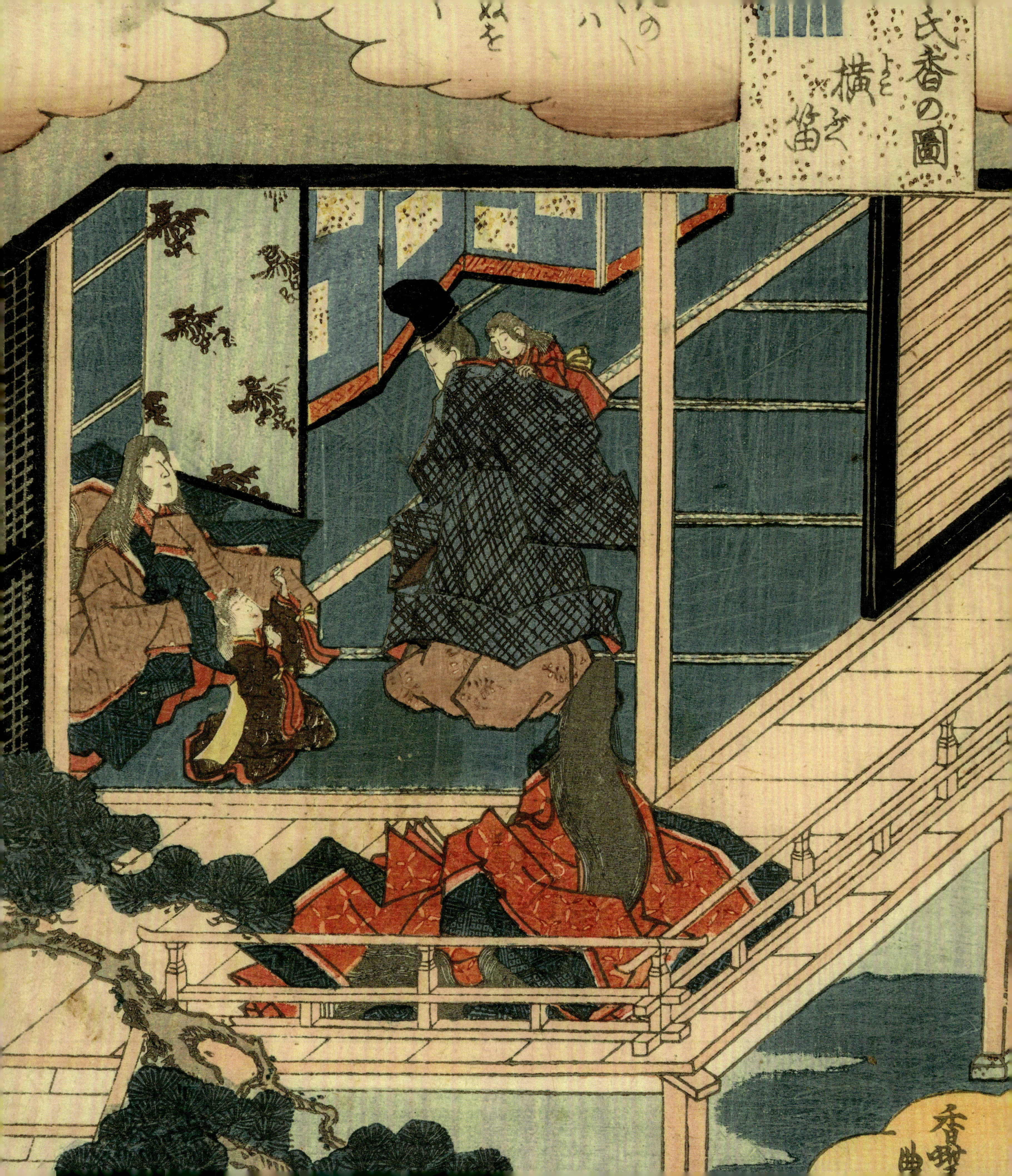

氏香の圖
横笛

In the *Genji Cards* series by Kunisada II, Ujimitsu (= Mitsuuji, Genji), the main character of *Ashikaga Robes*, holds the flute as he watches a dance by Kumoinojō and Kashiwanosuke (= Kashiwagi) (37D). The latter is still alive because, in this rearranged story line, the adultery with Mitsuai has not yet occurred.

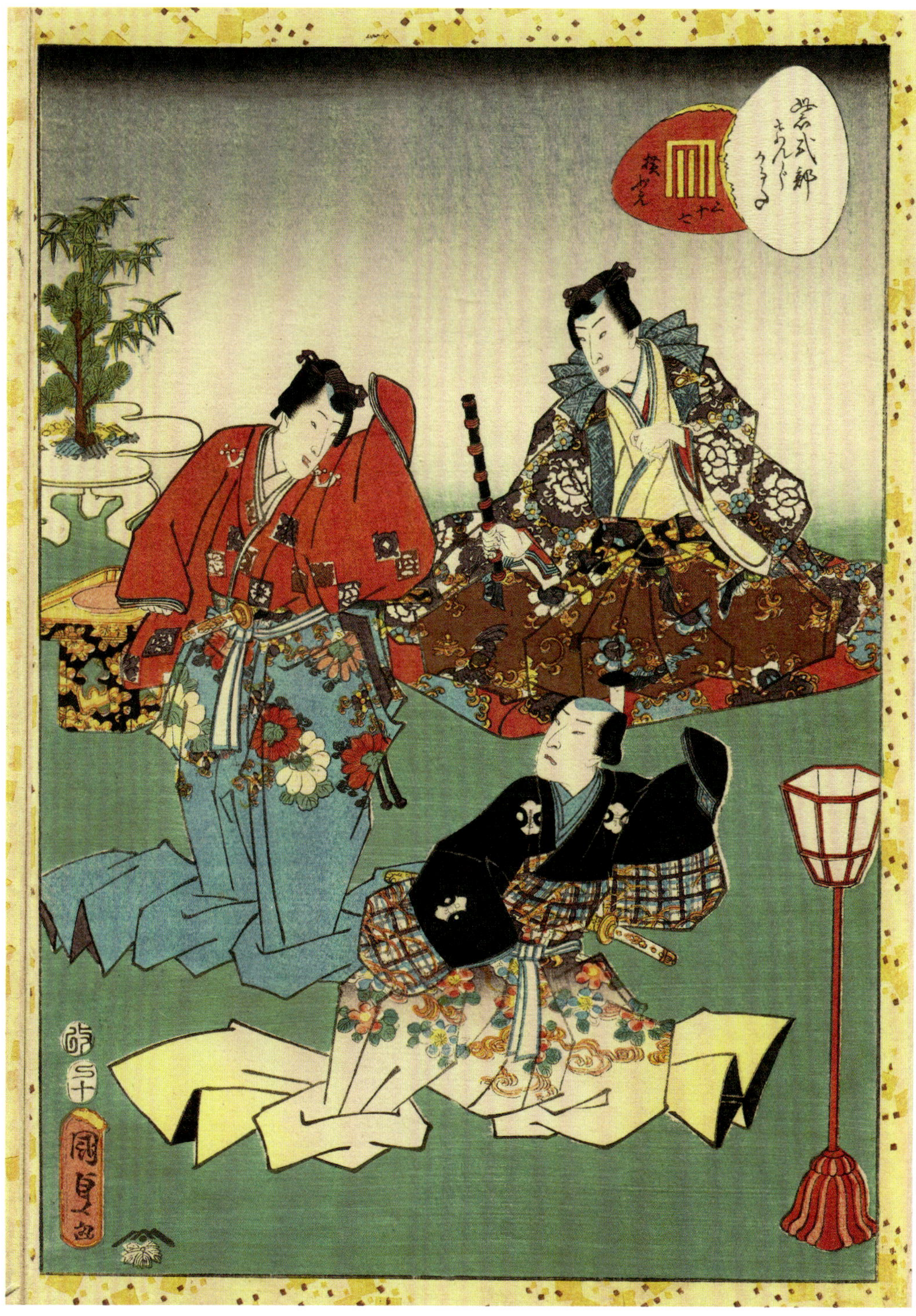

37D | Kunisada II, *Lady Murasaki's Genji Cards*, 1857

37A | (detail)

38

The Bell Cricket (Suzumushi)

This short chapter describes the elegant appointments of the chapel that Genji builds for the Third Princess within his palatial estate at Rokujō. He has a portion of the garden redone in the manner of a natural moor, with long grasses that he stocks with singing insects. On an autumn evening, he visits the Princess and plays the koto for her. They listen together to the melodious chirping of the insects and exchange poems; Genji's reply to the Princess is the poem chosen to represent the chapter.

The *Genji Incense* series shows Genji playing the koto for the Princess (38A). Her formerly floor-length hair was chopped to shoulder length when she took her preliminary vows as a Buddhist nun and here is covered with a blue scarf; if and when she takes higher vows, she will shave her head.

The illustration in the *Color Print Contest* series shows a young man and two girls in a wild garden with elaborate insect cages (38B). A similar, though not identical, scene opens chapter 20 of *Rustic Image*, in which the young people are releasing insects into the moor-like garden of the lady who is now a nun.

You may, for yourself,
have no wish but to be free
of this poor abode,
yet your sweet bell cricket song
for me never will grow old.

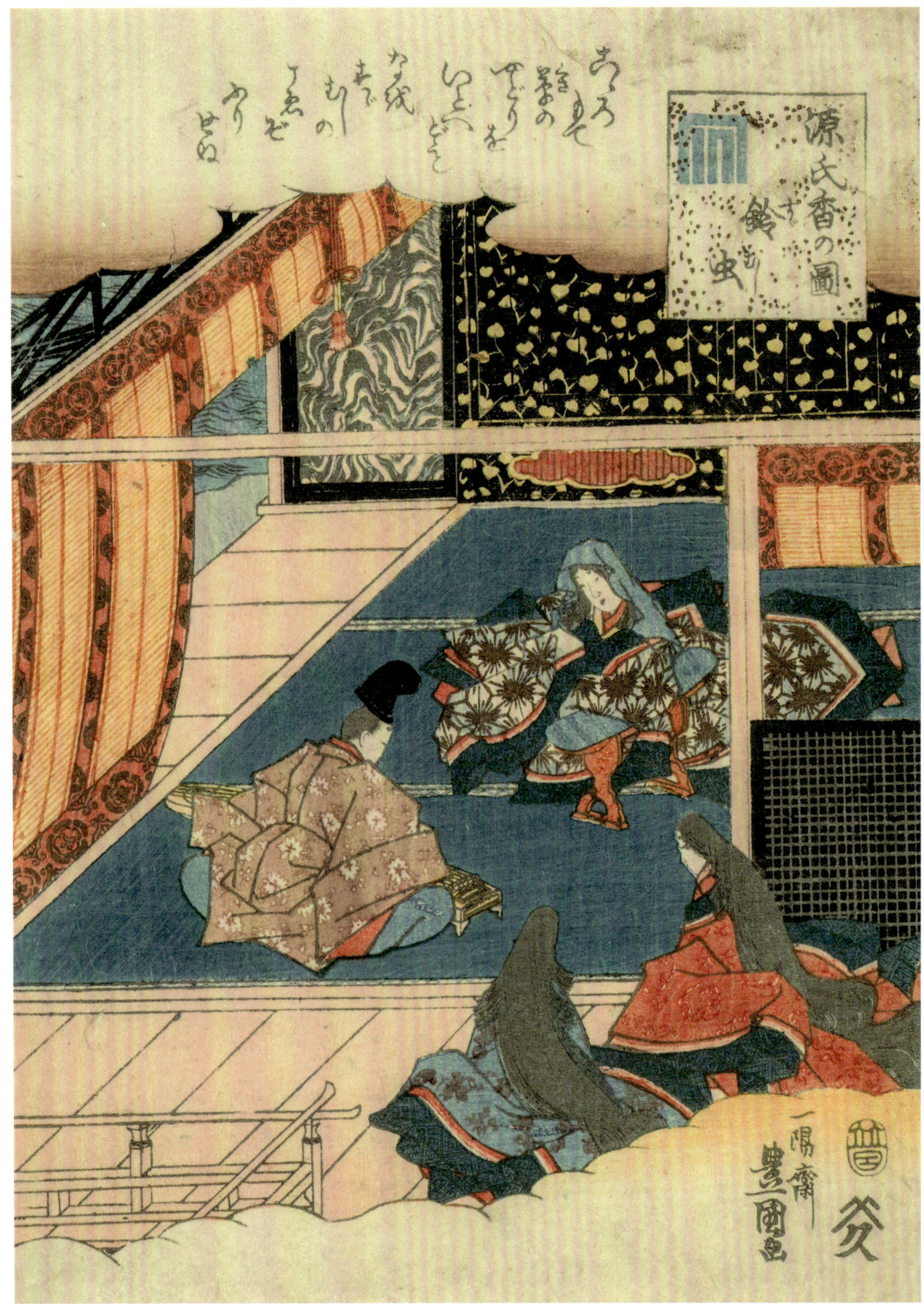

38A | Kunisada, *Genji Incense Pictures*, 1844–47

38B | Kunisada, *The Color Print Contest of a Modern Genji*, 1852

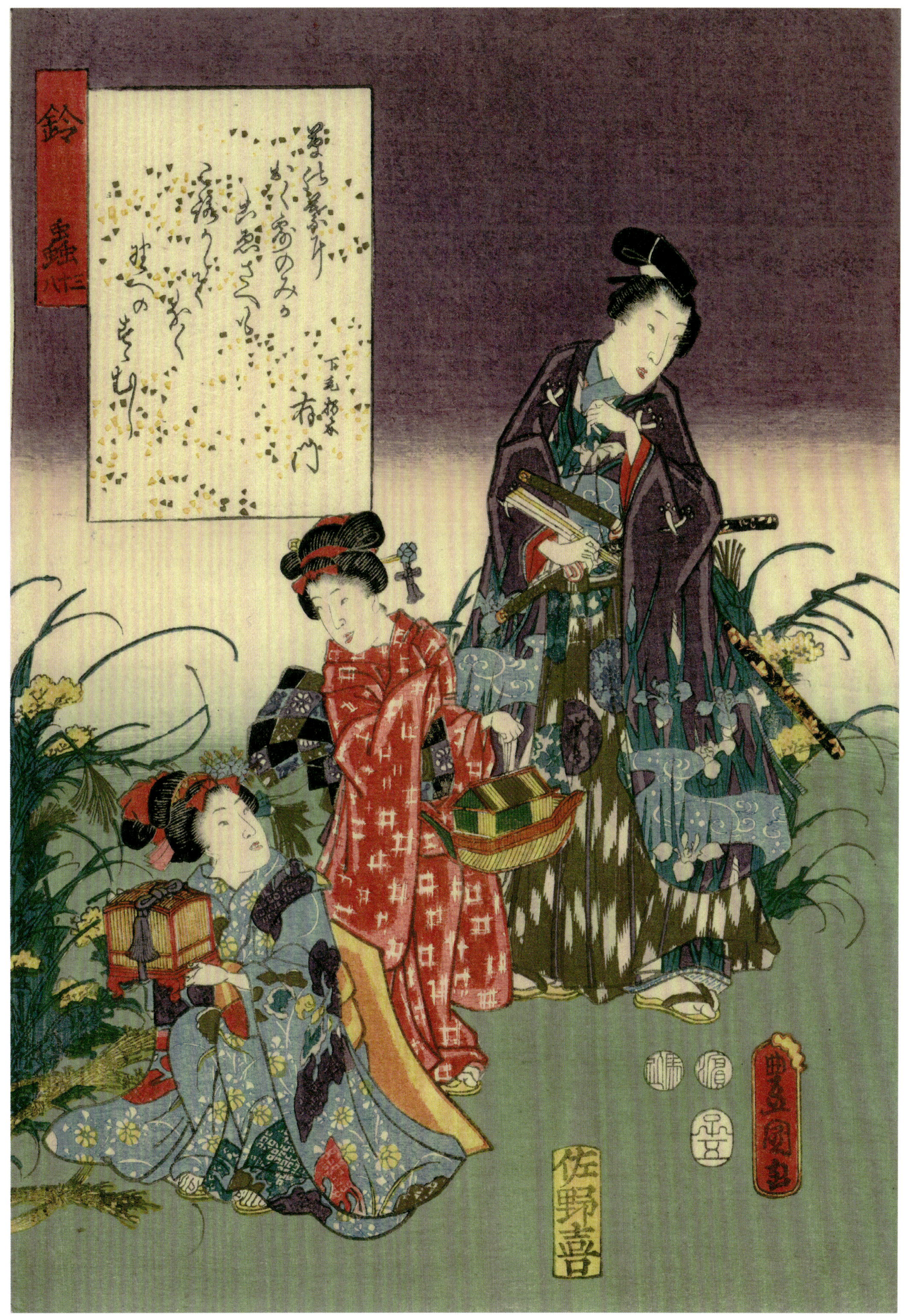
鈴蟲 八十二
豊国画
佐野喜

39

Evening Mist (Yūgiri)

Yūgiri is actively courting Kashiwagi's widow, Ochiba, but she resists his advances. When Ochiba's mother falls ill, the two women move together to a villa in Ono, a suburb of the capital. Yūgiri visits them there in autumn and tries, unsuccessfully, to use the rising mist as an excuse to spend the night. The poem that he composes gives the chapter its title and the character his nickname, Yūgiri (Evening Mist). The picture, however, shows a later episode in the chapter, after the death of the Princess's mother, due in part to her anxiety over the uncertainty of her daughter's future. Yūgiri visits Ono again and speaks with the lady-in-waiting Koshōshō, while deer cry in the garden outside the house (39A). The Princess herself, however, refuses to see him, since she blames him for the death of her mother.

Meanwhile, Yūgiri's wife Kumoinokari has learned of her husband's interest in another woman. After a heated argument with Yūgiri, she takes her children and goes home to her father, Tō no Chūjō. The chapter ends with Yūgiri on bad terms with both of the women in his life, but he does later manage to patch up his relationships with both of them; Kumoinokari and the children eventually return to his main house, and Ochiba moves into one of his other houses.

While such evening mists
as bring a mountain village
new melancholy
veil the sky, I cannot wish
to leave and set out for home.

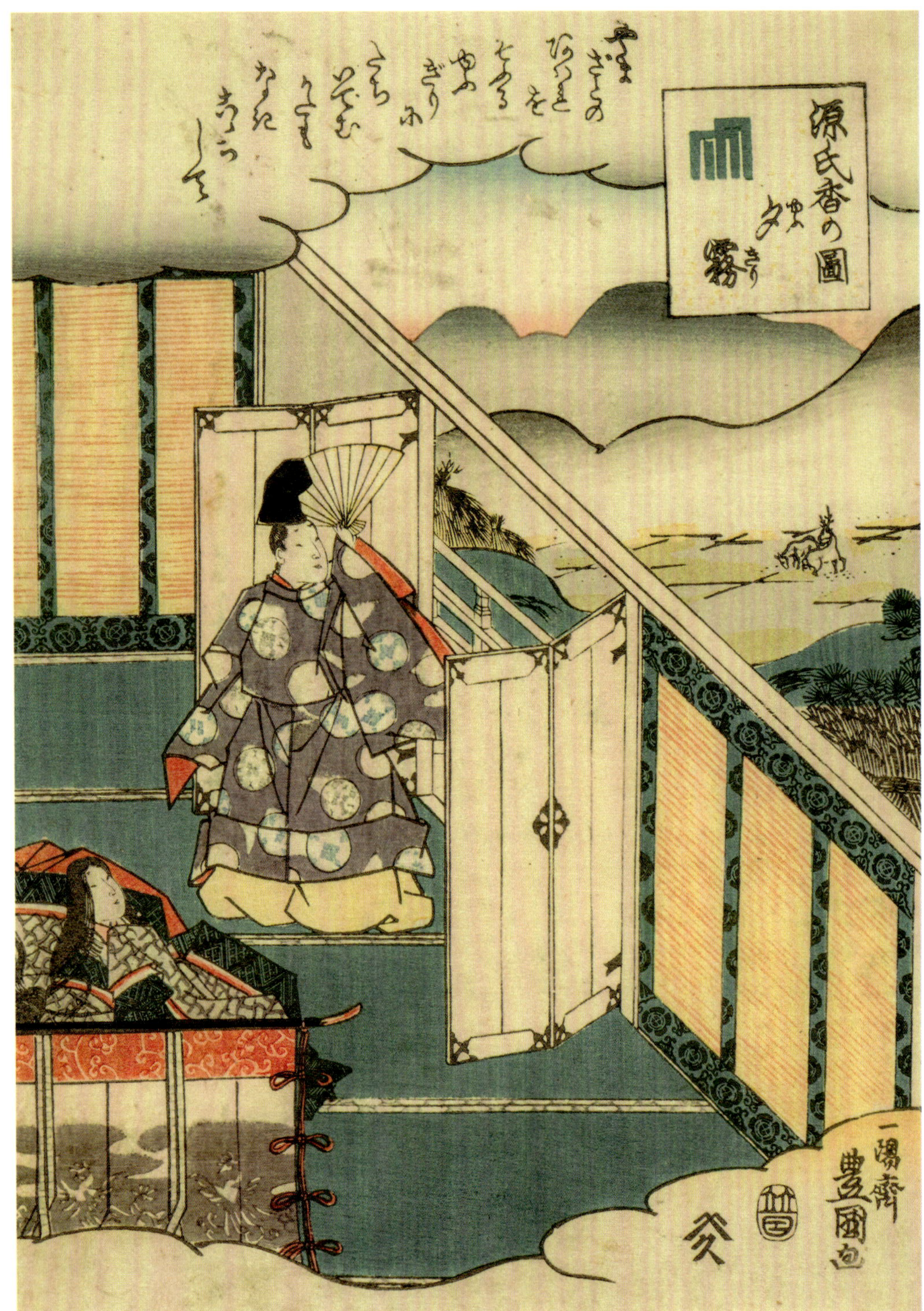

39A | Kunisada, *Genji Incense Pictures*, 1844–47

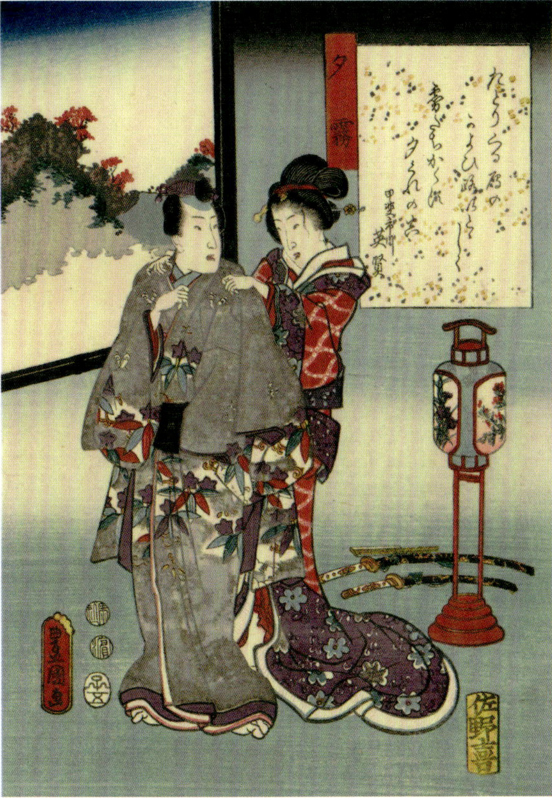

39B | Kunisada, *The Color Print Contest of a Modern Genji*, 1852

39C | Kunisada II, *Lady Murasaki's Genji Cards*, 1857

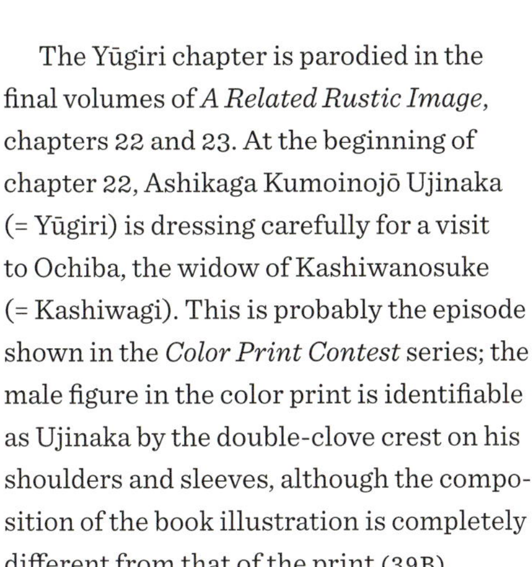

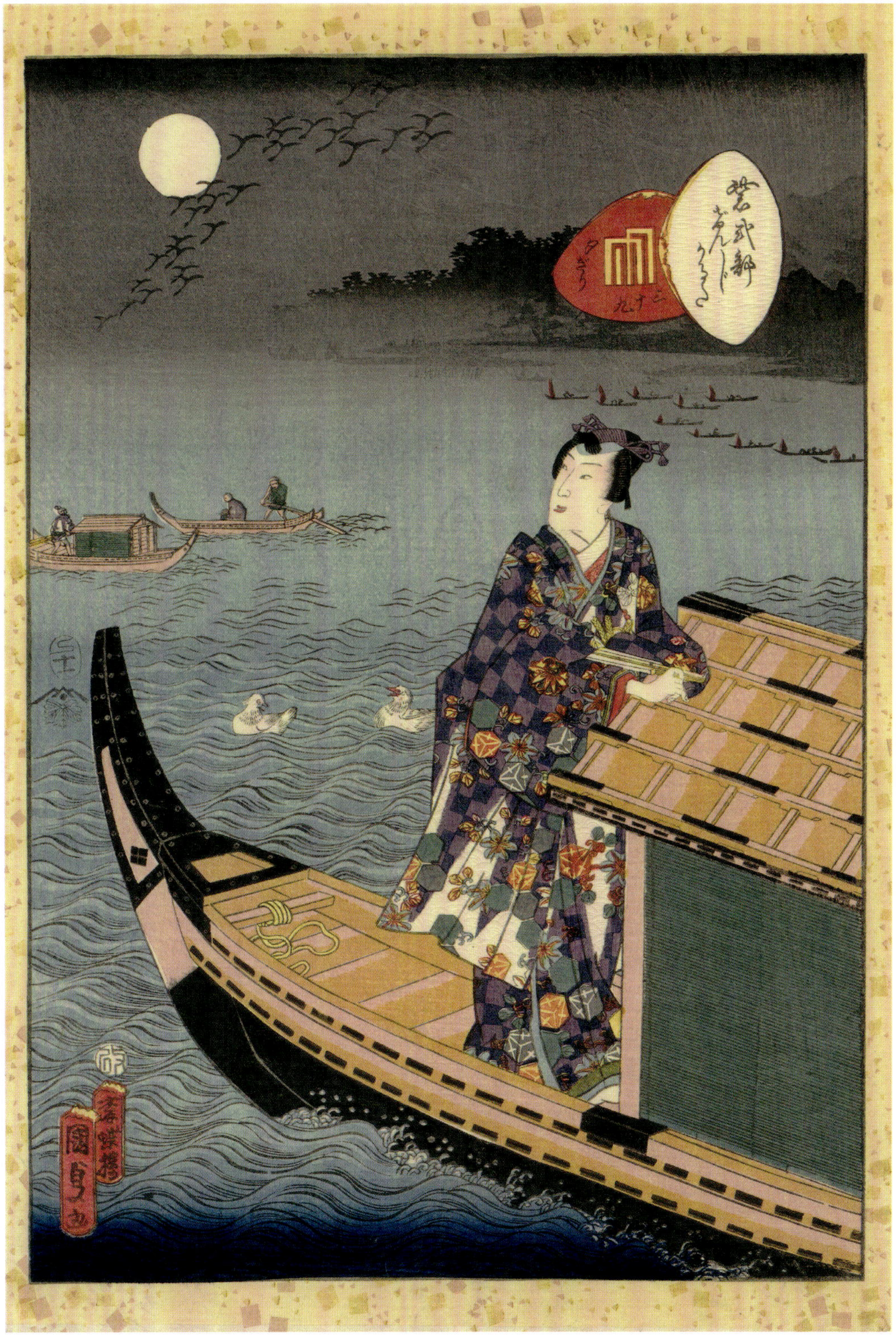

The Yūgiri chapter is parodied in the final volumes of *A Related Rustic Image*, chapters 22 and 23. At the beginning of chapter 22, Ashikaga Kumoinojō Ujinaka (= Yūgiri) is dressing carefully for a visit to Ochiba, the widow of Kashiwanosuke (= Kashiwagi). This is probably the episode shown in the *Color Print Contest* series; the male figure in the color print is identifiable as Ujinaka by the double-clove crest on his shoulders and sleeves, although the composition of the book illustration is completely different from that of the print (39B).

In the *Genji Cards* series, Kunisada II ignored the plot of the story and instead used the title theme to create a lovely image of romantic melancholy: Mitsuuji (or Terumoto), standing in a pleasure boat on a misty autumn evening, watches geese fly past the full moon (39C).

40

The Law (Minori)

Murasaki has never fully recovered from her earlier illness, and now she falls sick again and is not expected to recover. She wants to take vows as a nun, but Genji cannot bear to be parted from her. Instead, she commissions the copying of one thousand sutras, and in the spring, she holds a grand ceremony to dedicate the completed works. On this occasion she exchanges poems with some of Genji's other ladies; the chapter title, referring to the teachings of the Buddha, is from her poem addressed to Hanachirusato (see chapter 11).

The scene illustrated in the *Genji Incense* series is Murasaki's touching conversation with Prince Niou, a younger son of her beloved foster daughter, the Akashi Empress (40A). She tells the little boy that she will soon be leaving and asks him to look after the rose plum in the courtyard after she is gone, and to put its flowers on the altar sometimes.

Murasaki's health declines over the summer, and by autumn she is bedridden. She rallies long enough to enjoy one last visit from the Akashi Empress and her children, including Niou. On the following day she dies, and Genji is devastated. Yūgiri rises to the occasion, providing emotional support for his grieving father and handling such matters as the arrangement of the memorial services.

This is the last time rites
of mine will serve the Law,
yet I have great faith
they shall be to you and me
a bond that lasts many lives.

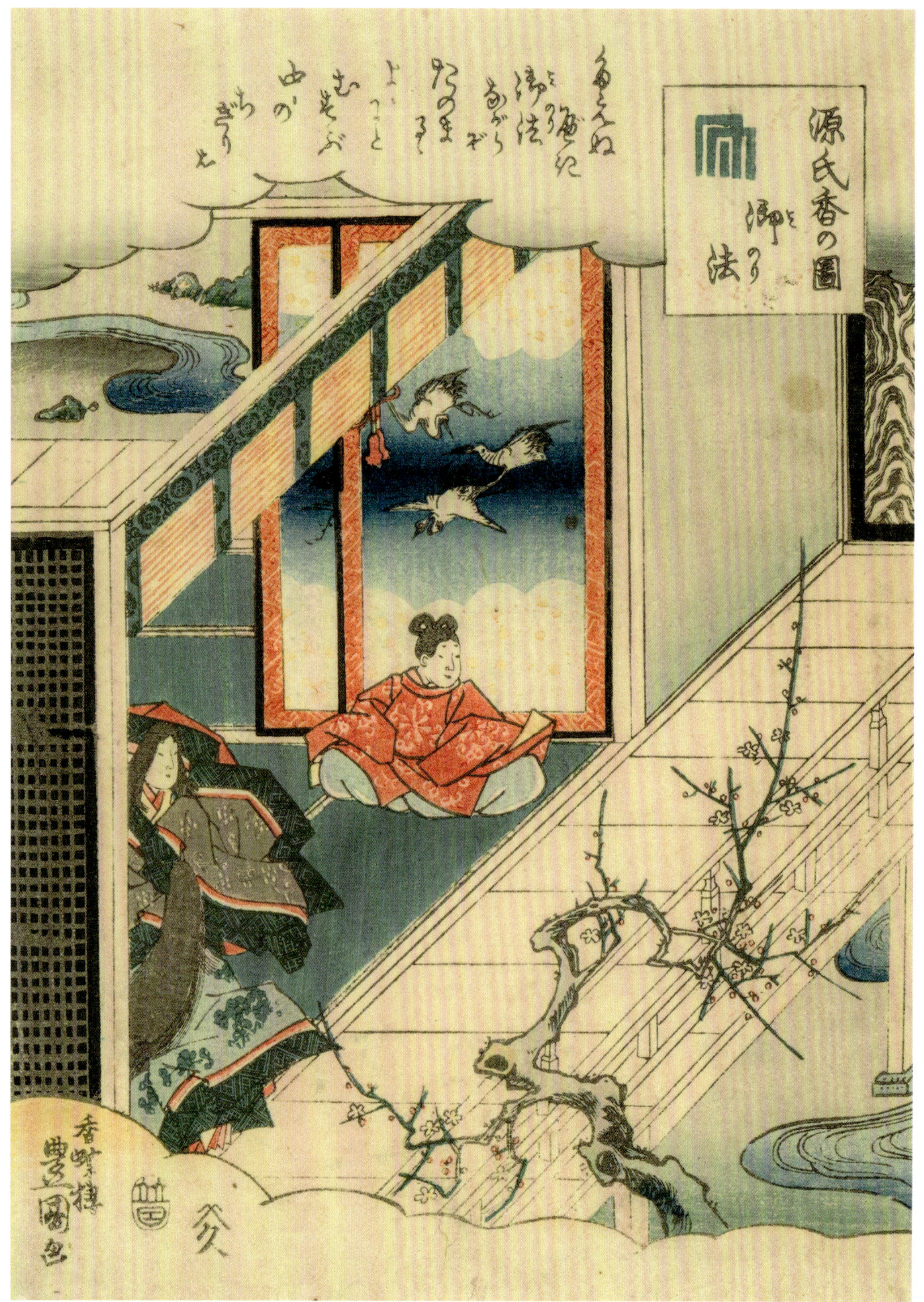

40A | Kunisada, *Genji Incense Pictures*, 1844–47

40B | Kunisada, *The Color Print Contest of a Modern Genji*, 1854

40C | Kunisada II and Hiroshige II, *Traces of Genji in Fifty-Four Chapters*, 1864

In the *Color Print Contest* series, Kunisada illustrates the chapter with an *Inaka Genji* version of the same scene he showed in *Genji Incense*: the dying Murasaki telling little Niou to look after her flowering trees when she is gone (40B). None of the four sequels to *Inaka Genji* cover chapters 40 and 41 of the original *Tale*; perhaps the authors and publishers feared that deaths of major characters would be unpopular with the reading public. This scene, however, appears as a flashback in chapter 1 of the third sequel, *Pale Purple Dawn at Uji* (*Usumurasaki Uji no akebono*), which takes up the last part of the story after the deaths of Genji and Murasaki.

Kunisada II and Hiroshige II, in their *Traces of Genji* series, play on the theme of Buddhist rites mentioned in the title poem, which is quoted in the fan-shaped inset by Hiroshige II in the upper part of the print. For the main image, Kunisada II repurposed an illustration by his teacher done for chapter 18 of *Rustic Image*. Terumoto (= Genji, Mitsuuji) visits his wife Lady Mitsuyo (= the Third Princess), now a Buddhist nun, and her baby Kaorinojō (= Kaoru), who grabs a bamboo shoot to use for teething (40C). This charming scene parodies the incident near the beginning of the Yokobue chapter (chapter 37) of the original *Tale of Genji*.

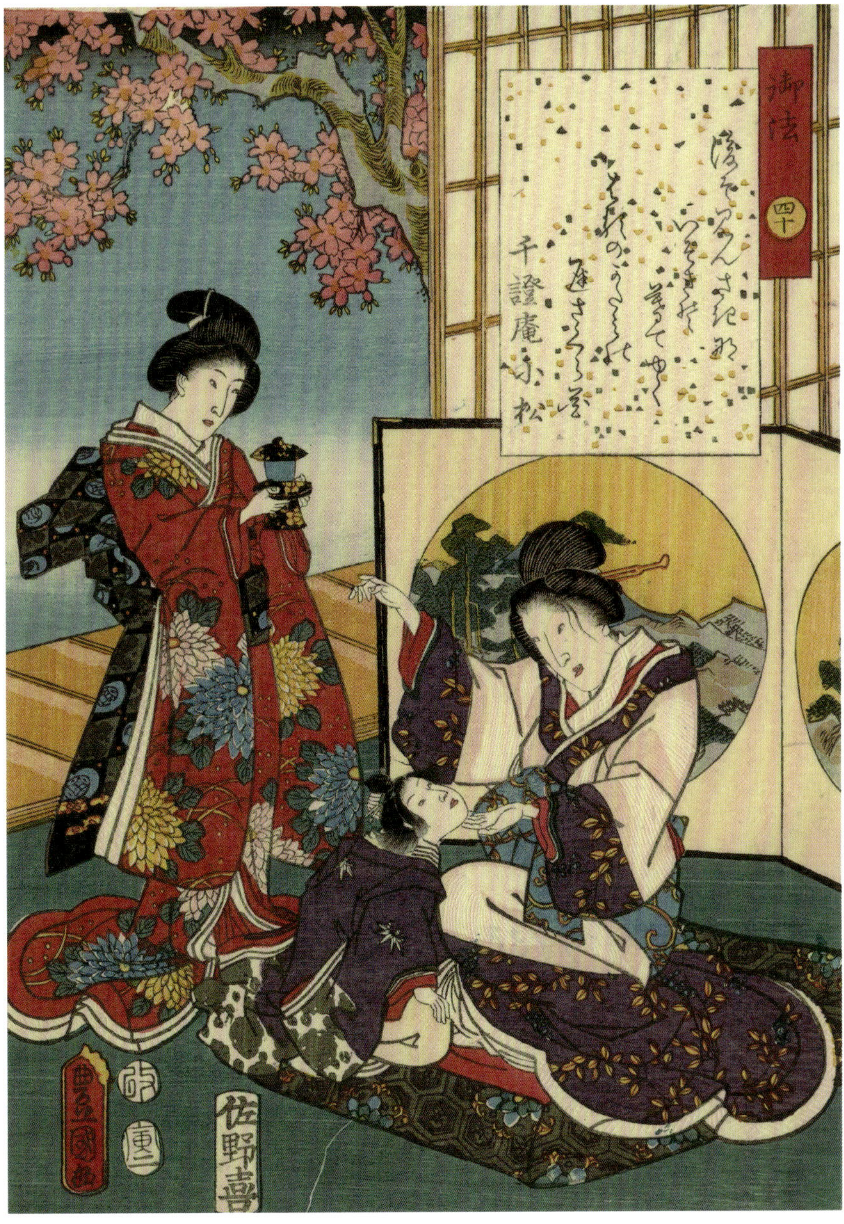

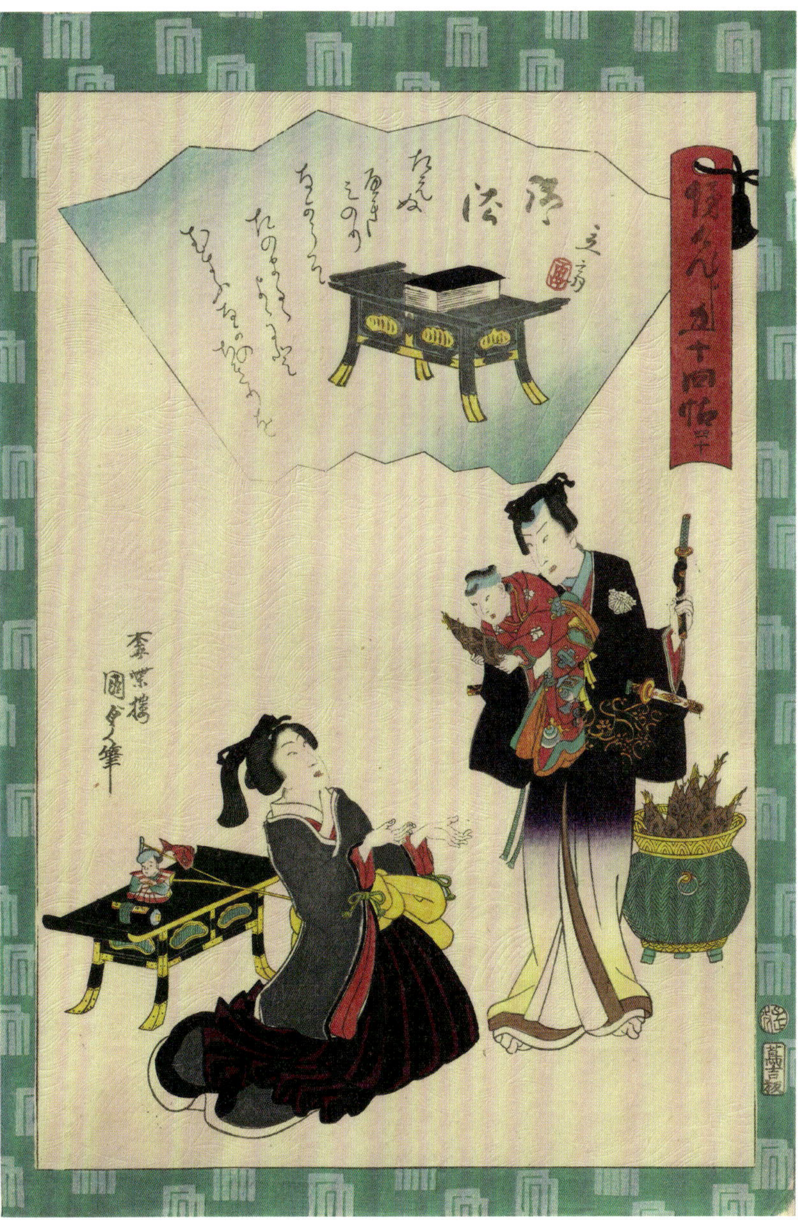

41

The Wizard (Maboroshi)

Genji mourns Murasaki deeply and thinks of her throughout the following year. The Akashi Empress has left Niou to keep his grandfather company, and in spring the little boy gathers flowering branches from the rose plum tree, just as Murasaki had told him to do in the previous chapter (41A). Genji considers taking Buddhist vows himself and retiring to a monastery, but in the end he decides not to.

In the autumn, Genji watches the flight of geese across the sky and composes the chapter title poem, a reference to the greatest love story in East Asian literature: the tale of the Tang Emperor Xuanzong and his consort Yang Guifei, as told in verse by Bai Juyi (772–846) in "The Song of Everlasting Sorrow," a long poem that became a classic favorite in Japan as well as China. In the poem, the emperor, grieving for his lost love after her tragic death, sends a Daoist wizard to search for her in the heavens; Genji imagines himself doing the same thing as he composes the chapter title poem. As New Year approaches, he thinks to himself that the coming year may be his last.

O seer who roams
the vastness of the heavens,
go and find for me
a soul I now seek in vain
even when I chance to dream.

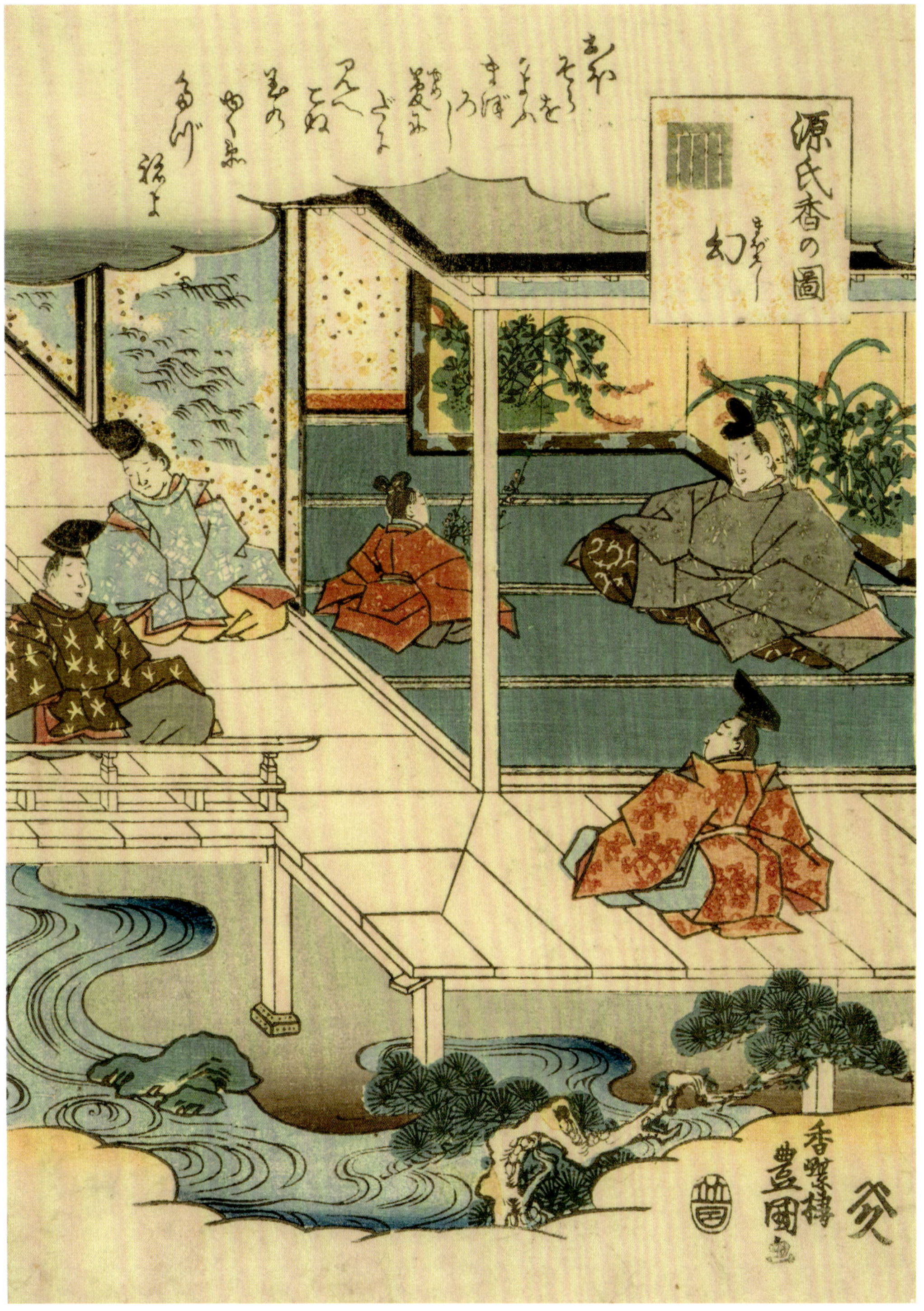

41A | Kunisada, *Genji Incense Pictures*, 1844–47

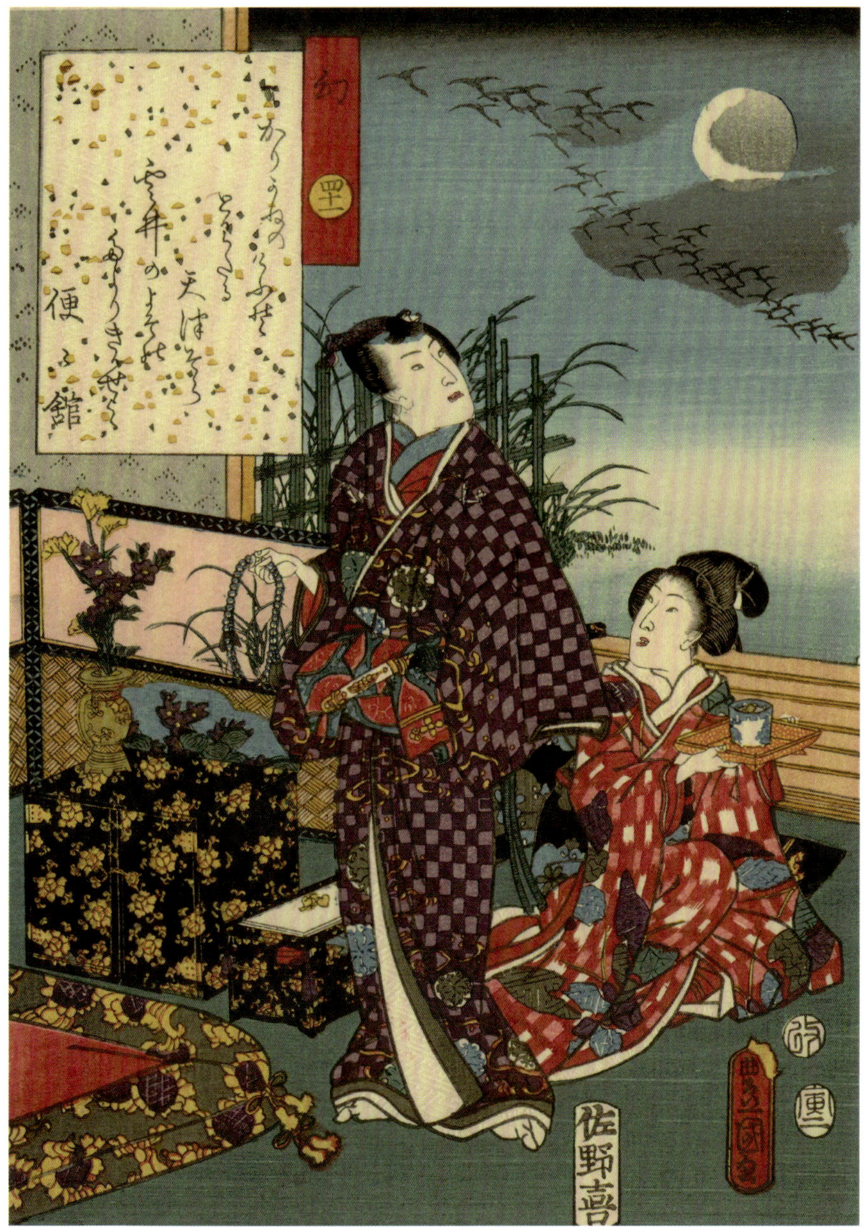

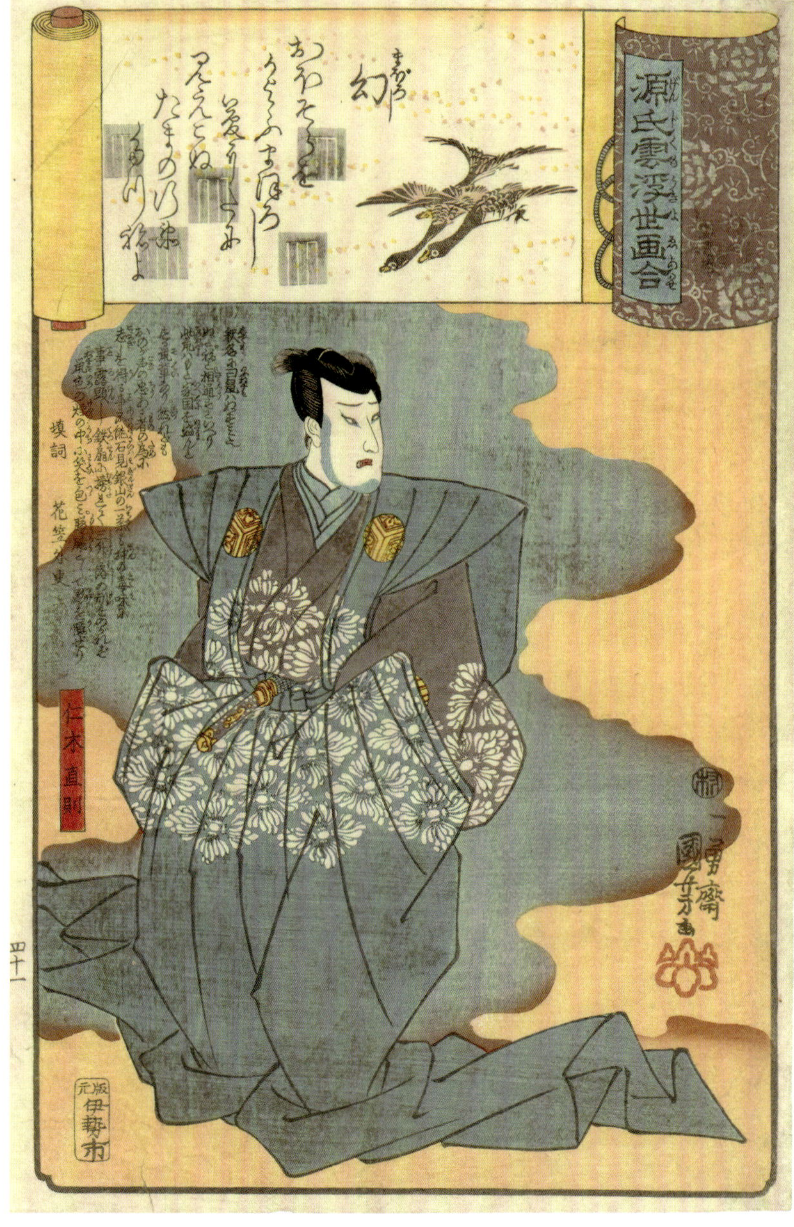

41B | Kunisada, *The Color Print Contest of a Modern Genji*, 1854

41C | Kuniyoshi, *Genji Clouds Matched with Ukiyo-e Pictures*, about 1845–46

While the *Genji Incense* series shows the earlier spring scene, the *Color Print Contest* design seems to be an *Inaka Genji* version of the scene in which the chapter title poem is composed, with the bereaved hero gazing sadly at the geese flying across the sky in autumn (41B). He holds a Buddhist rosary, and the female attendant beside him holds a tray with an incense burner.

Kuniyoshi, in the *Genji Clouds* series, depicted a literal wizard: the evil sorcerer Nikki Danjō Naonori, one of the most infamous villains of the kabuki stage, who can transform himself into a rat in order to spy on his enemies or steal small precious objects (41C). The handscroll depicted in the upper part of the print reproduces the chapter title poem, with a small illustration of flying geese.

42

The Perfumed Prince (Niou no miya)

Genji is now dead, and his children and grandchildren must carry on without him. Some later commentators speculated that there might be a missing chapter, giving this hypothetical chapter the title Hidden in the Clouds (Kumogakure); but the text believed to be the authentic original *Tale of Genji* simply moves from one chapter to the next with no description of Genji's last days. The two most important characters for the remainder of the book are Genji's grandson Niou, the little boy whose cheerful presence brightened Genji's final year, and his playmate Kaoru, the son of the Third Princess, who is believed to be Genji's child but is actually the product of the Princess's secret affair with the late Kashiwagi.

These two young men are now adults having their own romantic adventures. Both are extremely good-looking. Kaoru is blessed with natural pheromones that give him a rare, distinctive, very pleasant scent, while Niou contrives a similar effect through his mastery of incense and perfumes. Both of their nicknames, Kaoru and Niou, mean "fragrant."

What can it all mean,
and whom have I to question?
What is my secret,
when I myself do not know
whence I come or where I go?

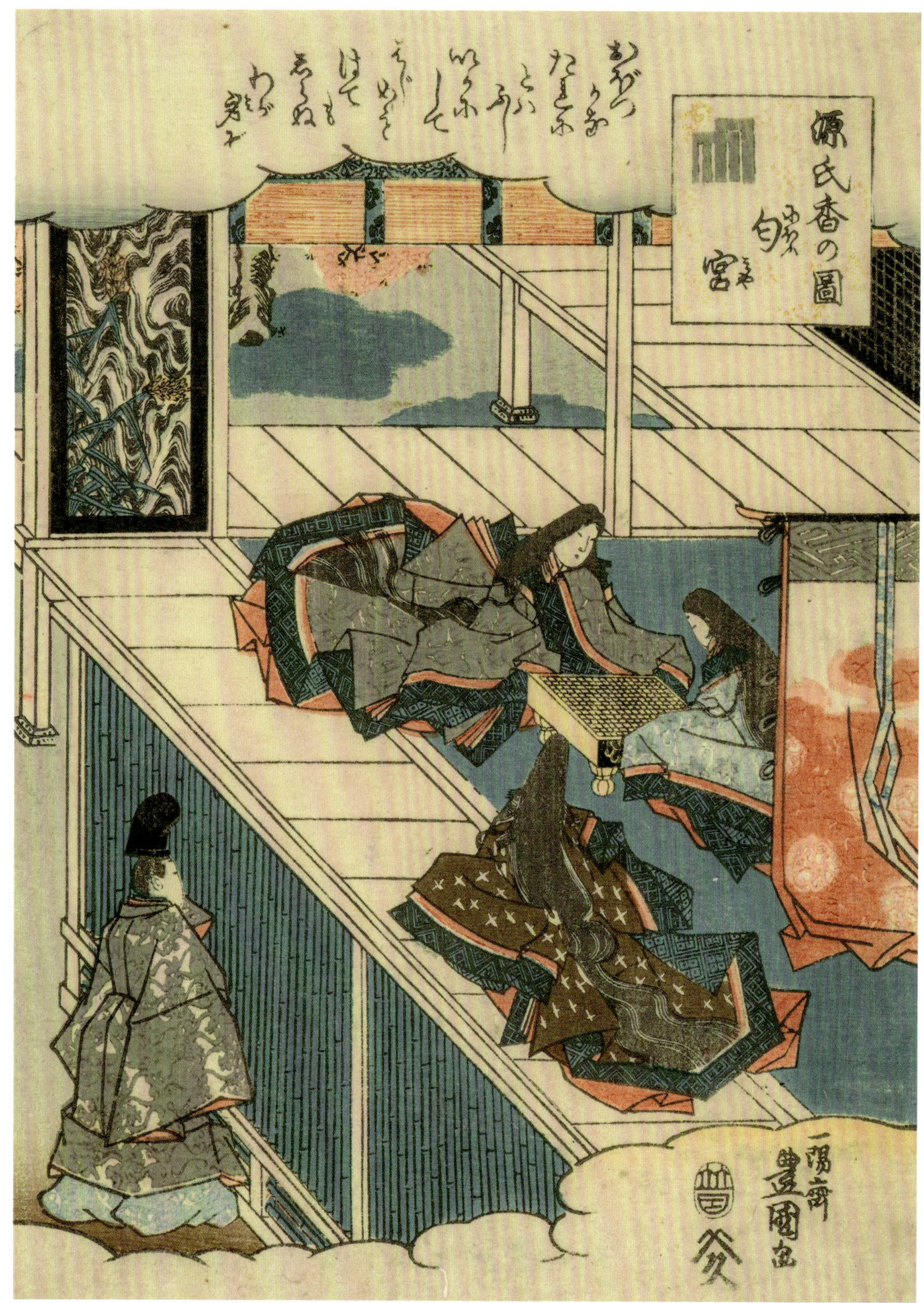

42A | Kunisada, *Genji Incense Pictures*, 1844–47

Although the chapter title is Niou's name, the only poem in the chapter is composed by Kaoru, who muses to himself about the mystery of his birth and his mother's surprising decision to become a nun. He has heard hints but does not yet know any details.

Most illustrations of this chapter show a party held by Yūgiri at Genji's old Rokujō mansion, which he has now inherited. Oddly, the illustration for the *Genji Incense* series shows a scene that does not occur in this chapter but rather in chapter 44: a young man secretly watching young women play a game of *go* (42A). The *Color Print Contest* series depicts a little boy with two female attendants at a cherry-blossom-viewing party, perhaps a reference to the privileged upbringing of the title character (42B).

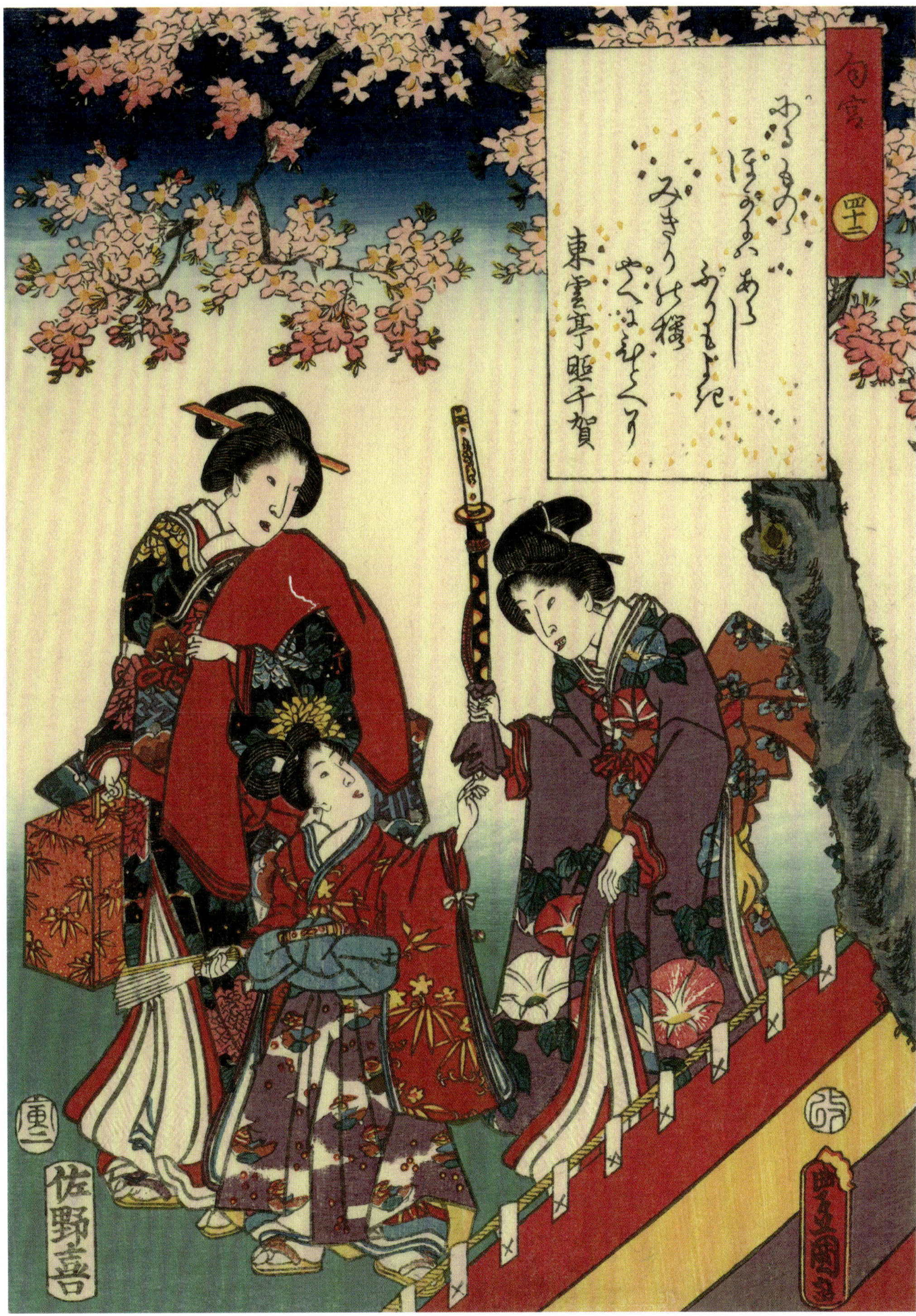

42B | Kunisada, *The Color Print Contest of a Modern Genji*, 1854

43

Red Plum (Kōbai)

The next two chapters of *The Tale of Genji*, Kōbai and Takekawa, are sometimes suspected of being interpolations by later writers because they are not closely connected to the ongoing plot developments of the *Tale*, but the majority of scholars believe that they are indeed by Murasaki Shikibu, who was simply trying to decide the direction in which she would now take her story.

Kōbai, who takes his name from this chapter, is the oldest surviving son of Tō no Chūjō and the head of the family now that his father and his older brother Kashiwagi are both dead. He is married to Makibashira (see chapter 31), the second marriage for both of them. Kōbai has two daughters by his first marriage and a son by Makibashira, but he also tries to be a good stepfather to Makibashira's daughter by her first marriage to Genji's cousin, the late Prince Hotaru (see chapter 25). Niou would be an ideal husband for any one of Kōbai's three girls, and so Kōbai has his young son deliver a branch of flowering plum to Niou, accompanied by the chapter title poem inviting him to visit their house.

When invitingly
the plum tree in my garden
perfumes every breeze,
O warbler, will you not come
to sport among those blossoms?

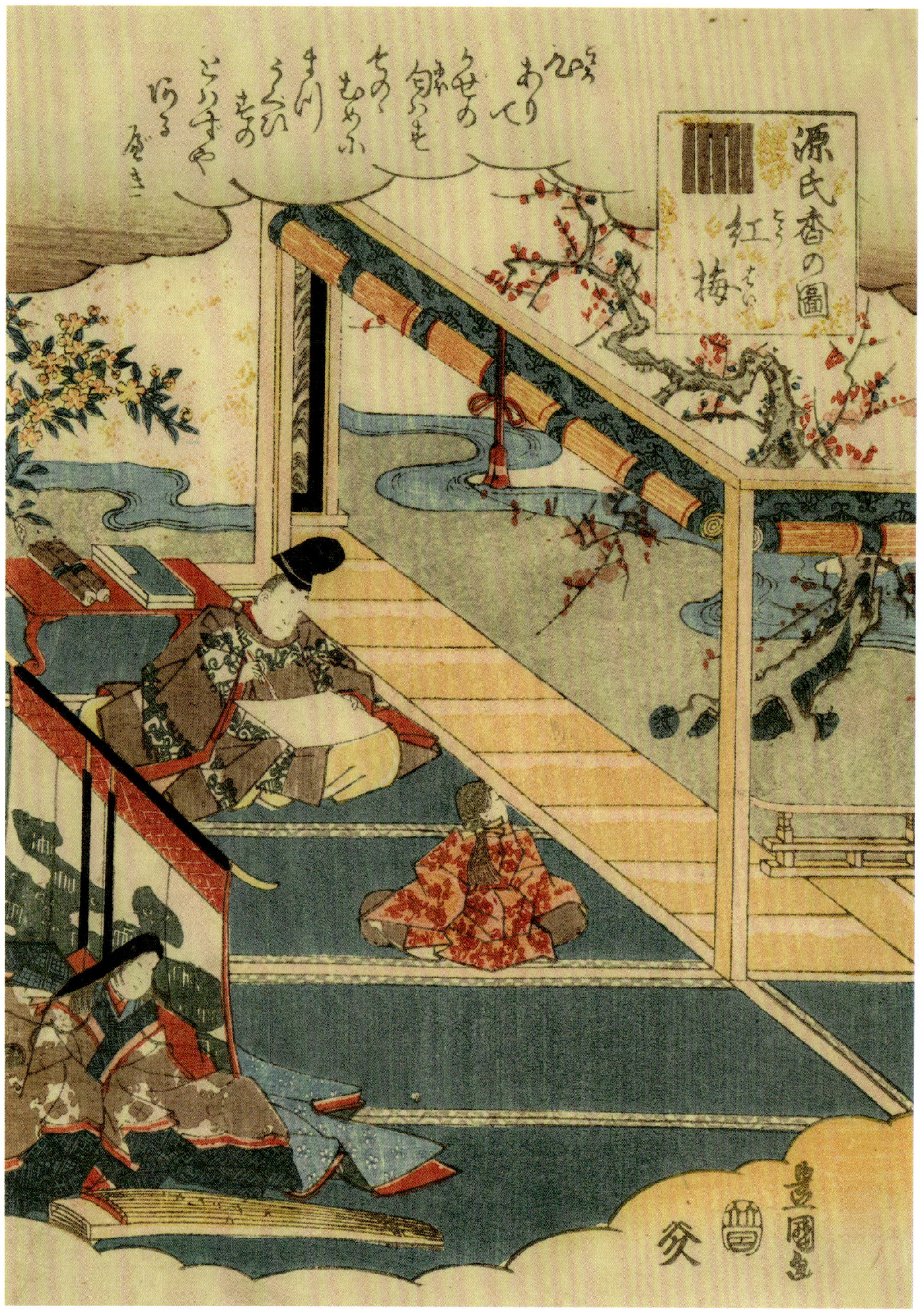

43A | Kunisada, *Genji Incense Pictures*, 1844–47

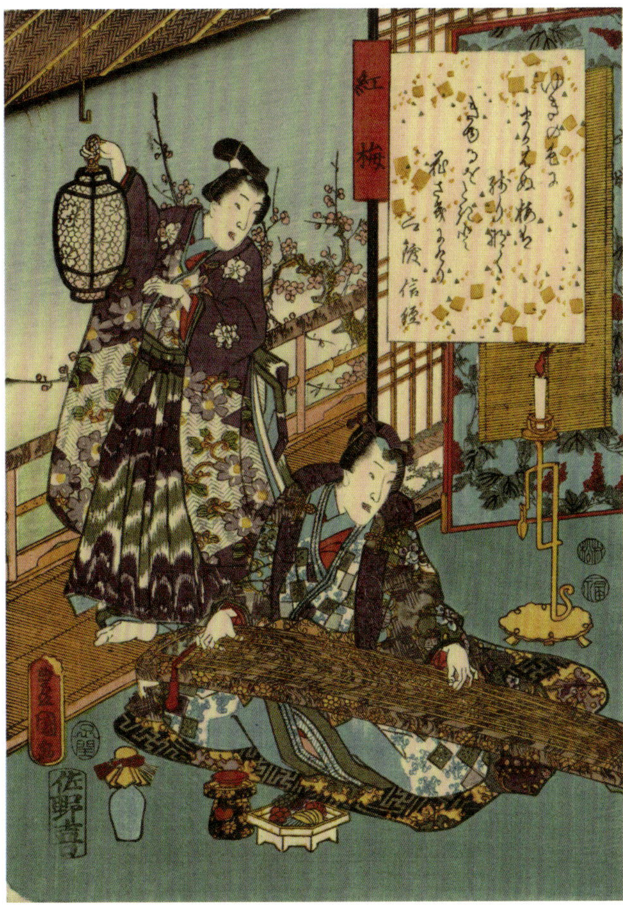

43B | Kunisada, *The Color Print Contest of a Modern Genji*, 1852

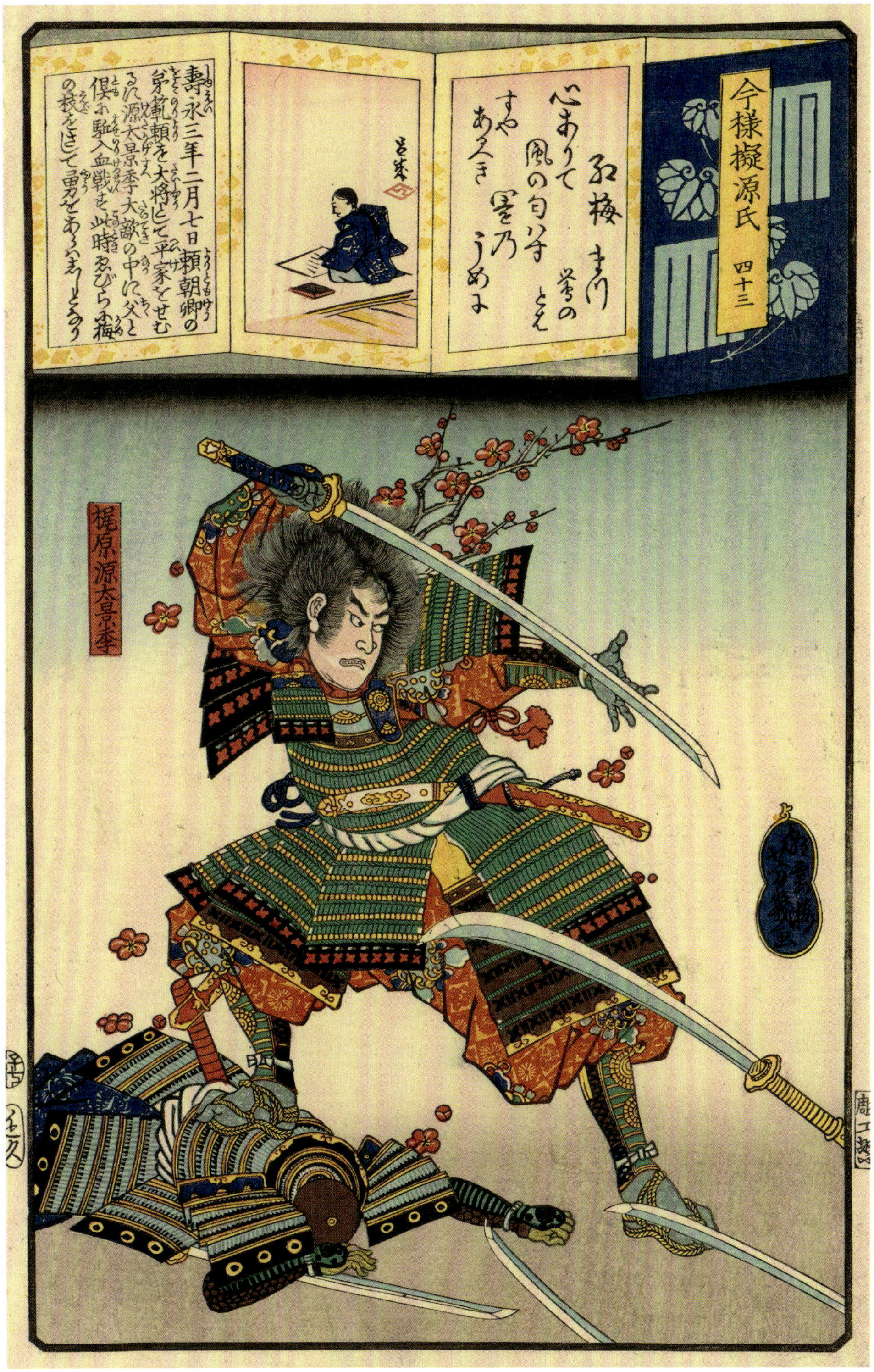

43C | Yoshiiku and Gengyo, *Modern Parodies of Genji*, 1864

The *Genji Incense* illustration of Kōbai writing the poem for his son to deliver is closely based on an illustration by Yamamoto Shunshō in the 1650 printed book *The Illustrated Tale of Genji* (*Eiri Genji monogatari*) (43A). A father-son motif is also suggested by the illustration in the *Color Print Contest* series, with an older man preparing to play the koto while an adolescent boy holds up a lantern (43B).

For his series of matching pictures, Yoshiiku compared the rose plum of the title to the emblem of the twelfth-century warrior Kajiwara Genta Kagesue, who once went into battle with a flowering plum branch tucked into his quiver, an incident so famous that it was dramatized in both nō and kabuki (43C).

44

Bamboo River (Takekawa)

This chapter shifts the focus from Niou to Kaoru as it follows the fortunes of the five children of Tamakazura after the death of their father, Higekuro. The chapter title refers to a song entitled “Bamboo River” that is sung at an impromptu New Year party hosted by Tamakazura when various guests, including Kaoru and a son of Yūgiri, pay holiday calls. The poem containing the title is written the next day by Kaoru to his friend, one of Tamakazura’s sons, who is expected to show it to his sisters as well. Kaoru is especially interested in the oldest sister, but in the end she marries the retired Reizei emperor (Genji’s secret son).

The most frequently illustrated scene in the chapter takes place in the spring, when Yūgiri’s son peeps at Tamakazura’s daughters as they enjoy a game of *go*. This may be the scene that Kunisada mistakenly used for the *Genji Incense* illustration of chapter 42, since no such scene occurs in that chapter.

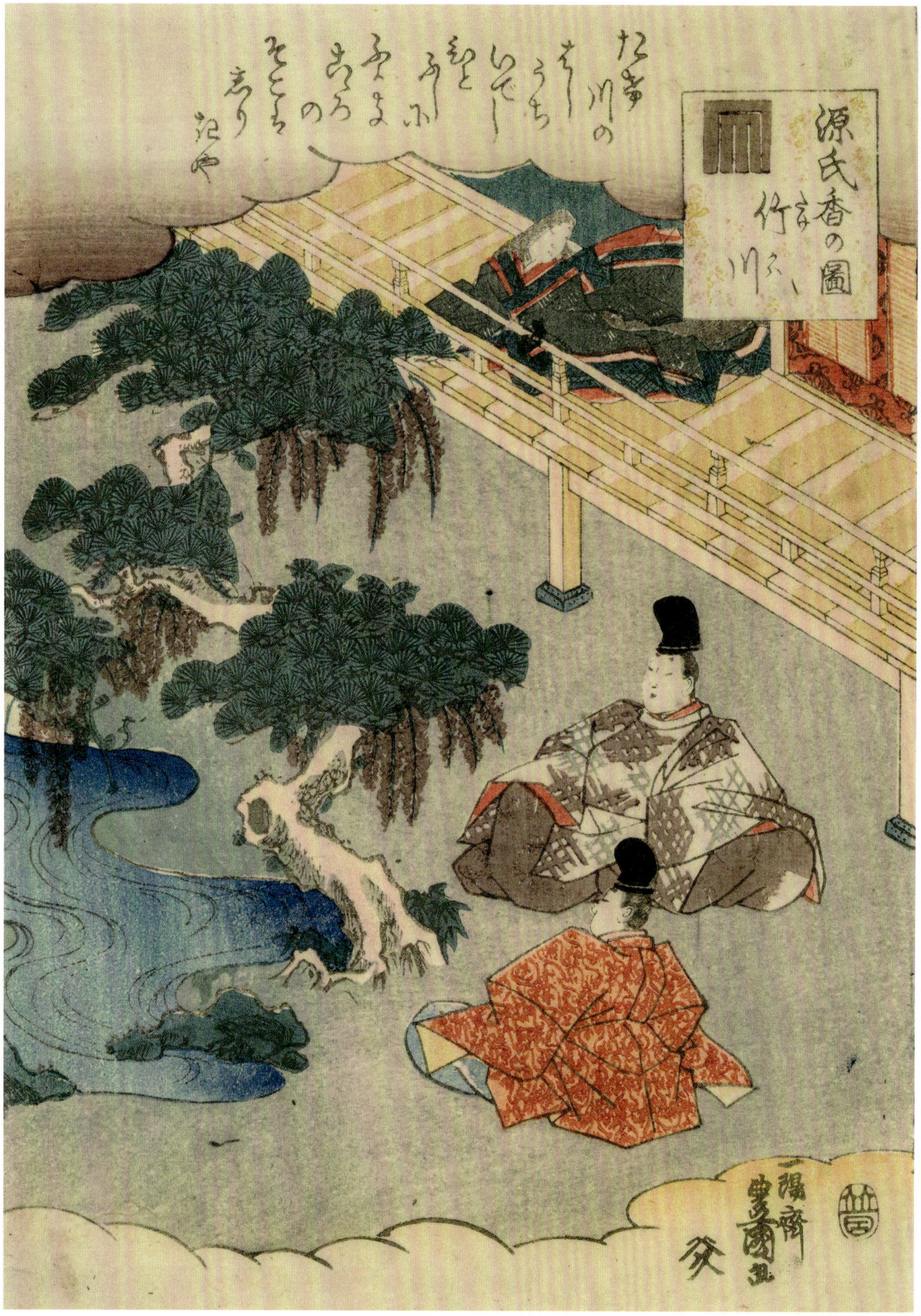

The measure of song
I made bold to give you all
on Bamboo River,
did you gather from its depths
the true bottom of my heart?

44A | Kunisada, *Genji Incense Pictures*, 1844–47

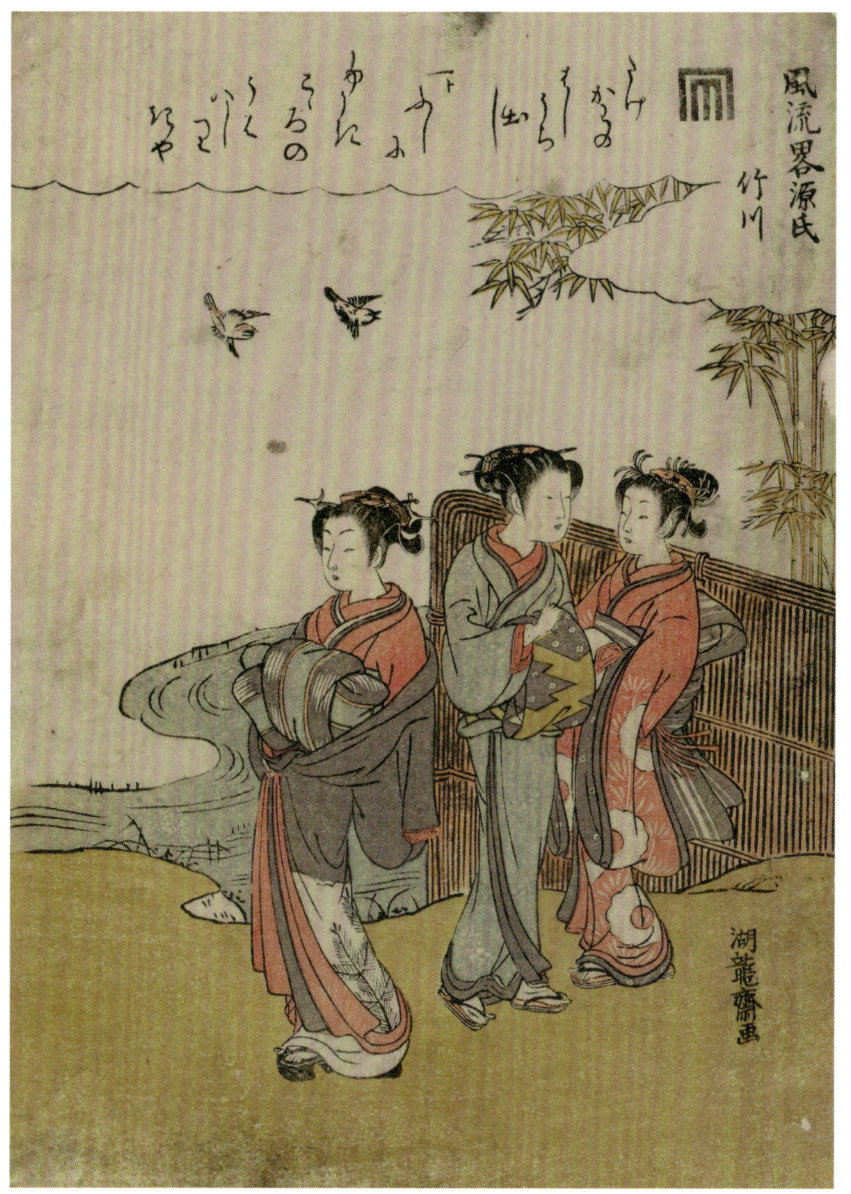

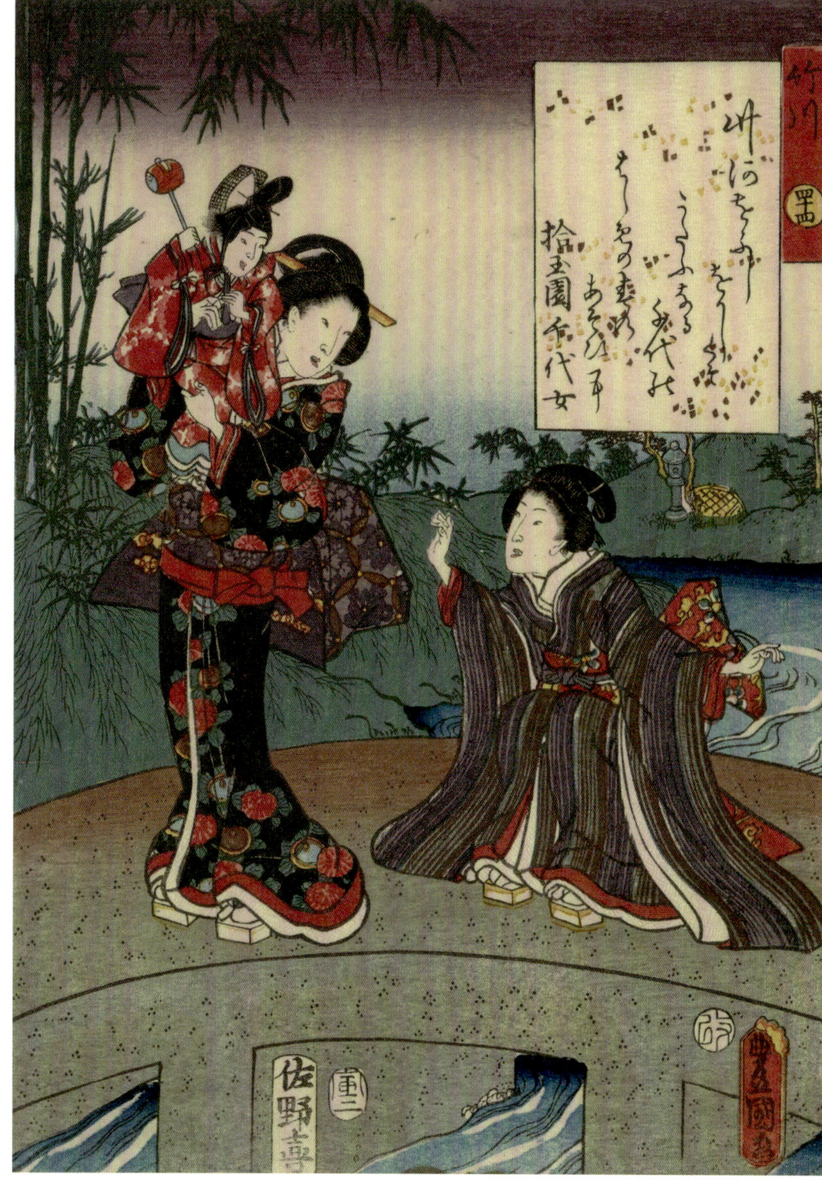

44B | Isoda Koryūsai, *Genji in Fashionable Modern Guise*, about 1770–72

44C | Kunisada, *The Color Print Contest of a Modern Genji*, 1854

Instead, the *Genji Incense* illustration for this chapter shows a somewhat later scene when Kaoru walks in the garden of the Reizei Palace with Tamakazura's son (44A). The two young men pause in front of the new lady's quarters to admire the wisteria growing on a pine tree there, and Kaoru composes a wistful poem noting the beauty of the flowers and the fact that they now hang too high for him. The picture is almost a mirror image of the 1650 book illustration of this scene, but with the addition of a lady-in-waiting on the veranda.

Koryūsai, in his updated parody series, simply used "bamboo river" as a theme and showed young women walking by a stream with bamboo growing beside it (44B). Kunisada himself took a similar approach for the *Color Print Contest* series, showing two women and an elaborately dressed baby boy on a garden bridge with bamboo growing nearby (44C).

45

The Lady of the Bridge (Hashihime)

The final ten chapters of *The Tale of Genji* can be read as an independent novel within the larger book. They are known as the Uji chapters because much of the plot centers on the town of Uji, not far from Kyoto, where many of the nobility had summer villas by the swift-flowing Uji River. Among the residents of Uji are the reclusive Eighth Prince, a half-brother of Genji, and his two beautiful young daughters, known as Agemaki (or Oigimi) and Kozeri (or Nakanokimi). Kaoru becomes a friend of the Eighth Prince and joins him in religious studies.

After several years of visits to Uji, one autumn night under a full moon he finally catches sight of the two daughters as they play their favorite instruments, the biwa and koto. This is the scene most often chosen by artists to illustrate the Hashihime chapter, but in the *Genji Incense* series Kunisada used it instead for the following chapter, Shiigamoto. He did use a parodic *Inaka Genji* version of it for the *Color Print Contest* series (45C).

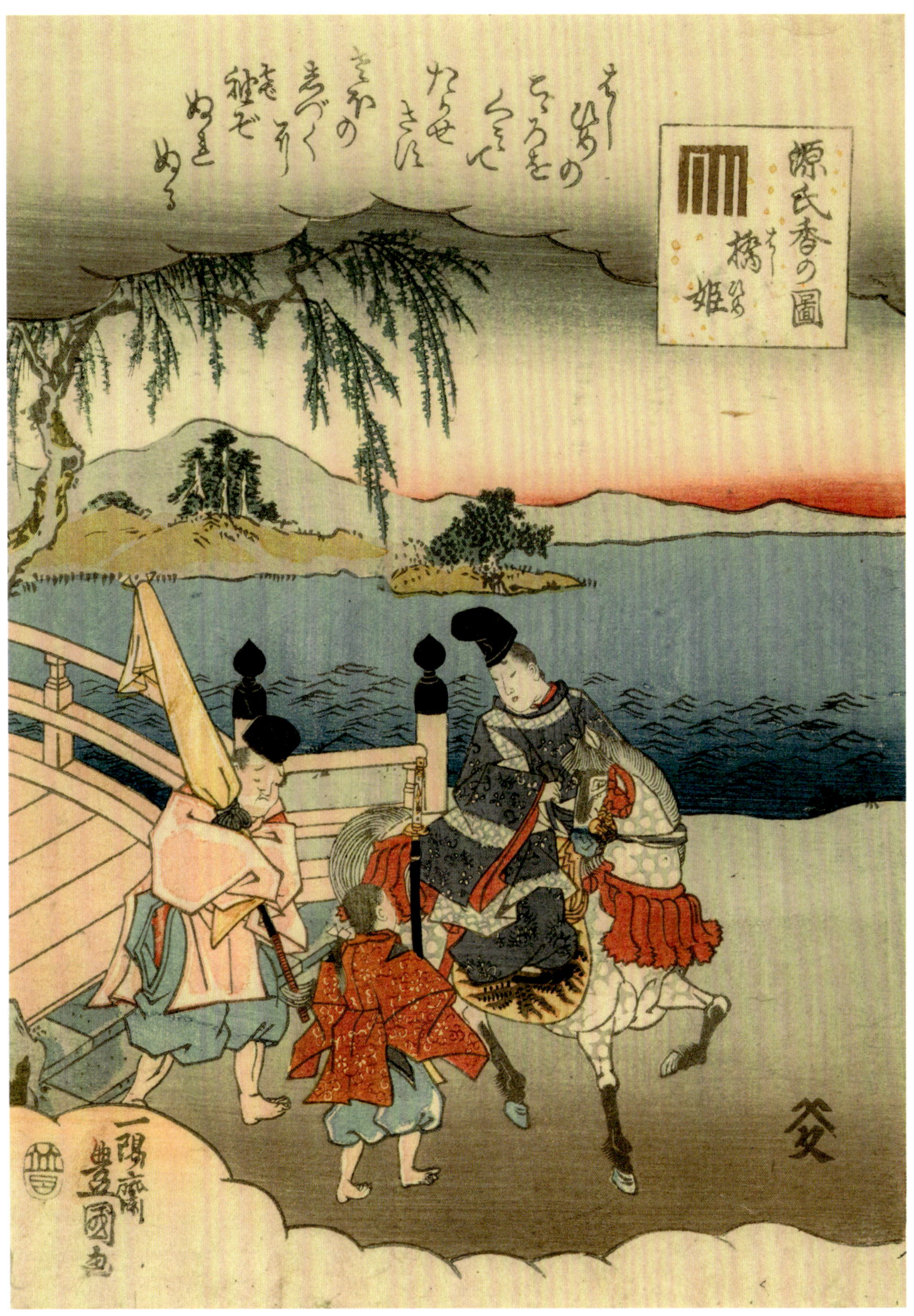

45A | Kunisada, *Genji Incense Pictures*, 1844–47

What drops wet these sleeves,
when the river boatman's oar,
skimming the shallows,
sounds out the most secret heart
of the Maiden of the Bridge.

45B | Yoshiiku, *Modern Parodies of Genji*, 1864

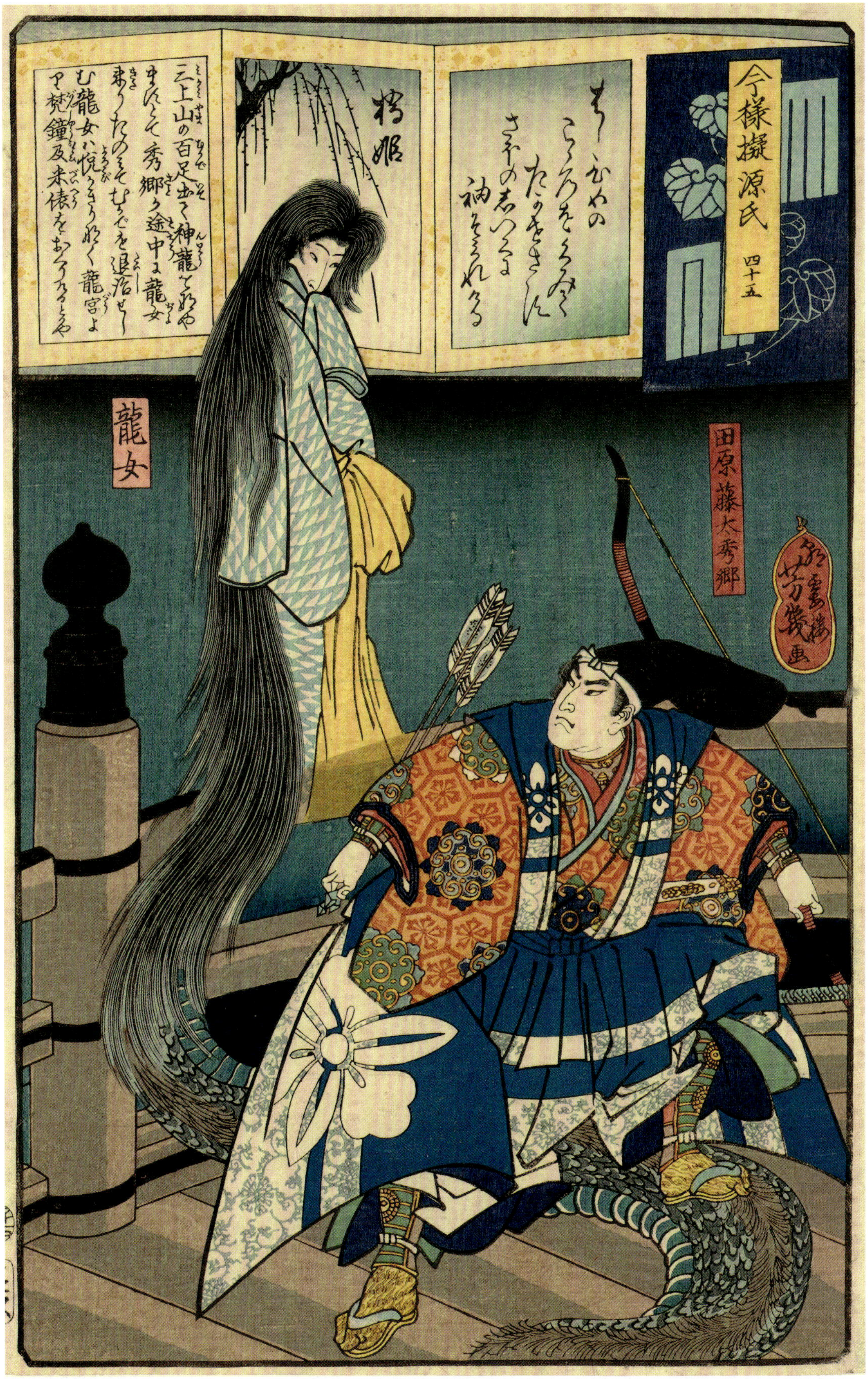

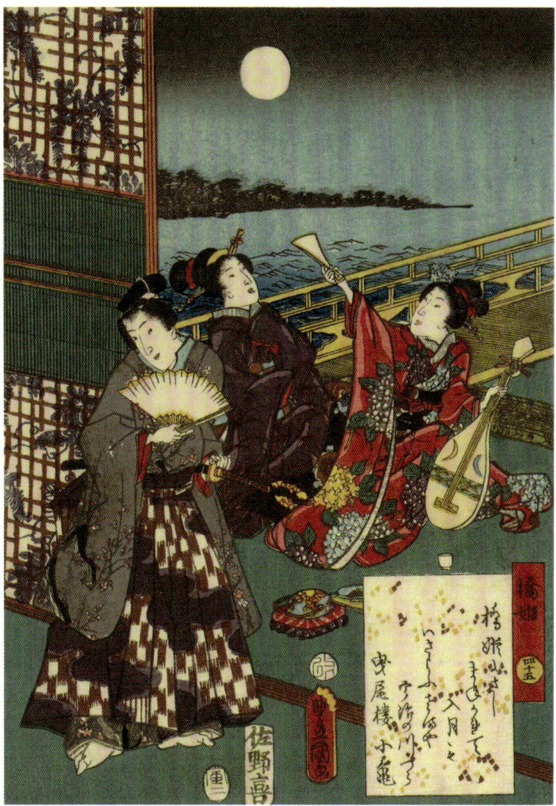

45C | Kunisada, *The Color Print Contest of a Modern Genji*, 1854

The chapter title poem, composed by Kaoru as he prepares to return to the capital, refers to the famous bridge at Uji and its spirit, the Lady of the Bridge, a goddess in some tales and a demon in others. The print from the *Genji Incense* series shows Kaoru beside the bridge, on his horse and accompanied by two attendants (45A). Yoshiiku, in his parody series, shows a hero actually meeting a ghostly woman on a bridge (45B). In Japanese folklore, bridges — because of their liminal status, neither in one place nor another — often serve as points of contact with the supernatural world. This is the legendary encounter between the tenth-century warrior Tawara Tōda and the Dragon Princess who came to ask for his help in defeating a giant centipede.

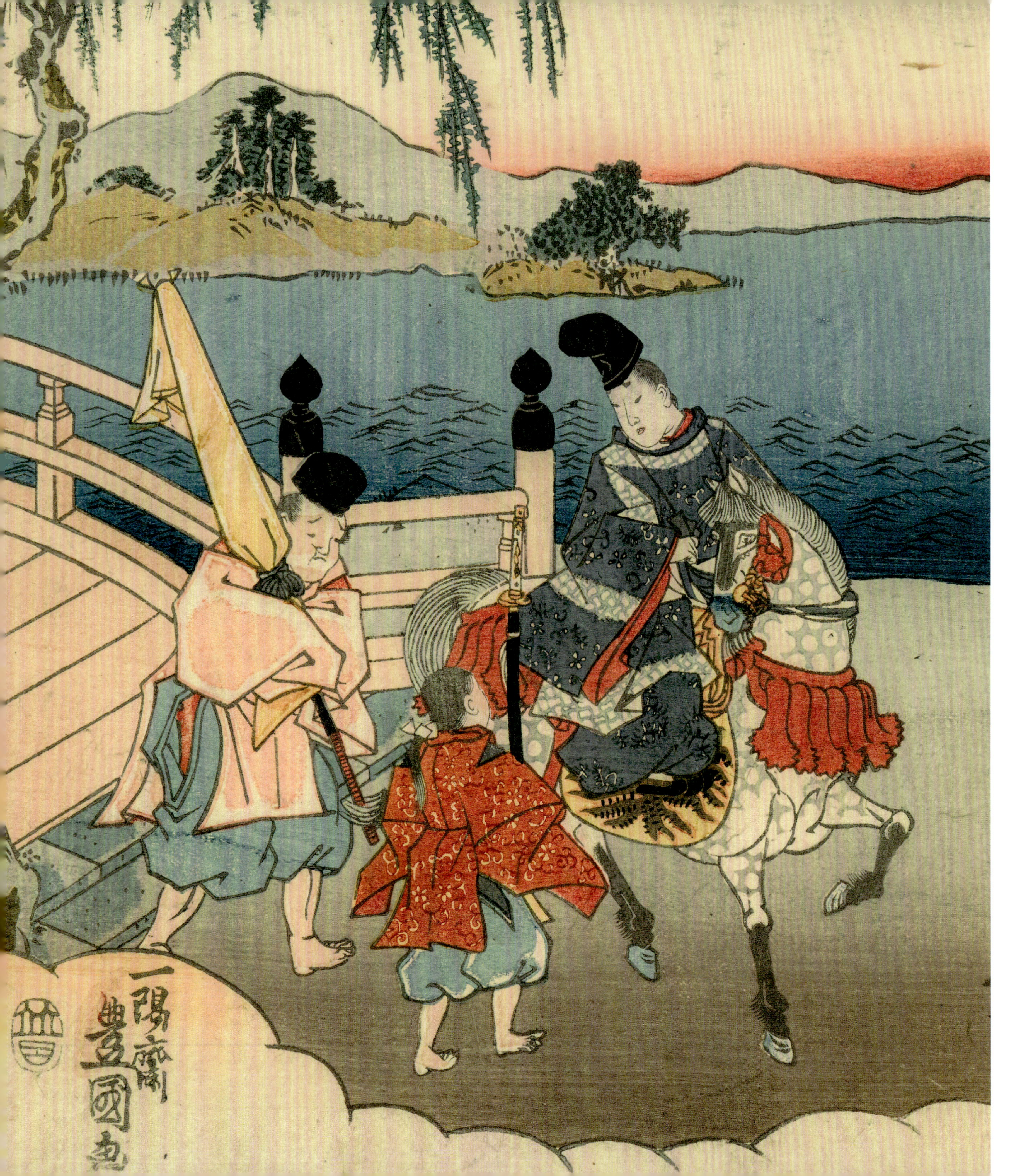
一陽齋豊國画

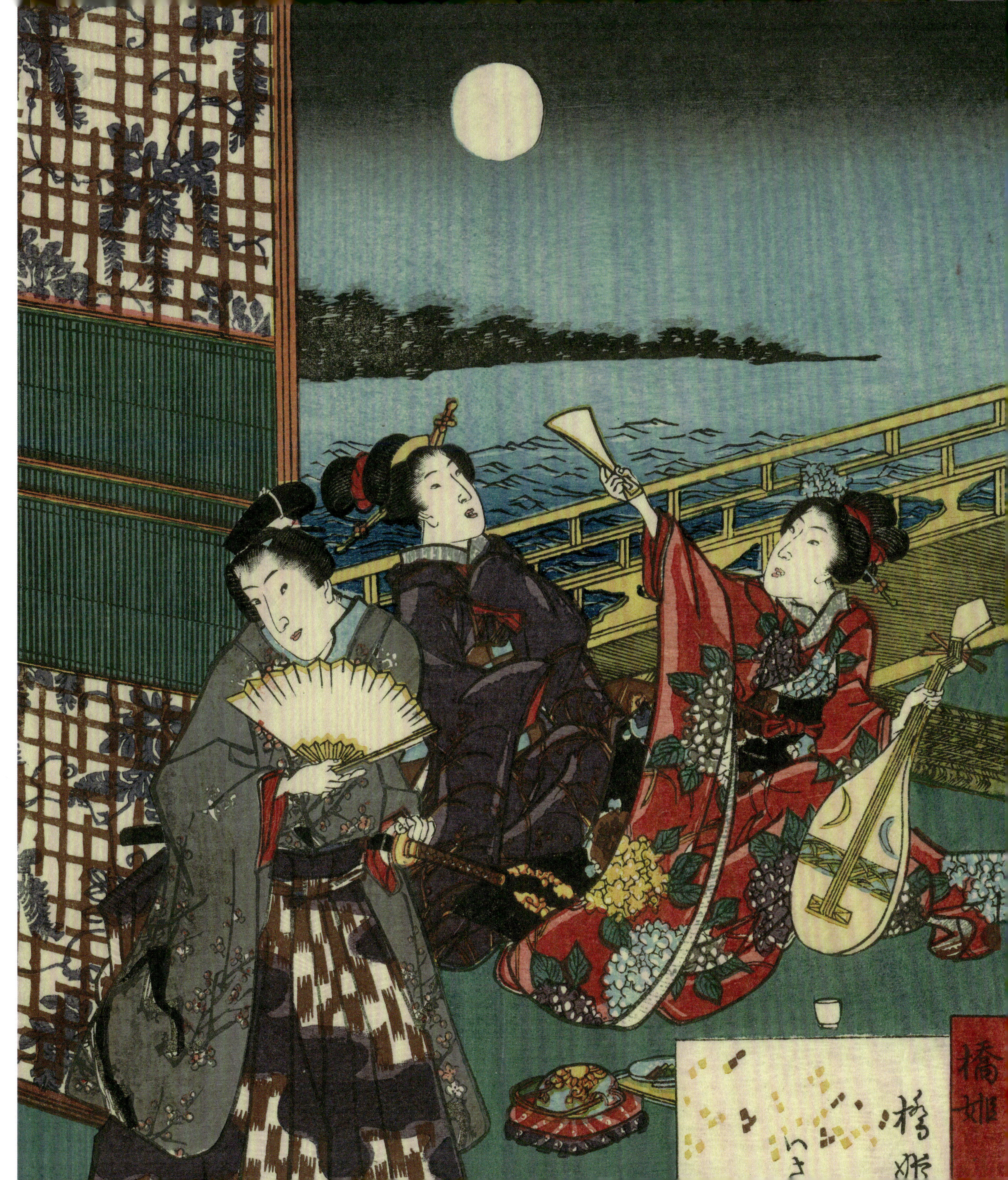
橋姫

46

Beneath the Oak (Shiigamoto)

Kaoru rashly tells his friend Prince Niou about the Uji sisters, and Niou also begins to cultivate their acquaintance, though without immediate results. Then the Eighth Prince goes on a religious retreat during which he falls ill and suddenly dies, leaving his daughters bereft. Kaoru mourns his friend and fellow student of religion and writes the chapter title poem as an expression of his grief.

At the end of the chapter, Kaoru visits Uji and at last catches a glimpse of the sisters in full daylight, confirming his feeling that although both girls are beautiful, it is the older one that he prefers. Kunisada may have had this incident in mind when he chose to illustrate the chapter with a scene of Kaoru peeping at the sisters (46A). However, the musical instruments make it clear that this is actually the famous scene from the previous chapter. As in the case of the depiction of the cat incident, a scene that occurs near the end of one chapter has been assigned to the next chapter instead; it is not clear whether Kunisada did this accidentally or deliberately.

The oak tree I sought
to give me happy refuge
under spreading shade
is no more, and where he lived
emptiness and silence reign.

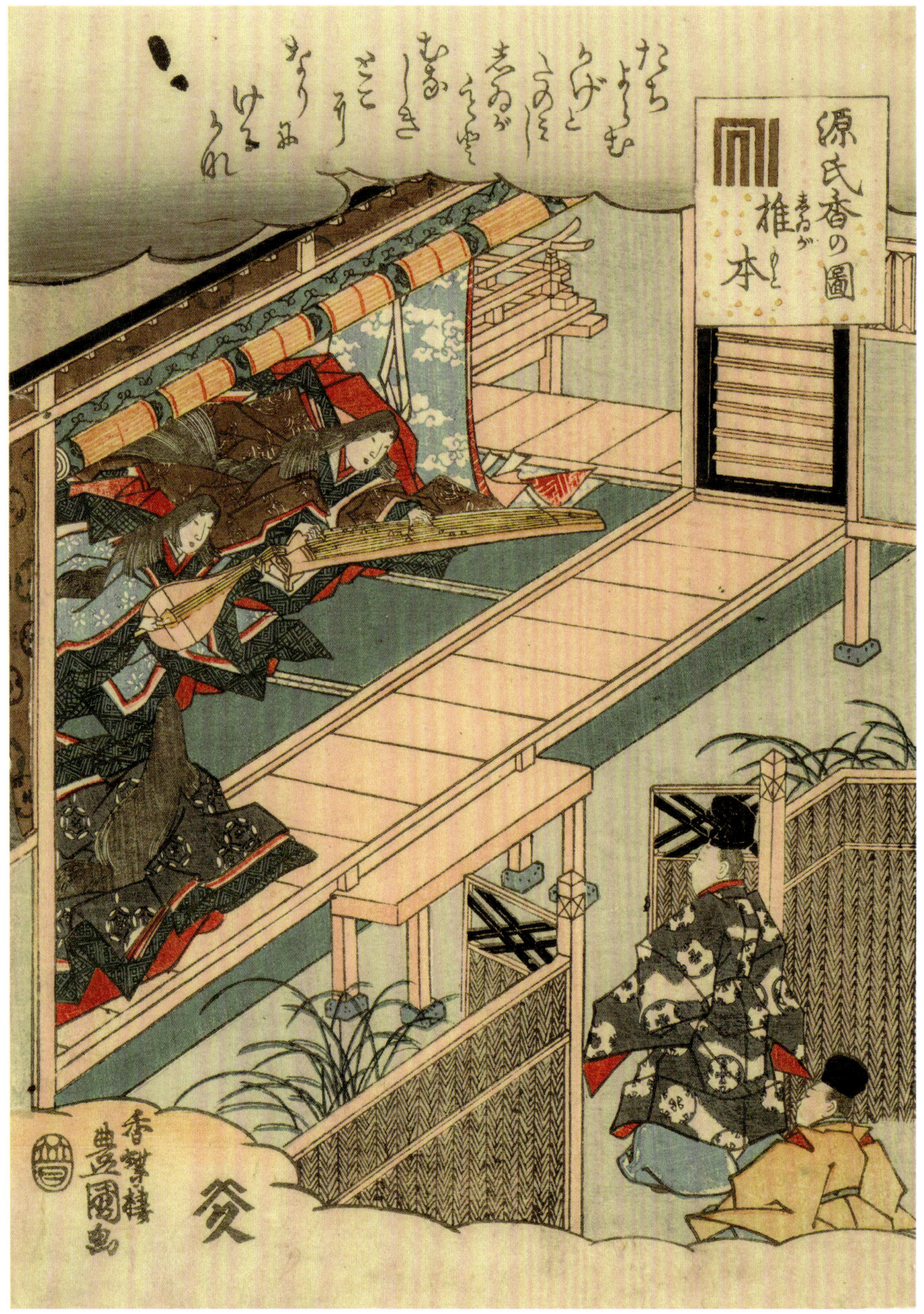

46A | Kunisada, *Genji Incense Pictures*, 1844–47

Kunisada's choice of illustration for this chapter in the *Color Print Contest* series is also puzzling, since it does not seem to refer to anything in chapter 2 of *Pale Purple Dawn*, even though that chapter is explicitly linked to Shiigamoto by the drawing of a Genji poem card in the frontispiece of the second volume. The print shows a spring scene, with cherry blossoms in full bloom (46B). A man of high rank walks along a bridge-like open corridor, accompanied by two women who carry flowering branches. He may represent the shogun Ashikaga Yoshizumi, the father of Niou's parody counterpart Ashikaga Hyōbunojō Ujisato.

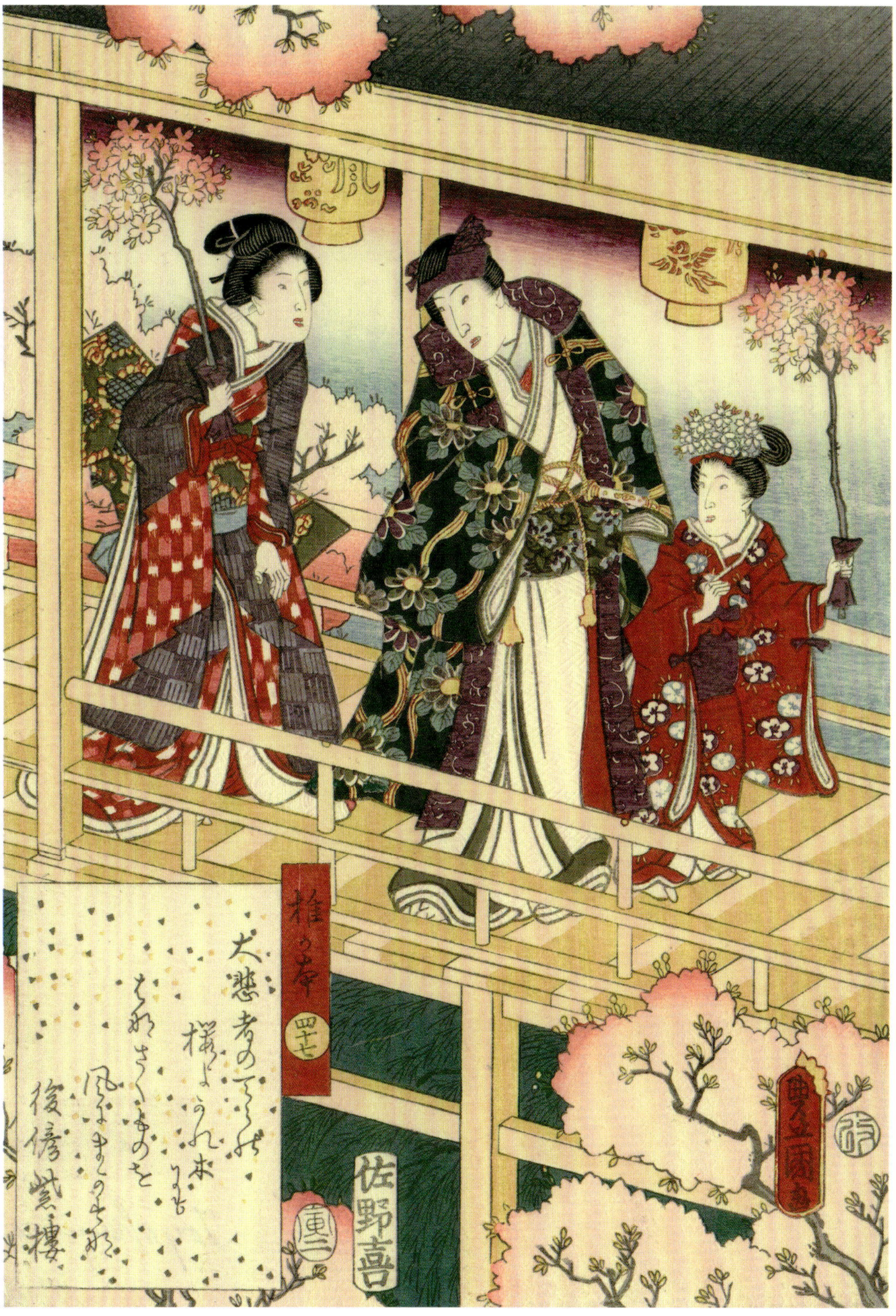

46B | Kunisada, *The Color Print Contest of a Modern Genji*, 1854

47

Trefoil Knots (Agemaki)

The title of this chapter is often used as a nickname for the older of the two daughters of the late Eighth Prince. The word agemaki refers to cords tied into a pattern of three loops, to be used as decorations for gifts such as the containers of incense that will be offered at the memorial service on the one-year anniversary of the Eighth Prince's death. Kaoru visits the sisters as they prepare for the event and composes the poem to express his steadfast love for Agemaki, who continues to refuse him because she wants him to marry her younger sister Kozeri (or Nakanokimi). In the end it is not Kaoru but Niou who marries Kozeri, with Kaoru's encouragement; but unfortunately for both sisters, Niou proves to be an unreliable husband.

The scene most often illustrated for this chapter, also chosen by Kunisada for the *Genji Incense* series, shows a gala autumn boating party arranged by Niou while he is staying at Yūgiri's villa across the river from the Eighth Prince's home. Watching through their blinds, the two sisters enjoy the music and admire the boats beautifully decorated with red leaves; the design in the *Genji Incense* series presents the event from their viewpoint (47A). Alas, Niou returns to the capital after the party without visiting Kozeri; and his imperial parents,

In these trefoil knots
may you secure forever
our eternal bond,
that our threads may always merge
in that one place where they meet.

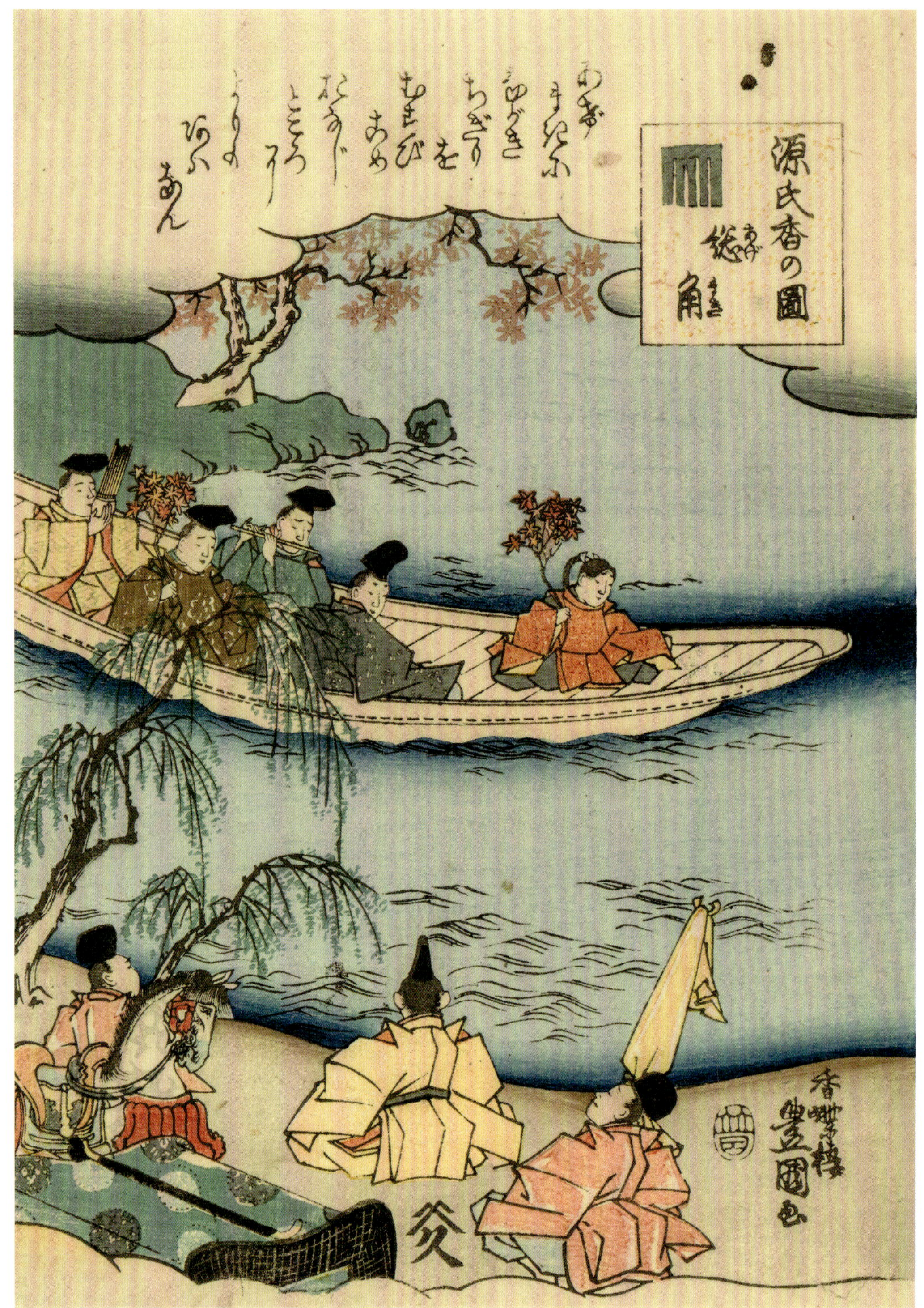

47A | Kunisada, *Genji Incense Pictures*, 1844–47

47B | Kunisada, *The Color Print Contest of a Modern Genji*, 1854

47C | Kunisada II and Hiroshige II, *Traces of Genji in Fifty-Four Chapters*, 1865

who disapprove of the Uji liaison, pressure him to take Yūgiri's sixth daughter as his primary wife. Agemaki, who feels responsible for her sister's welfare, is so distressed by Niou's neglectful behavior that she stops eating, becoming weaker and weaker. Kaoru learns of her condition and comes to her side, but it is too late.

For the *Color Print Contest* series, Kunisada seems to have ignored the parody plot and created a suitable illustration — a man and woman with reels of fine cord for making the decorative knots of the title — using elements from earlier parts of the story (47B). For example, the woman's short ponytail shows that she is a Buddhist nun, possibly Mitsuyo/Mitsuai (= the Third Princess). Similar to the handscrolls in Kuniyoshi's *Genji Clouds* series and the folding booklets in Yoshiiku's series of paired images, *Traces of Genji* by Kunisada II and Hiroshige II incorporates the chapter title poems from the original *Tale* depicted as fan-shaped paintings in the upper part of each sheet. Here, the poem is accompanied by a small illustration of the kind that might be seen on playing cards for the Genji poem game (see chapter 20, for example), showing one of the trefoil knots and reels of the colored cord used to make them (47C). In the main image, the decorative knots are used on the sleeves of a beautiful young lady from the world of *Inaka Genji*. An attendant offers her a bouquet, perhaps a gift from an admirer.

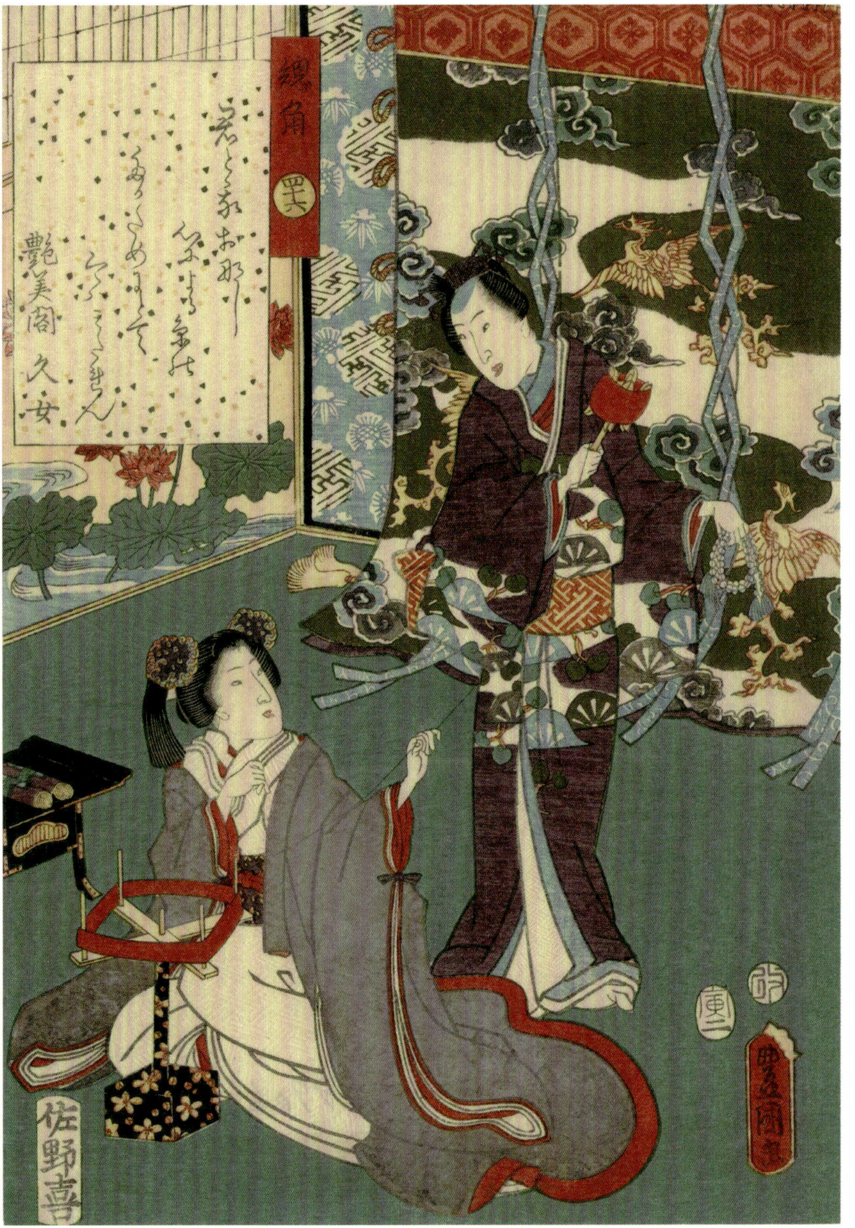

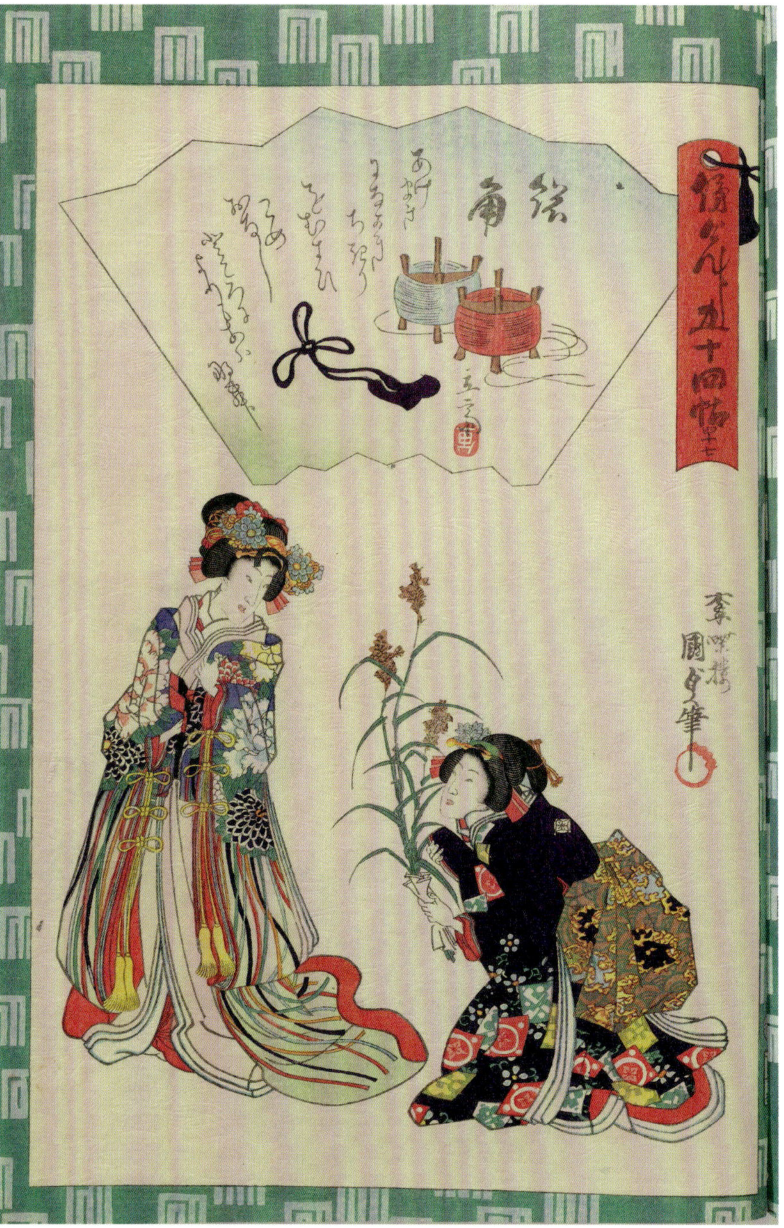

48

Fern Shoots (Sawarabi)

Kozeri, the second daughter and the last survivor of her family in the house at Uji, receives a gift of edible fern shoots (fiddleheads) from the abbot who was her late father's spiritual advisor; she is moved by his kindness and responds with the chapter title poem. Most illustrations of this chapter feature the tender greens in their basket, but for the *Genji Incense* series Kunisada chose a somewhat later scene, in which the ladies appear to be packing up their clothing and other possessions in preparation for the move to the city, where Niou will install Kozeri and her attendants in one of his own houses (48A). The Uji house will become a Buddhist temple. Kaoru visits Kozeri to help with the move and they reminisce sadly about old times.

As I am this spring,
who will enjoy them with me,
now that he is gone:
these bracken shoots from the hills,
picked in memory of him?

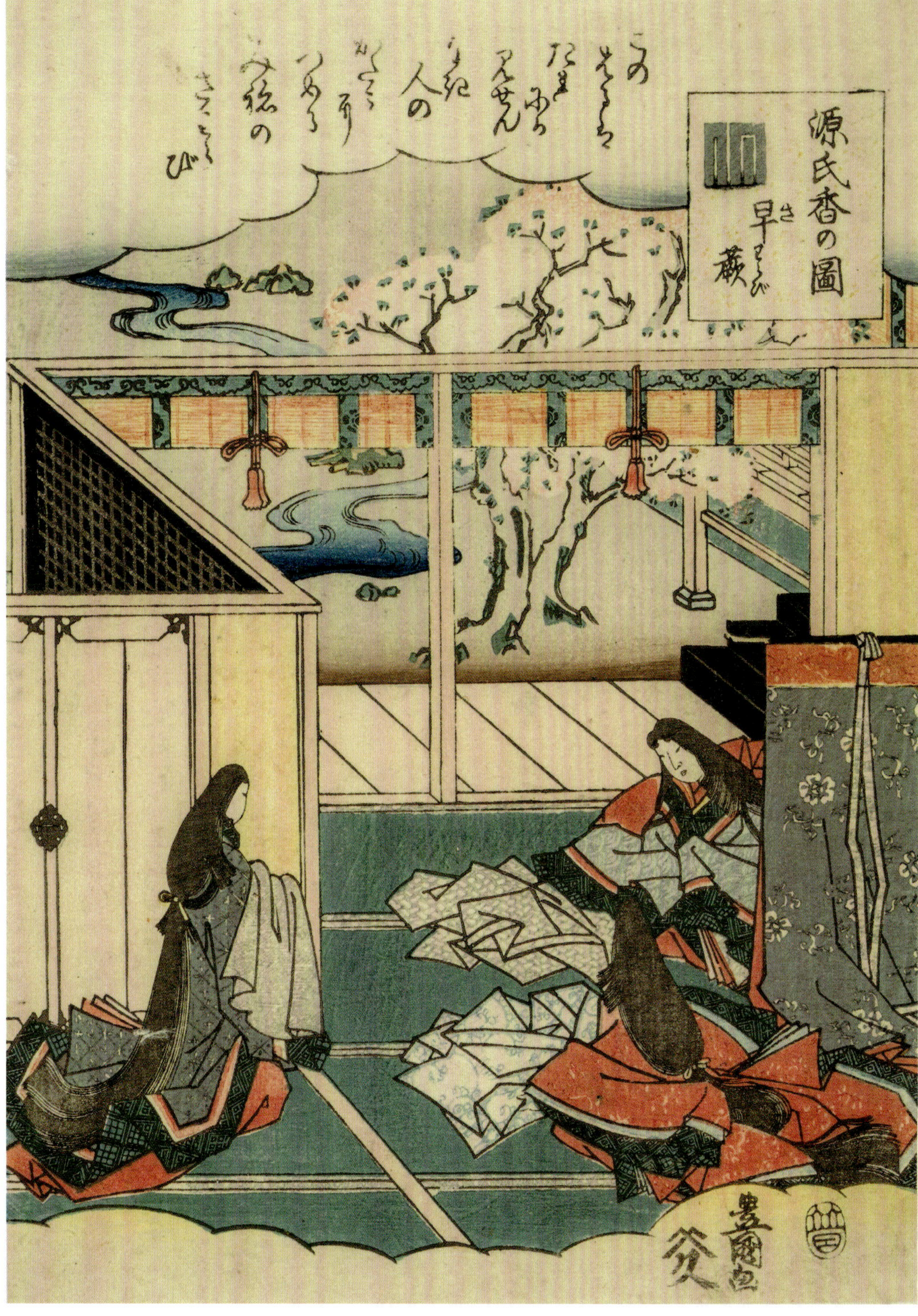

48A | Kunisada, *Genji Incense Pictures*, 1844–47

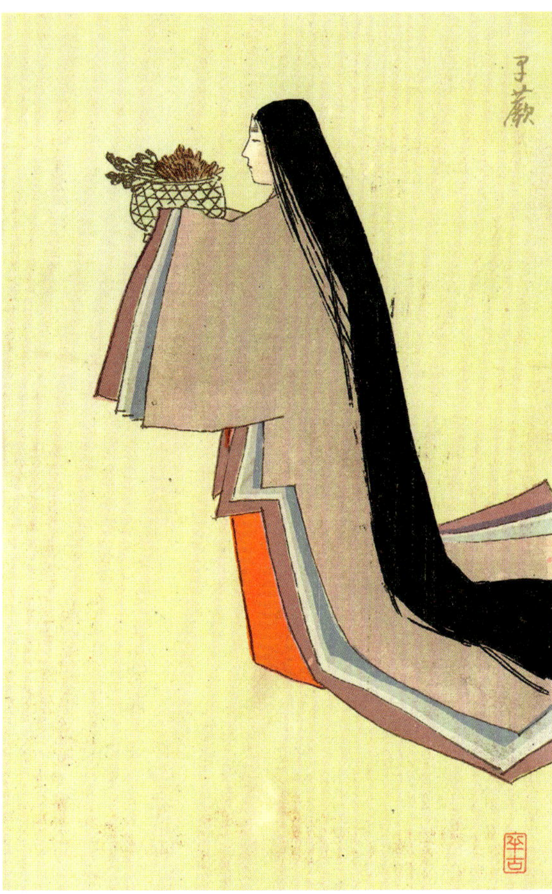

48B | Kajita Hanko, *The Tale of Genji*, 1905

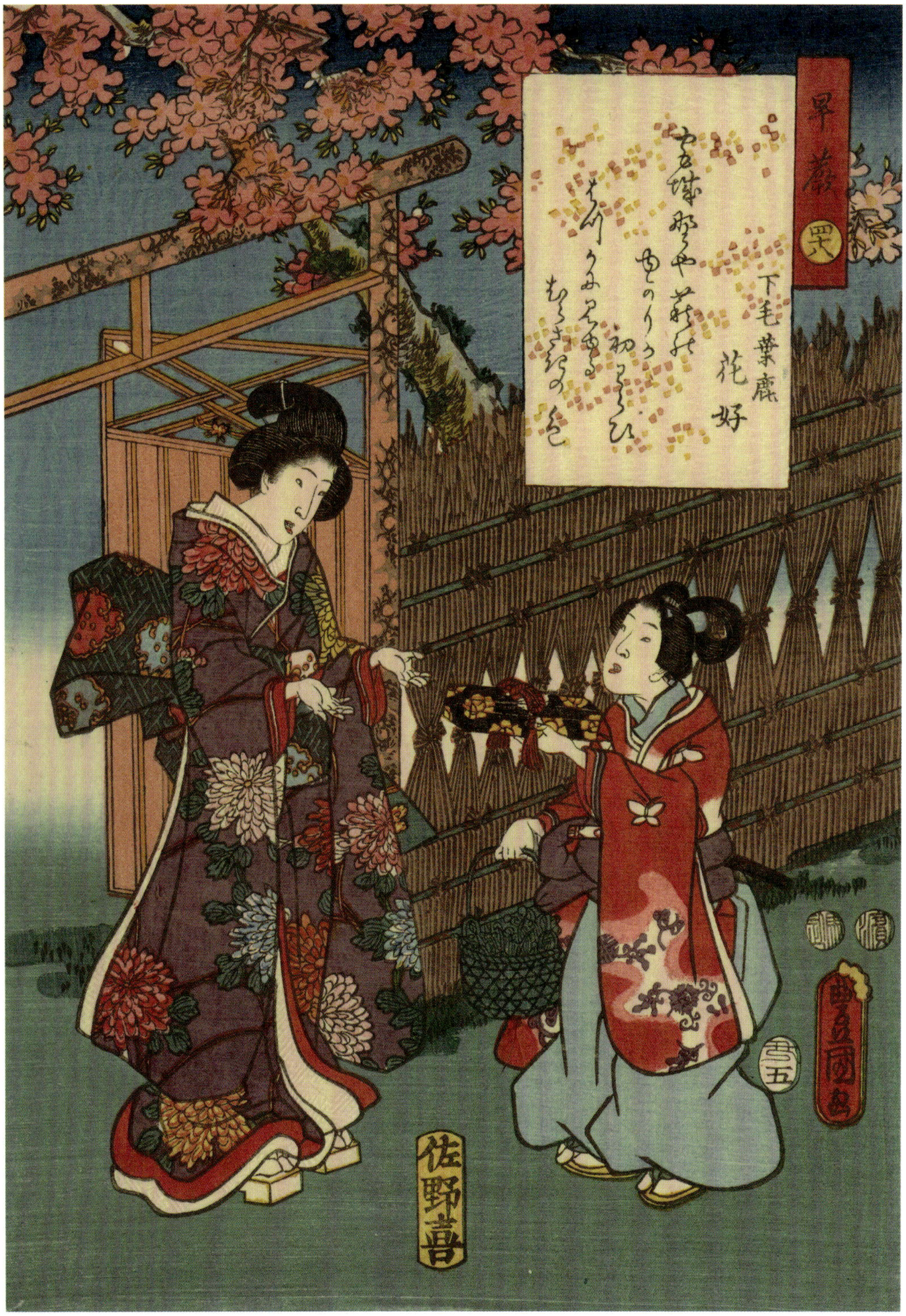

A lady-in-waiting, dressed in Heian courtly robes and carrying the basket of fern shoots, is featured in Kajita Hanko's design for an early twentieth-century postcard from his Genji series representing this chapter (48B). In the *Color Print Contest* series, Kunisada created an appropriate image in the *Inaka Genji* style, showing a temple pageboy delivering the basket of fern shoots together with a lacquered letter box containing the abbot's message and poem, to which the chapter title poem is a reply (48C). The very last part of the original *Tale of Genji*, from this chapter on, is not covered by any of the parody novels, and so illustrations of these final chapters must be either newly invented or recycled from earlier parts of the various *Inaka Genji* books.

48C | Kunisada, *The Color Print Contest of a Modern Genji*, 1853

49

The Ivy (Yadorigi)

Kaoru, still mourning Agemaki, is not yet officially married, and the reigning emperor (Niou's father) has an eligible daughter by a lady now deceased. When Kaoru visits the palace one autumn evening, the emperor invites him to play a game of *go*, loses to him, and then invites him to pick a chrysanthemum from the garden as a prize (49A). They exchange poems indicating that Kaoru understands the symbolism and is willing to accept the emperor's daughter as his wife. The corresponding print from the *Color Print Contest* series parodies this scene by showing a young man and woman gazing directly at each other, with the woman holding a pair of scissors as she prepares to snip a chrysanthemum blossom, distracting the man from his task of stringing a koto (49B).

Niou marries Yūgiri's daughter Rokuno-kimi, with elaborate celebrations, although he continues to care for Kozeri, who is now pregnant. Kaoru also visits her and hints that he regrets not having pursued her himself, as Agemaki wanted him to do. Kozeri deflects his awkward attentions to her by telling him of another lady who also resembles his lost love Agemaki: a third sister, or rather half-sister, by an unacknowledged lover of the Eighth Prince. This is the young woman who will later be known by the nickname Ukifune.

Did not memory
tell me I have lodged before
beneath these ivied trees,
ah, then, how forlorn this night,
spent lonely and far from home.

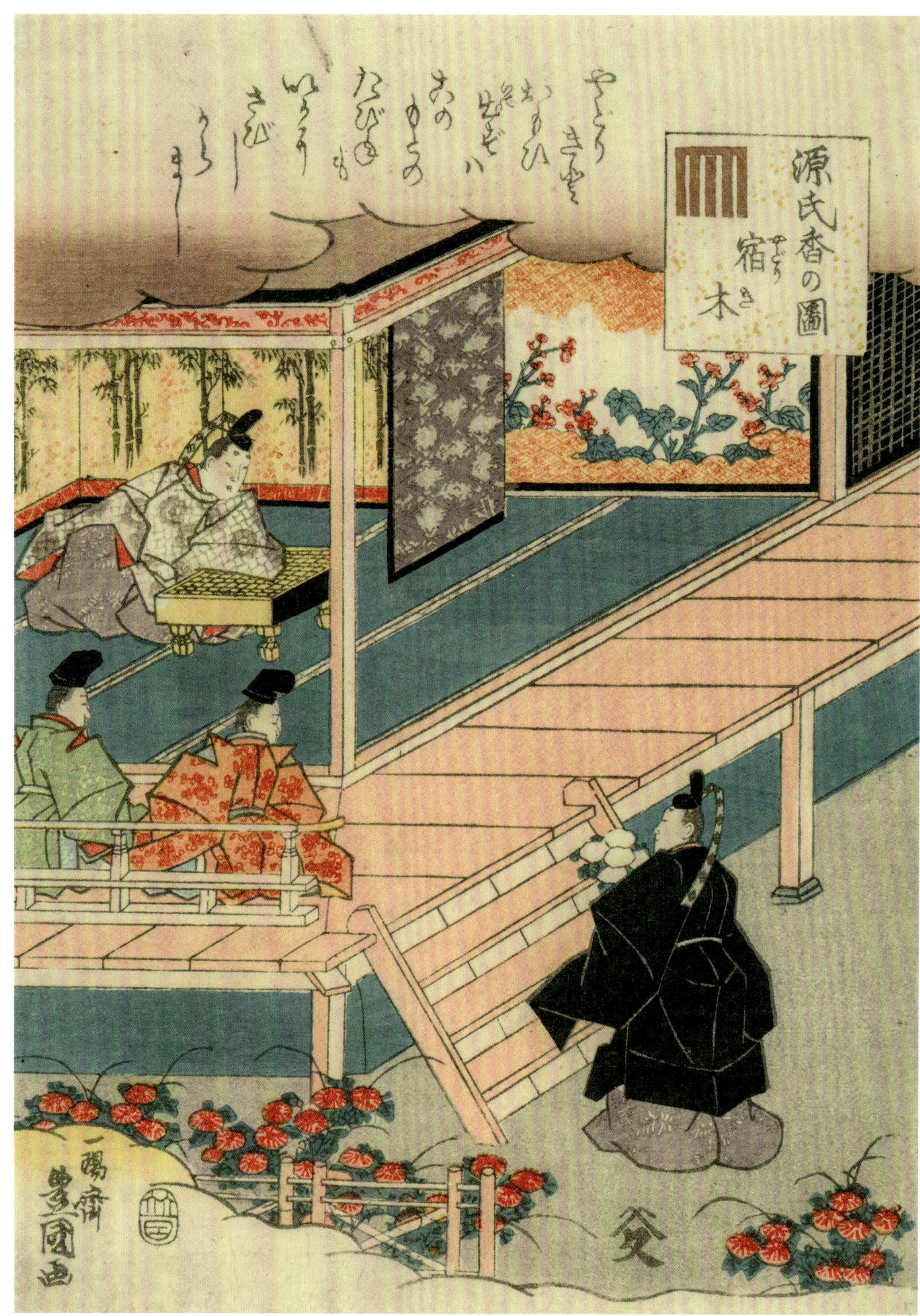

49A | Kunisada, *Genji Incense Pictures*, 1844–47

Kozeri gives birth to her baby, and Kaoru is duly married to the imperial princess. He is pleased with his new wife but still dreams of the Uji sisters. On another visit to Uji, he finally catches sight of Ukifune herself, who is staying there with her family on the way home after a pilgrimage.

Kuniyoshi used the title of this chapter for one of the triptychs in an *Inaka Genji* series playing on the five elements of East Asian cosmology, because the last character of yadorigi is the character for wood, one of the elements. The scene shown does not appear to refer to any actual plot elements in either the original *Tale* or the books in the *Inaka Genji* universe; instead, it is based on another bit of wordplay, since the first part of yadorigi suggests the theme of amayadori or "shelter from the rain." Mitsuuji (identified by his shrimp-tail hairstyle), a pageboy holding his sword, and a group of ladies gather under a tree during a shower, while two male servants hurry to join them (49C).

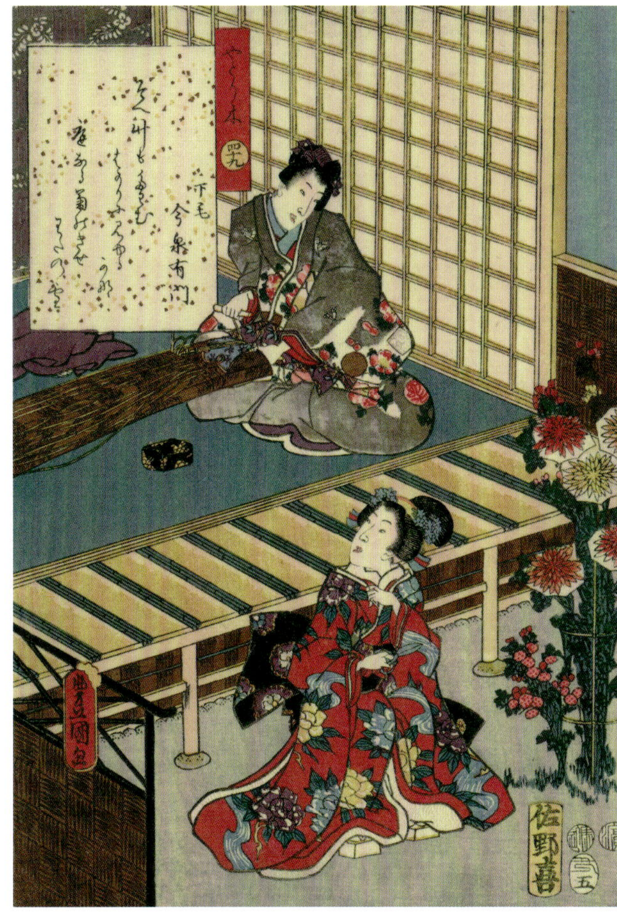

49B | Kunisada, *The Color Print Contest of a Modern Genji*, 1853

49C | Kuniyoshi, *Comparisons for the Five Elements*, 1847–52

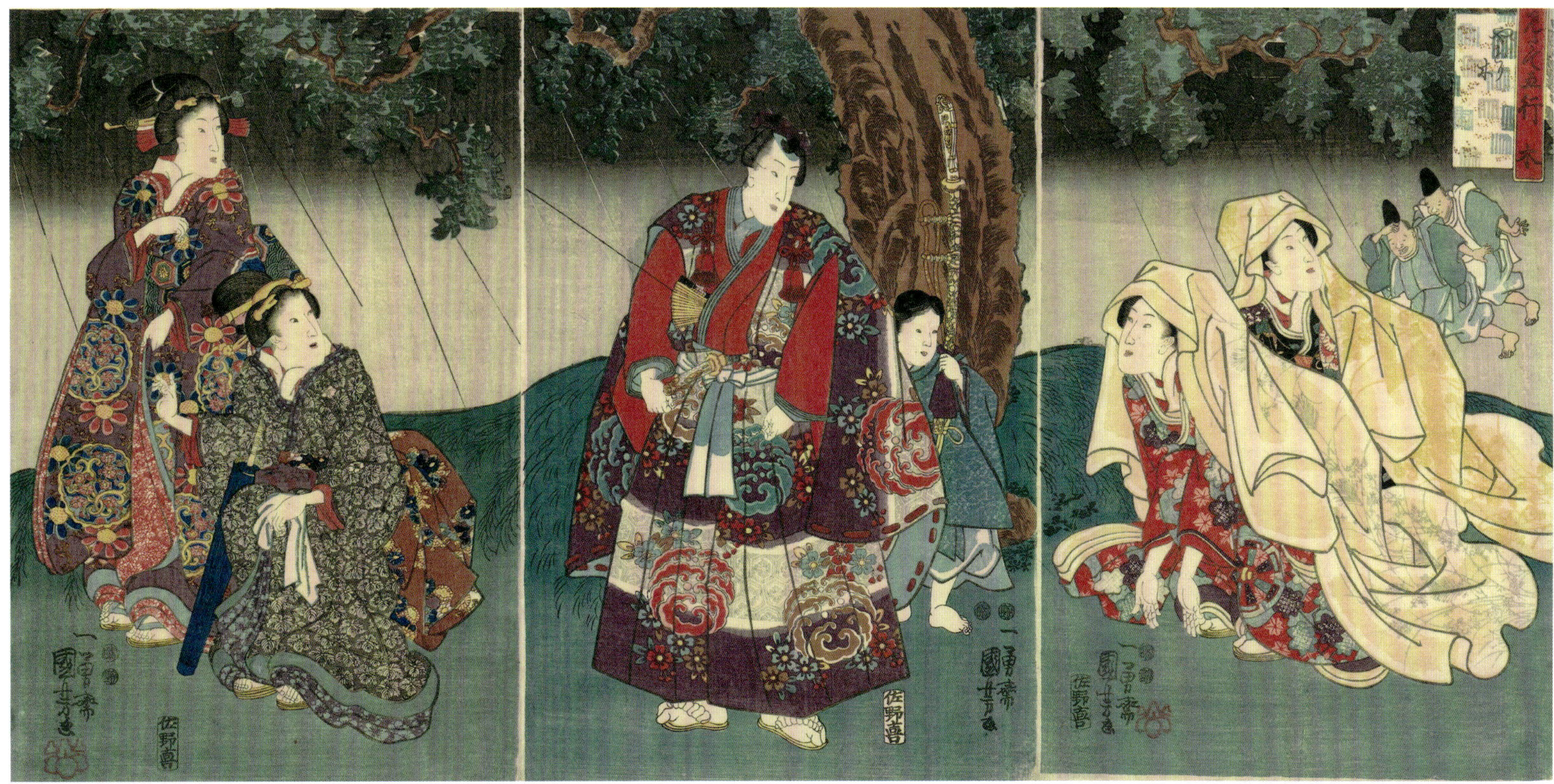

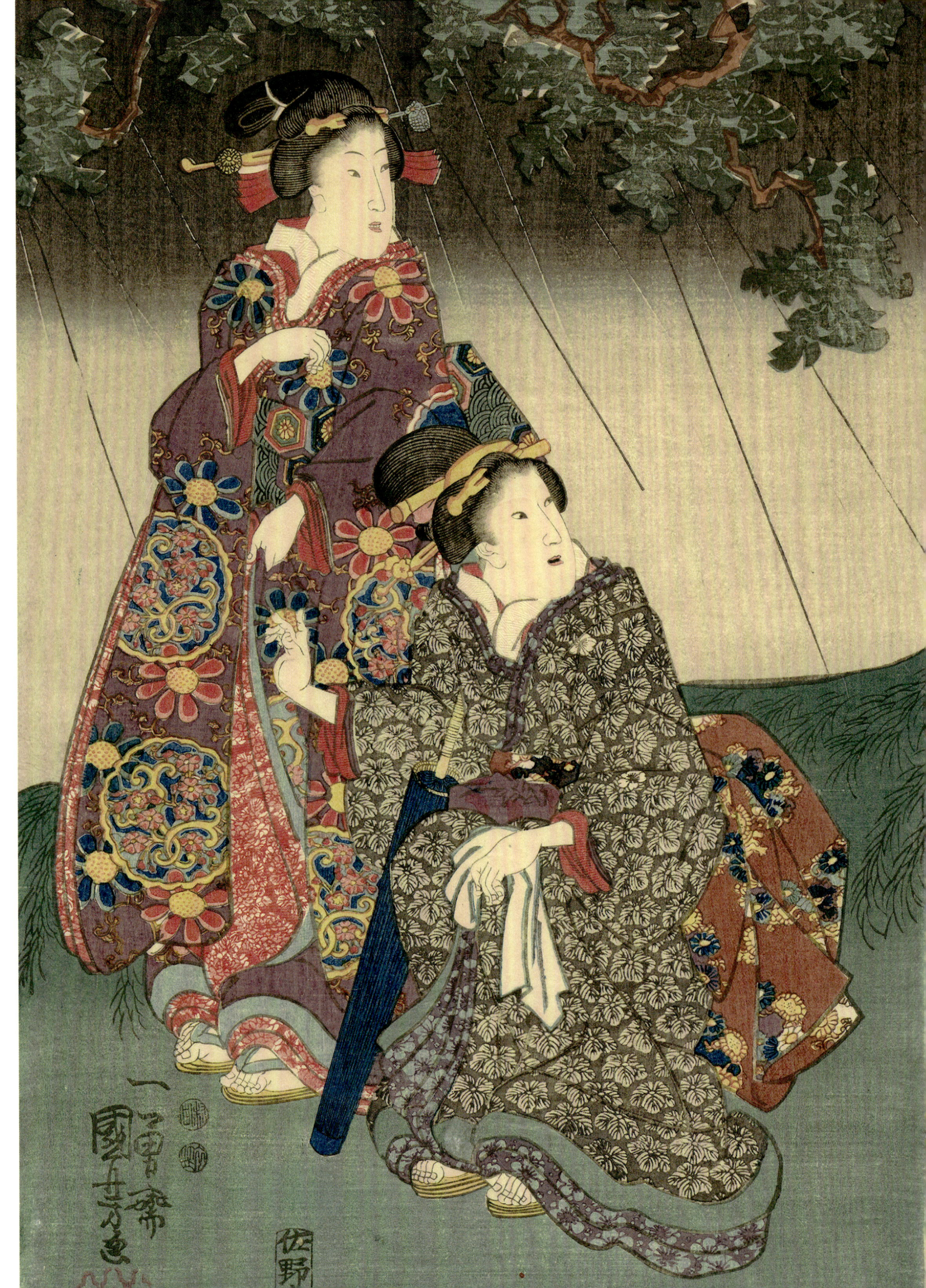
一勇斎國芳画
佐野

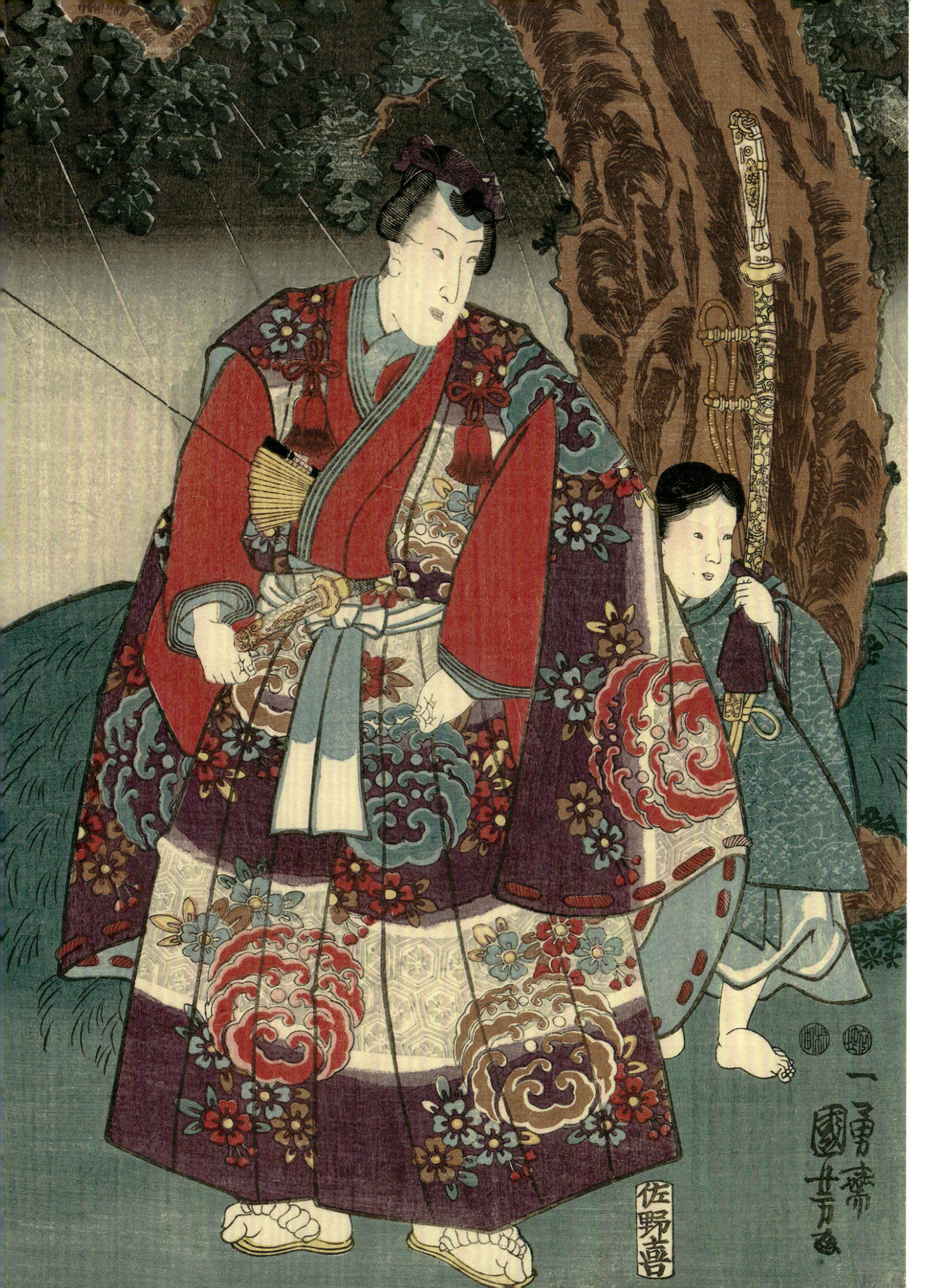

佐野喜
一勇斎國芳画

50

The Eastern Cottage (Azumaya)

At this point the focus of the narrative shifts to Ukifune. Following the affair with the Eighth Prince that resulted in the birth of her beautiful daughter, Ukifune's mother married a provincial governor and had several more children by him. Ukifune has a terrible experience when her fiancé jilts her in favor of her half-sister, with the connivance of the governor who favors his own child over his step-daughter. To help Ukifune recover from this sad disappointment, and take her out of a home situation where she is likely to be mistreated again, her mother arranges for her to go and stay with her married half-sister, Kozeri, whose little son is now crawling.

In Kozeri's house, however, Ukifune has other problems. When the opportunistic Niou spots an attractive newcomer in his wife's retinue, he does not hesitate to make advances toward her. The illustration in the *Genji Incense* series shows Ukifune attempting to cover her face with her fan, while Niou clutches at the hem of her robes, just as described in the book (50A). He is summoned to the imperial court before he can go any further, but Ukifune's mother and sister decide to move her to another, smaller house, the Eastern Cottage of the title. Kaoru finds Ukifune and succeeds in seducing her; he composes the chapter title

Are the weeds so thick
that they wholly bar your gate,
O eastern cottage —
too long, too long I waited
while the pouring rain came down!

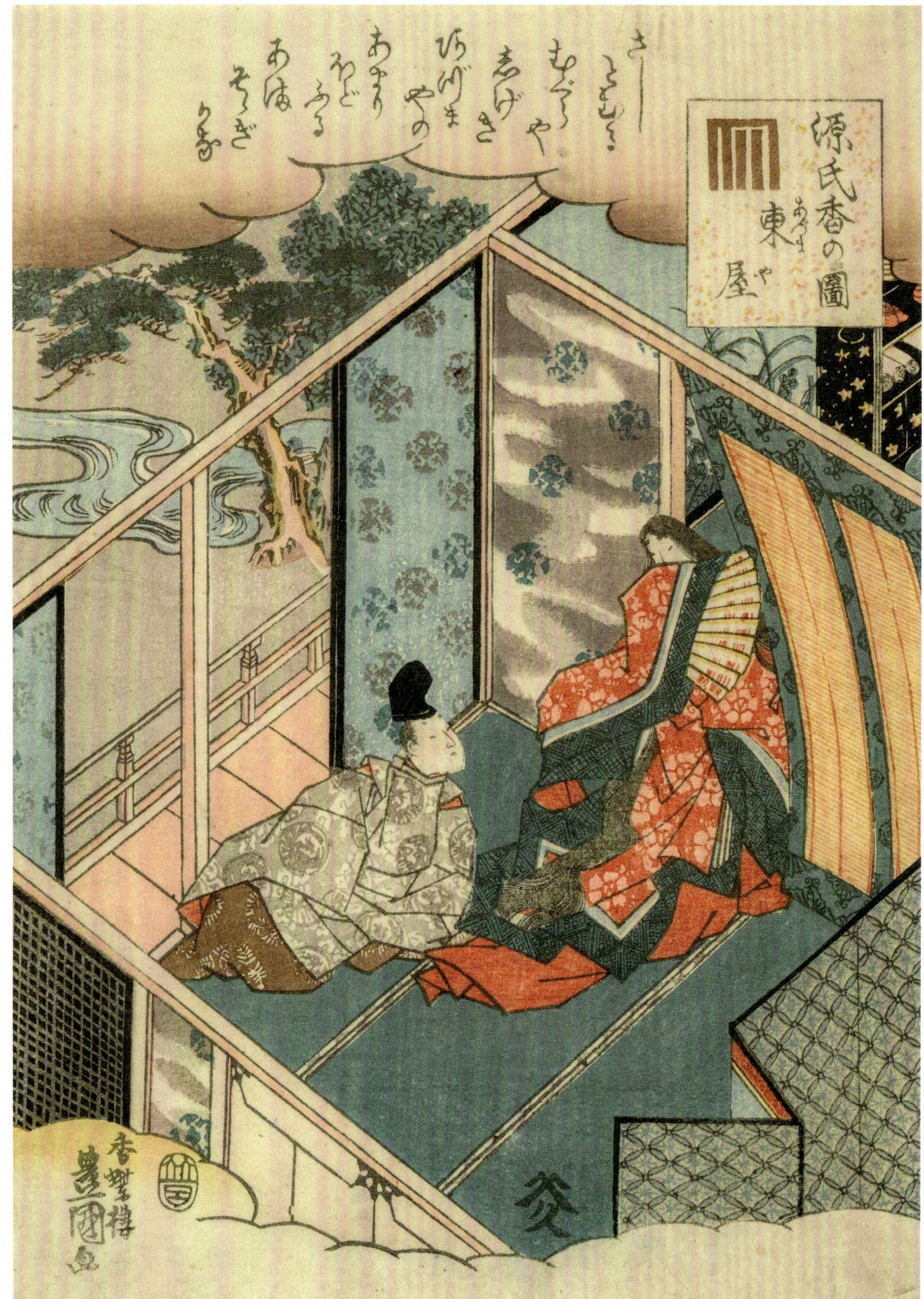

50A | Kunisada, *Genji Incense Pictures*, 1844–47

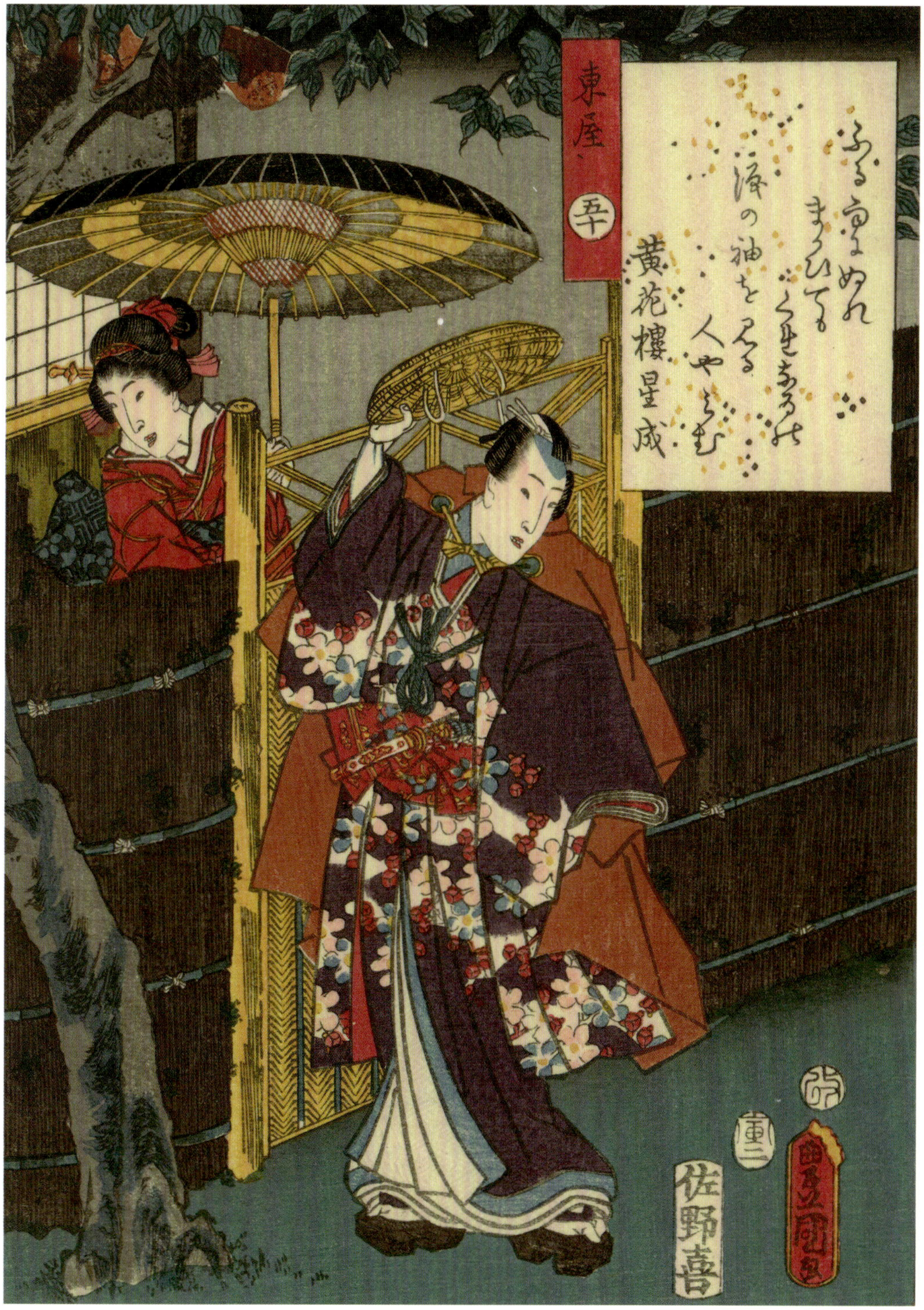

50B | Kunisada, *The Color Print Contest of a Modern Genji*, 1854

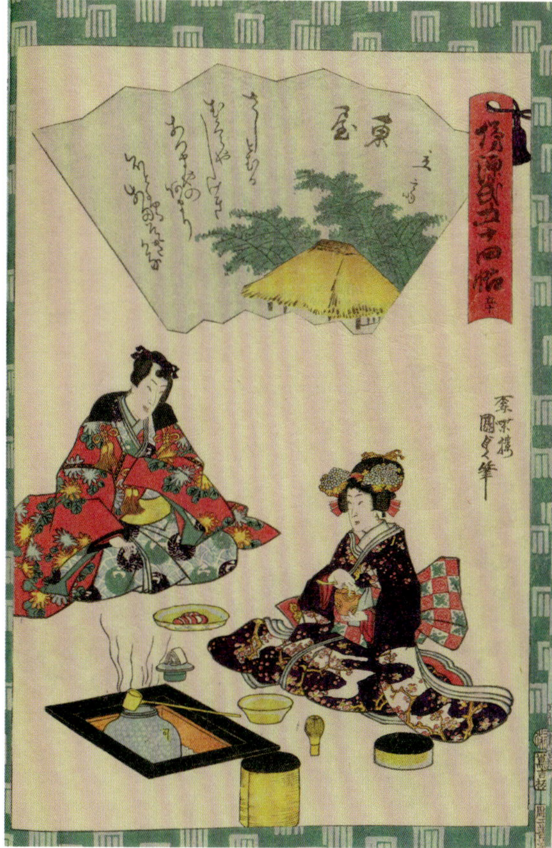

50C | Kunisada II and Hiroshige II, *Traces of Genji in Fifty-Four Chapters*, 1865

poem while waiting to be admitted to the Eastern Cottage. He then moves Ukifune to Uji and installs her in the old house there, enjoying her company while telling his wife that he is inspecting the new chapel.

Since this chapter is not included in the parody story, Kunisada illustrated it for the *Color Print Contest* series with a depiction of the title poem in *Inaka Genji* style: a man, presumably Kaorunosuke, arrives at a house on a rainy night and is admitted through the garden gate by a female attendant (50B). Kunisada II and Hiroshige II reimagined the Eastern Cottage itself as a small teahouse on the grounds of a large estate, showing Mitsuuji of *Inaka Genji* looking on approvingly as one of his ladies, perhaps Murasaki, performs a tea ceremony (50C).

51

A Drifting Boat (Ukifune)

This chapter contains the most frequently illustrated episode in the entire *Tale of Genji*. The scene of a couple in a boat, passing a snowy island, captures perfectly the mood of romantic melancholy that permeates the book.

When Ukifune sends New Year gifts to her sister Kozeri and the baby, Niou learns where Kaoru has hidden her and travels to Uji himself. Arriving at night, he poses as Kaoru and makes his way to Ukifune's bedroom. He is as smitten with her as Kaoru, and both men continue to visit frequently and send passionate letters. Ukifune cannot decide between them and becomes increasingly unhappy with the conflicting pressures put on her from various directions; her mother favors steady Kaoru, but her ladies-in-waiting prefer the dashing Niou. The two lovers soon find out about each other, and Ukifune worries that she may become a cause of trouble between the two men.

On one of Niou's visits, he takes Ukifune for a winter boat ride on the Uji River, accompanied by her personal attendant and the boatman who poles the boat, just as shown in the *Genji Incense* print (51A). As they pass the snow-covered Isle of Orange Trees, Ukifune is moved to compose a poem that expresses her anxiety about her situation, comparing herself to a helplessly

---

The enduring hue
of the Isle of Orange Trees
may well never change,
yet there is no knowing now
where this drifting boat is bound.

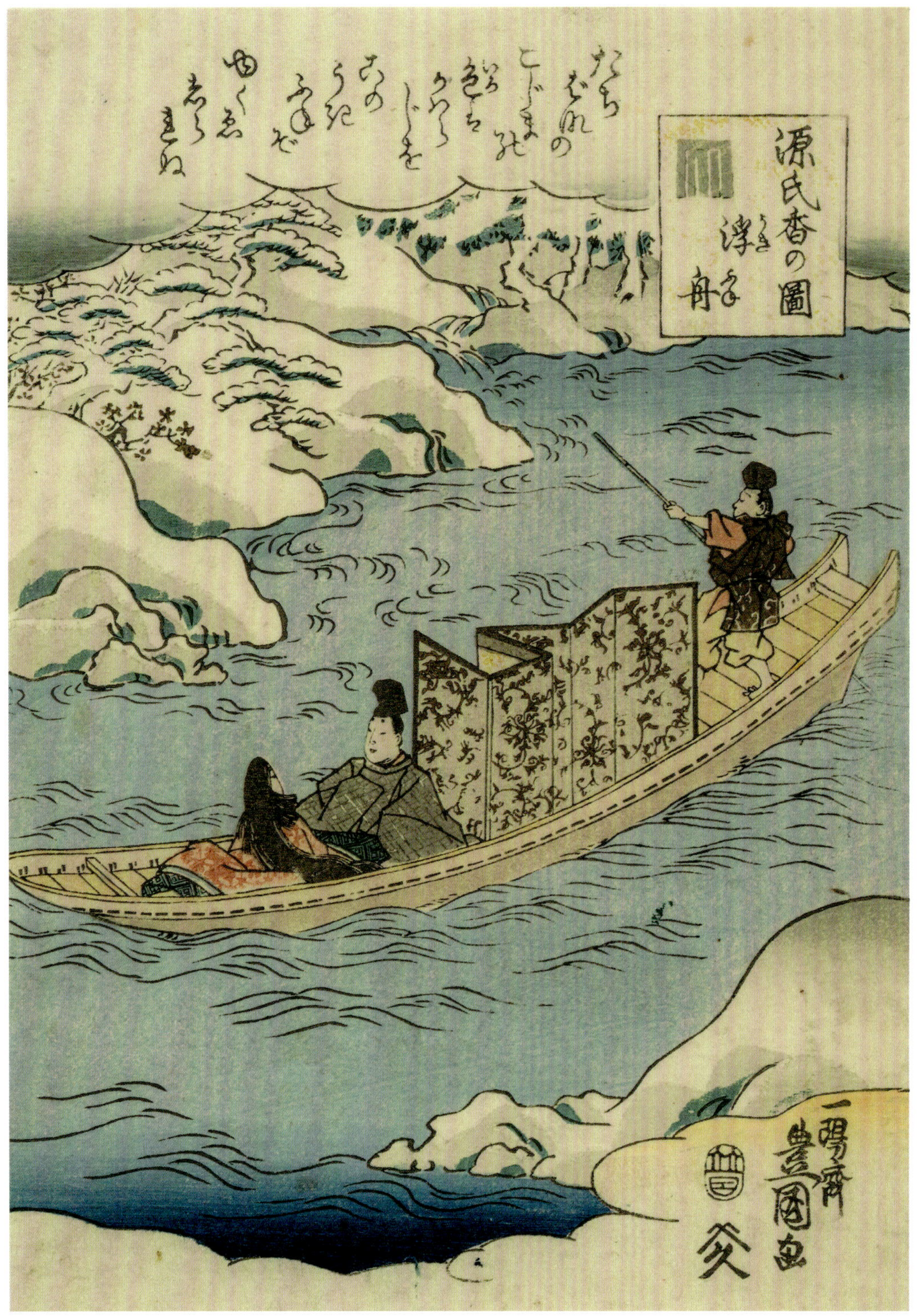

51A | Kunisada, *Genji Incense Pictures*, 1844–47

51B | Totoya Hokkei, *The Tale of Genji for the Akabane Club*, 1826

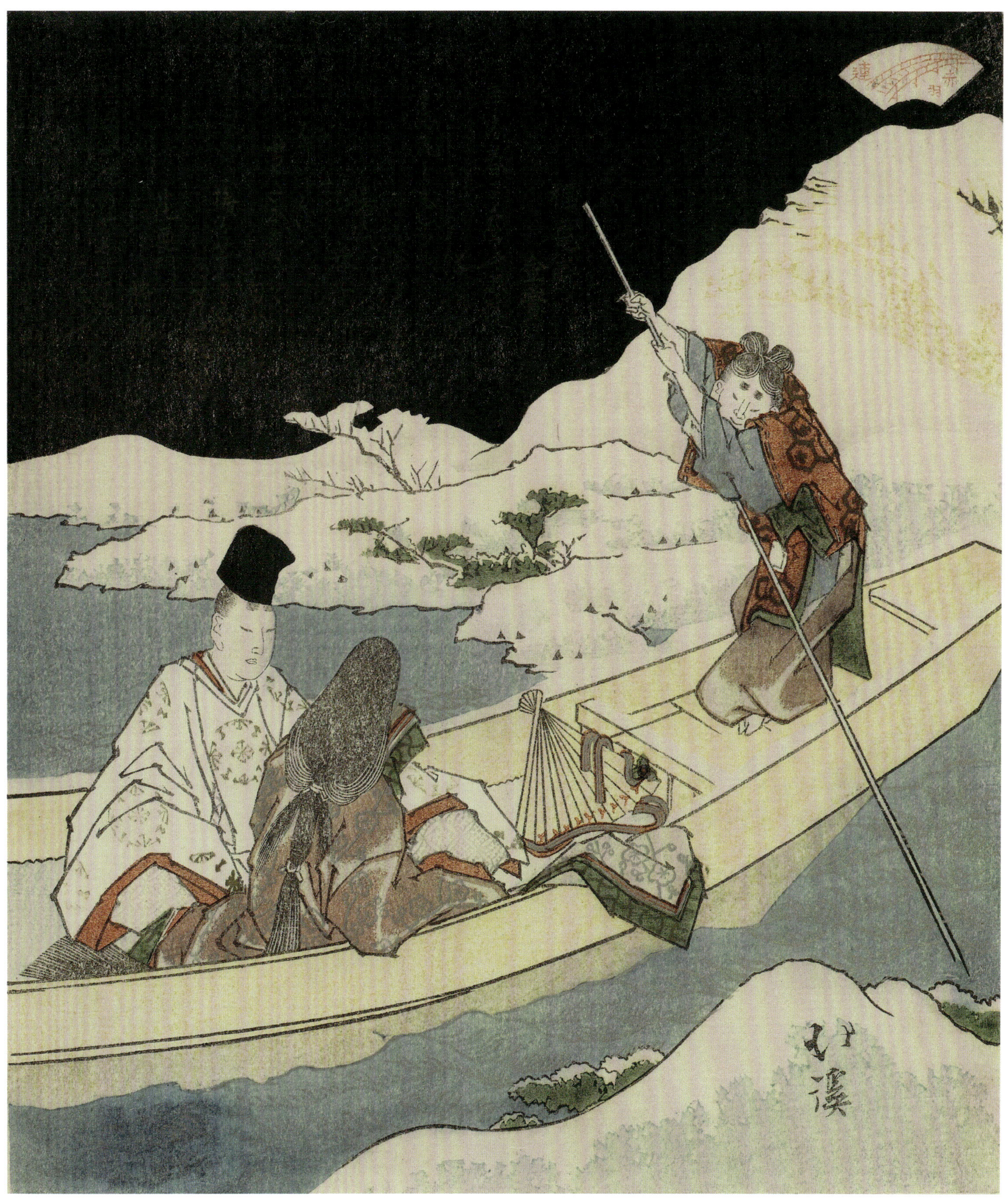
赤羽
連
北溪

drifting boat. Despite the romantic beauty of moments such as this, by the end of the chapter she has become so unhappy that she makes plans to die by throwing herself into the river.

The iconic boat scene is beautifully rendered in an unusual oval design (possibly intended for a fan) by Hiroshige, and an earlier surimono by Hokkei, both of which refer stylistically to the long tradition of elegant small album paintings of *The Tale of Genji* (51C, 51B). Okumura Masanobu, possibly the first artist to create modernized ukiyo-e parodies of Genji scenes (see chapter 6), designed a spectacular, extra-large hand-colored print explicitly referring to the Ukifune chapter, showing a contemporary couple enjoying a boat ride in moonlight, with a suggestive three-line haikai poem (51D).

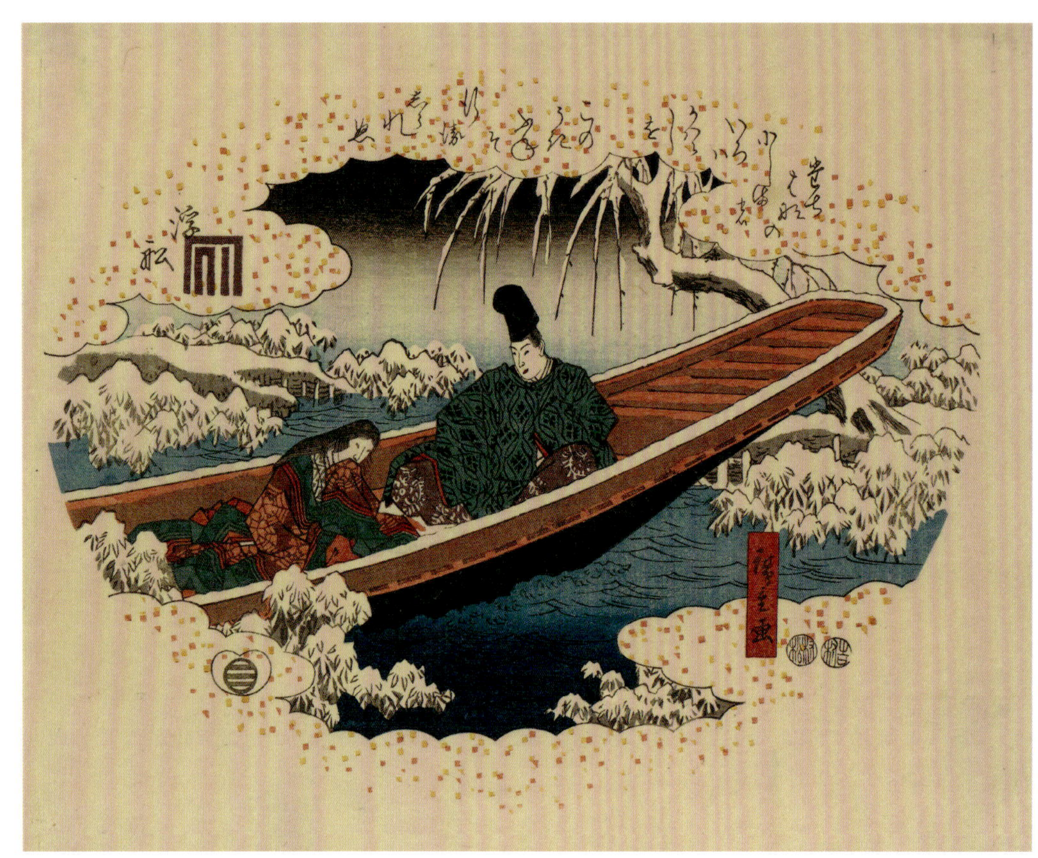

51C | Hiroshige, *Ukifune*, 1847–52

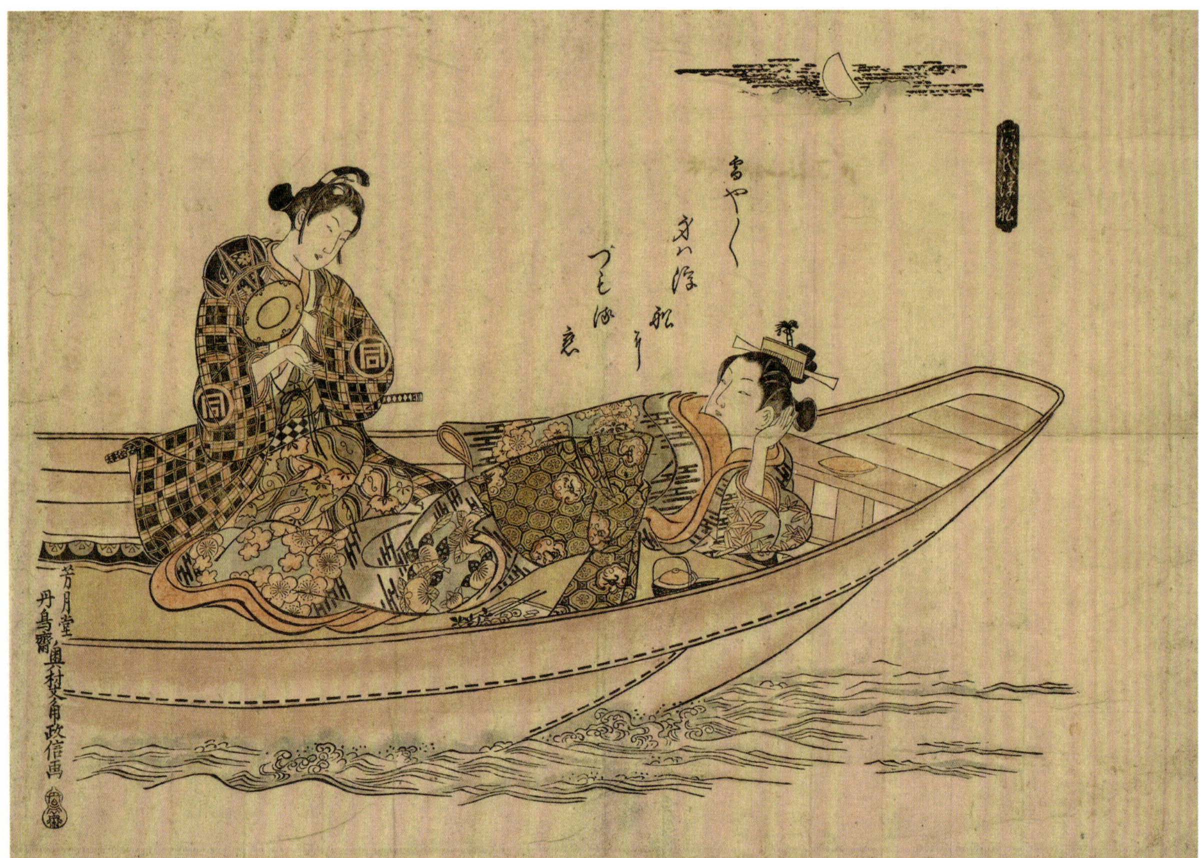

51D | Okumura Masanobu, *The Ukifune Chapter of The Tale of Genji*, 1740s

Pale Purple Dawn at Uji does not extend as far as the Ukifune chapter, but a preview illustration at the beginning of chapter 7, published in 1855, hints at the way the story might have been handled if it had continued further. Spread over a total of six pages is an elaborate illustration showing the daughters of Ashikaga Samanosuke Yoshikuni (= the Eighth Prince) and people associated with them, riding in a raft and a boat on the snowy river. The last two figures are "the courtesan Ukifune, actually Samanosuke's third daughter Fudeko" and Hyōbunojō Ujisato (= Niou). The Ukifune illustration in the *Color Print Contest* series, published in 1854, may have been an earlier version of this scene (51E). It shows a couple in a boat gazing fondly at each other, with a boatwoman holding an oar. All three are more sensibly dressed for winter than in the other versions: the couple wear warm hoods, and the boatwoman has a headscarf. The standing man is most likely Ujisato, and the woman is probably Fudeko. Her name, which includes the word for brush (fude), suggests the title of chapter 53, Tenarai (Writing Practice), also sometimes used as an alternate nickname for Ukifune.

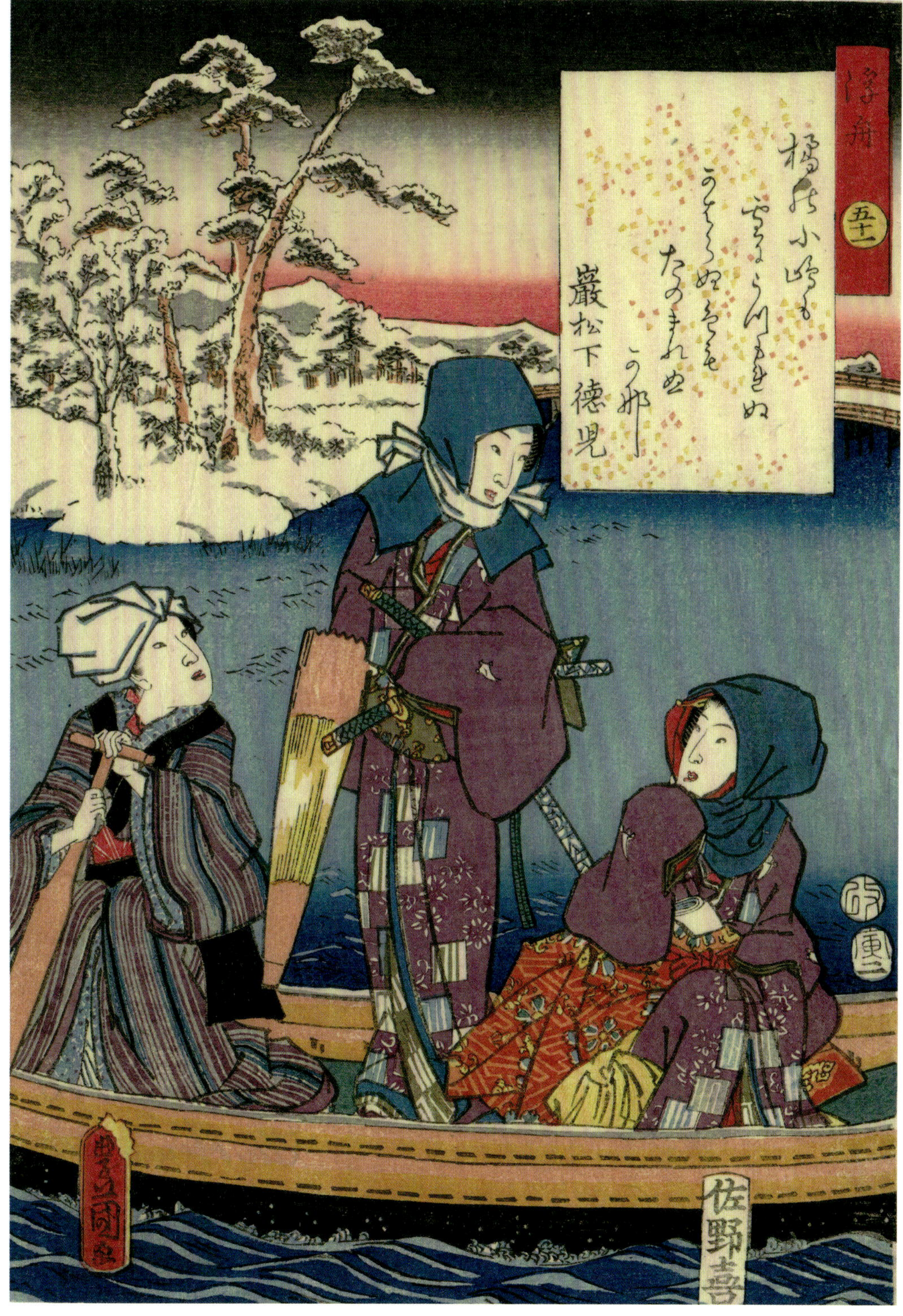

51E | Kunisada, *The Color Print Contest of a Modern Genji*, 1854

52

The Mayfly (Kagerō)

Ukifune has disappeared, leaving behind notes and poems that make her suicidal intentions all too clear. Assuming that her body has been swept away by the river, her flustered household staff claim at first that she died of a sudden illness. The *Genji Incense* illustration, based on the first illustration for this chapter in the 1650 illustrated book, shows a messenger, sent by Niou to try to find out what has really happened, conversing with an evasive lady-in-waiting, while inside the room another of Ukifune's ladies is weeping (52A). There is a hasty funeral with the cremation of an empty coffin, but eventually Niou and Kaoru learn the truth of the matter. Both of them mourn Ukifune deeply even as they console themselves through dalliances with other women. At the end of the chapter, Kaoru sits disconsolately on the veranda of the Rokujō mansion after another failed seduction attempt. Gazing at the insects in the garden while contemplating all that he has lost, he composes the chapter title poem.

In the context of Kaoru's poem, the insect named is the tiny mayfly, but the word kagerō can also refer to the dragonfly, which is similar in shape but larger. For his *Genji Clouds* series of matching images, Kuniyoshi played on the meaning of the title by showing a sumō wrestler named

---

There it is, just there,
yet ever beyond my reach,
till I look once more,
and it is gone, the mayfly,
never to be seen again.

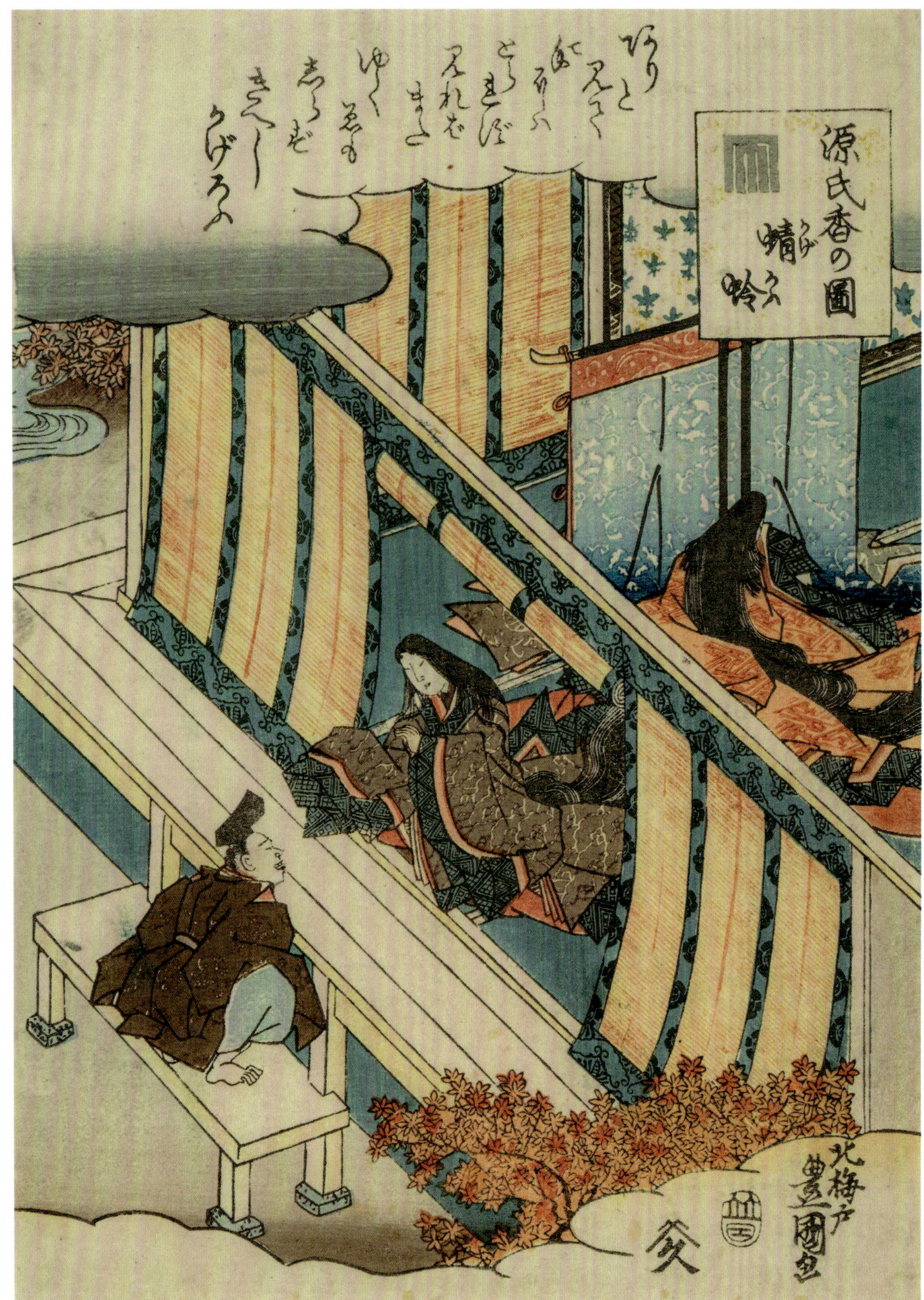

52A | Kunisada, *Genji Incense Pictures*, 1844–47

Akitsushima, a character in a popular kabuki play (52B). The wrestler's professional name, Akitsushima, means literally "Island of the Dragonfly" and is an archaic term for Japan. He wears the special hairstyle of wrestlers (without the shaven forehead that was standard for adult men), with warm winter robes concealing his massive body; he is so strong that he can bend a metal heating stove with just his right hand.

Kunisada also referred to insects in his design for the *Color Print Contest* series, showing a young man with a dragonfly painted on his fan and two little girls who seem to be hunting for insects on a summer night, using a long-handled fan that they hope the creatures will perch on (52C). The background view of a temple on a bluff overlooking a lake is, as the kyōka poem inscribed in the decorative panel at the upper left makes clear, none other than Ishiyama Temple, where Lady Murasaki is said to have begun writing the original *Tale of Genji*. The name Ishiyama, literally "Stone Mountain," refers to the unusual volcanic rocks that can be seen on the temple grounds, as shown in the print.

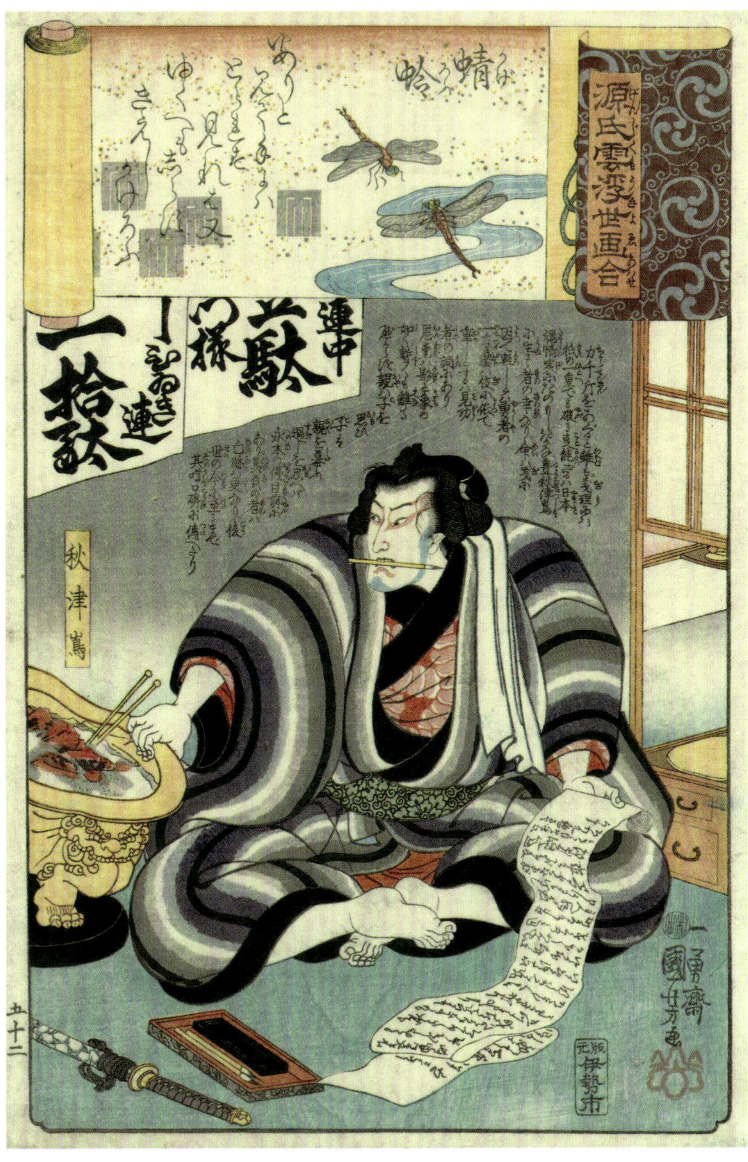

52B | Kuniyoshi, *Genji Clouds Matched with Ukiyo-e Pictures*, about 1845–46

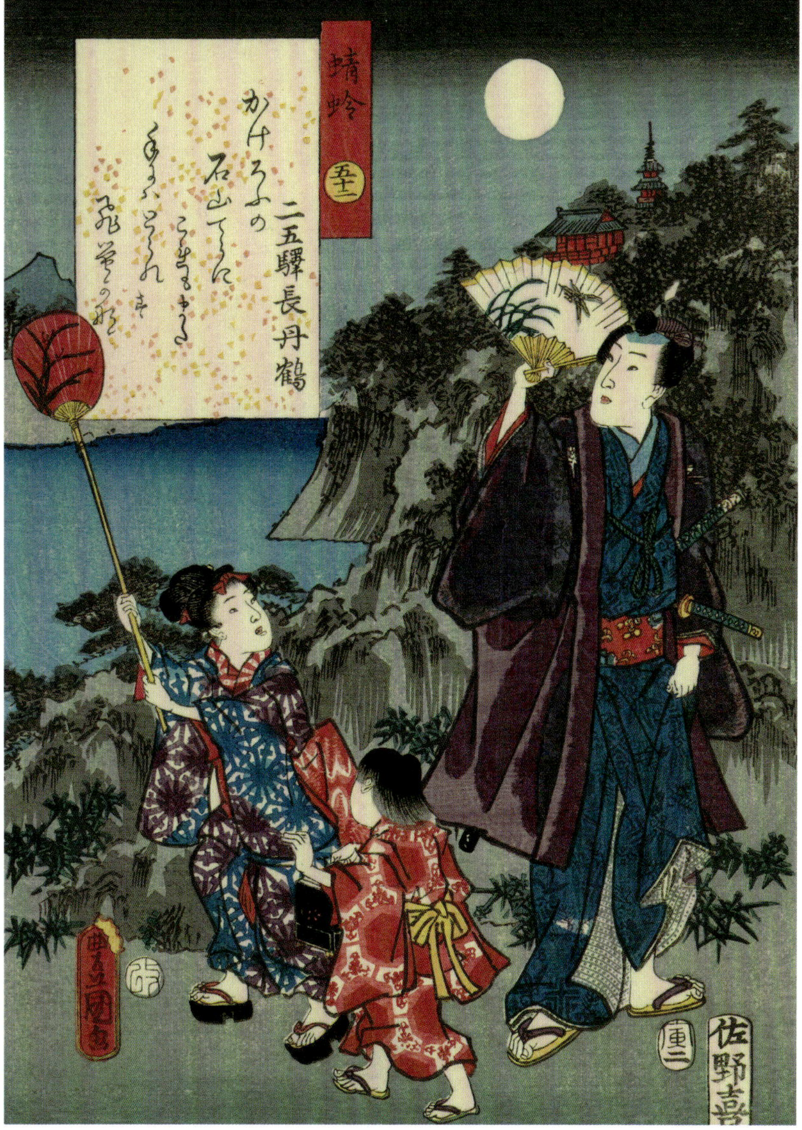

52C | Kunisada, *The Color Print Contest of a Modern Genji*, 1854

53

Writing Practice (Tenarai)

The elderly bishop of Yokawa and his sister, a nun who is mourning the recent death of her adult daughter, pass through Uji on their way home from a pilgrimage. There they find a disheveled young woman wandering in the woods, gravely ill and unable or unwilling to identify herself. It is of course Ukifune, who has apparently fallen into a fugue state before having been able to carry out her plan to drown herself in the river. The old people take her in and care for her, but she refuses to discuss her past. Instead she occupies herself with lengthy calligraphy practice, composing the chapter title poem for that purpose. It is now autumn, and outside the nun's house at Ono the farmers are hard at work bringing in the rice harvest (53A).

The nun comes to see Ukifune as a substitute for her lost daughter, and even tries to make a match for her with the daughter's husband. Ukifune insists on becoming a nun herself and at last persuades the bishop to cut her hair short and administer the vows. At the end of the chapter, Kaoru hears of the mysterious young woman at Ono and decides that he must go there and investigate.

Once again, Kunisada shows the same scene — with appropriate costumes for each story — for both the *Genji Incense* series and the *Color Print Contest* series. In the latter

Oh, who built that weir
across the river of tears,
when in its swift stream
I had cast myself to drown
and detained me in this life?

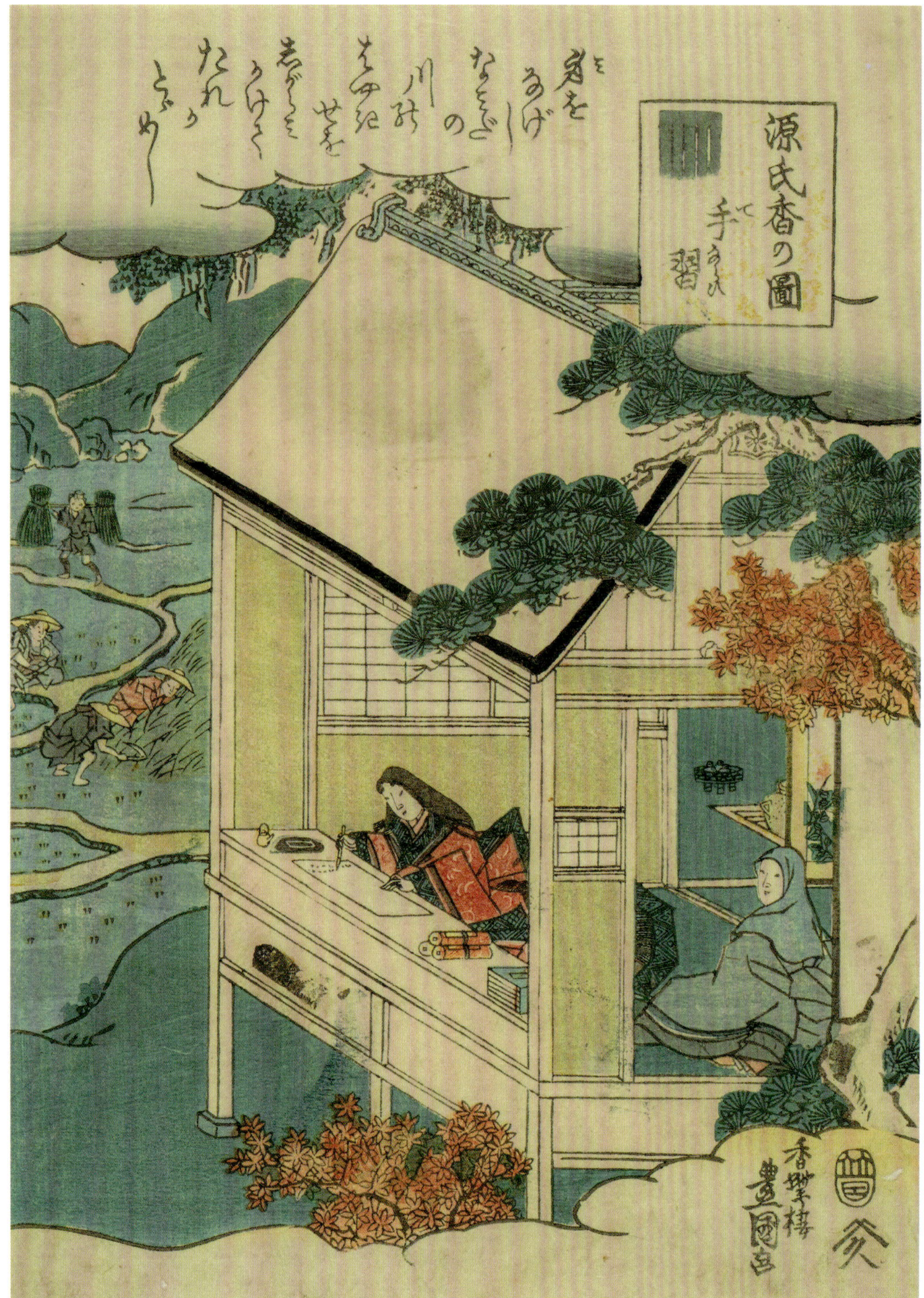

53A | Kunisada, *Genji Incense Pictures*, 1844–47

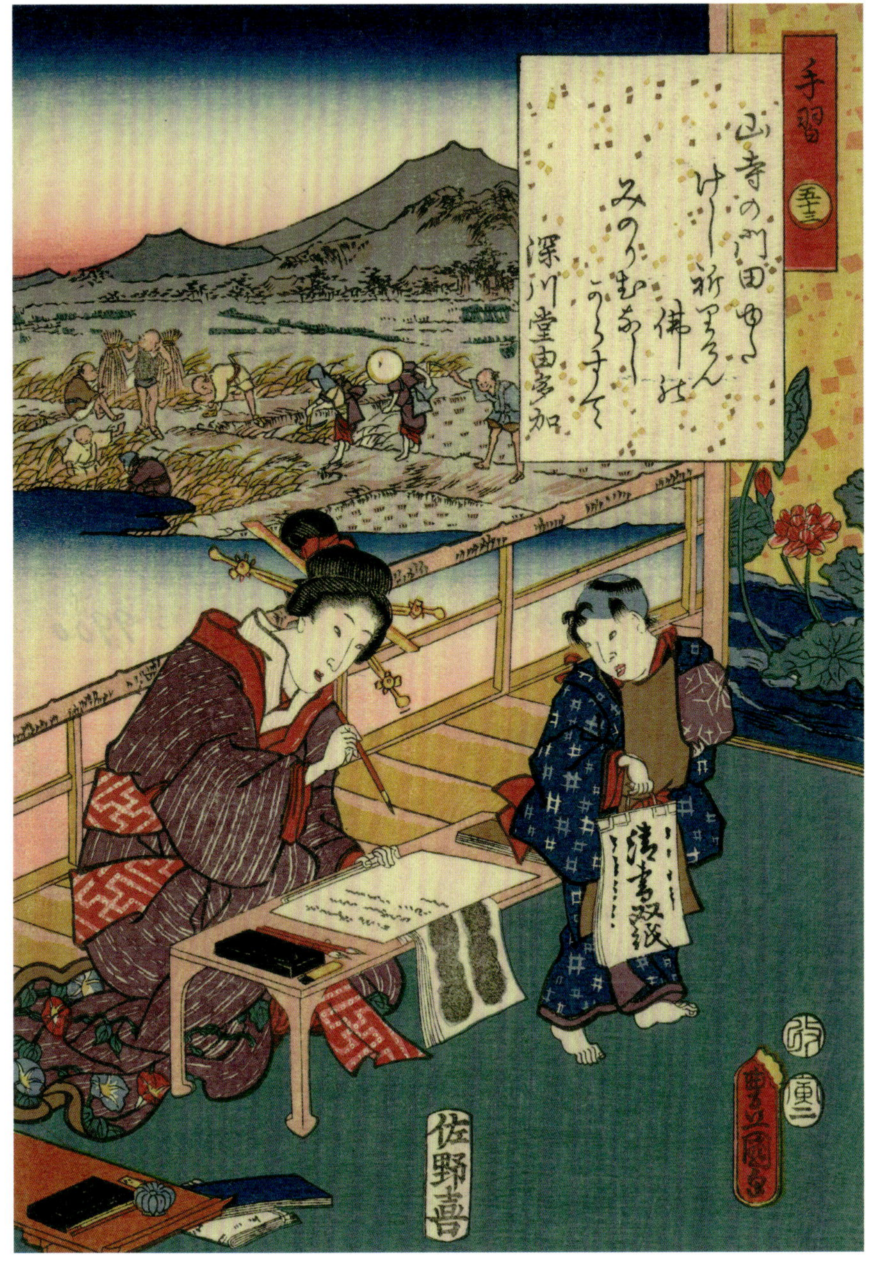

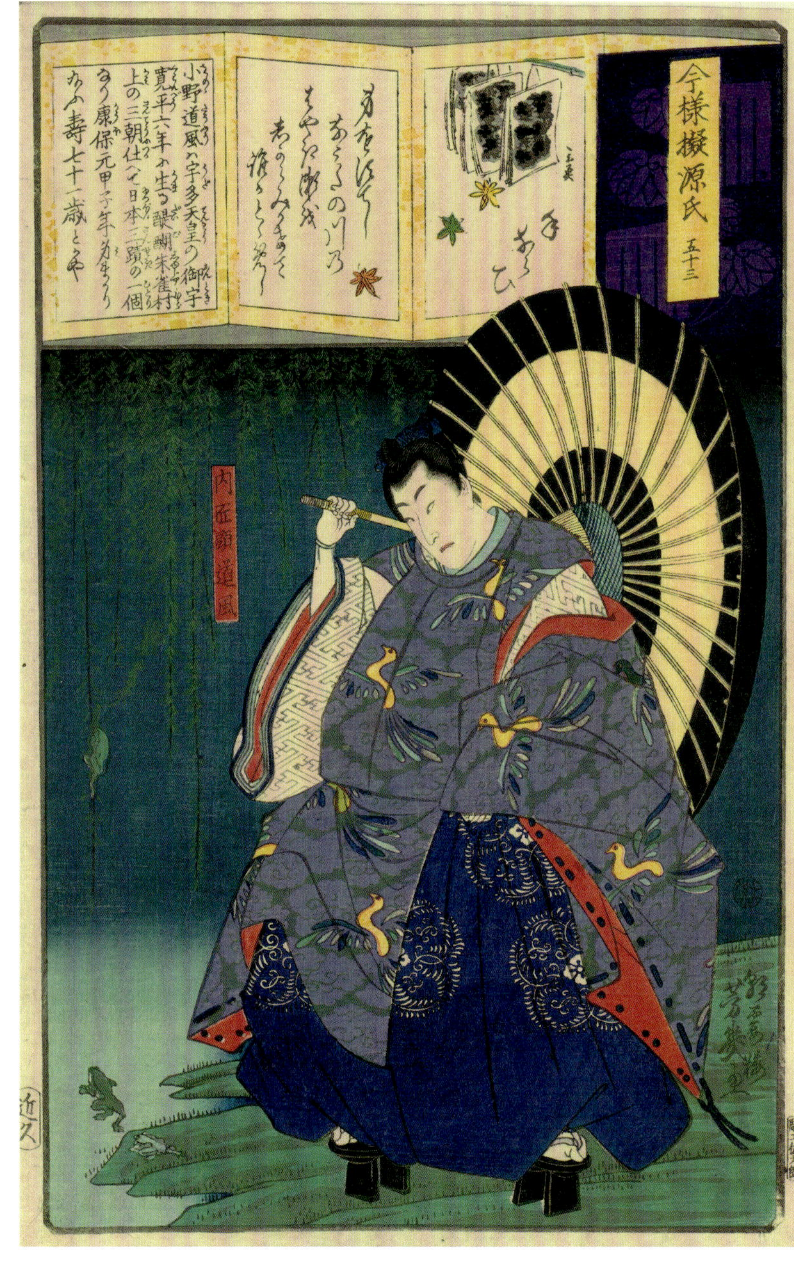

53B | Kunisada, *The Color Print Contest of a Modern Genji,* 1854

53C | Yoshiiku and Gengyo, *Modern Parodies of Genji,* 1864

work, he plays on the fact that during the Edo period, visual depictions of writing practice were strongly associated with young children (53B). He adds the figure of a child holding a writing-practice notebook; and he shows the young woman writing a poem at her desk with padding under the paper made up of old practice sheets thriftily recycled until the practice writing has become a solid black blur.

Similar practice sheets are shown in the inset of Yoshiiku's series of matching pictures (53C). The main image shows Ono no Tōfū (894–966), one of the most famous calligraphers in Japanese history. A well-known story related that he was once inspired by seeing a frog attempting to jump up to a hanging willow branch and trying over and over until at last, it succeeded.

54

The Floating Bridge of Dreams (Yume no ukihashi)

Kaoru visits the Bishop of Yokawa to learn more about the mysterious young woman living with the bishop's sister, who is almost certainly Ukifune. In the end he decides not to approach her directly but to send a letter through her young half-brother, with whom she used to be especially close. The boy delivers a cover letter from the bishop together with Kaoru's own letter, which contains the only poem in the chapter. The *Genji Incense* picture, like most illustrations of this chapter, shows the little brother waiting, in the hope of taking back a reply, while Ukifune reads Kaoru's letter (54A). Ukifune refuses to reply, to meet directly with her brother, or to discuss the past with anyone. Neither Kaoru nor the reader knows what may happen next.

The source of the chapter title is somewhat mysterious, since the exact phrase "Yume no ukihashi" (the floating bridge of dreams) is never actually used in the text, although it does occur in classical waka poetry. There are several references to dreams, as when Ukifune describes her past life as a nightmare; and as seen earlier, metaphorical bridges in general can suggest a dreamlike space between two worlds. The idea that all of life is an illusion, a dream from which we will awaken when we become

---

Following the path
I trusted would take me to
a teacher of the Law,
I lost my way and wandered
a mountain I never sought.

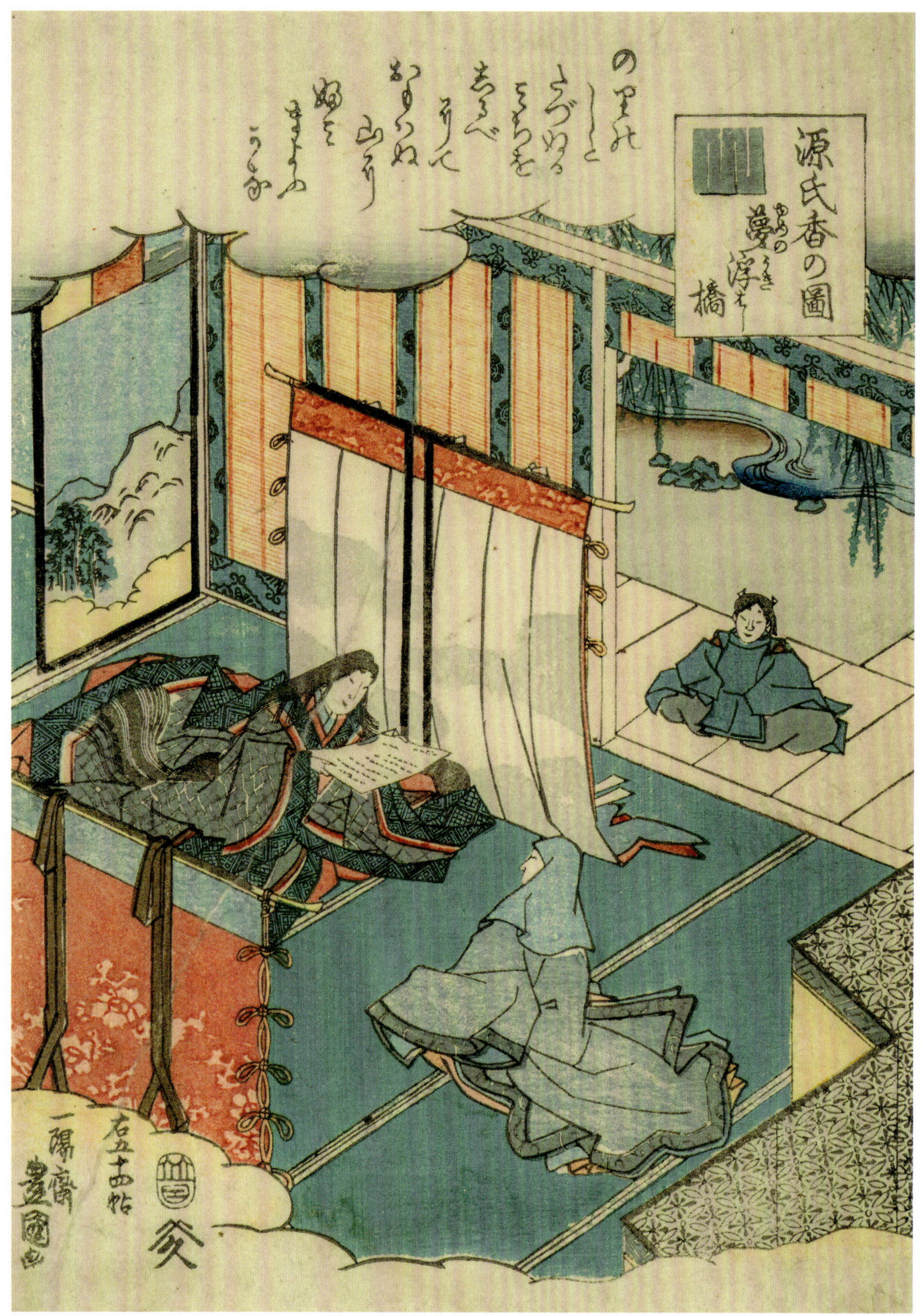

54A | Kunisada, *Genji Incense Pictures*, 1844–47

54B | (detail)

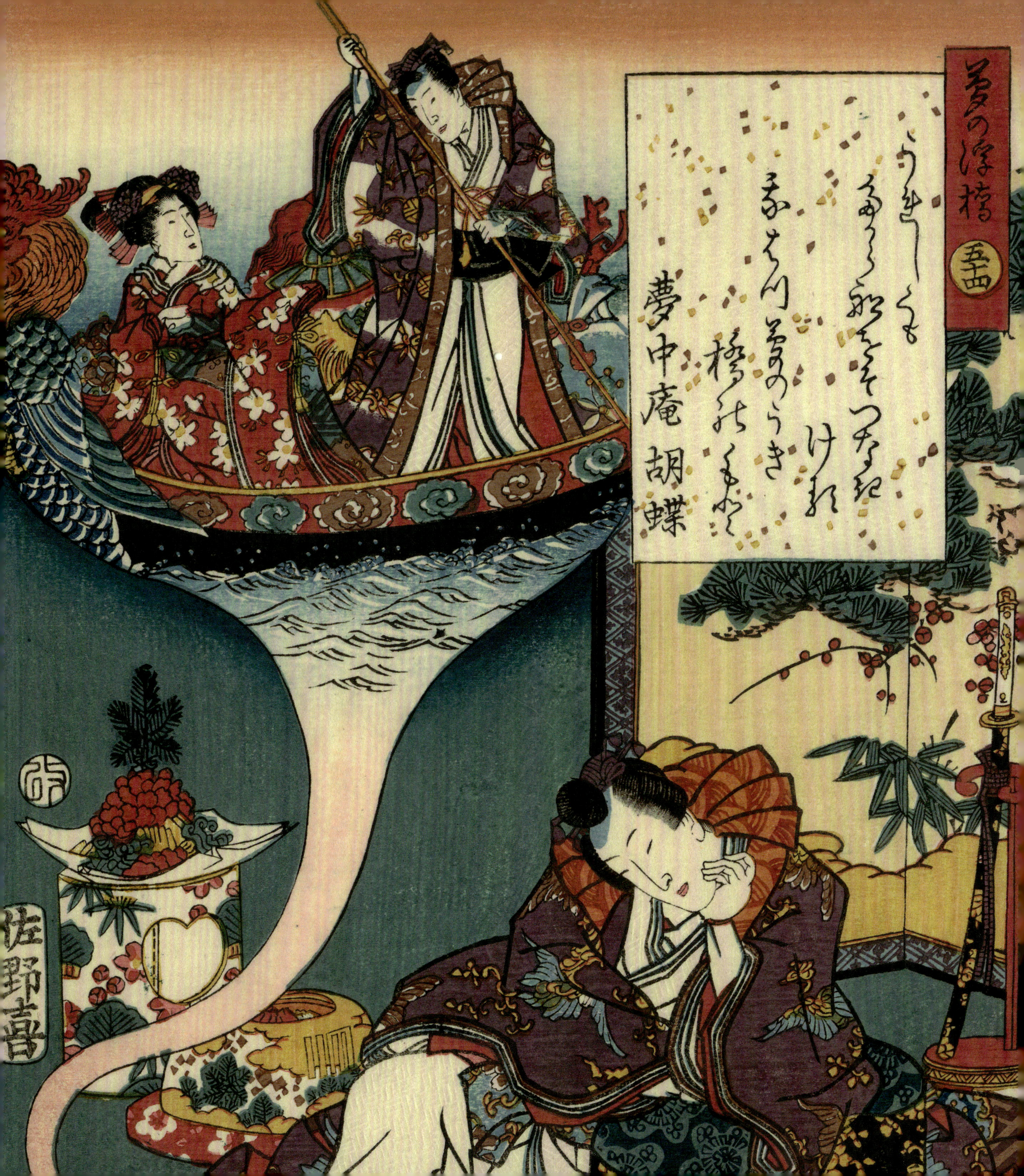
夢の浮橋
夢中庵胡蝶
佐野喜

enlightened, is very much in keeping with the Buddhist message that is one possible interpretation of *The Tale of Genji*.

The conclusions to the story imagined for the *Inaka Genji* universe take on a happy, festive tone, if perhaps a nostalgic one. Even if the lives of the characters remain unsettled within the text, the reader can celebrate the pleasure of finishing a long, emotionally satisfying story by reading it to the very end and thus, as the saying goes, crossing the Bridge of Dreams. Both Kunisada's design for the *Color Print Contest* series and the final print in the *Genji Cards* series by Kunisada II set the scene at New Year, by far the most important holiday of the year, when symbolic good-luck wishes abound.

In the *Color Print Contest* series, an elegantly dressed male figure who probably represents Mitsuuji's grandson Ujisato (= Niou) falls asleep leaning on an armrest, in front of a woodblock print showing the Treasure Boat (Takarabune) in which the Seven Gods of Good Fortune ride (54B). During the Edo period, sleeping with such a print under one's pillow at New Year was said to bring good dreams and hence good luck for the coming year. This dreamer sees the luxurious lifestyle of his illustrious forebear Mitsuuji (or Terumoto or Ujimitsu), who poles another Treasure Boat over the garden pond of his enormous mansion, accompanied by his true love Murasaki.

In the *Genji Cards* illustration by Kunisada II, Mitsuuji holds a sake dipper and is accompanied by a young boy and girl holding the festive decorations known as shimadai, cloud-shaped stands supporting miniature dioramas (54C). The girl holds a model of the legendary Isle of the Immortals (Mount Hōrai, or Penglai in the original Chinese), watched over by the orbs of the sun and moon, and inhabited by a crane and a tortoise, auspicious symbols of longevity. The boy holds a model of a dragon-prowed Treasure Boat containing lucky symbols.

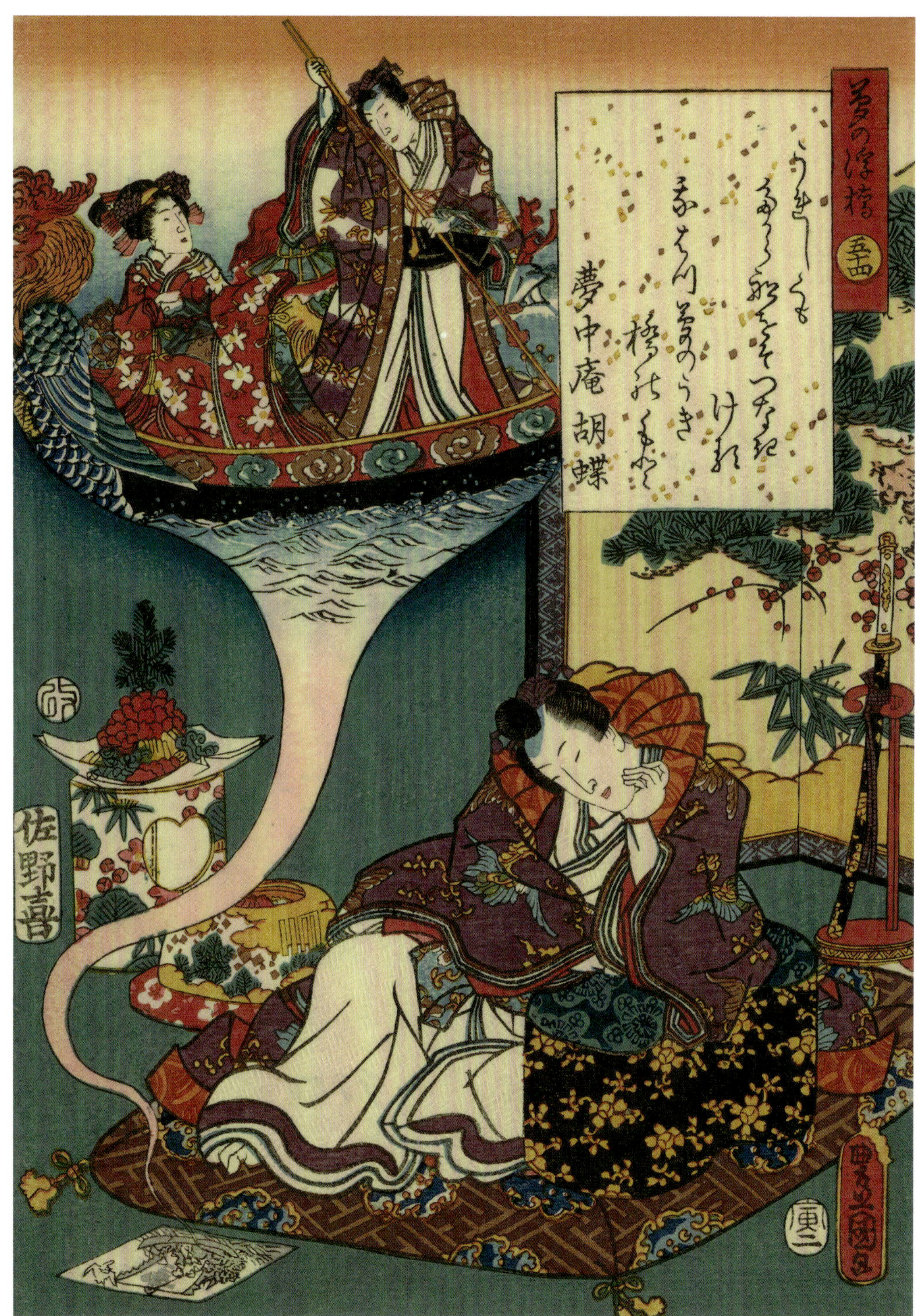

54B | Kunisada, *The Color Print Contest of a Modern Genji*, 1854

54C | Kunisada II, *Lady Murasaki's Genji Cards*, 1857

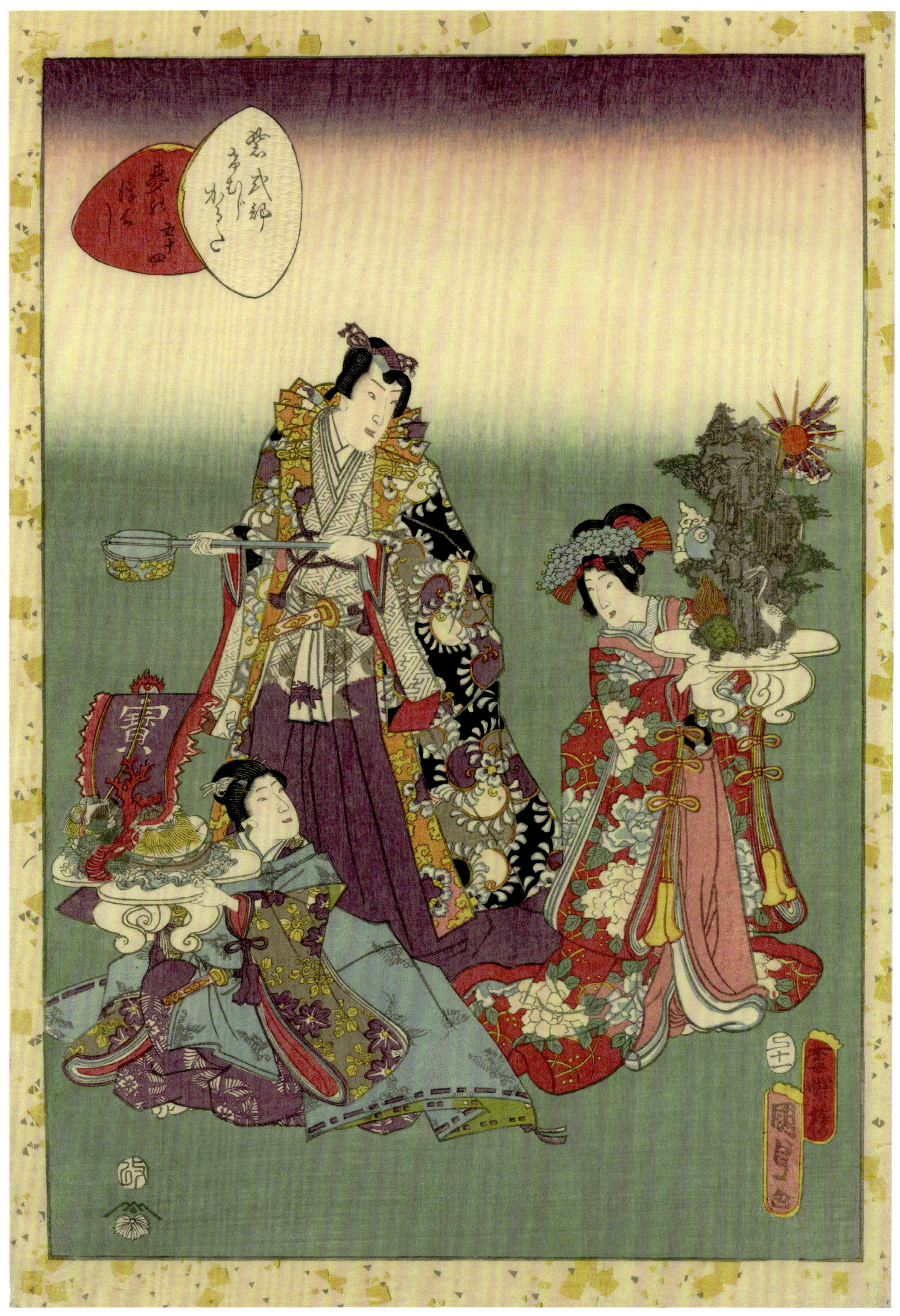
紫式部
げんじかるた
夢の浮橋 五十四

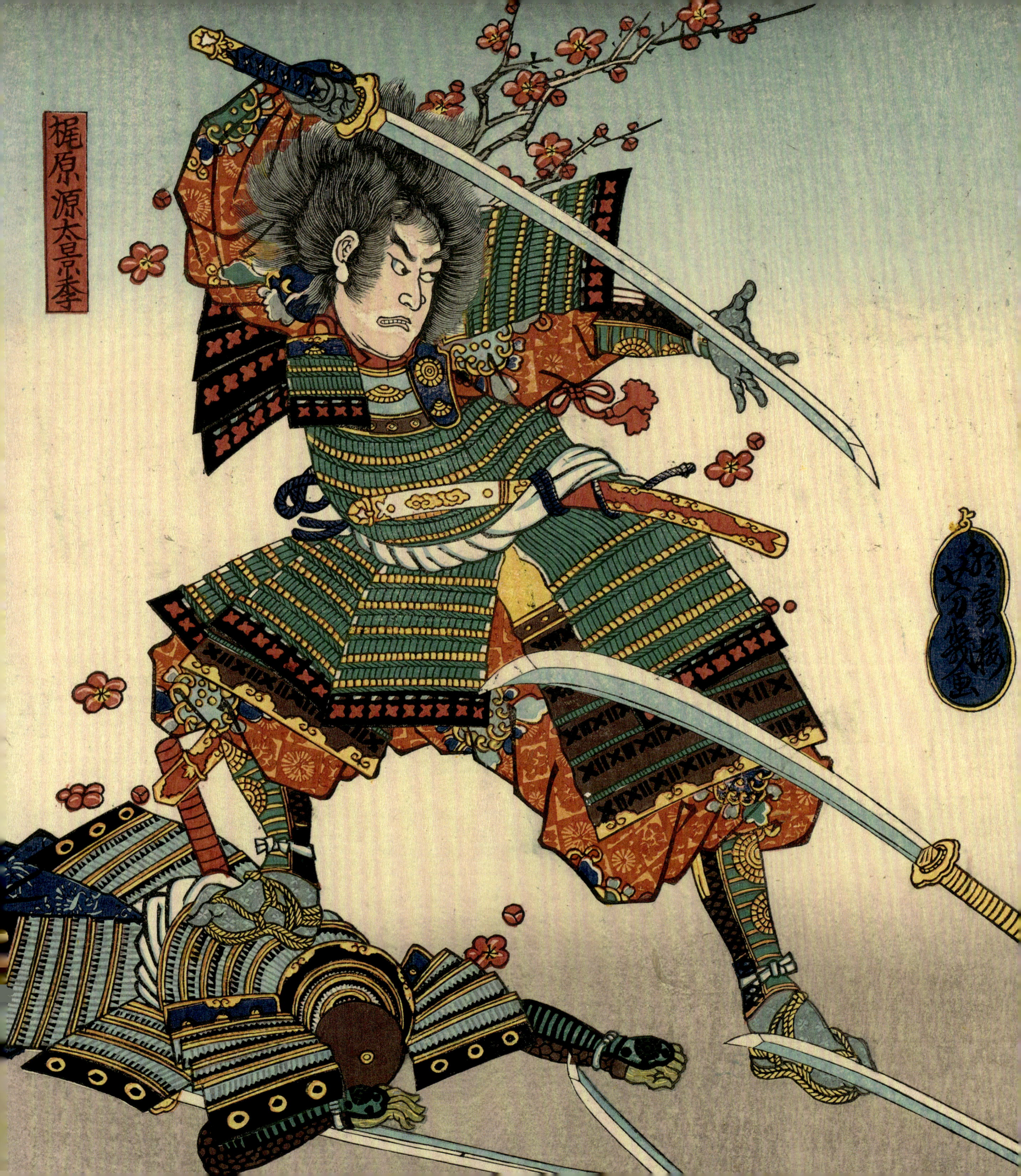
梶原源太景季

List of Illustrations

All works are in the collection of the Museum of Fine Arts, Boston. Unless otherwise stated, the format of each work is a vertical chūban (about 26 x 19 cm [10 1/4 x 7 1/2 in.]) and the medium is woodblock print (nishiki-e), ink and color on paper. Works attributed to Kunisada are by Utagawa Kunisada I (Toyokuni III) (1786–1864).

1 The Paulownia Courtyard (Kiritsubo)

1A Kunisada
Kiritsubo from the series *Genji Incense Pictures* (*Genji kō no zu*), 1844–47
Publisher: Yamamotoya Heikichi (Eikyūdō)
24.8 x 17.8 cm (9 3/4 x 7 in.)
Gift of the Anne Gordon Keidel Trust of June 2016, 2016.1532

1B Utagawa Hiroshige I (1797–1858)
Kiritsubo from the series *The Fifty-Four Chapters of the Tale of Genji* (*Genji monogatari gojūyojō*), 1852
Publisher: Iseya Kanekichi
Horizontal ōban; 24 x 37 cm (9 1/2 x 14 5/8 in.)
William S. and John T. Spaulding Collection, 21.9404

1C Kunisada
Kiritsubo from the series *The Color Print Contest of a Modern Genji* (*Ima Genji nishiki-e awase*), 1853
Publisher: Sanoya Kihei (Kikakudō)
25.6 x 18 cm (10 1/8 x 7 1/8 in.)
William Sturgis Bigelow Collection, 11.20809

2 The Broom Tree (Hahakigi)

2A Kunisada
Hahakigi from the series *Genji Incense Pictures* (*Genji kō no zu*), 1844–47
Publisher: Yamamotoya Heikichi (Eikyūdō)
24.9 x 17.8 cm (9 3/4 x 7 in.)
Gift of the Anne Gordon Keidel Trust of June 2016, 2016.1533

2B Kunisada
Parody of the Comparison of Women in The Tale of Genji (*Mitate Genji shinasadame*), 1855
Publisher: Ebisuya Shōshichi (Kinshōdō)
Vertical ōban diptych; 36.8 x 50.2 cm (14 1/2 x 19 3/4 in.)
William Sturgis Bigelow Collection, 11.43639a-b

2C Kunisada
Hahakigi from the series *The Color Print Contest of a Modern Genji* (*Ima Genji nishiki-e awase*), 1853
Publisher: Sanoya Kihei (Kikakudō)
26.2 x 18 cm (10 3/8 x 7 1/8 in.)
William Sturgis Bigelow Collection, 11.20851

3 The Shell of the Cicada (Utsusemi)

3A Kunisada
Utsusemi from the series *Genji Incense Pictures* (*Genji kō no zu*), 1844–47
Publisher: Yamamotoya Heikichi (Eikyūdō)
24.9 x 17.9 cm (9 3/4 x 7 in.)
Gift of the Anne Gordon Keidel Trust of June 2016, 2016.1534

3B Utagawa Hiroshige I (1797–1858)
Utsusemi from the series *The Fifty-Four Chapters of the Tale of Genji* (*Genji monogatari gojūyojō*), 1852
Publisher: Iseya Kanekichi
Horizontal ōban; 24.3 x 37.5 cm (9 5/8 x 14 3/4 in.)
William S. and John T. Spaulding Collection, 21.9406

3C Kunisada
Utsusemi from the series *The Color Print Contest of a Modern Genji* (*Ima Genji nishiki-e awase*), 1853
Publisher: Sanoya Kihei (Kikakudō)
25.8 x 18 cm (10 1/8 x 7 1/8 in.)
William Sturgis Bigelow Collection, 11.20914

3D Kunisada
Figures in Edo Purple: The Utsusemi Chapter (*Edo Murasaki sugata no Utsusemi*), 1847–52
Publisher: Sanoya Kihei (Kikakudō)
Vertical ōban triptych; 37.6 x 76.7 cm (14 3/4 x 30 1/4 in.)
William Sturgis Bigelow Collection, 11.15168, 11.15217, 11.15729

4 Evening Faces (Yūgao)

4A Kunisada
Yūgao from the series *Genji Incense Pictures* (*Genji kō no zu*), 1844–47
Publisher: Yamamotoya Heikichi (Eikyūdō)
24.7 x 17.9 cm (9 3/4 x 7 in.)
Gift of the Anne Gordon Keidel Trust of June 2016, 2016.1535

4B Suzuki Harunobu (1725–1770)
Parody of the Yūgao chapter of *The Tale of Genji*, about 1766
Vertical chūban diptych; 24.5 x 37.5 cm (9 5/8 x 14 3/4 in.)
Museum of Fine Arts, Boston — Worcester Art Museum exchange, made possible through the Special Korean Pottery Fund, Museum purchase with funds donated by contribution, and Smithsonian Institution — Chinese Expedition, 1923–24, 54.348-9

4C Kunisada
Yūgao from the series *The Color Print Contest of a Modern Genji* (*Ima Genji nishiki-e awase*), 1852
Publisher: Sanoya Kihei (Kikakudō)
25.7 x 18.1 cm (10 1/8 x 7 1/8 in.)
William Sturgis Bigelow Collection, 11.20798

4D Kunisada
Actors Ichikawa Kuzō II as Shinonome (R), Bandō Shūka I as Tasogare, Ōtani Tomomatsu I as Korekichi (C), Ichikawa Komazō VII as Akamatsu Tarō, and Ichikawa Danjūrō VIII as Ashikaga Jirō no kimi (L), 1851
Publisher: Yamamotoya Heikichi (Eikyūdō)
Vertical ōban triptych; 36.4 x 75.2 cm (14 3/8 x 29 5/8 in.)
William Sturgis Bigelow Collection, 11.44031a-c

4E Kunisada
Actors Bandō Shūka I as Tasogare (R), Ichikawa Danjūrō VIII as Ashikaga Jirō no kimi (C), and Fujikawa Kayū III as the Living Ghost of Akogi (Akogi no ikiryō) (L), 1851
Publisher: Yamadaya Shōjirō
Vertical ōban triptych; 36.4 x 74.7 cm (14 3/8 x 29 3/8 in.)
William Sturgis Bigelow Collection, 11.44063a-c

5 Young Lavender (Wakamurasaki)

5A Kunisada
Wakamurasaki from the series *Genji Incense Pictures* (*Genji kō no zu*), 1844–47
Publisher: Yamamotoya Heikichi (Eikyūdō)
24.9 x 17.8 cm (9 3/4 x 7 in.)
Gift of the Anne Gordon Keidel Trust of June 2016, 2016.1536

5B Utagawa Hiroshige I (1797–1858)
Wakamurasaki from the series *The Fifty-Four Chapters of the Tale of Genji* (*Genji monogatari gojūyojō*), 1852
Publisher: Iseya Kanekichi
Horizontal ōban; 23.3 x 37 cm (9 1/8 x 14 5/8 in.)
William S. and John T. Spaulding Collection, 21.9408

5C Kunisada
Wakamurasaki from the series *The Color Print Contest of a Modern Genji* (*Ima Genji nishiki-e awase*), 1853
Publisher: Sanoya Kihei (Kikakudō)
25.8 x 18 cm (10 1/8 x 7 1/8 in.)
William Sturgis Bigelow Collection, 11.20921

5D Kunisada
Mountain Scenery of Mount Kurama from the Book Inaka Genji by Tanehiko (*Tanehiko saku Inaka Genji no uchi Kurama-yama yama no kei*), 1830s
Publisher: Tsuruya Kiemon (Senkakudō)
Vertical ōban triptych; 37 x 77.4 cm (14 5/8 x 30 1/2 in.)
Nellie Parney Carter Collection — Bequest of Nellie Parney Carter, 34.418a-c

6 The Safflower (Suetsumuhana)

6A Kunisada
Suetsumuhana from the series *Genji Incense Pictures* (*Genji kō no zu*), 1844–47
Publisher: Yamamotoya Heikichi (Eikyūdō)
24.9 x 17.9 cm (9 3/4 x 7 in.)
Gift of the Anne Gordon Keidel Trust of June 2016, 2016.1537

6B Okumura Masanobu (1686–1764)
The Suetsumuhana Chapter from The Tale of Genji (*Genji Suetsumuhana*) from a series of Genji parodies, about 1710
Woodblock print (sumizuri-e); ink on paper
Horizontal ōban; 25.8 x 35 cm (10 1/8 x 13 3/4 in.)
William Sturgis Bigelow Collection, 11.13357

6C Kunisada
Suetsumuhana from the series *The Color Print Contest of a Modern Genji* (*Ima Genji nishiki-e awase*), 1852
Publisher: Sanoya Kihei (Kikakudō)
26 x 18.1 cm (10 1/4 x 7 1/8 in.)
William Sturgis Bigelow Collection, 11.20926

7 An Autumn Excursion (Momiji no ga)

7A Kunisada
Momiji no ga from the series *Genji Incense Pictures* (*Genji kō no zu*), 1844–47
Publisher: Yamamotoya Heikichi (Eikyūdō)
24.8 x 17.9 cm (9 3/4 x 7 in.)
Gift of the Anne Gordon Keidel Trust of June 2016, 2016.1538

7B Chōbunsai Eishi (1756–1829)
Momiji no ga from the series *Genji in Fashionable Modern Guise* (*Fūryū yatsushi Genji*), about 1792
Publisher: Izumiya Ichibei (Kansendō)
Vertical ōban triptych; 37.2 x 76.3 cm (14 5/8 x 30 in.)
William Sturgis Bigelow Collection, 11.14032, 11.14107, 11.14108

7C Kunisada
Momiji no ga from the series *The Color Print Contest of a Modern Genji* (*Ima Genji nishiki-e awase*), 1853
Publisher: Sanoya Kihei (Kikakudō)
26 x 18 cm (10 1/4 x 7 1/8 in.)
William Sturgis Bigelow Collection, 11.20925

7D Kunisada
Actors Bandō Hikosaburō IV as Asakura Tōgo, Onoe Kikujirō II as Jijo Katsuragi (R), Bandō Hikosaburō IV as Higashiyama Yoshimasa kō (C), Nakamura Tsuruzō I as Yamana Saburō, and Nakamura Fukusuke I as Ashikaga Mitsuuji (L), 1855
Publisher: Daikokuya Heikichi
Vertical ōban triptych; 37 x 75.5 cm (14 5/8 x 29 3/4 in.)
William Sturgis Bigelow Collection, 11.44195a-c

8 The Festival of the Cherry Blossoms (Hana no en)

8A Kunisada
Hana no en from the series *Genji Incense Pictures* (*Genji kō no zu*), 1844–47
Publisher: Yamamotoya Heikichi (Eikyūdō)
24.8 x 17.9 cm (9 3/4 x 7 in.)
Gift of the Anne Gordon Keidel Trust of June 2016, 2016.1539

8B Kunisada
Hana no en from the series *The Color Print Contest of a Modern Genji* (*Ima Genji nishiki-e awase*), 1852
Publisher: Sanoya Kihei (Kikakudō)
25.6 x 18 cm (10 1/8 x 7 1/8 in.)
William Sturgis Bigelow Collection, 11.20821

8C Kunisada
Hana no en from an untitled series of Genji pictures, 1852
Publisher: Hamadaya Tokubei
25.5 x 18.1 cm (10 1/8 x 7 1/8 in.)
William Sturgis Bigelow Collection, 11.21168

9 Heartvine (Aoi)

9A Kunisada
Aoi from the series *Genji Incense Pictures* (*Genji kō no zu*), 1844–47
Publisher: Yamamotoya Heikichi (Eikyūdō)
24.8 x 17.9 cm (9 3/4 x 7 in.)
Gift of the Anne Gordon Keidel Trust of June 2016, 2016.1540

9B Nishimura Shigenaga (1697?–1756)
Aoi from the series *Genji in Fifty-Four Sheets* (*Genji gojūyonmai no uchi*), about 1735
Publisher: Izumiya Gonshirō
Woodblock print (beni-e); ink on paper, with hand-applied and stenciled color and metallic powder
Horizontal hosoban; 15.9 x 32.9 cm (6 1/4 x 13 in.)
William Sturgis Bigelow Collection, 11.19129

9C Kunisada
Aoi from the series *The Color Print Contest of a Modern Genji* (*Ima Genji nishiki-e awase*), 1852
Publisher: Sanoya Kihei (Kikakudō)
26.2 x 18.1 cm (10 3/8 x 7 1/8 in.)
William Sturgis Bigelow Collection, 11.20844

10 The Sacred Tree (Sakaki)

10A Kunisada
Sakaki from the series *Genji Incense Pictures* (*Genji kō no zu*), 1844–47
Publisher: Yamamotoya Heikichi (Eikyūdō)
24.8 x 17.9 cm (9 3/4 x 7 in.)
Gift of the Anne Gordon Keidel Trust of June 2016, 2016.1541

10B Utagawa Toyokuni I (1769–1825)
Sakaki from the series *The Tale of Genji*, Edo period
23.3 x 17.9 cm (9 1/8 x 7 in.)
William Sturgis Bigelow Collection, 11.21014

10C Kunisada
Sakaki from the series *The Color Print Contest of a Modern Genji* (*Ima Genji nishiki-e awase*), 1853
Publisher: Sanoya Kihei (Kikakudō)
26 x 18 cm (10 1/4 x 7 1/8 in.)
William Sturgis Bigelow Collection, 11.20916

11 The Village of Falling Blossoms (Hanachirusato)

11A Kunisada
Hanachirusato from the series *Genji Incense Pictures* (*Genji kō no zu*), 1844–47
Publisher: Yamamotoya Heikichi (Eikyūdō)
24.7 x 17.9 cm (9 3/4 x 7 in.)
Gift of the Anne Gordon Keidel Trust of June 2016, 2016.1542

11B Kikukawa Eizan (1787–1867)
Clearing Weather of Hanachirusato (*Hanachirusato no seiran*): *Tsukasa of the Ōgiya, kamuro Ageha and Kochō* from the series *Eight Views of Genji* (*Genji hakkei*), about 1814–17
Publisher: Izumiya Ichibei (Kansendō)
Vertical ōban; 39 x 26 cm (15 3/8 x 10 1/4 in.)
William Sturgis Bigelow Collection, 11.17709

11C Kunisada
Hanachirusato from the series *The Color Print Contest of a Modern Genji* (*Ima Genji nishiki-e awase*), 1854
Publisher: Sanoya Kihei (Kikakudō)
25.7 x 18 cm (10 1/8 x 7 1/8 in.)
William Sturgis Bigelow Collection, 11.20824

12 Suma (Suma)

12A Kunisada
Suma from the series *Genji Incense Pictures* (*Genji kō no zu*), 1844–47
Publisher: Yamamotoya Heikichi (Eikyūdō)
24.8 x 17.9 cm (9 3/4 x 7 in.)
Gift of the Anne Gordon Keidel Trust of June 2016, 2016.1543

12B Chōbunsai Eishi (1756–1829)
Returning Sails at Suma (*Suma kihan*) from the series *Eight Views of Genji in the Floating World* (*Ukiyo Genji hakkei*), about 1797–99
Publisher: Nishimuraya Yohachi (Eijudō)
Vertical ōban; 38 x 24.7 cm (15 x 9 3/4 in.)
William S. and John T. Spaulding Collection, 21.4938

12c Kunisada
Suma from the series *The Color Print Contest of a Modern Genji* (*Ima Genji nishiki-e awase*), 1853
Publisher: Sanoya Kihei (Kikakudō)
26 x 18.2 cm (10 1/4 x 7 1/8 in.)
William Sturgis Bigelow Collection, 11.20857

13 Akashi (Akashi)

13A Kunisada
Akashi from the series *Genji Incense Pictures* (*Genji kō no zu*), 1844–47
Publisher: Yamamotoya Heikichi (Eikyūdō)
24.8 x 17.9 cm (9 3/4 x 7 in.)
Gift of the Anne Gordon Keidel Trust of June 2016, 2016.1544

13B Kunisada
Akashi from the series *The Color Print Contest of a Modern Genji* (*Ima Genji nishiki-e awase*), 1852
Publisher: Sanoya Kihei (Kikakudō)
26.1 x 18.1 cm (10 1/4 x 7 1/8 in.)
William Sturgis Bigelow Collection, 11.20852

13c Kunisada
Utagawa Hiroshige I (1797–1858)
Akashi from the series *Fashionable Genji* (*Fūryū Genji*), 1853
Publisher: Iseya Kanekichi
Vertical ōban triptych; 34.6 x 74.9 cm (13 5/8 x 29 1/2 in.)
William Sturgis Bigelow Collection, 11.26794, 11.26795, 11.29805

13D Kunisada
The Akashi Bathhouse (*Akashi-buro*), 1847–52
Publisher: Tsutaya Jūzaburō (Kōshodō)
Vertical ōban, two-tier hexaptych; 72.5 x 74.5 cm (28 1/2 x 29 3/8 in.)
William Sturgis Bigelow Collection, 11.26976-81

14 Channel Markers (Miotsukushi)

14A Kunisada
Miotsukushi from the series *Genji Incense Pictures* (*Genji kō no zu*), 1844–47
Publisher: Yamamotoya Heikichi (Eikyūdō)
24.9 x 17.9 cm (9 3/4 x 7 in.)
Gift of the Anne Gordon Keidel Trust of June 2016. 2016.1545

14B Unknown artist
Miotsukushi from an untitled series of *The Tale of Genji*, about 1836–37
Woodblock print (surimono); ink, color, and metallic pigment on paper
Shikishiban; 20.8 x 18.2 cm (8 1/4 x 7 1/8 in.)
William S. and John T. Spaulding Collection, 21.9268

14c Unknown artist
Miotsukushi from an untitled Genji postcard series, late Meiji–Taishō era
Collotype; color lithograph; ink and metallic pigment on card stock
8.8 x 13.8 cm (3 1/2 x 5 3/8 in.)
Leonard A. Lauder Collection of Japanese Postcards, 2002.19282

14D Kunisada
Miotsukushi from the series *The Color Print Contest of a Modern Genji* (*Ima Genji nishiki-e awase*), 1853
Publisher: Sanoya Kihei (Kikakudō)
26.2 x 18.3 cm (10 3/8 x 7 1/4 in.)
William Sturgis Bigelow Collection, 11.20853

15 The Wormwood Patch (Yomogiu)

15A Kunisada
Yomogiu from the series *Genji Incense Pictures* (*Genji kō no zu*), 1844–47
Publisher: Yamamotoya Heikichi (Eikyūdō)
24.8 x 17.9 cm (9 3/4 x 7 in.)
Gift of the Anne Gordon Keidel Trust of June 2016, 2016.1546

15B Kajita Hanko (1870–1917)
Yomogiu from the series *The Tale of Genji*, 1905
Publisher: Bun'endō
Color lithograph; ink and metallic pigment on coated card stock
13.8 x 8.8 cm (5 3/8 x 3 1/2 in.)
Leonard A. Lauder Collection of Japanese Postcards, 2002.966

15c Kunisada
Yomogiu from the series *The Color Print Contest of a Modern Genji* (*Ima Genji nishiki-e awase*), 1853
Publisher: Sanoya Kihei (Kikakudō)
26.1 x 18.2 cm (10 1/4 x 7 1/8 in.)
William Sturgis Bigelow Collection, 11.20843

16 The Gatehouse (Sekiya)

16A Kunisada
Sekiya from the series *Genji Incense Pictures* (*Genji kō no zu*), 1844–47
Publisher: Yamamotoya Heikichi (Eikyūdō)
24.7 x 17.9 cm (9 3/4 x 7 in.)
Gift of the Anne Gordon Keidel Trust of June 2016, 2016.1547

16B Kunisada
Sekiya from the series *The Color Print Contest of a Modern Genji* (*Ima Genji nishiki-e awase*), 1853
Publisher: Sanoya Kihei (Kikakudō)
25.6 x 18.1 cm (10 1/8 x 7 1/8 in.)
William Sturgis Bigelow Collection, 11.20829

16c Utagawa Kunisada II (Kunimasa III, Toyokuni IV) (1823–1880)
Sekiya from the series *Lady Murasaki's Genji Cards* (*Murasaki Shikibu Genji karuta*), 1857
Publisher: Tsutaya Kichizō (Kōeidō)
Vertical ōban; 37.3 x 25.3 cm (14 5/8 x 10 in.)
William Sturgis Bigelow Collection, 11.21746

17 The Picture Contest (Eawase)

17A Kunisada
Eawase from the series *Genji Incense Pictures* (*Genji kō no zu*), 1844–47
Publisher: Yamamotoya Heikichi (Eikyūdō)
24.8 x 17.9 cm (9 3/4 x 7 in.)
Gift of the Anne Gordon Keidel Trust of June 2016, 2016.1548

17B Kubo Shunman (1757–1820)
Eawase from the series *Twelve Designs from a Children's Genji for the Magaki Club* (*Magaki-ren Osana Genji jūni ban*), about 1801–18
Woodblock print (surimono); ink and color on paper
Yattsugiri; 19.5 x 13.7 cm (7 5/8 x 5 3/8 in.)
William Sturgis Bigelow Collection, 11.20765

17C Kunisada
Eawase from the series *The Color Print Contest of a Modern Genji* (*Ima Genji nishiki-e awase*), 1853
Publisher: Sanoya Kihei (Kikakudō)
25.7 x 18.1 cm (10 1/8 x 7 1/8 in.)
William Sturgis Bigelow Collection, 11.20830

17D Kunisada
Utagawa Hiroshige I (1797–1858)
View of Sagano (*Sagano fūkei*);
Eawase from the series *Fashionable Genji* (*Fūryū Genji*), 1853
Publisher: Iseya Kanekichi
Blockcutter: Yokokawa Takejirō (Hori Take)
Vertical ōban triptych; 36.8 x 76.1 cm (14 1/2 x 30 in.)
William Sturgis Bigelow Collection, 11.15184, 11.17146, 11.17153

18 The Wind in the Pines (Matsukaze)

18A Kunisada
Matsukaze from the series *Genji Incense Pictures* (*Genji kō no zu*), 1844–47
Publisher: Yamamotoya Heikichi (Eikyūdō)
24.8 x 17.7 cm (9 3/4 x 7 in.)
Gift of the Anne Gordon Keidel Trust of June 2016, 2016.1549

18B Chōbunsai Eishi (1756–1829)
Matsukaze from the series *Genji in Fashionable Modern Guise* (*Fūryū yatsushi Genji*), about 1792–93
Publisher: Izumiya Ichibei (Kansendō)
Vertical ōban triptych; 39 x 78.2 cm (15 3/8 x 30 3/4 in.)
William S. and John T. Spaulding Collection, 21.7371-3

18C Nishimura Shigenaga (1697?–1756)
Matsukaze from the series *Genji in Fifty-Four Sheets* (*Genji gojūyonmai no uchi*), about 1735
Publisher: Izumiya Gonshirō
Woodblock print (beni-e); ink on paper, with hand-applied and stenciled color and metallic powder
Horizontal hosoban; 16.2 x 33.8 cm (6 3/8 x 13 1/4 in.)
William Sturgis Bigelow Collection, 11.19132

18D Kunisada
Matsukaze from the series *The Color Print Contest of a Modern Genji* (*Ima Genji nishiki-e awase*), 1853
Publisher: Sanoya Kihei (Kikakudō)
25.9 x 18 cm (10 1/4 x 7 1/8 in.)
William Sturgis Bigelow Collection, 11.20850

19 Wisps of Cloud (Usugumo)

19A Kunisada
Usugumo from the series *Genji Incense Pictures* (*Genji kō no zu*), 1844–47
Publisher: Yamamotoya Heikichi (Eikyūdō)
24.9 x 17.9 cm (9 3/4 x 7 in.)
Gift of the Anne Gordon Keidel Trust of June 2016, 2016.1550

19B Kunisada
Usugumo from the series *The Color Print Contest of a Modern Genji* (*Ima Genji nishiki-e awase*), 1854
Publisher: Sanoya Kihei (Kikakudō)
25.6 x 18 cm (10 1/8 x 7 1/8 in.)
William Sturgis Bigelow Collection, 11.20832

19C Kunisada
Elegant Amusements of Eastern Genji (*Azuma Genji gayū no zu*), 1854
Publisher: Maruya Jinpachi (Marujin, Enjudō)
Vertical ōban triptych; 38.1 x 77.9 cm (15 x 30 5/8 in.)
William Sturgis Bigelow Collection, 11.15873-5

20 The Morning Glory (Asagao)

20A Kunisada
Asagao from the series *Genji Incense Pictures* (*Genji kō no zu*), 1844–47
24.9 x 17.9 cm (9 3/4 x 7 in.)
Gift of the Anne Gordon Keidel Trust of June 2016, 2016.1551

20B Kikukawa Eizan (1787–1867)
Asagao from the series *Eastern Figures Matched with The Tale of Genji* (*Azuma sugata Genji awase*), about 1818–23
Vertical ōban; 37.2 x 24.9 cm (14 5/8 x 9 3/4 in.)
William Sturgis Bigelow Collection, 11.17703

20C Kunisada
Asagao from the series *The Color Print Contest of a Modern Genji* (*Ima Genji nishiki-e awase*), 1852
Publisher: Sanoya Kihei (Kikakudō)
26 x 18 cm (10 1/4 x 7 1/8 in.)
William Sturgis Bigelow Collection, 11.20856

21 The Maiden (Otome)

21A Kunisada
Otome from the series *Genji Incense Pictures* (*Genji kō no zu*), 1844–47
Publisher: Yamamotoya Heikichi (Eikyūdō)
24.9 x 17.9 cm (9 3/4 x 7 in.)
Gift of the Anne Gordon Keidel Trust of June 2016, 2016.1552

21B Nishimura Shigenaga (1697?–1756)
Otome from the series *Genji in Fifty-Four Sheets* (*Genji gojūyonmai no uchi*), about 1735
Publisher: Izumiya Gonshirō
Woodblock print (beni-e); ink on paper, with hand-applied and stenciled color and metallic powder
Horizontal hosoban; 16.1 x 33.6 cm (6⅜ x 13¼ in.)
William Sturgis Bigelow Collection, 11.19141

21C Kunisada
Otome from the series *The Color Print Contest of a Modern Genji* (*Ima Genji nishiki-e awase*), 1854
25.6 x 18 cm (10⅛ x 7⅛ in.)
William Sturgis Bigelow Collection, 11.20877

22 The Jeweled Wreath (Tamakazura)

22A Kunisada
Tamakazura from the series *Genji Incense Pictures* (*Genji kō no zu*), 1844–47
Publisher: Yamamotoya Heikichi (Eikyūdō)
24.9 x 17.9 cm (9¾ x 7 in.)
Gift of the Anne Gordon Keidel Trust of June 2016, 2016.1553

22B Ryūryūkyo Shinsai (1764?–1820)
Tamakazura, Hatsune, Kochō from the series *The Tale of Genji* (*Genji monogatari*), about 1819–20
Woodblock print (surimono); ink, color, and metallic pigment on paper
Shikishiban; 20.9 x 18.6 cm (8¼ x 7⅜ in.)
William Sturgis Bigelow Collection, 11.20034

22C Kunisada
Tamakazura from the series *The Color Print Contest of a Modern Genji* (*Ima Genji nishiki-e awase*), 1852
Publisher: Sanoya Kihei (Kikakudō)
26 x 18.1 cm (10¼ x 7⅛ in.)
William Sturgis Bigelow Collection, 11.20847

23 The First Warbler (Hatsune)

23A Kunisada
Hatsune from the series *Genji Incense Pictures* (*Genji kō no zu*), 1844–47
Publisher: Yamamotoya Heikichi (Eikyūdō)
24.9 x 17.9 cm (9¾ x 7 in.)
Gift of the Anne Gordon Keidel Trust of June 2016, 2016.1554

23B Utagawa Toyokuni I (1769–1825)
Hatsune from the series *The Tale of Genji*, Edo period
23.1 x 18.2 cm (9⅛ x 7⅛ in.)
William Sturgis Bigelow Collection, 11.21017

23C Kunisada
Hatsune from the series *The Color Print Contest of a Modern Genji* (*Ima Genji nishiki-e awase*), 1852
Publisher: Sanoya Kihei (Kikakudō)
25.6 x 18 cm (10⅛ x 7⅛ in.)
William Sturgis Bigelow Collection, 11.20836

24 Butterflies (Kochō)

24A Kunisada
Kochō from the series *Genji Incense Pictures* (*Genji kō no zu*), 1844–47
Publisher: Yamamotoya Heikichi (Eikyūdō)
24.8 x 18 cm (9¾ x 7⅛ in.)
Gift of the Anne Gordon Keidel Trust of June 2016, 2016.1555

24B Utagawa Kuniyoshi (1797–1861)
Kochō: Abe no Yasuna from the series *Genji Clouds Matched with Ukiyo-e Pictures* (*Genji kumo ukiyo-e awase*), about 1845–46
Publisher: Iseya Ichibei
Vertical ōban; 36 x 23.9 cm (14⅛ x 9⅜ in.)
William Sturgis Bigelow Collection, 11.36527

24C Kunisada
Kochō from the series *The Color Print Contest of a Modern Genji* (*Ima Genji nishiki-e awase*), 1853
Publisher: Sanoya Kihei (Kikakudō)
25.7 x 18.1 cm (10⅛ x 7⅛ in.)
William Sturgis Bigelow Collection, 11.20837

25 The Firefly (Hotaru)

25A Kunisada
Hotaru from the series *Genji Incense Pictures* (*Genji kō no zu*), 1844–47
Publisher: Yamamotoya Heikichi (Eikyūdō)
24.9 x 17.9 cm (9¾ x 7 in.)
Gift of the Anne Gordon Keidel Trust of June 2016, 2016.1556

25B Ryūryūkyo Shinsai (1764?–1820)
Hotaru, Tokonatsu, Kagaribi from the series *The Tale of Genji* (*Genji monogatari*), about 1819–20
Woodblock print (surimono); ink, color, and metallic pigment on paper
Shikishiban; 20.2 x 18.3 cm (8 x 7¼ in.)
William S. and John T. Spaulding Collection, 21.9264

25C Kunisada
Hotaru from the series *The Color Print Contest of a Modern Genji* (*Ima Genji nishiki-e awase*), 1852
Publisher: Sanoya Kihei (Kikakudō)
25.7 x 18.1 cm (10⅛ x 7⅛ in.)
William Sturgis Bigelow Collection, 11.20838

26 The Wild Carnation (Tokonatsu)

26A Kunisada
Tokonatsu from the series *Genji Incense Pictures* (*Genji kō no zu*), 1844–47
Publisher: Yamamotoya Heikichi (Eikyūdō)
24.9 x 17.9 cm (9¾ x 7 in.)
Gift of the Anne Gordon Keidel Trust of June 2016, 2016.1557

26B Unknown artist
Tokonatsu from an untitled Genji series, late Meiji–Taishō era
Collotype; color lithograph; ink and metallic pigment on card stock
13.8 x 8.8 cm (5⅜ x 3½ in.)
Leonard A. Lauder Collection of Japanese Postcards, 2002.19285

26C Kunisada
Tokonatsu from the series *The Color Print Contest of a Modern Genji* (*Ima Genji nishiki-e awase*), 1852
Publisher: Sanoya Kihei (Kikakudō)
25.7 x 18 cm (10 1/8 x 7 1/8 in.)
William Sturgis Bigelow Collection, 11.20839

26D Utagawa Kunisada II (Kunimasa III, Toyokuni IV) (1823–1880)
Tokonatsu from the series *Lady Murasaki's Genji Cards* (*Murasaki Shikibu Genji karuta*), 1857
Publisher: Tsutaya Kichizō (Kōeidō)
Vertical ōban; 37.4 x 25.3 cm (14 3/4 x 10 in.)
William Sturgis Bigelow Collection, 11.21704

27 Garden Flares (Kagaribi)

27A Kunisada
Kagaribi from the series *Genji Incense Pictures* (*Genji kō no zu*), 1844–47
Publisher: Yamamotoya Heikichi (Eikyūdō)
24.8 x 17.9 cm (9 3/4 x 7 in.)
Gift of the Anne Gordon Keidel Trust of June 2016, 2016.1558

27B Chōkōsai Eishō (active 1780–1800)
Women in an iris garden; parody of the Kagaribi chapter of *The Tale of Genji*, about 1794–95
Publisher: Yamaguchiya Chūemon (Chūsuke)
Vertical ōban triptych; 38.5 x 75.5 cm (15 1/8 x 29 3/4 in.)
William S. and John T. Spaulding Collection, 21.7645-7

27C Kunisada
Kagaribi from the series *The Color Print Contest of a Modern Genji* (*Ima Genji nishiki-e awase*), 1853
Publisher: Sanoya Kihei (Kikakudō)
25.7 x 18.1 cm (10 1/8 x 7 1/8 in.)
William Sturgis Bigelow Collection, 11.20840

28 The Typhoon (Nowaki)

28A Kunisada
Nowaki from the series *Genji Incense Pictures* (*Genji kō no zu*), 1844–47
Publisher: Yamamotoya Heikichi (Eikyūdō)
24.8 x 17.9 cm (9 3/4 x 7 in.)
Gift of the Anne Gordon Keidel Trust of June 2016, 2016.1559

28B Isoda Koryūsai (1735–1790)
Nowaki from the series *Genji in Fashionable Modern Guise* (*Fūryū yatsushi Genji*), about 1770–72
22 x 15.9 cm (8 5/8 x 6 1/4 in.)
William Sturgis Bigelow Collection, 11.19752

28C Kunisada
Nowaki from the series *The Color Print Contest of a Modern Genji* (*Ima Genji nishiki-e awase*), 1852
Publisher: Sanoya Kihei (Kikakudō)
26.2 x 18.1 cm (10 3/8 x 7 1/8 in.)
William Sturgis Bigelow Collection, 11.20909

28D Utagawa Kunisada II (Kunimasa III, Toyokuni IV) (1823–1880)
Nowaki from the series *Lady Murasaki's Genji Cards* (*Murasaki Shikibu Genji karuta*), 1857
Publisher: Tsutaya Kichizō (Kōeidō)
Vertical ōban; 37.3 x 25.2 cm (14 5/8 x 9 7/8 in.)
William Sturgis Bigelow Collection, 11.21702

29 The Royal Outing (Miyuki)

29A Kunisada
Miyuki from the series *Genji Incense Pictures* (*Genji kō no zu*), 1844–47
Publisher: Yamamotoya Heikichi (Eikyūdō)
24.9 x 17.9 cm (9 3/4 x 7 in.)
Gift of the Anne Gordon Keidel Trust of June 2016, 2016.1560

29B Kunisada
Miyuki from the series *The Color Print Contest of a Modern Genji* (*Ima Genji nishiki-e awase*), 1853
Publisher: Sanoya Kihei (Kikakudō)
25.6 x 18 cm (10 1/8 x 7 1/8 in.)
William Sturgis Bigelow Collection, 11.20803

29C Kunisada
Miyuki from an untitled series of Genji pictures, 1852
Publisher: Hamadaya Tokubei
26 x 18.3 cm (10 1/4 x 7 1/4 in.)
William Sturgis Bigelow Collection, 11.21163

30 Purple Trousers (Fujibakama)

30A Kunisada
Fujibakama from the series *Genji Incense Pictures* (*Genji kō no zu*), 1844–47
Publisher: Yamamotoya Heikichi (Eikyūdō)
24.8 x 17.9 cm (9 3/4 x 7 in.)
Gift of the Anne Gordon Keidel Trust of June 2016, 2016.1561

30B Kunisada
Fujibakama from the series *The Color Print Contest of a Modern Genji* (*Ima Genji nishiki-e awase*), 1852
Publisher: Sanoya Kihei (Kikakudō)
26.3 x 18.1 cm (10 3/8 x 7 1/8 in.)
William Sturgis Bigelow Collection, 11.20855

30C Utagawa Kunisada II (Kunimasa III, Toyokuni IV) (1823–1880)
Fujibakama from the series *Lady Murasaki's Genji Cards* (*Murasaki Shikibu Genji karuta*), 1857
Publisher: Tsutaya Kichizō (Kōeidō)
Vertical ōban; 37.4 x 25.4 cm (14 3/4 x 10 in.)
William Sturgis Bigelow Collection, 11.21700

31 The Cypress Pillar (Makibashira)

31A Kunisada
Makibashira from the series *Genji Incense Pictures* (*Genji kō no zu*), 1844–47
Publisher: Yamamotoya Heikichi (Eikyūdō)
24.9 x 17.9 cm (9 3/4 x 7 in.)
Gift of the Anne Gordon Keidel Trust of June 2016, 2016.1562

31B Utagawa Yoshiiku (1833–1904)
Makibashira: Chinzei Hachirō Tametomo from the series *Modern Parodies of Genji* (*Imayō nazorae Genji*), 1864
Publisher: Ōmiya Kyūjirō (Kiyūdō)
Vertical ōban; 36 x 23.7 cm (14 1/8 x 9 3/8 in.)
William Sturgis Bigelow Collection, 11.41123

31C Kunisada
Makibashira from the series *The Color Print Contest of a Modern Genji* (*Ima Genji nishiki-e awase*), 1854
Publisher: Sanoya Kihei (Kikakudō)
25.6 x 18 cm (10 1/8 x 7 1/8 in.)
William Sturgis Bigelow Collection, 11.20873

31D Utagawa Kunisada II (Kunimasa III, Toyokuni IV) (1823–1880)
Makibashira from the series *Lady Murasaki's Genji Cards* (*Murasaki Shikibu Genji karuta*), 1857
Publisher: Tsutaya Kichizō (Kōeidō)
Vertical ōban; 37.3 x 25.4 cm (14 5/8 x 10 in.)
William Sturgis Bigelow Collection, 11.21699

32 A Branch of Plum (Umegae)

32A Kunisada
Umegae from the series *Genji Incense Pictures* (*Genji kō no zu*), 1844–47
Publisher: Yamamotoya Heikichi (Eikyūdō)
24.9 x 17.9 cm (9 3/4 x 7 in.)
Gift of the Anne Gordon Keidel Trust of June 2016, 2016.1563

32B Utagawa Hiroshige I (1797–1858)
Plum Garden at Kameido (*Mitate Umegae, Kameido umeyashiki*) from the series *Famous Places in Edo and Murasaki's Genji* (*Edo Murasaki meisho Genji*), 1843–47
Publisher: Ibaya Kyūbei
Vertical ōban; 33.5 x 22.6 cm (13 1/4 x 8 7/8 in.)
Gift of Miss Lucy T. Aldrich, 47.23

32C Kunisada
Umegae from the series *The Color Print Contest of a Modern Genji* (*Ima Genji nishiki-e awase*), 1854
Publisher: Sanoya Kihei (Kikakudō)
25.7 x 18.1 cm (10 1/8 x 7 1/8 in.)
William Sturgis Bigelow Collection, 11.20874

33 New Wisteria Leaves (Fuji no uraba)

33A Kunisada
Fuji no uraba from the series *Genji Incense Pictures* (*Genji kō no zu*), 1844–47
Publisher: Yamamotoya Heikichi (Eikyūdō)
24.8 x 17.9 cm (9 3/4 x 7 in.)
Gift of the Anne Gordon Keidel Trust of June 2016, 2016.1564

33B Chōbunsai Eishi (1756–1829)
Fuji no uraba from the series *Genji in Fashionable Modern Guise* (*Fūryū yatsushi Genji*), about 1791–94
Publisher: Izumiya Ichibei (Kansendō)
Vertical ōban triptych; 37.6 x 74.1 cm (14 3/4 x 29 1/8 in.)
William S. and John T. Spaulding Collection, 21.4856-8

33C Kunisada
Fuji no uraba from the series *The Color Print Contest of a Modern Genji* (*Ima Genji nishiki-e awase*), 1853
Publisher: Sanoya Kihei (Kikakudō)
26.1 x 18.1 cm (10 1/4 x 7 1/8 in.)
William Sturgis Bigelow Collection, 11.20946

34 Young Shoots, Part 1 (Wakana I)

34A Kunisada
Wakana no jō from the series *Genji Incense Pictures* (*Genji kō no zu*), 1844–47
Publisher: Yamamotoya Heikichi (Eikyūdō)
24.8 x 17.9 cm (9 3/4 x 7 in.)
Gift of the Anne Gordon Keidel Trust of June 2016, 2016.1565

34B Chōbunsai Eishi (1756–1829)
The Wakana Chapter, Part 1 (*Wakana no maki, jō*) from the series *Genji in Fashionable Modern Guise* (*Fūryū yatsushi Genji*), about 1790–91
Publisher: Izumiya Ichibei (Kansendō)
Vertical ōban triptych; 39 x 77.5 cm (15 3/8 x 30 1/2 in.)
William Sturgis Bigelow Collection, 11.14015, 11.14098, 11.14099

34C Kunisada
Wakana no jō from the series *The Color Print Contest of a Modern Genji* (*Ima Genji nishiki-e awase*), 1852
Publisher: Sanoya Kihei (Kikakudō)
25.9 x 18.1 cm (10 1/4 x 7 1/8 in.)
William Sturgis Bigelow Collection, 11.20846

34D Kunisada
Eastern Genji: The Wakana Chapter (*Azuma Genji Wakana no maki*), 1854
Publisher: Maruya Jinpachi (Marujin, Enjudō)
Vertical ōban triptych; 37.7 x 78 cm (14 7/8 x 30 3/4 in.)
William Sturgis Bigelow Collection, 11.15900-2

34E Kunisada
Utagawa Kuniteru II (Kunitsuna II) (1830–1874)
Cherry Blossoms at Genji's Rokujō Mansion (*Genji Rokujō no hana*), 1854
Publisher: Moriya Jihei (Kinshindō)
Vertical ōban triptych; 36.9 x 76.4 cm (14 1/2 x 30 1/8 in.)
William Sturgis Bigelow Collection, 11.15169, 11.15178, 11.15233

35 Young Shoots, Part 2 (Wakana II)

35A Kunisada
Wakana no ge from the series *Genji Incense Pictures* (*Genji kō no zu*), 1844–47
Publisher: Yamamotoya Heikichi (Eikyūdō)
24.9 x 17.9 cm (9 3/4 x 7 in.)
Gift of the Anne Gordon Keidel Trust of June 2016, 2016.1566

35B Utagawa Kuniyoshi (1797–1861)
Poem by Gonchūnagon Sadaie from the series *One Hundred Poems by One Hundred Poets* (*Hyakunin isshu no uchi*), about 1840–42
Publisher: Ehiko
Vertical ōban; 37.9 x 26.5 cm (14 7/8 x 10 3/8 in.)
William Sturgis Bigelow Collection, 11.16021

35C Kunisada
Wakana no ge from the series *The Color Print Contest of a Modern Genji* (*Ima Genji nishiki-e awase*), 1854
Publisher: Sanoya Kihei (Kikakudō)
25.6 x 18 cm (10 1/8 x 7 1/8 in.)
William Sturgis Bigelow Collection, 11.20871

36 The Oak Tree (Kashiwagi)

36A Kunisada
Kashiwagi from the series *Genji Incense Pictures* (*Genji kō no zu*), 1844–47
Publisher: Yamamotoya Heikichi (Eikyūdō)
24.9 x 17.9 cm (9 3/4 x 7 in.)
Gift of the Anne Gordon Keidel Trust of June 2016, 2016.1567

36B Isoda Koryūsai (1735–1790)
Kashiwagi from the series *Genji in Fashionable Modern Guise* (*Fūryū yatsushi Genji*), about 1770–72
22.1 x 15.9 cm (8 3/4 x 6 1/4 in.)
William Sturgis Bigelow Collection, 11.21800

36C Kunisada
Kashiwagi from the series *The Color Print Contest of a Modern Genji* (*Ima Genji nishiki-e awase*), 1854
Publisher: Sanoya Kihei (Kikakudō)
25.6 x 18.1 cm (10 1/8 x 7 1/8 in.)
William Sturgis Bigelow Collection, 11.20870

36D Utagawa Kunisada II (Kunimasa III, Toyokuni IV) (1823–1880)
Kashiwagi from the series *Lady Murasaki's Genji Cards* (*Murasaki Shikibu Genji karuta*), 1857
Publisher: Tsutaya Kichizō (Kōeidō)
Vertical ōban; 35.2 x 24.4 cm (13 7/8 x 9 5/8 in.)
William Sturgis Bigelow Collection, 11.44581

37 The Flute (Yokobue)

37A Kunisada
Yokobue from the series *Genji Incense Pictures* (*Genji kō no zu*), 1844–47
Publisher: Yamamotoya Heikichi (Eikyūdō)
24.9 x 17.9 cm (9 3/4 x 7 in.)
Gift of the Anne Gordon Keidel Trust of June 2016, 2016.1568

37B Kajita Hanko (1870–1917)
Yokobue from the series *The Tale of Genji*, 1905
Publisher: Bun'endō
Color lithograph; ink and metallic pigment on card stock
13.8 x 8.8 cm (5 3/8 x 3 1/2 in.)
Leonard A. Lauder Collection of Japanese Postcards, 2002.974

37C Kunisada
Yokobue from the series *The Color Print Contest of a Modern Genji* (*Ima Genji nishiki-e awase*), 1854
Publisher: Sanoya Kihei (Kikakudō)
25.7 x 18.1 cm (10 1/8 x 7 1/8 in.)
William Sturgis Bigelow Collection, 11.20869

37D Utagawa Kunisada II (Kunimasa III, Toyokuni IV) (1823–1880)
Yokobue from the series *Lady Murasaki's Genji Cards* (*Murasaki Shikibu Genji karuta*), 1857
Publisher: Tsutaya Kichizō (Kōeidō)
Vertical ōban; 35.2 x 24.4 cm (13 7/8 x 9 5/8 in.)
William Sturgis Bigelow Collection, 11.44582

38 The Bell Cricket (Suzumushi)

38A Kunisada
Suzumushi from the series *Genji Incense Pictures* (*Genji kō no zu*), 1844–47
Publisher: Yamamotoya Heikichi (Eikyūdō)
24.8 x 17.9 cm (9 3/4 x 7 in.)
Gift of the Anne Gordon Keidel Trust of June 2016, 2016.1569

38B Kunisada
Suzumushi from the series *The Color Print Contest of a Modern Genji* (*Ima Genji nishiki-e awase*), 1852
Publisher: Sanoya Kihei (Kikakudō)
25.6 x 18 cm (10 1/8 x 7 1/8 in.)
William Sturgis Bigelow Collection, 11.20792

39 Evening Mist (Yūgiri)

39A Kunisada
Yūgiri from the series *Genji Incense Pictures* (*Genji kō no zu*), 1844–47
Publisher: Yamamotoya Heikichi (Eikyūdō)
24.9 x 18 cm (9 3/4 x 7 1/8 in.)
Gift of the Anne Gordon Keidel Trust of June 2016, 2016.1570

39B Kunisada
Yūgiri from the series *The Color Print Contest of a Modern Genji* (*Ima Genji nishiki-e awase*), 1852
Publisher: Sanoya Kihei (Kikakudō)
25.8 x 18.1 cm (10 1/8 x 7 1/8 in.)
William Sturgis Bigelow Collection, 11.20849

39C Utagawa Kunisada II (Kunimasa III, Toyokuni IV) (1823–1880)
Yūgiri from the series *Lady Murasaki's Genji Cards* (*Murasaki Shikibu Genji karuta*), 1857
Publisher: Tsutaya Kichizō (Kōeidō)
Vertical ōban; 37.3 x 25.3 cm (14 5/8 x 10 in.)
William Sturgis Bigelow Collection, 11.21749

40 The Law (Minori)

40A Kunisada
Minori from the series *Genji Incense Pictures* (*Genji kō no zu*), 1844–47
Publisher: Yamamotoya Heikichi (Eikyūdō)
24.8 x 17.9 cm (9 3/4 x 7 in.)
Gift of the Anne Gordon Keidel Trust of June 2016, 2016.1571

40B Kunisada
Minori from the series *The Color Print Contest of a Modern Genji* (*Ima Genji nishiki-e awase*), 1854
Publisher: Sanoya Kihei (Kikakudō)
25.7 x 18 cm (10 1/8 x 7 1/8 in.)
William Sturgis Bigelow Collection, 11.20794

40C Utagawa Kunisada II (Kunimasa III, Toyokuni IV) (1823–1880)
Utagawa Hiroshige II (Shigenobu) (1826–1869)
Minori from the series *Traces of Genji in Fifty-Four Chapters* (*Omokage Genji gojūyojō*), 1864
Publisher: Tsutaya Kichizō (Kōeidō)
Vertical ōban; 37.5 x 25.4 cm (14 3/4 x 10 in.)
William Sturgis Bigelow Collection, 11.15554

41 The Wizard (Maboroshi)

41A Kunisada
Maboroshi from the series *Genji Incense Pictures* (*Genji kō no zu*), 1844–47
Publisher: Yamamotoya Heikichi (Eikyūdō)
24.7 x 17.9 cm (9 3/4 x 7 in.)
Gift of the Anne Gordon Keidel Trust of June 2016, 2016.1572

41B Kunisada
Maboroshi from the series *The Color Print Contest of a Modern Genji* (*Ima Genji nishiki-e awase*), 1854
Publisher: Sanoya Kihei (Kikakudō)
25.6 x 18.1 cm (10 1/8 x 7 1/8 in.)
William Sturgis Bigelow Collection, 11.20795

41C Utagawa Kuniyoshi (1797–1861)
Maboroshi: Nikki Naonori from the series *Genji Clouds Matched with Ukiyo-e Pictures* (*Genji kumo ukiyo-e awase*), about 1845–46
Publisher: Iseya Ichibei
Vertical ōban; 36.8 x 25 cm (14 1/2 x 9 7/8 in.)
William Sturgis Bigelow Collection, 11.36538

42 The Perfumed Prince (Niou no miya)

42A Kunisada
Niou no miya from the series *Genji Incense Pictures* (*Genji kō no zu*), 1844–47
Publisher: Yamamotoya Heikichi (Eikyūdō)
24.9 x 18 cm (9 3/4 x 7 1/8 in.)
Gift of the Anne Gordon Keidel Trust of June 2016, 2016.1573

42B Kunisada
Niou no miya from the series *The Color Print Contest of a Modern Genji* (*Ima Genji nishiki-e awase*), 1854
Publisher: Sanoya Kihei (Kikakudō)
25.7 x 18 cm (10 1/8 x 7 1/8 in.)
William Sturgis Bigelow Collection, 11.20917

43 Red Plum (Kōbai)

43A Kunisada
Kōbai from the series *Genji Incense Pictures* (*Genji kō no zu*), 1844–47
Publisher: Yamamotoya Heikichi (Eikyūdō)
24.9 x 17.9 cm (9 3/4 x 7 in.)
Gift of the Anne Gordon Keidel Trust of June 2016, 2016.1574

43B Kunisada
Kōbai from the series *The Color Print Contest of a Modern Genji* (*Ima Genji nishiki-e awase*), 1852
Publisher: Sanoya Kihei (Kikakudō)
25.8 x 18 cm (10 1/8 x 7 1/8 in.)
William Sturgis Bigelow Collection, 11.20918

43C Utagawa Yoshiiku (1833–1904)
Miyagi Gengyo (1817–1880)
Kōbai: Kajiwara Genta Kagesue from the series *Modern Parodies of Genji* (*Imayō nazorae Genji*), 1864
Publisher: Ōmiya Kyūjirō (Kiyūdō)
Vertical ōban; 36 x 23.7 cm (14 1/8 x 9 3/8 in.)
William Sturgis Bigelow Collection, 11.41128

44 Bamboo River (Takekawa)

44A Kunisada
Takekawa from the series *Genji Incense Pictures* (*Genji kō no zu*), 1844–47
Publisher: Yamamotoya Heikichi (Eikyūdō)
24.8 x 17.9 cm (9 3/4 x 7 in.)
Gift of the Anne Gordon Keidel Trust of June 2016, 2016.1575

44B Isoda Koryūsai (1735–1790)
Takekawa from the series *Genji in Fashionable Modern Guise* (*Fūryū yatsushi Genji*), about 1770–72
22 x 15.9 cm (8 5/8 x 6 1/4 in.)
William Sturgis Bigelow Collection, 11.19746

44C Kunisada
Takekawa from the series *The Color Print Contest of a Modern Genji* (*Ima Genji nishiki-e awase*), 1854
Publisher: Sanoya Kihei (Kikakudō)
25.7 x 18.1 cm (10 1/8 x 7 1/8 in.)
William Sturgis Bigelow Collection, 11.20867

45 The Lady of the Bridge (Hashihime)

45A Kunisada
Hashihime from the series *Genji Incense Pictures* (*Genji kō no zu*), 1844–47
Publisher: Yamamotoya Heikichi (Eikyūdō)
24.8 x 17.9 cm (9 3/4 x 7 in.)
Gift of the Anne Gordon Keidel Trust of June 2016, 2016.1576

45B Utagawa Yoshiiku (Japanese, 1833–1904)
Hashihime: Tawara Tōda Hidesato and the Dragon Woman (Ryūjo) from the series *Modern Parodies of Genji* (*Imayō nazorae Genji*), 1864
Publisher: Ōmiya Kyūjirō (Kiyūdō)
Vertical ōban; 36 x 23.7 cm (14 1/8 × 9 3/8 in.)
William Sturgis Bigelow Collection, 11.41130

45C Kunisada
Hashihime from the series *The Color Print Contest of a Modern Genji* (*Ima Genji nishiki-e awase*), 1854
Publisher: Sanoya Kihei (Kikakudō)
25.6 x 18.1 cm (10 1/8 x 7 1/8 in.)
William Sturgis Bigelow Collection, 11.20868

46 Beneath the Oak (Shiigamoto)

46A Kunisada
Shiigamoto from the series *Genji Incense Pictures* (*Genji kō no zu*), 1844–47
Publisher: Yamamotoya Heikichi (Eikyūdō)
24.7 x 17.9 cm (9 3/4 x 7 in.)
Gift of the Anne Gordon Keidel Trust of June 2016, 2016.1577

46B Kunisada
Shiigamoto from the series *The Color Print Contest of a Modern Genji* (*Ima Genji nishiki-e awase*), 1854
Publisher: Sanoya Kihei (Kikakudō)
25.7 x 18.1 cm (10 1/8 x 7 1/8 in.)
William Sturgis Bigelow Collection, 11.20962

47 Trefoil Knots (Agemaki)

47A Kunisada
Agemaki from the series *Genji Incense Pictures* (*Genji kō no zu*), 1844–47
Publisher: Yamamotoya Heikichi (Eikyūdō)
24.9 x 17.9 cm (9 3/4 x 7 in.)
Gift of the Anne Gordon Keidel Trust of June 2016, 2016.1578

47B Kunisada
Agemaki from the series *The Color Print Contest of a Modern Genji* (*Ima Genji nishiki-e awase*), 1854
Publisher: Sanoya Kihei (Kikakudō)
25.5 x 18.1 cm (10 x 7 1/8 in.)
William Sturgis Bigelow Collection, 11.20866

47C Utagawa Kunisada II (Kunimasa III, Toyokuni IV) (1823–1880)
Utagawa Hiroshige II (Shigenobu) (1826–1869)
Agemaki from the series *Traces of Genji in Fifty-Four Chapters* (*Omokage Genji gojūyojō*), 1865
Publisher: Tsutaya Kichizō (Kōeidō)
Vertical ōban; 36.9 x 25 cm (14 1/2 x 9 7/8 in.)
William Sturgis Bigelow Collection, 11.37391.47

48 Fern Shoots (Sawarabi)

48A Kunisada
Sawarabi from the series *Genji Incense Pictures* (*Genji kō no zu*), 1844–47
Publisher: Yamamotoya Heikichi (Eikyūdō)
24.8 x 17.9 cm (9 3/4 x 7 in.)
Gift of the Anne Gordon Keidel Trust of June 2016, 2016.1579

48B Kajita Hanko (1870–1917)
Sawarabi from the series *The Tale of Genji*, 1905
Publisher: Bun'endō
Color lithograph; ink metallic pigment on card stock
13.8 x 8.8 cm (5 3/8 x 3 1/2 in.)
Leonard A. Lauder Collection of Japanese Postcards, 2002.971

48C Kunisada
Sawarabi from the series *The Color Print Contest of a Modern Genji* (*Ima Genji nishiki-e awase*), 1853
Publisher: Sanoya Kihei (Kikakudō)
26.2 x 18 cm (10 3/8 x 7 1/8 in.)
William Sturgis Bigelow Collection, 11.20864

49 The Ivy (Yadorigi)

49A Kunisada
Yadorigi from the series *Genji Incense Pictures* (*Genji kō no zu*), 1844–47
Publisher: Yamamotoya Heikichi (Eikyūdō)
24.8 x 17.9 cm (9 3/4 x 7 in.)
Gift of the Anne Gordon Keidel Trust of June 2016, 2016.1580

49B Kunisada
Yadorigi from the series *The Color Print Contest of a Modern Genji* (*Ima Genji nishiki-e awase*), 1853
Publisher: Sanoya Kihei (Kikakudō)
26 x 18 cm (10 1/4 x 7 1/8 in.)
William Sturgis Bigelow Collection, 11.20863

49C Utagawa Kuniyoshi (1797–1861)
Wood (Ki): Yadorigi from the series *Comparisons for the Five Elements* (*Mitate gogyō*), 1847–52
Vertical ōban triptych; 37.8 x 76.5 cm (14 7/8 x 30 1/8 in.)
William Sturgis Bigelow Collection, 11.16065-7

50 The Eastern Cottage (Azumaya)

50A Kunisada
Azumaya from the series *Genji Incense Pictures* (*Genji kō no zu*), 1844–47
Publisher: Yamamotoya Heikichi (Eikyūdō)
24.8 x 17.9 cm (9 3/4 x 7 in.)
Gift of the Anne Gordon Keidel Trust of June 2016, 2016.1581

50B Kunisada
Azumaya from the series *The Color Print Contest of a Modern Genji* (*Ima Genji nishiki-e awase*), 1854
Publisher: Sanoya Kihei (Kikakudō)
25.7 x 18 cm (10 1/8 x 7 1/8 in.)
William Sturgis Bigelow Collection, 11.20819

50c Utagawa Kunisada II (Kunimasa III, Toyokuni IV) (1823–1880)
Utagawa Hiroshige II (Shigenobu) (1826–1869)
Azumaya from the series *Traces of Genji in Fifty-Four Chapters* (*Omokage Genji gojūyojō*), 1865
Publisher: Tsutaya Kichizō (Kōeidō)
Vertical ōban; 36.9 x 25 cm (14 1/2 x 9 7/8 in.)
William Sturgis Bigelow Collection, 11.37391.50

51 A Drifting Boat (Ukifune)

51a Kunisada
Ukifune from the series *Genji Incense Pictures* (*Genji kō no zu*), 1844–47
Publisher: Yamamotoya Heikichi (Eikyūdō)
24.8 x 17.9 cm (9 3/4 x 7 in.)
Gift of the Anne Gordon Keidel Trust of June 2016, 2016.1582

51b Totoya Hokkei (1780–1850)
The Ukifune chapter from *The Tale of Genji for the Akabane Club*, 1826
Woodblock print (surimono); ink, color, and metallic pigment on paper
Shikishiban; 21 x 18.3 cm (8 1/4 x 7 1/4 in.)
William Sturgis Bigelow Collection, 11.20609

51c Utagawa Hiroshige I (1797–1858)
Ukifune, 1847–52
Publisher: Ibaya Senzaburō (Dansendō)
Horizontal chūban; 22.5 x 27.7 cm (8 7/8 x 10 7/8 in.)
William S. and John T. Spaulding Collection, 21.10143

51d Okumura Masanobu (1686–1764)
The Ukifune Chapter of The Tale of Genji (*Genji Ukifune*), 1740s
Woodblock print (beni-e); ink on paper, with hand-applied color
Horizontal ōban; 33.1 x 47.5 cm (13 x 18 3/4 in.)
William S. and John T. Spaulding Collection, 21.6868

51e Kunisada
Ukifune from the series *The Color Print Contest of a Modern Genji* (*Ima Genji nishiki-e awase*), 1854
Publisher: Sanoya Kihei (Kikakudō)
25.6 x 18.2 cm (10 1/8 x 7 1/8 in.)
William Sturgis Bigelow Collection, 11.20953

52 The Mayfly (Kagerō)

52a Kunisada
Kagerō from the series *Genji Incense Pictures* (*Genji kō no zu*), 1844–47
Publisher: Yamamotoya Heikichi (Eikyūdō)
24.9 x 17.9 cm (9 3/4 x 7 in.)
Gift of the Anne Gordon Keidel Trust of June 2016, 2016.1583

52b Utagawa Kuniyoshi (1797–1861)
Kagerō: Akitsushima from the series *Genji Clouds Matched with Ukiyo-e Pictures* (*Genji kumo ukiyo-e awase*), about 1845–46
Publisher: Iseya Ichibei
36.8 x 25 cm (14 1/2 x 9 7/8 in.)
William Sturgis Bigelow Collection, 11.36545

52c Kunisada
Kagerō from the series *The Color Print Contest of a Modern Genji* (*Ima Genji nishiki-e awase*), 1854
Publisher: Sanoya Kihei (Kikakudō)
25.7 x 18.1 cm (10 1/8 x 7 1/8 in.)
William Sturgis Bigelow Collection, 11.20956

53 Writing Practice (Tenarai)

53a Kunisada
Tenarai from the series *Genji Incense Pictures* (*Genji kō no zu*), 1844–47
Publisher: Yamamotoya Heikichi (Eikyūdō)
24.9 x 17.9 cm (9 3/4 x 7 in.)
Gift of the Anne Gordon Keidel Trust of June 2016, 2016.1584

53b Kunisada
Tenarai from the series *The Color Print Contest of a Modern Genji* (*Ima Genji nishiki-e awase*), 1854
Publisher: Sanoya Kihei (Kikakudō)
25.7 x 18.1 cm (10 1/8 x 7 1/8 in.)
William Sturgis Bigelow Collection, 11.20860

53c Utagawa Yoshiiku (1833–1904)
Miyagi Gengyo (1817–1880)
Tenarai: Takumi no kami Tōfū from the series *Modern Parodies of Genji* (*Imayō nazorae Genji*), 1864
Publisher: Ōmiya Kyūjirō (Kiyūdō)
Vertical ōban; 36 x 23.4 cm (14 1/8 x 9 1/4 in.)
William Sturgis Bigelow Collection, 11.41138

54 The Floating Bridge of Dreams (Yume no ukihashi)

54a Kunisada
Yume no ukihashi from the series *Genji Incense Pictures* (*Genji kō no zu*), 1844–47
Publisher: Yamamotoya Heikichi (Eikyūdō)
24.8 x 17.9 cm (9 3/4 x 7 in.)
Gift of the Anne Gordon Keidel Trust of June 2016, 2016.1585

54b Kunisada
Yume no ukihashi from the series *The Color Print Contest of a Modern Genji* (*Ima Genji nishiki-e awase*), 1854
Publisher: Sanoya Kihei (Kikakudō)
25.6 x 18.1 cm (10 1/8 x 7 1/8 in.)
William Sturgis Bigelow Collection, 11.20811

54c Utagawa Kunisada II (Kunimasa III, Toyokuni IV) (1823–1880)
Yume no ukihashi from the series *Lady Murasaki's Genji Cards* (*Murasaki Shikibu Genji karuta*), 1857
Publisher: Tsutaya Kichizō (Kōeidō)
Vertical ōban; 37.4 x 25.2 cm (14 3/4 x 9 7/8 in.)
William Sturgis Bigelow Collection, 11.21722

Figure Illustrations

1 Torii Kiyomasu I (active about 1696–1716)
Woman reading the Akashi chapter of *The Tale of Genji*, about 1710s
Publisher: Igaya Kan'emon (Bunkidō)
Woodblock print (tan-e); ink on paper, with hand-applied color
Vertical ōban; 56 x 32.1 cm (22 x 12 5/8 in.)
Denman Waldo Ross Collection, 06.1334

2 Unknown artist
The picture contest from *The Tale of Genji*, 17th century
Album leaf; ink, color, and gold on paper
24.6 x 18.5 cm (9 5/8 x 7 1/4 in.)
William Sturgis Bigelow Collection, 11.7131

3 Torii Kiyonaga (1752–1815)
Child prodigy Gyokkashi Shima Eimo giving a reading lesson, about 1785
Publisher: Nishimuraya Yohachi (Eijudō)
Vertical ōban; 38 x 25.1 cm (14 15/16 x 9 7/8 in.)
Museum of Fine Arts, Boston — Worcester Art Museum exchange, made possible through the Weld Fund, 54.565

4 Hishikawa Moronobu (died 1694)
Picture Book of The Tale of Genji (*Genji Yamato-e kagami*), 1685
Publisher: Urokogataya
Woodblock printed book; ink on paper
Hanshibon; 22.4 x 15.5 cm (8 7/8 x 6 1/8 in.)
Source unidentified, 2006.1595

5 Hishikawa Moronobu (died 1694)
New Collection of Pictures of Beauties [*(Shinpan) Bijin e-zukushi*], about 1684–87
Woodblock printed book; ink on paper
Ōhon; 26.7 x 18.5 cm (10 1/2 x 7 1/4 in.)
William S. and John T. Spaulding Collection, 2006.1729.1-2

6 Okumura Masanobu (1686–1764)
Untitled album of prints of *The Tale of Genji*, about 1730s
Woodblock prints, mounted in album; ink on paper, with hand-applied color
Album page: 16.7 x 23.5 cm (6 5/8 x 9 1/4 in.)
Gift of Mrs. Jared K. Morse in memory of Charles J. Morse, 2011.788

7 Totoya Hokkei (1780–1850)
The Shell-Matching Game from the surimono series *Essays in Idleness* (*Tsurezure-gusa*), about 1831–32
Woodblock print (surimono); ink and color on paper
Shikishiban; 19.8 x 17.8 cm (7 3/4 x 7 in.)
William Sturgis Bigelow Collection, 11.25460

8 Toyohara Kunichika (1835–1900)
Suzumushi from the series *The Fifty-Four Chapters of The Tale of Genji in Modern Times* (*Genji gojūyojō*), 1884
Publisher: Takekawa Seikichi (Sawamuraya Seikichi)
Vertical ōban; 37.5 x 25 cm (14 3/4 x 9 7/8 in.)
William Sturgis Bigelow Collection, 11.16130

9 Kunisada
Shiigamoto from the series *Lingering Sentiments of a Late Collection of Genji* (*Genji goshū yojō*), 1859
Publisher: Ebisuya Shōshichi (Kinshōdō) (Japanese)
Vertical ōban diptych; 36.6 x 50.7 cm (14 3/8 x 20 in.)
Bequest of William Perkins Babcock, 00.1853a-b

Further Reading

English Translations of *The Tale of Genji* by Murasaki Shikibu

Arthur Waley. London: Allen & Unwin, 1925–1933.

Edward G. Seidensticker. New York: Knopf, 1976.

Royall Tyler. New York: Viking, 2001.

Dennis Washburn. New York: W. W. Norton, 2015.

References and Further Reading

Allen, Laura W. "Japanese Exemplars for a New Age: *Genji* Paintings from the Seventeenth-Century Tosa School." In *Critical Perspectives on Classicism in Japanese Painting, 1600–1700*, edited by Elizabeth Lillehoj, 99–132. Honolulu: University of Hawai'i Press, 2004.

Carpenter, John T., and Melissa McCormick, et al. *The Tale of Genji: A Japanese Classic Illuminated*. New York: The Metropolitan Museum of Art, 2019.

Clark, Timothy, Anne Nishimura Morse, and Louise E. Virgin, with Allen Hockley. *The Dawn of the Floating World, 1650–1765: Early Ukiyo-e Treasures from the Museum of Fine Arts, Boston*. London: Royal Academy of Arts, 2001.

Coats, Bruce A. "The Changing Face of 'The Twilight Beauty' (*Yūgao*) in Genji Prints." In *Genji's World in Japanese Woodblock Prints*, by Andreas Marks et al., 22–31. Claremont, Calif., and Leiden: Scripps College in association with Hotei Publishing, 2012.

Cranston, Edwin. *A Waka Anthology, Volume Two: Grasses of Remembrance*. Stanford: Stanford University Press, 2006.

Drake, Chris, trans. "A Country Genji by a Commoner Murasaki." In *Early Modern Japanese Literature: An Anthology, 1600–1900*, edited by Haruo Shirane, 801–42. New York: Columbia University Press, 2002.

Emmerich, Michael. *The Tale of Genji: Translation, Canonization, and World Literature*. New York: Columbia University Press, 2013.

Fukuda Kazuhiko, ed. *Enshoku Genji-e*. Tokyo: KK Bestsellers, 1991.

Haft, Alfred. *Aesthetic Strategies of the Floating World: Mitate, Yatsushi, and Fūryū in Early Modern Japanese Popular Culture*. Leiden: Brill, 2013.

Harper, Thomas, and Haruo Shirane, eds. *Reading "The Tale of Genji": Sources from the First Millennium*. New York: Columbia University Press, 2015.

Hockley, Allen. *The Prints of Isoda Koryūsai: Floating World Culture and Its Consumers in Eighteenth-century Japan*. Seattle and London: University of Washington Press, 2003.

Izzard, Sebastian, with essays by Thomas J. Rimer and John T. Carpenter. *Kunisada's World*. New York: Japan Society, Inc., in collaboration with the Ukiyo-e Society of America, 1993.

Kinoshita, Kyoko. "Evolving Iconographies of *The Tale of Genji*: Early Modern Interpretations of a *Yamato-e* Theme." In *The Tale of Genji: A Japanese Classic Illuminated*, by John T. Carpenter, Melissa McCormick, et al., 57–73. New York: The Metropolitan Museum of Art, 2019.

Kondo, Eiko. "Inaka Genji Series." In *Essays on Japanese Art Presented to Jack Hillier*, edited by Matthi Forrer, Neil K. Davey, and Jack R. Hillier, 78–93. London: Robert G. Sawers Publishing, 1982.

Kornicki, P. F. "Unsuitable Books for Women? 'Genji Monogatari' and 'Ise Monogatari' in Late Seventeenth Century Japan." *Monumenta Nipponica* 60, no. 2 (Summer 2009): 147–93.

Kyoto bunka hakubutsukan (Museum of Kyoto). *Yomu, miru, asobu Genji monogatari no sekai — Ukiyo-e kara Genji ishō made / Read, Look, Play: The World of "The Tale of Genji" — From Ukiyo-e Prints to the Design of Genji*. Kyoto: Kyoto bunka hakubutsukan, 2008.

Marks, Andreas. "A Country Genji: Kunisada's Single-sheet Genji Series." *Impressions* 27 (2006): 59–79.

Marks, Andreas, with Bruce A. Coats, Michael Emmerich, Susanne Formanek, Sepp Linhart, and Rhiannon Paget. *Genji's World in Japanese Woodblock Prints*. Claremont, Calif., and Leiden: Scripps College in association with Hotei Publishing, 2012.

Markus, Andrew Lawrence. *The Willow in Autumn: Ryūtei Tanehiko, 1783–1842*. Cambridge, Mass., and London: Council on East Asian Studies, Harvard University, and Harvard University Press, 1992.

McCormick, Melissa. *The Tale of Genji: A Visual Companion*. Princeton and Oxford: Princeton University Press, 2018.

Meech-Pekarik, Julia. "The Artist's View of Ukifune." In *Ukifune: Love in "The Tale of Genji,"* edited by Andrew Pekarik, 173–215. New York: Columbia University Press, 1982.

Mostow, Joshua. "Illustrated Classical Texts for Women in the Edo Period." In *The Female as Subject: Reading and Writing in Early Modern Japan*, edited by P. F. Kornicki, Mara Patessio, and G. G. Rowley, 59–85. Ann Arbor: Center for Japanese Studies, The University of Michigan, 2010.

Mostow, Joshua, trans. Kameda Kazuko. "Genji monogatari to jokunsho / Genji Monogatari and Jokunsho." In *Genji monogatari to Edo bunka, kashika sareru ga-zoku / Genji Monogatari and Edo Period Culture: Visualizing Ga and Zoku*, edited by Komine Kazuaki, Kojima Naoko, and Watanabe Kenji, 337–46. Tokyo: Shinwasha, 2008.

Murase, Miyeko. *Iconography of "The Tale of Genji": Genji Monogatari Ekotoba*. New York and Tokyo: Weatherhill, 1983.

Murase, Miyeko. *The Tale of Genji: Legends and Paintings*. New York: George Braziller, 2001.

Nakamachi, Keiko. "*Genji* Pictures from Momoyama Painting to Edo *Ukiyo-e*: Cultural Authority and New Horizons." In *Envisioning "The Tale of Genji": Media, Gender, and Cultural Production*, edited by Haruo Shirane, 177–210. New York: Columbia University Press, 2008.

Puette, William J. *Guide to "The Tale of Genji" by Murasaki Shikibu*. Rutland, Vermont, and Tokyo: Charles E. Tuttle Company, 1983.

Richardson, Donald M., and Teruo Tanonaka, trans., *The Rustic Genji of a Bogus Murasaki*. Winchester, Virgina, 1985.

Sakomura, Tomoko. "Japanese Games of Memory, Matching, and Identification." In *Asian Games: The Art of Contest*, edited by Colin Mackenzie and Irving Finkel, 252–71. New York: Asia Society, 2004.

Shirane, Haruo, ed. *Envisioning "The Tale of Genji": Media, Gender, and Cultural Production*. New York: Columbia University Press, 2008.

Suzuki Jūzō, ed. *Nise Murasaki inaka Genji* (*Shin Nihon koten bungaku taikei*, vols. 88–89). Tokyo: Iwanami shoten, 1995.

Thompson, Sarah E. "The Original Source (Accept No Substitutes!): Okumura Masanobu." In *Designed for Pleasure: The World of Edo Japan in Prints and Paintings, 1680–1860*, 57–79. Seattle and London: Asia Society and Japanese Art Society of America in association with University of Washington Press, 2008.

Thompson, Sarah E. "Poetry, Incense, Card Games, and Pictorial Narrative Coding in Early Modern Genji Pictures." In *Rethinking Visual Narratives from Asia*, edited by Alexandra Green, 109–25. Hong Kong: University of Hong Kong Press, 2013.

Tinios, Ellis. "Greater Than Utamaro: The Fame of Utagawa Kunisada / Utagawa Kunisada no hyōban — Utamaro o koeta ukiyoeshi." *Ukiyo-e geijutsu / Ukiyo-e Art* 171 (January 2016): 113–95 (English text) and 30–39 (Japanese translation). Translated by Kurahashi Masae.

Watanabe, Masako. "Edo no mitate-e to Onna San-no-miya, ga-zoku imeeji no hen'yō. / Onna San-no-miya and Edo Mitate-e: Changing Trends within Ga-zoku Images." In *Genji monogatari to Edo bunka, kashika sareru ga-zoku / Genji Monogatari and Edo Period Culture: Visualizing Ga and Zoku*, edited by Komine Kazuaki, Kojima Naoko, and Watanabe Kenji, 285–320. Tokyo: Shinwasha, 2008.

Waterhouse, David. *Images of Eighteenth-century Japan: Ukiyoe Prints from the Sir Edmund Walker Collection*. Toronto: Royal Ontario Museum, 1975.

Online Resources

WASEDA UNIVERSITY LIBRARY

https://archive.wul.waseda.ac.jp

Ashikaga Robes Hand-dyed in Purple (*Ashikaga-ginu tezome no Murasaki*), chapters 6–18 (complete)

The False Murasaki's Rustic Genji (*Nise Murasaki inaka Genji*), chapters 1–38 (complete)

Pale Purple Dawn at Uji (*Usumurasaki Uji no akebono*), chapters 1–8 (complete)

A Related Rustic Image (*Sono yukari hina no omokage*), chapters 1–23 (complete)

NATIONAL DIET LIBRARY

https://dl.ndl.go.jp

A Purple Story in Edo Tie-dyeing (*Edo kanoko Murasaki-zōshi*), chapter 1 (no other chapters known)

RITSUMEIKAN UNIVERSITY ART RESEARCH CENTER (ARC)

https://www.dh-jac.net/

The Color Print Contest of a Modern Genji (*Ima Genji nishiki-e awase*), complete series including title page and preface as well as transcriptions of poems

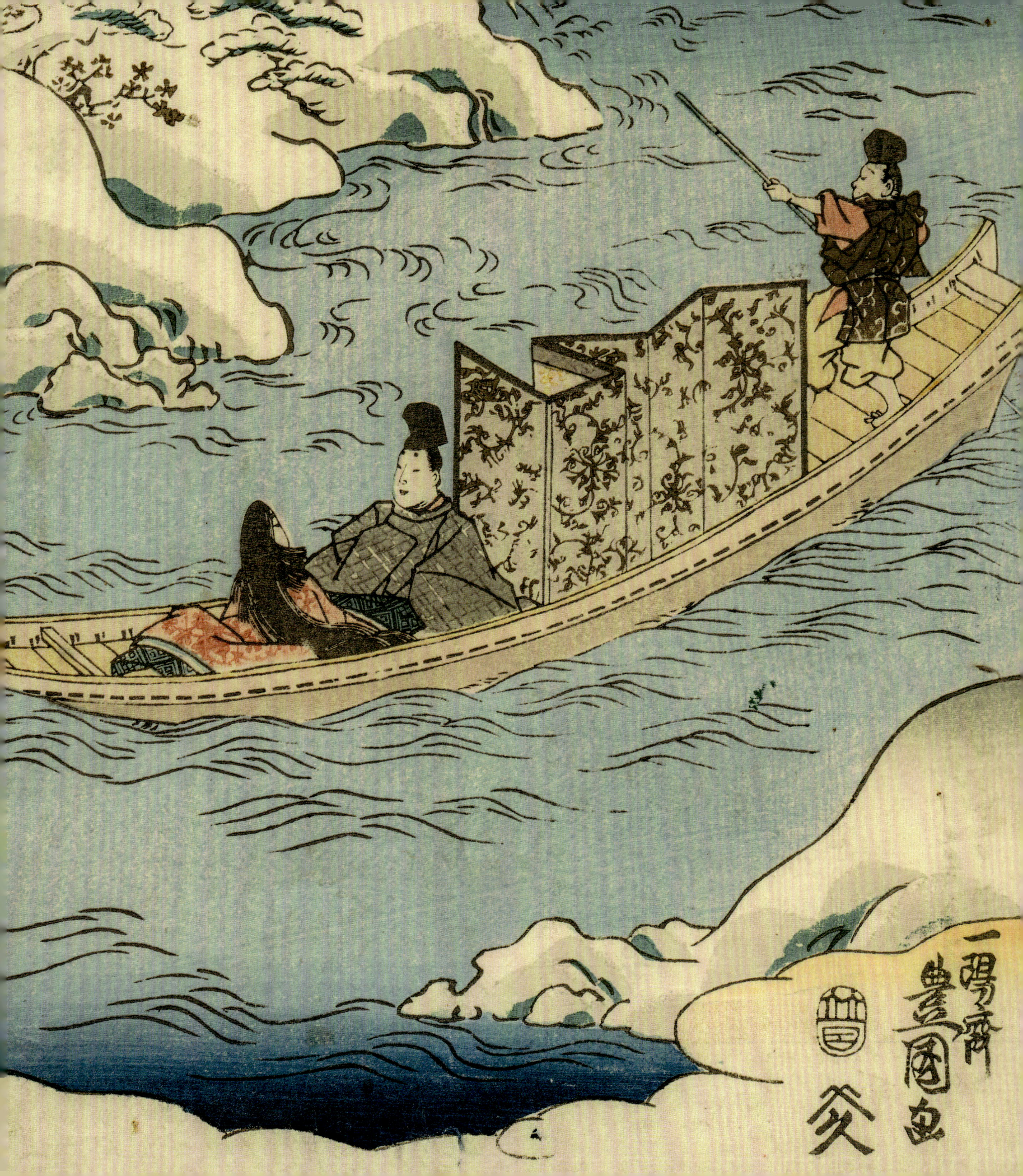
一陽斎豊国画

Acknowledgments

The idea for this book was sparked by a generous bequest in 2016 from an old friend of the Art of Asia Department at the MFA, Anne Gordon Keidel, who left us over seven hundred prints including the complete *Genji Incense* series. Anne worked for many years as a volunteer in the department, helping us to organize the old documents and correspondence that are an important record of the early days of Asian art studies in the U.S. I knew that she collected prints and had even visited her home to see some of them; but I had no idea that she planned to leave the collection to us, and so I was very touched by this final farewell gesture on her part. We think of her whenever we exhibit or publish her gifts.

For the translations of the poems associated with the fifty-four chapters of *The Tale of Genji*, reproduced in the *Genji Incense* series and a number of other Genji prints, we were fortunate to be given permission by Royall Tyler and his publisher for the use of his excellent translations. Reading these very accessible translations while studying the prints will, we hope, help our contemporary audience recreate the experience enjoyed by the first viewers of these works.

I am profoundly grateful to all of the authors of the publications listed in the References, the foundation on which this book is based. Any mistakes or misinterpretations of their work are my own. At the top of the list of the works that I consulted most often is *Genji's World* by Andreas Marks et al. (2012), with its essays on many different aspects of *Inaka Genji*, and an indispensable appendix listing all known Genji prints. The exhibition for which *Genji's World* served as a catalogue, organized by Bruce Coats at Scripps College and other venues, and featuring the spectacular collection of Paulette and Jack Lantz, greatly stimulated my own interest in *Inaka Genji* and was another source of inspiration for the present book.

My personal studies of Lady Murasaki's *Tale of Genji* date back to my days as a graduate student at Columbia, where I read (parts of) the original text with Edward Seidensticker, the author of what was at the time the most recent translation of the *Tale*, and investigated the pictorial tradition under the guidance of my own graduate advisor, Miyeko Murase, whose *Iconography of the Tale of Genji* (1983) is still, in my opinion, the most useful English-language guide to identifying specific scenes from the great classic as depicted in Japanese art over the centuries. I am also deeply indebted to the extensive work of my Columbia senpai Haruo Shirane on the reception of the *Tale*, particularly his two edited anthologies *Envisioning "The Tale of Genji"* (2008) and, with Thomas Harper, *Reading "The Tale of Genji"* (2015). The essay by Keiko Nakamachi in *Envisioning* was especially helpful. A gorgeous selection of Genji-inspired art of all kinds may be found in the catalogue of the 2019 exhibition at the Metropolitan Museum of Art, by John T. Carpenter, Melissa McCormick, et al., the most comprehensive pictorial presentation in English to date. Still more material is of course available in Japanese, and readers are strongly encouraged to check the bibliographies of the books and articles I have listed to find additional works of interest.

Research under pandemic conditions was greatly facilitated by the digital collections that have been made available in recent years by various Japanese libraries and other cultural institutions. In particular, I am grateful to the Waseda University Library, the National Diet Library, and the Art Research Center at Ritsumeikan University, all of which were essential to this project. Closer to home, I relied on online access to the MFA's own collection, which was made possible by the Japanese Print Access and Documentation Project (JPADP) of 2005 to 2010. Once again, I thank the dozens of MFA employees and volunteers who worked tirelessly to accession, photograph, and rehouse the prints; the visiting scholars from Japan and elsewhere who helped us to catalogue them; and the sources of the grant money that made it all possible, including an anonymous American organization, an anonymous Japanese organization, and the State Street Bank. All of the exhibitions and publications of Japanese prints that we have done since 2005 are due to the many people who supported and contributed to the JPADP.

Working with MFA Publications is always a pleasure. I greatly appreciate the insightful suggestions and ongoing moral support provided by editors Jennifer Snodgrass, who started the project with me, and Hope Stockton, who brought it to completion. Their cheerful attitudes even in difficult circumstances helped keep me going. Susan Marsh has once again provided a beautiful and eye-catching design, and the publication process has been ably directed by Debra LaKind. For support and encouragement of both the book and the author, I thank Christina Yu Yu, Matsutaro Shoriki Chair, Art of Asia.

Finally, I want to express my gratitude to the kind friends whose carefully organized, socially distanced social events kept me in touch with the rest of the human race during the quarantine: Pauline Webber and Philip Meredith, and Jo-Ann and Richard Pinkowitz. Many, many thanks for those very pleasant occasions.

Sarah E. Thompson
Curator, Japanese Art
Museum of Fine Arts, Boston

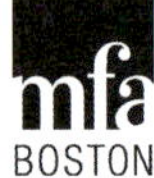

MFA Publications
Museum of Fine Arts, Boston
465 Huntington Avenue
Boston, Massachusetts 02115
www.mfa.org/publications

Generous support for this publication provided by the Andrew W. Mellon Publications Fund

ISBN: 978-0-87846-883-6
Library of Congress Control Number: 2021939902

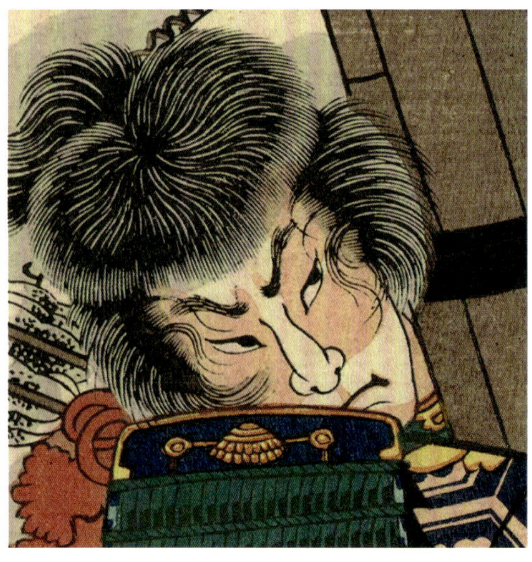

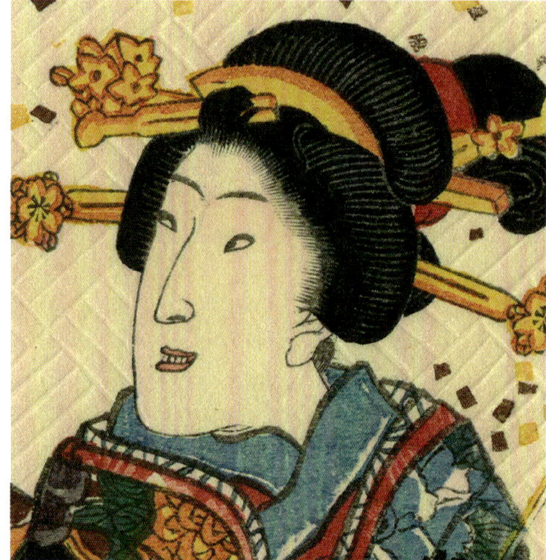

While the objects in this publication necessarily represent only a small portion of the MFA's holdings, the Museum is proud to be a leader within the American museum community in sharing the objects in its collection via its website. Currently, information about approximately 400,000 objects is available to the public worldwide. To learn more about the MFA's collections, including provenance, publication, and exhibition history, kindly visit www.mfa.org/collections.

For a complete listing of MFA publications, please contact the publisher at the above address, or call 617 369 4233.

Illustrations in this book were photographed by the Imaging Studios, Museum of Fine Arts, Boston, except where otherwise noted.

Editing and production by Hope Stockton
Proofread by Jessica Altholz Eber
Designed by Susan Marsh
Typeset by Matt Mayerchak in Sentinel, with Archer and Tungsten display (H&Co) and Meta Pro Thin display (FF)
Printed on 135 gsm Gardapat Kiara
Printed and bound at Graphicom, Verona, Italy

Distributed by
ARTBOOK | D.A.P.
75 Broad Street, Suite 630
New York, New York 10004
www.artbook.com

FIRST EDITION

Printed and bound in Italy
This book was printed on acid-free paper.

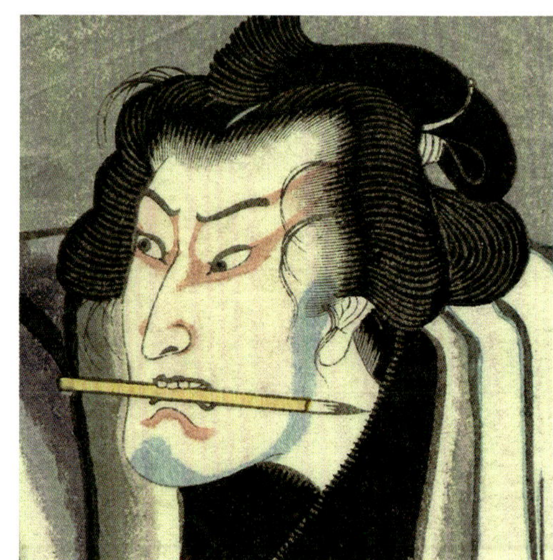